Fodor's

MONTANA AND WYOMING

Welcome to Montana and Wyoming

Big Sky Country is more than just a nickname: Montana has huge expanses of rugged country. It's a place to discover how beautiful the night sky can be and what "dark" truly is with limited city lights. While the days of the Wild West seem like history to many of us, Wyoming is still a land of cowboys and ranches. Even in high-end Jackson Hole, western attire mixes with ski gear. True to that frontier spirit, it's a land perfect for exploration. As you plan your travels, please confirm that places are still open and let us know when we need to make updates by writing to us at editors@fodors.com.

TOP REASONS TO GO

★ **Yellowstone National Park:** The world's oldest national park is filled with geothermal features and abundant wildlife.

★ **The Grand Tetons:** The magnificent mountains make the perfect photo backdrop but also offer great skiing in Jackson Hole.

★ **Skiing and Winter Sports:** You'll find abundant opportunities to enjoy the cold weather and abundant snowfall.

★ **Fly-Fishing:** Many rivers and lakes run through this country, one of the top regions for fly-fishing in the lower 48.

★ **Cowboy History:** Montana and Wyoming have been ranching country since the 19th century.

Contents

Fodor's Features

Contents

MAPS

Chapter 1

EXPERIENCE MONTANA AND WYOMING

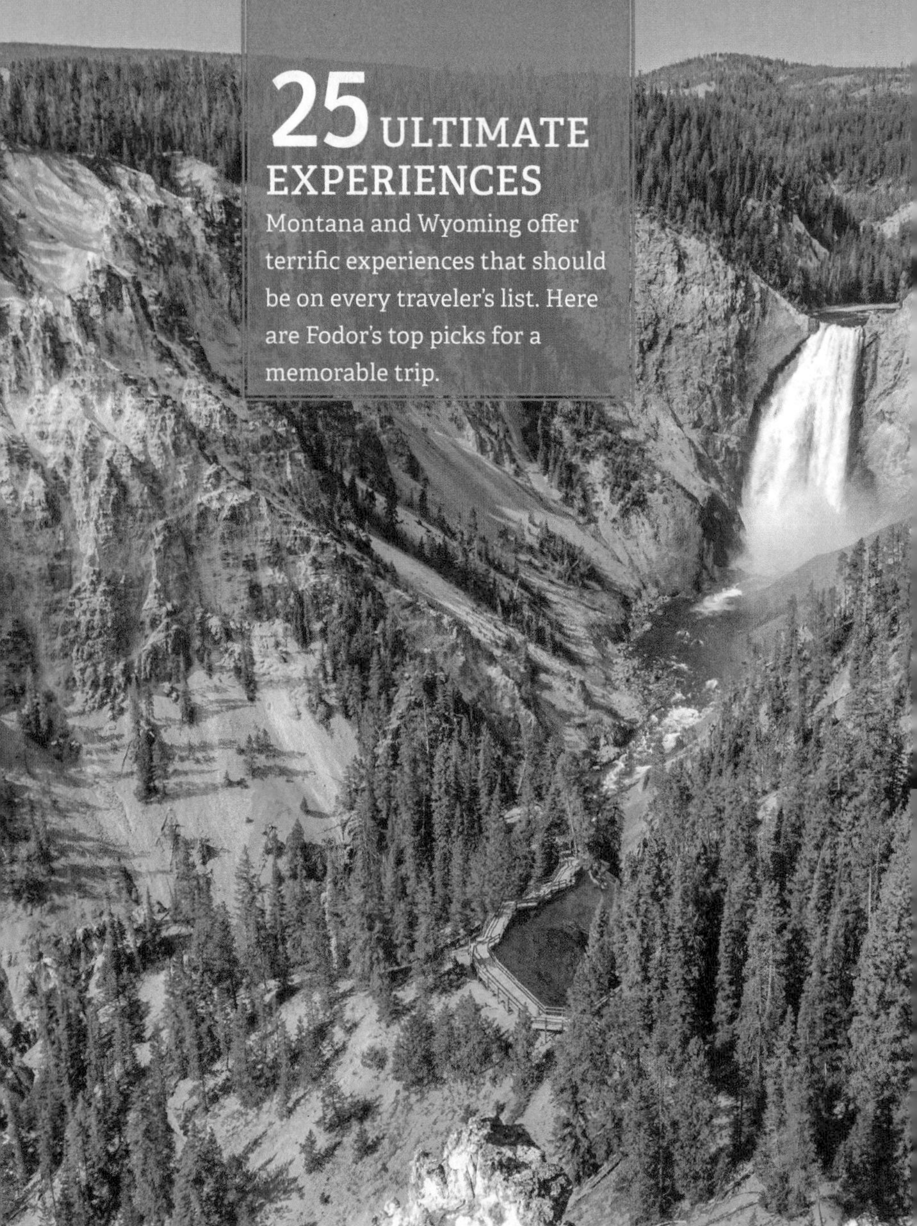

25 ULTIMATE EXPERIENCES

Montana and Wyoming offer terrific experiences that should be on every traveler's list. Here are Fodor's top picks for a memorable trip.

1 Listen to the Rush of Waterfalls in the Grand Canyon of Yellowstone

A 308-foot-high waterfall sits at the head of the Grand Canyon of Yellowstone National Park and further upstream is a 109-foot waterfall. Both are inside a spectacular 24-mile-long colorful canyon that is stunningly beautiful. *(Ch. 3)*

2 The Museum of the Rockies

The largest collection of dinosaur remains in the United States and the largest Tyrannosaurus skull ever discovered can be seen at this museum in Bozeman. *(Ch. 4)*

3 Canoe or Paddle Board on Lake McDonald

The largest lake in Glacier National Park is surrounded by glacier-carved peaks and can best be appreciated from a boat or a stand-up paddleboard. *(Ch. 5)*

4 See a Glacier

Grinnell Glacier is one of the most accessible glaciers in Glacier National Park; getting there involves two boat rides and a 7.6-mile round-trip hike, but the payoff is worth it. *(Ch. 5)*

5 Drive the Going-to-the-Sun Road

The scenic, historic road crosses the Continental Divide and is dotted with glaciers, waterfalls, mountains, and wildflowers; it's also a civil engineering landmark. *(Ch. 5)*

6 Experience Cat Skiing

Wyoming's Grand Targhee Resort is the perfect place to go off-piste. A snowcat will transport skiers to deep powder and breathtaking views of the Teton Range. *(Ch. 9)*

7 Saddle Up

Experience real cowboy life at a dude ranch. Round up cattle, pitch in at the stables, ride through magnificent scenery. Eaton's Ranch near Wolf Wyoming is the oldest dude ranch in America. *(Ch. 10)*

8 Search for Fossils at Fossil Butte

Wyoming's Fossil Butte National Monument is home to one of the largest deposits of freshwater fish fossils in the world, visible on a day tour or in the visitor center. *(Ch. 11)*

9 Enjoy a Soak in Bozeman Hot Springs

For more than 100 years, people have come to relax and rejuvenate near Yellowstone in Bozeman Hot Springs's nine pools and dry and wet saunas. *(Ch. 4)*

10 Mush a Team of Huskies

Explore the backcountry of northwest Montana by dogsled as early explorers once did. Ride in the warm sled or step behind it and be the musher. *(Ch. 6)*

11 Go Fly-Fishing on the Flathead River

Nothing compares to the thrill of catching a native cutthroat trout in the crystal clear waters of Montana's Flathead River near Glacier National Park. *(Ch. 6)*

12 Bike Mount Helena Ridge

One of 11 silver-level ride centers in the world, the Mount Helena Ridge Trail is the highlight of Helena's South Hills trail network. It's a mountain biking paradise. *(Ch. 4)*

13 Experience the World's Largest Outdoor Rodeo

Established in 1897, Cheyenne Frontier Days has grown into the world's largest outdoor rodeo competition and western celebration of the cowboy spirit. *(Ch. 11)*

14 Visit the National Museum of Wildlife Art

Built into a hillside overlooking the National Elk Refuge, the National Museum of Wildlife Art in Jackson houses more than 5,000 works from renowned artists. *(Ch. 9)*

15 Watch Old Faithful Erupt

Discovered in 1870, Yellowstone's Old Faithful geyser was named for its predictability. Eruptions happen about 20 times per day and vary in height between 100 to 180 feet. *(Ch. 3)*

16 Watch for Wildlife in America's Serengeti

In the northeastern corner of Yellowstone National Park, the Lamar Valley is renowned for wildlife, including bison, wolves, pronghorn, grizzly bears, bald eagles, and deer. *(Ch. 3)*

17 Experience the National Finals Skijoring Races

Since 1980, this has been the premiere event of the Red Lodge Winter Festival, where teams consisting of a horse, rider, and skier navigate a jumps and slalom gates at high speed. *(Ch. 4)*

18 Eat Huckleberry Pie

If Montana had an official state fruit, the wild huckleberry would definitely be in the running. When they're cooked in a flaky crust, it's epicurean magic. *(Ch. 5, 6)*

19 Ski Jackson Hole Mountain Resort

More than 2,500 acres of the best skiing and riding in North America await you. After a day carving up "cowboy powder," there's an incredible après ski scene to enjoy. *(Ch. 9)*

20 Cruise Through Grand Teton National Park

A sightseeing cruise on Jackson Lake gives you a unique perspective of Mount Moran. Some cruises also allow you to stop for a picnic on Elk Island. *(Ch. 8)*

21 Hit the Brew Trail in Billings

In the heart of downtown Billings you'll find six breweries, two distilleries, and a cider house. It's Montana's only walkable brewery trail, and it's a great place for a self-guided tour. *(Ch. 7)*

22 Drive the Beartooth Highway

The 68-mile-long scenic road is ruggedly beautiful. Tackling the switchbacks and the steep climb is worth it for the wonderful views of mountains, alpine meadows and sparkling lakes. *(Ch. 10)*

23 Visit the National Bison Range

One of the oldest wildlife refuges in America, the National Bison Range protects not only bison but also deer, elk, bighorn sheep, pronghorn, black bear, and 200 species of birds. *(Ch. 6)*

24 Experience River Tubing

Let the current take you on an exhilarating and refreshing journey. Tube rentals and river shuttles in Missoula make it easy to join the locals on the Blackfoot or Clark Fork River. *(Ch. 6)*

25 Visit Mammoth Hot Springs Terraces

Two terraced boardwalks pass through one of the most visually stunning areas of Yellowstone—an area with a complex of hot springs on a hill of travertine. *(Ch. 3)*

WHAT'S WHERE

1 Yellowstone National Park. Mountain men like John Colter and Jim Bridger knew Yellowstone was a wondrous place; today it remains just as alluring.

2 Bozeman, Helena, and Southwest Montana. Copper deposits made this region central to Montana's mining history, but its greatest treasures are its untamed forests and blue-ribbon trout streams.

3 Glacier National Park. The rugged mountains of Glacier draw 2 million visitors each year to hike its 730 miles of trails and take in the blues and emerald greens of its lakes and streams.

4 Missoula, Kalispell, and Northwest Montana. Flanked by the Bob Marshall Wilderness and watered by the lakes of the Seeley Valley, northwest Montana is a wild realm of nearly 3 million acres.

5 Great Falls, Billings, and the Montana Plains. East of the Rockies, the high plains of Montana and vast expanses of grassy prairie where cattle often outnumber

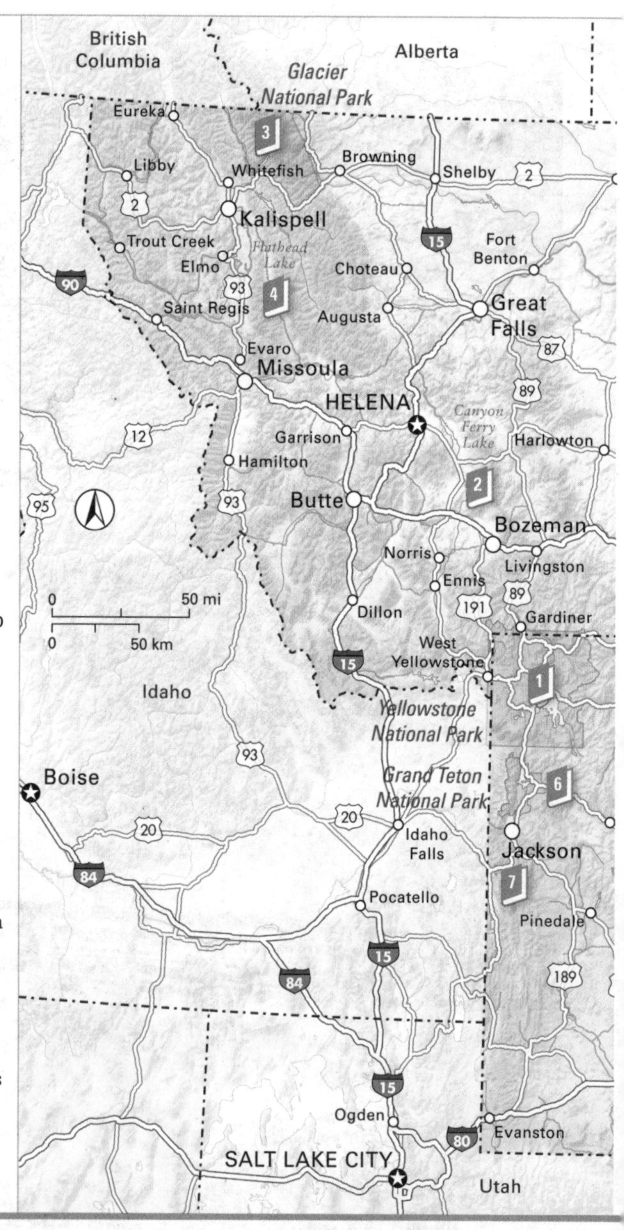

people, is an area rich with the history of America's last frontier.

6 Grand Teton National Park. You might think Grand Teton would suffer in comparison to Yellowstone, but the sight of the peaks rising out of Jackson Hole make the park its own spectacular destination.

7 Jackson and the Wind River Range. There's Jackson (the town) and Jackson Hole (the surrounding area); to the south is the Wind River range, home to the Wind River Reservation.

8 Cody, Sheridan, and Northern Wyoming. Northern Wyoming is divided almost exactly in half by the Big Horn Mountains. The wide-open plains of the Powder River Basin lie to the east. To the west is the Big Horn Basin, which is nearly as arid as a desert.

9 Cheyenne, Laramie, and Southern Wyoming. Southern Wyoming spans the wheat fields of the southeast, the lush meadows of the Platte River and Bridger valleys, and the wide-open sagebrush lands of the southwest. Cheyenne (the state capital) and Laramie are the largest towns.

Montana and Wyoming Today

Montana and Wyoming have a lot in common. They are two of the largest states in America by total land area, while also being two of the least populated states according to records of the United States Census Bureau. Cheyenne is the largest city in Wyoming; even still, its population is less than 65,000; Billings, the largest city in Montana, is larger, with a population estimate of 109,577. Simply put, however you look at it, there's a lot of wide-open space here and not that many people, and that explains a lot about what makes both states tick.

WILDERNESS AND WILDLIFE

With mountains, valleys, forests, deserts, grasslands, badlands, rivers, lakes, and canyons to explore, both states are ecologically diverse. The states have an abundance of federally protected lands, made up of national parks, national monuments, and national forests—including Yellowstone, which was the world's first national park, and the Bridger-Teton National Forest, the country's fifth-largest. The scenery is incredible, wildlife is abundant, and there are a vast number of recreational opportunities to enjoy. Both states are rich in natural resources that help sustain their respective economies.

The bison, Wyoming's state mammal, can be seen in many places throughout the two states. There are approximately 5,000 bison in Yellowstone National Park alone, and about 300 to 500 in the National Bison Range near Moiese, Montana. The grizzly bear is the state animal of Montana, and it's estimated that there are about 800 bears in the state: in Glacier National Park, Yellowstone National Park, and in other wilderness areas. Other animals of note include bighorn sheep, mountain goats, moose, elk, black bear, and pronghorn. Wyoming is home to one of the world's largest single herds of elk (typically more than 5,000 at the National Elk Refuge) and the world's largest population of pronghorn (now numbering some 400,000), which incidentally is the world's fastest hooved animal.

POLITICS

Wyoming has a long history of equality—so much so its official nickname is "the equality state." In 1869, Wyoming was the first territory to give women the right to vote. In 1870, Wyoming had the first female bailiff, the first female Justice of the Peace, and the first woman to serve on a grand jury. In 1920, the first woman voted in a presidential election. You can learn all about women and politics at The Wyoming House for Historic Women in Laramie, Wyoming. In recent years, Wyoming in particular has become more consistently Republican, with all its major office holders, Congressional representative, and a supermajority of legislators in both the state senate and house. Wyoming's single Congressional representative is Liz Cheney, the daughter of former Congressman and Vice President Dick Cheney; its senators are Cynthia Lummis and John Barrasso; the governor is Mark Gordon. Montana is slightly more politically diverse, with Republicans holding most but not all statewide offices; Montana still has one Democratic senator, Jon Tester, but its other senator, Steve Daines, and single Congressional representative, Matt Rosendale, are both Republicans, as is the governor, Greg Gianforte; both houses of its legislature have Republican majorities.

NATIVE AMERICANS IN MONTANA AND WYOMING

Montana is home to seven Native American reservations (governed by the Blackfeet, Chippewa Cree, Confederated Salish and Kootenai, Crow, Fort Belknap, Fort Peck, and Northern Cheyenne tribes) and the state-recognized Little Shell Chippewa Tribe. The Blackfeet Reservation and the Flathead Reservation rank in the top 10 for the largest Native American reservations in the United States by population. Although Wyoming was the historic home of five major tribes (the Arapaho, Cheyenne, Crow, Shoshone, and Ute), several other nomadic tribes came and went. Today, however, the state only has two recognized tribes: the Shoshone and Arapaho, both of whom live on the state's only Native American reservation—the Wind River Reservation. Named for its location in the Wind River Basin, it is the seventh-largest Native American reservation in the United States by area and the fifth-largest by population. The reservation was the setting for the 2017 film, *Wind River.* Throughout both states you'll find many indigenous historic sites. The Little Bighorn Battlefield National Monument in Montana and the Chief Joseph Scenic Byway in Wyoming both commemorate important battles between nomadic tribes and the U.S. Cavalry. There are many museums that feature Native American history and numerous sites throughout both states that are sacred to Native American people.

INDUSTRY

The oldest industries in Montana and Wyoming are ranching and farming, and agriculture is still vital to the economy of both states, but more so to Montana, where forestry and agriculture are the state's biggest industries. Mineral extraction and energy production are also important economic drivers. Wyoming is the eighth-largest oil producer in the United States, and mineral extraction is the state's biggest industry. The Powder River Basin and Green River Basin are important coal mining areas; the Salt Creek Field north of Casper is the state's most important center for oil and natural gas production.

Tourism brings a great deal of business to both states, with outdoor recreation as an area of growth. In Wyoming, tourism is the second most important industry; in Montana, it's the fifth. Wyoming welcomed 9.2 million overnight visitors in 2019, while almost 13 million tourists visited Montana in 2019. Tourist was down to both destinations due to the pandemic in 2020, but the drop was significantly less than in many other states that depend heavily on tourism, likely because many people come to both states for outdoor recreation.

Best of the West

LITTLE BIGHORN BATTLEFIELD NATIONAL MONUMENT

A visitor center, a museum, the 7th Cavalry Memorial, the Custer National Cemetery, and the Reno-Benteen Battlefield can all be seen at one of America's best-known historical landmarks in Crow Agency, Montana.

MONTANA STATE UNIVERSITY ANNUAL AMERICAN INDIAN COUNCIL POWWOW

With thousands of visitors and participants, the MSU American Indian Council Powwow in Bozeman is one of the largest powwows in Montana. It's a great place to experience Native American dancing, crafts and culture.

FORT LARAMIE NATIONAL HISTORIC SITE

Established in Wyoming in 1834, Fort Laramie grew into the largest military post on the Northern Plains before it was abandoned in 1890; just 14 miles northwest by car is the Oregon Trail Ruts National Historic Landmark.

MORMON ROW HISTORIC DISTRICT

Beginning in the 1890s, Mormon homesteaders established 27 homesteads north of Jackson, Wyoming, near Moose Junction. Photographers love to capture the historic buildings along Antelope Flats Road with the Teton Range in the background.

AMERICA'S FIRST DUDE RANCH

Eaton's Ranch sits on the eastern slopes of the Bighorn Mountains near Wolf, Wyoming. When it began welcoming visitors in 1904 as a place where urban folk could learn to rope, ride, and rodeo with weathered ranchers and professional cattle drivers, America's first dude ranch was born.

LIVINGSTON ROUNDUP

You haven't experienced the Wild West until you've been to a small-town rodeo. The Livingston Roundup has been held annually on July 4 weekend in Livingston, Montana, since the 1920s, attracting top cowboys and offering nightly fireworks. It's a PRCA-sanctioned event now.

World Championship Indian Relay Races in Sheridan, WY

WYOMING STATE FAIR
Since 1905, the Wyoming State Fair has been held in the old railroad town of Douglas, Wyoming, every August. It has thrilled visitors and locals alike with exhibits, carnival, live entertainment, rodeo, demolition derby, arm wrestling competitions, and more. If you come to the fair, don't forget to pay homage to the majestic beast commemorated in Jackalope Square (the pronghorn/jackrabbit hybrid was created here).

WORLD CHAMPIONSHIP INDIAN RELAY RACES
One rider, three horses, two holders, and a mugger make up a team for the World Championship Indian Relay Races in Sheridan, Wyoming, part of the annual Sheridan WYO Rodeo each year, along with a Native American Powwow and Dance. It's edge-of-your-seat excitement as riders race around a track switching horses twice.

MONTANA HISTORICAL SOCIETY MUSEUM
"Montana's Museum" lets you explore 12,000 years of the state's history in the state capital of Helena. In addition to its summer programs on folk music, Native American culture, and cowboys, it's also home to an incredible collection of Charles M. Russell art and historic photographs of Yellowstone by F. Jay Haynes.

LEWIS & CLARK NATIONAL HISTORIC TRAIL INTERPRETIVE CENTER
Built into a scenic bluff above the Missouri River in Great Falls, this Montana museum celebrates the 1804–06 Lewis and Clark Expedition's 8,000-mile journey across western North America.

Wild Wonders of Montana and Wyoming

HIGHLINE TRAIL

The 7.2-mile round-trip hike from Logan Pass to Haystack Pass traverses the western side of the Continental Divide in Glacier National Park. It offers incredible views of beautiful alpine meadows and expansive mountain vistas.

NATIONAL ELK REFUGE

The National Elk Refuge outside Jackson, Wyoming offers fantastic wildlife viewing year-round. It's a good place to see elk as well as bison, wolves, bighorn sheep, bald eagles, and trumpeter swans.

MEDICINE ROCKS STATE PARK

Listed on the National Register of Historic Places, the park in eastern Montana is known for its sandstone pillars that stand up to 80 feet tall and are marked with unusual holes, tunnels, and undulations. The giant rocks look a little like Swiss cheese. Theodore Roosevelt was struck by the area's beauty.

AMERICAN PRAIRIE RESERVE

Dark skies and vast grasslands make up this rugged and remote prairie reserve on Montana's Great Plains. It is one of the most remote areas in the lower 48 states. You need to be self-sufficient to stay here, but the reward is a chance to experience the beauty of the wild, unbroken prairie and its wildlife.

PRYOR MOUNTAIN WILD MUSTANG CENTER
Wild horses roam free in the Pryor Mountains near Lovell, Wyoming, and seeing them can be an experience of a lifetime. It is believed the wild mustangs at the center are descended from Spanish horses brought to the area by Native Americans.

MAKOSHIKA STATE PARK
Montana's largest state park has fascinating badlands that hide many fossils. The name "Makoshika" is derived from a Lakota phrase meaning "bad land" or "bad earth."

HAYDEN VALLEY
Make the Hayden Valley your first stop for wildlife-viewing in Yellowstone National Park. Centrally located, the broad valley is home to herds of bison, elk, grizzly bears and many birds.

THE CHINESE WALL
The Chinese Wall is a legendary multiday backpacking trip that leads to a 1,000 foot high limestone wall that stretches for miles along the Continental Divide in Montana's Bob Marshall Wilderness Complex.

CHIEF JOSEPH SCENIC BYWAY
WY 296 is an incredibly scenic, 47-mile drive that is a historically significant reminder of the Native American struggle. The roadway connects the town of Cody with the Beartooth Highway and the North-east Gate of Yellowstone National Park.

SEEDSKADEE NATIONAL WILDLIFE REFUGE COMPLEX
The Seedskadee National Wildlife Refuge Complex near Green River, provides habitat for more than 220 species of birds and other wildlife. It's one of the best birding spots in Wyoming.

10 Great Photo Ops

GARDEN OF ONE THOUSAND BUDDHAS
You don't expect to find a Buddhist shrine on a Native American reservation, but that's part of what makes the Garden of One Thousand Buddhas special. And yes—there really are 1,000 Buddhas in the 750 foot circular monument in Arlee, Montana.

DEVIL'S TOWER NATIONAL MONUMENT
Sacred to several Native American tribes, Devil's Tower is a stunning geologic feature scored with hundreds of parallel cracks that rises out of the prairie near Wyoming's Black Hills.

AVALANCHE LAKE
A moderate 4.5-mile hike brings you to this stunning backcountry lake on the west side of Glacier National Park. Bring your best camera because the reflections are incredible against a backdrop of mountains and waterfalls.

GRAND PRISMATIC SPRING
This multicolor spring in the Midway Geyser Basin north of Old Faithful—some 370 feet in diameter—is the most photographed thermal feature in Yellowstone National Park and the third-largest spring in the world. Its deep blue color surrounded by rings of orange and yellow make it instantly recognizable in photographs. Hike the Fairy Falls Trail to the overlook to get the best views.

OXBOW BEND
Made famous by photographer Ansel Adams, this bend on the Snake River has become one of the most photographed spots in Grand Teton National Park. If you're lucky, you may also spot sandhill cranes, trumpeter swans, and great blue herons. The quintessential photo is of a reflection of Mount Moran, usually seen in the calm early morning water.

MAMMOTH HOT SPRINGS
The intricate travertine formations are said to look like a cave turned inside out. This area in the northwestern corner of Yellowstone is one of the national park's most uniquely beautiful spots. If you have an hour to spare, take the Lower Terrace Interpretive Trail for views of bright, ornately terraced Minerva Spring. Alternatively, you can drive to the Lower Terrace Overlook on Upper Terrace Drive, but you still have to hike down to get the best views.

Grand Prismatic Spring

BIGHORN CANYON NATIONAL RECREATION AREA
The grandest canyon of the northern Rockies has colorful, 1,000-foot-high walls. Much of it is filled by a 60-mile-long lake, which was created when the Yellowtail Dam was built in the 1960s; today the steep canyon walls make for a marvelous photo op. In peak summer, you can rent a boat at one of the many marinas on the lake to get a good shot of the canyon walls.

POMPEYS PILLAR NATIONAL MONUMENT
In 1805, Captain William Clark carved his name in this 200-foot-high sandstone rock formation 30 miles east of Billings. Climb to the top of the mesa for the best views and to see the historic graffiti; it reads like a history book of the western frontier.

SNAKE RIVER OVERLOOK
A commanding view of the Teton Range can be seen from the roadside pullout on the main highway just north of Moose, Wyoming. Use your panoramic lens to capture the mountain peaks in the background.

WILD GOOSE ISLAND OVERLOOK
One of the most famous photo stops on the Going-to-the-Sun Road in Glacier National Park gives you the perfect view of this island rising out of Lake McDonald, which is surrounded by thick forests and majestic mountains. You can also see the island on a cruise from Lake Macdonald Lodge, but it's the drive high above the lake that offers the quintessential photography spot.

Montana and Wyoming with Kids

Whether you're hiking to a glacier, skipping rocks across a lake, or watching a geyser erupt right on schedule, Montana and Wyoming have unique adventures that make lasting family memories. Here are a few ideas to help you plan an awesome vacation with kids.

GET THE KIDS EXCITED

Involving your kids in age-appropriate planning of parts of the vacation gets them invested and excited. Even small children can help make decisions about the trip if you give them a list of optional activities and let them decide which ones to put on the itinerary. Here are some great children's books to educate and excite kids about exploring the key national parks in Montana and Wyoming.

A Weird and Wild Beauty: The Story of Yellowstone, the World's First National Park by Erin Peabody.

Yellowstone National Park for Kids, Preteens, and Teenagers: A Grande Guides Series Book for Children by Stephanie Del Grande.

What I Saw in Yellowstone: A Kid's Guide to the National Park by Durrae Johanek, photographs by Christopher Cauble.

What I Saw in Glacier: A Kid's Guide to the National Park by Ellen Horowitz, photographs by Christopher Cauble.

What I Saw in Grand Teton: A Kid's Guide to the National Park by Julie Gillum Lue, photographs by Christopher Cauble.

Junior Ranger Activity Book: Puzzles, Games, Facts, and Tons More Fun Inspired by the U.S. National Parks! by National Geographic Kids

OUTDOOR ADVENTURES

Most kids love getting outside and being active, and there are plenty of outdoor adventures to enjoy in Montana and Wyoming. Hiking, biking, horseback riding, whitewater rafting, boating, fishing, and wildlife watching are some of the activities families can enjoy together. You'll find playgrounds, community swimming pools, skateboard parks and other kid-friendly amenities in towns and cities throughout these states. Local tourism information centers can help you locate kid-friendly amenities in a particular area.

LEARNING IS FUN!

There are many opportunities to learn about nature, history and science in Montana and Wyoming. Here are a few of the best children's museums and kid-centric attractions to check out:

- Explorationworks, Helena, MT
- Montana Science Center, Bozeman, MT
- Children's Museum of Montana, Great Falls, MT
- Montana Natural History Center, Missoula, MT
- Wise Wonders Children's Museum, Billings, MT
- Buffalo Bill Historical Center, Cody, WY
- Lander Children's Museum, Lander, WY
- Teton Raptor Center, Wilson, WY
- Wyoming Dinosaur Center, Thermopolis, WY

What to Watch and Read Before Your Trip

AMERICAN SERENGETI: THE LAST BIG ANIMALS OF THE GREAT PLAINS

An award-winning examination of the animals that once roamed America's vast plains in abundance by outdoorsman and Professor Emeritus at the University of Montana Dan Flores.

A RIVER RUNS THROUGH IT

This 1992 film, directed by Robert Redford and starring Brad Pitt, may inspire you to take up fly-fishing. It's a deeply moving drama based on writer Norman Maclean's semi-autobiographical novella about life growing up in and around Missoula, Montana.

LEGENDS OF THE FALL

Set in the wilderness of Montana in the early 20th century, this 1994 historical drama, based on the novella of the same name by Jim Harrison, features an all-star cast including Brad Pitt, Anthony Hopkins, Aidan Quinn, Julia Ormond, and Henry Thomas. It tells the story of three brothers and how their lives are affected by love and war.

WIND RIVER

A U.S. Fish and Wildlife Service tracker (Jeremy Renner) and an FBI agent (Elizabeth Olsen) work together to solve a murder on the Wind River Reservation in Wyoming in this 2017 film written and directed by Taylor Sheridan.

UNFORGIVEN

For a taste of the Wild West complete with gunfighters, you can't beat this 1992 film. The story is set in the 1800s in the fictional town of Big Whiskey, Wyoming. Clint Eastwood directs and stars alongside Gene Hackman, Morgan Freeman, and Richard Harris.

THE HORSE WHISPERER

This 1995 bestselling novel by Nicholas Evans was made into a film by the same name in 1998, directed by and starring Robert Redford. Following an accident, a horse and its young rider are injured and severely traumatized, so the owner travels across the country to visit a "horse whisperer" on a Montana Ranch.

THE WHISTLING SEASON

In the autumn of 1909, widower Oliver Milliron hires Rose Llewellyn to be his housekeeper; she and her brother Morris Morgan end up in Marias Coulee, Montana, along with a slew of homesteaders lured by the promise of free land and a new life in this novel by Ivan Doig.

DECADE OF THE WOLF: RETURNING THE WILD TO YELLOWSTONE

This book provides an inside look at the Yellowstone Wolf Recovery Project. Project leader Douglas W. Smith and nature writer Gary Ferguson track the journey of 31 Canadian gray wolves released in Yellowstone National Park in 1995 and 1996.

THE STORIES OF YELLOWSTONE: ADVENTURE TALES FROM THE WORLD'S FIRST NATIONAL PARK

This book by M. Mark Miller covers the early history of Yellowstone from 1807, when John Colter first discovered the Yellowstone Plateau, to the 1920s golden age of tourist travel. The tales come from the letters, journals, and diaries of early visitors and tourists.

LETTERS FROM YELLOWSTONE

Diane Smith's engaging novel is set in Yellowstone in 1898 and offers a female perspective on its history. The plot centers on a young Cornell medical student who is invited to be the botanist for a Smithsonian-sponsored field study, although the study leader does not realize she is female when the invitation is extended.

Four Reasons to Visit Montana and Wyoming in Winter

There's a special kind of beauty to be found in Montana and Wyoming in winter when trees are frosty and mountains are covered in buckets of pristine white snow. It's also a time to enjoy unique outdoor activities, including some that can't be experienced anywhere else. Here are five great reasons to experience these states in winter.

SOME OF THE BEST SKIING IN NORTH AMERICA

Jaw-dropping terrain and dry light powder are key ingredients for a phenomenal ski experience and Wyoming and Montana have an abundance of both. There are many downhill ski resorts in both states. Jackson Hole Mountain Resort and Grand Targhee are two of the best in Wyoming; Big Sky Resort and Whitefish Mountain Resort are two that should not be missed in Montana. There are also many amazing backcountry and cross-country ski trails in both states.

INCREDIBLE ADVENTURES YOU CAN'T FIND ANYWHERE ELSE

Winter is prime time for adventure sports in Montana and Wyoming. Snowmobiling, ice climbing, winter hiking, snowshoeing, fat biking, ice fishing, and dogsledding are just a few of the amazing activities to be experienced. There are also adventures you can't find anywhere else like a horse-drawn sleigh ride in the National Elk Refuge, the National Finals Skijoring Races, and several fantastic winter festivals.

WINTER WILDLIFE WATCHING

While it's true that some animals hibernate in winter, there are many animals that are very active during the colder months. Winter is a good time to see bison, elk, moose, deer, pronghorn, and bighorn sheep. It's important to check road conditions before setting out: some roads close in winter, and others may become impassable in icy conditions. Top spots for viewing wildlife in winter include the National Elk Refuge, the National Bighorn Sheep Center, Grand Teton National Park, Yellowstone National Park, and Glacier National Park.

NATIONAL PARKS ARE BEAUTIFUL AND UNCROWDED IN WINTER

A winter visit to the national parks is a chance to experience these parks in a new light without crowds. Some areas of the national parks are closed in winter, so it's important to verify that the areas you plan to visit are open before setting out. Some area services may also be closed during the winter, but the payoff is a chance to experience the majesty of the parks when they are blanketed in snow and in some cases to have that beauty all to yourself.

Chapter 2

TRAVEL SMART

Updated by
Debbie Olsen

★ **CAPITALS:**
Helena, MT; Cheyenne, WY

POPULATION:
Montana: 1,068,778;
Wyoming: 578,759

LANGUAGE:
English

$ CURRENCY:
U.S. dollar

AREA CODE:
406 (MT), 307 (WY)

EMERGENCIES:
911

DRIVING:
On the right

ELECTRICITY:
120–220 v/60 cycles;
plugs have two or three rectangular prongs

TIME:
Mountain Time (2 hours behind New York)

WEB RESOURCES:
www.visitmt.com
travelwyoming.com

AIRPORTS:
Montana, Billings: BIL
Bozeman: BZN
Great Falls: GTF
Glacier Park: FCA
Missoula: MSO
Wyoming, Casper: CPR
Jackson Hole: JAC

Know Before You Go

WHEN THEY SAY "BIG SKY COUNTRY," THEY MEAN IT
Montana is the fourth-largest state by total land area, and Wyoming ranks as the tenth-largest state. It takes time to thoroughly explore these states, because there's so much territory to cover. Don't expect to see everything in a single weekend.

COVID-19
Having a lot of wide open space and a low population has its advantages in a pandemic. Wyoming is the least-populated state in the United States and Montana is also sparsely populated, but these states were still affected by COVID-19. At the peak of the pandemic, capacity restraints were placed on restaurants, bars, breweries, distilleries, and casinos. Restrictions were placed on some personal service businesses, mask mandates were put in place, and there were size limits on public gatherings. It is recommended that you review public health and travel advisories prior to your arrival and follow all public health orders during your visit.

PUBLIC TRANSPORTATION IS LIMITED
Public transportation is available in major cities and connecting major cities and towns, but there are some places in these states that simply don't have public transportation. Renting a car or driving your own vehicle is the most convenient way to get around—especially in rural areas and more remote communities. Vehicle rentals are available at airports, train stations, and in towns and cities throughout both states.

BE ON THE LOOKOUT FOR WILDLIFE
It's common to see wildlife on or near roadways inside the national parks and even in areas far from national parks. If you want to take a closer look at any wildlife while you're driving, slow down, turn on your hazard lights, and carefully pull over to the side of the road. Always stay inside the vehicle while you view it. Be conscious of other vehicles on the road and move on if a traffic jam develops. Stay inside your vehicle to observe and photograph wildlife, and never feed any wild animals. This is important for your own safety and for the health and well-being of the animals. Getting outside the vehicle can agitate an animal and cause the animal to become more habituated to humans. It can also cause an animal to become aggressive. If an animal injures a person, it may need to be put down by park staff or removed from the wild. Staying inside your vehicle protects the wildlife you are viewing and helps them stay wild.

PACK SOME BEAR SPRAY—YOU'RE IN BEAR COUNTRY
Montana and Wyoming are home to hundreds of bears. Seeing a black bear or a grizzly in their natural habitat is an extraordinary experience—as long as you do it safely. Whether you are hiking, camping, cycling, or enjoying any other outdoor activity in bear country, it is important to know what to do if you encounter a bear. Be bear aware, and follow bear-safety tips offered from the national parks. When you're camping, store food in a vehicle or in a bear box well away from your tent. Never hike alone. Make noise when you are hiking along trails. Bear attacks are rare, but the biggest danger comes from startling a bear. All campers and hikers in bear country should carry EPA-approved bear spray in an accessible location outside your pack and learn how to use it properly.

BOATING IN MONTANA AND WYOMING

Nonresidents launching watercraft in Montana must purchase a Vessel AIS (Aquatic Invasive Species) Prevention Pass; in Wyoming, an AIS decal must be purchased. This applies to motorized as well as nonmotorized watercraft such as rafts, kayaks, drift boats, catamarans, and sailboats. (In Wyoming, inflatable watercraft that are less than 10 feet in length are exempt from the AIS decal provision.) In both states, you can be fined if you fail to purchase the pass or decal. The purchase of these passes helps to fund the Aquatic Invasive Species prevention programs in the states.

HOW TO CHOOSE YOUR RIDE

The type of vehicle you rent depends on your intended itinerary. If you're planning to travel on backcountry or gravel roads, consider renting an SUV. If you're visiting the national parks, a higher vehicle can make wildlife viewing better—especially for children sitting in the backseat. A four-wheel-drive vehicle can be useful in winter, especially if you are traversing icy roads in mountainous areas.

SOME ATTRACTIONS AND BUSINESSES CLOSE IN WINTER

Winter is wonderful in Montana and Wyoming, but some areas, services, and roadways inside the national parks are closed or otherwise inaccessible in winter. Make sure the places you plan to visit are open before you go. In Yellowstone National Park, you can only access the park's interior and see the Old Faithful Geyser via a chartered snowcoach or a snowmobile. Be sure to reserve the snowcoach seat or a snowmobile rental well in advance of your visit, as they can sell out. Some accommodations inside the national parks are also closed during the winter. Similarly, many guest ranches, museums, and businesses far from the national parks also close in winter or have reduced hours. But there's plenty to see and do year-round in both states.

NATIONAL PARKS HAVE GREAT LEARNING PROGRAMS

Several nonprofit organizations run unique educational programs within the national parks. The Yellowstone Forever Institute, the Glacier Institute, and Teton Science Schools are some of the organizations that provide entertaining tours and experiences that help you learn about the national parks. Experiences may last a few hours or a few days and need to be booked in advance. The national park service also offers a free self-guided learning program for children called the junior ranger program. The junior ranger program does not need to be booked in advance.

PLAN FAR IN ADVANCE FOR PEAK SEASON TRAVEL

Book accommodations and car rentals well in advance (months ahead if you can), especially if you are traveling during the peak summer season. Hotels and vehicles sometimes sell out, and you may be disappointed if you don't plan ahead. Iconic properties like the Old Faithful Inn often book out 8 to 12 months in advance. Guided tours and excursions should also be booked in advance to avoid disappointment. Go early or late (after 5 pm) to popular sites in the national parks and you'll have a better chance of finding parking during the peak season.

Getting Here and Around

 Air

The best connections to Montana and often the shortest flights to Wyoming are through the Rockies hub cities Salt Lake City and Denver. Montana also receives transfer flights from Minneapolis, Seattle, and Phoenix. Rapid City Regional Airport has direct flights from Denver, Salt Lake City, Minneapolis, and Chicago; from there parts of northeastern Wyoming are within easy striking distance. Once you have made your way to Denver or Salt Lake City, you will still have one or two hours of flying time to reach your final airport destination. Many of the airports in these states are served by commuter flights that have frequent stops, though generally with very short layovers. There are no direct flights from New York to the area, and most itineraries from New York take between seven and nine hours. Likewise, you cannot fly direct from Los Angeles to Montana or Wyoming; it will take you four or five hours to get here from there.

At smaller airports you may need to be on hand only an hour before the flight. If you're traveling during snow season, allow extra time for the drive to the airport, as weather conditions can slow you down. If you'll be checking skis, arrive even earlier.

AIRPORTS

The major gateways in Montana include Missoula International Airport (MSO) and Glacier Park International Airport (GPI; in Kalispell); in Wyoming, Jackson Hole Airport (JAC), Cheyenne Regional Airport (CYS), Natrona County International Airport (CPR; in Casper), and Yellowstone Regional Airport (COD; in Cody); and in South Dakota, Rapid City Regional Airport (RAP), which is more convenient for some destinations in northeastern Wyoming. A flight to Denver International Airport (DEN) is sometimes much cheaper than a flight into Cheyenne, about two hours away by car, and there are regularly scheduled shuttles, too.

AIRPORT TRANSFERS

All airports listed in Montana, Wyoming, and South Dakota offer shuttle services, as well as taxis and rental cars, to nearby residences and lodging properties. Thrifty travelers prefer sharing a shuttle, which can often cut costs by half, to hiring a taxi. In general, shuttles and taxis will cost less here than in urban centers. For shuttles, establish a set price with your driver before you depart from the airport to avoid any surprises, and get contact information or establish a pickup time for your return to the airport at the conclusion of your trip. Don't forget to tip—generally about $2 per bag.

 Bus

There are three main options for public bus transportation in Montana and Wyoming. Greyhound covers both states with ten stops in Montana and ten in Wyoming. Jefferson Lines has 15 stops in Montana and three in Wyoming. Express Arrow also offers bus service in Wyoming with 10 stops in the state. But once you arrive at your destination, you'll almost certainly still need a car to get around.

 Car

You'll seldom be bored driving through the Rockies and plains, which offer some of the most spectacular vistas and challenging driving in the world. Montana's interstate system is driver-friendly, connecting soaring summits, rivers, glacial valleys, forests, lakes, and vast stretches of prairie, all capped by that endless "Big Sky." Wyoming's interstates link classic, open-range cowboy country and mountain-range vistas with state highways headed to the geothermal wonderland of Yellowstone National Park. In Wyoming everything is separated by vast distances, so be sure to leave each major city with a full tank of gas, and be prepared to see lots of wildlife and few other people.

Before setting out on any driving trip, it's important to make sure your vehicle is in top condition. It's best to have a complete tune-up. At the least, you should check the following: lights, including brake lights, backup lights, and emergency lights; tires, including the spare; oil; engine coolant; windshield-washer fluid; windshield-wiper blades; and brakes. For emergencies, take along flares or reflector triangles, jumper cables, an empty gas can, a fire extinguisher, a flashlight, a plastic tarp, blankets, water, and coins or a calling card for phone calls (cell phones don't always work in high mountain areas). In the Rockies and plains, as across the nation, gasoline costs fluctuate often.

BORDER CROSSINGS

Driving a car across the U.S.–Canadian border is simple. U.S. Citizens require a passport or a passport card. Citizens of other countries might also require a visa to enter Canada. Personal vehicles are allowed entry into the neighboring country, provided they are not to be left behind. Drivers must have owner registration and proof of insurance coverage handy. If the car isn't registered in your name, carry a letter from the owner that authorizes your use of the vehicle. Drivers in rental cars that are permitted to cross the border should bring along a copy of the rental contract, which should bear an endorsement saying that the vehicle is permitted to cross the border.

CAR RENTALS

Rates in most Montana and Wyoming cities run about $79 a day and about $554 per week for an economy car with air-conditioning, automatic transmission, and unlimited mileage. In resort areas such as Jackson or Kalispell, you'll usually find a variety of 4X4s and SUVs for rent, many of them with ski racks. Unless you plan to do a lot of mountain exploring, a four-wheel drive is usually needed only in winter, but if you do plan to venture onto any back roads, an SUV (about $115 a day) is the best bet because it will have higher clearance. Book your rental in advance to save money and avoid disappointment. Rentals can completely book out during peak travel times. Rates do not include tax on car rentals, which is 4% in Montana, 4% in Wyoming and 4.5% in South Dakota. If you rent from an airport location there may be an additional airport-concession fee.

Surcharges may apply if you're under 25 or if you take the car outside the area approved by the rental agency. You'll pay extra for child seats, which are compulsory for children under six years (under nine in Wyoming) and weighing less than 60 pounds and cost $10 to $15 a day, and usually for additional drivers (up to $25 a day, depending on location).

DRIVING

Roads range from multilane blacktop to barely traveled backcountry trails. Many twisting switchbacks are considerately marked with guardrails, but some primitive roads have a lane so narrow that you must back up to the edge of a steep cliff to make a turn. Scenic routes and lookout points are clearly marked, enabling you to slow down and pull over to take in the views.

Getting Here and Around

DRIVING IN SNOW

Highway driving through mountains and plains is safe and generally trouble-free even in cold weather. Although winter driving can present challenges, road maintenance is good and plowing is prompt. In mountain areas tire chains, studs, or snow tires are essential. If you're driving into high elevations, check the weather forecast and call for road conditions beforehand. Even main highways can close. Winter weather isn't confined to winter months in the high country, so be prepared: carry an emergency kit containing warm clothes, a flashlight, food and water, and blankets. It's also good to carry a cell phone, but be aware that the mountains, and distance from cell towers, can disrupt service. If you get stalled by deep snow, do not leave your car. Wait for help, running the engine only if needed (keep the exhaust clear, and occasionally open a window for fresh air). Assistance is never far away.

GASOLINE

Gas prices in Montana and Wyoming are fairly reasonable and quite comparable to other parts of the country. You'll find fuel stations in most communities. If you're traveling in more remote areas of these states, gas stations can be less common, so you should fill up whenever you can.

RULES OF THE ROAD

You'll find highways and the national parks crowded in summer, and almost deserted (and occasionally impassable) in winter. You may turn right at a red light after stopping if there is no sign saying otherwise and no oncoming traffic. When in doubt, wait for the green. Follow the posted speed limit, drive defensively, and make sure your gas tank is full. In Montana and Wyoming, the law requires that the driver and all passengers wear seat belts. Car seats are compulsory for children under six in Montana and under nine in Wyoming.

 Ride-Sharing

Uber and Lyft are the main ride-sharing services available in major cities in Montana and Wyoming. It's a good option for getting around these cities or for getting to the city from the airport. Ride-sharing is usually not available in smaller towns.

 Taxi

Taxi service is available in most major cities and can be useful for travelers on short trips within a metropolitan area. Some companies use fixed rates, while others use a meter. Fares are reasonable and you must phone the taxi company for pickup rather than hailing a cab from the street. Most taxi companies are open 24 hours.

 Train

Amtrak connects the Rockies and plains to both coasts and all major American cities. Trains run through northern Montana, with stops in Essex and Whitefish, near Glacier National Park. Connecting bus services to Yellowstone National Park are provided in the summer from Amtrak's stop in Pocatello, Idaho.

Essentials

Dining

Dining in Montana and Wyoming is generally casual. Menus are becoming more varied, with such regional specialties as trout, elk, or buffalo, but you can nearly always order a hamburger or a steak. Authentic ethnic food—other than Mexican—is hard to find outside of cities. Dinner hours are from 6 pm to 9 pm. Outside the large cities and resort towns in the high seasons, many restaurants close by 9 or 10 pm. The restaurants we list are the cream of the crop in each price category.

PAYING

Most restaurants take credit cards, but some smaller places still do not. It's worth asking. Waiters expect a 20% tip at high-end restaurants; some add an automatic gratuity for groups of six or more.

RESERVATIONS AND DRESS

Regardless of where you are, it's a good idea to make a reservation if you can. We mention them specifically only when reservations are essential (there's no other way you'll ever get a table) or when they are not accepted. (Large parties should always call ahead to check the reservations policy.) We mention dress only when men are required to wear a jacket or a jacket and tie.

MEALS AND MEALTIMES

You can find all types of cuisine in the major cities and resort towns, but don't forget to try native dishes such as trout, elk, and bison (the latter two have less fat than beef and are just as tasty); organic fruits and vegetables are also readily available. When in doubt, go for a steak, forever a Rocky Mountain and northern plains mainstay.

Rocky Mountain oysters, simply put, are bull testicles. They're generally served fried, although you can get them lots of different ways. You can find them all over the West, usually at down-home eateries, steak houses, and the like.

Unless otherwise noted, the restaurants listed in this guide are open daily for lunch and dinner.

SMOKING

Smoking is banned in all restaurants and bars in Montana. There is no state-wide smoking ban in Wyoming. Some Wyoming communities have banned smoking in indoor spaces while others leave it up to the business owner to decide whether or not smoking is allowed on their premises.

What It Costs

	$	$$	$$$	$$$$
AT DINNER	under $10	$10–$18	$19–$30	over $30

Health and Safety

COVID-19

A new novel coronavirus brought all travel to a virtual standstill in the first half of 2020. Although the illness is mild in most people, some experience severe and even life-threatening complications. Once travel started up again, albeit slowly and cautiously, travelers were asked to be particularly careful about hygiene and to avoid any unnecessary travel, especially if they are sick.

Older adults, especially those over 65, have a greater chance of having severe complications from COVID-19. The same is true for people with weaker immune systems or those living with some types of medical conditions, including diabetes, asthma, heart disease, cancer, HIV/AIDS,

Essentials

kidney disease, and liver disease. Starting two weeks before a trip, anyone planning to travel should be on the lookout for some of the following symptoms: cough, fever, chills, trouble breathing, muscle pain, sore throat, new loss of smell or taste. If you experience any of these symptoms, you should not travel at all.

And to protect yourself during travel, do your best to avoid contact with people showing symptoms. Wash your hands often with soap and water. Limit your time in public places, and, when you are out and about, wear a cloth face mask that covers your nose and mouth. Indeed, a mask may be required in some places, such as on an airplane or in a confined space like a theater, where you share the space with a lot of people. You may wish to bring extra supplies, such as disinfecting wipes, hand sanitizer (12-ounce bottles were allowed in carry-on luggage at this writing), and a first-aid kit with a thermometer.

Given how abruptly travel was curtailed in March 2020, it is wise to consider protecting yourself by purchasing a travel insurance policy that will reimburse you for any costs due to COVID-19-related cancellations. Not all travel insurance policies protect against pandemic-related cancellations, so always read the fine print.

OUTDOOR SAFETY

Many trails in the Rockies and northern plains are remote and sparsely traveled. In the high altitudes of the mountains, oxygen is scarce. Hikers, bikers, and riders should carry emergency supplies in their backpacks. Proper equipment includes a flashlight, a compass, waterproof matches, a first-aid kit, a knife, a cell phone with an extra battery (although you may have to climb atop a mountain ridge to find a signal), and a light plastic tarp for shelter. Backcountry skiers should add a repair kit, a blanket, an avalanche beacon, and a lightweight shovel to their lists. Always bring extra food and a canteen of water, as dehydration is a common occurrence at high altitudes. Never drink from streams or lakes, unless you boil the water first or purify it with tablets. Giardia, an intestinal parasite, may be present. It's a good idea to dress in layers as it can get cold at high altitudes—even in summer.

ALTITUDE

You may feel dizzy and weak and find yourself breathing heavily—signs that the thin mountain air isn't giving you your accustomed dose of oxygen. Take it easy and rest often for a few days until you're acclimatized. Throughout your stay drink plenty of water and watch your alcohol consumption. If you experience severe headaches and nausea, see a doctor. It is easy to go too high too fast. The remedy for altitude-related discomfort is to go down quickly into heavier air. Other altitude-related problems include dehydration and overexposure to the sun because of the thin air.

EXPOSURE

The high elevation, severe cold temperatures, and sometimes windy weather in Montana and Wyoming can often combine to create intense and dangerous outdoor conditions. In winter, exposure to wind and cold can quickly bring on hypothermia or frostbite. Protect yourself by dressing in layers, so you don't become overheated and then chilled. Any time of year, the region's clear air and high elevation make sunburn a particular risk. Always wear sunscreen, even when skies are overcast.

FLASH FLOODS

Flash floods can strike at any time and any place with little or no warning. Mountainous terrain can become dangerous when distant rains are channeled into gullies and ravines, turning a quiet streamside campsite or wash into a rampaging torrent in seconds. Similarly, desert terrain floods quickly when the land is unable to absorb heavy rain. Check weather reports before heading into the backcountry and be prepared to head for higher ground if the weather turns severe.

WILD ANIMALS

One of the most wonderful parts of the Rockies and plains is the abundant wildlife. And although a herd of grazing elk or a bighorn sheep high on a hillside is most certainly a Kodak moment, an encounter with a bear, an American bison, or a mountain lion is not. To avoid such a dangerous situation while hiking, make plenty of noise, keep dogs on a leash, and keep small children between adults. While camping, be sure to store all food, utensils, and clothing with food odors far away from your tent, preferably high in a tree (also far from your tent). If you do come across a bear or big cat, do not run. For bears, back away quietly; for lions, make yourself look as big as possible. In either case, be prepared to fend off the animal with loud noises, rocks, sticks, and so on. And as the saying goes, do not feed the bears—or any wild animals, whether they're dangerous or not.

When in the wilderness, give all animals their space and never attempt to feed any of them. If you want to take a photograph, use a long lens rather than a long sneak to approach closely. This is particularly important for winter visitors. Approaching an animal can cause it stress and affect its ability to survive the sometimes brutal climate. In all cases, remember that the animals have the right-of-way; this is their home, and you are the visitor.

Immunizations

There are no immunization requirements for visitors traveling to the United States for tourism.

Lodging

Accommodations in the Rockies and plains vary from posh resorts in ski areas such as Jackson Hole to basic chain hotels and independent motels. Dude and guest ranches often require a one-week minimum stay, and the cost is usually all-inclusive. Bed-and-breakfasts can be found throughout the Rockies and plains.

The lodgings we list are the cream of the crop in each price category. We list available facilities, but we don't specify whether they cost extra. When pricing accommodations, always ask what's included and what costs extra.

Most hotels and other lodgings can be booked online or over the phone with a credit card. However you book, get a confirmation in writing or via email and have it handy when you check in. Some mom-and-pop establishments still don't have websites (other than Facebook), but you might still be able to book on a third-party reservation site.

Be sure you understand the accommodation's cancellation policy. Some places allow you to cancel without any kind of penalty—even if you prepaid to secure a discounted rate—if you cancel at least 24 hours in advance. Others require you to cancel a week or more in advance or penalize you the cost of one night. Small inns and B&Bs are most likely to require you to cancel far in advance. Dude ranches are most likely to require a nonrefundable payment in advance of travel. Most hotels allow children under a certain age

Essentials

to stay in their parents' room at no extra charge, but others charge for them as extra adults; find out the cutoff age for discounts and the maximum number of guests allowed per room—including children and infants.

FACILITIES

You can assume that all rooms have private baths, phones, TVs, and air-conditioning, unless otherwise indicated. "Free breakfast" is noted when it is included in the rate, but it's not a typical perk at most Montana and Wyoming hotels (except for the limited-service chains that usually include it in the rates). There are a few hotels with pools, though some are indoors.

PARKING

In almost all cases throughout both states, parking is free, and only in a resort area like Jackson Hole's Teton Village will you have to pay a fee.

BED-AND-BREAKFASTS

Charm is the long suit of these establishments, which generally occupy a restored older building with some historical or architectural significance. They tend to be small, with fewer than 20 rooms. Breakfast is usually included in the rates, and sometimes there are other amenities and perks like afternoon tea service.

CABIN AND CONDO RENTALS

There are rental opportunities throughout Montana and Wyoming, with the best selection in resort areas such as Big Sky and Whitefish (Big Mountain), Montana, and Jackson and Cody, Wyoming. You'll find a variety of properties ranging from one-bedroom condos to multibedroom vacation homes. The widest selection is offered by developer-owner consortium.

GUEST RANCHES

If the thought of sitting around a campfire after a hard day on the range makes your heart beat faster, consider playing dude on a guest ranch. These range from wilderness-rimmed working ranches that accept guests and encourage them to pitch in with chores and other ranch activities to luxurious resorts on the fringes of small cities, with an upscale clientele, swimming pools, tennis courts, and a lively roster of horse-related activities such as breakfast rides, moonlight rides, and all-day trail rides. Rafting, fishing, tubing, and other activities are usually available; at working ranches you may even be able to participate in a cattle roundup. In winter, cross-country skiing and snowshoeing keep you busy. Lodgings can run the gamut from charmingly rustic cabins to the kind of deluxe quarters you expect at a first-class hotel. Meals may be gourmet or plain but hearty. Many ranches offer packages as well as children's and off-season rates. The various state tourism offices also have information on dude ranches. Many dude ranches require a nonrefundable deposit at booking and full nonrefundable payment 45 days prior to arrival (and some don't accept credit cards even though your weekly rate may be more than a thousand dollars). You can purchase cancellation insurance to protect you if you have to cancel your reservation for a covered reason.

RESORTS

Ski towns throughout the Rockies—including Big Sky and Whitefish in Montana and Jackson Hole in Wyoming—are home to dozens of resorts in all price ranges; the activities lacking in any individual property can usually be found in the town itself, in summer as well as winter. In the national parks there are both wonderfully rustic and luxurious resorts, such as Jackson Lake Lodge and Jenny Lake Lodge in Grand Teton National Park, Lake Yellowstone Hotel, and the Old Faithful Snow Lodge in Yellowstone, and Many Glacier Lodge in Glacier National Park.

LODGING PRICES

What it Costs			
$	$$	$$$	$$$$
FOR TWO PEOPLE			
under $80	$80–$130	$131–$200	over $200

Packing

Informality reigns in the mountains and on the plains: jeans, sport shirts, and T-shirts fit in almost everywhere, for both men and women. The few restaurants and performing-arts events where dressier outfits are required, usually in resorts and larger cities, are the exception.

If you plan to spend much time outdoors, and certainly if you go in winter, choose clothing appropriate for cold and wet weather. Cotton clothing, including denim—although fine on warm, dry days—can be uncomfortable when it gets wet and when the weather's cold: a better choice is clothing made of wool or any of a number of new synthetics that provide warmth without bulk and maintain their insulating properties even when wet.

In summer you'll want shorts during the day. But because early morning and evenings can be cold, and high-mountain passes windy, pack a sweater and a light jacket, and perhaps also a wool cap and gloves. Try layering—a T-shirt under another shirt under a jacket—and peel off layers as you go. For walks and hikes, you'll need sturdy footwear. To take you into the wilds, boots should have thick soles and plenty of ankle support; if your shoes are new and you plan to spend much time on the trail, break them in at home. Bring a day pack for short hikes, along with a canteen or water bottle, and don't forget rain gear, a hat, sunscreen, and insect repellent.

In winter prepare for subzero temperatures with good boots, warm socks and liners, long johns, a well-insulated jacket, and a warm hat and gloves. Dress in layers so you can add or remove clothes as the temperatures fluctuate.

If you attend dances and other events at Native American reservations, dress conservatively—skirts or long pants for women, long pants for men—or you may be asked to leave. Be aware that you should obtain permission before you take photographs of Native Americans or their programs such as powwow dances. Generally, at a powwow the dance master will announce when it is appropriate to take photos.

When traveling to mountain areas, remember that sunglasses and a sun hat are essential at high altitudes; the thinner atmosphere requires sunscreen with a greater SPF than you might need at lower elevations.

Passport

All visitors to the United States require a current passport that is valid for six months beyond your expected period of stay.

Montana borders Canada, and if you plan to enter that country, you need to present a passport or a passport card (which is less expensive than a passport and can

Essentials

be used for ground or water—but not air—passage between the United States and Canada, Mexico, and Caribbean nations). You need a valid passport or passport card to enter Waterton Lakes National Park in Canada (the park that borders Glacier National Park).

Taxes

Sales tax is 4% in Wyoming; Montana has no sales tax. Some areas have additional local sales and lodging taxes, which can be quite significant.

If you are crossing the border into Canada, be aware of Canada's goods and services tax (better known as the GST). This is a value-added tax of 7%, applicable on virtually every purchase except basic groceries and a small number of other items. Visitors to Canada, however, may claim a full rebate of the GST on any goods taken out of the country as well as on short-term accommodations. Rebates can be claimed either immediately on departure from Canada at participating duty-free shops or by mail within 60 days of leaving Canada. Rebate forms can be obtained from certain retailers, duty-free shops, and customs officials, or by going to the Canada Revenue Agency Website and searching for document GST176.

Tipping

It is customary to tip 15% at restaurants; 20% in resort towns is increasingly the norm. For coat checks and bellhops, $1 to $2 per coat or bag is the minimum. Taxi drivers expect 10% to 15%, depending on where you are. In resort towns, ski technicians, sandwich makers, coffee baristas, and the like also appreciate tips.

Tipping Guides for Montana and Wyoming

Bartender	$1–$5 per round of drinks, depending on the number of drinks
Bellhop	$1–$5 per bag, depending on the level of the hotel
Coat Check	$1–$2 per coat
Hotel Concierge	$5 or more, depending on the service
Hotel Doorstaff	$1–$5 for help with bags or hailing a cab
Hotel Maid	$2–$5 a day (in cash, preferably daily since cleaning staff may be different each day you stay)
Hotel Room Service Waiter	$1–$2 per delivery, even if a service charge has been added
Porter at Airport or Train Station	$1 per bag
Restroom Attendants	$1 or small change
Skycap at Airport	$1–$3 per bag checked
Spa Personnel	15%–20% of the cost of your service
Taxi Driver	15%–20%
Tour Guide	10%–15% of the cost of the tour, per person
Valet Parking Attendant	$2–$5, each time your car is brought to you
Waiter	15%–20%, with 20% being the norm at high-end restaurants; nothing additional if a service charge is added to the bill

U.S. Embassy/Consulate

All foreign governments have embassies in Washington, D.C., and most offer consular services in the embassy building.

Visa

Except for citizens of Canada and Bermuda, most visitors to the United States must have a visa. If you are from one of the 38 designated members of the Visa Waiver Program, then you only require an ESTA (Electronic System for Travel Authorization) as long as you are staying for 90 days or less. However, some changes were made in the Visa Waiver Program in 2015, and nationals of Visa-Waiver nations who have traveled to Iran, Iraq, Libya, Somalia, Sudan, Syria, or Yemen no longer qualify for ESTA. Also, if you have been denied a visa to visit the United States, your application for the ESTA program most likely will be denied.

Visitor Information

At each visitor center and highway welcome center you can obtain maps and information; most facilities have staff on hand to answer questions. You'll also find conveniences such as phones and restrooms.

MONTANA

The Montana Fish, Wildlife & Parks website has links to pages for outdoor-enthusiast information, including fishing and hunting licenses and permits, state parks and angler and hunter information, and a Montana Field Guide. The National Park Service website has links to information about Big Hole, Big Horn Canyon, Glacier National Park, Grant-Korhs Ranch, Little Bighorn Battlefield, the Lewis and Clark National Historic Trail, and Yellowstone National Park. Montana Travel, or Montana Kids.com, gives information about places that will make your family vacation kid approved. Montana Travel's Montana Big Sky Country's site has information on all the places for skiing, snowboarding, and snowmobiling, including a free winter-vacation-planning guide. Pacific Northwest Ski Areas Association provides weather conditions, information on upcoming events, snow reports, summer activities, and trip planning for Whitefish Mountain Resort and Big Mountain.

WYOMING

Wyoming Travel and Tourism's website has informative links to Wyoming's regions, visitor services, trip planning, state parks, and more. This extensive site has a great link for planning your trip to Yellowstone, links to statewide ski and snowmobiling resorts, and tips and links to sites for outdoor enthusiasts.

When to Go

Low Season: Low season in most destinations is winter (November through April).

Shoulder Season: Shoulder season is usually in late spring (May) and early fall (September to October).

High Season: Summer (June, July, and August) are the busiest times in both Montana and Wyoming, when there are many special events and festivals.

Great Itineraries

Into the Wild in Yellowstone and Grand Teton

5 days. This magnificent drive begins in Montana with a journey over the Beartooth Pass into Yellowstone National Park. Highlights include the Beartooth Highway, Yellowstone National Park, Grand Teton National Park, and Jackson Hole.

DAY 1: BILLINGS, MONTANA

1 day. Arrive in Billings, pick up your rental car so you can start exploring. Consider a visit and a tour of **Moss Mansion Museum.** Built in 1903, the mansion was designed by New York architect Henry Janeway Hardenbergh, the designer of the original Waldorf Astoria and Plaza hotels. There are several other fascinating historic sights a short drive from Billings including **Pictograph Cave State Park, Little Bighorn Battlefield National Monument,** and **Pompeys Pillar National Monument.** Billings has Montana's only **walkable brewery trail** and some good restaurants and accommodations. Drive up to **the Rimrocks** at sunset to take in the view of the Yellowstone Valley, the City of Billings, and the Beartooth Mountains in the distance.

DAY 2: BEARTOOTH HIGHWAY TO YELLOWSTONE NATIONAL PARK

1 day. The **Beartooth Highway** is one of the most breathtaking routes to Yellowstone National Park, offering magnificent scenery with views of more than 20 snowcapped peaks towering above 12,000 feet as well as high alpine meadows and sparkling lakes. From Billings, drive 63 miles southwest to Red Lodge and the start of the road. The Beartooth Highway is only 68 miles long, but you should give yourself at least three hours to make the journey. The steep road is full of switchbacks, and you'll want to stop often to take photographs. Watch for grizzlies and black bears, moose, elk, mountain goats, and wolves along the way. The landmark that gives the road its name is the **Bear's Tooth,** a jagged rock that resembles the tooth of a bear.

This route takes you through the tiny communities of **Cooke City** and **Silver Gate** before you reach the northeast gateway of Yellowstone National Park. Stop in Cooke City to fuel up your vehicle and yourself. There are several restaurants in the tiny community. The **Northeast Entrance Ranger Station** was constructed in 1934–35 and is a National Historic Landmark. Once you pass through the northeast entrance, you'll be in the heart of the **Lamar Valley,** one of the best places to see wildlife in the park. Watch for grizzlies, black bears, bison, and wolves. Stop to see **Tower Fall** and then continue driving toward Canyon. Take in the views of the **Grand Canyon of Yellowstone** on the **North and South rim drives,** stopping at viewpoints and overlooks along the way. Take an evening drive through the **Hayden Valley,** watching for birds and wildlife along the way. Dusk and dawn are prime times for wildlife watching. Then head to your chosen accommodation.

DAY 3: YELLOWSTONE NATIONAL PARK

1 day. Spend your second day exploring Yellowstone on the park's 142-mile **Grand Loop Road.** It passes nearly every major Yellowstone attraction, and you'll discover interpretive displays, overlooks, and short trails along the way. On your second day in the park, hike some trails, visit the geyser basins, and watch the wildlife. It's a good idea to stop at the **Old Faithful Visitor Education Center** to get the eruption times of the predictable geysers

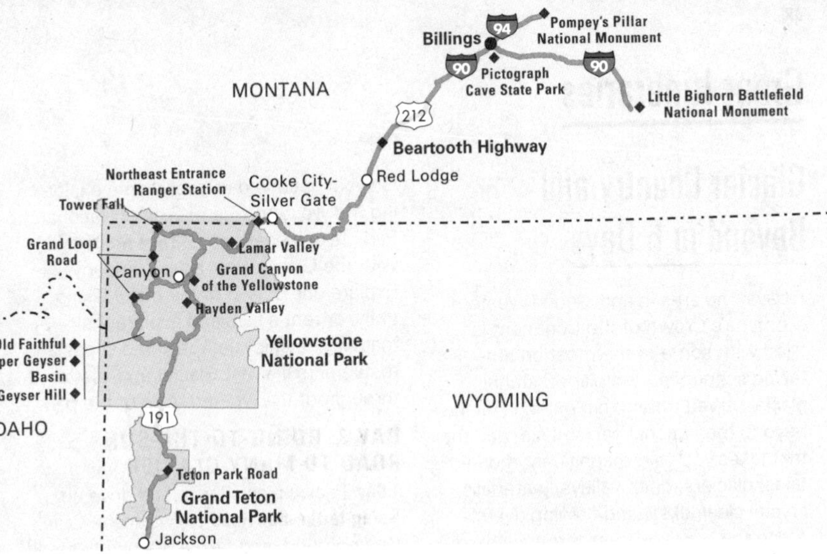

before you head to the **Upper Geyser Basin.** For your accommodations, you really can't go wrong with a stay at **Old Faithful Inn,** with its lodgepole-pine walls and ceiling beams, an immense volcanic rock fireplace, and green-tinted, etched windows.

DAY 4 AND 5: GRAND TETON NATIONAL PARK

2 days. Go on the 8:30 am ranger walk over **Geyser Hill** before you leave Yellowstone. Geyser Hill is at the heart of the world's largest concentration of geysers. The 1.25-mile guided interpretive walk takes about 90 minutes. The remainder of the final two days of your tour will be focused on experiencing Wyoming's other national treasure, **Grand Teton National Park.** Its northern boundary is 7 miles from Yellowstone's south entrance. The sheer ruggedness of the Tetons makes them seem imposing and unapproachable, but a drive on **Teton Park Road,** with frequent stops at scenic turnouts, will get you up close and personal with the peaks. Overnight in one of the park lodges, and spend your final day in the park hiking, horseback riding, or taking a river float trip before continuing south to **Jackson,** with its landmark elk-antler arches in the town square, fine dining, art galleries, museums, and eclectic shopping. After exploring Jackson, return your rental car to the **Jackson Hole Airport** and fly home. You could also consider flying home from the **Idaho Falls Airport,** a two-hour drive southwest of the Jackson Hole Airport.

Logistics

The Beartooth Highway is an All American Road that is traditionally open from Memorial Day though Columbus Day, but inclement weather can affect these opening dates. This scenic highway has many switchbacks as it climbs to 10,350 feet in Montana and 10,947 in Wyoming—the highest highway elevation in both states. It's a bucket-list drive.

If you want to stay in one of the historic hotels in Yellowstone or Grand Teton, make your reservations as far in advance as possible for the most popular hotels like the Old Faithful Inn. Some hotels book up to a year in advance.

Great Itineraries

Glacier Country and Beyond in 6 Days

6 days. The area in and around Western Montana's Crown of the Continent is filled with some of the most breathtaking scenery on the planet: stunning, glacial-carved terrain that extends well beyond the national parks. It's a road trip that takes you past magnificent mountains, glaciers, deep valleys, waterfalls, crystal clear lakes, and flowing rivers. Along the way, you pass through charming towns and cities and the land of two Tribal Nations. This is a loop itinerary, but it could be extended to include travel into other parts of Montana and Wyoming.

DAYS 1 AND 2: WEST GLACIER

2 days. Begin your journey in **Kalispell,** the location of the **Glacier Park International Airport.** From the airport, it's a 30-minute drive to the Western side of **Glacier National Park.** Make your way to **Apgar Village** at the edge of **Lake McDonald.** Grab a bite to eat in the village and explore the **Apgar Visitor Centre.** Walk along the shore of Lake McDonald and if time permits, rent a canoe, kayak, or paddleboard to enjoy a leisurely paddle. Next, take the 50-minute drive to **Polebridge,** a tiny unincorporated community without traditional electricity. Stop at the **Polebridge Mercantile and Bakery** and pick up a treat. Then make your way back to **West Glacier.** Stay overnight inside the park or in one of the many accommodations in the nearby village of West Glacier.

On your second day, spend time exploring the western side of Glacier National Park. Take a boat tour of **Lake McDonald** with the Glacier Park Boat Company. Explore one or two of the many hiking trails, or rent a bike and explore the roadways by bicycle. You'll find shops and restaurants in West Glacier and scattered throughout the western side of the park.

DAY 3: GOING-TO-THE-SUN ROAD TO MANY GLACIER

1 day. Pack a picnic lunch and drive up **Going-to-the-Sun Road** to Avalanche Creek Campground, and take a 30-minute stroll along the fragrant **Trail of the Cedars.** Hop back in the vehicle and continue driving up this amazingly scenic road. Stop at the summit and explore the **Logan Pass Visitor Center,** then take the 1.5-mile **Hidden Lake Nature Trail** up to prime wildlife-viewing spots. Have a picnic at the overlook. Afterward, continue driving east over the mountains. Stop at the **Jackson Glacier Overlook** to view one of the park's largest glaciers. Please note: the Going-to-the-Sun Road is generally closed from mid-September to mid-June. Next, drive to **Swiftcurrent Lake** and take in one of the prettiest views in the park. Enjoy dinner and stay two nights in this region, also known as **Many Glacier.** The Many Glacier Hotel and the Swiftcurrent Motor Inn are the two main accommodations here.

DAY 4: GRINNELL GLACIER HIKE

1 day. Spend the day hiking to the **Grinnell Glacier,** one of the most accessible glaciers in Glacier National Park. You can shorten the hike to 7.5 miles return if

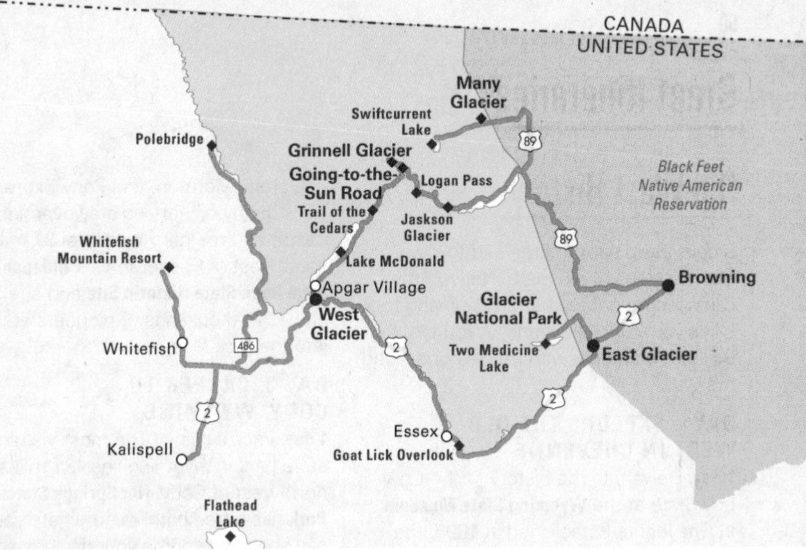

you travel by boat across **Swiftcurrent Lake** and **Josephine Lake** with Glacier Park Boats. The park service offers ranger-led hikes to Grinnell Glacier for a fee, but you need to book in advance.

DAY 5: BROWNING AND EAST GLACIER

1 day. Drive one hour southeast to **Browning** to visit the **Museum of the Plains Indian** and the unique shops on the **Blackfeet Indian Reservation.** Another 20-minute drive southwest and you'll be in **East Glacier Park Village.** Stop for lunch in the village, then drive to nearby **Two Medicine Lake.** You can take a boat tour on the lake and enjoy a naturalist-led hike to **Twin Falls** or just take in the view from the shore. You can also rent a boat or take the short 2.8-mile return hike to **Aster Falls.** Overnight in East Glacier Park Village or in **Essex,** a 35-minute drive southwest.

DAY 6: FLATHEAD VALLEY

1 day. Take your time and enjoy the scenery as you drive 90 miles southwest from East Glacier Park Village towards Kalispell. Be sure to stop at **Goat Lick Overlook** near **Essex.** It's common to see mountain goats at this natural mineral lick. You might also stop to enjoy a whitewater rafting or fly-fishing excursion on the Flathead River near the village of **West Glacier.** There are many attractions in the Flathead Valley region near **Kalispell.** It's a great region for mountain biking and road biking and there are excellent trails and rental shops. **Whitefish Mountain Resort** is a year-round destination with skiing in winter and a range of summer adventures to enjoy. You can also spend the day playing on beautiful **Flathead Lake.** There are plenty of restaurants, shops, and accommodations in the Flathead Valley.

Great Itineraries

Old West History

5 days. Step back in time and follow in the footsteps of pioneers, Native Americans and mountain men. This driving tour takes you from Cheyenne, Wyoming, to Billings, Montana, with many stops along the way.

DAY1: EXPLORE THE OLD WEST IN CHEYENNE

1 day. Delve into the history of the Cowboy State at the **Wyoming State Museum** in Cheyenne. Established in 1895, the museum contains a wide range of artifacts on two floors and admission is free. Then head over to **The Cowgirls of the West Museum & Emporium** to learn about the roles women played in taming the Wild West. If you're feeling adventurous for dinner, pop over to the **Bunkhouse Bar and Grill.** Some say they serve the best Rocky Mountain oysters (bull testicles) in the state.

DAY 2: CHEYENNE TO CASPER, WYOMING

1 day. Two important historic sites are found about 100 miles southeast of Cheyenne. At **Fort Laramie National Historic Site,** you can tour buildings dating back to 1849 and learn about the fur trade and the fort's role protecting and supplying emigrant wagon trains. **Oregon Trail Ruts State Historic Site** is about 16 miles northwest of Fort Laramie near **Guernsey.** Worn to a depth of up to five feet, these wagon ruts are some of the most impressive along the Oregon-California Trail. Next, head to **Casper, Wyoming** to visit the **National Historic Trails Interpretive Centre** to learn more about the Oregon, California, Mormon, and Pony Express Trails. Enjoy dinner and stay overnight in Casper. If time permits, travel 31 miles southwest of Casper to visit **Independence Rock State Historic Site** and see the names of thousands of pioneers etched into the rock face.

DAY 3: CASPER TO CODY, WYOMING

1 day. Pack a picnic! The most visited state park in Wyoming lies 131 miles northwest of Cody. **Hot Springs State Park** has a free bathhouse where you can soak and soothe your tired muscles in 104-degree water. There's beautiful scenery, and the Wyoming state bison herd is located inside the park. Once you've had your fill of hot springs and bison, head 85 miles northwest to **Cody, Wyoming** and the **Buffalo Bill Center of the West.** The center contains five museums that cover Plains Indian culture, western art, Yellowstone, firearms and the legend of Buffalo Bill. Stay two nights in Cody.

DAY 4: EAST YELLOWSTONE LOOP

1 day. Drive west from Cody on the **Buffalo Bill Scenic Byway** (U.S. 14-16-20). This scenic road follows the North Fork of the Shoshone River to the east entrance of **Yellowstone National Park.** It's a beautiful drive that takes you through the **Shoshone National Forest** and **East Yellowstone Valley.** Watch for wildlife along the way. Make a loop through the eastern half of the park to the northeast entrance. Be sure to stop at the **Fishing Bridge Visitor Center and Trailside Museum** to see vintage exhibits about the park and get maps, brochures, and information on your planned driving route and stops. This drive will take you past **Yellowstone Lake,** the **Grand Canyon of Yellowstone,** and **Tower Falls.** You will definitely want to stop along the way. After you exit the northeast entrance, take U.S. Hwy. 212 through the historic mining towns of **Silver Gate** and **Cooke City.** About 20 minutes outside Cooke City, turn onto Wyoming Hwy. 296, **The Chief Joseph Scenic Byway.** Just past the summit of **Dead Indian Pass,** turn south on Wyoming Hwy. 120 to return to Cody. This is one of the most beautiful scenic drives in the state, and you'll want to pull over often.

DAY 5: CODY TO BILLINGS AND BEYOND

1 day. Drive 113 miles northeast of Cody to see ancient indigenous pictographs in **Pictograph Cave State Park** just outside Billings, Montana. There are three main caves at this national historic landmark, and the oldest rock art is more than 2,000 years old. Next, drive 64 miles southeast to **Little Bighorn Battlefield National Monument,** the site of the Battle of the Little Bighorn in 1876. Learn about the clash of two vastly different cultures and the struggle of Native Americans to maintain their way of life. From here, drive 64 miles northwest to **Billings** for dinner and an overnight stay. Billings has good restaurants and accommodations, and it's home to Montana's only walkable brewery trail. If time permits, drive 30 minutes northeast of Billings to visit **Pompeys Pillar National Monument.** Carved in the rock are Native American petroglyphs as well as the signature of William Clark, co-leader of the Lewis and Clark Expedition.

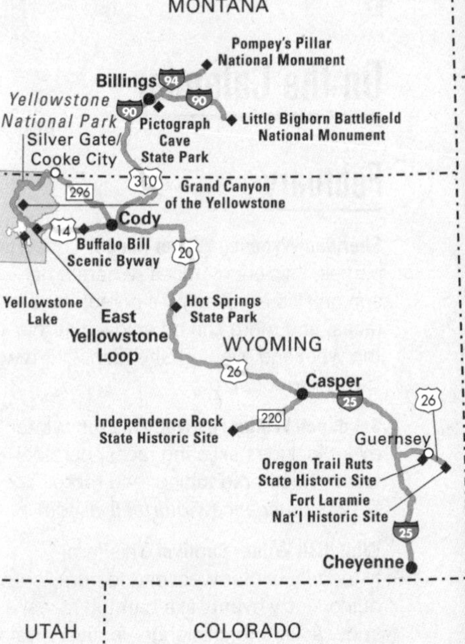

Logistics

The East Yellowstone Loop is an all-day drive that starts and ends in Cody and is 224 miles long without stops and side trips. Please note that parts of this route are under construction but should be fully open by May 2022. However, some of these roads are closed in winter.

Some travelers will find it cheaper and almost as convenient to fly into Denver, about two hours south of Cheyenne.

On the Calendar

February

Sheridan Wyoming Winter Rodeo. Concerts, parties, "skijoring" races (where a person on skis is pulled by a horse), fat bike races, and more can be enjoyed at this fun weekend event in Sheridan. 🌐 *www.wyowinterrodeo.org*

Sundance Winter Festival. This fun winter event includes skijoring races, barstool races, wild horse tubing, and more. 🌐 *www.sundancewinterfestival.com*

Whitefish Winter Carnival. This family-friendly winter weekend features quirky crazy events like bathtub races, a snow sculpture challenge, festival royalty, music, and much more in Whitefish, Montana. 🌐 *whitefishwintercarnival.com*

March

National Finals Skijoring Races. These outdoor skijoring races in Redlodge, Montana feature the best of the best in this exciting Nordic winter sport, where skiers are pulled behind horses at high speed on a winding course. 🌐 *redlodgeskijoring.com*

Wild West Wine Fest. Taste more than 100 different wines and beers from various vendors and distributors in downtown Sheridan. 🌐 *www.sheridanwyoming.org/festivals-events/wine-fest/*

May

Eaton's Horse Drive. Each May, a herd of more than 100 horses from Eaton's ranch are driven by cowboys through downtown Sheridan. 🌐 *www.sheridanwyoming.com/events/eatons-horse-drive*

Old West Days. A parade, an antler auction, a chili cook-off, a brewfest, and a music festival are all part of this multiday celebration in Jackson Hole. 🌐 *www.jacksonholechamber.com*

June

College National Finals Rodeo. The best of the best in college rodeo compete at the CNFR in Casper, Wyoming annually. 🌐 *cnfr.com*

Eastern Shoshone Indian Days. Enjoy three days of dance contests, drumming, and singing at this annual powwow on Wyoming's Wind River Reservation. 🌐 *windriver.org*

Friday Night Rodeos. From mid-June to mid-August, there's a rodeo every Friday night in Dubois, Wyoming. See bull riding, bronc riding, team roping, barrel racing, rodeo clowns, and calf roping. 🌐 *a3156843windriver.org/event/dubois-friday-night-rodeos/all/*

Headwaters Country Jam. Montana's largest country music and camping festival takes place in a natural outdoor amphitheater near Three Forks and features more than a dozen bands. 🌐 *headwaterscountryjam.com*

Lewis and Clark Festival. Historical reenactments, a Bluegrass concert, Native American dancers and drummers, children's activities, and more celebrate the Lewis and Clark Expedition in Great Falls, Montana. 🌐 *lewisandclarkfoundation.org*

Woodchoppers Jamboree and Rodeo. For more than 60 years, loggers have been competing for the title of Rocky Mountain Champion Lumberjack in Encampment, Wyoming. There's also a rodeo. 🌐 *www.woodchoppersjamboree.org*

July

Big Sky Country State Fair & Bozeman Roundup Ranch Rodeo. This traditional western fair has live music, a midway, children's activities, agricultural displays and a real ranch rodeo in Bozeman, Montana. 🌐 *406statefair.com*

Cheyenne Frontier Days. This 10-day festival celebrates Wyoming's western roots with a parade, rodeo, live music, a Native American Village, and more. 🌐 *cfdrodeo.com*

Cody Stampede Rodeo This rodeo began with Buffalo Bill and his Wild West Show. Since 1919, it has grown into an event that includes a stampede, a night rodeo, a parade, and more. 🌐 *codystampederodeo.com*

Evel Knievel Days. Evel Knievel's hometown of Butte, Montana holds an annual three-day celebration of the daredevil that features unique extreme sports spectacles and world record stunts. 🌐 *evelknieveldays.org*

Flathead Cherry Festival. Cherry pie, cherry-cooking contests, pit spitting contests, and local craft vendors are highlights of this fun family festival in Polson, Montana. 🌐 *flatheadcherryfestival.com*

Livingston Roundup. One of Montana's best small-town rodeos is held annually over the fourth of July weekend. It features big-name rodeo action, a parade, and nightly fireworks. 🌐 *livingstonroundup.com*

Montana Folk Festival. The largest free outdoor music festival in Montana features more than 20 acts performing across six stages in Uptown Butte. 🌐 *montanafolkfestival.com*

August

Montana Cowboy Poetry Gathering and Western Music Rendezvous. Music, poems, and a Western Art & Gear Show are just part of the festival fun in Lewistown, Montana. 🌐 *www.montanacowboypoetrygathering.com*

Sweet Pea Festival. A children's parade, Shakespeare in the Park, the Chalk Walk, entertainment, and food are highlights of this festival in Bozeman, Montana. 🌐 *sweetpeafestival.org*

Trout Creek Huckleberry Festival. For more than 40 years, the huckleberry festival has been held the second full weekend in August in Trout Creek, Montana. It's a home-spun craft festival with many family-friendly events. 🌐 *www.huckleberryfestival.com*

Wyoming State Fair and Rodeo. Since 1905, the four-day state agricultural fair and rodeo has been held in Douglas. 🌐 *wystatefair.com*

September

Balloon the Bighorns Hot Air Balloon Rally. This free weekend event sees hot air balloons soaring over the skies near Sheridan, Wyoming. 🌐 *www.sheridanwyoming.com*

Don King Days. Held in honor of a legendary saddle maker (not the boxing promoter), Don King Days celebrates classic equestrian events like polo, steer roping, and bronc riding in Sheridan, Wyoming. 🌐 *www.thebhec.org/donkingdays.htm*

Contacts

Air

AIRLINES Alaska Airlines. *800/252–7522* *www.alaskaair.com.* **Allegiant Air.** *800/432–3810, 702/505–8888* *www.allegiantair.com.* **American Airlines.** *Jackson Hole Airport, 1250 E. Airport Rd., Jackson* ⊕ *Located within Grand Teton National Park* *800/433–7300 for reservations only* *www.aa.com.* **Delta.** *800/221–1212* *www.delta.com.* **United.** *800/864–8331* *www.united.com.*

Bus

CONTACTS Express Arrow. *877/779–2999* *expressarrow.com.* **Greyhound Bus Lines.** *406/245–5116, 800/231–2222* *www.greyhound.com.*

Jefferson Lines *858/800–8898* *www.jeffersonlines.com.*

Camping

MONTANA CONTACTS Montana Fish, Wildlife & Parks. *406/444–2535* *fwp.mt.gov.* **U.S. Bureau of Land Management.** *406/896–5000* *www.blm.gov/mt/.* **U.S. Forest Service.** *406/329–3511* *www.fs.fed.us/r1.*

WYOMING CONTACTS Kemmerer District Bureau of Land Management. *307/828–4500* *www.blm.gov/office/kemmerer-field-office.* **Rawlins District Bureau of Land Management.** *307/328–4200* *www.blm.gov/office/rawlins-field-office.* **Rock Springs District Bureau of Land Management.** *307/352–0256* *www.blm.gov/office/rock-springs-field-office.* **U.S. Forest Service.** *303/275–5350* *www.fs.fed.us/r2.* **Wyoming Campground Association.** *307/655–2547* *www.campwyoming.org/.*

Car

MONTANA ROAD CONDITIONS Montana Department of Transportation. *800/226–7623* *www.mdt.mt.gov/travinfo.* **Montana Highway Patrol.** *406/444–3780* *www.doj.mt.gov/enforcement/highwaypatrol.*

WYOMING ROAD CONDITIONS Wyoming Department of Transportation. *307/777–4484, 307/772–0824 from outside Wyoming for road conditions, 888/996–7623 from within Wyoming for road conditions, 511 from a cell phone* *www.wyoroad.info/.* **Wyoming State Highway Patrol.** *888/996–7623, 800/442–9090* *dot.state.wy.us.*

Train

CONTACTS Amtrak. *800/872–7245* *www.amtrak.com.*

Visitor Information

Visitor information centers are located along major travel corridors in cities and towns. They provide information about area attractions and sites. Hours vary by location. Some are open year-round while others are open May through September. You can also get excellent tourism information and downloadable travel guides from the websites of state and local tourism information centers. **Montana**'s state tourism website is *visitmt.com.* In **Wyoming** it's *travelwyoming.com.*

Chapter 3

YELLOWSTONE NATIONAL PARK

3

Updated by
Andrew Collins

Camping ★★★★★ | Hotels ★★★★★ | Activities ★★★★☆ | Scenery ★★★★★ | Crowds ★★★★★

WELCOME TO YELLOWSTONE NATIONAL PARK

TOP REASONS TO GO

★ **Hot spots:** Thinner-than-normal crust depth and a huge magma chamber beneath the park explain Yellowstone's abundant geysers, steaming pools, hissing fumaroles, and bubbling mudpots.

★ **Bison sightings:** They're just one of many species that roam freely here (watch for moose and wolves, too). Seemingly docile, the bison make your heart race if you catch them stampeding across Lamar Valley.

★ **Hike for days:** Yellowstone has more than 900 miles of trails, along which you can summit a 10,000-foot peak, follow a trout-filled creek, or descend into the Grand Canyon of the Yellowstone.

★ **Lakefront leisure:** Here you can fish, boat, kayak, stargaze, bird-watch on black obsidian beaches, and stay in a grand historic hotel—just don't stray too far into the frigid water.

★ **Canyon adventures:** The Yellowstone River runs through the park, creating a deep yellow-tinged canyon with two impressive waterfalls.

1 **Mammoth Hot Springs.** This full-service area has an inn, restaurants, campsites, a visitor center, and general stores.

2 **Norris.** This is the hottest and most changeable part of Yellowstone National Park.

3 **Madison.** Here the Madison River is formed by the joining of the Gibbon and Firehole rivers. Anglers will find healthy stocks of brown and rainbow trout and mountain whitefish.

4 **Old Faithful.** Old Faithful erupts every 90 minutes or so. The geyser site is a full-service area with inns, restaurants, and general stores.

5 **Grant Village and West Thumb.** Named for President Ulysses S. Grant, Grant Village is on the western edge of Yellowstone Lake.

6 **Yellowstone Lake.** This is the largest body of water within the park. This is a full-service area.

7 **Canyon.** The Yellowstone River runs through the canyon, exposing geothermally altered rock.

8 **Tower-Roosevelt.** The least-visited area of the park is the place to go for horseback riding and animal sightings.

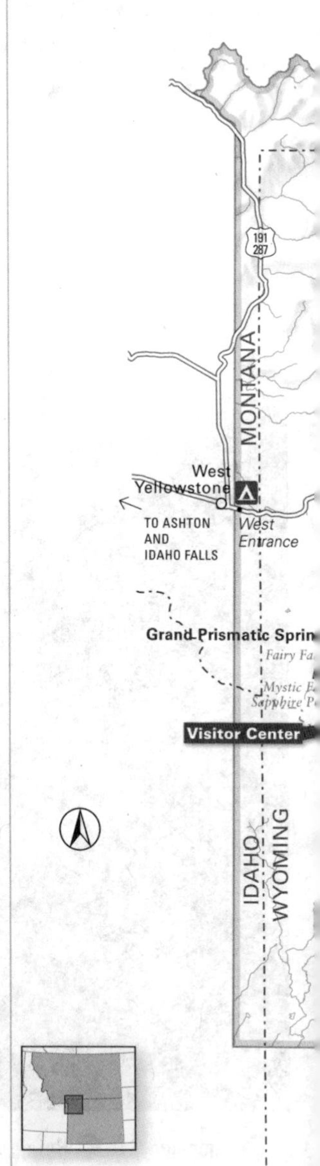

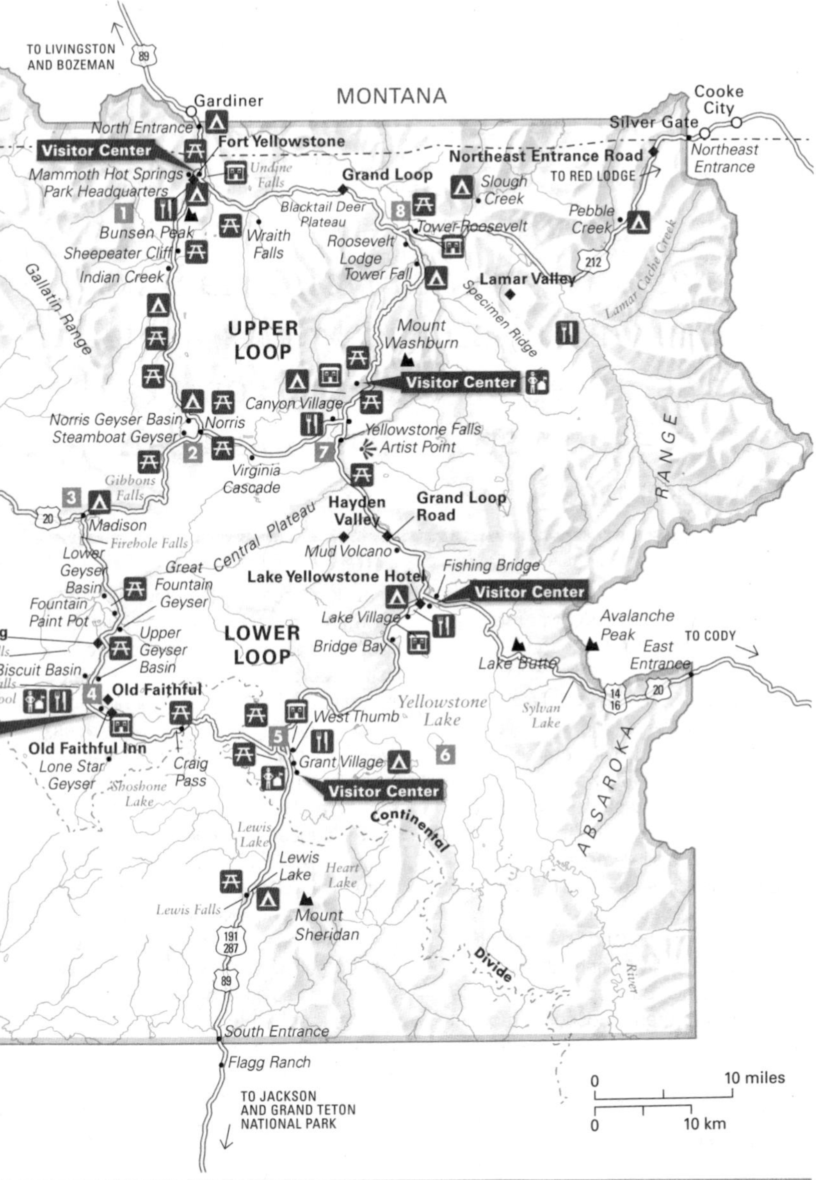

TO LIVINGSTON AND BOZEMAN
89
Gardiner
MONTANA
Cooke City
Silver Gate
North Entrance
Fort Yellowstone
Visitor Center
Mammoth Hot Springs
Park Headquarters
Undine Falls
Grand Loop
Northeast Entrance Road
TO RED LODGE
Northeast Entrance
Slough Creek
Blacktail Deer Plateau
Tower-Roosevelt
Pebble Creek
Bunsen Peak
Wraith Falls
Roosevelt Lodge
Sheepeater Cliff
Tower Fall
212
Indian Creek
Lamar Valley
Gallatin Range
Specimen Ridge
Lamar Cache Creek
UPPER LOOP
Mount Washburn
Visitor Center
Canyon Village
Norris Geyser Basin
Norris
Steamboat Geyser
Yellowstone Falls
Artist Point
Virginia Cascade
Gibbons Falls
RANGE
Hayden Valley
Grand Loop Road
20
Madison
Firehole Falls
Great Central Plateau
Mud Volcano
Lower Geyser Basin
Fountain Geyser
Lake Yellowstone Hotel
Fishing Bridge
Visitor Center
Fountain Paint Pot
Lake Village
Avalanche Peak
Upper Geyser Basin
LOWER LOOP
Bridge Bay
TO CODY
East Entrance
Lake Butte
Biscuit Basin
Old Faithful
Yellowstone Lake
Sylvan Lake
14 16
20
West Thumb
Old Faithful Inn
Lone Star Geyser
Craig Pass
Grant Village
Shoshone Lake
Visitor Center
Continental
ABSAROKA
Lewis Lake
Lewis Lake
Heart Lake
Lewis Falls
Mount Sheridan
191 287
Divide
River
89
South Entrance
Flagg Ranch
TO JACKSON AND GRAND TETON NATIONAL PARK
0
10 miles
0
10 km
1
2
3
4
5
6
7
8

A landscape of astonishing beauty that's captured the imagination of visitors for many generations, this magma-filled pressure cooker of a park contains the world's greatest concentration of geysers, mudpots, fumaroles, and hot springs. But Yellowstone's unparalleled diversity makes it truly special—here you'll also find a massive river canyon, meadows teeming with bison and wolves, a huge and pristine alpine lake, and some of the country's most striking national park architecture.

Yellowstone was established in 1872 by President Ulysses S. Grant as America's first national park. At 3,472 square miles, it's also the second largest national park in the Lower 48, trailing only Death Valley. It's named for the roaring, north-flowing river that indigenous Minnetaree inhabitants called Mi tse a-da-zi, or Yellow Rock River, for the yellow bluffs that flank it—early-19th-century French trappers adapted that name, calling the entire region Yellowstone. Only one small Shoshone band, the Sheepeaters, ever settled permanently on the land now framed by the park, but for thousands of years the Blackfeet, Crow, Bannock, Flathead, Nez Perce, and Northern Shoshone frequented the area for its plentiful wildlife.

Legendary mountain man John Colter, who arrived here in 1807, was the first white American known to explore the area. His descriptions of geysers and boiling rivers prompted some mapmakers to dub the uncharted region Colter's Hell. Reports by subsequent explorers and trappers continued to spread around the country over the next few decades, eventually spurring both privately and federally funded expeditions in the 1860s. The Hayden Geological Survey of 1871 produced the most detailed report yet, complete with the still-iconic photographs by William Henry Jackson and paintings by Thomas Moran. Members of Congress were so impressed that they felt compelled to preserve this awe-inspiring land as a national park, most of it in the then territory of Wyoming (with smaller sections in Montana and Idaho). For its first 45 years, the park was administered by the U.S. Army, whose Fort Yellowstone headquarters in Mammoth

AVERAGE HIGH/LOW TEMPERATURES					
JAN.	FEB.	MAR.	APR.	MAY	JUNE
30/10	33/12	42/17	49/28	60/32	71/41
JULY	AUG.	SEPT.	OCT.	NOV.	DEC.
81/45	79/45	67/37	56/30	38/22	30/12

Hot Springs remain a popular attraction. The National Park Service came into existence in 1916 and has been overseeing the park ever since.

Although enormous, Yellowstone National Park has been developed with a visitor-friendly logic that makes it surprisingly easy to explore. The five different entrances access 310 miles of picturesque paved roads, including the Grand Loop Road, which connects the park's most popular features. A network of historic villages with lodgings, restaurants, services, and well-maintained trails provides the opportunity for overnight stays in different sections of the park. And if you get an early start, it's possible to cover quite a lot of ground each day, especially during the longer days of summer.

That said, because there's so much to see, park lodgings book months in advance, and it can take two or three hours to travel between park entrances, it's wise to prepare a strategy before visiting. The park's geothermal features—including the geyser basins around Old Faithful and Norris and the western half of Yellowstone Lake—are a must, and they're mostly situated within or adjacent to Yellowstone Caldera, the still very active supervolcano whose three massive eruptions over the past 2.1 million years created the otherworldly landscape that makes the park so famous today. You can see much of the caldera in one long day, and each subsequent day in the park will allow you to enjoy other key attractions and activities: the Grand Canyon of the Yellowstone, Mammoth Hot Springs, Lamar Valley, and the many opportunities for viewing unusual geological features and mesmerizing wildlife, from lake cruises to snowcoach tours to both easy and rugged hikes.

Planning

When to Go

There are two major seasons in Yellowstone: summer (May–October), the only time when most of the park's roads are open to cars; and winter (mid-December–February), when over-snow travel—on snowmobiles, snowcoaches, and skis—delivers a fraction of the number of summer visitors to a frigid, bucolic sanctuary. Except for services at park headquarters at Mammoth Hot Springs, the park closes from mid-October to mid-December and from March to late April or early May.

You'll find the biggest crowds in July and August. If planning to visit at this time, book hotel accommodations inside or even near the park months in advance, and prepare for heavy traffic on park roads and parking areas. There are fewer people in the park the month or two before and after this peak season, but there are also fewer facilities open. In spring, there's also more rain, especially at lower elevations. Except for holiday weekends, there are few visitors in winter. Snow is possible year-round at high elevations.

FESTIVALS AND EVENTS

Cody Stampede Rodeo. The "Rodeo Capital of the World" has hosted the Stampede, one of the most important stops on the rodeo circuit, since 1919. The main event takes place at Cody Rodeo Grounds for several days around the July 4 holiday, and there are nightly performances at the Cody Nite Rodeo. 🌐 *www.codystampederodeo.com.*

Livingston Roundup Rodeo. Since the 1920s, the lively Montana town of Livingston has celebrated July 4 with riding, roping, bull-dogging, and barrel racing at the Roundup Rodeo. The revelry includes a parade, a three-day art show, and the crowning of the rodeo queen. 🌐 *www.livingstonroundup.com.*

Rendezvous Royale. Thomas Molesworth and his renowned Western furniture helped put Cody on the map when he moved here in the 1930s. This multiday festival held in late September celebrates his legacy with an art show, auctions, a quick-draw competition, and a major furniture exhibition. 🌐 *www.rendezvousroyale.org.*

Getting Here and Around

AIR

The closest airports to Yellowstone National Park served by most major airlines are in Cody, Wyoming, an hour from the East Entrance; Jackson, Wyoming, an hour from the South Entrance; and Bozeman, Montana, 90 minutes from the North and West entrances. Additionally, the tiny airport in West Yellowstone, Montana, just outside the park's west gate, has summer-only service on Delta from Salt Lake City.

CAR

Yellowstone is well away from the interstates—the nearest is Interstate 90, which passes through Livingston, Montana just 53 miles north of the park's North Entrance. You generally make your way here on scenic two-lane highways. Yellowstone has five road entrances. Many visitors arrive through the South Entrance, 57 miles north of Jackson and just 7 miles north of Grand Teton National Park. Other entrances are the East Entrance, 53 miles from Cody, Wyoming; the West Entrance at West Yellowstone, Montana (90 miles south of Bozeman), the North Entrance at Gardiner, Montana (80 miles south of Bozeman); and the Northeast Entrance at Cooke City, Montana, which can be reached from either Cody, Wyoming, via the Chief Joseph Scenic Highway (81 miles), or from Red Lodge, Montana, over the Beartooth Pass (67 miles). ■ **TIP→ You'll find gas stations at most of the main villages inside the park, although it's not a bad idea to fill your tank whenever you're outside Yellowstone, and gas is often cheaper in these areas.**

■ **TIP→ The best way to keep your bearings in Yellowstone is to remember that the major roads form a figure eight, known as the Grand Loop, which all entrance roads feed into. It doesn't matter at which point you begin, as you can hit most of the major attractions if you follow the entire route.**

The 466 miles of public roads in the park (310 miles of them paved) used to be riddled with potholes and hemmed in by narrow shoulders. But the park greatly upgraded its roads, and most are now smooth, if still narrow. Roadwork is likely every summer in some portion of the park. Remember, snow is possible at any time of year in almost all areas of the park. Also, never—under any circumstances—stop your car on the road any place that isn't designated. Instances of drivers blocking traffic and potentially causing accidents are rampant on park roads. Don't be a part of this problem.

Inspiration

The Yellowstone Story, by Aubrey L. Haines, is a classic, providing an illuminating and thorough history of the park, from prehistory to the present.

Decade of the Wolf, by Douglas Smith and Gary Ferguson, is the most comprehensive and gripping account of the reintroduction of wolves into the park in the 1990s.

A book that does a terrific job explaining the park's geological processes is Robert B. Smith and Lee J. Siegel's *Windows into the Earth: The Geologic Story of Yellowstone and Grand Teton National Parks.*

Lost in My Own Backyard, by Tim Cahill, is a hilarious account of one person's experiences in the park over more than 25 years.

Alston Chase's controversial *Playing God in Yellowstone* chronicles a century of government mismanagement in asserting that the National Park Service has ultimately damaged the park's ecosystem in its efforts to protect it.

Park Essentials

ACCESSIBILITY

Yellowstone has long been a National Park Service leader in providing access to visitors with disabilities. Restrooms with sinks and flush toilets designed for those in wheelchairs are in all developed areas except West Thumb, whose facilities are quite rustic. Accessible campsites and restrooms are at every park campground except Fishing Bridge RV Park. An accessible fishing platform is about 3½ miles west of Madison at Mt. Haynes Overlook. For more information, pick up a free copy of the *Visitor Guide to Accessible Features in Yellowstone National Park* at any visitor center.

PARK FEES AND PERMITS

Entrance fees of $35 per vehicle, $30 per motorcycle or snowmobile, or $20 per visitor 16 and older entering by foot, bike, ski, and so on, are good for seven days. See Activities for details on boating, camping, fishing, and horseback permits and fees.

PARK HOURS

At least some part of Yellowstone is open year-round, with 24-hour access. But many areas and entrances are closed in winter or during fall and spring shoulder seasons, and the exact times can vary depending on the weather, so it's important to check the park website for the latest details if you're planning to visit anytime from mid-October to early May. Conventional vehicles can always access the North Entrance at Gardiner, Montana, to Mammoth Hot Springs, and from Mammoth Hot Springs to the Northeast Entrance and the town of Cooke City (with no through-travel beyond Cooke City). Only over-snow vehicles can travel other parts of the park in winter. The park is in the Mountain time zone.

CELL PHONE RECEPTION

Most of the park's developed villages have (sometimes spotty) cell service, including Mammoth Hot Springs, West Yellowstone, Old Faithful, Grand Village, Lake Village, and Mt. Washburn. However, especially in the summer, crowds can overwhelm cellular capacity and greatly slow things down. Don't expect cell service on roads between these main developed areas or in the backcountry. There are public phones near visitor centers.

Hotels

Accommodations in the park continue to undergo significant upgrades, and overall, Yellowstone's lodgings are above average in quality and with rates that are comparable to many other national parks.

Yellowstone in One Day

If you have just one full day in the park, concentrate on the two biggest attractions: Old Faithful geyser and the Grand Canyon of the Yellowstone. En route between these places, you can see geothermal activity and most likely some wildlife.

Allow at least two hours to explore **Old Faithful** and the surrounding village. Eruptions occur approximately 90 minutes apart but can vary, so check with the visitor center for predicted times. Be sure to explore the surrounding geyser basin, including the 1½-mile **Geyser Hill Loop**, and **Old Faithful Inn**, from which you can watch the geyser erupt from the hotel's rear deck. A short drive north, make **Grand Prismatic Spring** in **Midway Geyser Basin** your can't-miss geothermal stop; farther north, near Madison, detour to the west along short **Firehole Canyon Drive** to see the Firehole River cut a small canyon and waterfall (Firehole Falls).

If arriving from the east, start with sunrise at **Lake Butte**, **Fishing Bridge**, and the wildlife-rich **Hayden Valley** as you loop through the park counterclockwise to Old Faithful. If you're entering through the North or Northeast Entrance, begin at dawn looking for wolves and other animals in **Lamar Valley**, then continue west to **Mammoth Hot Springs**, where you can walk the **Lower Terrace Interpretive Trail** past Liberty Cap and other strange, brightly colored travertine formations, before making your way south to Old Faithful. Keep an eye out for wildlife as you go—you're almost certain to see elk, bison, and possibly a bear. Once you've finished at Old Faithful, make your way east through Madison and Norris to **Canyon Village** to see the north or south rim of the **Grand Canyon of the Yellowstone** and its waterfalls. Alternatively, you could see the Canyon area earlier in the day and save Old Faithful for last—both of these areas are gorgeous at sunset.

Options range from a pair of magnificent historic hotels—the Old Faithful Inn and Lake Yellowstone Hotel—to simple cabins and utilitarian modern motels. Make reservations at least four months ahead for all park lodgings in July and August, although if planning a trip on shorter notice, it's still worth a try, as cancellations do happen. Old Faithful Snow Lodge and Mammoth Hot Springs Hotel are the only accommodations open in winter; rates are the same as in summer. There are no TVs in any park hotels. *Hotel reviews have been shortened. For full information, visit Fodors.com.*

Restaurants

The park's main developed areas all have at least one cafeteria or casual restaurant and typically a convenience store with limited groceries and deli items, but distances between these places can be considerable, and crowds during busy periods can result in long wait times for a table. For more flexibility and to be able to take advantage of the huge supply of park picnic areas, it's a good idea to fill a cooler with groceries in one of the larger towns outside the park. In addition to standard comfort fare—soups, salads, burgers, sandwiches, pizzas, ice cream—available in the park's casual eateries, you'll also encounter increasingly more sophisticated regional cuisine—with a focus on elk, bison, trout, and other game and seafood—at several more upscale restaurants, including the Old Faithful Inn, Lake Yellowstone Hotel, Grant Village Old Faithful Snow Lodge, and Mammoth Hotel dining rooms; reservations are advised, particularly in summer, at these venues. Given the park's remote location, prices at park restaurants can be a bit steep. *Restaurant reviews have been shortened. For full information, visit Fodors.com.*

PICNIC AREAS

You'll find more than 50 designated picnic areas in the park, ranging from secluded spots with a couple of tables to more popular stops with a dozen or more tables. **■TIP→ Keep an eye out for wildlife.** You never know when a herd of bison might decide to march through. If this happens, it's best to leave your food and move a safe distance away from them.

What It Costs

$	$$	$$$	$$$$
RESTAURANTS			
under $16	$16–$22	$22–$30	over $30
HOTELS			
under $150	$151–$225	$226–$300	over $300

Tours

★ Historic Yellow Bus Tours

BUS TOURS | FAMILY | Tours by park concessionaire Xanterra on restored bright-yellow buses from as far back as the 1930s offer more than a dozen itineraries throughout Yellowstone. It's an elegant way to learn about the park, and on warm days, the driver–tour narrator rolls back the convertible top. The tour lineup includes Evening Wildlife Encounters, Picture Perfect Photo Safari, and Wake Up to Wildlife, all longtime crowd-pleasers. Other tours, including some all-day ones that efficiently cover huge swaths of the park, are on newer buses. Tours depart from several park hotels. Xanterra also gives a variety of bus, boat, stagecoach, and other tours. ☎ *307/344–7311* 🌐 *www.yellowstonenationalparklodges.com* 🎫 *From $42.*

See Yellowstone

ADVENTURE TOURS | In summer this company conducts tours that might include day hiking in the backcountry, fly-fishing in Yellowstone, and horseback riding across wildflower meadows. The company also offers snowmobile and snowcoach excursions to Old Faithful and Lower Geyser Basin as well as cross-country skiing, snowshoeing, and dogsledding adventures. ✉ *211 Yellowstone Ave., West Yellowstone* ☎ *800/221–1151* 🌐 *www.seeyellowstone.com* 🎫 *From $95.*

Visitor Information

PARK CONTACT INFORMATION Yellowstone National Park. ☎ *307/344–7381* 🌐 *www.nps.gov/yell.*

Mammoth Hot Springs

6 miles south of Gardiner, 51 miles north of Old Faithful.

This park's northernmost community—which is just south of the North Entrance in Gardiner, Montana—is known for its massive natural travertine terraces, where mineral water flows continuously, building an ever-changing display. The entire complex of terraces, which is laced with boardwalks and pathways, is within walking distance of the area's historic village, which contains some charming mid-priced (by Yellowstone standards) lodging and dining options as well as the historic buildings of Fort Yellowstone,

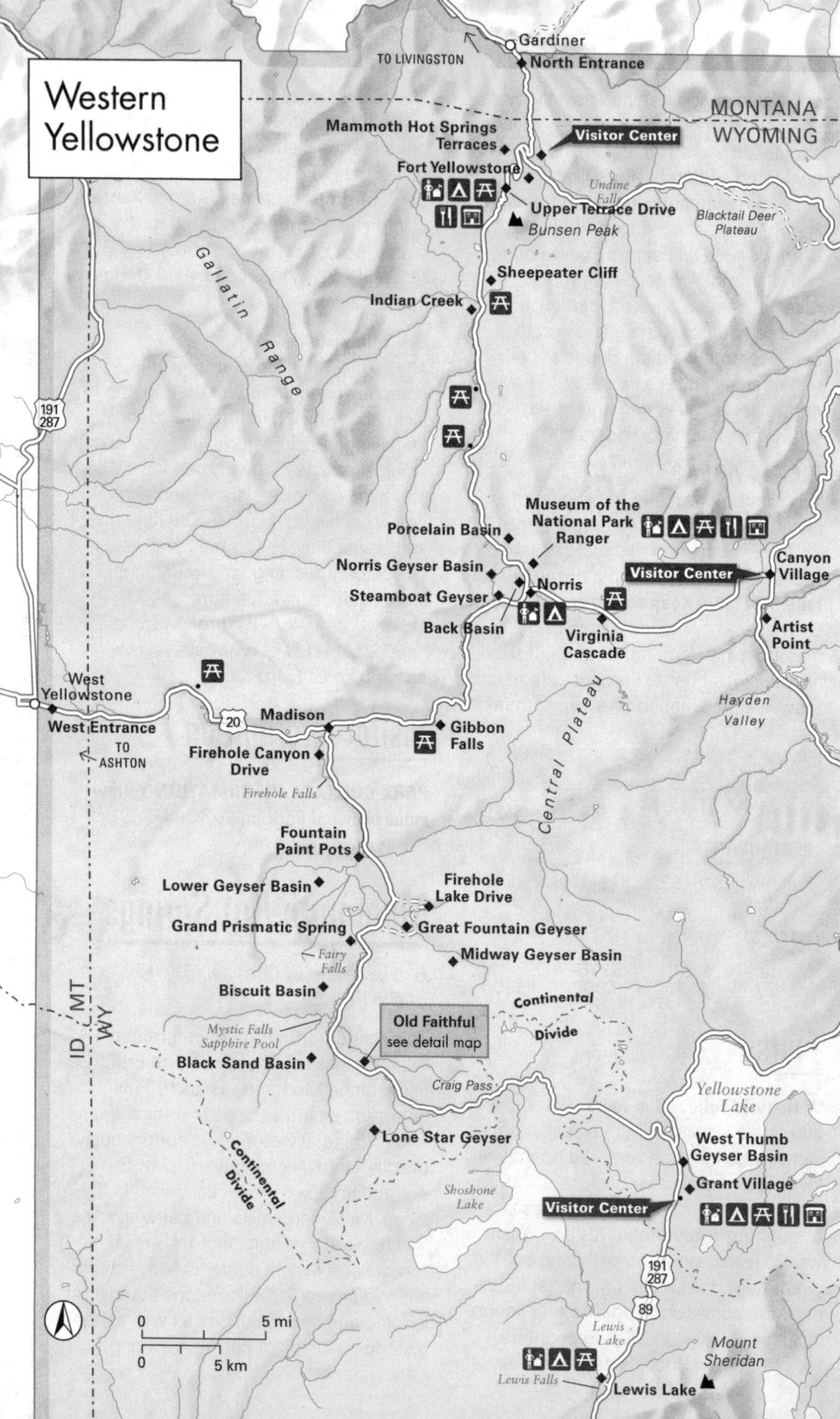
Western Yellowstone
Gardiner
TO LIVINGSTON
North Entrance
MONTANA
WYOMING
Mammoth Hot Springs Terraces
Visitor Center
Fort Yellowstone
Undine Falls
Upper Terrace Drive
Blacktail Deer Plateau
Bunsen Peak
Gallatin Range
Sheepeater Cliff
Indian Creek
191
287
Museum of the National Park Ranger
Porcelain Basin
Norris Geyser Basin
Norris
Visitor Center
Canyon Village
Steamboat Geyser
Back Basin
Virginia Cascade
Artist Point
West Yellowstone
West Entrance
TO ASHTON
20
Madison
Gibbon Falls
Firehole Canyon Drive
Firehole Falls
Central Plateau
Hayden Valley
Fountain Paint Pots
Lower Geyser Basin
Firehole Lake Drive
Grand Prismatic Spring
Great Fountain Geyser
Fairy Falls
Midway Geyser Basin
Biscuit Basin
Continental Divide
Old Faithful
see detail map
Mystic Falls
Sapphire Pool
Black Sand Basin
ID
MT
WY
Craig Pass
Yellowstone Lake
Lone Star Geyser
West Thumb Geyser Basin
Continental Divide
Grant Village
Shoshone Lake
Visitor Center
191
287
89
0
5 mi
0
5 km
Lewis Lake
Mount Sheridan
Lewis Falls
Lewis Lake

which are lovely to walk by. You will often see elk grazing in the village.

Sights

HISTORIC SIGHTS

★ Fort Yellowstone

MILITARY SITE | The oldest buildings here served as Fort Yellowstone from 1891 to 1918, when the U.S. Army managed the park. The redbrick buildings cluster around an open area reminiscent of a frontier-era parade ground. Pick up a self-guided tour map of the area from the Albright Visitors Center on Officers Row, and start your walking tour there. ✉ *Mammoth Hot Springs.*

SCENIC DRIVES

Upper Terrace Drive

SCENIC DRIVE | This popular 1½-mile drive at the top of the Mammoth Terraces will take you back into the woods, where you can see some impressive thermal features, among them White Elephant Back and Orange Spring Mound, that aren't visible from the main road. Park at the top of the Terraces for views of Fort Yellowstone, a short walk along the boardwalk to Canary Springs, or hike down into the Lower Terraces Area. RVs aren't permitted along this drive. ✉ *Grand Loop Rd.* ⏲ *Closed Dec.–Apr.*

SCENIC STOPS

★ Mammoth Hot Springs Terraces

BODY OF WATER | **FAMILY** | Multicolor travertine terraces formed by slowly escaping hot mineral water mark this unusual geological formation, one of the most remarkable sights in the park. You can explore the terraces via an elaborate network of boardwalks, the best of which is the Lower Terrace Interpretive Trail. If you head uphill from Liberty Cap, near the lower parking area, in a half-hour you'll pass bright and ornately terraced Minerva Spring, and in an hour you can make your way up to the Main Terrace Overlook and the side trail to Canary Spring. Along the way you might spot elk grazing nearby. Alternatively, you can drive up to the Main Terrace Overlook on Upper Terrace Drive and hike down to the Lower Terrace. Distances are fairly short amid these terraces, but give yourself at least a couple of hours to thoroughly explore them—especially if you enjoy taking lots of pictures. ✉ *Grand Loop Rd.*

TRAILS

Beaver Ponds Loop Trail

TRAIL | This 2½-hour, 5-mile loop starts at Liberty Cap in the busy Lower Terrace of Mammoth Hot Springs. Within minutes you'll find yourself amid the park's dense backcountry as you climb 400 feet through spruce and fir, passing several ponds and dams, as well as a glacier-carved moraine, before emerging on a windswept plain overlooking the Montana–Wyoming border. Look up to see Everts Peak to the east, Bunsen Peak to the south, and Sepulcher Mountain to the west. Your final descent into Mammoth Springs has great views of Mammoth Springs. *Moderate.* ✉ *Mammoth Hot Springs* ✥ *Trailhead: Lower Terrace parking area.*

★ Bunsen Peak Trail

TRAIL | Past the entrance to Bunsen Peak Road, this moderately challenging 4.4-mile round-trip trek climbs 1,280 feet to 8,527-foot Bunsen Peak for a dramatic panoramic view of Blacktail Plateau, Mammoth Hot Springs, the Gallatin Mountains, and the Yellowstone River valley. Allow about three hours. *Moderate–Difficult.* ✉ *Yellowstone National Park* ✥ *Trailhead: Grand Loop Rd., 1½ miles south of Mammoth Hot Springs.*

VISITOR CENTERS

Albright Visitor Center

INFO CENTER | **FAMILY** | Bachelor quarters for U.S. Army cavalry officers from 1909 to 1918, the carefully renovated red-roof visitor center is a great source for maps, advice, permits, and free Wi-Fi. This hefty stone structure also contains a bookstore and exhibits about the park's history, flora, and fauna, including displays of bears and wolves that kids love. ✉ *Grand Loop Rd., Mammoth Hot Springs* ☎ *307/344–2263* 🌐 *www.nps.gov/yell.*

Restaurants

Mammoth Hotel Dining Room

$$$ | **AMERICAN** | A wall of windows in the handsome art deco–style restaurant overlooks an expanse of green that was once a military parade and drill field. While enjoying breakfast, lunch, or dinner you might catch a glimpse of elk grazing on the lawn. **Known for:** bison burgers; creative appetizers; views of roaming elk. $ *Average main: $24* ✉ *305A Albright Ave., Mammoth Hot Springs* ☎ *307/344–7311, 866/439–7375* 🌐 *www.yellowstonenationalparklodges.com* ⏲ *Closed mid-Oct.–mid-Dec. and Mar.–late Apr.*

Mammoth Terrace Grill

$ | **AMERICAN** | **FAMILY** | Although the exterior looks rather elegant, this is actually the casual option at Mammoth Hot Springs, a good bet for simple fare like hot dogs, hamburgers, and chicken tenders. Continental breakfast is offered all day. **Known for:** biscuits and gravy in the morning; smoked-bison bratwurst sandwiches; pretty good beer and wine selection. $ *Average main: $9* ✉ *305B Albright Ave., Mammoth Hot Springs* ☎ *307/344–7311* 🌐 *www.yellowstonenationalparklodges.com* ⏲ *Closed mid-Oct.–late Apr.*

Hotels

★ **Mammoth Hot Springs Hotel and Cabins**

$$ | **HOTEL** | The rooms at this 1936 lodge are smaller and simpler than those at the park's other historic hotels, but this one is less expensive; the surrounding cabins look like tiny, genteel summer homes. **Pros:** good rates for a historic property; wake up to an elk bugling outside your window; cabins are among the park's nicest. **Cons:** least expensive rooms lack bathrooms; in one of the busier parts of the park; Wi-Fi is spotty. $ *Rooms from: $197* ✉ *2 Mammoth Hotel Ave.* ☎ *307/344–7311* 🌐 *www.yellowstonenationalparklodges.com* ⏲ *Closed mid-Oct.–mid Dec. and early Mar.–late Apr.* *216 rooms* *No meals.*

Norris

21 miles south of Mammoth Hot Springs, 13 miles west of Canyon Village.

The area at the western junction of the Upper and Lower Loops has the most active geyser basin in the park. The underground plumbing occasionally reaches such high temperatures—the ground itself has heated up in areas to nearly 200°F—that a portion of the basin is periodically closed for safety reasons. There are limited visitor services: two small museums, a bookstore, and a picnic area. The 21-mile span of Grand Loop Drive from Mammoth Hot Springs to Norris is quite dramatic, passing groves of aspens that explode with fall color just south from Upper Terrace Drive and traversing a hillside of giant boulders through the Golden Gate section. **■ TIP→ Ask rangers at the Norris Geyser Basin Museum when different geysers are expected to erupt and plan your walk accordingly.**

Sights

PICNIC AREAS

Gibbon Meadows

LOCAL INTEREST | **FAMILY** | You may see elk or buffalo along the Gibbon River from one of the several tables at this picturesque spot, which has a wheelchair-accessible pit toilet. ✉ *Grand Loop Rd.*

SCENIC STOPS

Museum of the National Park Ranger

MUSEUM | **FAMILY** | This historic ranger station housed soldiers from 1908 to 1918. The six-room log building is now an engaging museum where you can watch a movie telling the history of the National Park Service and visit with the retired rangers who volunteer here. Other exhibits relate to Army service in Yellowstone and early park rangers. ✉ *Norris Campground Rd.* ⏲ *Closed late Sept.–late May.*

Norris Geyser Basin

NATURE SITE | **FAMILY** | From the 1930 Norris Ranger Station, which houses a small museum that helps to explain the basin's geothermal activity, you can stroll a network of short boardwalk trails—some of them suitable for wheelchairs—to Porcelain Basin, Back Basin, and several geysers and other interesting and constantly evolving thermal features. ✉ *Grand Loop Rd. at Norris Canyon Rd.* 🌐 *www.nps.gov/yell* ⏲ *Ranger station closed mid-Oct.–mid-May.*

TRAILS

Back Basin–Porcelain Basin Loops

TRAIL | You can hike these two easy loops, which both leave from the Norris Ranger Station, in under two hours. The 1½-mile Back Basin loop passes Emerald Spring, Steamboat Geyser, Cistern Spring, and Echinus Geyser. The latter was long known as Norris's most dependable big geyser, but its schedule has become much more erratic. The ¾-mile Porcelain Basin loop leads past whitish geyserite stone and extremely active Whirligig and other small geysers. *Easy.* ✉ *Norris* ⊕ *Trailhead: at Grand Loop Rd. at Norris Canyon Rd.*

Madison

14 miles southwest of Norris, 15 miles east of West Yellowstone, Montana.

The area around the junction of the West Entrance Road and the Lower Loop is a good place to take a break as you travel through the park, because you will almost always see bison grazing along the Madison River, and elk are often in the area, too. The only visitor services in Madison are a small information station.

Sights

SCENIC DRIVES

★ Firehole Canyon Drive

SCENIC DRIVE | **FAMILY** | The 2-mile narrow asphalt road twists through a deep canyon of curving lava-rock formations and passes the 40-foot Firehole Falls, which are most scenic in the morning when you're not looking into the afternoon sun. In summer look for a sign marking a pullout and swimming hole. This is one of only two places in the park (Boiling River on the North Entrance Road is the other) where you can safely and legally swim in the thermally heated waters. Look for osprey and other raptors. ✉ *Yellowstone National Park* ⊕ *1 mile south of Madison junction, off Grand Loop Rd.* ⏲ *Closed early Nov.–early Apr.*

SCENIC STOPS

Gibbon Falls

BODY OF WATER | **FAMILY** | The water of this 84-foot fall on the Gibbon River rushes over the caldera rim. Driving east from Madison to Norris, you can see it on your right, but the angle is even better from the paved trail adjacent to the canyon's edge. ✉ *Yellowstone National Park* ⊕ *Grand Loop Rd., 4 miles east of Madison.*

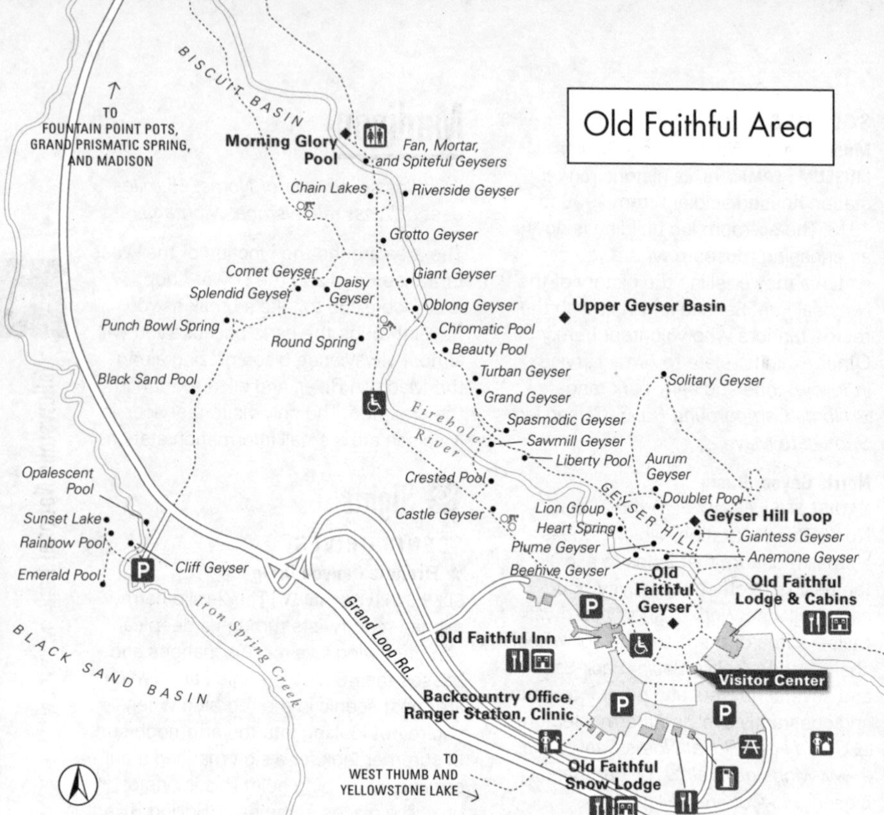

VISITOR CENTERS

Madison Information Station and Trailside Museum

INFO CENTER | **FAMILY** | In this handsome 1930s stone-and-timber structure, knowledgeable rangers share space with a store that sells books, maps, and learning aids, and a museum with exhibits on the thermal features in the vicinity. Spotting scopes are sometimes set up for viewing eagles, bison, and elk out the rear window. You can pick up backcountry camping and fishing permits, too. Picnic tables, toilets, and an amphitheater for summer-evening ranger programs are shared with the nearby campground. ✉ *Grand Loop Rd. at West Entrance Rd.* ☎ *307/344–2876* 🌐 *www.nps.gov/yell* ⏲ *Closed early Oct.–early June.*

Old Faithful

17 miles south of Madison, 40 miles west of Fishing Bridge Village.

The world's most famous geyser is the centerpiece of this area that includes one of the largest villages in the park and three prominent geyser basins: Upper, Midway, and Lower. The 1-square-mile Upper Geyser Basin is arguably the park's most famous draw, home to Old Faithful as well as 140 different geysers—one-fifth of the known geysers in the world. It's an excellent place to spend a day or more exploring, with a complex system of boardwalks and trails—some of them suitable for bikes—and equally extensive visitor services, including several lodging and dining choices, and a very fine visitor center. In winter you can dine and stay in this area and cross-country ski or snowshoe through the geyser basin. The smaller Midway and Lower geyser basins each have their own must-see features, including Grand Prismatic Spring and Fountain Paint Pots.

Sights

HISTORIC SIGHTS

★ Old Faithful Inn

HOTEL—SIGHT | **FAMILY** | It's hard to imagine how any work could be accomplished with snow and ice blanketing the region, but this truly iconic hotel was constructed over the course of a single winter. Completed in 1904, what's believed to be the world's largest log structure is one of the most recognizable, and impressive, buildings in the national park system. Even if you don't spend the night, walk through or take the free 45-minute guided tour to admire its massive open-beam lobby and rock fireplace. There are antique writing desks on the second-floor balcony. You can watch Old Faithful geyser from two second-floor decks. ✉ *3200 Old Faithful Inn Rd., Old Faithful* ☎ *307/344–7311* 🌐 *www.yellowstonenationalparklodges.com* ⏲ *Closed early Oct.–early May.*

PICNIC AREAS

Firehole River

LOCAL INTEREST | **FAMILY** | This scenic picnic area overlooks the roaring Firehole River, a place where you might see elk grazing along the river's banks. There's a pit toilet. ✉ *Grand Loop Rd., Madison.*

SCENIC DRIVES

Firehole Lake Drive

SCENIC DRIVE | This one-way, 3-mile-long road takes you past Great Fountain Geyser, which shoots out jets of water reaching as high as 200 feet about twice a day. Rangers' predictions provide a two-hour window of opportunity. Should you witness an eruption, you'll see waves of water cascading down the terraces that form the geyser's edges. ✉ *Firehole Lake Dr., Old Faithful* ⏲ *Closed early Nov.–early Apr.*

SCENIC STOPS

Biscuit Basin

NATURE SITE | A short drive north of Old Faithful and accessed via an easy ⅔-mile loop stroll, this basin is also the trailhead for the Mystic Falls Trail. The namesake "biscuit" formations were reduced to crumbs when Sapphire Pool erupted after the 1959 Hebgen Lake earthquake. Now, Sapphire is a calm, beautiful blue pool again, but that could change at any moment. ✉ *Grand Loop Rd., Old Faithful.*

Black Sand Basin

NATURE SITE | **FAMILY** | There are a dozen hot springs and geysers nearly opposite the cloverleaf entrance from Grand Loop Road to Old Faithful. Emerald Pool is one of the prettiest. It's an easy 1½-mile walk, ski, or bike ride from the Old Faithful area, or you can drive and park right in the middle of the basin. ✉ *Grand Loop Rd., Old Faithful.*

Geyser Hill Loop

TRAIL | **FAMILY** | Along the easy 1.3-mile Geyser Hill Loop boardwalk, accessed from the Old Faithful Boardwalk, you'll see active thermal features such as violent Giantess Geyser. Erupting only a few times each year (but sometimes going quiet for several years), Giantess spouts from 100 to 250 feet in the air for five to eight minutes once or twice hourly for a few to as long as 48 hours. Nearby Doublet Pool's two adjacent springs have complex ledges and deep blue waters that are highly photogenic. Starting as a gentle pool, Anemone Geyser overflows, bubbles, and finally erupts 10 feet or more, every three to eight minutes. The loop boardwalk brings you close to the action, making it especially fun for kids. ✉ *Old Faithful* ✣ *Trailhead: Old Faithful Visitor Center.*

A Good Tour: Old Faithful Area

Begin your tour at the impressive **Old Faithful Visitor Education Center.** Pick up the Old Faithful–area trail guide and check a bulletin board with the latest predictions for six geyser eruptions.

The Main Attraction

Concentrate first on the main attraction: **Old Faithful** spouts from 130 to 180 feet high approximately every 94 minutes. You don't need to jockey for position on the boardwalk directly in front of the visitor center to enjoy the geyser. It's impressive from any angle on the boardwalk surrounding it. The view from the second-floor deck of the **Old Faithful Inn** is glorious, too. Speaking of that famous, century-old structure, check out its massive log-construction interior.

Exploring the Basins

At Old Faithful Village you're in the heart of the **Upper Geyser Basin**, the densest concentration of geysers on Earth, with about 140 geysers within a square mile. Once you've watched Old Faithful erupt, explore the larger basin with a hike around **Geyser Hill**, where you may see wildlife as well as thermal features. Follow the trail north to the **Morning Glory Pool**, with its unique flower shape. Along this trail are Castle, Grand, and Riverside geysers. Return to the village and continue by car to **Black Sand Basin** or **Biscuit Basin.** At Biscuit Basin, follow the boardwalks to the trailhead for the Mystic Falls Trail, where you can get views of the Upper Geyser Basin.

Paint Pots and a Spring

Take a break from geyser watching with a packed lunch at the Whiskey Flat picnic area. Afterward, continue your drive toward **Lower Geyser Basin**, with its colorful **Fountain Paint Pots.** Then, on the way back to Old Faithful, stop at **Midway Geyser Basin**, where steaming runoff from the colorful 370-foot **Grand Prismatic Spring** crashes continuously into the Firehole River.

Relax and Celebrate

Relax and celebrate your day's accomplishments with dinner (reservations required) at the Old Faithful Inn, or enjoy drinks on the second floor.

★ Grand Prismatic Spring

NATURE SITE | FAMILY | You can reach Yellowstone's largest hot spring, 370 feet in diameter and arguably an even more dazzling sight than Old Faithful, by following a ⅓-mile boardwalk loop. The spring, in the Midway Geyser Basin, is deep blue in color, with yellow and orange rings formed by bacteria that give it the effect of a prism. For a stunning perspective, view it from the overlook along the Fairy Falls Trail. ✉ *Midway Geyser Basin, Grand Loop Rd.*

Lower Geyser Basin

NATURE SITE | With its mighty blasts of water shooting as high as 200 feet, the Great Fountain Geyser is this basin's superstar. When it spews, waves cascade down the terraces that form its edge. Check at the Old Faithful Visitor Center for predicted eruption times. Less impressive but more regular is White Dome Geyser, which shoots from a 20-foot-tall cone. You'll also find pink mudpots and blue pools at the basin's Fountain Paint Pots, a unique spot because visitors encounter all four of Yellowstone's hydrothermal features:

fumaroles, mudpots, hot springs, and geysers. ✉ *Grand Loop Rd.*

Midway Geyser Basin

NATURE SITE | Called "Hell's Half Acre" by writer Rudyard Kipling, Midway Geyser Basin contains the breathtaking Grand Prismatic Spring and is an even more interesting stop than Lower Geyser Basin. Boardwalks wind their way to the Excelsior Geyser, which deposits 4,000 gallons of vivid blue water per minute into the Firehole River. ✉ *Grand Loop Rd.*

Morning Glory Pool

NATURE SITE | Shaped somewhat like a morning glory, this pool once was a deep blue, but the color is no longer as striking as before due to tourists dropping coins and other debris into the hole. To reach the pool, follow the boardwalk past Geyser Hill Loop and stately Castle Geyser, which has the biggest cone in Yellowstone. Morning Glory is the inspiration for popular children's author Jan Brett's story *Hedgie Blasts Off*, in which a hedgehog travels to another planet to unclog a geyser damaged by space tourists' debris. ✉ *Yellowstone National Park* ✣ *North end of Upper Geyser Basin.*

★ Old Faithful

NATURE SITE | **FAMILY** | Almost every park visitor makes it a point to view the world's most famous geyser, at least once. Yellowstone's most predictable big geyser—although neither its largest nor most regular—sometimes shoots as high as 180 feet, but it averages 130 feet. The eruptions take place every 50–120 minutes, the average is around 94 minutes. Check the park website, visitor center, or the lobbies of the Old Faithful hotels for predicted times. You can view the eruption from a bench just yards away, from the dining room at the lodge cafeteria, or the second-floor deck of the Old Faithful Inn. The 1.6-mile loop hike to Observation Point yields yet another view—from above—of the geyser and the surrounding basin. ✉ *Grand Loop Rd.*

TRAILS

★ Fairy Falls Trail

TRAIL | Rewarding trekkers with the chance to view Grand Prismatic Spring from high up on a bluff and to gaze up at 200-foot-tall Fairy Falls cascade from a pool of mist down below, this mostly level 5.4-mile round-trip hike is one of the highlights of the Midway Geyser Basin. *Easy.* ✉ *Old Faithful* ✣ *Trailhead: Fairy Falls Trail parking lot, Midway Geyser Basin.*

Fountain Paint Pots Nature Trail

TRAIL | **FAMILY** | Take the ½-mile loop boardwalk to see the fumaroles (steam vents), blue pools, pink mudpots, and mini-geysers in this thermal area. The trail is popular, and sometimes a bit overcrowded, in summer and winter because it's so accessible. *Easy.* ✉ *Yellowstone National Park* ✣ *Trailhead: at Lower Geyser Basin.*

Lone Star Geyser

TRAIL | **FAMILY** | A little longer, at 4.8 miles round-trip, than many of the other trails in the vicinity of Upper Geyser Basin, this enjoyable ramble along a level, partially paved trail that parallels the Firehole River leads to an overlook where you can watch Lone Star Geyser erupt up to 45 feet into the sky. Eruptions take place every three hours or so,and the trail is also popular with cyclists. *Easy–Moderate.* ✣ *Trailhead: Just south of Kepler Cascades parking area, 3½ miles south of Old Faithful.*

Mystic Falls Trail

TRAIL | From the west end of Biscuit Basin boardwalk, this 2.4-mile round-trip trail climbs gently for a mile through heavily burned forest to the lava-rock base of 70-foot Mystic Falls. It then switchbacks up Madison Plateau to a lookout with the park's least-crowded view of Old Faithful and the Upper Geyser Basin. *Easy–Moderate.* ✉ *Old Faithful* ✣ *Trailhead: Biscuit Basin.*

★ **Observation Point Loop**

TRAIL | A 2-mile round-trip route leaves Geyser Hill Loop boardwalk and becomes a trail shortly after the Firehole River; it circles a picturesque overview of Geyser Hill with Old Faithful Inn as a backdrop. You may also see Castle Geyser erupting. Even when 1,000-plus people are crowded on the boardwalk to watch Old Faithful, expect to find fewer than a dozen here. *Easy–Moderate.* ✉ *Old Faithful* ✣ *Trailhead: Old Faithful Visitor Center.*

VISITOR CENTERS

★ **Old Faithful Visitor Education Center**

INFO CENTER | **FAMILY** | At this impressive, contemporary, LEED-certified visitor center that's a jewel of the national park system, you can check out the interactive exhibits and children's area, read the latest geyser-eruption predictions, and find out the schedules for ranger-led walks and talks. Backcountry and fishing permits are dispensed at the ranger station adjacent to the Old Faithful Snow Lodge, across the street. ✉ *Old Faithful Bypass Rd.* ☎ *307/344–2751* 🌐 *www.nps.gov/yell* ⏲ *Closed mid-Nov.–mid-Dec. and mid-Mar.–mid-Apr.*

Restaurants

Bear Paw Deli

$ | **AMERICAN** | **FAMILY** | You can grab a quick bite and not miss a geyser eruption at this snack shop in the Old Faithful Inn. Salmon, black-bean, and beef burgers as well as several sandwiches are available throughout the day, as is hand-dipped ice cream. **Known for:** inexpensive, no-frills meals; opens early, closes late (by park standards); great location by geyser. Ⓢ *Average main: $9* ✉ *3200 Old Faithful Inn Rd., Old Faithful* ☎ *307/344–7311* 🌐 *www.yellowstonenationalparklodges.com* ⏲ *Closed early Oct.–early May.*

★ **Old Faithful Inn Dining Room**

$$$ | **AMERICAN** | The Old Faithful Inn's original dining room—designed by Robert Reamer in 1903 and expanded by him in 1927—has lodgepole-pine walls and ceiling beams and a giant volcanic rock fireplace. Note the whimsical etched-glass panels that separate the dining room from the Bear Pit Lounge; the images of partying animals were commissioned by Reamer in 1933 to celebrate the end of Prohibition. **Known for:** gorgeous interior; buffet options offered at every meal; extensive wine list. Ⓢ *Average main: $24* ✉ *3200 Old Faithful Inn Rd., Old Faithful* ☎ *307/344–7311* 🌐 *www.yellowstonenationalparklodges.com* ⏲ *Closed early Oct.–early May.*

Old Faithful Snow Lodge Obsidian Dining Room

$$$ | **MODERN AMERICAN** | From the wood-and-leather chairs etched with animal figures to the intricate lighting fixtures that resemble snowcapped trees, there's ample Western atmosphere at this relatively intimate dining room inside the Old Faithful Snow Lodge. The huge windows give you a view of the Old Faithful area, and you can sometimes see the famous geyser as it erupts. **Known for:** hearty regional wild game dishes; open in winter; lounge offering microbrews and lighter fare. Ⓢ *Average main: $26* ✉ *2051 Snow Lodge Ave.* ☎ *307/344–7311* 🌐 *www.yellowstonenationalparklodges.com* ⏲ *Closed late-Oct.–mid-Dec. and Mar.–late Apr.*

Hotels

★ **Old Faithful Inn**

$$$ | **HOTEL** | **FAMILY** | Easily earning its National Historic Landmark status, this jewel of the national park system has been a favorite since the original Old House section opened in 1904—it's worth a visit whether or not you stay here. **Pros:** a one-of-a-kind property; rooms at a range of price points; incredible location near geyser. **Cons:** thin walls; waves of tourists in the lobby; least expensive rooms lack private baths.

Rooms from: $272 ✉ *3200 Old Faithful Inn Rd., Old Faithful* ☎ *307/344–7311* 🌐 *www.yellowstonenationalparklodges.com* ⏲ *Closed mid-Oct.–early May* 🛏 *329 rooms* 🍽 *No meals.*

Old Faithful Lodge Cabins

$$$ | **HOTEL** | There are no rooms inside the Old Faithful Lodge, but close to 100 rustic cabins can be found at the village's northeastern end. **Pros:** affordable; stone's throw from Old Faithful; services within walking distance. **Cons:** some cabins lack private bathrooms; pretty basic; few views from cabins. *Rooms from: $183* ✉ *725 Old Faithful Lodge Rd.* ☎ *307/344–7311* 🌐 *www.yellowstonenationalparklodges.com* ⏲ *Closed early Oct.–mid-May* 🛏 *96 cabins* 🍽 *No meals.*

Old Faithful Snow Lodge

$$$$ | **HOTEL** | This large, contemporary lodge brings back the grand tradition of park lodges by making good use of heavy timber beams and wrought-iron accents in its distinctive facade, guest rooms that combine traditional style with up-to-date amenities. **Pros:** the park's most modern hotel; inviting common spaces; open in both summer and winter. **Cons:** pricey, but you're paying for location; rooms don't have a ton of character; busy part of the park. *Rooms from: $324* ✉ *2051 Snow Lodge Ave., Old Faithful* ☎ *307/344–7311* 🌐 *www.yellowstonenationalparklodges.com* ⏲ *Closed late Oct.–mid-Dec. and mid-Mar.–late Apr.* 🛏 *100 rooms* 🍽 *No meals.*

Old Faithful Snow Lodge Cabins

$$$ | **HOTEL** | **FAMILY** | Just yards from Old Faithful, the Western Cabins feature bright interiors and a modern motel ambience, while the Frontier Cabins are simple pine structures. **Pros:** reasonably priced; close to geyser; open during winter. **Cons:** no amenities beyond the basics; small rooms; very rustic. *Rooms from: $233* ✉ *2051 Snow Lodge Ave., Old Faithful* ☎ *307/344–7311* 🌐 *www.yellowstonenationalparklodges.com* ⏲ *Closed late Oct.–mid-Dec., early Mar.–late Apr.* 🛏 *34 cabins* 🍽 *No meals.*

Shopping

Old Faithful Basin Store

FOOD/CANDY | **FAMILY** | Recognizable by the wooden "Hamilton's Store" sign over the entrance, this shop dates to 1897 and is the second-oldest building in the park. The old-fashioned soda fountain serves up all your ice-cream favorites, including beloved huckleberry shakes. ✉ *1 Old Faithful Loop Rd.* ☎ *307/545–7282* 🌐 *www.yellowstonevacations.com.*

Grant Village and West Thumb

22 miles southeast of Old Faithful, 78 miles north of Jackson.

Along the western edge of Yellowstone Lake, called the West Thumb, Grant Village is the first community you encounter if entering the park from the South Entrance. It has some basic lodging and dining facilities and other services, but the real draw here is the geothermal activity in the West Thumb Geyser Basin.

Sights

SCENIC DRIVES

South Entrance Road

SCENIC DRIVE | The sheer black lava walls and boulder-strewn landscape of the deep Lewis River canyon make this somewhat underrated drive toward Grand Teton National Park highly memorable. Turn into the parking area at the highway bridge for a close-up view of the spectacular Lewis River Falls, one of the park's most photographed sights. There are several pull-outs along the shore of Lewis Lake that are ideal for a picnic or just to stretch your legs. ✉ *Yellowstone National Park.*

"This was a magical moment that I captured at West Thumb Geyser Basin—the sunset reflecting off the rain clouds, steam rising from the geyser basin, and an elk drinking." —photo by Paul Stoloff, Fodors.com member

SCENIC STOPS

★ West Thumb Geyser Basin

NATURE SITE | FAMILY | The primary Yellowstone caldera was created by one massive volcanic eruption, but a later eruption formed the West Thumb, an unusual and particularly photogenic geyser basin because its active geothermal features are on the shore of Yellowstone Lake. Two boardwalks loop through the basin and showcase a number of sites, including the stunning blue-green Abyss Pool and Fishing Cone, where fishermen used to drop their freshly caught fish straight into boiling water without ever taking it off the hook. This area is popular in winter, when you can take advantage of the nearby warming hut and stroll around the geyser basin before continuing your trip via snowcoach or snowmobile. ✉ *Grand Loop Rd., West Thumb.*

VISITOR CENTERS

Grant Village Visitor Center

INFO CENTER | FAMILY | Exhibits at each visitor center describe a small piece of Yellowstone's history—the ones here provide details about the 1988 fire that burned more than a third of the park's total acreage and forced multiple federal agencies to reevaluate their fire-control policies. Watch an informative video, and learn about the 25,000 firefighters from across the United States who battled the blaze. Bathrooms and a backcountry office are here. ✉ *2 Grant Village Loop Rd., Grant Village* ☎ *307/242–2650* 🌐 *www.nps.gov/yell* 🕑 *Closed early Oct.–late May.*

West Thumb Information Station

INFO CENTER | This 1925 log cabin houses a bookstore and doubles as a warming hut in winter. There are restrooms in the parking area. In summer, check for informal ranger-led discussions beneath the old sequoia tree. ✉ *West Thumb Basin, West Thumb* ☎ *307/344–2650* 🌐 *www.nps.gov/yell* 🕑 *Closed early Oct.–late May.*

Restaurants

Grant Village Dining Room

$$$ | **AMERICAN** | Although the passable food here isn't the main event, the floor-to-ceiling windows of this waterfront restaurant provide dazzling views of Yellowstone Lake through the thick stand of pines. The pine-beam ceilings, cedar-shake walls, and contemporary decor lend the place a homey feel. **Known for:** sweeping water views; reliable breakfast fare; vanilla bean crème brûlée cheesecake. *Average main: $25 550 Sculpin La., Grant Village 307/344–7311 www.yellowstonenationalparklodges.com Closed Oct.–late May.*

Hotels

Grant Village Lodge

$$$ | **HOTEL** | Grant Village is an excellent location for touring the southern half of the park, but this 1980s lodge itself feels like a bit dormlike, its rooms furnished like their counterparts at a big-city motel, with beds, nightstands, and tables, and not much else. **Pros:** near Lake Yellowstone; many facilities nearby; closest Yellowstone lodge to Grand Teton. **Cons:** expensive for what you get; small rooms without character; spotty Wi-Fi. *Rooms from: $291 24 Rainbow Loop 307/344–7311 www.yellowstonenationalparklodges.com Closed late Sept.–late May 300 rooms No meals.*

Lake Yellowstone

22 miles northeast of West Thumb and Grant Village, 80 miles west of Cody.

In the park's southeastern quadrant, this section is closest to the East Entrance and is dominated by the tranquil beauty of massive Yellowstone Lake. One of the world's largest alpine bodies of water, the 132-square-mile Yellowstone Lake was formed when the glaciers that once covered the region melted and filled a caldera—a crater formed by a volcano. The lake has 141 miles of shoreline, along which you will often see moose, elk, waterfowl, and other wildlife. In winter you can sometimes see otters and coyotes stepping gingerly onto the ice at the lake's edge. Many visitors head here for the excellent fishing—streams flowing into the lake provide an abundant supply of trout. There are also three small villages near the northern tip of the lake: Fishing Bridge, which has a visitor center and the park's largest campground (you may see grizzly bears hunt for fish spawning or swimming near the lake's outlet to the Yellowstone River); Lake Village, home to the striking Lake Yellowstone Hotel and the more modest Lake Lodge; and Bridge Bay, which has a marina and boat launch.

Sights

HISTORIC SIGHTS

Lake Yellowstone Hotel

HOTEL—SIGHT | Completed in 1891 and meticulously restored in recent years, the oldest lodging in Yellowstone National Park is a splendid wedding cake of a building with a gorgeous setting on the water. Casual daytime visitors can lounge in white wicker chairs in the sunroom and watch the waters of Yellowstone Lake through massive windows. Robert Reamer, the architect of the Old Faithful Inn, added a columned entrance in 1903 to enhance the original facade of the hotel. *235 Yellowstone Lake Rd., Lake Village 307/344–7901 www.yellowstonenationalparklodges.com Closed late Sept.–mid-May.*

PICNIC AREAS

★ Sedge Bay

LOCAL INTEREST | **FAMILY** | On the northern end of this volcanic beach, look carefully for the large rock slabs pushed out of the lake bottom. Nearby trees offer shade

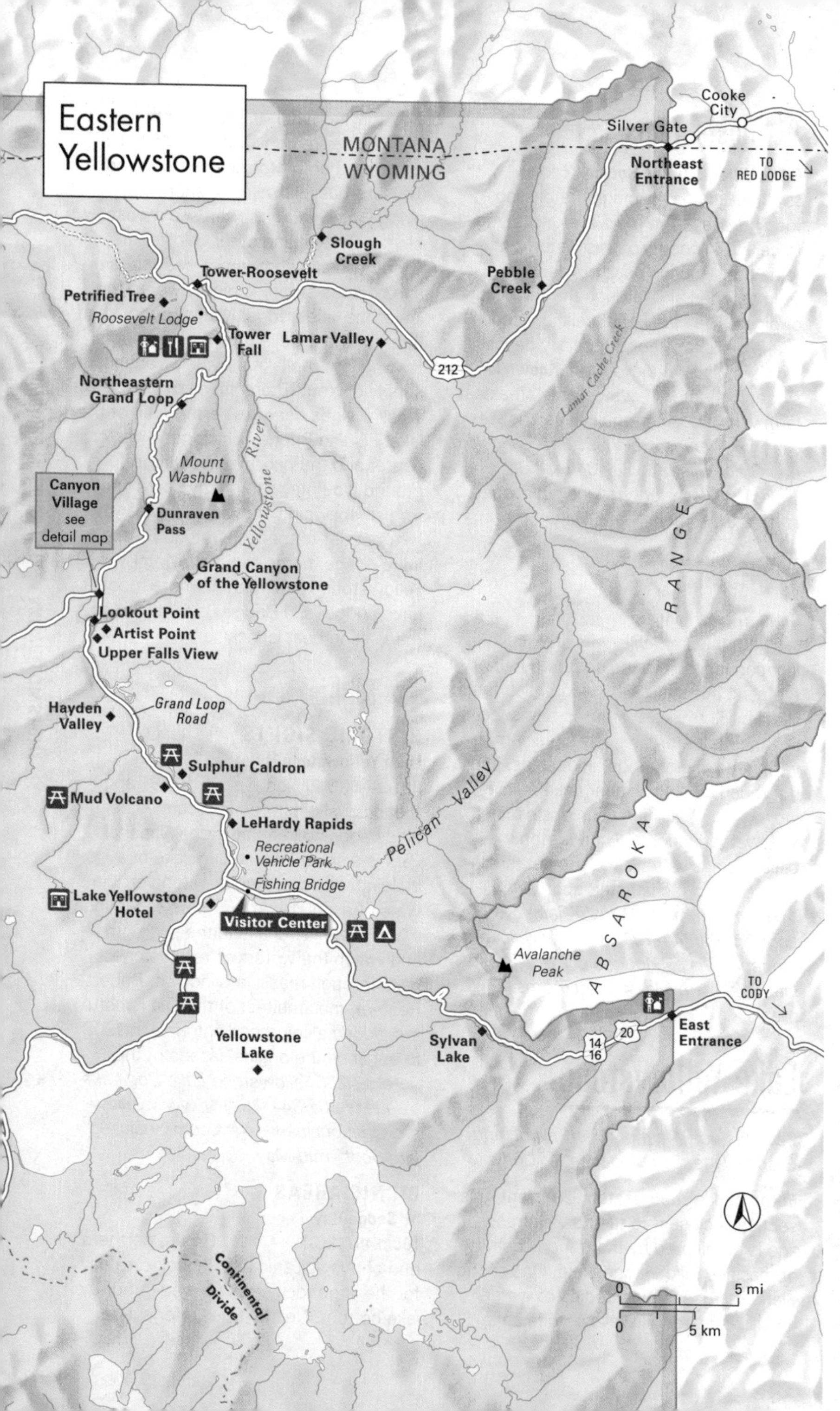

Eastern Yellowstone
MONTANA
WYOMING
Cooke City
Silver Gate
Northeast Entrance
TO RED LODGE
Slough Creek
Tower-Roosevelt
Pebble Creek
Petrified Tree
Roosevelt Lodge
Tower Fall
Lamar Valley
212
Lamar Cache Creek
Northeastern Grand Loop
Mount Washburn
Yellowstone River
Canyon Village see detail map
Dunraven Pass
Grand Canyon of the Yellowstone
Lookout Point
Artist Point
Upper Falls View
RANGE
Hayden Valley
Grand Loop Road
Sulphur Caldron
Mud Volcano
LeHardy Rapids
Pelican Valley
Recreational Vehicle Park
Fishing Bridge
Lake Yellowstone Hotel
Visitor Center
ABSAROKA
Avalanche Peak
TO CODY
Yellowstone Lake
Sylvan Lake
East Entrance
20
14
16
Continental Divide
0
5 mi
0
5 km

and a table, or you can hop onto the level rocks for an ideal lakeside picnic. You may see bubbles rising from the clear water around the rocks—these indicate an active underwater thermal feature. The only company you may have here could be crickets, birds, and bison. ✉ *East Entrance Rd.*

SCENIC DRIVES

★ Hayden Valley on Grand Loop Road

SCENIC DRIVE | Bison, bears, coyotes, wolves, and birds of prey all call Hayden Valley home almost year-round. Once part of Yellowstone Lake, the broad valley now contains peaceful meadows, rolling hills, and a serene stretch of the Yellowstone River. There are multiple turnouts and picnic areas on this 16-mile drive. Ask a ranger about "Grizzly Overlook," an unofficial site where wildlife watchers, including NPS rangers with spotting scopes for the public to use, congregate in summer. North of Mud Volcano are 11 unsigned turnouts. Look for the telltale timber railings, and be prepared to get caught in a traffic-stopping "bison jam" along the way. ✉ *Grand Loop Rd. between Canyon and Fishing Bridge* ⏲ *Closed early Nov.–early Apr.*

SCENIC STOPS

LeHardy Rapids

BODY OF WATER | Witness one of nature's epic battles as cutthroat trout migrate upstream by catapulting themselves out of the water to get over and around obstacles in the Yellowstone River. The ¼-mile forested loop takes you to the river's edge. Look for waterfowl and bears, which feed on the trout. ✉ *Fishing Bridge* ✣ *3 miles north of Fishing Bridge.*

TRAILS

★ Avalanche Peak Trail

TRAIL | On a busy day in summer, only a handful of parties will fill out the trail register at the Avalanche Peak trailhead, so if you're seeking solitude, this is your hike. Starting across from a parking area on the East Entrance Road, this rigorous 4.2-mile, four-hour round-trip climbs 2,150 feet to the peak's 10,566-foot summit, from which you'll see the rugged Absaroka Mountains running north and south. Look around the talus and tundra near the top of Avalanche Peak for alpine wildflowers and butterflies. From early September to late June, the trail is often impassable due to snow, and fall also can see grizzly bear activity. Stick to summer. *Difficult.* ✉ *Fishing Bridge* ✣ *Trailhead: 2 miles east of Sylvan Lake on north side of East Entrance Rd.*

Storm Point Trail

TRAIL | **FAMILY** | Well marked and mostly flat, this 2.3-mile loop leaves the south side of the road for a perfect beginner's hike out to Yellowstone Lake, particularly with a setting sun. The trail rounds the western edge of Indian Pond, then passes moose habitat on its way to Yellowstone Lake's Storm Point, named for its frequent afternoon windstorms and crashing waves. Heading west along the shore, you're likely to hear the shrill chirping of yellow-bellied marmots. Also look for ducks, pelicans, trumpeter swans, and bison. You'll pass several small beaches that kids enjoy exploring. *Easy.* ✉ *Fishing Bridge* ✣ *Trailhead: 3 miles east of Lake Junction on East Entrance Rd.*

VISITOR CENTERS

Fishing Bridge Visitor Center

INFO CENTER | **FAMILY** | If you can't distinguish between a Clark's nuthatch and an ermine (one's a bird, the other a weasel), check out the exhibits about the park's smaller wildlife at this distinctive stone-and-log building, built in 1931. Step out the back door to find yourself on one of the beautiful black obsidian beaches of Yellowstone Lake. Adjacent is one of the park's larger amphitheaters. Ranger presentations take place here nightly in summer. ✉ *East Entrance Rd.* ☎ *307/242–2450* 🌐 *www.nps.gov/yell* ⏲ *Closed early Sept.–late May.*

Continued on page 87

YELLOWSTONE'S GEOTHERMAL WONDERS

Steaming, bubbling, and erupting throughout the day like giant teapots.

Yellowstone's geothermal features are constantly putting on a show. The 10,000 hot springs, mud pots, and fumaroles, plus 500 or so active geysers within the park comprise more than half the entire world's thermal features. You'd need to search two or three other continents for as many geysers as you can see during a single afternoon around Old Faithful.

HEATING UP

Past eruptions of cataclysmic volcanoes brought about the steaming, vaporous landscape of Yellowstone today. The heat from the magma (molten rock) under the Yellowstone Caldera, an active volcano, continues to fuel the park's geyser basins, such as the Upper Geyser Basin, where more than 200 spouters cram into less than two square miles; and Norris, where water 1,000 feet below ground is 450° F. The complex underground plumbing in these geyser basins is affected by earthquakes and other subterranean hijinks that geologists are only beginning to understand. Some spouters spring to life, while others fall dormant with little or no warning.

HOT SPOT TIPS

■ **Stay on trails and boardwalks.** In some areas, like in Norris, water boils at temperatures of more than 200°. If you want to venture into the back country, where there are no boardwalks, consult a ranger first.

■ **Leave the area if you feel sick or dizzy.** You might be feeling this way due to overexposure to various thermal gases.

■ **These hot springs aren't for bathing.** The pH levels of some of these features are extremely acidic.

■ **They also aren't wishing wells.** In the past people threw hundreds of coins into the bright blue Morning Glory Pool. The coins clogged the pool's natural water vents, causing it to change to a sickly green color.

(left) Old Faithful. (above) Punch Bowl Spring.

HOW DO GEYSERS WORK?

A few main ingredients make geysers possible: abundant water, a heat source, a certain kind of plumbing system, and rock strong enough to withstand some serious pressure. The layout of any one geyser's underground plumbing may vary, but we know that below each vent is a system of fissures and chambers, with constrictions here and there that prevent hot water from rising to the surface. As the underground water heats up, these constrictions and the cooler surface water "cap" the whole system, keeping it from boiling over and ratcheting up the underground pressure. When a few steam bubbles eventually fight their way through the constrictions, the result is like uncapping a shaken-up soda bottle, when the released pressure causes the soda to spray.

FUN FACTS

- A cone geyser (like Lone Star Geyser in Yellowstone's backcountry) has a spout-like formation around its vent, formed by silica particles deposited during eruptions.
- A fountain geyser (like Daisy Geyser in the Old Faithful area) erupts from a vent submerged in a hot spring-like pool. Eruptions tend to be smaller and more sporadic.
- Yellowstone's tallest geyser is Steamboat, in Norris, shooting up to 350 feet high.
- When they erupt, geysers sometimes create rainbows amid their spray.

❶ RECHARGE STAGE

Groundwater accumulates in plumbing and is heated by the volcano. Some hot water flashes to steam and bubbles try to rise toward surface.

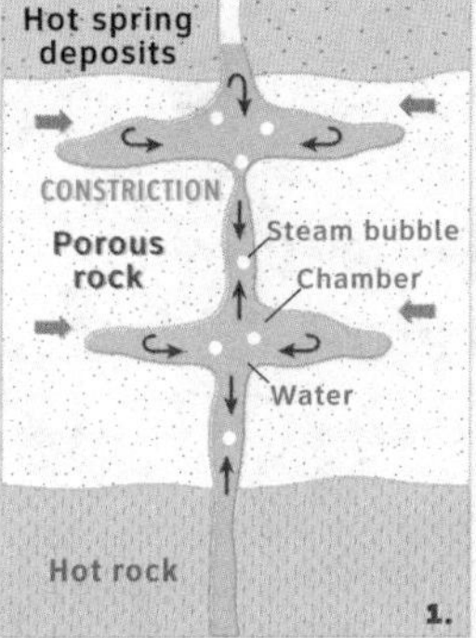

❷ PRELIMINARY ERUPTION STAGE

Pressure builds as steam bubbles clog at constriction. High pressure raises the boiling point, preventing superheated water from becoming steam.

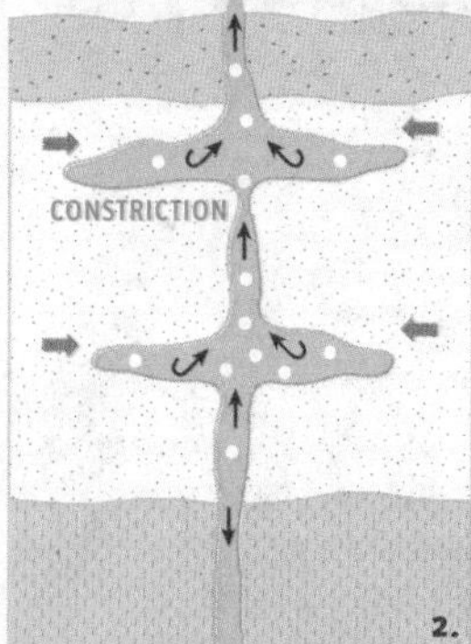

❸ ERUPTION STAGE

Bubbles squeeze through constriction, displacing surface water and relieving pressure. Trapped water flashes to steam, forcing water out of the chambers and causing a chain reaction.

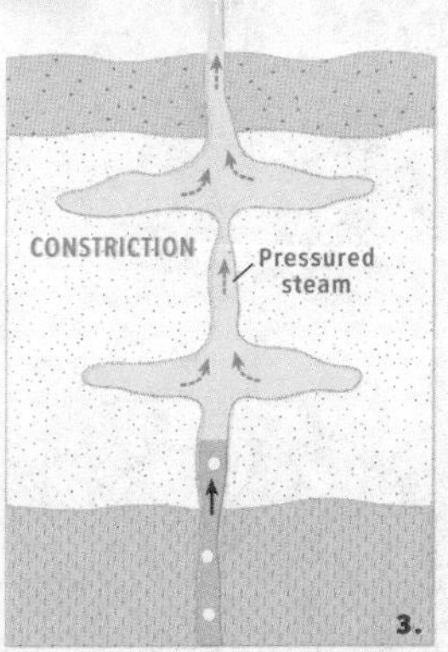

❹ RECOVERY STAGE

Eruption ends when the chambers are emptied or the temperature falls below boiling. Chambers begin to refill with ground water and the process begins again.

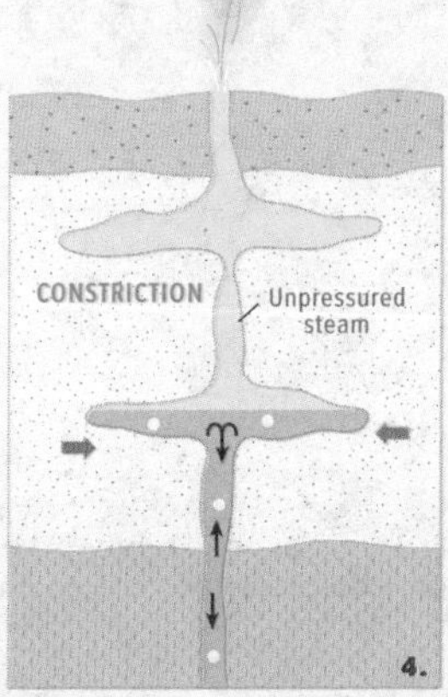

(left) Lone Star Geyser.

HOW DO HOT SPRINGS WORK?

Essentially, what keeps a hot spring from becoming a geyser is a lack of constriction in its underground plumbing. Like their more explosive cousins, hot springs consist of water that seeps into the earth, only to simmer its way back up through fissures after it's heated by hot volcanic rocks. Unlike in constricted geysers, water in a hot spring can circulate by convection. Rising hot water displaces cooling surface water, which then sinks underground to be heated and eventually rise again. Thus the whole mixture keeps itself at a gurgly equilibrium. As it rises, superheated water dissolves some subterranean minerals, depositing them at the surface to form the sculptural terraces that surround many hot springs.

The vivid colors that characterize hot springs and their terraces can be attributed alternately to minerals like sulfur and iron or to thermophiles. Thermophiles are microorganisms that thrive in extremely high temperatures. Blooming in thick bacterial mats, they convert light to energy, like plants, and their bright photosynthetic pigments help give hot springs their rainbow hues. Scientists suppose only a small percentage of Yellowstone's thermophiles have been identified. Still, these microbes have had a big impact on science. In 1965, a microorganism called Thermus aquaticus, or Taq, was discovered in the Lower Geyser Basin. From it, scientists extracted an enzyme that revolutionized molecular biology, ultimately making possible both DNA fingerprinting and the mapping of the human genome. NASA is among those performing research in the park today, studying thermophiles to gain insight on extraterrestrial life.

WHAT'S THAT SMELL?

Most people think hot springs smell like rotten eggs; some even say "burnt gunpowder" and "paper mill smoke-stack." Whatever simile you settle on, there's no question that hot springs and other thermal features stink to high heaven. Sulphur gases escaping from the volcano produce distinctive smells. Other gases are reduced to the stinky chemical hydrogen sulfide, which bubbles up to the surface. In high concentration, hydrogen sulfide can actually kill you, but the small amounts released by thermals can only kill your appetite. It's because hydrogen sulfide is often present in volcanic areas that we associate brimstone (or sulfur) with the underworld.

Did You Know?

Grand Prismatic Spring (pictured here) is the world's third-largest hot spring, at more than 370 feet across. The pool's vivid red and orange colors drizzle down its runoff channels, but from the boardwalk you can only glimpse a portion of these psychedelic tentacles. Thank the little guys: heat-loving microorganisms (bacteria and algae) tint the Grand Prismatic Spring with a rainbow of colors.

THE INNER WORKINGS OF HOT SPRINGS

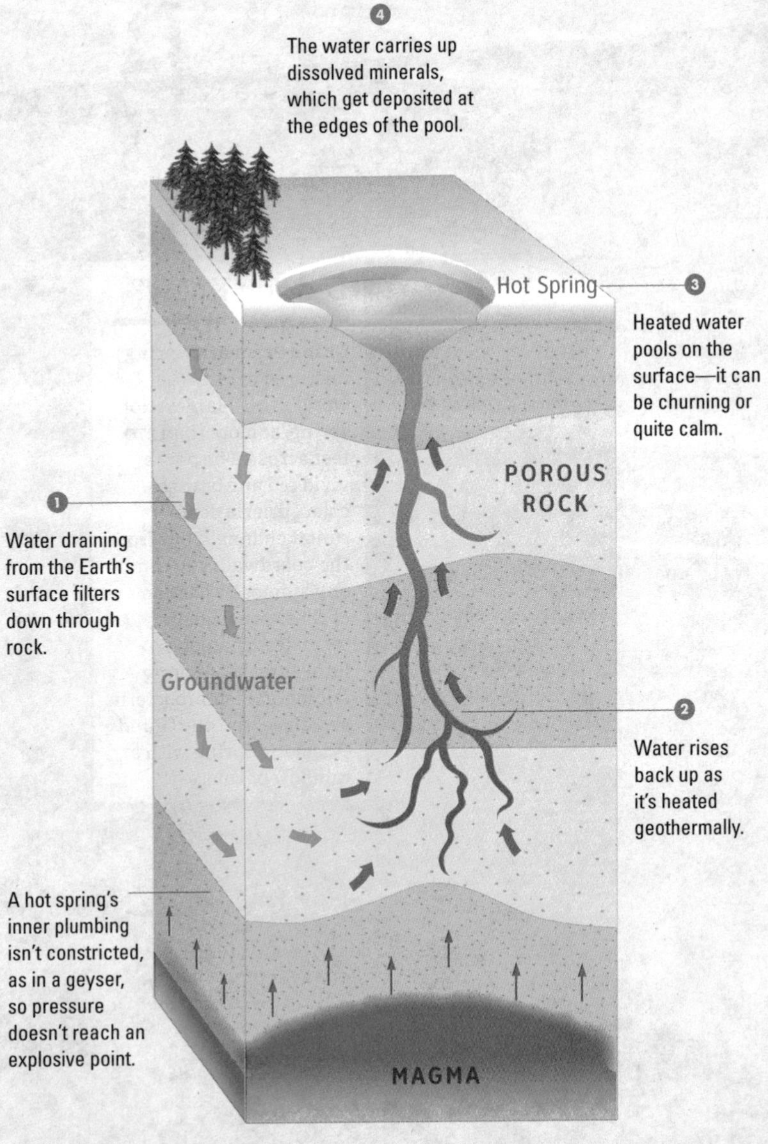

4 The water carries up dissolved minerals, which get deposited at the edges of the pool.

Hot Spring

3 Heated water pools on the surface—it can be churning or quite calm.

POROUS ROCK

1 Water draining from the Earth's surface filters down through rock.

Groundwater

2 Water rises back up as it's heated geothermally.

A hot spring's inner plumbing isn't constricted, as in a geyser, so pressure doesn't reach an explosive point.

MAGMA

WHAT ARE FUMAROLES?

Take away the water from a hot spring and you're left with steam and other gas, forming a fumarole. Often called steam vents, these noisy thermals occur when available water boils away before reaching the surface. All that escapes the vent is heat, vapor, and the whisper-roar of a giant, menacing teakettle. Fumaroles are often found on high ground. The gases expelled from fumaroles might include carbon dioxide, sulfur dioxide, and hydrogen sulfide. Some hot spots, like Red Spouter in the Lower Geyser Basin, can exhibit different behaviors depending on the seasonal water table, so what's a fumarole today could be a hot spring in a few months.

FUN FACTS

- The word fumarole comes from the Latin *fumus*, which means "smoke."
- Fumaroles are also known as steam vents and solfataras, from *sulpha terra*, Latin for "land of sulfur."
- Yellowstone's hottest fumarole is *Black Growler*, at Norris, which heats up to 280°F.
- About 4,000 fumaroles are in Yellowstone.

Fumarole

WHAT ARE MUD POTS?

Mud pots in Lower Geyser Basin.

Might as well say it up front: mud pots are great because their thick, bursting bubbles can sound like a chorus of rude noises or "greetings from the interior." That's why the few places they're found in Yellowstone are usually surrounded by gaggles of giggling visitors with video cameras rolling. A mud pot is basically just a hot spring where the water table results in a bubbling broth of water and clay. The acid gases react with surface rocks, breaking them down into silica and clay. As gases escape from below, bubbles swell and pop, flinging mud chunks onto the banks to form gloppy clay mounds. The mud's thickness varies with rainfall through the seasons.

FUN FACTS

- Mud pots have been nicknamed "paint pots" due to iron and other metals tinting the mud.
- The biggest cluster of mud pots in the park is in Pocket Basin in Lower Geyser Basin.
- Before it exploded in 1872, Mud Volcano was 30 feet tall by 30 feet wide.

PHOTOGRAPHY TIPS

- Set your alarm clock: generally, the best light for shooting the geothermal features is early in the morning. You'll avoid the thickest crowds then, too. The runner-up time is the late afternoon.

- Breezy days are good for photographing geysers, since the steam will be blown away from the jetting water. But avoid standing downwind or your view can be clouded with steam.
- If you get water from a thermal feature on your lens, dry it off as quickly as possible, because the water has a high mineral content that can damage your lens.

Thermal pool in the Rabbit Creek Thermal Area.

Restaurants

★ Lake Hotel Dining Room

$$$$ | MODERN AMERICAN | Opened in 1891, this double-colonnaded dining room off the lobby of the Lake Yellowstone Hotel is the park's most elegant dining spot, and with a menu that focuses on regional ingredients. Arrive early and enjoy a beverage and the view in the airy Reamer Lounge, which debuted as a sunroom in 1928. **Known for:** elegant, old-world ambience; the park's most sophisticated and creative cuisine; excellent wine list. *Average main: $31* *235 Yellowstone Lake Rd., Lake Village* *307/344–7311* *www.yellowstonenationalparklodges.com* *Closed early Oct.–early May.*

Wylie's Canteen at Lake Lodge

$ | AMERICAN | FAMILY | The former Lake Lodge Cafeteria was upgraded and rebranded as Wylie's Canteen in 2019 and still offers quick and casual bites with awe-inspiring Lake Yellowstone views, but the quality of food has improved. Try the breakfast burritos and breakfast sandwiches in the morning, or build-your-own burgers (bison, beef, chicken, Beyond Meat, or salmon), fried chicken, and salads later in the day. **Known for:** casual and affordable; wide variety of burgers; lake and meadow views. *Average main: $12* *459 Lake Village Rd.* *307/344–7311* *www.yellowstonenationalparklodges.com* *Closed Oct.–early June.*

Hotels

Lake Lodge Cabins

$$ | HOTEL | FAMILY | Located just up the lake shoreline from the grand Lake Yellowstone Hotel, this 1920 lodge is one of the park's homey, hidden treasures. **Pros:** lovely lakeside location; great lobby; good for families. **Cons:** no Wi-Fi in cabins (only in main lodge); few amenities; Pioneer cabins are particularly bare bones. *Rooms from: $170* *459 Lake Village Rd., Lake Village* *307/344–7311* *www.yellowstonenationalparklodges.com* *Closed late Sept.–early June* *186 cabins* *No meals.*

★ Lake Yellowstone Hotel

$$$ | HOTEL | Dating from 1891, the park's oldest lodge maintains an air of old-world refinement; just off the lobby, the spacious sun room offers priceless views of Yellowstone Lake at sunrise or sunset. **Pros:** relaxing atmosphere; the best views of any park lodging; charming old-world vibe. **Cons:** top rooms can be quite expensive; wired Internet, but no Wi-Fi; often books up months ahead. *Rooms from: $242* *235 Yellowstone Lake Rd., Lake Village* *307/344–7311* *www.yellowstonenationalparklodges.com* *Closed late Sept.–mid-May* *194 rooms* *No meals.*

Canyon

18 miles north of Lake Yellowstone Village, 33 miles southeast of Mammoth Hot Springs.

You'll find one of Yellowstone's largest villages—with myriad lodging, dining, and other services—in this area near the geographical center of the park, which is home to the justly famous Grand Canyon of the Yellowstone, through which the Yellowstone River has formed one of the most spectacular gorges in the world, with its steep canyon walls and waterfalls. The river's source is in the Absaroka Mountains, in the park's southeastern corner. From there it winds its way north through the heart of the park, entering Yellowstone Lake, then continuing northward under Fishing Ridge and through Hayden Valley. The stunning canyon is 23 miles long; most visitors clog the north and south rims to see its dramatic Upper and Lower Falls. The red-and-ocher canyon walls are topped by emerald-green forest. It's a feast of color. Keep an eye peeled for osprey, which nest in the canyon's spires and precarious trees.

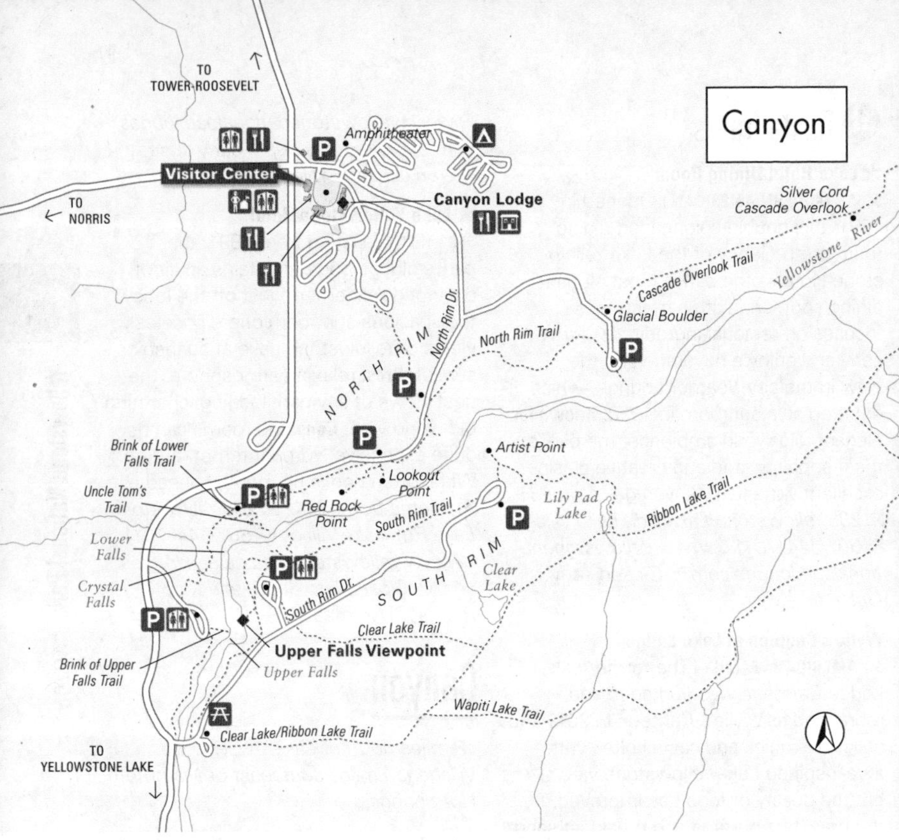

Sights

SCENIC STOPS

★ Artist Point

BODY OF WATER | An impressive view of the Lower Falls of the Yellowstone River can be had from this famous perch, which has two observation platforms, one accessible to wheelchairs. Rangers often give short talks on the lower platform. You can also access the South Rim Trail from here. ✉ *End of South Rim Rd.*

Lookout Point

BODY OF WATER | Midway on the North Rim Trail—also accessible via the one-way North Rim Drive—Lookout Point provides a view of the Grand Canyon of the Yellowstone. Follow the right-hand fork in the path to descend a steep trail, with an approximately 500-foot elevation change, for an eye-to-eye view of the falls from a ½ mile downstream. The best time to hike the trail is early morning, when sunlight reflects off the mist from the falls to create a rainbow. ✉ *Off North Rim Dr.*

TRAILS

Brink of the Lower Falls Trail

TRAIL | Especially scenic, this short but steep jaunt branches off of the North Rim Trail and can be accessed from either the Brink of the Upper Falls or Brink of the Lower Falls parking areas. The ½-mile one-way trail switchbacks 600 feet down to within a few yards of the top of the Yellowstone River's 308-foot Lower Falls. *Moderate.* ✉ *Yellowstone National Park* ✥ *Trailhead: North Rim Dr., just past junction with Grand Loop Rd.*

Mt. Washburn Trail

TRAIL | One of Yellowstone's most rewarding alpine hikes, the ascent to 10,259-foot Mt. Washburn can be approached from either the south leaving from the Dunraven Pass Trailhead or the north from the Chittenden Road Trailhead. The latter approach is a bit shorter (5.6 miles round-trip) but slightly steeper with a nearly 1,500-foot elevation gain, while from Dunraven Pass the hike switchbacks through bighorn sheep habitat and is about 6 miles round-trip, with a gain of just under 1,400 feet. Either way you'll be treated to panoramic views, and you can read interpretive exhibits in the small shelter at the summit (at the base of the fire tower). *Moderate–Difficult.* ✉ *Canyon Village* ✣ *Trailhead: Grand Loop Rd. at Dunraven Pass or Chittenden Rd.*

Mud Volcano Trail

TRAIL | **FAMILY** | This 0.6-mile loop hike in Hayden Valley curves gently around seething, sulfuric mudpots with such names as Sizzling Basin and Black Dragon's Cauldron, and around Mud Volcano itself. *Easy.* ✉ *Canyon* ✣ *Trailhead: Grand Loop Rd., 10 miles south of Canyon Village.*

North Rim Trail

TRAIL | **FAMILY** | Offering great views of the Grand Canyon of the Yellowstone, the 3-mile (each way) North Rim Trail runs from Inspiration Point to Chittenden Bridge. Particularly fetching is the ½-mile section of the North Rim Trail from the Brink of the Upper Falls parking area to Chittenden Bridge that hugs the rushing Yellowstone River as it approaches the canyon. This trail is paved and fully accessible between Lookout Point and Grand View, and it can be accessed at numerous points along North Rim Drive. *Moderate.* ✉ *Yellowstone National Park* ✣ *Trailhead: west side of Chittenden Bridge or Inspiration Point.*

Caution: A Wild Place

As you explore the park, keep this thought in mind: Yellowstone is not an amusement park. It is a wild place. The animals may seem docile or tame, but they are wild, and every year careless visitors are injured—sometimes even killed—when they venture too close. Particularly dangerous are female animals with their young, and bison, which can turn and charge in an instant. With bison, watch their tails: if standing up or crooked like a question mark, the animal is agitated.

Seven Mile Hole Trail

TRAIL | Give yourself the better part of a day (at least five hours) to tackle this challenging but generally uncrowded and peaceful 9.7-mile round-trip hike that begins near the North Rim's Inspiration Point, runs east for a while along the rim and then descends more than 1,000 feet to the banks of the roaring Yellowstone River. *Difficult.* ✉ *Yellowstone National Park* ✣ *Trailhead: Glacier Boulder pullout on road to Inspiration Point.*

★ South Rim Trail

TRAIL | **FAMILY** | Partly paved and fairly flat, this 1¾-mile trail along the south rim of the Grand Canyon of the Yellowstone affords impressive views and photo opportunities of the canyon and falls of the Yellowstone River. It starts at Chittenden Bridge, passes by magnificent Upper Falls View and Uncle Tom's Trail, and ends at Artist Point. Beyond Artist Point, you can continue your adventures for another 1.3 miles along a less-traveled and stunning trail to Point Sublime, or cut inland through high mountain meadows along the Clear Lake–Ribbon Lake Loop. You'll see fewer humans and possibly more wildlife in this more rugged backcountry, so carry bear spray. *Moderate.* ✉ *Canyon* ✥ *Trailhead: east side of Chittenden Bridge, off South Rim Dr.*

Uncle Tom's Trail

TRAIL | Accessed by the South Rim Drive, this spectacular and strenuous 700-step trail ½ mile east of Chittenden Bridge descends 500 feet from the parking area to the roaring base of the Lower Falls of the Yellowstone. Much of this walk is on steel sheeting, which can have a film of ice during early summer mornings or anytime in spring and fall. *Moderate–Difficult.* ✉ *Yellowstone National Park* ✥ *Trailhead: at South Rim Dr.*

VISITOR CENTERS

Canyon Visitor Center

INFO CENTER | **FAMILY** | This gleaming visitor center contains elaborate interactive exhibits for adults and kids. The focus here is on volcanoes and earthquakes and includes a room-size relief model of the park that illustrates eruptions, glaciers, and seismic activity. There are also exhibits about Native Americans and wildlife, including bison and wolves. The adjacent bookstore contains hundreds of books on the park, its history, and related science. ✉ *Canyon Village* ☎ *307/242–2550* 🌐 *www.nps.gov/yell* ⏲ *Closed mid-fall–late spring.*

Restaurants

Canyon Lodge Eatery

$ | **ECLECTIC** | **FAMILY** | Diners pack this mid-century-modern–inspired restaurant for casual breakfasts, as well as lunches and dinners that deviate from your standard national park fare. Design your own wok meal with veggies, meat, and toppings, or choose a protein and sauce on a three-item combo plate. **Known for:** more interesting than typical cafeteria-style fare; Asian-inspired wok stir-fries; lemon layer cake. $ *Average main: $15* ✉ *83B Lupine Ct.* ☎ *307/344–7311* 🌐 *www.yellowstonenationalparklodges.com* ⏲ *Closed mid-Oct.–late May.*

Hotels

Canyon Lodge & Cabins

$$ | **HOTEL** | **FAMILY** | You can choose from several different types of accommodations at this large, sprawling property near the Grand Canyon of the Yellowstone, which includes a modern and attractive lodge with smartly designed and sustainable rooms, the renovated pine-frame Western Cabins, and nicely updated rooms in the historic Dunraven and Cascade Lodge buildings. **Pros:** central to different parts of the park; eco-conscious design; pretty surroundings. **Cons:** spotty Wi-Fi; a bit pricey because of location; not much dining nearby. $ *Rooms from: $214* ✉ *41 Clover La., Canyon Village* ☎ *307/344–7311* 🌐 *www.yellowstonenationalparklodges.com* ⏲ *Closed mid-Oct.–mid-May* *590 units* *No meals.*

Tower-Roosevelt

20 miles north of Canyon Village, 33 miles west of Cooke City–Silver Gate.

The northeastern region of Yellowstone is the least visited part of the park, making it a great place to explore without running into as many people. Packs of wolves and herds of bison can often be spotted along the majestic drive through Lamar Valley.

Sights

SCENIC DRIVES

★ Northeast Entrance Road through Lamar Valley

SCENIC DRIVE | This 29-mile road has the richest landscape diversity of the five entrance roads. Just after you enter the park from Cooke City, Montana, you cut between 10,928-foot Abiathar Peak and the 10,404-foot Barronette Peak. Lamar Valley is home to hundreds of bison, and the rugged peaks and ridges adjacent to it shelter some of Yellowstone's most famous wolf packs. (Wolves were reintroduced to the park in the mid-1990s.) This is the park's best place for wolf- and bison-watching, especially in the early morning and early evening. As you exit Lamar Valley, the road crosses the Yellowstone River before leading you to the rustic Roosevelt Lodge. ✉ *Yellowstone National Park.*

Northeastern Grand Loop

SCENIC DRIVE | Commonly called Dunraven Pass, this 19-mile segment of Grand Loop Road climbs to nearly 9,000 feet as it passes some of the park's finest scenery, including views of backcountry hot springs and abundant wildflowers. Near Tower Falls, the road twists beneath a series of leaning basalt columns from 40 to 50 feet high. That behemoth to the east is 10,243-foot Mt. Washburn. ✉ *Between Canyon Junction and Tower Falls* ⏲ *Closed early Nov.–early Apr.*

SCENIC STOPS

Tower Fall

BODY OF WATER | **FAMILY** | This is one of the easiest waterfalls to see from the roadside; you can also view volcanic pinnacles here. Tower Creek plunges 132 feet at this waterfall to join the Yellowstone River. While a trail that used to go to the base of the falls has washed out, it will take trekkers down to the river. ✉ *Grand Loop Rd.*

TRAILS

Slough Creek Trail

TRAIL | Starting at Slough Creek Campground, this trail climbs steeply along a historic wagon trail for 1½ miles before reaching expansive meadows and prime fishing spots, where moose are common and grizzlies occasionally wander. Allow two or three hours for the full 3.4-mile round-trip hike. *Moderate.* ✉ *Yellowstone National Park* ✣ *Trailhead: Northeast Entrance Rd. at Slough Creek Campground.*

Trout Lake Trail

TRAIL | It takes just an hour or two to enjoy this slightly elevated but generally tame 1.2-mile round-trip hike in Lamar Valley that leads through meadows and stands of Douglas fir trees and then circumnavigates pretty Trout Lake, a favorite spot for fishing. *Easy.* ✉ *Yellowstone National Park* ✣ *Trailhead: Northeast Entrance Rd., just south of Pebble Creek Campground.*

Restaurants

Roosevelt Lodge Dining Room

$$ | **AMERICAN** | **FAMILY** | The menu at this atmospheric log cabin in a pine forest includes appropriately rustic options like skirt steak, mesquite-smoked chicken, and blackened ruby red trout, but you'll also find simpler comfort fare, like carnitas nachos and fried-green tomatoes. For a real adventure, make a reservation for the Roosevelt Old West Dinner Cookout, which includes a horseback trail ride or a stagecoach ride. **Known for:** updated cowboy cuisine; wild-game chili; rustic setting. [$] *Average main: $21* ✉ *100 Roosevelt Lodge Rd., Tower Junction* ☎ *307/344–7311* 🌐 *www.yellowstonenationalparklodges.com* ⏲ *Closed early Sept.–early June.*

Hotels

Roosevelt Lodge Cabins

$$ | **HOTEL** | Near the beautiful Lamar Valley in the park's north-central reaches, this simple lodge in a pine forest dates from the 1920s and surpasses some of the park's more expensive options when it comes to rustic tranquility. **Pros:** closest cabins to Lamar Valley and its world-famous wildlife; authentic western ranch feel; some cabins are quite affordable.

Cons: cabins are very close together; most cabins lack private bathrooms; cabins can be chilly at night. *Rooms from: $209* *100 Roosevelt Lodge Rd., Tower Junction* *307/344–7901* *www.YellowstoneNationalParkLodges.com* *Closed early Sept.–early June* *80 cabins* *No meals.*

Activities

In summer, hiking, boating, and fishing are the best ways to get out and enjoy the park. During the quieter winter seasons, snowmobiling and cross-country skiing are the activities of choice.

BOATING

Motorized boats are allowed only on Lewis Lake and Yellowstone Lake. Kayaking and canoeing are allowed on all lakes except Sylvan Lake, Eleanor Lake, Twin Lakes, and Beach Springs Lagoon. Most lakes are inaccessible by car, though, so accessing them requires long portages. Boating is not allowed on any river except the Lewis between Lewis Lake and Shoshone Lake, where nonmotorized boats are permitted.

You must purchase a permit for all boats—these are available at several points in the park, including Bridge Bay Ranger Station, Grant Village Backcountry Office, and Lewis Lake Ranger Station. The cost is $5 for a week, $10 for the season, for nonmotorized boats and floatables; and $10 for a week, $20 for the season, for all others. Boat permits issued in Grand Teton National Park are honored in Yellowstone, but owners must register their vessel in Yellowstone and obtain a no-charge Yellowstone validation sticker from a permit-issuing station. Rangers inspect all boats for aquatic invasive species before issuing a permit.

Bridge Bay Marina

BOATING | Watercraft, from rowboats to powerboats, can be rented for trips on Yellowstone Lake at this well-outfitted marina, which also provides shuttle boat rides to the backcountry and dock slip rentals. Additionally, you can rent 22-foot cabin cruisers with a guide. *Grand Loop Rd., Bridge Bay* *307/344–7311* *www.yellowstonenationalparklodges.com.*

Yellowstone Lake Scenic Cruises

BOATING | **FAMILY** | On one-hour cruises aboard the *Lake Queen II*, you'll learn about the park and the lake's history and have the chance to observe eagles, ospreys, and some of the park's big mammals along the shoreline. The vessel travels from Bridge Bay to Stevenson Island and back. Reservations are recommended. *Bridge Bay Marina, Bridge Bay* *307/344–7311* *www.yellowstonenationalparklodges.com* *$20.*

CAMPING

Yellowstone has a dozen frontcountry campgrounds—with more than 2,000 sites—throughout the park, in addition to more than 200 backcountry sites. Most campgrounds have flush toilets; some have coin-operated showers and laundry facilities. The campgrounds run by Yellowstone National Park Lodges—Bridge Bay, Canyon, Fishing Bridge RV Park, Grant Village, and Madison—accept bookings in advance (*307/344–7311* *www.yellowstonenationalparklodges.com*); nightly rates are $27 to $32 at most of these sites, except for Fishing Bridge RV Park, which costs $79 nightly. The rest of Yellowstone's campgrounds, operated by the National Park Service, are available on a first-come, first-served basis and have rates of $15 to $20. All camping outside designated campgrounds requires a backcountry permit. For trip dates between late May (Memorial Day) and September 10, the fee is $3 per person per night; there's no charge the rest of the year.

Bridge Bay Campground. The park's largest campground, Bridge Bay rests in a wooded grove above Yellowstone Lake and adjacent to the park's major marina—the views of the water and distant Absaroka Mountains are magnificent. ✉ *Grand Loop Rd., 3 miles southwest of Lake Village.*

Canyon Campground. A large campground with nearly 300 sites, Canyon Campground accommodates everyone from hiker/biker tent campers to large RVs. ✉ *North Rim Dr., Canyon Village.*

Fishing Bridge RV Park. It's more of a parking lot than a campground, but services like tank filling and emptying and full hookups make this a popular—though pricey—option among RVers. ✉ *Grand Loop Rd., 3 miles southwest of Lake Village.*

Grant Village Campground. The park's second-largest campground, with 430 sites, Grant Village has some sites with great views of Yellowstone Lake and is close to restaurants and other services. ✉ *South Entrance Rd., Grant Village.*

Indian Creek Campground. In a picturesque setting next to a creek, this campground is in the middle of a prime wildlife-viewing area. ✉ *Grand Loop Rd., 8 miles south of Mammoth Hot Springs.*

Lewis Lake Campground. Popular with visitors from Grand Teton, this nearest campground to the South Entrance is set among old pine trees on a bluff above beautiful and relatively uncrowded Lewis Lake. It's a quiet setting, and it has a boat launch. ✉ *South Entrance Rd., 6 miles south of Grant Village.*

Madison Campground. The largest National Park Service–operated campground, Madison has eight loops and nearly 300 sites. It's a good central location, handy for visiting the geysers in Norris and Old Faithful. ✉ *Grand Loop Rd., Madison.*

Mammoth Hot Springs Campground. At the base of a sagebrush-covered hillside, this campground can be crowded and noisy in the summer, but it's close to restaurants and some great attractions, and you may see bison, mule deer, and elk roaming the area. ✉ *North Entrance Rd., Mammoth Hot Springs.*

Norris Campground. Straddling the Gibbon River, this is a quiet, popular campground. A few of its walk-in sites rank among the most desirable in the park. ✉ *Grand Loop Rd., Norris.*

Pebble Creek. Beneath multiple 10,000-foot peaks (Thunderer, Barronette Peak, and Mt. Norris) the park's easternmost campground is set creekside in a forested canopy and is also close to the fun little hike to Trout Lake. ✉ *Northeast Entrance Rd., 22 miles east of Tower-Roosevelt Junction.*

Slough Creek. Down the park's most rewarding 2 miles of dirt road, Slough Creek is a gem. Nearly every site is adjacent to the creek, which is prized by anglers. ✉ *Northeast Entrance Rd., 10 miles east of Tower-Roosevelt Junction.*

Tower Falls. It's within hiking distance of the roaring waterfall, so this modest-size campground gets a lot of foot traffic but is in a somewhat remote part of the park. ✉ *Grand Loop Rd., 3 miles southeast of Tower-Roosevelt.*

EDUCATIONAL PROGRAMS

CLASSES AND SEMINARS

Yellowstone Forever

COLLEGE | **FAMILY** | Learn about the park's ecology, geology, history, and wildlife from park experts, including well-known geologists, biologists, and photographers. Classes generally take place on the north side of the park, around Mammoth Hot Springs, and last from a few hours to a few days, and rates are reasonable. Some programs are designed specifically for young people and families. ✉ *Gardiner* ☎ *406/848–2400* 🌐 *www.yellowstone.org.*

RANGER PROGRAMS

Yellowstone offers a busy schedule of guided hikes, talks, and campfire programs. For dates and times, check the park's *Yellowstone Today* newsletter, available at all entrances and visitor centers.

Daytime Walks and Talks

NATURE PRESERVE | FAMILY | Ranger-led walks are held at various locations throughout the summer. Winter programs and some walks are held at West Yellowstone, Old Faithful, and Mammoth. Check the website or park newspaper for details. 🌐 *www.nps.gov/yell.*

Evening Programs

TOUR—SIGHT | FAMILY | Gather around to hear tales about Yellowstone's fascinating history, with hour-long programs on topics ranging from the return of the bison to 19th-century photographers. Every major area hosts programs during the summer; check visitor centers or campground bulletin boards for updates. Winter programs are held at Mammoth and Old Faithful. 🌐 *www.nps.gov/yell.*

Junior Ranger Program

TOUR—SIGHT | FAMILY | Children ages 4 to 12 are eligible to earn patches and become Junior Rangers. Pick up a booklet at any visitor center for $3 and start the entertaining self-guided curriculum, or download it for free online. Kids five and older can also participate in the Young Scientist Program. Purchase a self-guiding booklet for $5 at the Canyon or Old Faithful visitor centers and solve a science mystery. 🌐 *www.nps.gov/yell.*

FISHING

Fishing season begins in late May on the Saturday of Memorial Day weekend and ends in November, and it's a highly popular activity in the park's many pristine lakes and rivers. Native cutthroat trout are among the prize catches, but four other varieties—brown, brook, lake, and rainbow—along with grayling and mountain whitefish inhabit Yellowstone's waters. Popular sportfishing opportunities include the Gardner and Yellowstone rivers as well as Soda Butte Creek, but the top fishing area is Madison River.

Yellowstone fishing permits cost $18 for three days, $25 for seven days, and $40 for the season. Anglers ages 15 and younger must have a (no-fee) permit or fish under direct supervision of an adult with a permit, which can be purchased at all ranger stations, visitor centers, and Yellowstone general stores. A state license is not needed to fish in the park.

Bridge Bay Marina Fishing Charters

FISHING | The park's largest concessionaire operates Yellowstone Lake fishing charters that can last from two to 12 hours, for up to six passengers. The fee includes gear. ✉ *Bridge Bay Marina, Bridge Bay* ☎ *307/344–7311* 🌐 *www.yellowstonenationalparklodges.com* 🎫 *From $103/hr.*

HIKING

Your most memorable Yellowstone moments will likely take place along a hiking trail. Encountering a gang of elk in the woods is unquestionably more exciting than watching them graze on the grasses of Mammoth Hot Springs Hotel. Hearing the creak of lodgepole pines on a breezy afternoon feels more authentic than listening to tourists chatter as you jockey for the best view of Old Faithful. Even a one-day visitor to Yellowstone can—and should—get off the roads and into the "wilderness." Because the park is a wild place, however, even a ½-mile walk on a trail puts you at the mercy of nature, so be sure to prepare yourself accordingly. As a guide on an Old Yellow Bus Tour said, "You don't have to fear the animals—just respect them."

No matter how short the hike, the following items are essential, not discretionary, especially if you're venturing into the backcountry and away from developed areas:

Bear spray. At $50 a can and sold in the park, it's not cheap, but it's a critical deterrent if you run into one. Learn how to use it, too.

Food and water. Your "meal" can be as simple as a protein bar and a bottle of water if you're hiking only a mile or two, but for hikes of an hour or longer, it's critical to head out with an ample supply of drinking water and a variety of snacks.

Appropriate clothing. Watch the forecast closely (available at every lodging office and visitor center). Bring a layer of clothing for the opposite extreme if you're hiking at least half the day. Yellowstone is known for fierce afternoon storms, so be ready with gloves, hat, and waterproof clothing.

Altitude awareness. Much of Yellowstone lies more than 7,500 feet above sea level. The most frequent incidents requiring medical attention are respiratory problems, not animal attacks. Be aware of your physical limitations—as well as those of your young children or elderly companions.

HORSEBACK RIDING

Reservations are recommended for horseback riding in the park. Don't worry about experience, as rangers estimate 90% of riders have not been on a horse in at least 10 years.

About 50 area outfitters lead horse-packing trips and trail rides into Yellowstone. Expect to pay from $250 to $400 per day for a backcountry trip, including meals, accommodations, and guides. A guide must accompany all horseback-riding trips.

Private stock can be brought into the park. Horses are not allowed in frontcountry campgrounds but are permitted in certain backcountry campsites. Day-use horseback riding does not require a permit, but overnight trips with stock are $5 per person per night with no cap.

★ Wilderness Pack Trips

HORSEBACK RIDING | FAMILY | Mike and Erin Thompson at Wilderness Pack Trips have led small group trips exclusively in Yellowstone National Park for many years. Popular destinations include the spectacular remote waterfalls and wildlife-rich regions often closed to the general public. Families are welcome for these excursions. Backcountry fishing trips and other day and overnight adventures can also be arranged. ✉ *172 E. River Rd., Emigrant* ☎ *406/581–5021* 🌐 *www.yellowstonepacktrips.com* 🎟 *From $375.*

Yellowstone National Park Lodges

HORSEBACK RIDING | FAMILY | The park's largest concessionaire offers one-hour horseback rides at Mammoth, and one- and two-hour rides at Tower-Roosevelt and Canyon Village. You can also book an Old West Dinner Cookout, which includes a ride. ☎ *307/344–7311* 🌐 *www.yellowstonenationalparklodges.com* 🎟 *From $55.*

SKIING, SNOWSHOEING, AND SNOWMOBILING

Yellowstone can be the coldest place in the continental United States in winter, with temperatures of –30°F not uncommon. Still, winter-sports enthusiasts flock here when the park opens for its winter season during the last week of December. Until early March, the roads teem with over-snow vehicles like snowmobiles and snowcoaches, and trails bristle with cross-country skiers and snowshoers. The Lone Star Geyser Trail near Old Faithful Village is a good one for skiing.

Snowmobiling is an exhilarating way to experience Yellowstone. It's also controversial: there's heated debate about the pollution and disruption to animal habitats. The number of riders per day is limited, and you must have a reservation, a guide, and a four-stroke engine, which are less polluting than the more common two-stroke variety. About a dozen companies are authorized to lead snowmobile excursions. Prices vary, as do itineraries and inclusions: ask about insurance, guides, taxes, park entrance fees, clothing, helmets, and meals.

Bear Den Ski Shops
SKIING/SNOWBOARDING | **FAMILY** | At Mammoth Hot Springs Hotel and Old Faithful Snow Lodge, these shops rent skis, gear, and snowshoes. Lessons, guided tours, and shuttles to trails are also available. ✉ *Mammoth Hot Springs, 1 Grand Loop Rd.* ☎ *307/344–7311* 🌐 *www.yellowstonenationalparklodges.com.*

Free Heel and Wheel
SKIING/SNOWBOARDING | This cross-country boutique outside the West Yellowstone entrance gate rents skis and other equipment and is a source for winter gear, sleds, snowshoes, and advice. Ski lessons and pull sleds for toting children are available. It also rents and repairs bicycles, and has an espresso bar to boot. ✉ *33 Yellowstone Ave., West Yellowstone* ☎ *406/646–7744* 🌐 *www.freeheelandwheel.com.*

Nearby Towns

Yellowstone National Park is itself a destination, and with its considerable size and wealth of lodging and dining options, it's easily possible—and sometimes the most enjoyable strategy—to spend nearly your entire visit within the park. That said, especially if visiting in summer without having made reservations far in advance, you may find it easier and less expensive to stay in one of the several nearby communities, which range from small villages with basic services to larger towns with swanky hotels, trendy restaurants, and the area's largest airports (which are in Cody, Jackson, and Bozeman).

In Montana, nearest to the North Entrance, are the small and bustling towns of **Gardiner,** just a short drive from Mammoth Hot Springs, and **Livingston,** a charmingly historic enclave about 53 miles north at the junction with Interstate 90. Just 25 miles west of Livingston via the interstate, the youthful and hip college town of **Bozeman** is one of the fastest-growing communities in the Rockies and a hub of art, shopping, dining, and outdoor attractions. Another popular Montana gateway, particularly in winter, is **West Yellowstone,** near the park's West Entrance. It's a small town without a ton of curb appeal, but there is a wealth of lodging and dining options. It's 50 miles south of the renowned ski resort community of **Big Sky.**

In Wyoming, because of its airport and its proximity to both Grand Teton and Yellowstone national parks, **Jackson**—the closest town to Yellowstone's South Entrance—is the region's busiest community in summer and has the widest selection of dining and lodging options (⇨ *see Grand Teton National Park for more information*). The Wild West town of **Cody** lies just an hour's drive from the East Entrance and is home to one of the best museums in the Rockies as well as a number of hotels, inns, and dude ranches.

Montana is again your best bet when entering through the park's Northeast Entrance. With both Yellowstone and the Absaroka-Beartooth Wilderness at its back door, the neighboring villages of **Cooke City–Silver Gate** are good places for hiking, horseback riding, mountain climbing, and other outdoor activities. Some 50 miles to the east of Cooke City and 60 miles southeast of Billings, the small resort town of **Red Lodge** is nestled against the foot of the pine-draped Absaroka-Beartooth Wilderness and popular with skiers, anglers, golfers, and horseback riders—it has more options for dining and lodging than Cooke City.

Gardiner

1 mile north of Yellowstone's North Entrance, 77 miles south of Bozeman.

As the only entrance to Yellowstone open the entire year, Gardiner (population 971) always feels like a hive of activity, with its quaint shops and smattering of good restaurants. The town's Roosevelt Arch has marked the park's North Entrance since 1903, when President Theodore Roosevelt dedicated it. The Yellowstone River slices through town, beckoning fishermen and rafters.

GETTING HERE AND AROUND

It's about an hour's drive from Interstate 90 and Livingston via U.S. 89, and a 15-minute drive to Mammoth Hot Springs.

Restaurants

Iron Horse Bar & Grill
$ | **AMERICAN** | Vintage advertisements, street signs, and gas-station memorabilia fill the interior of this rollicking roadhouse, but the heart of this place is the huge wooden deck overlooking the Yellowstone River and the mountains in the distance. The food is simple but hearty and well-seasoned—think elk tacos, bison burgers, and panfried rainbow trout. **Known for:** wooden deck with river views; comfort fare featuring local game; nice selection of craft beers. *Average main: $15 ✉ 212 Spring St., Gardiner ☎ 406/848–7888.*

Yellowstone Mine & Rusty Rail Lounge
$$ | **STEAKHOUSE** | **FAMILY** | Decorated with picks, shovels, and other mining equipment, this is a place for casual family-style dining. Locals come in for the steaks and seafood. **Known for:** low-key dining, year-round; steak-house staples; kitchen open later than at other local spots. *Average main: $18 ✉ Best Western by Mammoth Hot Springs, 901 Scott St. W, Gardiner ☎ 406/848–7336 ⊕ www.visitgardinermt.com/item/230-yellowstone-mine-restaurant-rusty-rail-lounge.*

Hotels

★ **Yellowstone Riverside Cottages**
$$ | **HOTEL** | **FAMILY** | Set on a pretty bend of the Yellowstone River in the heart of downtown Gardiner, this immaculate little compound of cottages, suites, and studios that sleep from two to six guests has kitchens or kitchenettes in every unit along with good Wi-Fi and private exterior entrances. **Pros:** good variety of room configurations; within walking distance of restaurants; short drive from Yellowstone's North Entrance. **Cons:** some rooms don't overlook river; no pets; can sometimes hear noise from rooms above. *Rooms from: $199 ✉ 521 Scott St. W, Gardiner ☎ 406/848–7719 ⊕ www.yellowstoneriversidecottages.com 17 rooms No meals.*

Yellowstone Village Inn and Suites
$$ | **HOTEL** | **FAMILY** | On the west end of Gardiner across from the Yellowstone River, this mid-range hotel provides a variety of room types and plenty of amenities to keep you entertained between day trips into Yellowstone. **Pros:** great location; heated indoor pool; some suites have full kitchens. **Cons:** Wi-Fi can be spotty; breakfast is continental; 15-minute walk to downtown core. *Rooms from: $220 ✉ 1102 Scott St. W, Gardiner ☎ 406/848–7417 ⊕ www.yellowstonevinn.com 45 rooms Free Breakfast.*

West Yellowstone

1 mile west of Yellowstone's West Entrance, 90 miles south of Bozeman.

This western gateway to the park is where the open plains of southwestern Montana and northeastern Idaho come together along the Madison River Valley. Affectionately known among winter recreationists as the "snowmobile capital of the world," this community of 1,400 has a rather bland downtown but is a good base for fishing, horseback riding, and downhill skiing and has a couple of noteworthy attractions that tap into the area's natural and cultural history.

GETTING HERE AND AROUND
Minutes from the park's West Entrance, the town of West Yellowstone is about a 90-minute drive from Bozeman. There's a small seasonal airport served by Delta in summer.

VISITOR INFORMATION Destination West Yellowstone. *30 Yellowstone Ave., West Yellowstone* *406/646–7701* *www.destinationyellowstone.com.*

Sights

★ Grizzly and Wolf Discovery Center
NATURE PRESERVE | FAMILY | Home to grizzlies and grey wolves, this nonprofit wildlife park provides an up-close look at Yellowstone's largest and most powerful predators. In summer, you can also view birds of prey, and the river otter exhibit is a hit with kids. The comprehensive "Bears: Imagination and Reality" exhibit compares myths about bears to what science has revealed about them. This is the only facility that formally tests bear-resistant products such as coolers and canisters in cooperation with state and federal agencies. *201 S. Canyon St., West Yellowstone* *406/646–7001, 800/257–2570* *www.grizzlydiscoveryctr.org* *$15.*

Museum of the Yellowstone
MUSEUM | FAMILY | West Yellowstone's 1909 Union Pacific Depot has been transformed into a museum dedicated to the modes of travel—from stagecoaches to planes—people employed to get to Yellowstone before World War II. Films provide insight on topics such as the fire that devastated Yellowstone in 1988 and the way earthquakes affect the area's hydrothermal features. *104 Yellowstone Ave., West Yellowstone* *406/646–1100* *www.museumoftheyellowstone.org* *$6* *Closed early Oct.–mid-May.*

Restaurants

Firehole Bar-B-Que
$ | BARBECUE | You'll find expertly prepared, slow-cooked, fall-off-the-bone barbecue in this no-frills barn-style restaurant a few blocks from Yellowstone's West Entrance. Order at the counter, then wait for your feast of tender brisket, pork, turkey, St. Louis–style ribs, or buffalo sausage to appear. **Known for:** smoked meats by the pound (perfect for park picnic supplies); smoked buffalo sausage links; house barbecue sauce available to go by the bottle. *Average main: $11* *120 Firehole Ave., West Yellowstone* *406/641–0020* *www.fireholebbqco.com.*

Madison Crossing Lounge
$$$ | MODERN AMERICAN | This handsome bistro and cocktail lounge set in part of West Yellowstone's 1918 former school building is an inviting spot for drinks—there's an encyclopedic wine, craft beer, and cocktail list—and appetizers. But if you're seeking a more substantial meal, consider the flat-iron steak with chimichurri sauce or a burger topped with smoked bacon and huckleberry-chipotle jam. **Known for:** nachos with bison chorizo; attractive fireplace-warmed dining room; creative cocktails. *Average main: $24* *121 Madison Ave., West*

Yellowstone ☎ 406/646–7621 ⊕ www.madisoncrossinglounge.com ⊙ Closed mid-Oct.–mid-Dec. No lunch.

Running Bear Pancake House

$ | **AMERICAN** | **FAMILY** | All the pies, muffins, and cinnamon rolls are made on the premises at this casual, family-friendly eatery. There are a lot of choices, but trust the name and go for the buttermilk or buckwheat pancakes topped with blueberries, strawberries, peaches, coconut, walnuts, or chocolate chips. **Known for:** several varieties of pancakes, plain and topped; espresso drinks using locally roasted beans; woodsy decor. [$] *Average main: $12 ✉ 538 Madison Ave., West Yellowstone ☎ 406/646–7703 ⊕ www.runningbearph.com ⊙ No dinner.*

Wild West Pizzeria and Saloon

$$ | **PIZZA** | **FAMILY** | Aaron and Megan Hecht make superb pizzas with crispy crusts, flavorful sauces, and memorable frontier names. Folks also come for the sandwiches, pasta dishes, and the live music hosted at the adjacent saloon. **Known for:** pizza sauce that's a family recipe; the Sitting Bull pie, topped with various meats; the Calamity Jane pie, with a white sauce, mushrooms, and other veggies. [$] *Average main: $16 ✉ 14 Madison Ave., West Yellowstone ☎ 406/646–4400 ⊕ www.wildwestpizza.com.*

Hotels

1872 Inn

$$$$ | **HOTEL** | This quieter, adult-oriented boutique hotel on the west side of downtown has warmly appointed rooms with leather chairs, custom wood furnishings, and Native American rugs and blankets. **Pros:** nicely designed bathrooms with heated towel racks and natural stone tiles; short walk from several restaurants; attractive common areas. **Cons:** not suitable for kids; expensive; no elevator. [$] *Rooms from: $379 ✉ 603 Yellowstone Ave., West Yellowstone ☎ 406/646–1025 ⊕ www.1872inn.com 18 rooms 🍽 Free Breakfast.*

★ Explorer Cabins at Yellowstone

$$$$ | **HOTEL** | **FAMILY** | Consisting of 50 warmly appointed, contemporary cabins set among five clusters across the street from West Yellowstone's Grizzly & Wolf Discovery Center, this family- and pet-friendly compound is an ideal base for visiting the national park. **Pros:** handy but quiet in-town location; friendly, helpful staff; most cabins can sleep 4 to 6 guests. **Cons:** no ovens or freezers in kitchenettes; cabins are close together; some cabins are a little cozy. [$] *Rooms from: $383 ✉ 250 S. Canyon St., West Yellowstone ☎ 877/600–4308 ⊕ www.yellowstonevacations.com 50 cabins 🍽 No meals.*

Three Bear Lodge

$$$$ | **HOTEL** | **FAMILY** | A towering stone fireplace and lots of natural wood greet guests in the lobby of this eco-friendly property. **Pros:** family-friendly; a block off the main drag; heated pool. **Cons:** no staff at front desk after 11 pm; some cabins are too cozy; free breakfast only in high season. [$] *Rooms from: $209 ✉ 217 Yellowstone Ave., West Yellowstone ☎ 406/646–7353, 800/646–7353 ⊕ www.threebearlodge.com 70 rooms 🍽 No meals.*

Cooke City–Silver Gate

2 miles east of Yellowstone's Northeast Entrance.

The tiny, neighboring communities of Cooke City and Silver Gate, are just outside the Northeast Entrance of Yellowstone and just west of the soaring Beartooth Mountains. This largely seasonal community that mostly shuts down from mid-October through early May has a handful of casual, Western-style lodgings and eateries and is a great little base camp for exploring Lamar Valley.

GETTING HERE AND AROUND

Year-round, you can get to these towns by traveling through Yellowstone's northern section from Mammoth Hot Springs past Tower Junction along Northeast Entrance Road—the drive from Gardiner takes about 90 minutes. In summer, you can continue east from town on U.S. 212 (the Beartooth Scenic Highway) to Red Lodge, which is also about a 90-minute drive.

Restaurants

★ **MontAsia**
$ | **ECLECTIC** | Make your way to this small log cabin with red trim for some of the tastiest and most interesting fare in the region, a fusion of Asian and Montana fare (hence the restaurant's name) prepared and served by a lovely, friendly family. Made-from-scratch chili and house-roasted chicken with fries and aioli appear on the same menu as pork-cabbage pot stickers with house-made ginger-soy sauce and rice noodles with tofu, nori, and Japanese sesame oil. **Known for:** outdoor seating with mountain views; Malaysian chicken rice; coconut shakes and chai brownies. *Average main: $15* ✉ *102 E. Main St., Cooke City-Silver Gate* ☎ *406/838–2382* *www.montasia.ninja* *Closed Wed.*

Hotels

Silver Gate Lodging
$$ | **RENTAL** | **FAMILY** | This friendly summer-only compound that offers everything from rustic but economical motel rooms to roomy cabins that can sleep up to 10 guests has the perfect location for exploring Lamar Valley—it's in tiny and tranquil Silver Gate, a mile from Yellowstone's Northeast Entrance. **Pros:** well-stocked general store; close proximity to Lamar Valley; good for families and larger groups. **Cons:** in a tiny town with few amenities; three-night minimum in high season; least-expensive units are quite small. *Rooms from: $160* ✉ *109 U.S. 212 W* ☎ *406/838–2371* *www.silvergatelodging.com* *Closed Nov.–Apr.* *30 rooms* *No meals.*

Chapter 4

BOZEMAN, HELENA, AND SOUTHWEST MONTANA

4

Updated by
Katie Jackson

Sights ★★★★★

Restaurants ★★★★☆

Hotels ★★★★☆

Shopping ★★★☆☆

Nightlife ★★☆☆☆

WELCOME TO BOZEMAN, HELENA, AND SOUTHWEST MONTANA

TOP REASONS TO GO

★ **Fishing:** Fly-fishing the gorgeous Gallatin River.

★ **The Beartooth Highway:** For a scenic and exhilarating drive, the Beartooth Highway can't be topped.

★ **State Capitol Building, Helena:** from Charlie Russell's Lewis and Clark painting to the Goddess of Liberty crowning the copper dome, the capitol is a masterpiece.

★ **Fossils:** The Museum of the Rockies houses the largest collection of North American dinosaur fossils.

★ **Skiing:** "The biggest skiing in America" at Big Sky Ski Resort.

By land, this region constitutes about 1/7th of the state. It's best to fly into Bozeman, which has the most flights. Helena is 100 miles northwest, and the southwestern corner of the state, near the ghost town of Bannack, is 140 miles from Bozeman.

1 Bozeman. The mecca for all things outdoors is also the home to Montana State University. It's one of the fastest-growing and diverse communities in Montana.

2 Helena. This gold-mining camp turned capital city once had more millionaires per capita than any other place in the country.

3 Red Lodge. The gateway to the Beartooth Mountains sits at the foot of the Absaroka-Beartooth Wilderness. It's now a modest mountain resort town popular with travelers to Yellowstone.

4 Big Timber. This small, remote community is a great base for exploring the Crazy Mountains; it's also a center for fly-fishing on the Yellowstone River.

5 Livingston. This gateway to Paradise Valley was originally a railroad town; now it's a popular gateway to Yellowstone National Park and is also one of the filming locations for *A River Runs Through It.*

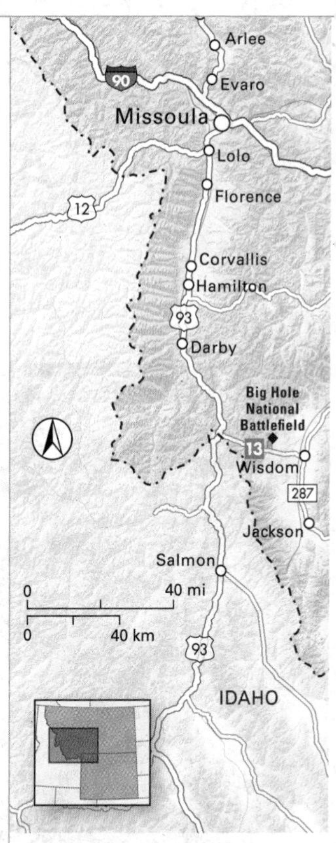

6 Three Forks. Home to the headwaters of the Missouri River, this historic town figured prominently in the Lewis and Clark expedition.

7 Big Sky. Montana's answer to Aspen and the Alps is one of the country's biggest ski resorts.

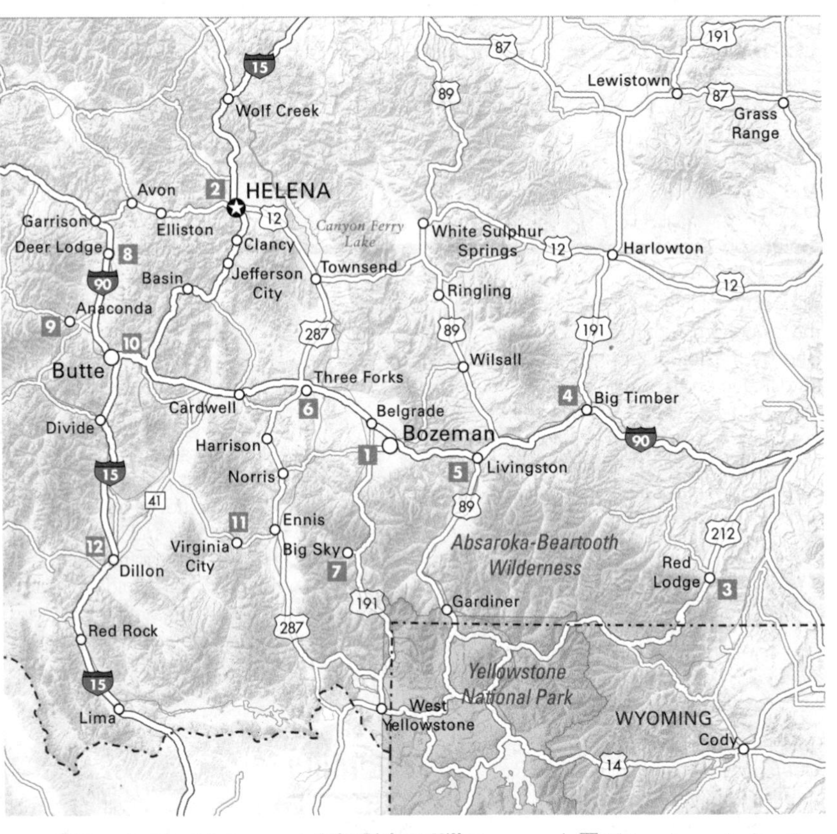

8 Deer Lodge. A former cattle ranch turned museum town draws visitors to its historic buildings.

9 Anaconda. One of the world's largest copper smelting plants is the centerpiece for this small town, the gateway to the Anaconda-Pintler Wilderness.

10 Butte. "The Mining City" was once deemed "The Richest Hill on Earth." Many ornate historic buildings remain from this era; the town's biggest annual draw is its St. Patrick's Day parade.

11 Virginia City. The tiny town was once the Montana territorial capital. This living time capsule of an Old West mining town, and its nearby neighbor Nevada City, serve as a reminder of the Gold Rush days.

12 Dillon. An agricultural hot spot has emerged as an outdoor recreation hub with excellent fishing on the nearby Beaverhead River.

13 Big Hole National Battlefield. This battlefield stands very much as it did in the late 19th century, memorializing the site where the U.S. Army fought the Nez Perce.

Glistening, glaciated, and grand, the Absarokas, Crazies, Gallatins, and other mountains send cooling summer winds to roil among the grasslands and forests of southwest Montana. This is a wild place inhabited by hundreds of animal species.

Abundant wildlife is a daily sight, from the pronghorn sprinting across grasslands to the 10,000-strong northern elk herd in and north of Yellowstone National Park. Bald eagles and ospreys perch in tall snags along the rivers, watching for fish. White-tailed and mule deer spring over fences (and across roads, so watch out when driving). Golden eagles hunt above hay fields. Riparian areas come alive in spring with ducks, geese, pelicans, and great blue herons. The south-central area known as Yellowstone Country shares the topography, wildlife, rivers, and recreational opportunities of its namesake national park.

Critters outnumber people in southwest Montana, which should come as no surprise when you consider that some counties have fewer than one person per square mile. The region's ranches are measured in the thousands of acres, though they are bordered by ranchettes of fewer than 20 acres around the towns of Bozeman and Red Lodge. But even the most densely populated area, Yellowstone County, has only about 61 people per square mile. That leaves thousands of square miles in the region wide open for exploration. Hiking, fishing, mountain biking, and rock climbing are popular outdoor activities in summer, and in winter the thick pillows of snow make skiing and snowmobiling conditions near perfect.

Southwest Montana's human history reaches back only about 12,000 years, and the non–Native American presence dates back only 200 years. Yet this place is full of exciting tales and trails, from the path followed by the Lewis and Clark Expedition to the Bozeman and Nez Perce trails. To the west, in Montana's southwesternmost corner, is Gold West Country, which includes the gold-rush town of Helena. Roadside signs along various routes in the region indicate the sites of battles, travels, and travails.

Planning

Getting Here and Around

AIR

Several daily flights link Bozeman's Yellowstone International Airport to Denver, Los Angeles, Minneapolis, Salt Lake City, and Seattle. Butte Airport has service from Salt Lake City. Helena Airport has service from Minneapolis, Denver, Seattle, and Salt Lake City. Note that major air carriers tend to use smaller planes to serve the area.

AIRPORTS Bert Mooney Airport. ✉ *101 Airport Rd., Butte* ☎ *406/494–3771* 🌐 *www.butteairport.com.* **Bozeman Yellowstone International Airport.** ✉ *850 Gallatin Field Rd., Belgrade* ☎ *406/388–8321* 🌐 *www.bozemanairport.com.* **Helena Airport.** ✉ *2850 Mercer Loop, Helena* ☎ *406/442–2821* 🌐 *www.helenaairport.com.*

CAR

Although rideshare services like Uber and Lyft exist in Bozeman and Helena, they will only get you so far. A private vehicle is almost a necessity to explore southwest Montana, as it allows you to appreciate the grandeur of the area. Wide-open terrain affords startling vistas of mountains and prairies, where you're likely to see abundant wildlife. I–90 is the major east–west artery through the region; I–15 is the major north–south route. Most of the other routes here are paved and in good shape, but be prepared for gravel and dirt roads the farther off the beaten path you go. Driving through the mountains in winter can be challenging, so a four-wheel-drive vehicle, available from most car-rental agencies, is best.

Major routes are paved and well maintained, but there are many gravel and dirt roads off the beaten track. When heading into remote regions, be sure to fill up the gas tank, and check road reports for construction delays or passes that may close in severe winter weather. Always carry a flashlight, drinking water and some food, a first-aid kit, and emergency overnight gear (a sleeping bag and extra, warm clothing). Most important, make sure someone is aware of your travel plans. While driving, be prepared for animals crossing roads, livestock on open ranges along the highway, and other hazards such as high winds and dust or snowstorms. When driving in the mountains in winter, make sure you have tire chains, studs, or snow tires.

Hotels

Lodging varies from national chain hotels to mom-and-pop motor inns. More and more guest ranches are inviting lodgers, historic hotels are being restored, and new bed-and-breakfasts are opening their doors. If you plan to visit in summer or during the ski season (December–mid-March), it's best to reserve rooms far in advance.

CAMPING

There are numerous campsites throughout the region, and they vary from rustic (with pit toilets) to relatively plush (with cabins and heated swimming pools). When camping, ask about bears in the area and whether or not food must be stored inside a hard-sided vehicle (not a tent).

Planning Your Time

For the best tour of southwest Montana, drive the unforgettable roadways that seem to reach the top of the world, making frequent stops in historic towns and parks. Drive up the Beartooth Pass from Red Lodge and, between late May and early October, hike along myriad trails right from the highway. Stop in Big Timber to sample small-town Western life, ride a white-water raft on the Stillwater River, or fly-fish the Yellowstone River with a knowledgeable outfitter. From Livingston, home to several museums, drive south into ever more beautiful countryside, through the Paradise Valley toward Yellowstone National Park. A float trip on this section of the Yellowstone, combined with a stay at Chico Hot Springs or Sage Lodge, is the stuff of which great memories are made.

In summer in Virginia City, Ennis, or Three Forks, return to gold-rush days along the historic streets or live for today with a fly rod in hand and a creel waiting to be filled beside you. Trail rides, float trips, steam trains—not to mention long walks in the long-gone footsteps of Lewis and Clark, Sacajawea, and a few thousand forgotten trappers, traders, cavalry soldiers, and Native Americans—all await you around these towns.

Bozeman, Big Sky, and the Gallatin Canyon are premier destinations in any season, with more than enough museums, galleries, historic sites, and scenic stops to fill your itinerary. Southwest Montana offers ample opportunities for outdoor recreation even when the snow flies. In places like Big Sky, Bridger Bowl, and the Gallatin National Forest you can experience some of the best skiing and snowmobiling in the United States, and after a day on the slopes or the trails plunge into the hot springs in Bozeman, Butte, or Boulder.

In making the most of your time, pause to breathe in the air filtered through a few million pines, to listen to the sounds of nature all around, to feel the chill of a mountain stream or the welcome warmth of a thermal spring. Small moments like these stick with you and become the kind of memories that will beckon you back to this high, wide, and handsome land.

Restaurants

This is ranch country, so expect numerous Angus-steer steak houses. Many restaurants also serve bison meat and various vegetarian meals, but you'll find few ethnic dishes. Restaurants here are decidedly casual: blue jeans, crisp shirts, and cowboy boots are dressy for the region.

HOTEL AND RESTAURANT PRICES

Restaurant and hotel reviews have been shortened. For full information, visit Fodors.com.

What it Costs

$	$$	$$$	$$$$
RESTAURANTS			
under $10	$10–$18	$19–$30	over $30
HOTELS			
under $80	$80–$130	$131–$200	over $200

When to Go

December through March is the best time to visit for skiers, snowboarders, snowshoers, and people who love winter. Summer draws even more visitors. That's not to say that southwest Montana gets crowded, but you may find more peace and quiet in spring and fall, when warm days and cool nights offer pleasant vacationing under the Big Sky.

Temperatures will drop below freezing in winter (and in fall and spring in the mountains) and jump into the 80s and 90s in summer. The weather can change quickly, particularly in the mountains and in the front range area north of Helena, and temperatures have been known to vary by as much as 70°F within a few hours, bringing winds, thunderstorms, and the like.

Bozeman

This recreation capital offers everything from trout fishing to white-water river rafting to backcountry mountain biking to skiing. The arts have also flowered in Bozeman, the home of Montana State University. The mix of cowboys, professors, students, skiers, and celebrities makes it one of the more diverse communities in the northern Rockies as well as one of the fastest-growing towns in Montana.

Bozeman has a strong Western heritage, readily evident at local museums, downtown galleries, and even the airport. In 1864 a trader named John Bozeman led his wagon train through this valley en route to the booming goldfields of Virginia City and southwest Montana. For several years this was the site of Fort Ellis, established to protect settlers making their way west along the Bozeman Trail, which extended into Montana Territory.

GETTING HERE AND AROUND

Several daily flights link Bozeman's Yellowstone International Airport to Dallas, Denver, Los Angeles, Minneapolis, Salt Lake City, and Seattle.

The bright yellow **Streamline buses** (☎ *406/587–2434* 🌐 *www.streamlinebus.com*) offer free weekday and Saturday service between downtown, Montana State University, Bozeman Deaconess Hospital, and outlying shopping areas, as well as late-night service Thursday, Friday, and Saturday and a route to and from Livingston. Free two-hour parking is available on and near Main Street; there's also a parking garage between Tracy and Black avenues on East Mendenhall Street.

You can easily maneuver in downtown Bozeman's mix of Old West bars, saddle shops, upscale stores and restaurants, and espresso cafés on foot or by bicycle. To appreciate the town's diversity, stroll the residential area near the university, where mansions, bungalows, and every style in between coexist side by side. A vehicle is necessary—in winter, a four-wheel-drive vehicle is best—to explore the parks, trails, and recreation areas in the mountain ranges surrounding Bozeman.

VISITOR INFORMATION

Free maps for self-guided historical walking tours are available at the Bozeman Area Chamber of Commerce.

CONTACTS Bozeman Area Chamber of Commerce. ✉ *2000 Commerce Way* ☎ *406/586–5421* 🌐 *www.bozemanchamber.com.*

Sights

Bozeman Hot Springs

HOT SPRINGS | You can soak for an hour or a day at Bozeman Hot Springs, which offer 12 pools (including both indoor pools and outdoor pools), a sauna, spa, fitness center, and juice bar. ✉ *81123 Gallatin Rd.* ✣ *Hwy. 191, 5 miles west of Bozeman at Four Corners Junction off Huffine La. and U.S. 191* ☎ *406/586–6492* 🌐 *www.bozemanhotsprings.co* 🎫 *$17.*

Emerson Center for the Arts and Culture

ARTS VENUE | A school until 1992, this 1920 Gothic Revival brick building now houses around 40 galleries, studios, and classrooms, plus a performing-arts hall. You can watch craftspeople at work, purchase artwork, take a class, or catch a performance here, plus enjoy a tasty lunch or dinner at the on-site Sidewall Pizza Company. All tenants maintain individual hours. Contact them directly for details. ✉ *111 S. Grand Ave.* ☎ *406/587–9797* 🌐 *www.theemerson.org* 🎫 *Free* 🕒 *Closed weekends.*

Gallatin History Museum

MUSEUM | West of downtown, this redbrick former jail, built in 1911, serves as a reminder of the rough-and-tumble days of the past. Inside, the Gallatin Historical Society displays Native American artifacts, a model of Fort Ellis, a life-size reconstruction of an 1870s log cabin, a research library, photo archives, and a bookstore. ✉ *317 W. Main St.* ☎ *406/522–8122* 🌐 *www.gallatinhistorymuseum.org* 🎫 *$8* 🕒 *Closed Sun. and Mon.*

★ **Museum of the Rockies**

MUSEUM | **FAMILY** | Here you'll find a celebration of the history of the Rockies region, with exhibits ranging from prehistory to pioneers, plus a planetarium with laser shows. Most renowned is the museum's Siebel Dinosaur Complex housing one of the world's largest dinosaur fossil collections along with the largest-known T-rex skull, a Mesozoic Media

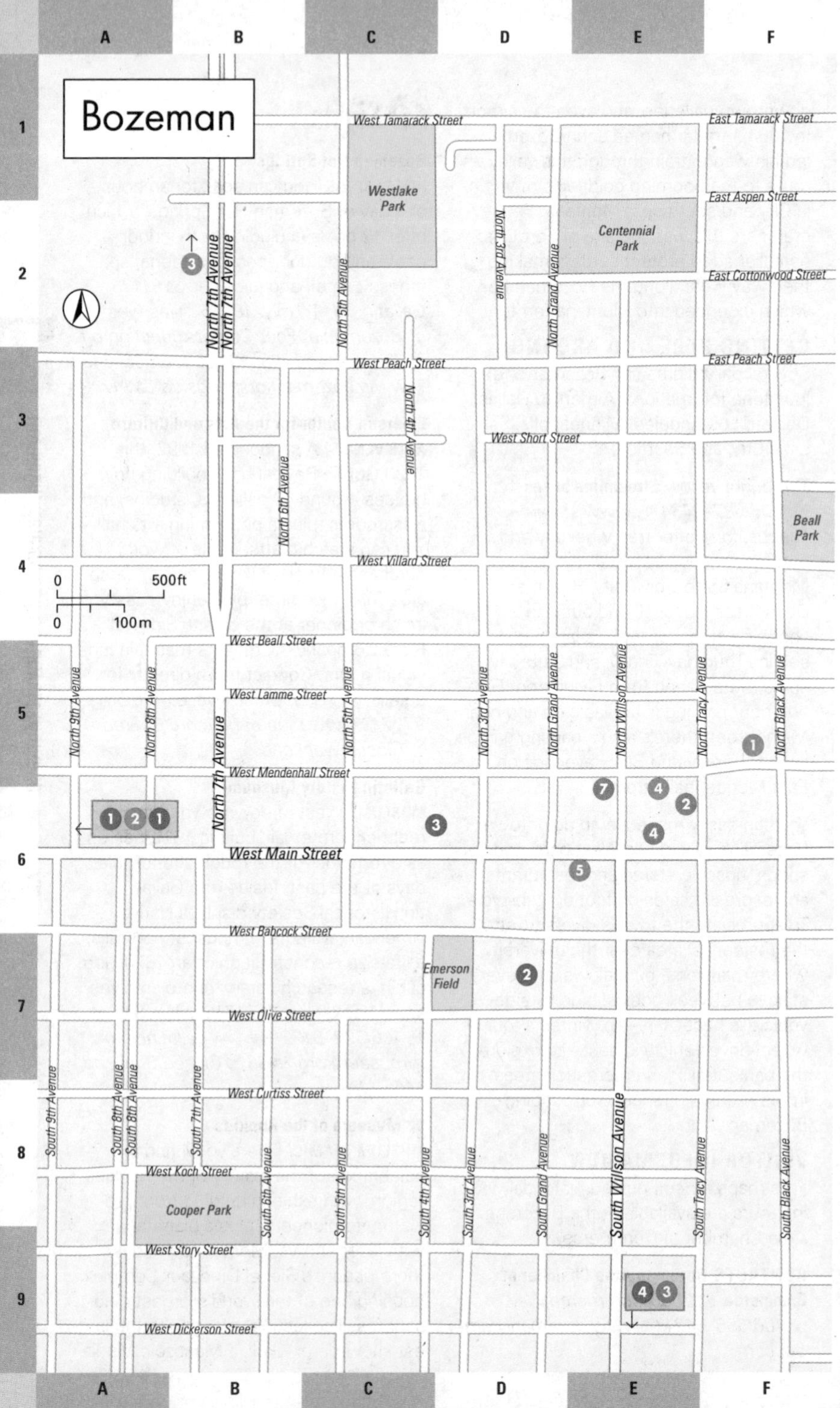

Bozeman
A
B
C
D
E
F
1
2
3
4
5
6
7
8
9
0
500ft
100m
West Tamarack Street
East Tamarack Street
Westlake Park
East Aspen Street
Centennial Park
East Cottonwood Street
North 7th Avenue
North 5th Avenue
North 3rd Avenue
North Grand Avenue
West Peach Street
East Peach Street
North 4th Avenue
West Short Street
North 6th Avenue
Beall Park
West Villard Street
West Beall Street
West Lamme Street
North 9th Avenue
North 8th Avenue
North Willson Avenue
North Tracy Avenue
North Black Avenue
West Mendenhall Street
West Main Street
West Babcock Street
Emerson Field
West Olive Street
West Curtiss Street
South 9th Avenue
South 8th Avenue
South 7th Avenue
South 6th Avenue
South 5th Avenue
South 4th Avenue
South 3rd Avenue
South Grand Avenue
South Willson Avenue
South Tracy Avenue
South Black Avenue
West Koch Street
Cooper Park
West Story Street
West Dickerson Street

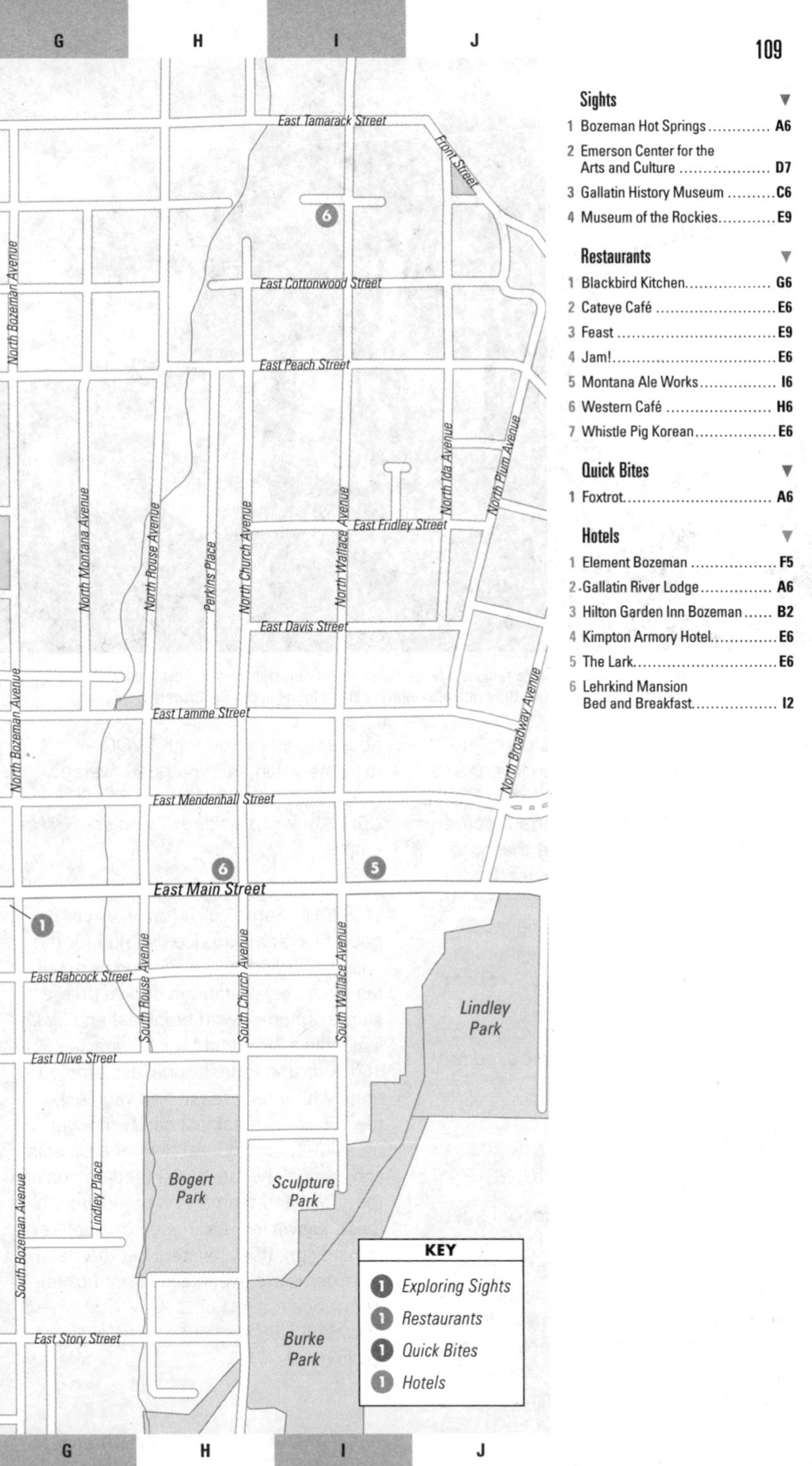

Sights

1 Bozeman Hot Springs **A6**
2 Emerson Center for the Arts and Culture **D7**
3 Gallatin History Museuem **C6**
4 Museum of the Rockies........... **E9**

Restaurants

1 Blackbird Kitchen.................. **G6**
2 Cateye Café **E6**
3 Feast **E9**
4 Jam!................................... **E6**
5 Montana Ale Works................ **I6**
6 Western Café **H6**
7 Whistle Pig Korean................ **E6**

Quick Bites

1 Foxtrot.............................. **A6**

Hotels

1 Element Bozeman **F5**
2 Gallatin River Lodge.............. **A6**
3 Hilton Garden Inn Bozeman...... **B2**
4 Kimpton Armory Hotel............. **E6**
5 The Lark.............................. **E6**
6 Lehrkind Mansion Bed and Breakfast................. **I2**

The Museum of the Rockies houses a famously large collection of dinosaur fossils. This bronze statue of "Big Mike" sits outside the museum; the original skeleton can be found in the Smithsonian.

Center, and a Hall of Giants complete with sound effects. Children love the hands-on science activities in the Explore Yellowstone Martin Children's Discovery Center and (in the summer) the living history farm. Tinsley Homestead, with home-crafts demonstrations, including butter churning, weaving, and blacksmithing is open Wednesday through Sunday. ✉ *600 W. Kagy Blvd.* ✣ *South end of university campus* ☎ *406/994–2251* 🌐 *www.museumoftherockies.org* 🎟 *$13* 🕓 *Tinsley Homstead closed Mon. and Tues.*

Restaurants

Blackbird Kitchen

$$$ | ITALIAN | Ground zero for unforgettable authentic Italian food in Bozeman, Blackbird Kitchen offers almost as many antipasti options as wine options. After your antipasti, choose from salads, pizzas, pastas, and meat entrées like lamb shank and crispy pork belly. **Known for:** a creative one-page menu; mind-blowing house bread served with EVOO; extremely thin-crust pizza. $ *Average main: $22* ✉ *140 E. Main St.* ☎ *406/586–0010* 🌐 *www.blackbirdkitchen.com* 🕓 *No lunch.*

Cateye Café

$$ | DINER | Some call it funky; all call it good food at a fair price. Named for the shape of Grandma's glasses, this small family-owned restaurant serves up a sense of humor with breakfast and lunch, including a "Purrfect Lunch" special; "Look for the Catastrophe" (scrambled eggs with taters, toast, and veggies); the "Felix" (a breakfast sandwich with prosciutto, roasted red pepper aioli, spinach, gouda cheese, and a fried egg on a torta roll); and the banana bread French toast. **Known for:** really good drip coffee; tomato jam; its consistent cat theme (restrooms are even called litter boxes). $ *Average main: $12* ✉ *23 N. Tracy Ave.* ☎ *406/587–8844* 🌐 *www.cateyecafe.com* 🕓 *No dinner.*

A Dark Day in Bozeman

At 8:12 am on March 5, 2009, a natural gas leak sparked an explosion that would forever change the landscape of Bozeman's Main Street. The blast was heard blocks away, and windows were shattered as far down as the Baxter Hotel on West Main Street. By the time the fire and ash settled, one life had been lost, half a historic city block had been leveled, two buildings were structurally damaged, and nine businesses were displaced. It happened at a time of economic uncertainty, and the community wondered what, if anything, would fill the void.

Things may not ever be the same, but there were signs of recovery in short order. Montana Trails Gallery relocated. The iconic Rockin' R Bar and American Legion rebuilt in their former locations.

Bozeman's **Gallatin History Museum** (✉ *317 W. Main St.* ☎ *406/522–8122* 🌐 *www.gallatinhistorymuseum.org*) featured an exhibit called *The Block That Was Rocked*, explaining the events of the tragic day.

Feast

$$$$ | **AMERICAN** | Feast is one of only a handful of restaurants in Montana serving up a daily dose of ceviche, bison carpaccio, and other raw bar specialties. Crabs, shrimp, oysters, scallops: if a fisherman can catch it, Feast serves it. **Known for:** outstanding, attentive servers; crispy brussel sprouts; an upscale yet unassuming atmosphere. [$] *Average main: $34* ✉ *270 W. Kagy, Suite C* ☎ *406/577–2377* 🌐 *www.feastbozeman.com* ⏲ *No lunch.*

Jam!

$$ | **MODERN AMERICAN** | Colorful murals, high ceilings, and exposed air ducts create a mod-industrial ambience in this bustling downtown café that serves breakfast all day as well as a selection of tasty lunch items. Specialties include the crab cake Benedict and challah bread French toast stuffed with jam-infused mascarpone cheese. **Known for:** mimosas and brunch cocktails; bacon–smoked bacon burgers; both sweet and savory crepes. [$] *Average main: $13* ✉ *25 W. Main St.* ☎ *406/585–1761* 🌐 *www.jamon-main.com* ⏲ *No dinner.*

Montana Ale Works

$$$ | **ECLECTIC** | A cavernous brick building, the former Northern Pacific Railroad depot houses a full bar with a huge selection of Montana microbrews, and a restaurant with a choice of quiet or boisterous seating areas. In addition to 40-plus beers on tap, Ale Works serves bison burgers, bison pot stickers, hand-cut steaks, sandwiches, fish tacos, and seasonal salads. **Known for:** always having a good crowd; truffle fries worth the upgrade; no sampling of beers. [$] *Average main: $21* ✉ *611 E. Main St.* ☎ *406/587–7700* 🌐 *www.montanaale-works.com* ⏲ *No lunch.*

Western Café

$ | **DINER** | A deer head, often sporting sunglasses, surveys the cowboys and families that pack the counter stools and tables at this down-home breakfast and lunch spot. Peruse the local paper as you work your way through biscuits and gravy, eggs with corned-beef hash, or pork chops. **Known for:** a wait on the weekends; amazing chicken fried steak; the best cinnamon rolls in the state. [$] *Average main: $9* ✉ *443 E. Main St.* ☎ *406/587–0436* 🌐 *www.thewesternca-fe.com* ⏲ *No dinner.*

★ Whistle Pig Korean
$$ | **KOREAN** | A welcome addition to Bozeman's growing selection of international restaurants, this cozy, dimly lighted Korean eatery serves delectable pork-kimchi buns, fried tofu dumplings, and bibimbap with bulgogi beef. Be sure to save room for a house-made Korean street doughnut. **Known for:** cucumber kimchi; Kalbi barbecued short ribs; short but sweet list of interesting beer and wine. *Average main: $12* *25 N. Willson Ave.* *406/404–1224* *www.whistlepigkorean.com* *Closed Sun. and Mon. No lunch.*

 Coffee and Quick Bites

Foxtrot
$ | **CAFÉ** | This dapper counter-service café in Bozeman's eco-friendly Market Building roasts small-batch Guatemalan coffee and serves a selection of beer, wine, and cocktails, too. It's also a good bet for flavorful breakfast and lunch fare, from veggie scrambles to healthy power bowls. **Known for:** stellar espresso drinks; airy, modern design; biscuits with pork shoulder and Dijon-creme gravy. *Average main: $9* *The Market Bldg., 730 Boardwalk Ave.* *406/551–7438* *www.foxtrotbzn.com* *No dinner.*

Hotels

Element Bozeman
$$$ | **HOTEL** | This dog-friendly LEED-certified extended stay hotel is conveniently located one block off Main Street. **Pros:** free airport shuttle; complimentary bicycles; 24-hour pantry. **Cons:** small pool; no hot tub; on-site parking is $5. *Rooms from: $159* *25 E. Mendenhall St.* *406/582–4972* *www.marriott.com* *104 rooms* *Free breakfast.*

Gallatin River Lodge
$$$$ | **B&B/INN** | On the property of a 20-acre ranch, this full-service, year-round fly-fishing lodge has private access on the Gallatin, for which it is named. **Pros:** lodge earns praise for its delicious dinners; idyllic setting; top-notch fly-fishing guides. **Cons:** if fly-fishing isn't your thing, not the best choice; airport transfers aren't always included; can be a bit pricey. *Rooms from: $375* *9105 Thorpe Rd.* *406/388–0148, 888/387–0148* *www.grlodge.com* *12 rooms* *Free breakfast.*

Hilton Garden Inn Bozeman
$$$ | **HOTEL** | This comfortable property with a friendly staff is a 10-minute drive from downtown and 15 minutes from the airport. **Pros:** decor a step up from usual chain hotel look; staff helpful and pleasant; free airport shuttle. **Cons:** located in busy mall area; it's not pet-friendly; the pool is on the smaller side. *Rooms from: $136* *2023 Commerce Way* *406/582–9900* *www.hiltongarden-inn3.hilton.com* *123 rooms* *No meals.*

★ Kimpton Armory Hotel
$$$$ | **HOTEL** | With a striking art deco design, this gorgeous nine-story hotel opened in Bozeman's former armory building in 2020, providing urban accommodations and amenities in an appealing downtown location that's within day-tripping distance of Big Sky skiing and Yellowstone National Park adventures. **Pros:** great pool and fitness center; fantastic restaurant and rooftop bar; heart of downtown dining and shopping district. **Cons:** can be pricey at busy times; expensive valet-only parking; busy downtown location. *Rooms from: $250* *24 W. Mendenhall St.* *406/551–7700, 833/549–0847* *www.armoryhotelbzn.com* *122 rooms* *No meals.*

The Lark
$$$ | **HOTEL** | The Lark may be one of Bozeman's newest hotels, but as one of its first boutique hotels, it's also one of the city's most needed hotels, conveniently located on Main Street within walking distance of dozens of shops and restaurants. **Pros:** it's dog-friendly; staff is young, hip, and always happy to

share hiking tips; downtown Bozeman is outside your front door. **Cons:** no complimentary on-site parking; rooms could use curtains that block more light; can be loud since it's on Main Street. *Rooms from: $150* *122 W. Main St.* *406/624–3070, 866/464–1000* *www.larkbozeman.com* *67 rooms* *No meals.*

★ **Lehrkind Mansion Bed and Breakfast**
$$$ | **B&B/INN** | Built in 1897 for a wealthy master brewer, this B&B's gables, bays, and corner tower exemplify Queen Anne architecture. **Pros:** grand oak staircase and carefully selected antique furnishings; proprietors are former Yellowstone National Park rangers who are happy to relate sightseeing itineraries as well as the history of the home; located a few blocks from bustling Main Street, so it's quiet. **Cons:** opt for Garden House if stairs are a problem; breakfast at set time; not pet-friendly. *Rooms from: $160* *719 N. Wallace Ave.* *406/585–6932, 800/992–6932* *www.bozemanbedandbreakfast.com* *9 rooms* *Free breakfast.*

Nightlife

Plonk
WINE BARS—NIGHTLIFE | Cowboy boots, Carhartt jackets, and upscale urban garb mingle amiably at Plonk. Though technically a wine bar, this trendy place also serves dinner, and has a full bar serving classy cocktails and local microbrews. *29 E. Main St.* *406/587–2170* *www.plonkwine.com.*

Rocking R Bar
BARS/PUBS | Every college town has "that bar," and in Bozeman it's the Rockin R Bar, where students, locals, and visitors watch the big game. If you're not an MSU fan, enter at your own risk. *211 E. Main St.* *406/587–9355* *www.rockingrbar.com.*

Sky Shed
BARS/PUBS | This stunning rooftop bar above the new Kimpton Armory Hotel features views of four different mountain ranges. Get cozy with a spiced cocktail around one of the outdoor fire pits or the fireplace inside. *24 W. Mendenhall St.* *406/551–7703* *www.skyshedbar.com.*

Performing Arts

Bozeman Symphony Society
MUSIC | This group runs a year-round concert series, often featuring talented university students and traveling artists. Performances take place at the Willson Auditorium. *1001 W. Oak St., Suite 110* *406/585–9774* *www.bozemansymphony.org.*

Shakespeare in the Parks
THEATER | During the summer months, this university-based touring theater troupe performs Shakespeare plays in some 61 rural communities throughout Montana and nearby states. *Black Box Theater, Visual Communications Bldg., MSU* *Corner of Bobcat Circle and W. Grant St.* *406/994–3303* *www.shakespeareintheparks.org* *Free.*

Shopping

Country Bookshelf
BOOKS/STATIONERY | The two levels of Country Bookshelf house a large Montana and Western section, including many autographed works, as well as more general offerings. They'll ship all over the world. *28 W. Main St.* *406/587–0166* *www.countrybookshelf.com.*

Montana Trails Gallery
ART GALLERIES | Since 1993, this gallery has been where Montana's finest artists go to see and be seen. Stop by to browse a private collection or purchase an original souvenir. *7 W. Main St.* *406/586–2166* *www.montanatrails.com.*

Northern Lights Trading Co.

SPORTING GOODS | Outdoor wear, Onewheels, and boating gear are sold at Northern Lights Trading Co. The shop also rents out canoes, fishing equipment, kayaks, and rafts. It's closed Sunday and Monday. ✉ *8358 Huffline Lane, Unit C* ☎ *406/586–6029* 🌐 *www.northernlightstrading.com.*

Schnee's

SPORTING GOODS | In business since 1946 Schnee's sports two rooms filled with fishing gear and Western gear including its signature Pac boots made in Schnee's Bozeman boot factory. ✉ *35 E. Main St.* ☎ *800/922–1562* 🌐 *www.schnees.com.*

Activities

BIKING

Bozeman bike shops can supply all the equipment, repairs, and info that bike addicts might wish.

Bangtail Bicycle Shop

BICYCLING | This full-service shop sells bikes, gear, and maps. ✉ *137 E. Main St.* ☎ *406/587–4905* 🌐 *www.bangtailbikes.com* ⏲ *Closed Sun.*

Chalet Sports

BICYCLING | This sports shop rents mountain and road bikes in the summer, and snowshoes, cross-country skis, and downhill skis in the winter. ✉ *108 W. Main* ☎ *406/587–4595* 🌐 *www.chaletsportsmt.com.*

Summit Bike & Ski

BICYCLING | The staff at Summit Bike & Ski sells bikes, supplies, maps, and biking guidebooks. They don't do rentals. ✉ *26 S. Grand Ave.* ☎ *406/587–1064* 🌐 *www.summitbikeandski.com* ⏲ *Closed Sun. in summer; closed Sun. and Mon. in winter.*

FISHING

The River's Edge

FISHING | The full-service fly-fishing shop is the only retailer in the world with the entire line of Simms Fishing Products. Come in for yesterday's fishing report, today's bait, or to arrange tomorrow's guided trip. ✉ *612 E. Main St., Suite A* ☎ *406/586–5373* 🌐 *www.theriversedge.com.*

SKIING

Bridger Bowl

SKIING/SNOWBOARDING | **FAMILY** | Located 20 minutes from downtown Bozeman, Bridger Bowl is known for skiing in "cold smoke," light, dry powder. The terrain, from steep, rocky chutes to gentle slopes and meadows, is the headline act at this community-owned mountain, where lift tickets ($63) are almost half the price of those at upscale resorts. One quad, one double, and six triple chair lifts access 75 named runs covering more than 2,000 acres. There are also hundreds of expert-only terrain, reached by the Schlasman's lift; skiers are required to carry avalanche transceivers. The mountain is open early December–early April. Fresh powder on the mountain? Look for a flashing blue beacon atop the former Baxter Hotel on Main Street. ✉ *15795 Bridger Canyon Rd.* ☎ *406/587–2111* 🌐 *www.bridgerbowl.com.*

Crosscut Mountain Sports Center

SKIING/SNOWBOARDING | This nonprofit Nordic center maintains 27 miles of groomed trails perfect for cross-country skiing, snowshoeing, fat-biking, and even biathlon training. Passes are required; lessons and rentals are available as well. The season runs from early December to late March, depending on trail conditions. Dogs are welcome on Monday, Wednesday, and Saturday afternoon. ✉ *16621 Bridger Canyon Rd.* ☎ *406/586–9690* 🌐 *www.crosscutmt.org* ☞ *Day passes from $25.*

Helena

Montana's state capital is a city of 33,000, with 30 city parks, several museums, and a thriving arts community. The southern part of the city, near the state capitol and neighboring museums, mansions, and parks, is hilly and thick, with lush greenery in summer. This quiet town started as a rowdy mining camp in 1864 and became a banking and commerce center in the Montana Territory. At the turn of the 20th century Helena had more millionaires per capita than any other town in the country. Some of that wealth came from ground now occupied by Main Street: called Last Chance Gulch, it was the first of several gulches that yielded more than $15 million in gold during the late 1800s. With statehood came a fight between the towns of Anaconda and Helena over which would be the capital. In a notoriously corrupt campaign in which both sides bought votes, Helena won. The iron ball of urban renewal has since robbed the town of much of its history, but Helena still has ornate brick-and-granite historic buildings along Last Chance Gulch.

GETTING HERE AND AROUND

Helena Airport has service from Denver, Seattle, and Salt Lake City. The downtown historic area has a pedestrian-only mall on Last Chance Gulch with shops, microbreweries, coffeehouses, galleries, and restaurants. There are several historic sights here that you can see on foot, but other sights are spread out in the city and best accessed by car. While Helena has Uber and Lyft, drivers can be few and far between during busy times.

TOURS

Last Chance Train Tour

BUS TOURS | Out in front of the Montana Historical Society, catch the Last Chance Train Tour for an hour-long tour through historic neighborhoods of miners' mansions on the west side to the site where four miners made their first gold discovery on the gulch. Tours run from June through mid-September at select times depending on the week and month. ✉ *225 N. Roberts St.* ☎ *406/442–1023* 🌐 *lctours.com* 🎟 *$10* 🕓 *Closed Sun.*

VISITOR INFORMATION

CONTACTS Helena Area Chamber of Commerce. ✉ *225 N. Cruse Ave., Suite A* ☎ *406/442–4120* 🌐 *www.helenachamber.com.*

Sights

Atlas Building

BUILDING | Stylized flames lap at dancing salamanders on the rooftop of this restored 1889 neo-Romanesque building, which a statue of Atlas appears to be hoisting on his shoulders. Once an insurance building, it's now home to Ocean Spirit Massage. ✉ *7 N. Last Chance Gulch* 🎟 *Free.*

Cathedral of St. Helena

RELIGIOUS SITE | Modeled after the cathedral in Vienna, Austria, this Gothic Revival building has stained-glass windows from Bavaria and 230-foot-tall twin spires that are visible from most places in the city. Construction began in 1908 and was completed six years later. Note the white-marble altars, statues of Carrara marble, and gold leaf decorating the sanctuary. Free guided tours are given between 1 and 3 pm Tuesday–Thursday in the summer (Memorial Day–Labor Day). Call for guided tours for 10 or more during other months of the year. ✉ *530 N. Ewing St.* ☎ *406/442–5825* 🌐 *www.sthelenas.org* 🎟 *Donations accepted.*

ExplorationWorks

MUSEUM | **FAMILY** | Rotating exhibits and interactive permanent displays—which include "Waterways to the Future" and "Montana Outdoors"—are the main attractions at Helena's beloved children's science museum. ✉ *995 Carousel Way* ☎ *406/457–1800* 🌐 *www.explorationworks.org* 🎟 *$8* 🕓 *Closed Mon.*

A
B
C
D
E
F
1
2
3
4
5
6
7
8
9
Leslie Avenue
Wilder Avenue
North Benton Avenue
Centennial / Bausch Park
N. Last Chance Gulch St.
N. Last Chance Gulch St.
Memorial Park
Memorial Drive
12
West Lyndale Avenue
West Lyndale Avenue
17th Street
East 16th Street
East 15th Street
East 14th Street
Helena Avenue
Madison Avenue
Dearborn Avenue
North Benton Avenue
North Park Avenue
North Last Chance Gulch Street
North Jackson Street
Getchell Street
Front Street
W. 13th St.
Flowerree Street
Gilbert Street
Neill Avenue
Hill Park
Power Street
Logan Street
North Warren Street
North Ewing Street
North Rodney Street
12th Avenue
North Davis Street
Holter Street
North Park Avenue
Fuller Avenue
N. Last Chance Gulch St.
11th Avenue
West Lawrence Street
East Lawrence Street
Clarke Street
9th Avenue
11th Avenue
8th Avenue
9th Avenue
7th Avenue
South Benton Ave.
North Jackson Street
N. Cruse Avenue
North Warren Street
6th Avenue
8th Avenue
South Howie St.
Jefferson Street
5th Avenue
North Rodney Street
North Beattie Street
6th Avenue
Raleigh Street
North Hoback Street
South Park Avenue
5th Avenue
S. Cruse Street
East Broadway Street
North Davis Street
Breckenridge Street
Fire Tower Park
East Broadway Street
Hillsdale Street
Highland Street
Pine Street
South Rodney Street
South Davis Street
State Street
Blake Street
Chaucer Street
Dale Harris Park
3rd Street
South Beattie Street
0
1,000 ft
0
200 m

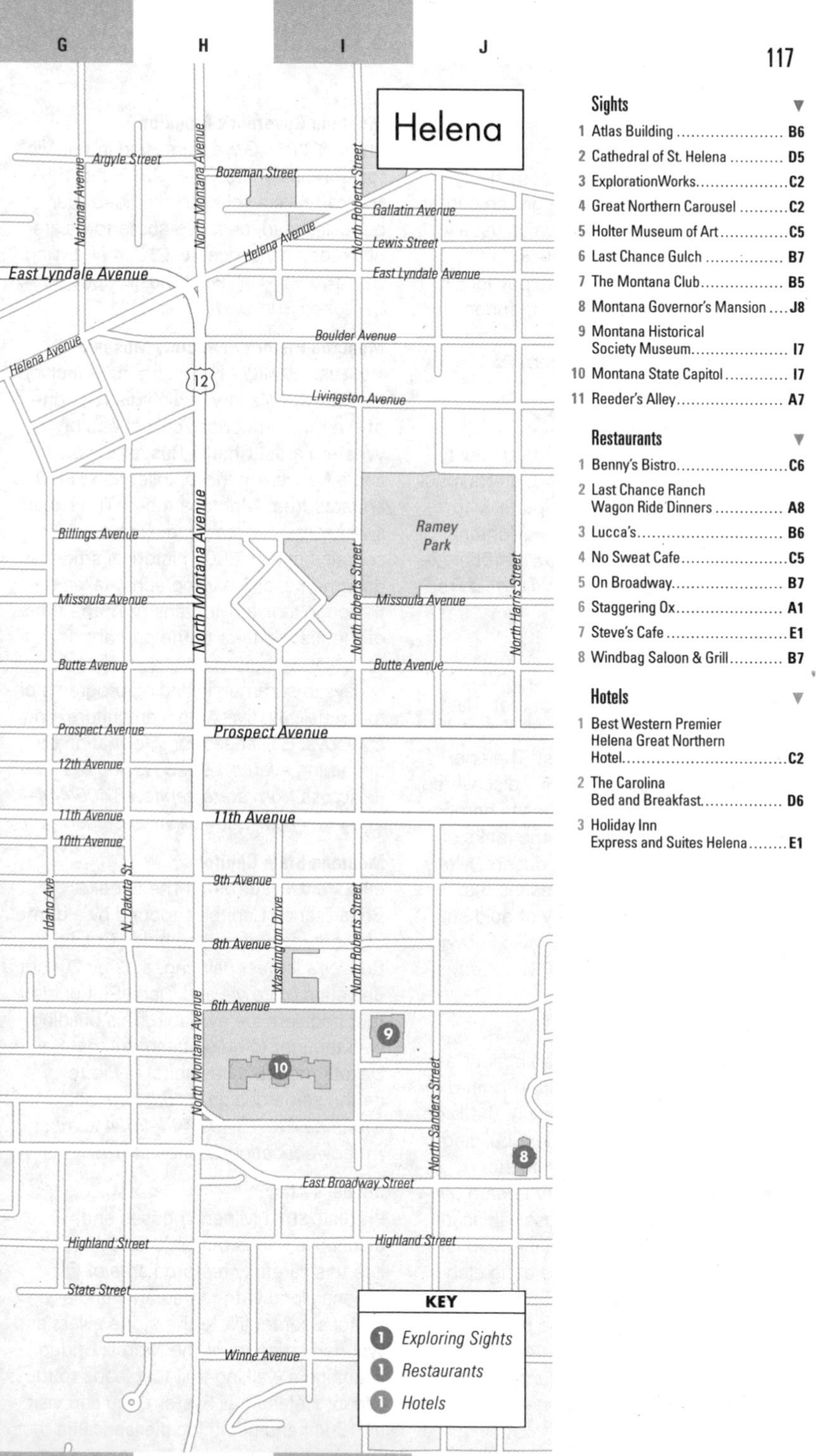

Sights

1 Atlas Building **B6**
2 Cathedral of St. Helena **D5**
3 ExplorationWorks.................. **C2**
4 Great Northern Carousel **C2**
5 Holter Museum of Art.............. **C5**
6 Last Chance Gulch **B7**
7 The Montana Club.................. **B5**
8 Montana Governor's Mansion **J8**
9 Montana Historical Society Museum.................. **I7**
10 Montana State Capitol **I7**
11 Reeder's Alley..................... **A7**

Restaurants

1 Benny's Bistro...................... **C6**
2 Last Chance Ranch Wagon Ride Dinners **A8**
3 Lucca's.............................. **B6**
4 No Sweat Cafe...................... **C5**
5 On Broadway........................ **B7**
6 Staggering Ox....................... **A1**
7 Steve's Cafe **E1**
8 Windbag Saloon & Grill............ **B7**

Hotels

1 Best Western Premier Helena Great Northern Hotel.................................. **C2**
2 The Carolina Bed and Breakfast................ **D6**
3 Holiday Inn Express and Suites Helena........ **E1**

Great Northern Carousel

CAROUSEL | FAMILY | Hand-carved grizzly bears, mountain goats, bighorn sheep, and river otters gallop through the center of town on this carousel, which usually operates most afternoons (except on major holidays). You can also buy locally made premium ice cream and fudge here. ✉ *989 Carousel Way* ☎ *406/457–5353* 🌐 *www.gncarousel.com* 🎟 *$2* ⏲ *Closed Mon. and Tues.*

Holter Museum of Art

MUSEUM | Displays at this 17,000-square-foot museum include folk art, crafts, photography, painting, and sculpture, with an emphasis on homegrown Montana artists. ✉ *12 E. Lawrence St.* ☎ *406/442–6400* 🌐 *www.holtermuseum.org* 🎟 *Free* ⏲ *Closed Mon.*

Last Chance Gulch

HISTORIC SITE | Four down-and-out prospectors designated this spot their "last chance" after they'd followed played-out gold strikes across the West. Their perseverance paid off when they discovered the first of several gold deposits here, which propelled Helena to the ranks of Montana's leading gold producers. Many of the mansions and businesses that resulted from the discovery of gold still stand on this historic route, also known as Main Street. ✉ *Helena* 🌐 *www.downtownhelena.com.*

The Montana Club

BUILDING | Built in 1905 by architect Cass Gilbert, who also designed the United States Supreme Court Building, the Montana Club was once the tallest building in the state. It's notable for its stone archways and contemporary I-beam construction underneath its classical facade. Founded in 1885, the Montana Club is the oldest continuously operating club between Minneapolis and Seattle. Once private, it's now open to the public for dinner and Sunday brunch. ✉ *24 W. 6th Ave.* ☎ *406/442–5980* 🌐 *montanaclub.coop* 🎟 *Free* ⏲ *Closed Mon.–Wed.*

Montana Governor's Mansion

HISTORIC SITE | Governors lived in this Victorian mansion between 1913 and 1959. You can take a scheduled guided tour, but call ahead, because some tours are unexpectedly canceled. ✉ *304 N. Ewing St.* ☎ *406/444–2694* 🌐 *mhs.mt.gov* 🎟 *$4* ⏲ *Closed Sun. and Mon.*

Montana Historical Society Museum

MUSEUM | FAMILY | Highlights here include the MacKay Gallery, which displays one of the most important collections of Western artist Charlie Russell's work, and a Native American collection of 6,000 artifacts from Montana tribes. The expansive Montana Homeland exhibit, which contains nearly 2,000 historical artifacts, documents, and photographs, takes a thorough look at Montana from the time of the first settlers to the present. The venue also hosts special events and family days in summer, including programs on folk music, Native American culture, and cowboys. Call ahead for information on upcoming events. ✉ *225 N. Roberts St.* ✣ *Across from state capitol* ☎ *406/444–2694* 🌐 *mhs.mt.gov* 🎟 *$5* ⏲ *Closed Sun.*

Montana State Capitol

GOVERNMENT BUILDING | The Greek Renaissance Capitol is topped by a dome of Montana copper and holds Charlie Russell's largest painting, a 12-by-25-foot depiction of Lewis and Clark. Self-guided-tour booklets are available. This building was thought to be so beautiful that South Dakota modeled its capitol in Pierre on the same design. ✉ *6th Ave. and Montana Ave.* ☎ *406/444–2694* 🌐 *mhs.mt.gov/education/Capitol* 🎟 *Free.*

Reeder's Alley

HISTORIC SITE | Miners' houses and distinctive shops built in the 1870s line this carefully restored area of Old Helena along with restaurants and a visitor's center. Note the stone pillars and wooden stringers of the Morelli Bridge, spanning a walking trail that leads to the Mount Helena Trail System. You can visit an 1864 hand-hewn log **pioneer cabin** that

The Montana State Capitol, crowned with a copper dome, also displays Charles Russell's largest painting, which depicts Lewis and Clark.

now houses a museum of the gold-rush days of the 1860s; this is Helena's oldest surviving home. ✉ *212 S. Park Ave.* ✣ *Near south end of Last Chance Gulch* ☎ *406/422–4727* 🌐 *www.reedersalley.com.*

Restaurants

Benny's Bistro
$$$ | CONTEMPORARY | The art deco–inspired interior, often filled with live jazz music, is a hallmark of this small but spacious restaurant, which started out serving comfort food but has branched into tapas and more exotic, internationally influenced but locally sourced fare. Favorites include the creamy tomato soup with fresh rosemary and the apple-tizer: black pepper feta and Flathead Lake apples drizzled with Montana honey. **Known for:** Montana-grown proteins; using paper straws and no styrofoam; excellent curries for Montana. $ *Average main: $24* ✉ *108 E. 6th Ave.* ☎ *406/443–0105* 🌐 *www.bennyshelena.com* ⏲ *Closed Sun. and Mon.*

Last Chance Ranch Wagon Ride Dinners
$$$$ | AMERICAN | Get a true taste of Montana during this all-you-can-eat prime-rib dinner, which follows a horse-drawn wagon ride through high mountain forest. The private forested plot feels like backcountry. **Known for:** Grizzly Gulch succotash; entertainment by Bruce Anfinson, "Montana's Musical Ambassador"; huge horses (they're draft horses). $ *Average main: $100* ✉ *2884 Grizzly Gulch Dr.* ✣ *Transportation from Helena to ranch, 8 miles southwest of town, is included in price* ☎ *406/442–2884* 🌐 *www.lastchanceranch.biz* ⏲ *Closed Oct.–May. No lunch.*

Lucca's
$$$ | ITALIAN | You're a guest of honor at this cozy Italian eatery tucked into the north end of the walking mall. With only 54 seats, dinner is intimate and elegant, and this regularly ranks among the best restaurants in Helena. **Known for:** everything being made from scratch; half-price wines on Wednesday; reservations essential. $ *Average main: $30*

On the Trail of Lewis and Clark

America's greatest adventure began with the stroke of a pen, when in 1803 President Thomas Jefferson purchased the vast Louisiana Territory from cash-strapped France, effectively doubling the size of the United States. The land, stretching from the Gulf of Mexico to Canada and from the Mississippi River to the Rockies, was unmapped and virtually unknown to outsiders.

To understand what his $16 million had bought, Jefferson appointed a secret "Corps of Discovery" to venture west, make contact with native peoples, chart the landscape, and observe the growing British presence in the Pacific Northwest. The group would be headed by Jefferson's personal secretary, Meriwether Lewis, and another intrepid explorer, William Clark.

Time in Montana

On May 14, 1804, Lewis and Clark set out from St. Louis on their expedition with a party of 45 seasoned soldiers, scouts, interpreters, and others, poling up the Missouri River in well-stocked flatboats and keelboats. After wintering with the Mandans in North Dakota, the corps continued upriver in canoes and keelboats as soon as ice jams had cleared the waterway.

They entered what is now Montana on April 27, 1805, and followed the Missouri to its Montana headwaters—the confluence of the Jefferson, Madison, and Gallatin rivers. After they reached the Continental Divide, Shoshone Indians helped them cross the Rockies. The party then followed the Snake, Clearwater, and Columbia rivers, reaching the Pacific Ocean that fall.

On the return trip, the expedition split into two groups in Montana and explored several rivers, including the Yellowstone. The explorers arrived back in St. Louis on September 23, 1806, having traveled more than 8,000 miles. They had spent more than a quarter of their time in Montana, where much of the land they observed remains unchanged today.

Following in Their Footsteps

If you want to trace Lewis and Clark's path, the best place to start is the Lewis and Clark National Historic Trail Interpretive Center in Great Falls, where the 200-year-old adventure unfolds before you. Nearby Giant Springs State Park marks the place where Clark discovered a large fountain or spring during an 18-mile portage around a series of waterfalls.

Missouri Headwaters State Park near Three Forks preserves the spot where the explorers traced the river to its origin. The Lolo Pass Visitor Center, on U.S. 12 at the Montana-Idaho border, also interprets the expedition.

Another way to connect with Lewis and Clark history is a boat tour on the Mighty Mo. Several operators offer tours at Gates of the Mountains, north of Helena off I–15, and also at the White Cliffs area of the Upper Missouri National Wild and Scenic River below Fort Benton. A canoe rental and shuttle service on the Missouri near Loma gives you a self-guided option. And look for Lewis and Clark Trail signs along state, U.S., and interstate highways that follow the expedition's route.

56 N. Last Chance Gulch 406/457–8311 www.luccasitalian.com Closed Mon. and Tues. No lunch.

No Sweat Cafe

$ | **AMERICAN** | Wooden booths give this cozy restaurant an old-time, casual feel. Potatoes figure heavily into the breakfast menu, in items such as the Bakery Ladies' Special: potatoes and sausage, green onions, and cheese. **Known for:** half-portions available; a wait, especially Sunday; no cell phones allowed. *Average main: $9 427 N. Last Chance Gulch 406/442–6954 No credit cards Closed Mon. No dinner.*

On Broadway

$$$ | **ITALIAN** | Wooden booths, discreet lighting, and brick walls contribute to the comfortable ambience at this family-owned Italian restaurant, known for its generous portions and long-term staff. Popular menu items include rib-eye steak, pasta puttanesca (sautéed Greek olives, artichoke hearts, red bell peppers, red onions, capers, and pine nuts tossed in linguine), and the breaded Chicken Broadway, topped with mozzarella and served with a side of pesto linguine. **Known for:** no reservations; good seafood for a landlocked state; decadent creamy Parmesan dressing. *Average main: $25 106 E. Broadway 406/443–1929 www.onbroadwayinhelena.com Closed Sun. No lunch.*

Staggering Ox

$ | **FAST FOOD** | The creative deli sandwiches here have even more creative, often political, names. Try the Capitol Complex (loaded with different deli meats and cheese), or the Nuke (ham, turkey, roast beef, and three cheeses). **Known for:** the smell of freshly baked bread; homemade sauces you can buy by the container; interesting sandwich names like ISIS Crisis and Swingin' Single. *Average main: $9 Lundy Center, 400 Euclid Ave. 406/443–1729 www.staggeringox.com.*

Steve's Cafe

$$ | **AMERICAN** | Consistently voted Helena's, and even Montana's, "best breakfast," Steve's has been so successful since it debuted in 2009 that it opened a second location at 630 North Montana Avenue in 2013. Family-owned and operated, Steve's uses eggs from the local Hutterites, three sausages made without preservatives on-site, huckleberries from Montana, and Yukon Gold potatoes from Idaho. **Known for:** homemade chili, which you can even get in an omelet; secret menu; weekly stuffed French toast specials. *Average main: $10 1225 E. Custer Ave. 406/444–5010 www.stevescafe.com No dinner.*

Windbag Saloon & Grill

$$ | **AMERICAN** | This pub-style restaurant in the heart of downtown is housed in a historic building dating back to 1882. While it's a family restaurant, it's named for the political debates you're likely to hear while dining on burgers, sandwiches, mac and cheeses, and wings. **Known for:** cocktails made with fresh fruit puree; infamous "Death by Chicken" hot sauce; a funnel cake dessert served as fries. *Average main: $14 19 S. Last Chance Gulch 406/443–3520 www.windbag406.com.*

Hotels

Best Western Premier Helena Great Northern Hotel

$$$ | **HOTEL** | Located across the street from Carroll College, this full-service hotel with convention facilities is considered to be one of the nicest hotels in the state and it often hosts faculty and visiting speakers. **Pros:** rooms are clean and modern for a chain; walking distance to Great Northern Carousel; better-than-average buffet breakfast. **Cons:** seems pricey for Montana; fills up fast when events are in town; not right off the interstate. *Rooms from: $170 835 Great Northern Blvd. 406/457–5500*

www.bestwestern.com *100 rooms* *Free breakfast.*

The Carolina Bed and Breakfast

$$$ | **B&B/INN** | This hospitality gem is in Helena's historic district; larger than most B&Bs, its guests enjoy extra amenities like toiletries, complimentary beverages, luxury linens, and down pillows. **Pros:** one of the rooms has a shower with a chair; the Corak room has a California king bed; furniture and decor is better than most B&Bs. **Cons:** although a crib is available, it's not really a kid-friendly place; the latest breakfast sitting is 9; the larger rooms are upstairs. *Rooms from: $145* *309 N. Ewing St.* *406/422–0418* *www.carolinab-b.net* *10 rooms* *Free breakfast.*

Holiday Inn Express and Suites Helena

$$ | **HOTEL** | This hotel is staffed with pleasant locals who know the region and just may share a favorite fishing spot with you. **Pros:** conveniently located near the interstate and shopping; reasonably priced; on-site business center. **Cons:** offers a typical chain-hotel experience; pool and hot tub is often broken; mini-refrigerators not in every room. *Rooms from: $130* *3170 N. Sanders St.* *406/442–7500* *www.ihg.com* *87 rooms* *Free breakfast.*

Nightlife

Hap's Bar

BARS/PUBS | Since 1935 (for nearly a century now), this neighborhood bar has been a popular gathering place for Helena's night owls. Expect locals playing pool, karoake (often on Saturday), and if you need clean clothes, the bar owns a laundromat next door. *1505 Railroad Ave.* *406/443–2804* *hapsbar.net.*

The Hawthorn

WINE BARS—NIGHTLIFE | Half tasting room and half bottle shop, The Hawthorn is a place for both socializing and stocking up. Grab a seat at the bar and sample wines, cheeses, and even small-batch beers. In the winter warm up with their famous mulled wine. *46 N. Last Chance Gulch* *406/422–4622* *www.thehawthorn-wine.com.*

Performing Arts

Alive at Five

MUSIC | June through mid-August, live music plays in downtown parks and plazas Wednesday evening from 5:30 to 8:30 as part of the Alive at Five series. The type of music and the venues vary, but it's always free and good family fun. *Helena* *406/447–1535.*

The Myrna Loy

ARTS CENTERS | In a remodeled historic stone jail, The Myrna Loy—named after the Montana-born actress—hosts live performances by nationally and internationally recognized musicians and dance troupes. Foreign and independent films are shown in the auditorium and screening room *15 N. Ewing St.* *406/443–0287* *www.themyrnaloy.com.*

Shopping

Archie Bray Foundation

CERAMICS/GLASSWARE | Since 1951, many of the nation's best ceramic artists have come to work in residency at the Archie Bray Foundation. Wander near the five antiquated, 8-foot-high, dome-shape brick kilns on a self-guided walking tour and visit the gift shop, which sells work produced by foundation artists. Call first in case it's by appointment only that day; the gallery is closed on weekends. *2915 Country Club Ave.* *406/443–3502* *www.archiebray.org.*

The Base Camp

SPORTING GOODS | Find everything you need for outdoor recreation at The Base Camp, a longtime outfitter that rents camping gear, stand-up paddleboards, and cross-country ski equipment. They also offer clothing, books, maps, and are considered footwear specialists. *5*

W. Broadway ☎ *406/443–5360* 🌐 *www.thebasecamp.com.*

Montana Book and Toy Company
BOOKS/STATIONERY | A refreshing stop in the historic center of town, the independent Montana Book and Toy Company lines its shelves with regional and hard-to-find books, toys, games, and gifts. ✉ *331 N. Last Chance Gulch* ☎ *406/443–0260* 🌐 *www.mtbookco.com* ⏲ *Closed Sun.*

Parrot Confectionery
FOOD/CANDY | **FAMILY** | For an old-fashioned sweet treat, pull up a stool at the Parrot Confectionery, a soda fountain and candy store built in the 1920s that sells everything from chocolate malts with homemade ice cream to hand-dipped chocolates and a regional favorite, cherry phosphates. ✉ *42 N. Last Chance Gulch* ☎ *406/442–1470* 🌐 *www.parrotchocolate.com* ⏲ *Closed Sun.*

Activities

To stretch your legs, consider taking an hour-long hike to the top of Mt. Helena, which towers over the Last Chance Gulch pedestrian mall on the west edge of town. From the summit, you'll have panoramic views of the city, the Helena Valley, and the Rocky Mountains to the west.

BICYCLING

Helena is quickly gaining a reputation as a go-to place for mountain biking, in no small part because of the free **Saturday shuttle service** (🌐 *ww.downtownhelena.com*, mid-June–mid-September) from Last Chance Gulch to Mount Helena's Ridge Trail, providing easy access to 8 miles of downhill single-track back to town. Other trails such as the Birdseye Loop and the Helena Valley Loop lead to mining towns and thick forests.

Helena Bicycle Club
BICYCLING | To find out more about bike routes, check the website of the Helena Bicycle Club. ✉ *P.O. Box 4682* 🌐 *www.helenabicycleclub.org.*

Great Divide Cyclery
BICYCLING | This shop rents full-suspension mountain bikes as well as gravel bikes. ✉ *336 N. Jackson* ☎ *406/443–5188* 🌐 *www.greatdividecyclery.com.*

Helena National Forest
BICYCLING | The Helena National Forest can provide bike route information by phone. ✉ *Helena* ☎ *406/449–5201* 🌐 *www.fs.usda.gov.*

BOATING

Canyon Ferry Recreation Area
BOATING | The more than 75 miles of shoreline of the Canyon Ferry Recreation Area make a great place to fish, boat, sail, camp, and watch wildlife. The Missouri River once flowed freely here, before the dam created a lake. ✉ *Hwy. 284, Townsend* ☎ *406/475–3310* 🌐 *www.recreation.gov.*

Gates of the Mountains
BOATING | In their travels on the Missouri River, Lewis and Clark made note of towering limestone cliffs. Gates of the Mountains boat tours take you past these same great stone walls, which rise 1,200 feet above the river. ✉ *3131 Gates of the Mountains Rd.* ✣ *Off I–15, 20 miles north of Helena* ☎ *406/458–5241* 🌐 *www.gatesofthemountains.com.*

Kim's Marina, RV Park and Store
BOATING | You can rent pontoon boats, fishing boats, kayaks, and paddleboards from Kim's Marina, RV Park and Store. ✉ *8015 Canyon Ferry Rd.* ✣ *2 miles east of dam on Hwy. 284* ☎ *406/475–3723* 🌐 *www.kimsmarina.com.*

CAMPING

Cromwell-Dixon Campground. High above Helena on MacDonald Pass at 6,320 feet, this forested spot on the Continental Divide is frequented by migrating birds in spring and fall. ✉ *MacDonald Pass, U.S. 12, 15 miles west of Helena* ☎ *406/449–5490.*

FISHING

Montana Waters Outfitting
FISHING | Experienced anglers offer half-day, full-day, and multiday guided fishing tours. They even offer jet boat tours led by a licensed U.S. Coast Guard Captain. ✉ *3885 Kismet Dr.* ☎ *406/465–6833* 🌐 *montanawatersoutfitting.com.*

Red Lodge

60 miles southwest of Billings via I–90 and U.S. 212; 60 miles northwest of Cody via WY120Rte.120/MT72 Rte. 72 and Rte. 308.

Nestled against the foot of the pine-draped Absaroka-Beartooth Wilderness, this little burg is listed on the National Register of Historic Places and has become a modest mountain resort town, complete with a ski area, trout fishing, access to backcountry hiking, horseback riding, and a golf course. Red Lodge was named for the Crow custom of marking their tepee lodges with paintings of red earth. It became a town in the late 1880s, when the Northern Pacific Railroad laid tracks here to take coal back to Billings. One of Red Lodge's most colorful characters from this time was former sheriff "Liver Eatin'" Jeremiah Johnston, the subject of much Western lore and an eponymous movie starring Robert Redford. This area is a favored stopover for motorcyclists and others heading over the Beartooth Highway to Yellowstone National Park. Free brochures for self-guided historical walking tours of the town and driving tours of the county are available at the chamber of commerce and the museum.

FESTIVALS

The folks in Red Lodge, all 2,300 of them, relish festivals. For a complete list and exact dates, contact the Red Lodge Area Chamber of Commerce.

Each August the **Festival of Nations,** billed as the oldest festival in Montana, celebrates the varied heritages of early settlers, many of whom migrated to work in now-defunct coal mines. The weekend festival includes ethnic music, food, and dance.

July 4 weekend means the **Home of Champions Rodeo** (🌐 *www.redlodgerodeo.com*) has come to town. Now in its ninth decade, this three-day event sees many of the country's rodeo greats taking part in all the usual events. Some also join in the Saturday parade along the town's main street.

GETTING HERE AND AROUND

You need a car to get to Red Lodge. Once you're here, shops, galleries, and restaurants are walkable from most lodging facilities. There is no public transportation, and there is only one taxi (as in vehicle, not company). There are also no traffic lights or parking meters, but there are plenty of stop signs. When passing through Joliet on U.S. 212, obey the frequently changing speed-limit signs to the letter. The nearest airport is in Billings.

VISITOR INFORMATION

Red Lodge Area Chamber of Commerce
✉ *601 N. Broadway* ☎ *406/446–1718* 🌐 *www.redlodgechamber.org.*

Sights

★ Beartooth Highway
SCENIC DRIVE | Driving south from Red Lodge along the 68-mile Beartooth Highway (U.S. 212) will take you over the precipitous 11,000-foot Beartooth Pass as the road winds its way through lush alpine country to the "back door" of Yellowstone National Park. With multiple steep climbs and switchbacks, this National Scenic Byway was a feat of 1930s engineering. The highway is usually open from late May to mid-October, but snow can close it at any time of the year. You'll find trailheads for several good hikes along the route. ✉ *U.S. 212* 🌐 *www.beartoothhighway.com* ⏲ *Closed mid-Oct.–late May.*

The 68-mile Beartooth Highway passes through some spectacular scenery on its route from Red Lodge to Yellowstone National Park, including beautiful Gardiner Lake.

Carbon County Historical Society and Museum

MUSEUM | Established to showcase a prominent family's rodeo artifacts, this community museum now chronicles the area's mining history as well as the cultural legacy of Native Americans and homesteaders. The new (2019) Festival of Nations exhibit is a great addition. ✉ *224 N. Broadway* ☎ *406/446–3667* 🌐 *www.carboncountyhistory.com* 🎫 *$7* 🕐 *Closed Sun. and Mon.*

Charles Ringer Studio & Gallery

MUSEUM | Along Highway 212 in Joliet you'll find the Charles Ringer Studio & Gallery. Ringer's metal kinetic sculptures, from the huge and strange to the small and lovely, are in collections around the world, including that of former president Bill Clinton. ✉ *418 E. Front Ave., Joliet* ☎ *406/962–3705* 🌐 *www.charlesringer.com.*

Yellowstone Wildlife Sanctuary

NATURE PRESERVE | **FAMILY** | See eye-to-eye with mountain lions, black bears, bobcats, coyotes, and bison at this non-profit center sheltering injured animals that cannot be released in the wild. Year-round educational programs are offered, and there is a summer camp for children. ✉ *615 E. 2nd St.* ☎ *406/446–1133* 🌐 *www.yellowstonewildlifesanctuary.org* 🎫 *$10* 🕐 *Closed Tues.*

Restaurants

Bogart's

$$ | **ECLECTIC** | **FAMILY** | This longtime local favorite for Mexican food, margaritas, specialty pizzas, and burgers is set inside a handsome historic downtown building but has a modern, rustic, real-Montana feel. Good bets from the Mexican side of the menu include pork chile verde burritos and mahi-mahi fish tacos, while the Surfing Pig (with Canadian bacon, grilled shrimp, pineapple, mozzarella, and barbecue sauce) is a favorite among the pizzas. **Known for:** friendly, laid-back vibe; good kids' menu; jalapeño-mango margaritas.

$ *Average main: $15* ✉ *11 S. Broadway* ☎ *406/446–1784* 🌐 *www.bogarts.fun.*

Carbon County Steakhouse

$$$ | **STEAKHOUSE** | Saddles, saddle blankets, bridles, and other cowboy and ranch paraphernalia prepare you for the certified Angus beef from the grill, perhaps in the form of a hearty Cowboy Coffee Ribeye, charbroiled with a spiced rum coffee sauce. Seared fresh mussels (from Prince Edward Island) are a local favorite. **Known for:** extra crispy duck drumettes; memorable bison meatballs; attentive, accommodating servers. $ *Average main: $30* ✉ *121 S. Broadway* ☎ *406/446–4025* 🌐 *www.carboncountysteakhouse.com* ⏲ *Closed Mon. and Tues.*

Foster and Logan's Pub & Grill

$$ | **AMERICAN** | Multiple TVs, each tuned to a different sport, line the brick walls of this friendly place. The bar claims 20 beers on tap, the better to enjoy what locals call the town's best hamburgers and other hearty pub fare. **Known for:** attracting a younger crowd; really good Reubens; being open to substitutions. $ *Average main: $13* ✉ *17 S. Broadway* ☎ *406/446–9080.*

★ Piccola Cucina at Ox Pasture

$$$ | **SICILIAN** | In this stylish little storefront eatery—the lone Montana outpost of a group of hip Sicilian restaurants in New York City—you can savor some of the best Italian food in the Rockies, along with an exceptional selection of wines. The cooking here ranges from old-school classics like eggplant Parmesan and spaghetti with clams to more ambitious fare, such as whole grilled sea bass. **Known for:** locally sourced ingredients; urban, contemporary decor; pistachio crème brûlée. $ *Average main: $22* ✉ *7 Broadway N* ☎ *406/446–1212* 🌐 *www.oxpasture.com* ⏲ *Closed Mon. and Nov.–Apr.*

Sam's Taproom and Kitchen

$$ | **AMERICAN** | The culinary cousin of Red Lodge Ales, Sam's Taproom and Kitchen serves lunch and dinner as well as beer brewed on-site (just on the other side of the wall, in fact). It specializes in hot sandwiches including panini, grilled cheese, and baked sammies. **Known for:** always having a good crowd; at least a handful of hand-crafted ciders; the pulled-pork special served on a pretzel bun. $ *Average main: $10* ✉ *1445 Broadway Ave. N* ☎ *406/446–0234* 🌐 *www.redlodgeales.com.*

Hotels

Gallagher's Irish Rose B&B

$$$ | **B&B/INN** | A large stone fireplace serves as the focal point of the living room, and gas or electric stoves or fireplaces lend a cozy feel to each guest room, as do quilts and artwork, both by the owners. **Pros:** food products organically grown; easy walk to shops, galleries, and restaurants; the rooms look better in person. **Cons:** stairs pose a problem for some; no parking, but street parking plentiful nearby; located on the main street so traffic (from bikers) can be loud. $ *Rooms from: $135* ✉ *302 S. Broadway* ☎ *406/446–0303* 🌐 *www.irishrosehost.com* ⏲ *Closed Oct., Nov., and Apr.* *3 rooms* *Free breakfast.*

Pollard Hotel

$$$ | **HOTEL** | Plenty of legendary characters, including Buffalo Bill and Calamity Jane, have stayed at this 1893 landmark in the heart of Red Lodge's historic district—Ernest Hemingway even mentioned the place in *For Whom the Bell Tolls*. Guns have been banned in the hotel ever since Harry Longabaugh, aka the Sundance Kid, brandished one when he robbed a bank on the corner. **Pros:** you can tell the staff loves their jobs; loads of legends and historic charm; great new on-site restaurant serving breakfast and dinner. **Cons:** breakfast not included

unless you opt for the B&B rate; nearly two hours from Yellowstone; old-fashioned vibe isn't to everyone's taste. *Rooms from: $139* ✉ *2 N. Broadway* ☎ *406/446–0001* 🌐 *www.thepollardhotel.com* *39 rooms* *No meals.*

Nightlife

Bear Creek Saloon & Steakhouse
BARS/PUBS | Sit back with a beer and a steak while you watch the Bear Creek Downs' Pig Races at the Bear Creek Saloon & Steakhouse. Oinkers in numbered jerseys streak around an outdoor oval while patrons bet on their favorites; proceeds fund local scholarships. The races take place summer evenings at 7, Thursday through Sunday. ✉ *108 W. Main St., Bearcreek* *7 miles east of Red Lodge on Hwy. 308* ☎ *406/446–3481*.

Shopping

ART GALLERIES

Carbon County Arts Guild & Depot Gallery
ART GALLERIES | Located in an 1889 train depot, the Carbon County Arts Guild & Depot Gallery showcases paintings and sculptures by Western artists. ✉ *11 W. 8th St.* ☎ *406/446–1370* 🌐 *www.carboncountydepotgallery.org*.

Coleman Gallery and Studio
ART GALLERIES | The Coleman Gallery and Studio features works by photographer Merv Coleman. Natural scenery and wildlife are his specialties. ✉ *223 S. Broadway* ☎ *406/446–1228* 🌐 *www.mervcoleman.com*.

Kevin Red Star Gallery
ART GALLERIES | Internationally recognized painter Kevin Red Star, whose works draw on his Crow heritage, displays his oils, acrylics, lithographs, and etchings at Kevin Red Star Gallery. Red Star's works are in the permanent collections of the Smithsonian Institution, the Institute of American Indian Art, and the Pierre Cardin Collection in Paris. ✉ *19 S. 1st St., Roberts* ☎ *406/445–2549* 🌐 *www.kevinredstar.com*.

Red Lodge Clay Center
ART GALLERIES | This center promotes local, regional, and national ceramic artists. Exhibits change monthly. ✉ *123 S. Broadway* ☎ *406/446–3993* 🌐 *www.redlodgeclaycenter.com*.

CANDY

Montana Candy Emporium
FOOD/CANDY | Pick up a paper bag and fill it from the bushel baskets overflowing with what once was called "penny candy" at the Montana Candy Emporium. ✉ *7 S. Broadway* ☎ *406/446–1119* 🌐 *www.montanacandyemporium.net*.

GIFTS

Hometown Sisters
GIFTS/SOUVENIRS | Even if the word "cute" isn't in your vocabulary, it will be after you step foot in this boutique owned and managed by sisters Chelsea and Courtney. They were born and raised in Red Lodge and have an eye for everything from graphic tees to soaps and earrings. ✉ *208 S. Broadway* ☎ *406/445–3334*.

Sylvan Peak Enterprises
SPORTING GOODS | Sylvan Peak Enterprises carries a large selection of top-quality mountain-country dry goods, hiking gear, locally-made fleece jackets, hats, and kids' togs. In the winter, they rent cross country skis and offer info on local Nordic trail conditions. ✉ *9 S. Broadway* ☎ *406/446–1770* 🌐 *www.sylvanpeak.com*.

Activities

CAMPING

Greenough Campground and Lake. Pine trees, a small trout-stocked lake, and gentle hiking trails provide summer respite at Greenough, one of a dozen U.S. Forest Service campgrounds in the Red Lodge vicinity. There's fishing in Greenough Lake ¼ mile from the campground. ✉ *10½ miles south of Red Lodge on U.S. 212, then 1 mile west on Hwy. 421, Beartooth Ranger District, Red Lodge* ☎ *406/446–2103.*

Red Lodge KOA. With its heated pool (open from Memorial Day to Labor Day), playground, trout-filled brook, and access to Rock Creek for fishing, this tidy campground is ideal for families. Sites are along the banks of small creeks and among shady willows and pine trees. Reservations are essential in July. ✉ *7464 U.S. 212, 4 miles north of Red Lodge* ☎ *406/446–2364, 800/562–7540.*

DOWNHILL SKIING

Red Lodge Mountain

SKIING/SNOWBOARDING | There are 70 runs on 1,600 acres at Red Lodge Mountain, all in the Custer National Forest. The family-friendly resort has a 2,400-foot vertical drop, a large beginner area, plenty of groomed intermediate terrain, and 30 acres of extreme chute skiing. Slopes are accessed by two high-speed quads, one triple, three double chairs, and a magic carpet surface lift. Full-day lift tickets cost a bit more on holidays. The season runs from late November through early April. **Facilities:** 70 runs; 1,600 acres; 2,400-foot vertical drop; 6 lifts. ✉ *305 Ski Run Rd.* ☎ *406/446–2610, 800/444–8977* 🌐 *www.redlodgemountain.com* 🎫 *Lift ticket averages $55.*

NORDIC SKIING

Red Lodge Nordic Ski Center

SKIING/SNOWBOARDING | Escape to the solitude of forests along some 9 miles of groomed trails at the base of the Beartooth Mountains. You also can experience on- and off-trail backcountry skiing and snowboarding. Trails are maintained by volunteers, and there is no lodge. Sign in and pay at the kiosk. ✉ *Red Lodge* ✣ *1 mile from town on Hwy. 78, then 2 miles west on Fox Trail* ☎ *406/425–0698* 🌐 *www.beartoothtrails.org* 🎫 *$5.*

FISHING

Montana Trout Scout

FISHING | This place owned by the enthusiastic Craig Beam conducts fly-fishing float trips and wade fishing on local streams and rivers such as the Yellowstone, Clark's Fork, Stillwater, and Rock Creek. ✉ *213 W. 9th St.* ☎ *406/855–3058* 🌐 *montanatroutscout.wordpress.com.*

WHITE-WATER RAFTING

Adventure Whitewater

WHITE-WATER RAFTING | The Stillwater River's foaming white water flows from the Absaroka-Beartooth Wilderness, providing exhilarating rafting from mild to wild with Adventure Whitewater. ✉ *1 N. Stillwater Rd., Absaroka* ☎ *406/446–3061, 800/897–3061* 🌐 *www.adventure-whitewater.com.*

Big Timber

88 miles northwest of Red Lodge via Hwy. 78 north and I–90 west; 81 miles west of Billings via I–90.

People come to Big Timber for its small-town (population 1,700) Western ambience, to fly-fish the blue-ribbon trout streams, float the Yellowstone River, or unwind in front of the Crazy Mountains (so called because a homesteader supposedly went crazy from living in such a remote setting). South of town you can follow the Boulder River in its mad dash out of the Absaroka-Beartooth Wilderness. This journey along Highway 298 will take you into wild country, with craggy peaks rising on either side of a lush, ranch-filled valley.

GETTING HERE AND AROUND

To get around, you'll need a vehicle, as there is no public transportation. There are also no parking meters. The nearest airport is Billings.

VISITOR INFORMATION

CONTACTS Sweet Grass Chamber of Commerce. ✉ *1350 Hwy. 10 W, Big Timber* ☎ *406/932–5131* 🌐 *www.bigtimber.com.*

Sights

Crazy Mountain Museum
MUSEUM | The small but well-organized Crazy Mountain Museum houses exhibits on Big Timber's history and people, as well as the Crazy Mountains. Highlights include the famous Cremer Rodeo, sheep and wool exhibits, a collection of chaps and cattle brands, and a room dedicated to pioneers that includes artifacts dating from the late 1890s. An early-20th-century schoolhouse and a Norwegian stabbur, or storehouse, also stand on the grounds. ✉ *2 S. Frontage Rd., Big Timber* ✣ *Exit 367 off I–90* ☎ *406/932–5126* 🌐 *www.crazymountain-museum.com* 🎫 *Donations accepted.*

Greycliff Prairie Dog Town State Park
NATURE PRESERVE | **FAMILY** | The comical critters at Greycliff Prairie Dog Town State Park pop out of their underground homes, stand upright, sound their chirping alarms, and dash to another hole. Explorers Meriwether Lewis and William Clark referred to these "barking squirrels" in their journals. At this 98-acre protected habitat you can catch the action from your car. ✉ *Old U.S. Hwy. 10, Greycliff* ✣ *I–90, Exit 377* ☎ *406/445–2326* 🌐 *fwp.mt.gov* 🎫 *$8 for out-of-state vehicles.*

Natural Bridge State Monument
NATURE SITE | At Natural Bridge State Monument the Boulder River disappears underground, creating a natural bridge, then reappears as roaring falls in the Boulder River canyon. Hiking trails and interpretive signs explain how this geologic wonder occurred. The Main Boulder Ranger Station, a few miles past the bridge, is one of the oldest in the United States and is now an interpretive center. ✉ *Hwy. 298, Big Timber* ✣ *27 miles south of Big Timber* ☎ *406/222–1892* 🌐 *www.fs.usda.gov* 🎫 *Free.*

Yellowstone River Trout Hatchery
NATURE PRESERVE | Drop by the Yellowstone River Trout Hatchery, a five-minute drive from the town center, to view and learn about cutthroat trout. The best time to visit the hatchery is in spring, when you can see the fingerlings. ✉ *Fairgrounds Rd., Big Timber* ☎ *406/932–4434* 🎫 *Free.*

Restaurants

Iron Star Pizza Company
$$ | **PIZZA** | Stop by Iron Star Pizza Company for pizza, wings, and specialty subs. There are also several tempting fried items on the menu. **Known for:** a spicy pizza sauce so good you'll want the recipe; happy, helpful employees; a great take-out option in a town with no fast food chains. 💲 *Average main: $14* ✉ *101 Bramble St., Big Timber* ☎ *406/932–5998* 🌐 *www.bigtimberpizza.com* 🕘 *Closed Sun.*

Thirsty Turtle Burgers & BBQ
$$ | **BURGER** | This is the busiest restaurant in town, and rightfully so. The family-owned and family-friendly establishment serves an impressive selection of burgers, sammies, and house-smoked BBQ. **Known for:** the "Gut Buster Challenge" where diners have 30 minutes to eat 4½ pounds of food; one of the only halibut burgers you'll find in Montana; no substitutions, so don't even bother asking. 💲 *Average main: $11* ✉ *37 McLeod St., Big Timber* ☎ *406/932–3330* 🌐 *thirstyturtlemt.com.*

Hotels

Grand Hotel
$ | **B&B/INN** | Fine dining and an 1890s saloon are two of the attractions of this classic Western hotel, listed on the National Register of Historic Places, in downtown Big Timber. **Pros:** virtually

Greycliff Prairie Dog Town State Park protects a large colony of endangered black-tailed prairie dogs covering some 98 acres.

shrieks once-grand Old West; restaurant decor and food still qualify as grand; very reasonable prices. **Cons:** claw-foot tubs in hallway baths notwithstanding, the dearth of en suite facilities won't please all; on a given day the "chef's choice" breakfast might not coincide with guest's choice; beds are smaller than most hotel beds. *Rooms from: $99 139 McLeod St., Big Timber 406/932–4459 thegrand-hotel.com 14 rooms Free breakfast.*

The Homestead Bed & Breakfast

$$$ | **HOTEL** | There's nothing rustic about this homestead. **Pros:** quiet neighborhood; most bathrooms are quite large; owner Nancy is beyond accommodating. **Cons:** the town offers few dining options; no parking lot, but street parking is no problem; return guests book a year in advance so it can be hard to get a room in the summer. *Rooms from: $150 614 McLeod St., Big Timber 406/932–3033 4 rooms Free breakfast.*

Nightlife

Holly's Road Kill Saloon

BARS/PUBS | The name may evoke unsavory images, but that doesn't stop bikers, fly-fishing anglers, ranchers, and curious tourists from filling Holly's Road Kill Saloon. Beer, burgers, and Road Kill T-shirts are big sellers. Disclaimer: it's one of those rare establishments resisting the mask policy, so enter at your own risk as long as COVID-19 is still raging. *1557 Boulder Rd., McLeod U.S. 298, 15 miles south of Big Timber 406/932–6174.*

Shopping

Crazy Woman Trading Montana

JEWELRY/ACCESSORIES | This one-stop shop for women's clothing, jewelry, and kitchen supplies sells a lot of self-branded merchandise. (Here in the shadow of the Crazy Mountains, being crazy is a good thing.) *214 McLeod St., Big Timber 406/932–6073* *www.crazywomantradingmontana.com* *Closed Mon. and Tues.*

Dave Hodges Fine Art

ART GALLERIES | At Dave Hodges Fine Art, you'll find bronze sculptures of horses, wildlife, and cowboys by this internationally known artist. Western-theme paintings and Navajo weavings also are displayed. *122 McLeod St., Big Timber* *406/932–6834* *www.hodgesfineart.com.*

Activities

CAMPING

Halfmoon Campground. At the end of a dusty road leading into the lovely Crazy Mountains, this respite with tent and trailer sites (up to 32 feet) is ideal for scenic picnicking, hiking, and fishing. Be aware that the altitude is 6,400 feet. *11 miles north of Big Timber on U.S. 191, then 12 miles west on Big Timber Canyon Rd.* *406/932–5155* *www.fs.fed.us* *12 sites.*

West Boulder Campground and Cabin. Shady and cool, this remote setting is known for good fishing, access to the Absaroka-Beartooth Wilderness, and quiet camping. The three-room cabin has five single beds, electricity, a woodstove, and potable water in summer. Reservations, available through National Reservation Service, are essential for the cabin and are not accepted for the campsites. *11 miles north of Big Timber on U.S. 191, then 12 miles west on Big Timber Canyon Rd.* *877/444–6777* *www.recreation.gov* *10 tent sites, 1 cabin.*

FISHING

Big Timber Fly Fishing

FISHING | A love of fly-fishing brought Big Timber Fly Fishing co-owners, Rachel and Doug, together many years ago. In addition to lessons and guided fishing trips, they offer scenic floats, too. *Big Timber* *406/930–1038* *www.bigtimberflyfishing.com.*

The Running of the Sheep

Great Montana Sheep Drive. The annual one-day **Great Montana Sheep Drive**, held the Sunday of Labor Day weekend, celebrates the sturdy Montana-bred sheep and the state's agriculture history with humor. In addition to the sheep run (the sheep are let loose down the main street, sort of like the bulls in Pamplona, Spain, only a lot tamer), you can see a parade of antique cars and enjoy live music and games all day. *Reed Point* *I–90, Exit 392, 25 miles west of Big Timber* *406/322–4505* *stillwatercountychamber.com.*

Sweetcast Angler

FISHING | Big Timber's sole fly shop also offers trips with guides, all of whom come from the Big Timber area. They help anglers explore the Yellowstone, Boulder, and Stillwater rivers. *119 W. 1st Ave., Big Timber* *406/932–4469* *www.sweetcastangler.com.*

HORSEBACK RIDING

Montana Bunkhouses Working Ranch Vacations LLC

HORSEBACK RIDING | Montana Bunkhouses Working Ranch Vacations LLC is an organization of more than 20 ranches working cooperatively on the European agro-tourism model to give visitors a nongussied-up ranching experience. At least three are in the Big Timber area. Join the rancher in his daily tasks, take part in cattle drives, go for a trail ride, head for the nearest trout stream, or just relax. Accommodations range from ranch houses to remote cabins to bunkhouses. *Big Timber* *406/222–6101* *www.montanaworkingranches.com.*

Livingston

35 miles west of Big Timber via I–90; 116 miles west of Billings via I–90.

The stunning mountain backdrop to the town of Livingston was once Crow territory, and a chief called Arapooish said about it, "The Crow country is good country. The Great Spirit has put it in exactly the right place. When you are in it, you fare well; when you go out of it, you fare worse."

Livingston, along the banks of the beautiful Yellowstone River, was built to serve the railroad and the settlers it brought. The railroad still runs through this town of around 7,800, but now tourism and outdoor sports dominate the scene. Many writers and artists call Livingston home, and there are some 15 art galleries here. Robert Redford chose the town, with its turn-of-the-20th-century flavor, to film parts of the movie *A River Runs Through It.*

GETTING HERE AND AROUND

Livingston is reachable by I–90 from the east and west, and U.S. 89 from the north and south. The historic section, with its restaurants and attractions, is compact and walkable. There is one taxi company, but not one parking meter. The nearest airport is in Bozeman.

MAJOR EVENTS

Since the 1920s cowboys and cowgirls have ridden and roped at the annual **Livingston Roundup Rodeo** (🌐 *www.livingstonroundup.com*), held at the Park County Fairgrounds for three days in early July (usually the days leading up to July 4). Participants descend on Livingston from around the United States and Canada to draw more than 10,000 spectators.

Since the 1950s the **Wilsall Rodeo** has been showcasing cowboy and cowgirl events in mid-June. This ranching community is at the base of the Crazy Mountains, 35 miles east of Livingston.

Sights

Livingston Depot Center
MUSEUM | The 1902 Livingston Depot Center is situated in the former Northern Pacific depot, which served as the gateway to Yellowstone for the park's first 25 years. In the summer months it's now a museum with displays centered on Western and railroad history. ✉ *200 W. Park St., Livingston* ☎ *406/222–2300* 🌐 *www.livingstondepot.org* 🎟 *$5.*

Paradise Valley Loop
SCENIC DRIVE | A drive on this loop takes you along the spectacular Yellowstone River for a short way and then past historic churches, schoolhouses, hot springs, and expansive ranches, all below the peaks of the Absaroka-Beartooth Wilderness. ✉ *U.S. 89, Livingston* ✣ *From Livingston, head 3 miles south on U.S. 89, turn east onto E. River Rd., and follow it 32 miles, over Yellowstone River, and through tiny towns of Pine Creek, Pray, Chico, and Emigrant and back to U.S. 89.*

Yellowstone Gateway Museum
MUSEUM | The Yellowstone Gateway Museum, on the north side of town in a turn-of-the-20th-century schoolhouse, holds an eclectic collection, including finds from a 10,000-year-old Native American dig site, a flag fragment associated with the Battle of the Little Bighorn, and a Native cultures interpretive exhibit. Outdoor displays include an old caboose, a sheep wagon, a stagecoach, and other pioneer memorabilia. ✉ *118 W. Chinook St., Livingston* ☎ *406/222–4184* 🌐 *www.yellowstonegatewaymuseum.org* 🎟 *$5* ⏲ *Closed Sun.–Tues.*

Yellowstone River
BODY OF WATER | Just south of Livingston and north of Yellowstone National Park, the Yellowstone River comes roaring down the Yellowstone Plateau and flows through Paradise Valley. A dozen fishing access sites are found in this area, some with primitive public campsites

The section of Yellowstone River running through Paradise Valley near Livingston, which is just north of Yellowstone National Park, is a popular destination for fishing, rafting, and canoeing.

(available on a first-come, first-served basis). In addition to trout fishing, rafting and canoeing are popular here. With snowcapped peaks, soaring eagles, and an abundance of wildlife, a float on this section of the Yellowstone is a lifetime experience. U.S. 89 follows the west bank of the river, and East River Road runs along the east side. ✉ *U.S. 89, Livingston.*

Restaurants

Faye's Cafe

$$ | **AMERICAN** | The collaborative chef's choice concept at this cute artsy café is unique to say the least. Instead of a traditional menu, diners pick adjectives and nouns that speak to them off a chalkboard with dozens of words. **Known for:** the chef is happy to accommodate for food allergies; fragrant hot tea sweetened with local honey; irresistible huckleberry bacon. [$] *Average main: $16* ✉ *Shane Lalani Center for the Arts, 415 E. Lewis, Room 104, Livingston* ☎ *406/223–7481* ⊕ *sarahfayemontana.com* ⊙ *No lunch or dinner.*

Gil's Goods

$$ | **PIZZA** | Although it's most famous for its wood-fired pizza (made with 36-hour naturally fermented dough), Gil's Goods also serves salads, burgers, and sandwiches, including a Nashville hot chicken special. It also boasts a full bar and pretty extensive beer and wine list for a casual establishment. **Known for:** homemade breads, available for sale by the loaf; can be loud and a bit hectic during rush hour; sidewalk seating for prime people-watching in the summer. [$] *Average main: $14* ✉ *207 W. Park St., Livingston* ☎ *406/222–9463* ⊕ *gilsgoods.com* ⊙ *Closed Tues.*

The Grill at Sage Lodge

$$$$ | **STEAKHOUSE** | Don't be fooled by its name: The Grill at Sage Lodge is a high-end contemporary steak house where you come for the food but stay for the view (or vice versa). Steaks are all grass-fed and range from a 16-ounce oxtail to a 32-ounce Porterhouse that will

set you back a pretty penny. **Known for:** being quite pricey; a special five-course chef's choice menu; hit-and-miss food and service depending on how busy they are. *Average main: $75 55 Sage Lodge Dr., Pray 855/400–0505 www.sagelodge.com/grill Closed Mon. and Tues. No lunch.*

Montana's Rib & Chop House

$$$ | **STEAKHOUSE** | Here, in the middle of cattle country, you can expect the juiciest, tenderest steaks—such as the hand-cut rib eye—all made from certified Angus beef. Jambalaya, salmon, and baby back ribs marinated for 24 hours are also on the menu. It's a small chain, but a local one in Montana, Wyoming, Utah, and Colorado. **Known for:** servers who write their names upside down on the paper tablecloths; kids meals served in classic car cutout boxes; surprisingly good margaritas for a steak house. *Average main: $22 305 E. Park St., Livingston 406/222–9200 www.ribandchophouse.com.*

★ **Mustang Fresh Food**

$$$ | **MODERN AMERICAN** | Creative, contemporary regional American fare is the specialty at this romantic little bistro set inside an arresting historic downtown storefront with high pressed-tin ceilings and teal banquette seats. The menu rotates according to what's fresh but might feature pan-seared halibut with a clementine gremolata, or roasted baby carrots with a sumac-cashew sauce. **Known for:** locally, seasonally sourced cuisine; excellent vegetarian options; lemon cheesecake with salted caramel. *Average main: $24 112 N. Main St., Livingston 406/222–8884 www.mustangfreshfood.com Closed Sun.*

Yellowstone Valley Grill

$$$$ | **AMERICAN** | There are no Michelin star-rated restaurants in Montana, but this place comes close. With creative specialties like northern Thai bison larb, adobo-cured Kurobuta pork chop, and for dessert Oaxacan chocolate truffle, your taste buds won't be disappointed. **Known for:** beautiful river views; being one of the best places in Montana for sashimi; inventive food. *Average main: $40 Yellowstone Valley Lodge, 3840 Hwy. 89 S, Livingston 406/333–4787 www.yellowstonevalleylodge.com/dining Closed Mon. No lunch.*

Hotels

B Bar Ranch

$$$$ | **RESORT** | In winter, when 2- to 6 feet of snow blanket this 9,000-acre working cattle ranch, guests enjoy spectacular adventures in cross-country skiing and wildlife tracking. **Pros:** a rare chance to enjoy winter ranch activities near Yellowstone; owners' strong commitment to ecology is evident; it's a great place to see grizzlies (bring binoculars). **Cons:** ranch access involves travel on gravel roads; limited cell phone service and Wi-Fi is slow; no cross-country ski rentals; guests must bring their own. *Rooms from: $335 818 Tom Miner Creek Rd., Emigrant 406/848–7729 www.bbar.com 13 units All-inclusive.*

Chico Hot Springs Resort & Day Spa

$$ | **RESORT** | **FAMILY** | This rambling, quirky spa hotel opened in 1900, offering guests leisurely soaks in its 96°F–103°F hot-spring pools and accommodations with views of 10,920-foot Emigrant Peak and the Absaroka-Beartooth Wilderness beyond. **Pros:** restaurant is a destination in itself; so pet-friendly the gift shop sells homemade dog biscuits; beautiful, quiet setting amid nature. **Cons:** remote; the least expensive rooms share a bath; sometimes books up with weddings. *Rooms from: $115 163 Chico Rd., Pray 406/333–4933 www.chicohotsprings.com 110 rooms No meals.*

Mountain Sky Guest Ranch

$$$$ | **RESORT** | This full-service guest-ranch resort in the middle of scenic Paradise Valley and 30 miles north of Yellowstone National Park is a family favorite. **Pros:** variety, preparation, and abundance of food win raves; plenty of cabins; nannies are welcome at a lower, flat rate. **Cons:** big (100% occupancy means 90 guests); long minimum stay requirement (7 nights); expensive rates. *Rooms from: $4490 480 Big Creek Rd., Emigrant U.S. 89 S, then west 4½ miles on Big Creek Rd. 406/333–4911 www.mountainsky.com Closed Nov.–Apr. 33 cabins All meals.*

★ The Murray Hotel

$$$ | **HOTEL** | Even cowboys love soft pillows, which is one reason so many of them favor this 1904 town centerpiece, whose floors have seen silver-tipped cowboy boots, fly-fishing waders, and the polished heels of Hollywood celebrities. **Pros:** easy stroll to shops and galleries; metal beds, claw-foot tubs, and pedestal sinks maintain period ambience; great bar and restaurant. **Cons:** elevator requires an operator; some areas show their age; thin walls. *Rooms from: $139 201 W. Park St., Livingston 406/222–1350 www.murrayhotel.com 30 rooms No meals.*

Sage Lodge

$$$$ | **HOTEL** | Paradise Valley's most luxurious property opened in 2018, and it's hard to top your first impression: the two-story open floor plan A-frame lobby with views of Emigrant Peak. **Pros:** gorgeous view, worthy of a national park; in-room fireplaces; abundance of included activities. **Cons:** located in a very windy valley; the service in the restaurant can be hit or miss depending on how busy they are; high pet fee ($75). *Rooms from: $225 55 Sage Lodge Dr., Pray 855/400–0505 www.sagelodge.com 34 rooms, 4 houses No meals.*

Yellowstone Valley Lodge

$$$$ | **HOTEL** | Offering more of a well-appointed practical base than an exclusive luxury lodge experience, these comfortable cabins are about 16 miles south of Livingston and about 40 minutes north of Yellowstone National Park. **Pros:** unbeatable location and scenic backdrop; has a fantastic restaurant and filling breakfast; dog-friendly. **Cons:** mosquitoes can be bad in the summer; cottages look a bit dated from the outside; patios are semi-private. *Rooms from: $265 3840 Hwy. 89 S, Livingston 406/333–4787 www.yellowstonevalleylodge.com 15 cabins Free breakfast.*

 Nightlife

Murray Bar

BARS/PUBS | Locals voted the jukebox at the Murray Bar the best in town, and its staff the friendliest. There's live music most weekends. *The Murray Hotel, 201 W. Park St., Livingston 406/222–9463 www.themurraybar.com.*

The Owl Lounge

BARS/PUBS | Drop by this giant brick building on the corner for happy hour from 4 to 6 every day except Sunday. The Owl Lounge serves beer, wine, and specialty martinis, including the Snowy Owl: pinnacle whipped strawberry vodka, cranberry juice, and cream. It closes at midnight. *110 N. 2nd St., Livingston 406/333–2601 www.theowllounge.com.*

Pine Creek Cafe

MUSIC CLUBS | Friday and Saturday evening June through September, the Pine Creek Cafe serves live music, food, beer, and wine under the stars. The fun starts at 7:30. During winter, the music moves inside. Friday is open-mike night starting at 7:30. *2496 E. River Rd., Livingston About 12 miles from town 406/222–3628 www.pinecreeklodgemontana.com Closed Mon. and Tues. No lunch.*

Performing Arts

THEATER

Blue Slipper Theatre

THEATER | The historic district's Blue Slipper Theatre presents various full-length productions, including one-act plays, popular melodramas, and an annual Christmas variety show. ✉ *113 E. Callender St., Livingston* ☎ *406/222–7720* 🌐 *www.blueslipper.com.*

Shopping

Livingston's beauty has inspired a number of artists, as evidenced by the many fine-art galleries in town.

Dan Bailey's Outdoor Company

SPORTING GOODS | In addition to selling outdoor clothing, boots, and bicycles, Dan Bailey's rents cross-country skis, backcountry skis, and mountain bikes. The friendly staff is happy to help mountain bikers, hikers, and skiers with trail maps, directions, and repairs. ✉ *209 W. Park St., Livingston* ☎ *406/222–1673* 🌐 *www.danbaileys.com.*

High Trash Boutique

CLOTHING | Don't judge a boutique by its name. This is a trove of treasures, including vintage clothing, boots, and all things chic, including menswear. ✉ *113 S. Main St., Livingston* ☎ *406/544–1766.*

Montana Brewery Shop

LOCAL SPECIALTIES | Selling souvenirs, including apparel, from more than 20 breweries across the state, this is a must-stop for the beer enthusiast. ✉ *108 W. Callender St., Livingston* ☎ *406/333–2530* 🌐 *www.mtbreweryshop.com* ⏲ *Closed Sun.–Tues.*

Sax and Fryer

BOOKS/STATIONERY | The floorboards creak as you walk through Sax and Fryer, an old-time bookstore specializing in Western literature, especially books by Montana authors. It's the oldest store in Livingston. ✉ *109 W. Callender St., Livingston* ☎ *406/222–1421* ⏲ *Closed Sun.*

Visions West Contemporary

ART GALLERIES | This is the place to look for contemporary Western and wildlife art, including numerous works on the fly-fishing theme, from paintings and bronzes to hand-carved flies. ✉ *108 S. Main St., Livingston* ☎ *406/222–0337* 🌐 *www.visionswestcontemporary.com* ⏲ *Closed Sun.*

Activities

The Yellowstone River and its tributary streams draw fly-fishers from around the globe for Yellowstone cutthroat, brown, and rainbow trout. Hiking trails lead into remote accesses of surrounding peaks, often snowcapped through June.

BOATING

Rowdy River Guides

BOATING | River enthusiast Rowdy Nelson runs this outfitting business, which specializes in 2½-hour relaxing floats on the Yellowstone River. He also offers full-day and sunset floats. Every trip is private, and trips run from May through September. ✉ *5237 U.S. Hwy. 89, #7, Livingston* ☎ *406/223–3380* 🌐 *www.rowdyriverguides.com.*

Rubber Ducky River Rentals

BOATING | Boaters eager to explore the Yellowstone River will find a one-stop shop at Rubber Ducky River Rentals. The store rents everything you need for a day on the river including guiding and pickup and drop-off services. Call for a reservation. ✉ *15 Mt. Baldy Dr., Livingston* ☎ *406/222–3746* 🌐 *www.rubberduckyrentals.com.*

CAMPING

Paradise Valley/Livingston KOA. Set among willows, cottonwoods, and small evergreens, this full-service campground is well situated along the banks of the Yellowstone River, 40 miles north of Yellowstone National Park. Pull-throughs

Welcome to Fly-Fishing Heaven

Montana has the best rainbow, brown, and brook trout fishing in the country. This is the land of *A River Runs Through It*, the acclaimed Norman Maclean novel that most people know as a movie. Although the book is set in Missoula, the movie was filmed in the trout-fishing mecca of southwest Montana, and the Gallatin River played the role of Maclean's beloved Big Blackfoot. Several rivers run through the region, notably the Madison, Gallatin, and Yellowstone (more or less parallel to one another, flowing north of Yellowstone National Park), as well as the Big Hole River to the west. All are easily accessible from major roads, which means that in summer you might have to drive a ways to find a fishing hole to call your own.

If you're only a casual angler, all you'll really need is a basic rod and reel, some simple tackle (hooks, sinkers, floaters, and extra line) and a few worms, which can all be bought at most outfitting and sporting-goods stores for less than $60. Many non-fly-fishers use open-face reels with lightweight line and spinners, which makes for a nice fight when they connect with trout. If you would like to try your hand at the more elegant stylings of fly-fishing, hire a local guide. Not only will he show you the good fishing holes, but a knowledgeable outfitter can teach you how not to work waters into a froth. Many guide services will provide you with fly-fishing equipment for the day.

accommodate RVs up to 90 feet. It's popular with families, who enjoy the heated pool in the summer; reserve ahead. ✉ *10 miles south of Livingston on U.S. 89, then ½ mile east on Pine Creek Rd.* ☎ *406/222–0992, 800/562–2805.*

Pine Creek Campground. A thick growth of pine trees surrounds this Paradise Valley campground at the base of the mountains. It's near the trailhead for hikes to Pine Creek Waterfalls and into the Absaroka-Beartooth Wilderness. ✉ *10 miles south of Livingston on U.S. 89, then 6 miles east on Pine Creek Rd.* ☎ *406/222–1892, 877/444–6777.*

FISHING

★ Dan Bailey's Fly Shop

FISHING | The fishing experts at this world-renowned shop can help you find the right fly, tackle, and outdoor clothing. For the best fishing, ask about their guided trips in the summer. ✉ *209 W. Park St., Livingston* ☎ *406/222–1673* 🌐 *www.danbaileys.com.*

George Anderson's Yellowstone Angler

FISHING | This tackle shop and guide service specializes in catch-and-release fly-fishing float trips on the Yellowstone River, wade trips on spring creeks, access to private lakes, and fly-casting instruction. ✉ *5256 U.S. 89 S, Livingston* ☎ *406/222–7130* 🌐 *www.yellowstoneangler.com.*

HORSEBACK RIDING

Bear Paw Outfitters

HORSEBACK RIDING | This family-owned outfit run by 4th-, 5th-, and 6th-generation Montanans specializes in half- and full-day rides and pack trips in Paradise Valley, the Absaroka-Beartooth Wilderness, and Yellowstone National Park. You can also ride for just an hour. ✉ *136 Deep Creek Rd., Livingston* ☎ *406/222–6642* 🌐 *www.bearpawoutfittersmt.com.*

Rockin' HK Outfitters

HORSEBACK RIDING | This company will customize your multiday pack trip into the backcountry of Yellowstone National Park. The focus can be on fly-fishing or photography, as well as the riding experience itself. ✉ *Chico Hot Springs, 163 Chico Rd., Pray* ✣ *17 miles south of Livingston* ☎ *406/333–4933* 🌐 *www.rockinhk.com.*

Three Forks

51 miles west of Livingston via I–90; 29 miles west of Bozeman via I–90.

Although the scenery in Three Forks is striking, it's the historic sites that make this place worth a visit. Sacajawea (circa 1786–1812) traveled in the area with her Shoshone family before she was kidnapped as a child by a rival tribe, the Hidatsas. Five years later she returned as part of the Lewis and Clark expedition. In 1805 they arrived at the forks (of the Madison, Jefferson, and Gallatin rivers), now in Missouri Headwaters State Park, looking for the river that would lead them to the Continental Divide. A plaque in the city park commemorates her contribution to the expedition's success.

GETTING HERE AND AROUND

The town of Three Forks is easily walkable, but you'll want a car to reach the Headwaters and Buffalo Jump areas. There's ample free parking downtown. The nearest airport is Bozeman Yellowstone International Airport.

Sights

Headwaters Heritage Museum

MUSEUM | Thousands of local historical artifacts are on display in the Headwaters Heritage Museum, including a small anvil and all that is left of a trading post, Fort Three Forks, established in 1810.

Thousands of local historical artifacts are on display in the Headwaters Heritage Museum, including a small anvil and all that is left of a trading post, Fort Three Forks, established in 1810. ✉ *202 S. Main* ☎ *406/285–4778* 🌐 *www.tfhistory.org* ⏲ *Closed Oct.–May.*

Lewis and Clark Caverns

CAVE | **FAMILY** | The Lewis and Clark Caverns, Montana's oldest state park, hold some of the most beautiful underground landscapes in the nation. Two-hour tours lead through narrow passages and vaulted chambers past colorful, intriguingly varied limestone formations. The temperature stays in the 50s year-round; jackets and rubber-sole shoes are recommended. Note that the hike to the cavern entrance is mild. A campground sits at the lower end of the park. ✉ *25 Lewis & Clark Caverns Rd.* ✣ *Hwy. 2, 19 miles west of Three Forks* ☎ *406/287–3541* 🌐 *stateparks.mt.gov* 🎟 *$8 per out-of-state vehicle.*

Madison Buffalo Jump

NATIVE SITE | Within the Madison Buffalo Jump historic site is a cliff where Plains Indians stampeded bison to their deaths for more than 2,000 years, until European guns and horses arrived in the West. An interpretive center explains how the technique enabled Native Americans to gather food and hides. Picnic areas provide a restful break from touring. Be on the lookout for rattlesnakes here, and avoid wandering off the paths. ✉ *6990 Buffalo Jump Rd.* ✣ *5 miles east of Three Forks on I–90, exiting at Logan, then 7 miles south on Buffalo Jump Rd.* ☎ *406/285–3610* 🌐 *stateparks.mt.gov* 🎟 *$8 per out-of-state vehicle, includes admission to Missouri Headwaters State Park.*

Missouri Headwaters State Park

NATIONAL/STATE PARK | The Madison, Jefferson, and Gallatin rivers come together to form the mighty Missouri River within Missouri Headwaters State Park, a National Historic Landmark. At 2,340 miles, the Missouri is the country's longest river. Lewis and Clark named the three forks after Secretary of the Treasury

Albert Gallatin, Secretary of State James Madison, and President Thomas Jefferson. The park has historical exhibits, interpretive signs, picnic sites, hiking trails, and camping. ✉ *1585 Trident Rd.* ✣ *3 miles northeast of Three Forks on I–90, exit at Three Forks off-ramp, then go east on 205 and 3 miles north on 286* ☎ *406/285–3610* 🌐 *stateparks.mt.gov.*

Restaurants

Wheat Montana
$ | **CAFÉ** | At Wheat Montana's Three Forks headquarters and flagship restaurant/store, you can enjoy tasty sandwiches, freshly baked bread, and pastries. You can even purchase grind-your-own flour from their Prairie Gold Whole Wheat. **Known for:** cinnamon rolls the size of your head; a long, fast-moving line during lunch; Italian sodas. $ *Average main: $10* ✉ *10778 Hwy. 287* ✣ *I–90 at Exit 274* ☎ *406/285–3614* 🌐 *www.wheatmontana.com.*

Hotels

Grey Cliffs Ranch
$$$$ | **ALL-INCLUSIVE** | **FAMILY** | Located on a 5,000-acre working ranch with world-class fly-fishing access, this striking luxury lodge just 30 minutes from downtown Bozeman is often used as a vacation home for its owners. **Pros:** unrivaled views of the surrounding mountain ranges; feels like you're staying in a well-equipped luxury home; serves superb, locally sourced dishes. **Cons:** the location is remote so cell phone service is iffy; off a gravel road and requires an AWD vehicle in the winter; personal alcohol is not allowed. $ *Rooms from: $385* ✉ *1915 Lakota Dr.* ☎ *406/285–6512* 🌐 *www.greycliffsranch.com* *7 suites* *All-inclusive.*

Activities

BOATING

Canoeing House and Guide Service
BOATING | In addition to arranging guided fly-fishing float trips, **Canoeing House and Guide Service** rents canoes and kayaks. ✉ *11227 U.S. 287* ☎ *406/285–3488.*

CAMPING

Missouri Headwaters State Park. Tent and trailer sites are strewn among the cottonwood trees of the campground at this park. Three pavilions detail the Lewis and Clark adventure through the area, and 4 miles of trails lead visitors through meadows and to vista points along the rivers. Reservations are taken only for groups. ✉ *4 miles northeast of Three Forks on Hwy. 205, then north on Hwy. 286* ☎ *406/994–4042* 🌐 *www.fwp.mt.gov* *17 sites.*

Big Sky

75 miles southeast of Three Forks via I–90 and then U.S. 191; 43 miles southwest of Bozeman via I–90, then U.S. 191.

The region known as "Big Sky" is actually three areas: the Mountain Village at the top of the 9-mile-long Lone Mountain Trail (Highway 64); the Meadow Village, 3 miles west of Highway 191 on Lone Mountain Trail; and the area around the intersection of Highway 191 and Lone Mountain Trail.

GETTING HERE AND AROUND

Bozeman has the nearest airport. Uber exists here, but it's hard to find drivers, so it's best to have your own vehicle. **Skyline Bus** (🌐 *www.skylinebus.com*) offers year-round rides between these areas, the three distinct sections of Big Sky, as well as routes to Bozeman and back.

AIRPORT TRANSFERS Karst Stage. ✉ *511 N. Wallace Ave., Bozeman* ☎ *406/556–3500* 🌐 *www.karststage.com.*

Sights

Big Sky Resort

RESORT—SIGHT | The name of Lone Peak, the mountain that looms over the isolated community beneath Big Sky, is a good way to describe one of the most remote ski resorts in the country. Here you can ski a true wilderness. With nearly 6,000 skiable acres, it's the second-largest ski resort in the U.S. Yellowstone National Park is visible from the upper mountain ski runs, as are 11 mountain ranges in three states. The park's western entrance at West Yellowstone is about 50 miles away, along a route frequented by elk, moose, and bison (use caution when driving U.S. 191).

Conceived in the 1970s by national TV newscaster Chet Huntley, the resort area is the solitary node of civilization in otherwise undeveloped country, between Bozeman and West Yellowstone. Getting here invariably means a flight to Bozeman and about an hour's drive to the resort through Gallatin Canyon, a narrow gorge of rock walls, forest, and the frothing Gallatin River.

This is not to suggest that Big Sky is primitive. Indeed, being just a few decades old and growing rapidly, the resort is quite modern in its design and amenities. You won't find crowds among all this rugged nature, but you will discover that all the perks of a major summer and ski vacation spot are readily available in Big Sky's three distinct villages. One is in the Gallatin Canyon area along the Gallatin River and U.S. 191. Another, Meadow Village, radiates from the 18-hole Big Sky Golf Course. The third enclave, 9 miles west of U.S. 191, is the full-service ski resort itself, overlooking rugged wilderness areas and Yellowstone National Park.

Major real-estate developments around Big Sky have started to impinge upon the resort-in-the-wild atmosphere with exclusive developments such as Spanish Peaks and the gated Yellowstone Club. Still, outdoor pleasures abound. In addition to skiing, golfing, hiking, horseback riding, ziplining, and other activities, Big Sky hosts many festivals, musical events, races, and tournaments. ✉ *50 Big Sky Resort Rd., Big Sky* ☎ *800/548–4486* 🌐 *www.bigskyresort.com.*

Historic Crail Ranch

FARM/RANCH | In 1902 Frank Crail picked this spot for the headquarters of his 960-acre homestead and cattle ranch. Now the Historic Crail Ranch makes a pleasant picnic spot in the midst of Big Sky's Meadow Village area. Guided tours take place on weekends June through September. To get here, drive west on Big Sky Spur Road, make a right on Little Coyote, go past the chapel, and make a left onto Spotted Elk Road in Meadow Village. ✉ *2100 Spotted Elk Rd., Big Sky* ☎ *406/993–2112* 🎫 *Free.*

Restaurants

Buck's T-4 Lodge and Restaurant

$$$$ | **STEAKHOUSE** | Within a historic log lodge and bar, this restaurant is known for its dinners of seafood, wild game, and hand-cut Montana steaks. **Known for:** extensive wine list recognized by Wine Spectator; two-fisted sandwiches; Moscow mules served in souvenir mugs. 💲 *Average main: $35* ✉ *46625 Gallatin Rd., Big Sky* ☎ *406/995–4111* 🌐 *www.buckst4.com.*

By Word of Mouth

$$$ | **AMERICAN** | At night this restaurant fills with the boisterous merrymaking of the après-ski crowd—particularly Friday night, when a throng gathers for an all-you-can-eat fish fry. The menu includes Asian soba noodles, grilled rainbow trout, and lamb burger blended with mint chimicurri. **Known for:** the adult happy meal: burger, draft beer and pineapple vodka shot; a Montana-theme old-fashioned cocktail featuring chokecherry liquor; poutine featuring hand-cut garlic fries. *$ Average main: $24 ✉ 77 Aspen Leaf Dr., Big Sky ☎ 406/995–2992 🌐 www.bywombywordofmouth.com ⏲ Closed weekends.*

Horn & Cantle

$$$$ | **AMERICAN** | Fine dining in Big Sky doesn't get any finer than here, where shareable feasts include the splurge-worthy tomahawk bone-in rib eye and braised bison short ribs. Mains include everything from veal schnitzel to vegan enchiladas. **Known for:** truffle fries served with harissa ketchup; chocolate chip cookie skillets; fried chicken so good you'd swear you're in the South. *$ Average main: $35 ✉ 750 Lone Mountain Ranch Rd., Big Sky ☎ 406/995–4644 🌐 www.hornandcantle.com ⏲ Closed Wed.*

Montana Dinner Yurt

$$$$ | **EUROPEAN** | For a unique dining experience, rendezvous upstairs in the Snowcrest building in Mountain Village to ride a snowcat into the pristine land of Big Sky for a meal under the stars. While the chef prepares French onion soup, filet mignon, garlic mashed potatoes, and chocolate fondue with fresh fruit and pound cake, you can sled on hills under the light of the moon or relax around a bonfire. **Known for:** a cold snowcat ride, so dress warm; using Toblerone instead of cheap chocolate; a fillet that cuts with a spoon. *$ Average main: $175 ✉ Big Sky ☎ 406/995–3880 🌐 www.bigskyyurt.com.*

Coffee and Quick Bites

Blue Moon Bakery

$$ | **AMERICAN** | Blue Moon Bakery sets out a tempting array of scones, muffins, cakes, and cookies. They also serve sizeable sandwiches and gourmet pizza. **Known for:** pizza crust with notes of garlic butter and Parmesan; a welcoming staff with excellent service; homemade cream cheese. *$ Average main: $11 ✉ 120 Big Pine Dr., Big Sky ☎ 406/995–2305 🌐 www.bigskybluemoonbakery.com.*

Hungry Moose

$$ | **AMERICAN** | Hungry Moose serves deli sandwiches as well as basic grocery items. **Known for:** a long, but fast-moving line; hand-dipped ice cream from a Montana creamery; being the best place to get hiking snacks. *$ Average main: $10 ✉ Town Center, 209 Aspen Leaf Dr., Big Sky ☎ 406/995–3045 🌐 www.hungry-moose.com.*

Wrap Shack

$$ | **AMERICAN** | Westfork Meadows has several tasty eat-in or take-out spots. At Wrap Shack wraps start out the size of a pizza, and stuffed, aren't a whole lot smaller. **Known for:** tasty margaritas and mojitos; "rolling 'em fat"; awesome tacos. *$ Average main: $10 ✉ 2815 Aspen Leaf Dr., Big Sky ☎ 406/995–3099.*

Hotels

Buck's T-4 Lodge

$$$ | **HOTEL** | Named for the original owner, the hotel dates back to 1946, when it was used as a hunting camp, so there's a considerable nostalgia factor at work here. **Pros:** has a great restaurant on-site; rooms are spread out over several buildings so you have more privacy; location is convenient for visiting Big Sky and Yellowstone. **Cons:** furnishings and decor are dated; getting hot water in the shower can take time; at least 20 minutes from the après ski scene. *$ Rooms from: $169 ✉ 46625 Gallatin Rd., Big Sky ☎ 406/995–4111 🌐 www.buckst4.com ⇨ 72 rooms 🍽 Free breakfast.*

The Lodge at Big Sky

$$$ | **HOTEL** | The Great Room at this pet-friendly Mountain Village property has the requisite stone fireplace topped by a bronze cowboy sculpture, and a wall of windows overlooking 11,000-foot Lone Peak. **Pros:** four hot tubs and heated indoor pool; good rates for mountaintop property; slopeside ski access. **Cons:**

furnishings and decor on the boring side; some guest rooms have limited views; popular for events and conventions. *Rooms from: $169 Mountain Village, 75 Sitting Bull Rd., Big Sky 406/995–7858, 888/995–7858 www.lodgeatbigsky.com 130 rooms Free breakfast.*

Lone Mountain Ranch

$$$$ | **HOTEL** | Three-night to one-week packages include seasonal activities such as naturalist-guided trips to Yellowstone, cross-country ski passes, and kids' camps in the summer. **Pros:** guests praise the cozy lodgings; wide variety of adventure and nature-oriented activities; on-site restaurant is a destination in itself. **Cons:** not a working ranch; older cabins are pretty rustic for the price; service can be slow. *Rooms from: $950 750 Lone Mountain Ranch Rd., Big Sky 406/995–4644 www.lonemountainranch.com Closed Oct., Nov., Apr., and May 25 cabins All-inclusive.*

Montage Big Sky

$$$$ | **RESORT** | The first five-star hotel in the region, Montage Big Sky just opened its doors in 2021. **Pros:** unparalleled luxury for the area; access to an 18-hole Tom Weiskopf–designed golf course; mountain views in every direction. **Cons:** prices are high; lacks local character; not within walking distance of Mountain Village. *Rooms from: $795 995 Settlement Dr., Big Sky 866/551–8244 www.montagehotels.com 150 rooms No meals.*

★ Rainbow Ranch Lodge

$$$ | **HOTEL** | The Rainbow Ranch Lodge's original 1919 main building has been painstakingly restored to its original glory after a 2008 fire, while guests stay in two separate room sections, and special events are held in the barn. **Pros:** guest room decks overlook the river; great use of wood, even in baths; close to a popular 3.5-mile walking loop. **Cons:** situated along highway rather than in resort area; the restaurant can be unavailable if there's a wedding; some of the rooms are pretty outdated. *Rooms from: $200 42950 Gallatin Rd., Big Sky 406/995–4132 www.rainbowranchbigsky.com 21 rooms Free breakfast.*

Summit at Big Sky

$$$$ | **HOTEL** | Along with having an absolute prime location at the foot of Big Sky's chairlifts, the Summit Hotel now has bragging rights for having hosted the First Family during President Obama's August 2009 visit to Montana. **Pros:** all the facilities one could wish for; near slopes, shops, and restaurants; undergoing a multimillion dollar renovation so things are new. **Cons:** some miss the intimacy of smaller properties; attracts conventions; check-in isn't until 5 pm. *Rooms from: $295 60 Big Sky Resort Rd., Big Sky 800/548–4486 www.bigskyresort.com Closed mid-Apr., May, Oct., and Nov. 213 rooms Free breakfast.*

Nightlife

Corral

MUSIC CLUBS | Some weekends the Corral rocks to regional live bands. Other entertainment comes from quirky bartenders, pool-table bets, and legions of skiers, snowmobilers, and locals in for the Montana brews. *42895 Gallatin Rd., Big Sky 406/995–4249.*

Montana Jack

MUSIC CLUBS | Enjoy live music where the dancing often spills out onto the deck. *The Exchange at Big Sky, 52 Big Sky Resort Rd., Big Sky 406/995–5786 bigskyresort.com/dining/montana-jack.*

Westward Social

GATHERING PLACES | Opened in January 2020, this new late-night hot spot is perfect for after-hours après ski activities. It even hosts the Montana Stein Hoisting Championship. *The Exchange at Big Sky, 52 Big Sky Resort Rd., Big Sky 406/995–5723 bigskyresort.com/resort-dining/westward-social.*

Performing Arts

Music in the Mountains

CONCERTS | The Music in the Mountains summer concert series showcases such headliners as Taj Mahal, Willie Nelson, and the Bozeman Symphony Orchestra in outdoor venues. ✉ *Center Stage at Town Center Park, Big Sky* ☎ *406/995–2742* 🌐 *www.bigskyarts.org.*

Shopping

Big Sky Sports

SPORTING GOODS | Top-of-the-line ski and snowboard equipment and outerwear are sold at Big Sky Sports. ✉ *50 Big Sky Resort Rd., Big Sky* ☎ *406/995–5840* 🕒 *Closed when resort is closed for season.*

Gallatin River Gallery

ART GALLERIES | Gallatin River Gallery, the first contemporary gallery in Big Sky, sells one-of-a-kind jewelry, paintings, sculptures, and photography from international, national, and local artists. Call for an appointment. ✉ *114 Ousel Falls Rd., Big Sky* ☎ *406/995–2909.*

Horse of a Different Color

HOUSEHOLD ITEMS/FURNITURE | Sort of like a local Anthropologie, minus the apparel, the boutique sells candles, home goods, kitchen accessories, and the most beautiful little boxes. ✉ *50 Meadow Village Dr., Big Sky* ☎ *406/995–3113* 🌐 *www.horsebigsky.com.*

Activities

CAMPING

Greek Creek Campground. This Forest Service campground with RV and tent sites snuggles up to the Gallatin River under a canopy of tall evergreens. ✉ *U.S. 191, 30 miles south of Bozeman* ☎ *877/444–6777* 🌐 *www.recreation.gov* *14 sites.*

DOWNHILL SKIING AND SNOWBOARDING

For many years the attitude of more advanced skiers toward Big Sky was "big deal." There wasn't nearly enough challenging skiing to keep expert skiers interested for long, and certainly not for an entire ski week. As a remedy, the Big Sky people strung up the Challenger chairlift, one of the steepest in the country, and then installed a tram to the summit of Lone Peak, providing access to an array of steep chutes, open bowls, and at least one scary-steep couloir. The tram also gave Big Sky the right to claim the second-greatest vertical drop—4,350 feet—of any resort in the country.

None of that, however, has diminished Big Sky's otherwise easy-skiing reputation. There is still a good deal of intermediate and lower-intermediate terrain, a combination of wide-open bowl skiing higher up and trail skiing lower down. Additionally, there are 85 km (51 miles) of groomed cross-country skiing trails nearby at Lone Mountain Ranch.

The other plus about skiing Big Sky is its wide variety of exposures. Many of the ski areas here are built on north-facing slopes, where snow usually stays fresher longer, protected from the sun. In addition to these, Big Sky also has plenty of runs facing south and east, and the differing snow textures that result make for more interesting skiing.

Lift tickets cost $165 during peak season (January) and drop to $74 by mid-April. Multiday tickets (up to 10 days) offer savings of up to $9 per day. Kids 10 and under ski free. "The Biggest Skiing in America" lift ticket ($94) allows access to both Big Sky Resort and Moonlight Basin, which make up the largest connected skiable terrain in the United States (5,500 acres).

FACILITIES

Overview: 4,350-foot vertical drop; 5,850 skiable acres; 300 runs on 4 mountains; 15% beginner, 25% intermediate, 42% advanced, 18% expert; 1 aerial tram, 1 high-speed 8-seat, 2 high-speed 6-seats, 5 high-speed quads, 3 quads, 9 triples, 5 doubles, and 12 surface lifts.

LESSONS AND PROGRAMS

Big Sky Ski school

SKIING/SNOWBOARDING | **FAMILY** | Half-day adult group-lesson rates start at $126. Special clinics including racing camps and adaptive programs are also available. There's also a ski school just for kids—whether they're first-timers or speedsters—with enthusiastic instructors. There are two locations; Mountain Village and Madison Base. ✉ *Big Sky* ☎ *406/995–5743.*

RENTALS

Big Sky Sports Rentals

SKIING/SNOWBOARDING | The resort's **Big Sky SportsRentals** at the base of the mountain offers ski and snowboard rental packages for $56, and high-performance packages for $85. ✉ *Big Sky* ☎ *406/995–5841.*

Gallatin Alpine Sports

SKIING/SNOWBOARDING | At **Gallatin Alpine Sports** rentals start at $21 with discounts for multidays; performance skis start at $38 and demos, $57. ✉ *169 Snowy Mountain Circle, Big Sky* ☎ *406/995–2313.*

FISHING

Rivers such as the Gallatin, which runs along U.S. 191, the Madison (one valley west), and the Yellowstone (one valley east) have made southwest Montana famous among fly-fishers, most of whom visit during the nonwinter months.

East Slope Outdoors

FISHING | **East Slope Outdoors** arranges guides for winter and summer fly-fishing. You can also rent or buy flies, rods and reels, clothing, and gifts here. ✉ *44 Town Center Ave., Big Sky* ☎ *406/995–4369* 🌐 *www.eastslopeoutdoors.com.*

Gallatin River Guides

FISHING | Flies, rods and reels, clothing, equipment rentals, and guides are available at **Gallatin River Guides.** ✉ *47430 Gallatin Rd., Big Sky* ☎ *406/995–2290* 🌐 *www.montanaflyfishing.com.*

Wild Trout Outfitters

FISHING | **Wild Trout Outfitters** offers fly-fishing instruction, half-day and full-day fishing trips, float-tube fishing, and drift boat trips with stops for wade fishing at prime runs. ✉ *47530 Gallatin Rd., Gallatin Gateway* ☎ *406/995–2975* 🌐 *www.wildtroutoutfitters.com.*

HORSEBACK RIDING

Canyon Adventures

HORSEBACK RIDING | **Canyon Adventures** leads one- and two-hour trail rides May through September in the Gallatin Canyon. There's also a ride-and-raft combo. ✉ *47200 Gallatin Rd., Big Sky* ☎ *406/995–4450* 🌐 *www.canyonadventuresmontana.com.*

Jake's Horses

HORSEBACK RIDING | **FAMILY** | This outfitter will take you on one- to six-hour rides along mountainous trails on Forest Service lands year-round. Summer dinner rides and multiday pack trips inside Yellowstone National Park are also available. ✉ *200 Beaver Creek Rd., Gallatin Gateway* ☎ *406/995–4630* 🌐 *www.jakeshorses.com.*

KIDS' ACTIVITIES

Lone Mountain Ranch

CAMPING—SPORTS-OUTDOORS | **FAMILY** | The kids-only Outdoor Youth Adventures program at **Lone Mountain Ranch** is offered June through August. It's for ages 4 to 12. ✉ *750 Lone Mountain Ranch Rd., Big Sky* ✣ *4 miles west of U.S. 191 on Lone Mountain Trail, Hwy. 64 and ½ mile down gravel Lone Mountain Ranch Rd.* ☎ *406/995–4644* 🌐 *www.lonemountainranch.com.*

The Gallatin River runs mostly along U.S. 191 from the northwest corner of Yellowstone National Park to just outside Bozeman and is considered one of Montana's most scenic rivers.

NORDIC SKIING

Lone Mountain Ranch

SKIING/SNOWBOARDING | **Lone Mountain Ranch** is a rare bird in cross-country and snowshoeing circles. Not only are there 85 km (51 miles) of groomed trails, but the network is superb, with everything from a flat, open, golf-course layout to tree-lined trails with as much as 1,600 feet of elevation gain (and loss). Much of the trail network provides a genuine sense of woodsy mountain seclusion. If there is a drawback, it's that moose sometimes wander onto the trails. ✉ *750 Lone Mountain Ranch Rd., Big Sky* ☎ *406/995–4644* 🌐 *www.lonemountain-ranch.com.*

RAFTING

Geyser Whitewater Expeditions

WHITE-WATER RAFTING | **Geyser Whitewater Expeditions** has guided raft trips on the Gallatin River. ✉ *46651 Gallatin Rd., Big Sky* ☎ *406/995–4989* 🌐 *www.raftmon-tana.com.*

Montana Whitewater

WHITE-WATER RAFTING | **Montana White-water** arranges half- or full-day rafting trips on the Gallatin, Madison, and Yellowstone rivers. The company also offers paddle-and-saddle combos and ziplining. ✉ *63960 Gallatin Rd., Big Sky* ☎ *406/763–4465* 🌐 *www.montanawhite-water.com.*

SNOWMOBILING

Far and away the most popular nonskiing activity in the region is snowmobiling into and around Yellowstone National Park. West Yellowstone, about 50 miles south of Big Sky on U.S. 191, prides itself on being the Snowmobile Capital of the World. The most popular excursion is the 60-mile round-trip between West Yellow-stone and Old Faithful; the park allows in a few hundred commercially guided snowmobiles each day.

Canyon Adventures

SNOW SPORTS | **Canyon Adventures** arranges snowmobiling excursions December

Hitting the Slopes

It's called "cold smoke"—the exceedingly light, dry snow that falls on the mountains of southwest Montana—and it doesn't go to waste. All told, the region has six downhill ski areas and more than 390 km (245 miles) of cross-country trails. The season generally begins in late November or early December and runs through early to mid-April.

Downhill ski areas such as Bridger Bowl, Discovery, Moonlight Basin, Maverick, and Red Lodge Mountain are family-friendly, inexpensive, and relatively uncrowded. For steep skiers, one of the country's largest resorts, Big Sky, has more than 500 turns on a single slope; it's also a fine mountain for beginner and intermediate skiers.

The cross-country tracks of Lone Mountain Ranch stand out among the 40 or 50 trails in southwest Montana. They're groomed daily and are track-set for both classic and skate skiing. Backcountry skiing has no limits, with hundreds of thousands of skiable acres on public land.

through April, depending on snow conditions. ✉ *47200 Gallatin Rd., Big Sky* ☎ *406/994–4450* 🌐 *www.canyonadventuresmontana.com.*

SNOWSHOEING

At **Big Sky Resort** (✉ *50 Big Sky Resort Rd.* ☎ *406/995–5769*), you can rent snowshoes and hire a guide at the Basecamp office. Or bring your own and snowshoe through Big Sky Rentals for use on the resort's 2-mile Moose Tracks trail, which winds through aspen groves. You can rent snowshoes through Big Sky Rentals for use on the resort's 2-mile Moose Tracks trail, which wends through aspen groves.

Quiet and picturesque snowshoe trails lead through the woods and meadows of **Lone Mountain Ranch** (✉ *4 miles on Lone Mountain Trail, Hwy. 64, and ½ mile down gravel ranch road* ☎ *406/995–4644, 800/514–4644*), where you can get a trail map and rent snowshoes and poles.

Deer Lodge

60 miles southwest of Helena via U.S. 12 and I–90; 80 miles southeast of Missoula via I–90; 60 miles northwest of Butte via I–90.

Deer Lodge, a quiet community of 3,000 residents, maintains a complex of history museums in and near its old state penitentiary. Many locals make their living by ranching, which came to the 55-mile-long Deer Lodge Valley in 1862, when John Grant built the area's first cabin and began a cattle operation, selling beef to miners. Ranching remained the primary industry as the town of Deer Lodge developed. Its name derives from a 40-foot-high geothermal mound that used to emit steam from its top; Native Americans thought it resembled a large medicine lodge. The minerals and water attracted deer, and so the Native Americans named the place Deer Lodge. The mound is hidden behind trees and buildings at the Warm Springs State Hospital.

GETTING HERE AND AROUND

Deer Lodge is small and easily walkable, with most of the attractions on or near Main Street. There's plenty of free on-street parking. The nearest airports are in Helena and Butte.

Sights

A single admission charge ($15) grants you access to the Old Montana Prison Museum, the Montana Auto Museum, the Frontier Montana Museum, and Yesterday's Playthings.

Frontier Montana Museum

MUSEUM | The Frontier Montana Museum displays hats, saddles, spurs, chaps, and all things cowboy. Also here are Civil War items, Native American artifacts, and Desert John's Saloon, complete with whiskey memorabilia. ✉ *1106 Main St.* ☎ *406/846–3111* 🌐 *www.pcmaf.org* 🎫 *$15 (includes Old Prison Museum, Powell County Museum, Yesterday's Playthings, and Montana Auto Museum)* ⏲ *Closed Oct.–Apr.*

Grant-Kohrs Ranch National Historic Site

HISTORIC SITE | **FAMILY** | Guided or self-guided tours of the 1,600-acre Grant-Kohrs Ranch National Historic Site, a working cattle ranch run by the National Park Service, provide insight into ranching life in the 1860s. You can learn about roping steers, watch blacksmithing demonstrations, and bounce along in a covered wagon. ✉ *266 Warren La.* ✥ *½ mile off I–90* ☎ *406/846–2070* 🌐 *www.nps.gov* 🎫 *Free.*

Montana Auto Museum

MUSEUM | The Montana Auto Museum is a car buff's delight. Displays include more than 160 vintage Mopars, Chevys, Fords, and Studebakers dating from 1903 to the 1970s, including such rarities as a 1886 Benz Replica. ✉ *1106 Main St.* ☎ *406/846–3111* 🌐 *www.pcmaf.org* 🎫 *$15 (includes Old Prison Museum, Frontier Montana Museum, Powell County Museum, and Yesterday's Playthings).*

Old Montana Prison Museum

MUSEUM | Built in 1871, the old Montana Territorial Prison did not shut down until 1979. It's now where you can enter cells and learn about early Montana law. Also on display is the gallows tree taken from town to town in territorial days to hang convicted prisoners. ✉ *1106 Main St.* ☎ *406/846–3111* 🌐 *www.pcmaf.org* 🎫 *$15 (includes Frontier Montana Museum, Powell County Museum, Yesterday's Playthings, and Montana Auto Museum).*

Powell County Museum

MUSEUM | The Powell County Museum focuses on local history; it includes a hand-carved wood folk-art collection, photographs, mining memorabilia, and vintage furniture and household items. ✉ *1106 Main St.* ☎ *406/846–1694* 🌐 *www.pcmaf.org* 🎫 *$15 (includes Old Prison Museum, Frontier Montana Museum, Yesterday's Playthings, and Montana Auto Museum)* ⏲ *Closed Oct.–Apr.*

Yesterday's Playthings

MUSEUM | Whimsical old toys including model trains, dolls, and Hotwheels Cars inhabit Yesterday's Playthings. Admission here grants you access to the Montana Auto Museum, Frontier Montana Museum, and Old Montana Prison Museum. ✉ *1106 Main St.* ☎ *406/846–3111* 🌐 *www.pcmaf.org* 🎫 *$15 (includes Old Prison Museum, Frontier Montana Museum, Powell County Museum, and Montana Auto Museum)* ⏲ *Closed Oct.–Apr.*

Restaurants

Broken Arrow Steakhouse

$$$ | **AMERICAN** | Your quintessential small town establishment, this small-town steak house is a no-frills place with simply decent steaks and shrimp, yet it's some of the best food in Deer Lodge. What it lacks in industry accolades it makes up for with local character. **Known for:** above-average cheeseburgers; being busy since it advertises the town's best steaks; quick service for a sit-down restaurant. *Average main: $22* ✉ *317 N. Main St.* ☎ *406/846–3400.*

Hotels

Travelodge by Wyndham
$ | **HOTEL** | This budget-friendly property located right off I–90 is also pet-friendly. **Pros:** surprisingly helpful staff for a basic hotel; can be flexible with check-in time; large rooms. **Cons:** parking lot can seem sketchy; it's an older motel; could use a deep cleaning. *Rooms from: $52* ✉ *1150 N. Main St.* ☎ *406/545–2858* 🌐 *www.wyndhamhotels.com* *58 rooms* *Free breakfast.*

Western Big Sky Inn
$ | **HOTEL** | This pet-friendly, mom-and-pop motor inn is right off I–90 and within walking distance of the Grant-Kohrs Ranch National Historic Site. **Pros:** very budget-friendly; cleaner than most motels; fast food and groceries within walking-distance. **Cons:** hair dryers and irons are only available on request; dated furniture and decor; no hot tub, pool, or fitness center. *Rooms from: $50* ✉ *210 N. Main St.* ☎ *406/846–2590* 🌐 *www.westernbigskyinn.com* *20 rooms* *Free breakfast.*

Shopping

Quilters Corner, Etc.
CRAFTS | Handmade quilts and quilting materials fill Quilters Corner, Etc., in the historic Larabie Brothers Bank building, the first Deer Lodge bank. ✉ *401 S. Main St.* ☎ *406/846–3096.*

Territorial Antiques and Uniques
ANTIQUES/COLLECTIBLES | Territorial Antiques and Uniques sells porcelain dolls, china, lamps, and furnishings. ✉ *300 Maryland Ave.* ☎ *406/846–1400* *Closed Sun.*

Activities

CAMPING

Indian Creek Campground. Set among brush and flats, this campground along tiny Indian Creek has large campsites, plus cable TV hookups and Wi-Fi. It's a good idea to make reservations. ✉ *745 Maverick La., Deer Lodge* ☎ *406/846–4848* *51 full hookups, 10 partial hookups, 10 tent sites.*

Anaconda

22 miles south of Deer Lodge via I–90; 24 miles west of Butte via I–90 and Rte. 1.

Nicknamed the Smelter City, Anaconda is a window on the age of the copper barons, who ran this town from the 1880s through the 1950s. A number of sites preserve traces of Anaconda's rough-and-tumble history, including the dormant 585-foot smokestack, visible for miles, of the copper-smelting works around which the town was built. Copper is no longer the chief industry here, but even the Jack Nicklaus–designed golf course uses smelter-tailings slag for sand traps. Anaconda is also an ideal spot for fishing and hiking, and it sits at the base of the rugged Pintler Mountains, popular for cross-country skiing, downhill skiing, and backcountry adventures.

GETTING HERE AND AROUND

Anaconda is motorist- and pedestrian-friendly; streets are uncrowded, and parking is free.

Sights

Anaconda-Pintler Wilderness
NATURE PRESERVE | Overlapping three ranger districts of the Beaverhead-Deerlodge National Forest, the 159,000-acre Anaconda-Pintler wilderness area extends more than 30 miles along the Continental Divide to the southwest of Anaconda. Elevations range from 5,400 feet near

the Bitterroot River to 10,793 feet at the summit of West Goat Peak. Glaciation formed many spectacular cirques, U-shape valleys, and glacial moraines in the foothills. The habitat supports mountain lions, deer, elk, moose, bears, and many smaller animals and birds. About 280 miles of Forest Service trails cross the area. If you hike or ride horseback along the Continental Divide, at times you can view the Mission Mountains to the northwest and the mountains marking the Idaho-Montana border to the southwest. If you want to explore the wilderness, you must obtain a detailed map and register your plans with a Forest Service office. Stock forage is scarce, so if you're riding a horse, bring concentrated feed pellets. Note that no motorized travel is permitted in the wilderness area. There are more than 20 access points to the area, including popular ones at Moose Lake, Georgetown Lake, and the East Fork of the Bitterroot River. ✉ *Anaconda* ✣ *Access to East Fork of Bitterroot River via U.S. 93* ☎ *406/683–3900* 🎫 *Free.*

Anaconda Smoke Stack State Park
NATIONAL/STATE PARK | At 585 feet tall, "the Stack" at Anaconda Smoke Stack State Park is a solid reminder of the important role the Anaconda Copper Company played in the area's development. Built in 1919, the stack, one of the tallest freestanding brick structures in the world, is listed on the National Register of Historic Places. Smelting operations ceased in 1980. There's a viewing and interpretive area with displays and historical information, but you cannot access the smokestack itself. ✉ *100 Anaconda Smelter Rd.* ☎ *406/287–3541* 🌐 *www.fwp.mt.gov* 🎫 *$8 per out-of-state vehicle.*

Anaconda Visitor Center
INFO CENTER | The Anaconda Visitor Center, in a replica railroad depot, displays memorabilia of the town's copper history. Here you can board a 1936 **Vintage Bus** for a tour of historic Anaconda (offered summer weekdays at 10 am). ✉ *306 E. Park Ave.* ☎ *406/563–2400* 🌐 *www.discoveranaconda.com* 🎫 *Visitor center free, bus tour $10* 🕒 *No bus tours on weekends and mid-Sept.–mid-May.*

Copper Village Museum and Art Center
MUSEUM | The Copper Village Museum and Art Center houses displays on the area's history along with local artwork. The center also hosts musical performances and special events. ✉ *401 E. Commercial St.* ☎ *406/563–2422* 🌐 *www.cvmac.org* 🎫 *Free* 🕒 *Closed Sat.–Mon.*

Pintler Scenic Highway
SCENIC DRIVE | The 64 miles of mountain road on this highway pass a ghost town, historic burgs, and Georgetown Lake. The road begins in Anaconda and ends on I–90 at Drummond, backdropped by the 159,000-acre Anaconda-Pintler Wilderness. ✉ *Anaconda* ☎ *406/563–2400 for information on highway.*

Restaurants

Barclay II
$$$ | **STEAKHOUSE** | This supper club and lounge is known for its steak and seafood. Folks come especially for the huge set meal of tenderloin typically served with salad, shrimp cocktail, breadsticks, spaghetti, salami and cheese, and ice cream. **Known for:** huckleberry ice cream; large portions; steak so good it doesn't need sauce. 💲 *Average main: $25* ✉ *1300 E. Commercial Ave.* ☎ *406/563–5541* 🕒 *Closed Mon. No lunch.*

Hotels

Fairmont Hot Springs Resort
$$$ | **RESORT** | **FAMILY** | This resort between Anaconda and Butte is a great option for families. **Pros:** pools are huge and great for any age; close to Discovery Area and Georgetown Lake; tons of on-site activities so kids are never bored. **Cons:** can

be noisy; detractors point to outdated facilities and lackluster food; $15 each for additional guests in a room (two included in the rate). *Rooms from: $200* *1500 Fairmont Rd.* *406/797–3241* *www.fairmontmontana.com* *153 rooms* *No meals.*

The Ranch at Rock Creek
$$$$ | **RESORT** | Even if it's no longer the most expensive property in the United States, The Ranch at Rock Creek is still a bucket-list vacation destination. **Pros:** unrivalled luxury; all horse rides are private; surreal setting. **Cons:** pricey; pretty remote, even for Montana; ranch is very spread out. *Rooms from: $1000* *79 Carriage House La., Phillipsburg* *877/786–1545* *www.theranchatrock-creek.com* *29 rooms* *All-inclusive.*

Seven Gables Resort
$$ | **RESORT** | At Georgetown Lake, this simple, clean lodge has views of the Pintler Mountains and is 4 miles from skiing and across the road from fishing. **Pros:** convenient to fishing; fair prices; amazing lake views. **Cons:** miles from most services; food service can be slow; breakfast not included. *Rooms from: $100* *150 Southern Cross Rd.* *406/563–5052* *www.7gablesresort.com* *10 rooms* *No meals.*

Performing Arts

Washoe Theatre
FILM | The classic art deco Washoe Theatre, built in 1931, was ranked by the Smithsonian as the fifth-most-beautiful theater in the nation. Murals and ornamentation in silver, copper, and gold leaf are some of the highlights of this theater, which is open nightly for movies and other events. In 2013, the theater updated its 35-mm film projector to a digital projector enabling it to play 3D movies. *305 Main St.* *406/563–6161.*

Activities

BICYCLING

Sven's Bicycles of Anaconda
BICYCLING | Check with **Sven's Bicycles of Anaconda** for local advice, including the best mountain-biking routes, from back roads to challenging mile-high trails. In winter Sven's rents ice skates, and offers ski and snowboard tunes and repairs. *106 E. Commercial Ave.* *406/563–7988.*

CAMPING

Lost Creek State Park Campground. A short trail at this scenic recreation area leads to the Lost Creek Falls. Views of limestone cliffs rising 1,200 feet above the canyon floor, and frequent sightings of bighorn sheep and mountain goats are some of the attractions of this park. The campground has hiking trails and creek fishing. *5750 Lost Creek Rd., 1½ mile east of Anaconda on Hwy. 1, then 2 miles north on Hwy. 273, then 6 miles west* *406/287–3541* *25 sites.*

CROSS-COUNTRY SKIING

Mt. Haggin Cross-Country Ski Trails
SKIING/SNOWBOARDING | Beautifully groomed skate and classic-ski trails climb nearly to the Continental Divide at the Mt. Haggin Cross-Country Ski Trails area, the state's largest wildlife management area, with more than 54,000 acres. Twenty-five kilometers of trails are maintained by volunteers from the Mile High Nordic Ski Club. There's a warming hut but there are no services. Information is available at Sven's Bicycles at Hickory Street and Commercial Avenue. To get to the area from Anaconda, head southwest on Highway 1, cross the railroad tracks, and look for the sign to Wisdom; from here make a left onto Highway 274 and follow it for 11 miles to the parking area. *Anaconda* *406/832–3229* *milehighnordic.org.*

DOWNHILL SKIING

Discovery Ski Area

SKIING/SNOWBOARDING | Powder skiing at **Discovery Ski Area**, an inexpensive family resort, offers thrills on the extreme steeps and extensive beginner and intermediate runs. ✉ *Hwy. 1* ✣ *23 miles northwest of Anaconda at Georgetown Lake* ☎ *406/563–2184* 🌐 *www.skidiscovery.com.*

Butte

30 miles east of Anaconda via Hwy. 1 and I–90; 79 miles northwest of Virginia City via Hwy. 287 and Hwy. 55; 68 miles south of Helena via I–15.

Dubbed the "Richest Hill on Earth," Butte was once a wealthy and rollicking copper-, gold-, and silver-mining town. During its heyday, 100,000 people from around the world lived here; by 1880 Butte had generated about $22 billion in mineral wealth. The revived historic district, Uptown Butte, is now a National Historic Landmark area. Numerous ornate buildings recall the Old West, and several museums preserve the town's past. Today about 35,000 people live in the Butte–Silver Bow County area. The city maintains a strong Irish flavor, and its St. Patrick's Day parade is one of the nation's most notorious.

GETTING HERE AND AROUND

Uptown Butte's attractions are easily accessible on foot, but you'll want some kind of motorized vehicle if you'll be staying in The Flats south of I–90. A **municipal bus** (🌐 *buttebus.org*) plies five routes within the city. Other than during St. Patrick's Day and other festivals, free parking is plentiful. Delta/Skywest is currently the only major carrier operating out of Butte's Bert Mooney Airport, offering three flights a day to and from Salt Lake City.

TOURS

Butte Trolley Tours

GUIDED TOURS | You can catch narrated tours on a red trolley ($20 for adults) at the **Butte–Silver Bow Chamber of Commerce**, just off I–90 at Exit 126. Tours are about two hours. You also can pick up free information about the area and take a stroll down the scenic Blacktail Creek Walking Path. ✉ *1000 George St.* ☎ *406/723–3177* 🌐 *www.buttechambersite.org.*

Old Butte Historical Adventures

GUIDED TOURS | For a behind-the-scenes look at the shadier side of Butte's heyday, Old Butte Historical Adventures leads guided walking tours to underground speakeasies, brothels of the Red Light District, and the former city jail, known as the "Butte Bastille." Tours are offered year-round, by appointment only. ✉ *117 N. Main St.* ☎ *406/498–3424* 🌐 *www.buttetour.info* 🎫 *$20* ⏲ *Closed Sun.*

Sights

Berkeley Open Pit Mine

MINE | Thanks to old mining waste, Butte has the dubious distinction as the location of the largest toxic-waste site in the country. Some underground copper mines were dug up in the 1950s, creating the site which stretches 1½ by 1 mile, reaches 1,600 feet deep, and is filled with toxic water some 800 feet deep. A viewing platform allows you to look into the now-abandoned mammoth pit where more than 20 billion pounds of copper, 704 million ounces of silver, and 3 million ounces of gold were extracted from the Butte mining district. ✉ *Continental Dr.* ✣ *At Park St.* ☎ *406/723–3177* 🎫 *$2* ⏲ *Closed Dec.–Feb.*

Clark Chateau Museum

HOUSE | The Clark Chateau Museum, an elegant 1898 four-story Victorian mansion that was built by William Clark as a wedding gift for his son Charles, is open for self-guided and guided tours. Call ahead to reserve your spot. The house, a replica of one wing of the Chateau de Chenonceau in France's Loire Valley, displays 18th- and 19th-century furniture, textiles, and collectibles as well as artwork. ✉ *321 W. Broadway* ☎ *406/565–5600* 🎫 *$7* ⊙ *Closed Mon.–Wed. Closed weekdays Oct.–Apr.*

Copper King Mansion

HOUSE | William Clark, one of Butte's richest copper barons, built the Copper King Mansion between 1884 and 1888. Tours of the house take in the hand-carved oak paneling, nine original fireplaces, antiques, a lavish ballroom, and frescoes. The house doubles as a B&B. ✉ *219 W. Granite St.* ☎ *406/782–7580* 🌐 *www.thecopperkingmansion.com* 🎫 *$10.*

Mai Wah Museum

MUSEUM | The Mai Wah Museum contains exhibits on the history of the Chinese and other Asian settlers of Butte. The two historic buildings it occupies were constructed to house Chinese-owned businesses: the Wah Chong Tai Company and the Mai Wah Noodle Parlor. ✉ *17 W. Mercury St.* ☎ *406/723–3231* 🌐 *www.maiwah.org* 🎫 *$8* ⊙ *Closed Sun. and Mon.*

Mineral Museum

MUSEUM | More than 1,300 mineral specimens are displayed at Montana Tech University's Mineral Museum, including a 27½-troy-ounce gold nugget and a massive Ni-Fe meteorite, which was discovered in Beaverhead County. ✉ *1300 W. Park St.* ☎ *406/496–4414* 🌐 *www.mbmg.mtech.edu* 🎫 *Free* ⊙ *Closed weekends mid-Sept.–mid-June.*

Our Lady of the Rockies

RELIGIOUS SITE | Keeping watch over Butte is Our Lady of the Rockies, on the Continental Divide. The 90-foot-tall, 80-ton statue of the Virgin Mary is lighted at night. For a 2½-hour bus tour, stop by the visitor center, run by a nonprofit, nondenominational organization. Reservations are required, so call ahead. ✉ *Butte Plaza Mall, 3100 Harrison Ave.* ☎ *406/782–1221* 🌐 *www.ourladyoftherockies.net* 🎫 *$22* ⊙ *Closed Nov.–May.*

Sheepshead Recreation Area

NATURE PRESERVE | At this designated Wildlife Viewing Area you might glimpse elk, deer, moose, waterfowl, and birds of prey. The area is wheelchair-accessible, and offers paved walking trails, a fishing dock, picnic tables, a rentable pavilion, horseshoe pits, and drinking water. ✉ *Butte* ✥ *13 miles north of Butte on I–15 to Exit 138, Elk Park, west on Forest Service Rd. 442, follow signs for 6 miles* ☎ *406/494–2147* 🎫 *Free* ⊙ *Closed Labor Day–mid-June.*

Restaurants

Hanging Five Restaurant

$$ | AMERICAN | This beloved diner has been feeding the Butte masses, especially after mass, since the mid-1990s. The staff is friendly, the hash browns are plentiful, and the menu is exactly what you'd expect to see in a diner. **Known for:** comfortable booth seating; blueberry streusel French toast; huge portions, served hot. [$] *Average main: $10* ✉ *2110 Harvard Ave.* ☎ *406/494–4309.*

Metals Sports Bar & Grill

$$ | AMERICAN | Housed in a former bank that was designed by Cass Gilbert in 1906, this busy sports bar is rich in history and still boasts the original vault and marble tellers' counters. The food is typical pub fare: nachos, burgers, pizza, and fried food. **Known for:** a great place to watch the big game; decor so cool it's almost distracting; good selection (20) of draft beers. [$] *Average main: $16* ✉ *8 W. Park St.* ☎ *406/782–5534* 🌐 *www.metalssportsbarandgrill.com.*

★ Uptown Café

$$$$ | CONTEMPORARY | Fresh seafood, steaks, poultry, and pasta are served in this elegant restaurant that's one of southwest Montana's finest eateries.

Try the scallops Provençal, sauteed with tomatoes, feta cheese,and garlic. **Known for:** best-selling pecan ball dessert; amazing clams; five-course meals. *Average main: $40 47 E. Broadway 406/723–4735 uptowncafe.com.*

 Coffee and Quick Bites

Town Talk Bakery

$$ | **BAKERY** | No visit to Butte is complete without trying a pasty, the traditional miner's dinner of meat, potatoes, and onion baked inside a pastry shell. This bakery is one of the best of several eateries that serve these pocket-size meals; they also sell doughnuts, cookies, cakes, and breads, all cash-only. **Known for:** amazing maple bars; doughnuts selling out early; strong coffee. *Average main: $10 611 E. Front St. 406/782–4985 No credit cards Closed Sun. and Mon. No lunch or dinner.*

 Hotels

Best Western Butte Plaza Inn

$ | **HOTEL** | Butte's largest hotel is convenient to shopping, sports events, and the interstates. **Pros:** no surprises; decent breakfast bar; full-service restaurant attached. **Cons:** generic; can be loud; not walking distance to the Uptown Butte sights. *Rooms from: $86 2900 Harrison Ave. 406/494–3500 www.bestwestern.com 134 rooms Free breakfast.*

Copper King Mansion Bed and Breakfast

$$$ | **B&B/INN** | Completed in 1888 as the home of notorious Copper King William Andrews Clark, the mansion remains much in its original state, and is the only privately owned mansion in Montana accessible to the public through seasonal tours. **Pros:** where else can you live like a Copper King? The furniture, the stories, and the history are all genuine and first-rate; central downtown location; free guided tour. **Cons:** even kings get hot without air-conditioning; no pets; some rooms have a shared bathroom. *Rooms from: $150 219 W. Granite St. 406/782–7580 www.thecopperkingmansion.com 5 rooms Free breakfast.*

Hotel Finlen

$$ | **HOTEL** | In continuous operation since it opened in 1924, Finlen, with its lobby of ornate chandeliers and pillars, stands in testament to Butte's heyday, when the hotel played host to the likes of Charles Lindbergh and Mrs. Herbert Hoover. **Pros:** elegant, historic lobby; excellent value; best location in Uptown Butte. **Cons:** not all rooms have views; small parking lot; tiny bathrooms. *Rooms from: $95 100 E. Broadway 406/723–5461 56 rooms No meals.*

★ **Toad Hall Manor Bed and Breakfast**

$$$ | **B&B/INN** | Built as a private home in the early 1990s, this mansion has a historic feel thanks to hardwood accents, marble tile, and a classic redbrick exterior. **Pros:** the gourmet breakfast is taken very seriously; the theme is unique; the 2-bedroom suite has a private elevator. **Cons:** only four rooms, so you need to book well in advance; low ceilings might be hard for tall guests; hosts might be too friendly for most introverts. *Rooms from: $165 1 Green La. 406/494–2625 www.toadhallmanor.com 4 rooms Free breakfast.*

 Shopping

Beautiful Things on Broadway

ANTIQUES/COLLECTIBLES | Owner Rick loves Native American artifacts, but he's also quite the collector of very high-end pieces including contemporary furniture. Stop by during store hours, or call for an appointment. *27 W. Broadway 406/697–1500 Closed Sun. and Mon.*

Second Edition Books

BOOKS/STATIONERY | One of Montana's largest bookstores, Second Edition Books, buys, sells, and trades books on many different subjects but specializes in hard-to-find regional tomes. ✉ *112 S. Montana St.* ☎ *406/723–5108* ⏲ *Closed Sun.*

Uptown Butte Farmers' Market
OUTDOOR/FLEA/GREEN MARKETS | While visiting the historic district, stop at the Uptown Butte Farmers' Market for fresh garden produce, fruit, flowers, baked goods, and local crafts. It's open Saturday in summer from 8 to 1. ✉ *Butte ✣ W. Park St. between Main and Dakota Sts.* ☎ *406/497–6464.*

CAMPING

Butte KOA. This large and grassy campsite with cottonwood trees has a playground and allows fishing in the on-site Silver Bow Creek. It's next to the Butte visitor center and is easily accessed from the interstate. It's a good idea to reserve ahead. ✉ *1601 Kaw Ave., off I–90 at Exit 126* ☎ *406/782–8080* 🌐 *www.koa.com* *100 RV site (full or partial hookups), 27 tent sites, 4 cabins.*

FISHING

The StoneFly
FISHING | The StoneFly has all the gear needed for fly-fishing. Co-owners Chris and Mike and their guides make sure visiting anglers have an unforgettable time fishing Butte's waters. ✉ *2205 Amherst Ave.* ☎ *406/494–0707* 🌐 *www.thestonefly.com.*

HORSEBACK RIDING

Cargill Outfitters
HORSEBACK RIDING | **Cargill Outfitters**, which is just over the Continental Divide, 20 minutes east of Butte, offers two-hour to full-day horseback trips into the Highland Mountain range. ✉ *40 Cedar Hills Rd., Whitehall* ☎ *406/494–2960* 🌐 *www.ironwheel.com.*

ICE SKATING

U.S. High Altitude Sports Center
ICE SKATING | You can speed-skate on ice at the **U.S. High Altitude Sports Center** with international speed skaters or beginners. The ice track is open for general ice skating as well; call for times. Skate rentals are available. ✉ *34 Olympic Way* ☎ *406/494–4018.*

Virginia City

72 miles southeast of Butte via Hwys. 2, 41, and 287; 68 miles southwest of Bozeman via Rte. 84, U.S. 287, and Rte. 287.

Remnants of Montana's frontier days, Virginia City and its smaller neighbor, Nevada City, are two of the state's standout attractions. Boardwalks pass in front of partially restored historic buildings, and 19th-century goods stock the stores. Virginia City prospered when miners stampeded into Montana Territory after the 1863 discovery of gold. The diggings were rich in Alder Gulch, and Virginia City eventually became Montana's second territorial capital. Enticed by the city's wealth, criminals came to prey on the miners. In turn, vigilance committees held lightning-fast trials and strung up the bad guys. The outlaws were buried atop Boot Hill, overlooking town.

Fourteen miles east of Virginia City is Ennis. In addition to being a hub of ranching in the area, this tiny town sits among some of the best trout streams in the West. People come from around the world for the area's blue-ribbon fishing, particularly in the area of Beartrap Canyon. Welcoming you to town is a sign that reads: "840 people, 11,000,000 trout." One of the town's biggest annual events and consistently rated among the most exciting and challenging rodeos in Montana, the July 3 and 4 **Ennis Rodeo** attracts top cowpokes.

GETTING HERE AND AROUND

Virginia City is easily walkable; the smaller Nevada City is 1 mile west on Highway 287. Except during busiest times, free parking is readily available on Wallace Street or nearby side streets.

TOURS

Scenic Nevada City Train Ride

TRAIN TOURS | Enjoy a scenic 20-minute locomotive ride between Virginia City and Nevada City on weekends from late May through late September. ✉ *Virginia City* ☎ *406/843–5247, 406/843–5247* 🌐 *www.virginiacitymt.com* 🎟 *$10.*

VISITOR INFORMATION

CONTACTS Virginia City Depot Visitor Center. ✉ *413 W. Wallace St.* ☎ *406/843–5247* 🌐 *www.virginiacitymt.com.*

Sights

Beartrap Canyon

CANYON | In this part of the Lee Metcalf Wilderness you can hike, fish, and go white-water rafting on the Madison River. A picnic area and access to Trail Creek are at the head of the canyon below Ennis Lake. To get here, drive north out of Ennis on U.S. 287 to the town of McAllister and turn right down a bumpy dirt road (no number), which takes you around to the north side of the lake across the dam. Turn left after the dam onto an unmarked road and drive across the river to the Trail Creek access point. ✉ *Ennis* ☎ *406/683–8000* 🎟 *Free.*

Boot Hill

CEMETERY | After they were hanged by vigilantes, the outlaws who preyed on miners ended up in graves at Boot Hill cemetery. Have a look at the old markers and take in the hill's view. ✉ *Virginia City* ✣ *From Wallace St. turn north on Spencer St. and follow signs for "Road Agents' Graves"* ☎ *406/843–5247* 🌐 *www.historicmt.org.*

Ennis National Fish Hatchery

FISH HATCHERY | Each year at the Ennis National Fish Hatchery six strains of rainbow trout produce 23 million eggs used to stock streams throughout the United States. ✉ *180 Fish Hatchery Rd., Ennis* ☎ *406/682–4847* 🌐 *www.fws.gov* 🎟 *Free.*

Nevada City Old Town

HISTORIC SITE | The living-history Nevada City Old Town down the road from Virginia City, preserves the town as it was at the turn of the 20th century, with restored buildings, thousands of artifacts from the gold-rush era, and weekend demonstrations. Included in the collection is the **Depuis House,** from the PBS television series *Frontier House.* ✉ *U.S. 287* ✣ *1½ miles west of Virginia City* ☎ *406/843–5247* 🌐 *www.virginiacitymt.com* 🎟 *$12* ⏲ *Closed Labor Day–Memorial Day.*

Norris Hot Springs

HOT SPRINGS | For a bit of relaxation, nothing beats soaking in the natural hot water of the Norris Hot Springs pool. Live musical acts perform on the poolside stage Friday through Sunday nights. There's a $2 cover charge for music. ✉ *42 Norris Rd., Norris* ✣ *16 miles north of Ennis on U.S. 287, then ¼ mile east through town, or 33 miles west of Bozeman on Hwy. 84* ☎ *406/685–3303* 🌐 *www.norrishotsprings.com* 🎟 *Free; to soak it's $8* ⏲ *Closed Mon.–Thurs.*

Thompson-Hickman Memorial Museum

MUSEUM | The eclectic assortment of items dating from 1860 to 1900 at the Thompson-Hickman Memorial Museum includes a petrified wedding cake, the eponymous limb of "Club Foot" George Lane, rifles, and numerous photographs. The collection is made up of the heirlooms of three local families. The local library is upstairs. ✉ *Wallace St.* ☎ *406/843–5238* ⏲ *Closed Labor Day–Memorial Day.*

Just down the road from Virginia City, Nevada City was a Gold Rush–era town that is preserved just as it was at the turn of the 20th century.

Restaurants

Continental Divide
$$$$ | **CONTEMPORARY** | This bistro-style restaurant is a pleasant surprise in an area with numerous steak houses. Among the specials are Thai curry salmon, wild game chili, and duck ramen. **Known for:** incredible wine menu; filling up quickly, so make a reservation far in advance; outdoor deck with nice views. *Average main: $34 ✉ 47 Geyser St., Ennis ✣ 1½ miles north of Ennis on Hwy. 287 ☎ 406/682–7600 ⏲ Closed Jan. No lunch.*

Coffee and Quick Bites

Star Bakery Restaurant
$ | **BAKERY** | Opened in 1863, Star Bakery made beer and bread for area miners. Open almost continually ever since, it's now a popular bakery managed by a schoolteacher. **Known for:** cheese and ham croissants; memorable cinnamon rolls; amazing pies. *Average main: $5 ✉ 1576 MT-287 ☎ 406/369–8169 ⏲ Closed Labor Day–Memorial Day.*

Hotels

Fairweather Inn
$$ | **HOTEL** | Virginia City's Fairweather Inn is a classic Western-Victorian hotel with balconies in the heart of the area's gold-mining country. **Pros:** historic hotel; convenient location; comfortable rooms. **Cons:** no king beds; some rooms have shared bath; Wi-Fi is iffy. *Rooms from: $120 ✉ 305 W. Wallace St. ☎ 406/843–5377 🌐 www.aldergulchaccommodations.com ⏲ Closed Sept. 15–mid-May 15 rooms No meals.*

Fan Mountain Inn
$$ | **HOTEL** | This simple but clean family motel has wonderful views of the Madison Range and is within walking distance of downtown shops and galleries. **Pros:** good location; reasonably priced; pet-friendly. **Cons:** very basic—just a place to rest your head; exterior door entry; fills up during fishing season. *Rooms from:*

$85 ✉ *204 N. Main St., Ennis* ☎ *406/682–5266, 406/682–5200* 🌐 *www.fanmountaininn.com* *27 rooms* *No meals.*

Just an Experience B&B

$$ | **B&B/INN** | This rustic, yet comfy, B&B is perfect for exploring nearby Nevada City, which is within walking distance. **Pros:** tamales for breakfast; great back deck for socializing with other guests; cute cabins with lofts for the kids. **Cons:** only five rooms/cabins so they go quickly; not in downtown Virginia City; bathrooms in the main house are on the smaller side. *Rooms from: $120* ✉ *1570 MT-287 N* ☎ *406/843–5402* 🌐 *www.justanexperience.com* *5 rooms* *Free breakfast.*

Upper Canyon Outfitters

$$$ | **RENTAL** | Along with cattle herding, hunting, and fly-fishing adventures, this secluded guest ranch offers rooms in its spacious Western-style lodge or kitchen-equipped log cabins. **Pros:** an all-inclusive Western experience; family-owned and operated; amazing guides. **Cons:** a far cry from Disneyland; far from Virginia City; lots of hunters during hunting season. *Rooms from: $200* ✉ *2149 Upper Ruby Rd.* *35 miles southwest of Virginia City* ☎ *406/842–5884* 🌐 *www.ucomontana.com* *Closed Dec.–May* *12 rooms* *All-inclusive.*

Nightlife

Bale of Hay Saloon

BARS/PUBS | With flags and fresh flowers hanging outside its wooden storefront, it's easy to see the Bale of Hay Saloon takes pride in its business. Although it's a saloon (it looks like it was taken from Tombstone), it's relatively family-friendly, the food is good, and kids aren't shunned. In the summer (the saloon is open from Memorial Day to Labor Day), enjoy live music and drinking on the outdoor patio. ✉ *344 W.E. Wallace* ☎ *406/843–5700.*

Brewery Follies

CABARET | For a no-holds-barred, singing comedy cabaret, leave the kids at home and hit the bawdy Brewery Follies (ages 13 and up); shows take place daily Memorial Day through Labor Day. ✉ *H.S. Gilbert Brewery Bldg., 201 E. Wallace* ☎ *800/829–2969* 🌐 *www.breweryfollies.net.*

Long Branch Saloon

BARS/PUBS | The very definition of a dive bar, the Long Branch Saloon in nearby Ennis doesn't disappoint if that's what you're in the mood for. It's busy for a few reasons: friendly servers, consistent hours (open every day), funny bumper stickers, big steaks, and an even bigger crowd. ✉ *124 Main St., Ennis* ☎ *406/682–7370.*

Performing Arts

Virginia City Opera House

THEATER | The historic Opera House is the oldest continuously operating summer theater in the West, in operation since 1949. Early June through early September, the theater hosts an amusing vaudeville show by the Virginia City Players. Shows are Tuesday through Thursday at 4, Friday and Saturday at 7. Weekend matinees are at 2. ✉ *338 W. Wallace St.* ☎ *800/829–2969* *From $25.*

Shopping

Rank's Mercantile

GIFTS/SOUVENIRS | Opened in 1864, Rank's Mercantile is Montana's oldest continuously operating store. Period clothing, books, toys, gifts, and groceries are for sale here. ✉ *211 W. Wallace St.* ☎ *406/843–5454* 🌐 *www.ranksmercantile.com.*

RiverStone Gallery

ART GALLERIES—ARTS | The RiverStone Gallery displays original paintings, sculptures, pottery, and contemporary jewelry by Western artists. ✉ *319 E. Main St., Ennis* ☎ *406/682–5768.*

CAMPING

Ennis RV Village. An 8-acre wetlands park with hiking trails is adjacent to this RV park, with views of the Madison, Gravelly, and Tobacco Root ranges. Reservations are recommended. ✉ *15 Geyser St., just off Hwy. 287, 1 mile north of Ennis* ☎ *406/682–5272, 866/682–5272* 🌐 *www.ennisrv.com* *90 sites.*

Rambling Moose RV Park. It's a good idea to reserve ahead at this RV park, which also has grassy campsites and cabins. Open May through September. ✉ *Hwy. 287, ¼ mile east of Virginia City* ☎ *406/843–5493* 🌐 *www.virginiacityrvpark.com* *27 RV sites with hookups, 2 tent sites.*

FISHING

In these parts, Ennis, 14 miles east of Virginia City, is known for its fishing.

Hooked Outfitting

FISHING | Hooked Outfitting offers full-day floats and wading trips on the Madison. Owner and lead guide Captain Garrett Blackburn is one of the best in the West, and abroad. In the winter he guides in Patagonia. ✉ *Ennis* ☎ *406/625–3967* 🌐 *www.hookedoutfitting.com.*

Tackle Shop

FISHING | The **Tackle Shop** offers guided float and wade fishing on the Madison, Big Hole, and other rivers. The full-service Orvis fly shop also sells luggage, clothing, and fishing accessories. ✉ *127 E. Main St., Ennis* ☎ *800/808–2832* 🌐 *www.thetackleshop.com.*

HORSEBACK RIDING

Bar 88 Horses

HORSEBACK RIDING | Ride the dusty trails on half- and full-day adventures in the Beaverhead National Forest. Owners Jeff and Shylea Wingard operate out of Ennis, east of Virginia City. ✉ *Ennis* ☎ *406/682–4827.*

Dillon

65 miles south of Butte via I–90 west and I–15 south.

Blue-ribbon trout fishing on the Beaverhead River attracts thousands of anglers here year-round. A capital of southwest Montana's ranch country, Dillon began as a cattle- and wool-shipping point between Utah and the goldfields of Montana. From the mid-1860s until the early 1900s cattle and sheep remained the primary cargo shipped out of here on the Union Pacific Railroad.

Everyone is a cowboy for the annual Dillon Jaycee Labor Day Rodeo and Parade, which has been staged here since 1914; it's the biggest annual draw. Among the activities that take place at this weeklong celebration leading up to Labor Day are a fair, rodeo, and concert.

GETTING HERE AND AROUND

Dillon's downtown area is easily accessed on foot, and there's plenty of free parking in town. From Dillon you can hike and mountain-bike into the nearby Ruby and Tendoy mountains.

Bannack State Historic Park

HISTORIC SITE | Bannack was Montana's first territorial capital and the site of the state's first major gold strike, on July 28, 1862, at Grasshopper Creek. Now this frontier boomtown has historic structures lining the main street, and picnic and camping spots. It was here that the notorious renegade Sheriff Henry Plummer and two of his deputies were caught and executed by vigilantes for murder and robbery. A re-creation of the gallows on which Plummer was hanged still stands. Rumors persist that Plummer's stash of stolen gold was hidden somewhere in the mountains near here and never found. Bannack Days, the third weekend in July, celebrates life in Montana's first

Bannack was Montana Territory's first capital; today it's just a ghost town and popular state park, with its historic structures still intact.

territorial capital with plenty of exciting reenactments and pioneer-theme events ($5/person). ✉ *Bannack* ✣ *Bannack is 24 miles west of Dillon* ☎ *406/834–3413* 🌐 *www.bannack.org* 🎫 *$8 per out-of-state vehicle.*

Beaverhead County Museum

MUSEUM | The Beaverhead County Museum exhibits Native American artifacts, ranching and mining memorabilia, a homesteader's cabin, agricultural artifacts, a one-room schoolhouse, a Lewis and Clark diorama, a model train, a research center, and a boardwalk imprinted with the area's ranch brands. ✉ *15 S. Montana St.* ☎ *406/683–5027* 🎫 *$3* 🕒 *Closed weekends and Oct.–May.*

Clark's Lookout State Park

NATIONAL/STATE PARK | William Clark of the Lewis and Clark Expedition climbed to the top of this limestone bluff in 1805 and took three compass readings. The maps he made from these readings became an important resource for future travelers. A ¼-mile gravel loop trail takes visitors to the top of the bluff, where interpretive signs include a replica of Clark's sketched map of the area. ✉ *25 Clark's Lookout Rd.* ✣ *1 mile north of Dillon on Hwy. 91* ☎ *406/834–3413* 🌐 *stateparks.mt.gov* 🎫 *Free.*

Pioneer Mountain Scenic Byway

SCENIC DRIVE | Mountains, meadows, lodgepole-pine forests, and willow-edged streams line this road, which runs north–south between U.S. 278 (west of Bannack) and Highway 43. Headed north, the byway skirts the Maverick Mountain Ski Area and Elkhorn Hot Springs and ends at the town of Wise River on the Big Hole River. In the winter it's closed to car traffic but popular with snowmobilers. ✉ *420 Barrett St., Bannack* ✣ *Bannack is 24 miles west of Dillon* ☎ *406/683–3900* 🕒 *Closed Dec. 1–May 15.*

Red Rock Lakes National Wildlife Refuge

NATURE PRESERVE | In the undeveloped and remote Centennial Valley, this almost-50,000-acre refuge shelters moose, deer, and antelope, but is primarily a sanctuary for 230 species of birds, including trumpeter swans. Once threatened with extinction, these elegant birds have survived thanks to refuge protection; today they build their nests and winter here among the 16,500 acres of lakes and marshes. ✉ *27650B S. Valley Rd., Lima* ✣ *60 miles south of Dillon on I–15 to Monida; follow signs east 28 miles on gravel road* ☎ *406/276–3536* 🌐 *www.fws.gov* 🎟 *Free.*

Sparky's Garage

$$ | **AMERICAN** | Since 2002, Sparky's has been whetting the appetite of locals and travelers alike with delicious appetizers (cheese curds, Southern fried pickles, and the "lugnutz"—deep-fried salmon wontons), salads, burgers and more. While you wait for your food, take a look at the cool classic decor including the fun vintage signs. **Known for:** a classic garage theme; big selection of craft beers; excellent ribs for a sports bar. $ *Average main: $11* ✉ *420 E. Poindexter St.* ☎ *406/683–2828* 🌐 *www.sparkysrestaurant.com.*

Coffee and Quick Bites

Sweetwater Coffee

$$ | **CONTEMPORARY** | This warm and friendly coffee shop offers salads, sandwiches, and pasta along with its espresso drinks. Try the French toast breakfast sandwich. **Known for:** fresh-squeezed lemonade; most things made from scratch; cute atmosphere with local artwork. $ *Average main: $13* ✉ *24 S. Idaho St.* ☎ *406/683–4141* ▭ *No credit cards* ⏲ *Closed weekends.*

FairBridge Inn Express, Dillon

$$ | **HOTEL** | This hotel is affordable, clean, and quiet, and has an indoor heated pool and hot tub. **Pros:** has guest laundry; indoor pool; not overpriced—it's one of the nicer places to stay in Dillon. **Cons:** feels like a typical chain hotel; close to the freeway so noise can be an issue; breakfast is hot but nothing special. $ *Rooms from: $110* ✉ *580 Sinclair St.* ☎ *406/683–3636* 🌐 *www.fairbridgeinns.com* *58 rooms* 🍽 *Free breakfast.*

Goose Down Ranch

$$$ | **RENTAL** | Darling cabins, one log and one clapboard, and a carriage house have mountain views all around and are near the famed Poindexter Slough blue-ribbon fly-fishing spot on the Beaverhead River. **Pros:** great fishing; full-service cabins; wonderful hosts. **Cons:** only three rentals means advance reservations are essential; one of the bedrooms is a loft; the carriage house is above a garage. $ *Rooms from: $150* ✉ *2405 Carrigan La.* ☎ *406/683–6704* 🌐 *www.goosedown-ranch.com* *3 units* 🍽 *No meals.*

The Grasshopper Inn

$$ | **B&B/INN** | In the spectacular Pioneer Mountains, this mountain B&B is ideally situated for snowmobiling, hiking, and fishing. **Pros:** cozy, secluded getaway; reasonably priced; rooms have thoughtful touches like USB ports and blackout curtains. **Cons:** miles from services; pet fee is $25; no on-site bar or restaurant. $ *Rooms from: $115* ✉ *9601 Pioneer Scenic Byway, Polaris* ✣ *45 miles west of Dillon* ☎ *406/834–3456* 🌐 *www.thegrasshopper-inn.com* *9 rooms* 🍽 *Free breakfast.*

Cathy Weber–Artmaker

GIFTS/SOUVENIRS | Original paintings of flowers, dragonflies, sticks, stones, skulls, bones, and other scenes from nature are for sale at the Cathy Weber–Artmaker studio. ✉ *26 N. Idaho St.* ☎ *406/683–5493* ⏲ *Closed Sun.*

Big Hole National Battlefield commerates one of the fiercest and most tragic confrontations between the Nez Perce and U.S. Army.

Activities

CAMPING

Dillon KOA. Pine, aspen, and birch trees shade this campground on the banks of the Beaverhead River. The campground, which is on the edge of Dillon, has views of the Pioneer Mountains and other peaks. ⊠ *735 W. Park St.* ☎ *406/683–2749* 🌐 *www.koa.com* ⛺ *18 sites with full hookups, 43 sites with partial hookups, 34 tent sites, 4 cabins.*

FISHING

Backcountry Angler

FISHING | Whether they're discussing nymphs, caddis flies, or crane flies, the guides of **Backcountry Angler** know the art of fly-fishing. They lead overnight fishing-lodging trips, plus wade- and float-fishing day adventures. ⊠ *426 S. Atlantic St.* ☎ *406/683–3462* 🌐 *www.backcountryangler.com.*

HORSEBACK RIDING

Centennial Outfitters

HORSEBACK RIDING | Horse and mule day rides and pack trips traverse the Continental Divide and the Lima Peaks with **Centennial Outfitters**. ⊠ *27 S. Valley Rd., Lima* ☎ *406/660–7088* 🌐 *www.centennialoutfitters.com.*

SKIING

Maverick Mountain Ski Area

SKIING/SNOWBOARDING | **FAMILY** | A fun family attraction, **Maverick Mountain Ski Area** has a top elevation of 8,820 feet, a vertical drop of 2,020 feet, and 24 runs. Lessons and ski and snowboard rentals and sales are available for kids and adults. Note: it's only open Thursday–Sunday. ⊠ *1600 Maverick Mountain Rd.* ✣ *40 miles west of Dillon in Polaris* ☎ *406/834–3454* 🌐 *www.skimaverick.com.*

Big Hole National Battlefield

60 miles northwest of Bannock via Hwy. 278 northwest and Hwy. 43 west; 87 miles southwest of Butte via I–90 west, I–15 south, and Hwy. 43 west.

GETTING HERE AND AROUND

Big Hole is 6,300 feet above sea level, so you may need to slow your pace while walking its trails; visitors are encouraged to drink plenty of fluids. Nearest facilities are in Wisdom, 10 miles east of the battlefield, which has a gas station, store, and restaurants.

Sights

Big Hole National Battlefield

MEMORIAL | The visitor center overlooks meadows where one of the West's most tragic stories played out. In 1877 Nez Perce warriors in central Idaho killed some white settlers as retribution for earlier killings by whites. Knowing the U.S. Army would make no distinction between the guilty and the innocent, several hundred Nez Perce fled, beginning a 1,500-mile, five-month odyssey known as the Nez Perce Trail. The fugitives engaged 10 separate U.S. commands in 13 battles and skirmishes. One of the fiercest of these was at Big Hole, where both sides suffered losses. The Big Hole battlefield remains as it was when the battle unfolded; tepee poles erected by the park service mark the site of a Nez Perce village and serve as haunting reminders of what transpired here. Ranger-led programs take place daily in summer; group tours can be arranged with advance request. The park stays open for winter snowshoeing (the visitor center has a few pairs) and cross-country skiing (bring your own equipment) on a groomed trail through the battlefield's sites. The annual commemoration of the Battle of Big Hole takes place every August and includes ceremonies, traditional music, demonstrations, and cavalry exhibitions. It's one of 38 sites in four states that make up the **Nez Perce National Historic Park** (*208/843–7001, www.nps.gov/nepe*), which follows the historic Nez Perce Trail. *✉ 16425 Hwy. 43 W ⊕ 10 miles west of Wisdom ☎ 406/689–3155 🌐 www.nps.gov 🎫 Free.*

Hotels

Jackson Hot Springs Lodge

$$$ | **RESORT** | William Clark (of Lewis and Clark) cooked his dinner in the hot springs near the site of this spacious log lodge decorated with elk antlers, a stuffed mountain lion, and other critters. **Pros:** first-class dining; relaxing pool; classic Western lodge. **Cons:** online payments are nonrefundable; facilities in need of upkeep; Wi-Fi only in the lobby. *$ Rooms from: $140 ✉ 108 Jardine Ave., Jackson ⊕ 30 miles northwest of Big Hole ☎ 406/834–3151 🌐 www.jackson-hotsprings.com ⏲ Closed Tues. and Wed. in winter 🛏 18 rooms 🍴 No meals.*

★ Triple Creek Ranch

$$$$ | **HOTEL** | Lavishly appointed log cabins sit amid 1.6 million acres of Montana's Bitterroot National Forest, providing a wonderful sense of heritage with log post beds, Western-theme quilts, spectacular photos, and world-class artworks, not to mention blissful isolation and excellent food. **Pros:** superb farm-to-table cuisine; romantic setting (no kids allowed); incredible workshops, from cooking to photography. **Cons:** no cell service (but Wi-Fi is available); not family-friendly; off-ranch activities pricey. *$ Rooms from: $1700 ✉ 5551 W. Fork Rd., Darby ☎ 406/821–4600 🌐 www.triplecreekranch.com ⏲ Closed mid-Mar.–mid-Apr. and mid-Nov.–mid-Dec. 🛏 30 cabins 🍴 All-inclusive.*

Chapter 5

GLACIER AND WATERTON LAKES NATIONAL PARKS

Updated by
Debbie Olsen

Camping
★★★★★

Hotels
★★★☆☆

Activities
★★★★★

Scenery
★★★★☆

Crowds
★★☆☆☆

WELCOME TO GLACIER AND WATERTON LAKES NATIONAL PARKS

TOP REASONS TO GO

★ **Witness the Divide:** The rugged mountains that weave their way through Glacier and Waterton along the Continental Divide seem to have glaciers in every hollow melting into tiny streams, raging rivers, and icy-cold mountain lakes.

★ **Just hike it:** Hundreds of miles of trails of all levels of difficulty lace the park, from flat and easy half-hour strolls to steep, strenuous all-day hikes.

★ **Go to the sun:** Crossing the Continental Divide at the 6,646-foot-high Logan Pass, Glacier's Going-to-the-Sun Road is a spectacular drive.

★ **View the wildlife:** This is one of the few places in North America where all native carnivores, including grizzlies, black bears, coyotes, and wolves, still survive.

★ **See glaciers while you still can:** Approximately 150 glaciers were present in Glacier National Park in 1850; by 2010, there were only 25 left.

1 **Western Glacier National Park.** Known to the Kootenai people as "sacred dancing lake," Lake McDonald is the largest glacial water basin lake in Glacier National Park and a highlight of its western reaches.

2 **Along the Going-to-the-Sun Road.** At 6,646 feet, Logan Pass is the highest point on, and very much a highlight of, Glacier National Park's famous (and famously beautiful) Going-to-the-Sun Road. From mid-June to mid-October, a 1½-mile boardwalk leads to an overlook that crosses an area filled with lush meadows and wildflowers.

3 **Eastern Glacier National Park.** St. Mary Lake and Many Glacier are the major highlights of the eastern side of Glacier National Park. Grinnell Glacier, the most accessible glacier in the park, is reached via a hike that begins near Swiftcurrent Lake in the Many Glacier region.

4 **Waterton Lakes National Park.** The Canadian national park is the meeting of two worlds: the flatlands of the prairie and the abrupt upthrust of the mountains. The park is also home to a vast array of wildlife, spectacular scenery, and wonderful hiking trails.

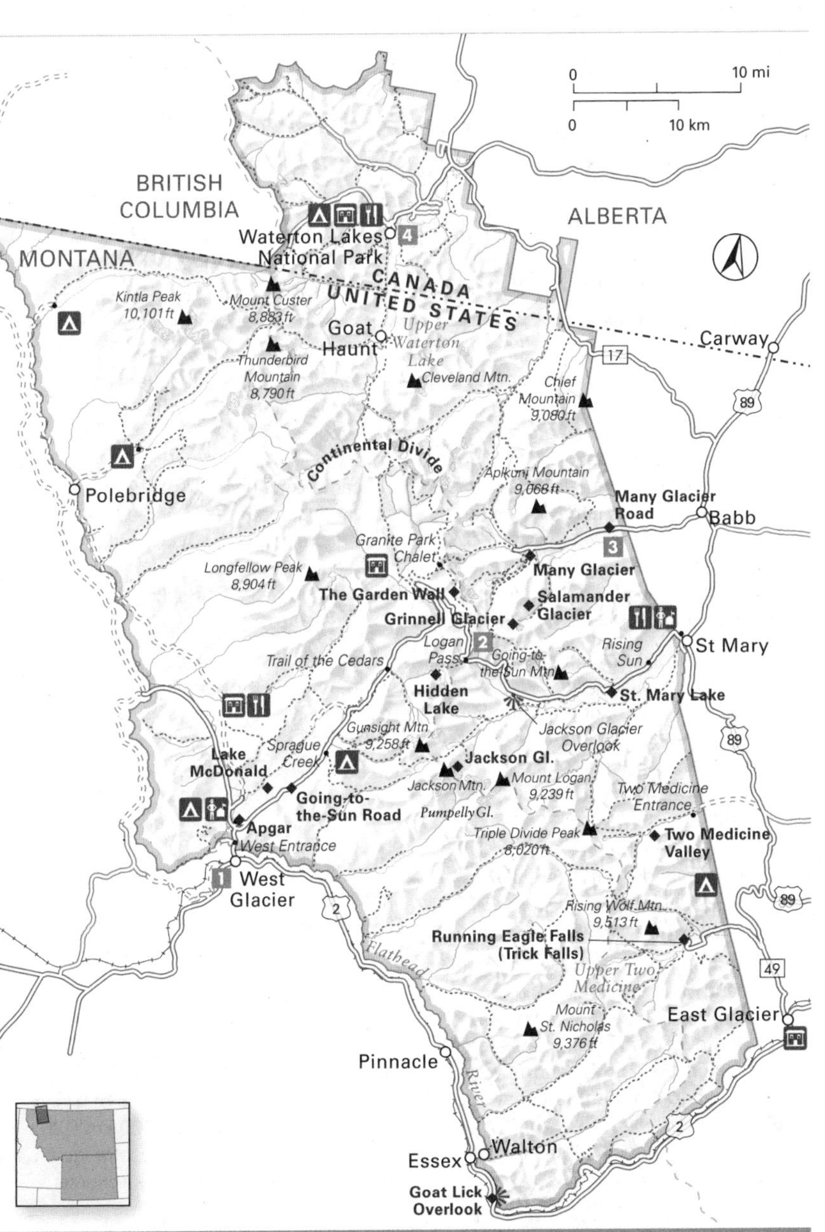

0
10 mi
0
10 km
BRITISH COLUMBIA
ALBERTA
MONTANA
CANADA
UNITED STATES
Waterton Lakes National Park
4
Kintla Peak 10,101 ft
Mount Custer 8,883 ft
Goat Haunt
Upper Waterton Lake
Carway
17
Thunderbird Mountain 8,790 ft
Cleveland Mtn.
Chief Mountain 9,080 ft
89
Continental Divide
Apikuni Mountain 9,068 ft
Polebridge
Many Glacier Road
Babb
3
Granite Park Chalet
Longfellow Peak 8,904 ft
Many Glacier
The Garden Wall
Salamander Glacier
Grinnell Glacier
Logan Pass
2
Rising Sun
St Mary
Trail of the Cedars
Going-to-the-Sun Mtn
Hidden Lake
St. Mary Lake
Jackson Glacier Overlook
Gunsight Mtn 9,258 ft
Lake McDonald
Sprague Creek
Jackson Gl.
Jackson Mtn.
Mount Logan 9,239 ft
Two Medicine Entrance
Going-to-the-Sun Road
Pumpelly Gl.
Apgar
West Entrance
Triple Divide Peak 8,020 ft
Two Medicine Valley
1
West Glacier
2
Rising Wolf Mtn 9,513 ft
Running Eagle Falls (Trick Falls)
Flathead
Upper Two Medicine
49
Mount St. Nicholas 9,376 ft
East Glacier
Pinnacle
River
Walton
Essex
Goat Lick Overlook

The astonishing landscapes at the crown of the continent know no boundaries. Here, the rugged, glacier-carved mountains span the border between the United States and Canada to form the International Peace Park, which consists of two national parks: Glacier in Montana and Waterton Lakes in Alberta.

The scenery in these parks is unparalleled: craggy peaks, thick coniferous forests, deep lakes, gleaming glaciers, wildflower-carpeted meadows, and too many stunning waterfalls to count. The animals roaming the terrain include everything from ungulates such as deer, elk, bighorn sheep, mountain goats, and moose to carnivores like mountain lions, black bears, and grizzlies.

Evidence of human use in this area dates back over 10,000 years, with the Blackfeet, Salish, and Kootenai peoples inhabiting the region long before the first Europeans came. The completion of the Great Northern Railway in 1891 allowed more people to visit and settle this region of Montana. By the late 1800s, people began to realize the land had value far beyond mining, agricultural, or other commercial endeavors.

Renowned conservationist George Bird Grinnell and other influential leaders lobbied for nearly a decade to have the so-called Crown of the Continent protected as a national park. Their efforts were rewarded when President Taft set aside 1,583 square miles (4,100 square km) to create Glacier, America's 10th national park, on May 11, 1910.

On May 30, 1895, a 140-square-km (54-square-mile) area of what is now Waterton Lakes National Park was first protected as a Dominion Forest Park. It became a national park in 1930, and today it encompasses 505 square km (195 square miles). It was Canada's fourth national park and is the smallest of those in the Canadian Rockies.

The idea of creating an International Peace Park was conceived and promoted by the Cardston Rotary Club and was unanimously endorsed in a meeting of Alberta and Montana Rotary clubs in 1931. On June 18, 1932, the two parks were officially united, establishing the world's first International Peace Park—an enduring symbol of the harmony and friendship between the United States and Canada. On December 6, 1995, the Glacier-Waterton International Peace Park was designated a UNESCO World Heritage Site.

These parks are a nature-lover's dream, filled with magnificent mountains, glaciers, lakes, and forests. There are more than 700 miles (1,127 km) of hiking trails in Glacier and another 200 km (120 miles) in Waterton Lakes. These range in difficulty from easy strolls to strenuous day hikes to multiday backpacking adventures. Other popular activities include fishing, boating, paddleboarding, cycling, mountaineering, climbing, cross-country skiing, and wildlife watching. Glacier's Going-to-the-Sun Road is considered one of the most beautiful drives on the planet, and Waterton's Crypt Lake Hike has been ranked one of the world's most thrilling. If these parks aren't on your bucket list, they should be.

Planning

When to Go

Of the 2 million annual visitors to Glacier and 400,000 to Waterton, most come between July and mid-September, when the streams are flowing, wildlife is roaming, and naturalist programs are fully underway. Snow removal on the alpine portion of Going-to-the-Sun Road is usually completed by mid-June; the opening of Logan Pass at the road's summit marks the summer opening of Glacier. Canada's Victoria Day in late May marks the beginning of the season in Waterton. Spring and fall are quieter.

FESTIVALS AND EVENTS

Canada Day. On July 1, all guests get into the national parks free of charge in honor of Canada's birthday. Waterton also has special activities for families such as treasure hunts and evening theater programs.

Montana Dragon Boat Festival. Held on Flathead Lake, this captivating event features 95 teams of 20 paddlers each racing 46-foot-long Hong Kong–style boats. 🌐 *www.montanadragonboat.com.*

NW Montana Antique Threshing Bee. Steam threshing machines, steam plows, antique tractors, and engines flex muscles in the Parade of Power, organized by the Northwest Montana Antique Power Association in Kalispell. Participants challenge friends and neighbors to tractor barrel races and shingle-making events, while children of all ages enjoy miniature steam-train rides, music, food, and entertainment.

Ski Fest. This annual celebration of cross-country skiing is a great way to introduce newcomers to kick-and-glide skiing. Equipment demonstrations, free ski lessons, and family activities are scheduled at the Izaak Walton Inn in Essex, Montana, and free trail passes are dispensed. 🌐 *www.izaakwaltoninn.com.*

Summer Concert Series. Running each Thursday from mid-June to early August, the series is held in the Don Lawrence Amphitheater at Marantette Park in Columbia Falls. Types of music vary, but the Don Lawrence Big Band performs every year.

Waterton Wildflower Festival. Wildflower walks, horseback rides, hikes, watercolor workshops, photography classes, and family events help visitors and locals celebrate the annual blooming of Waterton's bountiful wildflowers. 🌐 *www.watertonwildflowers.com.*

Waterton Wildlife Weekend. Wildlife viewing is at its best in Waterton during the fall. The weekend's events include viewing on foot, on horseback, and by boat. There are also photography, drawing, and sketching courses. 🌐 *www.watertonwildlife.com.*

Whitefish Winter Carnival. For more than 60 years this February fest has been the scene of lively activities, including a grand parade with more than 100 entries, a torchlight parade on skis, fireworks, a penguin dip, and other family-friendly activities. 🌐 *www.whitefishwintercarnival.com.*

GLACIER AVERAGE HIGH/LOW TEMPERATURES IN FAHRENHEIT					
JAN.	**FEB.**	**MAR.**	**APR.**	**MAY**	**JUNE**
28/15	35/19	42/23	53/30	64/37	71/44
JULY	**AUG.**	**SEPT.**	**OCT.**	**NOV.**	**DEC.**
79/47	78/46	67/39	53/32	37/25	30/18

GLACIER AVERAGE HIGH/LOW TEMPERATURES IN CELSIUS					
JAN.	**FEB.**	**MAR.**	**APR.**	**MAY**	**JUNE**
-2/-9	2/-7	6/-5	12/-1	18/3	22/7
JULY	**AUG.**	**SEPT.**	**OCT.**	**NOV.**	**DEC.**
26/8	26/8	19/4	12/0	3/-4	-1/-8

WATERTON AVERAGE HIGH/LOW TEMPERATURES IN CELSIUS					
JAN.	**FEB.**	**MAR.**	**APR.**	**MAY**	**JUNE**
0/-11	1/-10	6/-6	10/-2	15/3	19/6
JULY	**AUG.**	**SEPT.**	**OCT.**	**NOV.**	**DEC.**
23/8	22/7	17/3	12/1	3/-6	1/-9

WATERTON AVERAGE HIGH/LOW TEMPERATURES IN FAHRENHEIT					
JAN.	**FEB.**	**MAR.**	**APR.**	**MAY**	**JUNE**
32/12	34/14	42/22	50/29	59/37	66/43
JULY	**AUG.**	**SEPT.**	**OCT.**	**NOV.**	**DEC.**
73/46	72/44	63/38	53/33	38/22	33/15

Getting Here and Around

AIR

The nearest airports to Glacier are in Kalispell (25 miles) and Great Falls (157 miles), both in Montana. The nearest airport to Waterton Lakes is in Calgary (271 km [168 miles]).

Glacier Park International Airport
Five major airlines fly into Glacier Park International Airport (FCA) and service the national park and the Flathead Valley region. ✉ *4170 Hwy. 2 E, Kalispell* ☎ *406/257–5994* 🌐 *iflyglacier.com.*

BUS

Glacier National Park operates a free hop-on, hop-off shuttle along the Going-to-the-Sun Road from July through early September. The shuttle runs from Apgar to St. Mary Visitor Center; park visitor centers have departure information.

CAR

On the western side of Glacier National Park, U.S. 2 goes to West Glacier. At the park's northwestern edge, North Fork Road connects to Polebridge. On the park's east side, U.S. 2 goes to East Glacier and Highway 49 reaches to Two Medicine. U.S. 89 accesses St. Mary, and U.S. Route 3 connects to Many Glacier. Take the Chief Mountain Highway (Highway 17) to access Waterton Lakes in summer or U.S. 89 to Alberta Highway 2 through Cardston and then west via Highway 5 any time of the year.

In both parks, repeated freezing and thawing can cause roads—either gravel or paved—to deteriorate, so drive slowly. In summer, road reconstruction is part of the park experience as crews take advantage of the few warm months to complete projects. At any time of the year, anticipate that rocks and wildlife may be just around the bend. Gasoline is available along most paved roads. Scenic pull-outs are frequent; watch for other vehicles pulling in or out, and watch for children in parking areas. Most development and services center on Lake McDonald in the west and St. Mary Lake in the east.

BORDER CROSSINGS

A passport is required of everyone crossing the Canadian–U.S. border. When you arrive at the border crossing, customs officers will ask for information such as where you are going and where you are from. You and your vehicle are subject to random search. Firearms are prohibited, except hunting rifles, which require permission you must obtain in advance. Soil, seeds, meat, and many fruits are also prohibited. Kids traveling with only one parent need a notarized letter from the other parent giving permission to enter Canada or the United States. If you are traveling with pets, you need proof of up-to-date immunizations to cross the border in either direction. Citizens from most countries (Canada, Mexico, and Bermuda are exceptions) entering the United States from Canada must pay $6 (cash only) at the border for a required I–94 or I–94W Arrival-Departure Record form, to be returned to border officials when leaving the United States. Contact United States Customs (☎ *406/335–2611* 🌐 *www.cbp.gov*) or the Canada Border Services Agency (☎ *403/344–3767* 🌐 *www.cbsa-asfc.gc.ca*) for more information.

TRAIN

Montana's Amtrak stations are all on the *Empire Builder* route that connects Glacier National Park with Chicago and Portland/Seattle. The main stops near the park are at East Glacier Park Village, West Glacier, Essex, and Whitefish. From the stations, you can rent a car.

Inspiration

Bear Attacks: Their Causes and Avoidance, by Stephen Herrero, explores what we know about grizzly and black bears, how to avoid an incident, what to do if a bear attacks, and what the future holds for these fascinating creatures.

Charles Waterton, 1782–1865: Traveller and Conservationis, by Julia Blackburn, provides insight on Charles Waterton, the eccentric British naturalist and explorer who was one of the first conservationists of the modern age. The Waterton Lakes were named in his honor by Lieutenant Thomas Blakiston, a member of the Palliser Expedition.

Fools Crow, by James Welch and first published in 1986, is a fictional but fascinating look at what life was like for Native Americans living in this region of Montana before Glacier became a national park.

The Melting World: A Journey Across America's Vanishing Glaciers, is by Christopher White, who traveled to Montana to chronicle the work of Dan Fagre, a climate scientist and ecologist, who has spent years monitoring ice sheets in Glacier National Park.

The Wild Inside: A Novel of Suspense, by Christine Carbo, is the first in the Glacier Mystery Series of four crime novels that are set in Glacier National Park. Enjoy wonderful descriptions of the Rocky Mountains as officers follow the trail of a killer deep into the wilderness.

Park Essentials

ACCESSIBILITY

All visitor centers are wheelchair accessible, and most of the campgrounds and picnic areas are paved, with extended-length picnic tables and accessible restrooms. Three of Glacier's nature trails are wheelchair accessible: the Trail of the Cedars, Running Eagle Falls, and the Oberlin Bend Trail, just west of Logan Pass. In Waterton, the Linnet Lake Trail, Waterton Townsite Trail, Cameron Lake day-use area, and the International Peace Park Pavilion are wheelchair accessible.

PARK FEES AND PERMITS

Entrance fees for Glacier are $35 per vehicle in the summer and $25 per vehicle in the winter. The fee for motorcycles is $30 during peak season and $15 November 1–April 30. Entrance fees are good for seven days, or you can purchase a Glacier National Park annual pass for $70. An America the Beautiful Pass is $80 and covers entrance to national parks and other federal recreation sites for one year. Free entrance to the park is offered on Martin Luther King Jr. Day, the first day of national park week, National Park Service Birthday, National Public Lands Day, and Veteran's Day. A day pass to Waterton Lakes is C$7.90 for an individual or C$16 per seven people per vehicle, and a Parks Canada Discovery Pass costs C$69.19 for an individual or C$139.40 for a family and provides unlimited admission to Canada's national parks and historic sites for one year. Youth 17 and under receive free admission to all Canadian national parks and historic sites. Free entrance is offered on Canada Day (July 1). *Passes to Glacier and Waterton must be purchased separately.*

At Glacier, the required backcountry permit is $7 per person per day from the Apgar Backcountry Permit Center after mid-April for the upcoming summer. Reservations cost $40. On the park's official website (🌐 *www.nps.gov/glac/planyourvisit/backcountry.htm*), you can find the latest backcountry information and a form that can be faxed to the backcountry office.

Waterton requires backcountry camping permits for use of its backcountry camping spots, with reservations available up to 90 days ahead at the visitor reception center. The fee is C$10.02 per person per night. A nonrefundable reservation fee of $11.96 is also charged. There is no charge for children ages 16 and under. Consult the park website or phone the visitor reception center (☎ *403/859–5133*) to find out which campgrounds are open and the condition of camping sites.

PARK HOURS

The parks are open year-round, but many roads and facilities close from October through May. The parks are in the Mountain time zone.

CELL PHONE RECEPTION

Cell phone coverage is improving, but, in mountainous terrain, it is common to have poor reception. Cell service is best available in West Glacier or St. Mary in Glacier National Park and in the Waterton Townsite in Waterton Lakes National Park. Find pay phones at Avalanche Campground, Glacier Highland Motel and Store, Apgar, St. Mary Visitor Center, Two Medicine Camp Store, and all lodges except Granite Park Chalet and Sperry Chalet. Several pay phones are also available in the townsite of Waterton Lakes National Park.

Hotels

Lodgings in the parks tend to be rustic and simple, though there are a few grand lodges. Some modern accommodations have pools, hot tubs, boat rentals, guided excursions, and fine dining. The supply of rooms within both parks is limited, but the prices are relatively reasonable. It's best to reserve well in advance, especially for July and August. *Hotel reviews have been shortened. For full information, visit Fodors.com.*

RESTAURANTS

Steak houses serving certified Angus beef are typical of the region; in recent years, resort communities have diversified their menus to include bison, venison, elk, moose, trout, and gluten-free and vegetarian options. Small cafés offer hearty, inexpensive meals and perhaps the chance to chat with locals. In Montana, huckleberries appear on many menus. Attire everywhere is casual. *Restaurant reviews have been shortened. For full information, visit Fodors.com.*

What It Costs in U.S. Dollars

	$	$$	$$$	$$$$
RESTAURANTS				
	under $13	$13–$20	$21–$30	over $30
HOTELS				
	under $100	$100–$150	$151–$200	over $200

What It Costs in Canadian Dollars

	$	$$	$$$	$$$$
RESTAURANTS				
	under C$15	C$15–C$20	C$21–C$25	over C$25
HOTELS				
	under C$150	C$150–C$200	C$201–C$250	over C$250

Tours

Dark Sky Guides

GUIDED TOURS | A Night Sky Discovery Tour is the most popular offering from this tour company. Hike to a viewing spot, and learn about the legends associated wth constellations from a knowledgeable guide. See stars close up with powerful telescopes. The company also conducts twilight wildlife walks and starry skies strolls. ✉ *Box 56, Waterton Lakes National Park* 🌐 *darkskyguides.ca* 🎫 *From C$20 per person.*

Red Bus Tours

BUS TOURS | Glacier National Park Lodges operates driver-narrated bus tours that cover most areas of the park that are accessible by road. The tour of Going-to-the-Sun Road, a favorite, is conducted in vintage, 1936, red buses with roll-back tops—photo opportunities are plentiful. In addition to tours, which last from a few hours to a full day, hiker shuttles and transfers from the West Glacier train station to Lake McDonald Lodge or the Village Inn are available. You can catch your tour from the doorstep of Glacier Park Lodge or a few steps from Apgar Village Lodge, West Glacier Village, Motel Lake McDonald, and St. Mary Village. Reservations are essential. ☎ *855/733-4522, 303/265-7010* 🌐 *www.glaciernationalparklodges.com/red-bus-tours* 🎫 *Tours from $55; shuttles from $6.*

Sun Tours

BUS TOURS | Tour the park in an air-conditioned coach, and learn from Native American guides who concentrate on how Glacier's features are relevant to the Blackfeet Nation, past and present. These tours depart from East Glacier and the St. Mary Visitor Center. ✉ *29 Glacier Ave., East Glacier Park* ☎ *406/732-9220, 800/786-9220* 🌐 *www.glaciersuntours.com* 🎫 *From $50.*

Visitor Information

PARK CONTACT INFORMATION Glacier Country Montana. ✉ *140 N. Higgens Ave., Suite 204, Missoula* ☎ *800/338-5072* 🌐 *www.glaciermt.com.* **Glacier National Park.** ☎ *406/888-7800* 🌐 *www.nps.gov/glac.* **Waterton Lakes Chamber of Commerce.** 🌐 *www.mywaterton.ca.* **Waterton Lakes National Park.** ☎ *403/859-5133, 403/859-2224 year-round* 🌐 *www.pc.gc.ca/waterton.*

Glacier National Park

The massive peaks of the Continental Divide in northwest Montana are the backbone of Glacier National Park and its sister park in Canada, Waterton Lakes, which together make up the International Peace Park. From their slopes, melting snow and alpine glaciers yield the headwaters of rivers that flow west to the Pacific Ocean, north to the Arctic Ocean, and southeast to the Atlantic Ocean via the Gulf of Mexico. Coniferous forests, thickly vegetated stream bottoms, and green-carpeted meadows provide homes and sustenance for all kinds of wildlife.

Western Glacier National Park

35 miles northeast from Kalispell to the Apgar Visitor Center via U.S. Route 2.

The western side of the park is closest to the airport in the city of Kalispell and has the most amenities. Highlights include the bustling village of West Glacier, Apgar Village, Lake McDonald, and the tiny community of Polebridge. West Glacier Village is just over 2 miles from the Apgar Visitor Center.

HISTORIC SIGHTS

Apgar

TOWN | FAMILY | On the southwest end of Lake McDonald, this tiny village has a few stores, an ice-cream shop, motels, ranger buildings, a campground, and a historic schoolhouse. A store called the Montana House is open year-round, but except for the weekend-only visitor center, no other services remain open from November to mid-May. Across the street from the visitor center, **Apgar Discovery Cabin** is filled with animal posters, kids' activities, and maps. ✉ *2 miles north of west entrance, Glacier National Park* ☎ *406/888–7939.*

PICNIC AREAS

Fish Creek

RESTAURANT—SIGHT | In a forested area adjacent to Lake McDonald, this picnic area has tables, drinking water, and restrooms. Nearby there's a swimming area and several trailheads. ✉ *Glacier National Park* ↔ *Off Camas Rd. before Fish Creek Campground, 4 miles northwest of west entrance.*

Sprague Creek

RESTAURANT—SIGHT | This picnic site on Lake McDonald's eastern shore has tables, restrooms, and drinking water in summer. ✉ *Glacier National Park* ↔ *Off Going-to-the-Sun Rd., adjacent to Sprague Creek Campground, 9 miles northeast of west entrance.*

SCENIC DRIVES

Apgar Village to Polebridge (Camas Road and North Fork Road)

SCENIC DRIVE | The 25-mile journey to the tiny community of Polebridge involves travel along a gravel road that has a few potholes, but the scenery along the north fork of the Flathead River makes up for the bumpy ride. Be on the lookout for wildlife, and be sure to stop for a snack at the Polebridge Mercantile and Bakery.

West Glacier Village to East Glacier Park Village (US-2 E)

SCENIC DRIVE | A paved, 57-mile, two-lane highway follows the middle fork of the Flathead River and connects West Glacier with East Glacier. Enjoy lovely mountain views, stop at Goat Lick to look for mountain goats, or consider having lunch at the Izaak Walton Inn in Essex.

SCENIC STOPS

Goat Lick Overlook

VIEWPOINT | Mountain goats frequent this natural salt lick on a cliff above the middle fork of the Flathead River. Watch the wildlife from an observation stand. ✉ *U.S. 2, 29 miles southeast of West Glacier Village, Glacier National Park.*

Glacier in One Day

It's hard to beat the **Going-to-the-Sun Road** for a one-day trip in Glacier National Park. This itinerary takes you from west to east—if you're starting from St. Mary, take the tour backward. First, however, call the Glacier Park Boat Company (☎ 406/257–2426) to make a reservation for a boat tour on **St. Mary Lake** in the east or **Lake McDonald**, in the west, depending on your trip's end point. Then drive up Going-to-the-Sun Road to **Avalanche Creek Campground** for a 30-minute stroll along the fragrant **Trail of the Cedars.** Afterward, continue driving up—you can see views of waterfalls and wildlife to the left and an awe-inspiring, precipitous drop to the right. At the summit, **Logan Pass**, your arduous climb is rewarded with a gorgeous view of immense peaks, sometimes complemented by the sight of a mountain goat. Stop in at the **Logan Pass Visitor Center**, then take the 1½-mile **Hidden Lake Nature Trail** up to prime wildlife-viewing spots. Have a picnic at the overlook above Hidden Lake. In the afternoon, continue driving east over the mountains. Stop at the **Jackson Glacier Overlook** to view one of the park's largest glaciers. Continue down; eventually the forest thins, the vistas grow broader, and a gradual transition to the high plains begins. When you reach **Rising Sun Campground**, take the one-hour St. Mary Lake boat tour to St. Mary Falls. The Going-to-the-Sun Road is generally closed from mid-September to mid-June.

Lake McDonald

BODY OF WATER | This beautiful, 10-mile-long lake, the parks' largest, is accessible year-round from Going-to-the-Sun Road. Cruise to the middle for a view of the surrounding glacier-clad mountains. You can fish and horseback ride at either end, and in winter, snowshoe and cross-country ski. ✉ *2 miles north of west entrance, Glacier National Park.*

Polebridge

TOWN | On the banks of the North Fork of the Flathead River on Glacier National Park's western edge, this tiny community (population 25) has just one store, one restaurant and saloon, one camp store, and one hostel, yet it is a gem in the wilderness. You can see where a massive wildfire burned up to some of the buildings in 1988 and how quickly new growth has advanced. The entrance station, staffed in summer only, is the gateway to Bowman and Kintla lakes, as well as Logging and Quartz lakes, which are in the backcountry and accessible only by hiking trails. The bakery at the Polebridge Mercantile store is amazing, with huckleberry macaroons or bear claws and hot, gooey cinnamon buns. ✉ *Polebridge.*

TRAILS

Rocky Point Nature Trail

TRAIL | Enjoy fantastic mountain and lake views on this family-friendly, 1.9-mile trail along the western shore of Lake McDonald. *Easy.* ✥ *Trailhead: near Fish Creek Campground.*

VISITOR CENTERS

Apgar Visitor Center

INFO CENTER | **FAMILY** | This is a great first stop if you're entering the park from the west. Here you can get all kinds of information, including maps, permits, books, and the *Junior Ranger* newspaper, and you can check out displays that will help you plan your tour of the park. There is a variety of ranger-led programs including free snowshoe walks in winter.

Snowshoes can be rented for $2 at the visitor center. ✉ *2 miles north of West Glacier in Apgar Village, Glacier National Park* ☎ *406/888–7800.*

Travel Alberta West Glacier Information Center

INFO CENTER | Plan your visit to the Canadian side of the International Peace Park with the help of travel experts at this visitor center in West Glacier. You'll find maps, pamphlets, displays, and bathroom facilities here. ✉ *125 Going-to-the-Sun Rd., West Glacier* ☎ *406/888–5743* ⏲ *Mid-Sept.–mid-May.*

Restaurants

Lake McDonald Lodge Restaurants

$$$ | AMERICAN | In Russell's Fireside Dining Room, take in a great view of the lake while enjoying standards such as pasta, steak, wild game, and salmon; delicious salads; or local favorites like the huckleberry elk burger or the Montana rainbow trout. Many ingredients are locally sourced, and there is a nice selection of cocktails, wine, and craft beer. **Known for:** incredible views of Lake McDonald; hearty regional fare at main restaurant, pizza and burgers at smaller eateries; breakfast and (on request) box lunches in main restaurant. *$ Average main: $22* ✉ *Glacier National Park* ✣ *Going-to-the-Sun Rd., 10 miles north of Apgar* ☎ *406/888–5431, 406/892–2525* 🌐 *www.glaciernationalparklodges.com/dining/lake-mcdonald-lodge* ⏲ *Closed early Oct.–early June.*

Hotels

★ Lake McDonald Lodge

$$$ | HOTEL | On the shores of Lake McDonald, near Apgar and West Glacier, this historic lodge—where public spaces feature massive timbers, stone fireplaces, and animal trophies—is an ideal base for exploring the park's western side. **Pros:** lakeside setting; historic property; close to Apgar, West Glacier, and Going-to-the-Sun Road. **Cons:** rustic; no TV (except in suites) and limited Wi-Fi; small bathrooms. *$ Rooms from: $200* ✉ *Going-to-the-Sun Rd., Glacier National Park* ☎ *855/733–4522, 406/888–5431* 🌐 *www.glaciernationalparklodges.com* *80 units* *No meals.*

Village Inn

$$$ | HOTEL | Listen to waves gently lap the shores of beautiful Lake McDonald at this motel, which is on the National Register of Historic Places and was fully renovated in recent years, so all its rooms have Wi-Fi, new beds, and furnishings that fit with the historic style. **Pros:** great views; convenient Apgar village location; kitchenettes in some rooms. **Cons:** rustic motel; no a/c; no in-room phones. *$ Rooms from: $165* ✉ *Apgar Village, Glacier National Park* ☎ *855/733–4522* 🌐 *www.glaciernationalparklodges.com* ⏲ *Closed Oct. 2–late May* *36 rooms* *No meals.*

Along the Going-to-the-Sun Road

50 miles between Glacier National Park's western and eastern reaches.

The Going-to-the-Sun Road, one of the nation's most beautiful drives, connects Lake McDonald on the western side of Glacier with St. Mary Lake on the east. Turnoffs provide views of the high country and glacier-carved valleys. Consider making the ride in one of the vintage red buses operated by Glacier National Park Lodges (☎ *844/868–7474*). Drivers double as guides, and they can roll back the tops of the vehicles for better views. Logan Pass, elevation 6,646 feet (2,026 meters), sits at the Continental Divide, the highest point on the Going-to-the-Sun Road.

Sights

PICNIC AREAS

Avalanche Creek

RESTAURANT—SIGHT | This picnic area is near two popular day hikes. There are tables, restrooms, and drinking water, and shuttle transfers are available in summer. ✉ *Glacier National Park* ⊕ *Across from Avalanche Creek Campground, off Going-to-the-Sun Rd., 25 km (15.7 miles) northeast of west entrance.*

SCENIC STOPS

The Garden Wall

NATURE SITE | An abrupt and jagged wall of rock juts above the road and is visible for about 10 miles as it follows Logan Creek from just past Avalanche Creek Campground to Logan Pass. ✉ *Going-to-the-Sun Rd., 24–34 miles northeast of West Glacier, Glacier National Park.*

Jackson Glacier Overlook

VIEWPOINT | On the eastern side of the Continental Divide, you come into view of Jackson Glacier looming in a rocky pass across the upper St. Mary River valley. If it isn't covered with snow, you'll see sharp peaks of ice. The glacier is shrinking and may disappear in another 100 years. ✉ *5 miles east of Logan Pass, Glacier National Park.*

Logan Pass

SCENIC DRIVE | At 6,646 feet, this is the park's highest point accessible by motor vehicle. Crowded in July and August, it offers unparalleled views of both sides of the Continental Divide. Mountain goats, bighorn sheep, and grizzly bears frequent the area. The Logan Pass Visitor Center is just east of the pass. ✉ *34 miles east of West Glacier, 18 miles west of St. Mary, Glacier National Park.*

TRAILS

Avalanche Lake Trail

TRAIL | From Avalanche Creek Campground, take this 3-mile trail leading to mountain-ringed Avalanche Lake. The walk is only moderately difficult (it ascends 730 feet), making this one of the park's most accessible backcountry lakes. Crowds fill the parking area and trail during July and August and on sunny weekends in May and June. *Moderate.* ✉ *Glacier National Park* ⊕ *Trailhead: across from Avalanche Creek Campground, 15 miles north of Apgar on Going-to-the-Sun Rd.*

Baring Falls

TRAIL | **FAMILY** | For a nice family hike, try the 1.3-mile path from the Sun Point parking area. It leads to a spruce and Douglas fir woods; cross a log bridge over Baring Creek and you arrive at the base of gushing Baring Falls. *Easy.* ✉ *Glacier National Park* ⊕ *Trailhead 11 miles east of Logan Pass on Going-to-the-Sun Rd., at Sun Point parking area.*

Hidden Lake Nature Trail

TRAIL | Hidden Lake Overlook is an easy, 1½-mile hike from the Logan Pass Visitor Center. Along the way, you'll pass through beautiful alpine meadows known as the Hanging Gardens. Enjoy incredible views of Hidden Lake, Bearhat Mountain, Mt. Cannon, Fusillade Mountain, Gunsight Mountain, and Sperry Glacier. It's common to see mountain goats near the overlook. If you want a challenge, continue hiking all the way down to the edge of the lake—a moderate 5.4-mile round-trip hike. *Easy to moderate.* ✉ *Glacier National Park* ⊕ *Trailhead: behind Logan Pass Visitor Center.*

★ Highline Trail

TRAIL | From the Logan Pass parking lot, hike north along the Garden Wall and just below the craggy Continental Divide. Wildflowers dominate the 7.6 miles to Granite Park Chalet, a National Historic Landmark, where hikers with reservations can overnight. Return to Logan Pass along the same trail or hike down 4½ miles (a 2,500-foot descent) on the Loop Trail. *Moderate.* ✉ *Glacier National Park* ⊕ *Trailhead: at Logan Pass Visitor Center.*

Trail of the Cedars

TRAIL | FAMILY | This ½-mile boardwalk loop through an ancient cedar and hemlock forest is a favorite of families with small children and people with disabilities (it's wheelchair accessible). Interpretive signs describe the habitat and natural history. *Easy.* ✉ *Glacier National Park* ⊕ *Trailhead: across from Avalanche Creek Campground, 15 miles north of Apgar on Going-to-the-Sun Rd.*

VISITOR CENTERS

Logan Pass Visitor Center

INFO CENTER | Built of stone, this center stands sturdy against the severe weather that forces it to close in winter. When it's open, rangers give 10-minute talks on the alpine environment and offer a variety of activities including guided hikes. You can get advice from them and buy books and maps. ✉ *Going-to-the-Sun Rd., Glacier National Park* ⊕ *34 miles east of West Glacier, 18 miles west of St. Mary* ☎ *406/888–7800.*

Hotels

Granite Park Chalet

$$ | B&B/INN | Early tourists used to ride horses 7 to 9 miles through the park each day and stay at a different chalet each night; today, the only way to reach the Granite Park, one of two such chalets that's still standing (Sperry is the other), is via hiking trails. **Pros:** beautiful scenery; secluded; historic lodging. **Cons:** difficult to access; rustic; far from services (and you must bring your own food and water). $ *Rooms from: $115* ✉ *Going-to-the-Sun Rd., Glacier National Park* ⊕ *7.6 miles south of Logan Pass* ☎ *888/345–2649* 🌐 *www.graniteparkchalet.com* ⏲ *Closed mid-Sept.–late June* *12 rooms* 🍴 *No meals.*

Eastern Glacier National Park

Via U.S. routes 2 and 89, St. Mary is 130 miles northeast of Kalispell and 97 miles northeast of Apgar; via the Going-to-the-Sun Road, it's roughly 50 miles between Apgar and St. Mary.

The park's eastern end has historical and cultural significance to the Blackfeet Nation, and much of this region is on tribal lands. East Glacier Park Village is the hub with shops, restaurants, and hotels. Two Medicine Lake, St. Mary Lake, and Swiftcurrent Lake are scenic highlights of this area. The eastern end of the Going-to-the-Sun Road is near the tiny community of St. Mary on the western border of the Blackfeet Indian Reservation.

Sights

PICNIC AREAS

Rising Sun

RESTAURANT—SIGHT | In a cottonwood grove adjacent to St. Mary Lake, this area has tables, restrooms, and drinking water in summer. ✉ *Glacier National Park* ⊕ *Off Going-to-the-Sun Rd., 6 miles southwest of St. Mary Visitor Center.*

SCENIC DRIVES

East Glacier Park Village to Two Medicine Lake and Saint Mary Lake

SCENIC DRIVE | You'll see the striking contrast of prairies and mountains as you travel northwest from East Glacier Park Village to Two Medicine Lake on MT-49. Once you turn onto Two Medicine Road, you'll be heading straight toward snowcapped peaks and lovely Two Medicine Lake. From there, head back out to MT-49 and then to US-89 North to make your way to the town of St. Mary and then onto the Going-to-the-Sun Road to reach St. Mary Lake, the park's second largest. The entire route is 49 miles one-way. End the drive with an additional

The scenic, 50-mile Going-to-the-Sun Road takes about two hours to drive, depending on how often you stop.

stop at Swiftcurrent Lake, and you'll cover about 75 miles total. ✉ *Glacier National Park.*

SCENIC STOPS

Running Eagle Falls (Trick Falls)

BODY OF WATER | Cascading near Two Medicine, these are actually two different waterfalls from two different sources. In spring, when the water level is high, the upper falls join the lower falls for a 40-foot drop into Two Medicine River; in summer, the upper falls dry up, revealing the lower 20-foot falls that start midway down the precipice. ✉ *2 miles east of Two Medicine entrance, Glacier National Park.*

St. Mary Lake

BODY OF WATER | When the breezes calm, the park's second-largest lake mirrors the snowcapped granite peaks that line the St. Mary Valley. To get a good look at the beautiful scenery, follow the Sun Point Nature Trail (closed for renovation in 2016) along the lake's shore. The hike is 1 mile each way. ✉ *1 mile west of St. Mary, Glacier National Park.*

Swiftcurrent Lake

BODY OF WATER | The Many Glacier Hotel is perched on the shores of Swiftcurrent Lake. The views here are some of the park's prettiest, taking in the mountains that rise more than 3,000 feet immediately west of the lake. Scenic boat tours ply the waters and transport hikers to trails that lead to other lakes and glaciers in the park's Many Glacier region.

Two Medicine Valley

NATURE SITE | Rugged, often windy, and always beautiful, the valley is a remote 9-mile drive from Highway 49 and is surrounded by some of the park's most stark, rocky peaks. Near the valley's lake you can rent a canoe, take a narrated boat tour, camp, and hike. Bears frequent the area. The road is closed from late October through late May. ✉ *Two Medicine entrance, 9 miles east of Hwy. 49, Glacier National Park* ☎ *406/888–7800, 406/257–2426 boat tours.*

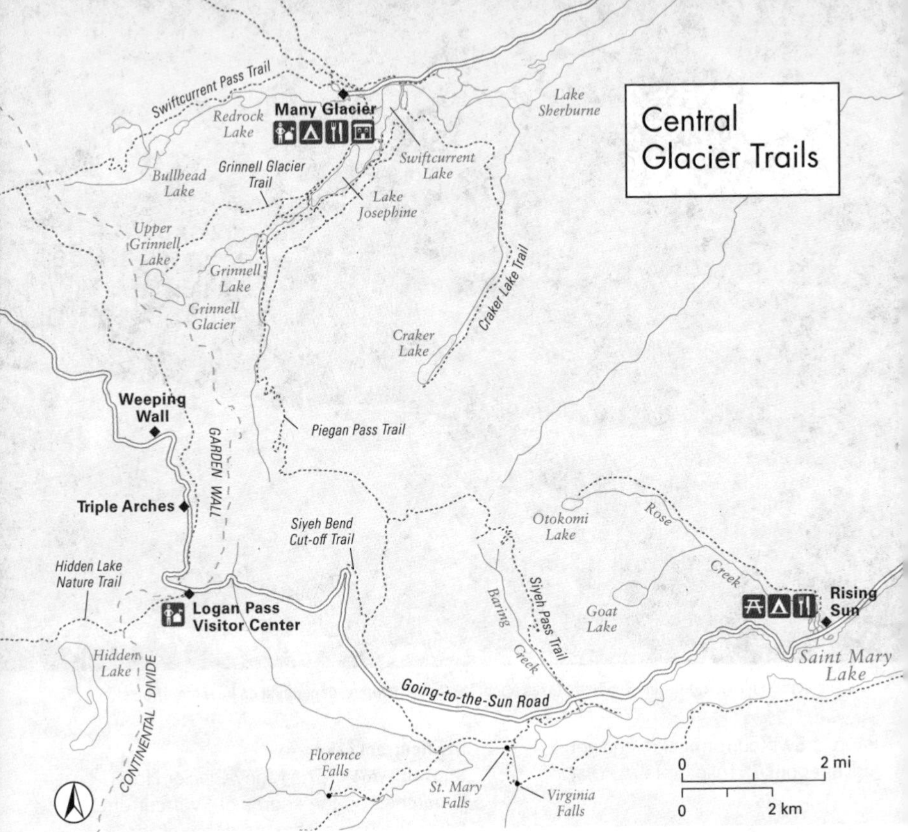

TRAILS

Grinnell Glacier Trail

TRAIL | In 1926, one giant ice mass broke apart to create the Salamander and Grinnell glaciers, which have been shrinking ever since. The 5½-mile trail to Grinnell Glacier, the park's most accessible, is marked by several spectacular viewpoints. You start at Swiftcurrent Lake's picnic area, climb a moraine to Lake Josephine, then climb to the Grinnell Glacier overlook. Halfway up, turn around to see the prairie land to the northeast. You can cut about 2 miles (each way) off the hike by taking scenic boat rides across Swiftcurrent Lake and Lake Josephine. From July to mid-September, a ranger-led hike departs from the Many Glacier Hotel boat dock on most mornings at 8:30. *Difficult.* ✉ *Glacier National Park* ✣ *Trailheads: Swiftcurrent Lake picnic area or Lake Josephine boat dock.*

Iceberg Lake Trail

TRAIL | This moderately strenuous, 9-mile, round-trip hike passes the gushing Ptarmigan Falls, then climbs to its namesake, where icebergs bob in the chilly mountain loch. Mountain goats hang out on sheer cliffs above, bighorn sheep graze in the high mountain meadows, and grizzly bears dig for glacier lily bulbs, grubs, and other delicacies. Rangers lead hikes here almost daily in summer, leaving at 8:30 am. *Moderate.* ✉ *Glacier National Park* ✣ *Trailhead: at Swiftcurrent Inn parking lot, off Many Glacier Rd.*

Sun Point Nature Trail

TRAIL | A stunning waterfall awaits at the end of this well-groomed, 1.3-mile trail along the cliffs and shores of picturesque St. Mary Lake. You can hike one-way and take a boat transfer back. *Easy.* ✉ *Glacier National Park* ✣ *Trailhead: 11 miles east of Logan Pass on Going-to-the-Sun Rd., at Sun Point parking area.*

VISITOR CENTERS

St. Mary Visitor Center

INFO CENTER | Glacier's largest visitor complex has a huge relief map of the park's peaks and valleys and screens a 15-minute orientation video. Exhibits help visitors understand the park from the perspective of its original inhabitants—the Blackfeet, Salish, Kootenai, and Pend d'Orielle peoples. Rangers conduct evening presentations in summer, and the auditorium hosts Native America Speaks programs. The center also has books and maps for sale, backcountry camping permits, and large viewing windows facing the 10-mile-long St. Mary Lake. ✉ *Going-to-the-Sun Rd., off U.S. 89, Glacier National Park* ☎ *406/732–7750.*

Restaurants

Ptarmigan Dining Room

$$$ | **AMERICAN** | The picturesque Ptarmigan's massive windows afford stunning views of Grinnell Point over Swiftcurrent Lake. Known for using regional, sustainably sourced ingredients, the restaurant specializes in dishes such as house-smoked Montana trout, braised bison short ribs, and roasted duck with Flathead cherry chutney. **Known for:** exceptional views; gluten-free and vegetarian options amid the regional fish-and-game mix; huckleberry cobbler (and margaritas!). $ *Average main: $28* ✉ *Many Glacier Rd., Glacier National Park* ☎ *303/265–7010* 🌐 *www.glaciernationalparklodges.com* ⏲ *Closed late Sept.–early June.*

Hotels

Many Glacier Hotel

$$$$ | **HOTEL** | On Swiftcurrent Lake in the park's northeastern section, this is the most isolated of the grand hotels, and—especially if you are able to book a lake-view balcony room—among the most scenic. **Pros:** stunning views from lodge; secluded; good hiking trails nearby. **Cons:** rustic rooms; no TV, limited Internet; the road leading to the lodge is very rough. $ *Rooms from: $207* ✉ *Many Glacier Rd., Glacier National Park* ✣ *12 miles west of Babb* ☎ *855/733–4522, 406/732–4411* 🌐 *www.glaciernationalparklodges.com* ⏲ *Closed mid-Sept.–mid-June* *214 rooms* *No meals.*

Activities

BIKING

Cyclists in Glacier must stay on roads or bike routes and are not permitted on hiking trails or in the backcountry. The one-lane, unpaved Inside North Fork Road from Apgar to Polebridge is well suited to mountain bikers. Two Medicine Road is an intermediate paved route, with a mild grade at the beginning, becoming steeper as you approach Two Medicine Campground. Much of the western half of Going-to-the-Sun Road is closed to bikes from 11 am to 4 pm. Other restrictions apply during peak traffic periods and road construction. Many cyclists enjoy the Going-to-the-Sun Road prior to its opening to vehicular traffic in mid-June. You cannot cycle all the way over the pass in early June, but you can cycle as far as the road is plowed and ride back down without encountering much traffic besides a few snowplows and construction vehicles. You can find thrilling off-road trails just outside the park in Whitefish, which is the closest place to rent bikes.

Glacier Cyclery

BICYCLING | Daily and weekly bike rentals of touring, road, and mountain bikes for all ages and skill levels are available here. The shop also sells bikes, equipment, and attire, and does repairs. Information about local trails is available on its website and in the store. ✉ *326 2nd St. E, Whitefish* ☎ *406/862–6446* 🌐 *www.glaciercyclery.com* 🎫 *From $30.*

Great Northern Cycle & Ski

BICYCLING | You can rent road and mountain bikes from this outfitter, which also services and repairs bikes and sells cycling and skiing attire and gear. ✉ *328 Central Ave., Whitefish* ☎ *406/862–5321* 🌐 *www.gncycleski.com* 🎫 *From $75.*

BOATING AND RAFTING

Glacier has many stunning lakes and rivers, and boating is a popular park activity. Many rafting companies provide adventures along the border of the park on the Middle and North Forks of the Flathead River. The Middle Fork has some excellent white water, while the North Fork has both slow- and fast-moving sections. If you bring your own raft or kayak—watercraft such as Sea-Doos or Jet Skis are not allowed in the park—stop at the Hungry Horse Ranger Station in the Flathead National Forest near West Glacier to obtain a permit. Consider starting at Ousel Creek and floating to West Glacier on the Middle Fork of the Flathead River.

Glacier Park Boat Company

BOATING | This company conducts 45- to 90-minute tours of five lakes. A Lake McDonald cruise takes you from the dock at Lake McDonald Lodge to the middle of the lake for an unparalleled view of the Continental Divide's Garden Wall. The Many Glacier tours on Swiftcurrent Lake and Lake Josephine depart from Many Glacier Hotel and provide views of the Continental Divide. Two Medicine Lake cruises leave from the dock near the ranger station and lead to several trails. St. Mary Lake cruises leave from the launch near the Rising Sun Campground and head to Red Eagle Mountain and other spots. You can also rent small watercraft at Apgar, Lake McDonald, Two Medicine, and Many Glacier. ☎ *406/257–2426* 🌐 *www.glacierparkboats.com* 🎫 *Tours from $22.25, rentals from $15.*

Great Northern Whitewater

BOATING | Sign up for daylong or multiday white-water, kayaking, and fishing trips, or look into the outfitter's River School, where you can learn how to paddleboard, kayak, or even become a rafting guide. This company also rents Swiss-style chalets with views of Glacier's peaks. ✉ *12127 U.S. 2 E, Glacier National Park* ✣ *1 mile south of West Glacier* ☎ *406/387–5340, 800/735–7897* 🌐 *www.greatnorthernresort.com* 🎫 *From $60.*

Wild River Adventures

BOATING | Brave the white water in an inflatable kayak or a traditional raft or enjoy a scenic float with these guys, who will paddle you over the Middle Fork of the Flathead, and peddle you tall tales all the while. They also conduct trail rides and scenic fishing trips on rivers around Glacier National Park. ✉ *11900 U.S. 2 E, 1 mile west of West Glacier, Glacier National Park* ☎ *406/387–9453, 800/700–7056* 🌐 *www.riverwild.com* 🎫 *From $58.*

CAMPING

There are several major campgrounds in Glacier National Park, and excellent backcountry sites for backpackers. Reservations for St. Mary campground are available through the National Park Reservation Service (☎ *877/444–6777 or 518/885–3639* 🌐 *www.recreation.gov*). Reservations may be made up to five months in advance.

Apgar Campground. This popular and large campground on the southern shore of Lake McDonald in the park's western reaches has many activities and services. ✉ *Apgar Rd.* ☎ *406/888–7800.*

Avalanche Creek Campground. This peaceful campground on Going-to-the-Sun Road is shaded by huge red cedars and bordered by Avalanche Creek. ✉ *15.7 miles from west entrance on Going-to-the-Sun Rd.* ☎ *406/888–7800.*

Kintla Lake Campground. Beautiful and remote, this is a trout fisherman's dream. ✉ *14 miles north of Polebridge Ranger Station on Inside North Fork Rd.*

Many Glacier Campground. One of the most beautiful spots in the park is also a favorite for bears. ✉ *Next to Swiftcurrent Motor Inn on Many Glacier Rd.*

Sprague Creek Campground. This sometimes noisy roadside campground for tents, RVs, and truck campers (no towed units) offers spectacular views of the lake and sunsets, and there's fishing from shore. ✉ *Going-to-the-Sun Rd., 1 mile south of Lake McDonald Lodge* ☎ *406/888–7800.*

St. Mary Campground. This large, grassy spot alongside the lake and stream has mountain views and cool breezes. ✉ *Roughly 1 mile from St. Mary entrance to Going-to-the-Sun Rd.* ☎ *406/888–7800.*

EDUCATIONAL PROGRAMS

Glacier Institute

TOUR—SIGHT | **FAMILY** | Based near West Glacier at the Field Camp and on the remote western boundary at the Big Creek Outdoor Education Center, this learning institute offers an array of field courses for kids and adults. Year-round, experts in wildlife biology, native plants, and river ecology lead treks into Glacier's backcountry on daylong and multiday programs. The Youth Adventure Series for children ages 6 to 11 features one-day naturalist courses; preteens and teens can take weeklong trips. Three-day family camps for ages seven and up are also on offer. ✉ *137 Main St., Kalispell* ☎ *406/755–1211, 406/755–7154* 🌐 *www.glacierinstitute.org* 🎫 *From $70.*

★ Ranger-led Activities

TOUR—SIGHT | **FAMILY** | Free ranger-led programs, most of them held daily from July to early September, include guided hikes, group walks, evening talks, historical tours, gaze-at-the-stars parties, and naturalist discussions. For the Native America Speaks program, tribal members share their history and culture through stories, poetry, music, and dance. In winter, guided, two-hour snowshoe treks take place in the Apgar area. Among the activities for children is the **Junior Ranger Program,** for which children between ages 6 and 12 complete fun educational tasks to become Junior Rangers. ☎ *406/888–7800* 🌐 *www.nps.gov/glac/planyourvisit/ranger-led-activities.htm* 🎫 *Free.*

FISHING

Within Glacier there's an almost unlimited range of fishing possibilities, with catch-and-release encouraged. You can fish in most waters of the park, but the best fishing is generally in the least accessible spots. A license is not required inside the park, but you must stop by a park office to pick up a copy of the regulations. The season runs from the third Saturday in May through November. Several companies offer guided fishing trips. ■ **TIP→ Fishing on both the North Fork and the Middle Fork of the Flathead River requires a Montana conservation license ($10), an AIS Prevention Pass ($15), and a Montana fishing license ($25 for two consecutive days or $86 for a season).** They are available at most convenience stores, sports shops, and from the Montana Department of Fish, Wildlife, and Parks (☎ *406/752–5501* 🌐 *www.fwp.mt.gov*).

HIKING

With more than 730 miles of marked trails, Glacier is a hiker's paradise. Trail maps are available at all visitor centers and entrance stations. Before hiking, ask about trail closures due to bear or mountain lion activity. Never hike alone. For backcountry hiking, pick up a permit from park headquarters or the Apgar

Backcountry Permit Center (☎ *406/888–7939*) near Glacier's west entrance.

Glacier Guides

HIKING/WALKING | The exclusive backpacking guide service in Glacier National Park can arrange guided full- or multiday hikes. All are customized to match the skill level of the hikers, and they include stops to identify plants, animals, and habitats. ✉ *11970 U.S. 2 E, West Glacier* ☎ *406/387–5555, 800/521–7238* 🌐 *www.glacierguides.com* 🎫 *From $53.*

HORSEBACK RIDING

Horses are permitted on many trails within the parks; check for seasonal exceptions. Horseback riding is prohibited on paved roads. You can pick up a brochure with suggested routes and lists of outfitters from any visitor center or entrance station. The Sperry Chalet Trail to the view of Sperry Glacier above Lake McDonald is a tough 7-mile climb.

Glacier Gateway Trailrides

HORSEBACK RIDING | On this East Glacier company's trips, a Blackfoot cowboy guides riders on Blackfeet Nation land adjacent to the Two Medicine area of Glacier National Park. Rides, from an hour to all day, climb through aspen groves to high-country views of Dancing Lady and Bison mountains. Special cattle-drive rides are also offered. Riders must be seven or older, and reservations are essential. ✉ *520 3rd Ave. Hwy 49, East Glacier Park* ☎ *406/226–4408 in season, 406/338–5560 off season, 406/226–4409 fax* 🎫 *From $70.*

Swan Mountain Outfitters

HORSEBACK RIDING | The only outfitter that offers horseback riding inside the park, Swan begins its treks at Apgar, Lake McDonald, Many Glacier, and West Glacier. Trips for beginning to advanced riders cover both flat and mountainous terrain. Fishing can also be included, and this operator also offers one- or multiday llama pack trips. Riders must be seven or older and weigh less than 250 pounds. Reservations are essential. ✉ *Coram* ☎ *877/888–5557 central reservations, 406/387–4405 Apgar Corral* 🌐 *www.swanmountainglacier.com* 🎫 *From $50.*

MULTISPORT OUTFITTERS

Glacier Guides and Montana Raft Company

WHITE-WATER RAFTING | Take a raft trip through the Wild-and-Scenic–designated white water of the Middle Fork of the Flathead and combine it with a hike, horseback ride, or barbecue. Other offerings include guided hikes and bike rides, fly-fishing trips, and multiday adventures. The company also offers bike (including e-bike) rentals and fly-fishing lessons. ✉ *11970 U.S. 2 E, 1 mile west of West Glacier, Glacier National Park* ☎ *406/387–5555, 800/521–7238* 🌐 *www.glacierguides.com* 🎫 *From $53.*

Glacier Raft Company and Outdoor Center

BOATING | In addition to running fishing trips, family float rides, saddle-and-paddle adventures, kayak trips, and high-adrenaline white-water adventure rafting excursions, this outfitter will set you up with camping, backpacking, and fishing gear. There's also a full-service fly-fishing shop and outdoor store. You can stay in one of 13 log cabins or a glacier-view home. ✉ *12400 U.S 2 E, West Glacier* ☎ *406/888–5454, 800/235–6781* 🌐 *www.glacierraftco.com* 🎫 *From $65.*

SKIING AND SNOWSHOEING

Cross-country skiing and snowshoeing are increasingly popular in the park. Glacier distributes a free pamphlet entitled *Ski Trails of Glacier National Park,* with 16 noted trails. You can start at Lake McDonald Lodge and ski cross-country up Going-to-the-Sun Road. The 2½-mile Apgar Natural Trail is popular with snowshoers. No restaurants are open in winter in Glacier, but you can pop into Montana House (🌐 *montanahouse.info*) for hot cider, coffee, cookies, and a little shopping. The park website (🌐 *home.nps.gov/applications/glac/ski/xcski.htm*) has ski trail maps.

Glacier Adventure Guides
KIING/SNOWBOARDING | This outfit leads full- and multiday guided snowshoe trips on scenic winter trails. On overnight trips, you stay in igloos and snow caves. In summer, the company conducts guided hiking and rock-climbing adventures outside the park. ✉ *Glacier National Park* ☎ *877/735–9514, 406/892–2173* 🌐 *www.glacieradventureguides.com* 🎫 *From $180.*

Izaak Walton Inn
SKIING/SNOWBOARDING | Just outside the southern edge of the park, this inn has more than 30 miles of groomed cross-country ski trails on its property. It offers equipment rentals and lessons, as well as guided ski and snowshoe tours inside the park. Inn guests can ski for free, but others must purchase a ski pass. The inn is one of the few places in the area that is both open in winter and accessible by Amtrak train, which saves you the worry of driving on icy mountain roads. ✉ *290 Izaak Walton Inn Rd., Essex* ✥ *Off U.S. 2* ☎ *406/888–5700* 🌐 *www.izaakwaltoninn.com/activities/winter-activities* 🎫 *From $15.*

Waterton Lakes National Park

A World Heritage Site, Waterton Lakes National Park represents the meeting of two worlds—the flatlands of the prairie and the abrupt upthrust of the mountains—squeezing an unusual mix of wildlife, flora, and climate zones into its 505 square km (200 square miles). The quaint alpine town of Waterton lies just off the shore of Upper Waterton Lake, and the historic Prince of Wales Hotel sits high on a hill overlooking it all. The park is quieter than most of the other Rocky Mountain parks, but it is just as beautiful and diverse. Visitors coming from Glacier National Park typically reach Waterton via the seasonal Chief Mountain Highway border crossing, 67 miles northwest of East Glacier Park Village. It's also possible to access the park via the border crossing at Carway, which is open year-round.

Shrinking Glaciers

The effects of climate change are on full display at Glacier National Park. In 1850, there were approximately 150 glaciers here; as of 2010, only 25 remained. Some climate scientists predict that by 2050 even these will be gone.

In September 2017, the Kenow Wildfire burned 19,303 hectares (47,698 acres) of parkland, greatly affecting park infrastructure, including more than 80% of its hiking trail network. Through the efforts of brave firefighters, the townsite was virtually untouched. In 2018, the Boundary Wildfire burned the Boundary Creek Valley region in Glacier National Park and blazed across the U.S.–Canada border into Waterton Lakes National Park. Wildfires play an important role in a forest ecosystem, though, and the park is already recovering. Check the website to learn the status of trails before heading out.

Sights

HISTORIC SIGHTS

First Oil Well in Western Canada
HISTORIC SITE | Alberta is known worldwide for its oil and gas production, and the first oil well in western Canada was established in 1902 in what is now the park. Stop at this National Historic Site to explore the wellheads, drilling equipment, and remains of the Oil City boomtown. ✉ *Waterton Lakes National Park* ✥ *Watch for sign 7.7 km (4.8 miles) up the Akamina Pkwy.* 🎫 *Free.*

Waterton in One Day

Begin your day with a stop at the **Waterton Information Centre** to pick up free maps and information about interpretive programs and schedules.

Stop at the **Bear's Hump Trailhead,** where you can enjoy a short and invigorating, 1.4-km (0.9-mile) hike to a beautiful scenic overlook. Afterward, drive up the hill to the historic **Prince of Wales Hotel** to enjoy the view from the hillside behind the hotel.

Next, visit **Waterton Townsite** for an early lunch. Afterward, walk the easy 3-km (2-mile) **Townsite Loop Trail,** stopping to view **Cameron Falls** and explore the trail behind the falls. Learn more about the International Peace Park and its flora and fauna by reading the interpretive signs at Peace Park Point near the marina.

End the day with a scenic two-hour **Waterton Inter-Nation Shoreline Cruise** across the border to **Goat Haunt Ranger Station** and back.

Prince of Wales Hotel

HISTORIC SITE | Named for the prince who later became King Edward VIII, this hotel was constructed between 1926 and 1927 and was designated a National Historic Site in 1995. Take in the magnificent view from the ridge outside the hotel, or pop inside to enjoy the vista from the comfort of the expansive lobby, where afternoon tea is served. ✉ *Off Hwy. 5, Waterton Lakes National Park* ☎ *848/868–7474, 403/236–3400* 🌐 *www.glacierparkcollection.com/lodging/prince-of-wales-hotel* 🎫 *Free* 🕙 *Closed late-Sept.–mid-May.*

PICNIC AREAS

Waterton's picnic sites are in some of the most scenic areas of the park. All are equipped with tables and washroom facilities, and most have a water source nearby. Some sites are equipped with barbecues or outdoor fire pits, and you can buy firewood in the village.

Cameron Bay

RESTAURANT—SIGHT | There are several picnic shelters along Upper Waterton Lake in the Cameron Bay area. These lakefront sites are equipped with tables, water taps, and wood-burning stoves. ✉ *Waterton Townsite* ✥ *Along Upper Waterton Lake.*

SCENIC DRIVES

Akamina Parkway

BODY OF WATER | Take this winding, 16-km (10-mile) road up to Cameron Lake, but drive slowly and watch for wildlife: it's common to see bears along the way. At the lake you will find a relatively flat, paved, 1.6-km (1-mile) trail that hugs the western shore and makes a nice walk. Bring your binoculars. Grizzly bears are often spotted on the lower slopes of the mountains at the far end of the lake. ✉ *Waterton Lakes National Park.*

Red Rock Parkway

SCENIC DRIVE | The 15-km (9-mile) route takes you from the prairie up the Blakiston Valley to Red Rock Canyon, where water has cut through the earth, exposing red sedimentary rock. It's common to see bears just off the road, especially in autumn, when the berries are ripe. ✉ *Waterton Lakes National Park.*

SCENIC STOPS

Cameron Lake

BODY OF WATER | The jewel of Waterton, Cameron Lake sits in a land of glacially carved cirques (steep-walled basins). In summer, hundreds of varieties of alpine wildflowers fill the area, including 22 kinds of wild orchids. Canoes, rowboats, kayaks, and fishing gear can be rented here. ✉ *Akamina Pkwy., 13 km (8 miles) southwest of Waterton Townsite, Waterton Lakes National Park.*

Goat Haunt Ranger Station

NATURE PRESERVE | Reached only by foot trail, private boat, or tour boat from Waterton Townsite, this spot on the U.S. end of Waterton Lake is the stomping ground for mountain goats, moose, grizzlies, and black bears. It is also the official border crossing for the U.S.side of Waterton Lake. In recent years, the crossing has not been staffed by U.S. Customs personnel, and, consequently, tour boats do not allow passengers to disembark at Goat Haunt as they once did. If you want to explore the trails on this end of the lake, you will need to hike or paddle in on your own. Check in before arrival by using the CBP ROAM app. Visitors to this area must carry their passports and proof of ROAM trip approval.The hikes on the U.S. side of the lake were unaffected by the wildfires of recent years. ✉ *Southern end of Waterton Lake, Waterton Lakes National Park* ☎ *403/859–2362* 🌐 *www.watertoncruise.com* 🎫 *Tour boat C$51.*

Waterton Townsite

TOWN | In roughly the park's geographic center, this low-key townsite swells with tourists in summer, and restaurants and shops open to serve them. In winter only a few motels are open, and services are limited. ✉ *Waterton Townsite.*

TRAILS

Bear's Hump Trail

TRAIL | This steep, 2.8-km (1.4-mile) trail climbs to an overlook with a great view of Upper Waterton Lake and the townsite. *Moderate.* ✉ *Waterton Lakes National Park* ✥ *Trailhead: across from Prince of Wales access road. Behind site of old visitor information center.*

Bertha Lake Trail

TRAIL | This 11.4-km (7.1-mile) round-trip trail leads from Waterton Townsite through a Douglas fir forest to a beautiful overlook of Upper Waterton Lake, and on to Lower Bertha Falls. From there, a steeper climb takes you past Upper Bertha Falls to Bertha Lake. In June, the wildflowers along the trail are stunning. *Moderate.* ✉ *Waterton Lakes National Park* ✥ *Trailhead: at parking lot off Evergreen Ave., west of Townsite Campground.*

Blakiston Falls

TRAIL | A 2-km (1.2-mi) round-trip hike will take you from Red Rock Canyon to Blakiston Falls. Several viewpoints overlook the falls. *Easy* ✉ *Waterton Lakes National Park* ✥ *Trailhead: at Red Rock Canyon lower parking lot. Cross the bridge over Red Rock Creek, then turn left across the bridge over Bauerman Creek, and turn right to follow the trail.*

Cameron Lake Shore Trail

TRAIL | **FAMILY** | Relatively flat and paved, this 1.6-km (1-mile) one-way trail offers a peaceful hike. Look for wildflowers along the shoreline and grizzlies on the lower slopes of the mountains at the far end of the lake. *Easy.* ✉ *Waterton Lakes National Park* ✥ *Trailhead: at lakeshore in front of parking lot, 13 km (8 miles) southwest of Waterton Townsite.*

Crandell Lake Trail

TRAIL | This 2½-km (1½-mile) trail winds through fragrant pine forest, ending at a popular mountain lake. *Easy.* ✉ *Waterton Lakes National Park* ✥ *Trailhead: about halfway up Akamina Pkwy.*

★ Crypt Lake Trail

TRAIL | Awe-inspiring and strenuous, this 17.2-km (11-mile) round-trip trail is one of the most stunning hikes in the Canadian

Rockies. Conquering the trail involves taking a boat taxi across Waterton Lake, climbing 700 meters (2,300 feet), crawling through a tunnel nearly 30 meters (100 feet) long, and scrambling across a sheer rock face. The reward, and well worth it: views of a 183-meter (600-foot) cascading waterfall and the turquoise waters of Crypt Lake. This hike was completely untouched by the wildfires of recent years. *Difficult.* ✉ *Waterton Lakes National Park* ✥ *Trailhead: at Crypt Landing, accessed by ferry from Waterton Townsite.*

VISITOR CENTERS

Waterton Information Centre

INFO CENTER | The original Waterton Information Centre was destroyed by the Kenow Wildfire in 2017, and a new building is under construction. Until it's finished, the visitor center is in the Lion's Hall in the Waterton Townsite. Stop in to pick up brochures, maps, and books. You can also pick up the booklet for the free Xplorer Program for kids between ages 6 and 11. Park interpreters are on hand to answer questions and give directions. ✉ *Waterton Rd., before townsite, Waterton Lakes National Park* ☎ *403/859–5133.*

Restaurants

Lakeside Chophouse

$$$$ | STEAKHOUSE | Grab a window seat or a spot on the patio to enjoy the spectacular view from Waterton's only lakefront restaurant. This is the place in the park for a steak dinner—locally produced Alberta beef plays a starring role on the globally inspired menu. **Known for:** great steaks; lakefront views; all-day service. $ *Average main: C$29* ✉ *Bayshore Inn, 111 Waterton Ave., Waterton Townsite* ☎ *888/527–9555, 403/859–2211* 🌐 *www.bayshoreinn.com.*

Thirsty Bear Kitchen & Bar

$$ | AMERICAN | Waterton's only gastropub is the place for live music most weekends and casual eats anytime. The nachos here are the best in town, and there's a wide selection of burgers, sandwiches, and wraps—all served with salad or fries. **Known for:** live music and a dance floor; great casual dining; fun atmosphere with big-screen TVs, pool tables, and foosball. $ *Average main: C$20* ✉ *111 Waterton Ave., Waterton Townsite* ☎ *403/859–2211 Ext. 309* 🌐 *www.thirstybearwaterton.com* ⊙ *Closed mid-Oct.–mid-May.*

Wieners of Waterton

$ | HOT DOG | FAMILY | If there is such a thing as a gourmet hot dog, then this is the place to find it. The buns here are baked fresh daily, and the all-beef wieners and smokies are sourced locally with one exception: the genuine Nathan's dogs are shipped from New York City. **Known for:** gourmet hot dogs; interesting toppings; fun menu. $ *Average main: C$9* ✉ *301 Wildflower Ave., Waterton Townsite* ☎ *403/859–0007* 🌐 *www.wienersofwaterton.com* ⊙ *Closed Oct.–Apr.*

Hotels

Bayshore Inn

$$$$ | HOTEL | Right in town and on the shores of Waterton Lake, this inn has a lot going for it: lovely views, the only on-site spa in Waterton, multiple dining options, and easy access to many services. **Pros:** only lakefront accommodation in Waterton; plenty of on-site amenities; great townsite location. **Cons:** older-style hotel; rustic motor inn; can sometimes hear noise between rooms. $ *Rooms from: C$269* ✉ *111 Waterton Ave., Waterton Townsite* ☎ *888/527–9555, 403/859–2211* 🌐 *www.bayshoreinn.com* ⊙ *Closed mid-Oct.–Apr.* 🛏 *70 rooms* 🍽 *No meals.*

Bear Mountain Motel

$ | HOTEL | This classic, 1960s motel offers a variety of affordable accommodations that have painted cinder-block walls, wood-beam ceilings, and small bathrooms with shower stalls. **Pros:** most affordable accommodation in Waterton; clean, comfortable, and very basic; family-run motel right in townsite. **Cons:** noise can be an issue with the old cinder-block construction; closed in winter; no in-room coffee or tea (available in main office). *Rooms from: C$149* *208 Mount View Rd., Waterton Townsite* *403/859–2366* *bearmountainmotel.com* *Closed Oct.–Apr.* *36 rooms* *No meals.*

Prince of Wales Hotel

$$$$ | **HOTEL** | A high steeple crowns this iconic, 1920s hotel, which is fantastically ornamented with eaves, balconies, and turrets; is perched between two lakes with a high-mountain backdrop; and has a lobby where two-story windows capture the views. **Pros:** spectacular valley and townsite views; historic property; bellmen wear kilts. **Cons:** very rustic rooms; no TVs; no a/c. *Rooms from: C$259* *Off Hwy. 5, Waterton Lakes National Park* *Turn left at marked access road at top of hill just before village* *844/868–7474, 403/859–2231* *www.glacierparkcollection.com/lodging/prince-of-wales-hotel* *Closed late Sept.–mid-May* *86 rooms* *No meals.*

Waterton Glacier Suites

$$$$ | **HOTEL** | In the heart of the townsite, this all-suite property is within walking distance of restaurants, shopping, and the dock on beautiful Waterton Lake. **Pros:** modern suites with mini-refrigerators and a/c; open year-round; convenient location. **Cons:** no views; pullout sofas uncomfortable; no on-site breakfast. *Rooms from: C$319* *107 Wildflower Ave., Waterton Townsite* *403/859–2004, 866/621–3330* *www.watertonsuites.com* *26 rooms* *No meals.*

Activities

The park contains numerous short hikes for day-trippers and some longer treks for backpackers. Upper and Middle Waterton and Cameron lakes provide peaceful havens for boaters. A tour boat cruises Upper Waterton Lake, crossing the U.S.–Canada border, and the winds that rake across that lake create an exciting ride for windsurfers—bring a wet suit, though; the water remains numbingly cold throughout summer.

BIKING

Bikes are allowed on some trails, such as the 3-km (2-mile) **Townsite Loop Trail.** A great family bike trail is the paved, 6.9-km (4.3-mile) one-way **Kootenai Brown Trail,** which edges the lakes and leads from the townsite to the park gates. A ride on mildly sloping **Red Rock Canyon Road** isn't too difficult (once you get past the first hill). The **Crandell Loop** trail provides a slightly more challenging ride for mountain bikers.

Blakiston and Company

BICYCLING | Rent electric bikes, canoes, kayaks, and stand-up paddleboards through this company. *102 Mountain Rd., Waterton Townsite* *800/456–0772* *www.blakistonandcompany.com.*

Pat's Waterton

BICYCLING | **FAMILY** | Choose from surrey, mountain, and e-bikes or motorized scooters at Pat's, which also rents tennis rackets, strollers, coolers, life jackets, hiking poles, bear spray, and binoculars. *224 Mt. View Rd., Waterton Townsite* *403/859–2266* *www.patswaterton.com* *From $15.*

BOATING

Nonmotorized boats can be rented at Cameron Lake in summer; private craft can be used on Upper and Middle Waterton lakes.

Cameron Lake Boat Rentals
BOATING | Rent canoes, kayaks, rowboats, pedal boats, and stand-up paddleboards right at the docks on Cameron Lake. You can also buy tackle and rent fishing rods. ✉ *Waterton Lakes National Park* ✣ *At the boat docks at Cameron Lake, 16 km (10 miles) southwest of the townsite* ☎ *403/627–6443* 🌐 *www.cameronlake-boatrentals.com.*

Waterton Inter-Nation Shoreline Cruise Co.
BOATING | This company's two-hour round-trip boat tour along Upper Waterton Lake from Waterton Townsite to Goat Haunt Ranger Station is one of the most popular activities in Waterton. The narrated tour passes scenic bays, sheer cliffs, and snow-clad peaks. This company also offers a shuttle service for the Crypt Lake and Vimy Peak hikes. ✉ *Waterton Townsite Marina, northwest corner of Waterton Lake near Bayshore Inn, Waterton Lakes National Park* ☎ *403/859–2362, 403/859–2362* 🌐 *www.watertoncruise.com* 🎟 *C$55.*

CAMPING

Parks Canada operates a handful of campgrounds (though one of them, the Crandell, was destroyed by the 2017 wildfire) that range from fully serviced to unserviced sites. There are also some backcountry campsites. Visitors can prebook campsites for a fee of C$11 online or C$13.50 by phone. The reservation service is available at 🌐 *www.reservation.parkscanada.gc.ca* or by phone at ☎ *877/737–3783.*

Waterton Townsite Campground. Though the campground is busy and windy, sites here are grassy and flat with access to kitchen shelters and have views down the lake into the U.S. part of the Peace Park. ✉ *Waterton and Vimy Aves.* ☎ *877/737–3783.*

EDUCATIONAL PROGRAMS

Evening interpretive programs at Waterton Lakes National Park are offered from late June until Labor Day at the Falls Theatre, near Cameron Falls, and the townsite campground. These one-hour sessions begin at 8. A guided International Peace Park hike is held every Wednesday and Saturday in July and August. The 14-km (9-mile) hike begins at the Bertha trailhead and is led by Canadian and American park interpreters. You eat lunch at the International Border before continuing on to Goat Haunt in Glacier National Park, Montana, and returning to Waterton via boat. A fee is charged for the return boat trip. You must preregister for this hike at the Waterton Information Centre.

HIKING

There are 225 km (191 miles) of trails in Waterton Lakes that range in difficulty from short strolls to strenuous treks. Some trails connect with the trail systems of Glacier and British Columbia's Akamina-Kishenina Provincial Park. The wildflowers in June are particularly stunning along most trails. In 2017, the Kenow Wildfire damaged more than 80% of the trails in Waterton Lakes National Park. The Crypt Lake and the hikes on the U.S. side of the lake that depart from the Goat Haunt Ranger Station were unaffected by the fire. Trails in other parts of the park received varying amounts of damage. Consult the park website for the latest trail reports. *Hiking Glacier and Waterton National Parks,* by Erik Molvar, has detailed information including pictures and GPS-compatible maps for 60 of the best hiking trails in both parks.

HORSEBACK RIDING

Rolling hills, grasslands, and rugged mountains make riding in Waterton Lakes a real pleasure. Scenery, wildlife, and wildflowers are easily viewed from the saddle, and horses are permitted on many park trails.

Family Fun

Opportunities for family fun at Glacier and Waterton include canoeing, climbing, hiking, biking, and touring.

Canoe Lake McDonald. Rent a canoe and paddle around the lake. If you work up a sweat, jump in. *Glacier.*

Climb Bear's Hump. This 2.8-km (1.7-mile) trail winds up a mountainside to an overlook with a great view of Upper Waterton Lake and the townsite. *Waterton.*

Hike Hidden Lake Nature Trail. A 2.4-km (1½-mile) trail runs uphill from Logan Pass to the Hidden Lake Overlook, yielding beautiful views of the lake and McDonald Valley. In spring, ribbons of water pour off the rocks surrounding the lake. A boardwalk protects the abundant wildflowers and spongy tundra on the way. *Glacier.*

Surrey Around Town. Rent a surrey bike at Pat's Waterton store and pedal around the townsite. A surrey bike has a flat seat and a canopy and can hold up to three people. *Waterton.*

Tour Going-to-the Sun in a Vintage Bus. With amazing vistas and many stops for photo ops, the Going-to-the-Sun Road tour in a vintage bus is a beloved park tradition. *Glacier.*

Alpine Stables

HORSEBACK RIDING | At these family-owned stables you can arrange hour-long trail rides and full-day guided excursions within the park, as well as multiday pack trips through the Rockies and foothills. They are open May through September. ✉ *Waterton Lakes National Park* ☎ *403/859–2462, 403/653–2449* 🌐 *www.alpinestables.com* 🎫 *From C$45.*

Nearby Towns

You could easily spend a week exploring Waterton and Glacier, but you may wish to take advantage of hotels, restaurants, sights, and outfitters in nearby towns. Outside Glacier National Park's western reaches and 2½ miles south of the Apgar Visitor Center is the gateway community of **West Glacier;** 27 miles to its southeast is **Essex.** Slightly farther afield to the southwest of West Glacier are **Columbia Falls** and **Whitefish.** Just over 40 miles southeast of the St. Mary Visitor Center on the east side of the park is the gateway of **East Glacier Park Village.** To the northeast, roughly midway between the visitor center and East Glacier, is the interesting town of **Browning.** Note that there are Amtrak stations in Whitefish, West Glacier, Essex, East Glacier Park Village, and Browning.

West Glacier

2½ miles south of Glacier National Park's Apgar Visitor Center.

The green waters of the Flathead River's Middle Fork and several top-notch outfitters make West Glacier an ideal base for river sports such as rafting, kayaking and fishing. West Glacier is one of the stops on Amtrak's nortthern route, so you can get there by train or by motor vehicle. Some accommodations and shops are open in winter, and there are snowshoe and cross-country ski trails nearby.

VISITOR INFORMATION

Glacier Area Information Center

Located in the Belton Train Depot in West Glacier, the Glacier National Park Conservancy's historic bookstore and gift shop doubles as an information center. It is open daily from Memorial Day through Labor Day. ✉ *12544 U.S. Hwy. 2 E, West Glacier* ☎ *406/888–5756* 🌐 *glacier.org.*

★ Belton Chalet Grill Dining Room

$$$$ | **AMERICAN** | The hotel's handsome restaurant still has its original wainscoting and leaded-glass windows, but in fine weather, ask to dine on the deck outside to watch the sun set behind the mountains. Bison meat loaf has been a signature dish for years, but you'll also find other unique dishes like confit duck leg with flathead cherries; house-made fettuccine with fennel, olives, and shitake mushrooms; or lamb with huckleberry jus. **Known for:** bison meat loaf; berry crisp; top-notch food. Ⓢ *Average main: $32* ✉ *12575 U.S. Hwy. 2 E, next to railroad station, West Glacier* ☎ *406/888–5000, 844/868–7474 toll free* 🌐 *www.glacierparkcollection.com/lodging/belton-chalet/dining* ⏲ *Closed early Oct.–early Dec. and late Mar.–late May. Closed Mon.–Thurs. early Dec.–late Mar. (brunch only on Sun. Dec.–Mar.). No lunch.*

Josephine's Bar & Kitchen

$ | **AMERICAN** | This seasonal restaurant and bar—named for Josephine Doody, "the bootleg lady of Glacier National Park"—is a very casual spot: you order at a window beside the bar, and they bring the food to your table. For a starter, consider the fried green tomatoes with truffle caper aioli balsamic reduction; unique and delicious sandwich options include a prime rib with red onion marmalade, a smoked trout cake po' boy, and a bison gyro served in a warm pita. **Known for:** innovative cocktails; fried green tomatoes; local hangout. Ⓢ *Average main: $12* ✉ *10245 Hwy. 2 E, Coram* ☎ *406/300–4755* 🌐 *www.josephinesbar.com* ⏲ *Closed mid-Oct.–mid-May.*

Belton Chalet

$$$ | **HOTEL** | This carefully restored, 1910 railroad hotel, the original winter headquarters for the park, has a great location just outside the West Glacier entrance and cozy, bright rooms with period furnishings and original woodwork. **Pros:** excellent restaurant; wraparound decks with lovely views; historic property. **Cons:** train noise; rustic; no a/c or TVs. Ⓢ *Rooms from: $200* ✉ *12575 U.S. Hwy. 2 E, West Glacier* ☎ *406/888–5000, 888/235–8665, 406/888-5005* 🌐 *www.beltonchalet.com* *27 rooms* *Breakfast.*

Glacier Guides Lodge

$$$$ | **HOTEL** | Tucked away in a forested canyon, this rustic, eco-friendly lodge is within walking distance of downtown restaurants and other amenities. **Pros:** secluded location in West Glacier; delicious, included breakfast; mini-refrigerators in rooms. **Cons:** difficult to find; Wi-Fi can be slow; maximum 2 people per guest room. Ⓢ *Rooms from: $259* ✉ *120 Highline Blvd., West Glacier* ☎ *800/521–7238 toll free, 406/387–5555* 🌐 *glacierguides.com/lodging/glacier-guides-lodge* ⏲ *Closed mid-Oct.–Apr.* *13 units* *Free Breakfast.*

Glacier Outdoor Center Cabins

$$$$ | **RENTAL** | **FAMILY** | Five minutes from the entrance to West Glacier, these cozy two-bedroom cabins can accommodate up to 10 people and have living rooms, barbecues, private decks, and fully equipped kitchens. **Pros:** great for families; can accommodate large groups; kitchens in cabins. **Cons:** outside the townsite; no restaurant; on the pricey side. Ⓢ *Rooms from: $299* ✉ *12400 U.S. 2 E, West Glacier* ☎ *800/235–6781,*

406/888–5454, *www.glacierraftco.com* *Cabins closed Nov.–Apr.; lodge and sister Homestead property open year-round* *26 units* *No meals.*

Essex

27 miles southeast of West Glacier; 29 miles southeast of Apgar Visitor Center.

You can reach Essex by car or by train, as the tiny, unincorporated community is the site of the main rail terminal for park visitors. The historic Izaak Walton Inn sits right beside the tracks, and you can rent vehicles through its front desk (with advance reservations). Hiking and cross-country ski trails in the Great Bear Wilderness are nearby, as is the Walton Goat Lick Overlook, a great place to watch mountain goats. Beyond all this, there aren't many amenities or services.

Hotels

Izaak Walton Inn

$$$ | **HOTEL** | This historic lodge just south of Glacier National Park is popular with railway buffs: not only was it originally built to house rail workers (and has the industry memorabilia decor to prove it), but its lodging options include refurbished train cars, cabooses, and even a locomotive in addition to classic lodge rooms and family cabins. **Pros:** good location between East and West Glacier; Amtrak station right beside the inn; fun railway theme. **Cons:** train noise can be a problem; no phones or TVs in rooms; no cell reception and Wi-Fi signal is weak. *Rooms from: $169* *290 Izaak Walton Inn Rd., off U.S. Hwy. 2, Essex* *406/888–5700, 406/888–5200* *www.izaakwaltoninn.com* *48 units* *No meals.*

Browning

28 miles southeast of Glacier National Park's St. Mary Visitor Center.

Browning is the center of the Blackfeet Nation, whose name is thought to derive from the color of its members' painted or dyed black moccasins. At 1.5 million acres, the Blackfeet Indian Reservation is home to Montana's largest tribe by population, with about 13,000 enrolled members. The city's main attractions are the Museum of the Plains Indian, the Blackfeet Heritage Center and Art Gallery, Glacier Peaks Casino, and the Pikuni Gift Shop. If you want to really experience the culture, visit during the annual North American Indian Days celebration, which is held the second weekend in July, or during Heart Butte Indian Days the second weekend in August.

VISITOR INFORMATION

Blackfeet Country Visitor Information. *16 Old Person Rd., Browning* *406/338–7406* *blackfeetcountry.com.*

Sights

Museum of the Plains Indian

MUSEUM | The impressive collection of Blackfeet artifacts at this museum includes clothing, saddlebags, and artwork. *19 Museum Loop, Browning* *406/338–2230* *www.doi.gov/iacb/museum-plains-indian* *$5 June–Sept., free Oct.–May.*

East Glacier Park Village

13½ miles southwest of Browning; 42 miles southeast of St. Mary Visitor Center.

Early tourists to Glacier National Park first stopped in East Glacier, where the Great Northern Railway had established a station. Although most people coming from the east now enter by car, some still make the journey on Amtrak's *Empire Builder* train from Whitefish. With quiet, secluded surroundings and the lovely Glacier Park Lodge, East Glacier makes a great base for exploring the national park. You can golf on the oldest green grass golf course in Montana, enjoy a variety of dining options, and explore hundreds of miles of hiking trails.

VISITOR INFORMATION

East Glacier Chamber of Commerce. *909 Hwy. 49 N, East Glacier Park 406/226-4403.*

Restaurants

Serrano's

$$ | **MEXICAN** | Mexican food in Montana! After a day on the dusty trail, Serrano's is a treat whether dining inside or on the back patio. **Known for:** excellent Mexican food; fabulous margaritas; huckleberry carrot cake. *Average main: $15 29 Dawson Ave., East Glacier Park 406/226-9392 www.serranosmexican.com Closed Oct.–Apr.*

Summit Mountain Steakhouse

$$$ | **STEAKHOUSE** | The slightly off-the-beaten-track drive to this steak house southwest of East Glacier is well worth it. The small dining room has large windows with mountain views that are shared by an outdoor patio with additional seating. **Known for:** grilled steaks and handmade hamburgers; huckleberry cheesecake; great views. *Average main: $26 16900 U.S. 2 W, East Glacier Park 406/226-9319 www.summitmtnlodge.com Closed Mon. Closed mid-Sept.–mid-June. No lunch No credit cards.*

Hotels

Glacier Park Lodge

$$$ | **HOTEL** | Just east of the park, across from the Amtrak station, this beautiful full-service hotel built in 1913 is supported by 500- to 800-year-old fir and 3-foot-thick cedar logs. **Pros:** golf course; scenic location; lots of activities. **Cons:** small bathrooms; no elevator; no a/c or TV. *Rooms from: $179 Off U.S. 2, East Glacier Park 406/892-2525, 844/868-7474 www.glacierparkcollection.com/lodging/glacier-park-lodge Closed late Sept.–May 161 rooms No meals.*

Chapter 6

MISSOULA, KALISPELL, AND NORTHWEST MONTANA

Updated by
Jeff Gailus

Sights	Restaurants	Hotels	Shopping	Nightlife
★★★☆☆	★★★☆☆	★★★☆☆	★★☆☆☆	★★☆☆☆

WELCOME TO MISSOULA, KALISPELL, AND NORTHWEST MONTANA

TOP REASONS TO GO

★ **Dive into downtown Missoula:** The city's thriving historic core is teeming with cultural events, eateries, concerts, craft breweries, festivals, boutiques, and farmers' markets.

★ **Enjoy the great outdoors at Big Mountain:** Its picturesque slopes are awash in wildflowers in summer and entertain skiers and snowboarders in winter.

★ **Bring on the bison:** The National Bison Range comes alive in the spring with all the new babies.

★ **Get wet at Flathead Lake:** Even if you only dip your toes into the crystalline waters, the spectacular views at this mountain-lined lake are sure to please.

★ **Take the road less traveled:** Ride a horse, ski, or hike into the beautiful, unspoiled backcountry.

Much of the region's population is concentrated in the Bitterroot, Missoula, Mission, and Flathead valleys. Missoula, home of the University of Montana, is the business and shopping center full of good restaurants and breweries. In friendly towns such as Hamilton, Stevensville, Kalispell, Polson, and Whitefish you'll find well-preserved historic sites and small yet resourceful museums. However, civilization here perches on the edge of seemingly endless wilderness: visit this part of the world for its wildlife, water, and natural beauty.

1 **Flathead Reservation.** Home to the Salish and Kootenai tribes.

2 **Flathead Lake.** Largest freshwater lake west of the Mississippi River.

3 **Kalispell.** Heart of the Flathead Valley.

4 **Whitefish.** Summer and winter recreation destination.

5 **Columbia Falls.** Gateway to Glacier National Park.

6 **Seeley Lake.** Paddle the Clearwater Canoe Trail.

7 **Holland Lake.** Crystal-clear water in a majestic setting.

8 **Bob Marshall Wilderness.** 1.5 million acres of untrammeled nature.

9 **Missoula.** Cultural center of northwest Montana.

10 **Stevensville.** Quaint town on the beautiful Bitterroot River.

11 **Hamilton.** Home of the Daly Mansion.

12 **Darby.** A small mountain town with a big rodeo.

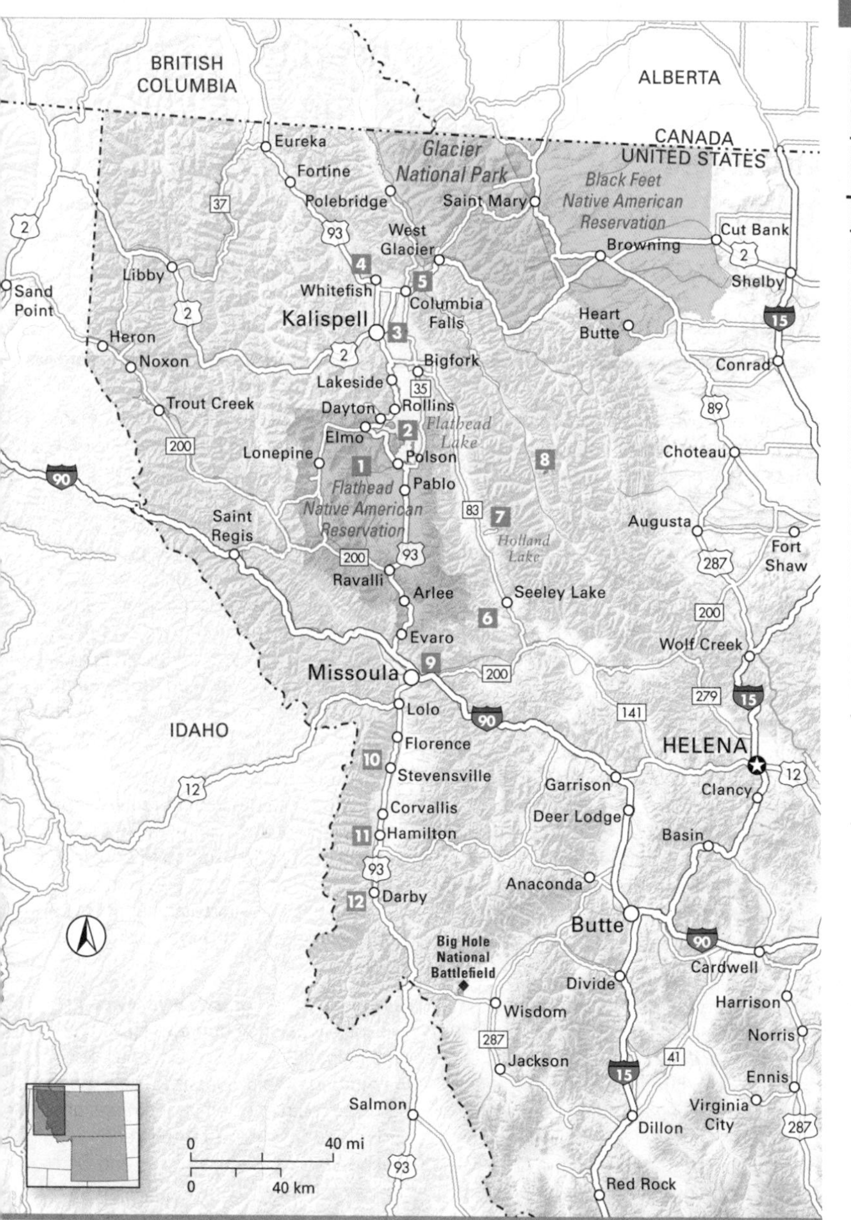
BRITISH COLUMBIA
ALBERTA
CANADA
UNITED STATES
Glacier National Park
Black Feet Native American Reservation
Eureka
Fortine
Polebridge
Saint Mary
West Glacier
Browning
Cut Bank
Shelby
Libby
Sand Point
Whitefish
Columbia Falls
Kalispell
Heart Butte
Heron
Noxon
Bigfork
Conrad
Lakeside
Trout Creek
Dayton
Rollins
Flathead Lake
Elmo
Lonepine
Polson
Choteau
Flathead Native American Reservation
Pablo
Saint Regis
Holland Lake
Augusta
Fort Shaw
Ravalli
Arlee
Seeley Lake
Evaro
Wolf Creek
Missoula
Lolo
IDAHO
Florence
HELENA
Stevensville
Garrison
Clancy
Corvallis
Deer Lodge
Hamilton
Basin
Anaconda
Darby
Butte
Big Hole National Battlefield
Cardwell
Divide
Wisdom
Harrison
Norris
Jackson
Ennis
Salmon
Virginia City
Dillon
Red Rock
0
40 mi
0
40 km
1
2
3
4
5
6
7
8
9
10
11
12
2
37
93
35
83
89
200
90
287
279
15
141
12
41

With more than 6 million acres of public land, northwest Montana might be America's largest outdoor destination. In the summer, travelers head to the many lakes and forests for hiking and water activities. In winter the land settles under a blanket of snow and the water under sheets of ice, creating a winter-sports paradise, particularly for skiers.

The region's rivers, streams, lakes, and mountains attract outdoor adventurers, but once here, they discover playhouses, art galleries, craft breweries, and summer festivals and rodeos. In winter visitors seek out northwest Montana's six ski areas and scores of cross-country ski trails. But some of the best times to visit are the shoulder seasons, particularly in September, when there are fewer crowds and gorgeous days.

Between the Canadian border and Missoula, tree-lined lakes and snowy peaks punctuate glaciated valleys scoured out by ice sheets some 12,000 years ago. A growing destination for golf, boating, skiing, and other outdoor recreation, the fertile **Flathead and Mission Valleys** support ranching and farming, and are becoming known for some of the state's best restaurants.

Squeezed between two magnificent mountain ranges the glacially formed **Seeley–Swan Valley** is littered with lakes, sprinkled with homesteads, and frosted with snow for five months of the year. One road, Highway 83, winds along an 80-mile course that follows the Clearwater and Swan rivers, popular for boating and fishing—both winter ice fishing and summer trout fishing. Several trailheads lead into the Bob Marshall Wilderness from the Swan Valley. Modern amenities are as sparse as the population. Only about 2,000 people reside here year-round, so you are much more likely to encounter a dozen deer than a dozen humans. Summer visitors fill campgrounds and the few guest lodges. Besides snowmobiling and cross-country skiing, winters bring snow, drippy weather, and low clouds, but that doesn't keep anyone indoors.

The metropolitan area of **Missoula,** with a population of approximately 75,000, is the largest concentration of people in the region. Home of the University of Montana, it's a business and shopping center and offers many arts and cultural attractions.

This history-filled **Bitterroot Valley** south of Missoula was once home to Nez Perce who helped Lewis and Clark find their way through the mountains. The expedition's campsites, plus historic mansions and missions, are scattered in and around Stevensville, Hamilton, and Darby, towns founded by early settlers attracted by temperate weather and fertile soil. The valley is named for the state flower, the delicate pink rosette-shape bitterroot, which blooms in late spring; its roots were a staple of the Salish Indian diet.

Planning

Getting Here and Around

AIR

Northwest Montana has two principal airports: Missoula International, on U.S. 93 just west of Missoula, and Glacier Park International, 8 miles northeast of Kalispell and 11 miles southeast of Whitefish on U.S. 2. Both are serviced by major airlines; if you're coming from outside the Rockies area, the odds are that you'll have a connecting flight through a larger hub such as Denver, Salt Lake City, Minneapolis/St. Paul, Phoenix, or Calgary, Alberta.

CONTACTS Glacier Park International Airport. ✉ *4170 U.S. 2 E, Kalispell* ☎ *406/257–5994* 🌐 *www.iflyglacier.com.* **Missoula International Airport.** ✉ *5225 W. Broadway, Missoula* ☎ *406/728–4381* 🌐 *www.flymissoula.com.*

CAR

Of Montana's 75,000 miles of public roads, there are certainly more gravel and dirt roads than paved. Many of the unpaved routes are in good shape, yet you'll need to slow down and, as on any Montana road, be on the lookout for wildlife, open-range livestock, farm equipment, unexpected hazards such as cattle-crossing guards, and changing weather and road conditions. Snow can fall any month of the year. In more remote areas, carry an emergency kit with water, snacks, extra clothing, and flashlights. Gasoline is available along most paved roads. However, if you are traveling in more remote areas, be sure to gas up before leaving town. In mountainous terrain it's unlikely that you will have cell-phone reception.

TRAIN

Amtrak chugs across the Highline and the northwest part of the state, stopping in East Glacier, West Glacier, and Whitefish daily. Amtrak offers travel packages to get you to Glacier National Park and other northwest Montana destinations.

CONTACTS Amtrak. ✉ *500 Depot St., Whitefish* ☎ *800/872–7245* 🌐 *www.amtrakvacations.com.*

Hotels

From massive log lodges to historic bed-and-breakfasts to chain hotels, you'll find the range of lodging options here that you'd expect from a region that makes a business of catering to tourists. Many historic lodges and cabins do not offer air-conditioning, but in general you won't miss it, since summers here are never humid and temperatures rarely reach 90°F and can get downright cold at night. During ski season and the summer vacation months, reservations are necessary. Some hotels are open only in summer and early fall.

CAMPING

Campgrounds across the region vary from no-services, remote state or federal campsites, to upscale commercial operations. Forest service cabins and former fire towers are also great alternatives. During July and August it's best to reserve a camp spot. Ask locally about bears, and whether food must be stored inside a hard-sided vehicle or a bear-proof cooler (not a tent). Avoid leaving pets alone at campgrounds because of wildlife confrontations, and because it's against the rules at most campgrounds. The easiest way to locate and reserve campsites, cabins, and fire towers is through **Reserve America** 🌐 *www.reserveamerica.com.*

Planning Your Time

Among the best in the state, northwest Montana's six alpine ski areas are led by the Whitefish Mountain Resort at Big Mountain in the Flathead Valley. If you come in summer, be sure to take a chairlift ride to the top: from there you can see the Canadian Rockies, the peaks of Glacier, and the valley. You can also ride the bike park, take the zipline, or clamber through the aerial adventure park. Nearby, railroad fans and history buffs will appreciate Whitefish's Stumptown Historical Museum and Kalispell's Northwest Montana Historical Museum, both crammed full of local history, plus a few humorous exhibits. Water lovers find ample room for all kinds of sports on Flathead Lake, the West's largest natural freshwater lake. Artsy types should stop in Bigfork, on the lake's northeast shore, where galleries dominate the main street and eateries are often galleries, too.

If your travels include Missoula, you can figure out the lay of the land via a short hike to the M on the mountainside above the University of Montana's Washington-Grizzly Football Stadium. From here you'll see the Clark Fork River, downtown's Missoula Art Museum, and, way off to the west, the Rocky Mountain Elk Foundation Wildlife Visitor Center. Take time to wander along the riverfront paths and explore the historic downtown core, where boutiques, craft breweries, cultural events, and eateries abound.

In the forested Bitterroot Valley, where many travelers follow Lewis and Clark's trail, stop at Traveler's Rest State Park for perspective on the expedition. Plan on floating and fishing the Bitterroot and other local rivers, and in early July watch the Senior Pro Rodeo if you're in Hamilton. At one of the valley's guest ranches, be sure to sign up for a trail ride into the Bitterroot or Selway wilderness areas and along surrounding U.S. Forest Service trails. Wherever you go, don't forget your cowboy hat and your "howdy."

Restaurants

Although Montana generally isn't known for elegant dining, several sophisticated restaurants are tucked away among the tamaracks and cedars, where professionally trained chefs bring herbed nuances and wide-ranging cultural influences to their menus. More typical of the region are steak houses featuring certified Angus beef; in recent years, particularly in resort communities, these institutions have diversified their menus to include bison meat, fresh fish, and savory vegetarian options. Small cafés offer hearty, inexpensive meals, and you can pick up on local history through photographs and artwork on walls and conversation with the local denizens. Attire everywhere is decidedly casual: blue jeans, a clean shirt, and cowboy boots or flip-flops are dress-up for most Montana restaurants.

Restaurant and hotel reviews have been shortened. For full information, visit Fodors.com.

HOTEL AND RESTAURANT COSTS

What it Costs			
$	**$$**	**$$$**	**$$$$**
RESTAURANTS			
under $10	$10–$18	$19–$30	over $30
HOTELS			
under $80	$80–$130	$131–$200	over $200

When to Go

Most visitors to northwest Montana come in July and August, enticed by lakes, rivers, golf courses, trails, and fresh mountain air. Arts festivals, rodeos, powwows, and farmers' markets fill the summer calendar. Even during this busiest season, though, you're unlikely to feel cramped among Montana's wide-open spaces. Winter is the second peak season; deep snows attract snowboarders and skiers to the region's six alpine ski areas. It's also an excellent time to explore cross-country-skiing and snowshoe trails through the light, fluffy snow.

Spring and fall are the quiet seasons, but they're becoming increasingly popular. In spring, wildlife-sightings include newborn elk calves, fawns, and an occasional bear cub. Mountain air cools the nights, and the occasional late-spring storm can cloak the region in snow, if only for a day. Fall's dry, warm days and blessedly cool nights offer the best of weather; there are few other tourists, and most attractions are still open. Lodgings offer off-season rates and there are no crowds, unless it's at a local high-school event, where nearly the entire town shows up. No matter the time of year, keep in mind that weather in this part of the world can change rapidly. Be prepared with extra clothing.

Flathead Reservation

20 miles north of Missoula via U.S. 93.

Home to the Confederated Salish and Kootenai Tribes, this 1.2-million-acre reservation is also a fascinating historical sight. Archaeological evidence indicates that Native Americans were here some 14,000 years ago, but it wasn't until the 1700s that the Kootenai, Salish, and Pend d'Oreille shared common hunting grounds in this area. The people hunted bison, descendants of which you can see at the National Bison Range. When Catholic "Black Robes" arrived to convert the native Americans, they built the St. Ignatius Mission. The tribes hold a fishing tournament called **Mack Days** every spring and fall, where up to $50,000 in cash prizes are awarded for catching Flathead Lake's prodigious lake trout.

GETTING HERE AND AROUND

The southern border to the reservation is a quick 20-minute drive on U.S. Highway 93 from Missoula International Airport. Glacier International Airport is 35 miles to the north.

VISITOR INFORMATION

Of the approximately 7,7533 enrolled tribal members of the Confederated Salish and Kootenai Tribes, about 5,000 live on the reservation, which is interspersed with non–Native American ranches and other property. Both tribes celebrate their heritage during the annual July 4 celebration, which draws Native Americans from all over the West.

CONTACTS Confederated Salish and Kootenai Tribes. *42487 Complex Blvd. ☎ 406/675–2700, 406/657–0160, 888/835–8766 🌐 www.csktribes.org.*

Fort Connah

HISTORIC SITE | Established in 1846 as the last Hudson Bay Company trading post built in the United States, Fort Connah was used by fur traders until 1871. Of the original three buildings, one remains today; it's believed to be the oldest building still standing in Montana. You can't go inside, but a historical marker details events and inhabitants. ✉ *U.S. 93 at Post Creek* ✣ *Between St. Ignatius and Charlo* ☎ *406/676–5541, 406/745-4336* 🌐 *www.visitmt.com.*

Garden of One Thousand Buddhas

RELIGIOUS SITE | You might not expect to find a Buddhist temple in the middle of the Flathead Reservation, but if you find yourself in or near Arlee, which is about 27 miles north of Missoula, this garden is worth a stop if only for the magnificent photo op of 1,000 Buddha statues in a beautiful, picturesque public garden attached to the Ewan Buddhist Institute. While the garden is open year-round, tours are offered only from April through

October. ✉ *34756 White Coyote Rd., Arlee* 🌐 *ewam.org* 🎫 *Free.*

★ National Bison Range

NATURE PRESERVE | The Red Sleep Mountain Drive, a 19-mile loop road, allows close-up views of bison, elk, pronghorn, deer, and mountain sheep. The gravel road rises 2,000 feet and takes about two hours to complete; you're required to begin the drive no later than 6 pm and to finish before the gate closes at dark. The 19,000-acre refuge at the foot of the Mission Mountains was established in 1908 by Theodore Roosevelt. Today the Confederated Salish and Kootenai Tribes own the refuge and manage the herd of approximately 350 to 500 bison. A visitor center explains the history, habits, and habitat of the bison. To reach the bison range, follow the signs west, then north from the junction of U.S. 93 and Route 200 in Ravalli. ✉ *58355 Bison Range Rd., Moiese* ☎ *406/644–2211* 🌐 *www.fws.gov/bisonrange* 🎫 *$5 per vehicle.*

Ninepipe National Wildlife Refuge

NATURE PRESERVE | Sprawling Ninepipe National Wildlife Refuge is the place for birdwatchers. This 2,000-acre wetland complex in the shadow of the Mission Mountains is home to everything from marsh hawks to kestrels to red-winged blackbirds. Flanking both sides of U.S. 93 are rookeries for double-crested cormorants and great blue herons; bald eagles fish here in the winter. Roads (including U.S. 93, where stopping is prohibited within the boundaries) through the center of the refuge are closed March through mid-July during nesting season, but you can drive along the periphery throughout the year. Maps are available from the nearby National Bison Range, which manages Ninepipe. ✉ *58355 Bison Range Rd.* ☎ *406/644–2211* 🌐 *www.fws.gov.*

Three Chiefs Culture Center

MUSEUM | The center (formerly The People's Center) allows you to experience the rich cultural heritage of the Salish, Kootenai, and Pend d'Oreille people. The People's Center includes artifacts, photographs, and recordings, runs educational programs, and includes guided interpretive tours, outdoor traditional lodges, and annual festivals. A gift shop sells both traditional and nontraditional work by local artists and craftspeople. ✉ *53253 U.S. 93 W, Pablo* ✣ *6 miles south of Polson* ☎ *406/675–0160* 🌐 *threechiefs.org* 🎫 *$5* ⏲ *Closed weekends.*

St. Ignatius Mission

RELIGIOUS SITE | The St. Ignatius Mission—a church, cabin, and collection of other buildings—was built in the 1890s with bricks made of local clay by missionaries and Native Americans. The 61 murals on the walls and ceilings of the church were used to teach Bible stories to the Indians. In the St. Ignatius Mission Museum (an old log cabin) there's an exhibit of early artifacts and arts and crafts. The mission is still a functioning church; Mass is offered every Sunday morning in the rectory. To reach the mission from St. Ignatius, take Main Street south to Mission Drive. ✉ *300 Bear Track Ave.* ☎ *406/745–2768.*

Symes Hot Springs Hotel and Mineral Baths

HOT SPRINGS | Truly a unique find on the western edge of the Flathead Indian Reservation, this rustic 1928 hotel has hot mineral pools from continuously flowing springs, spa treatments, massage, and live music on weekends. In the restaurant, steak, seafood, and pasta satisfy hungry soakers. The hotel itself isn't a standout, though the rates are reasonable. Several historic hot springs in the area attracted Native Americans for centuries. ✉ *209 Wall St., Hot Springs* ☎ *406/741–2361* 🌐 *www.symeshotsprings.com* 🎫 *Pools and baths $10.*

Restaurants

Allentown Restaurant

$$$ | STEAKHOUSE | On the edge of the Ninepipe National Wildlife Refuge, the

The National Bison Range protects a herd of not only 500 bison but also pronghorn, elk, deer, and over 200 bird species.

lodge has views of the snow-tipped Mission Mountains and native-grass-edged wetlands full of birds. The restaurant is open seven days a week, and dinners include local Double R Ranch beef steaks, seafood, and specials like baby back ribs. **Known for:** good food and outstanding views; nice spot to stop after exploring Ninepipes National Wildlife Refuge; great patio allows outdoor dining beside a private kettle pond. *Average main:* ✉ *Ninepipes Lodge, 69286 U.S. Hwy. 93, Charlo* ☎ *406/644–2588* 🌐 *www.ninepipeslodge.com.*

Hotels

Cheff Guest Ranch and Outfitters

$$$ | **RENTAL** | This 20,000-acre working cattle ranch at the base of the Mission Mountains lets you take part in ranching life in summer and conducts pack trips from September through November while staying in one of their fully equipped cabins. **Pros:** the Cheffs have been taking care of folks for a long time, and are excellent hosts; horses and mules are some of the best in the outfitting world, and they do a good job matching a rider's skill with the right horse; you can arrange multiday pack trips into the Bob Marshall Wilderness. **Cons:** a significant drive coming from either Kalispell or Missoula; though well-appointed, the cabins are a little on the small size; cabins are self-catering. *Rooms from: $165* ✉ *30888 Eagle Pass Trail, Charlo* ☎ *406/644–2557* 🌐 *www.cheffranch.com* *2 cabins* *No meals.*

Shopping

Flathead Indian Museum and Trading Post

LOCAL SPECIALTIES | The Flathead Indian Museum and Trading Post has an extensive collection of authentic artifacts from local Native American tribes. On sale are blankets, arts, crafts, local beadwork, books, maps, and gifts. ✉ *32621 U.S. Hwy. 93, St. Ignatius* ☎ *406/745–2951.*

Zimmer Tackle

SPORTING GOODS | Dick Zimmer is a local legend who has been fishing the

Flathead Valley for decades. He makes his own lures and jigs and can set you up with all the gear and information you'll need to catch fish of all kinds, from 20-pound lake trout and pike to smaller perch and kokanee. ✉ *35933 Carlyle La., Pablo* ☎ *406/675–0068* 🌐 *www.zimmerttackle.com/.*

CAMPING

Mission Meadows RV Park. Tucked away beneath shady pines, this conveniently located RV park is near the bison range and fishing. Tucked away beneath shady pines, this conveniently located RV park is near the bison range and fishing. ✉ *44457 Mission Meadow Dr., 2 miles north of Ronan* ☎ *406/676–5182, 406/676–0854* 🌐 *www.missionmeadowscamping.com/* *120 sites.*

Flathead Lake

12 miles north of Ronan via U.S. 93.

The 370-foot-deep Flathead Lake, with 180 miles of shoreline, is the largest natural freshwater lake in the western United States. It's a wonderful—and popular—place for sailing, fishing, camping and swimming. Wildhorse Island State Park is home to bighorn sheep and other wildlife; the 2,165-acre island can be reached only by boat, which can be rented. Cherry groves line the lake's shores, and toward the end of July farmers harvest them and sell cherries at roadside stands along the two highways that encircle the lake.

GETTING HERE AND AROUND

Seven miles south of Kalispell the road splits, and you can choose which route along the lake you would like to take. U.S. Highway 93 is the more traveled, winding along the west side of the lake through the towns of Lakeside and Polson. Montana Highway 35 goes through the town of Bigfork and along the east side of the lake, where most of the cherry orchards are.

VISITOR INFORMATION

CONTACTS Bigfork Chamber of Commerce. ✣ *8155 MT-35,* ☎ *406/837–5888* 🌐 *www.bigfork.org.* **Flathead Convention and Visitor Bureau.** ✉ *15 Depot Park, Suite 1, Kalispell* ☎ *406/756–9091* 🌐 *www.fcvb.org/.*

Bigfork Art & Cultural Center

MUSEUM | The rotating exhibits at Bigfork Art & Cultural Center display bronzes, paintings, and works in other mediums by Montana artists. ✉ *525 Electric Ave., Bigfork* ☎ *406/837–6927* 🌐 *baccbigfork.org* *Free (donations accepted)* ⏲ *Closed Sun. and Mon.*

Mission Mountain Winery

WINERY/DISTILLERY | Between the Bitteroot Valley and the Flathead Valley, Highway 93 winds its way around the west side of Flathead Lake. Known for the two-lane, often slow-going traffic, this route has many places to stop and drink in the mountain backdrop that frames the lake. Along the way, wine lovers should check out the family-owned Mission Mountain Winery, where you can sample wines from Montana's first bonded winery. The pinot noir and pinot gris, both from grapes grown in the property's vineyard, are award-winners. ✉ *82420 Hwy. 93, Dayton* ✣ *23 miles north of Polson* ☎ *406/849–5524* 🌐 *www.missionmountainwinery.com* ⏲ *Closed Nov.–Apr.*

Mission Mountains Wilderness Complex

NATURE PRESERVE | From much of the Mission Valley and Flathead Indian Reservation you can see the Mission Mountains, on which there's a 73,877-acre wilderness area full of hiking, camping, and fishing opportunities. The area is probably best known for the 1,000-foot drops of Elizabeth and Mission falls. Glorious McDonald Peak looms at 9,280

Big Country, Brief History

Scraped by receding glaciers and chiseled by weather, the landscape of northwest Montana has a long history, but the region's human history is relatively recent. The earliest Native Americans probably settled here between 10,000 and 12,000 years ago, or traveled through in search of bison herds east of the Rockies. Today the Confederated Salish and Kootenai Tribes live on the Flathead Reservation, spread out across the Mission and Flathead valleys; their People's Center is one of the state's best displays of native culture and history.

Explorers such as David Thompson and Lewis & Clark looked at but mostly didn't touch the riches—timber, wild game, and emerald lakes—of northwest Montana, and more permanent white settlers didn't arrive until the railroad arrived and Montana became a state in 1889. Many of the frontier communities are only now celebrating centennial anniversaries. Even so, the area claims some of Montana's oldest structures, such as St. Mary's Mission, the first Catholic mission in the Northwest, and Fort Connah, a Hudson's Bay Company fur-trading post. Three railroads laid track through Glacier Country, leaving in their wake elegant train stations and a heritage of rail travel.

Historic sites throughout northwest Montana offer a glimpse back at the rough-and-tumble old days, but the wild lands and wildlife are what you'll write home about. On the National Bison Range you'll see descendants of the last few free-roaming American bison. Watch for birds of prey wherever you go. From the Lee Metcalf National Wildlife Refuge to the Bob Marshall Wilderness to Glacier National Park, elk, bighorn sheep, mountain goats, and bears thrive. All of these critters are living reminders of centuries of Montana history.

feet; it's a favorite of grizzly bears, who gather on the snowfields to eat swarms of cutworm moths and ladybugs. Try the Mission Reservoir Trail for a relatively easy hike up a beautiful valley. Those who aren't tribal members must obtain a recreation permit to hike, fish, and camp here among the mountain lions, lynx, wolverines, black bears, and grizzlies. Recreational permits are available at local grocery and sporting-goods stores and most gas stations. Call the Confederated Salish and Kootenai Tribes at the number below for camping permits and information on the recreation permits. ✉ *St. Ignatius* ☎ *406/675–2700* 🎫 *Recreational permit $25.*

Polson

TOWN | Polson, a quiet community of 4,000 on the southwest corner of Flathead Lake, sits under the morning shadow of the jagged Mission Mountains. It's the largest town on the Flathead Indian Reservation. Picnic spots, lake access, and playgrounds are found at Boettcher, Sacajawea, and Riverside parks. Some other parks are for tribal members only; signs identify picnic areas that are closed to the public. Plan on attending the two-day Flathead Cherry Festival in mid-July to get your fill of the area's famous cherries. ✉ *Polson.*

Restaurants

Betty's Diner
$ | **AMERICAN** | A classic 1950s American diner on the south end of the lake near Polson, Betty's is a favorite among locals and visitors alike. Decorated with old signs and other Americana artifacts, it serves classics like biscuits and gravy, homemade milkshakes, and signature Betty pancakes. **Known for:** fast, friendly service in a fun atmosphere; can handle big groups with ease; tasty, juicy burgers, especially the cajun Breezy burger, with green chillies and pepperjack cheese. *Average main: $8* ✉ *49779 U.S. Hwy. 93, Polson* ☎ *406/883–1717* 🌐 *www.page70.com/bettysdiner/* ⏲ *No dinner.*

Flathead Lake Brewing Co. Pubhouse
$$ | **AMERICAN** | On top of 16 selections of house-brewed beer you'll find a typical pub menu upstairs in the Pubhouse and deep-dish pizza downstairs in the cellar. This is a popular place in both summer and winter, with nice views of the lake from the open-air decks. **Known for:** large portions of hearty pub food; stupendous views of Flathead Lake; a dozen or so craft brews made locally. *Average main: $15* ✉ *116 Holt Dr., Bigfork* ☎ *406/837–2004* 🌐 *flatheadlakebrewing.com.*

Saketome Sushi
$$$ | **SUSHI** | Sakatome is easily the best sushi restaurant in Montana. Owner Drake Doepke creates great flavors with unique combinations of local and exotic ingredients, and he only uses the freshest fish not found on the Seafood Watch list. **Known for:** good wine selection and delicious craft cocktails made with local spirits; food that is as beautiful as it is tasty; great ambience with funky aesthetics. *Average main: $25* ✉ *459 Electric Ave., Suite I, Bigfork* ☎ *406/837–1128* 🌐 *www.saketomesushi.com* ⏲ *No lunch.*

Traditions Restaurant at the Bigfork Inn
$$$ | **EUROPEAN** | The Swiss-chalet style of the Bigfork Inn is reminiscent of the lodges in nearby Glacier National Park. Inside, you'll find a lively atmosphere, with seating for more than 200 patrons between the main dining room, library, deck (summer), balcony, and two private rooms. **Known for:** the owner is a friendly fourth-generation French chef; pie and crème brûlée made with local huckleberries; rare opportunity for good European food in Montana. *Average main: $30* ✉ *604 Electric Ave., Bigfork* ☎ *406/837–6680* 🌐 *www.bigforkinn.com* ⏲ *Closed Mon. and Tues.*

Hotels

For lodging at the base of Whitefish Mountain Resort, contact **Central Reservations** (☎ *800/858–4152*), which handles everything from upscale Kandahar Lodge to dormitory-like Hibernation House, and various new-and-chic to older-yet-updated condominiums.

Averill's Flathead Lake Lodge
$$$$ | **ALL-INCLUSIVE** | **FAMILY** | Since 1945 Averill's has been providing families a wholesome and active Western getaway. **Pros:** watching large herds of horses being turned out to pasture at end of day is breathtaking; well-kept facility with excellent food; tons of activities, including waterskiing, fly-fishing lessons, and shooting sporting clays. **Cons:** sign on the east side of Highway 35 can easily be missed; price makes this facility out of reach of most travelers; 7-day minimum. *Rooms from: $1178* ✉ *150 Flathead Lodge Rd., Bigfork* ☎ *406/837–4391* 🌐 *www.flatheadlakelodge.com* *46 rooms* *All-inclusive* ☞ *7-day minimum.*

Bridge Street Cottages
$$$$ | **RENTAL** | Located in a grove of old Ponderosa pines on the banks of the Swan River, these well-appointed cottages are an excellent place to stay any season of the year. **Pros:** well-appointed

digs with comfy beds; community BBQ and laundry facilities on-site; staff are friendly, welcoming, and helpful. **Cons:** cabins are pretty close together; TVs are a little outdated; most units have only kitchenettes. *Rooms from: $240 309 Bridge St., Bigfork 406/837–2785 www.bridgestreetcottages.com 13 cottages No meals.*

Mountain Lake Lodge

$$$$ | **HOTEL** | This resort, perched above Flathead Lake, offers 30 well-appointed suites surrounding an outdoor pool on meticulously groomed grounds. **Pros:** beautiful facility with stunning views; two good on-site eateries; near craft cocktails and live music at The Raven. **Cons:** too far to walk to downtown Bigfork; no direct access to the lake; rooms a little outdated. *Rooms from: $300 14735 Sylvan Dr., Bigfork At Hwy. 35 mile marker 26.5 406/837–3800, 877/823–4923 toll-free www.mountainlakelodge.com 30 rooms No meals.*

Swan River Inn

$$$ | **HOTEL** | Situated in downtown Bigfork with views overlooking Bigfork Bay, the Swan River Inn has eight opulent suites in a 19th-century building. **Pros:** all except one room have great views of the bay; terrific location for all the restaurants, shops, and entertainment in Bigfork; lakeside solitude at the south property. **Cons:** downtown Bigfork is a busy place in summer; rates are fairly expensive; some guests complain about cleanliness. *Rooms from: $145 360 Grand Ave., Bigfork 406/837–2328 www.swanriverinn.com 16 rooms No meals.*

Performing Arts

Bigfork Summer Playhouse

THEATER | Mid-May through early September, the repertory group Bigfork Summer Playhouse presents Broadway musicals and comedies every night except Sunday in the Bigfork Center for the Performing Arts. Tickets are available online and by mail beginning in April, and by phone starting mid-May. Children's workshops and theater are held in the same facility. *526 Electric Ave., Bigfork 406/837–4886 www.bigforksummerplayhouse.com $32.*

Port Polson Players

THEATER | Enjoy summer theater with the Port Polson Players. The high-quality amateur troupe puts on musicals, comedies, and dramas in a beautiful 1930s log theater. *32 Golf Course Dr., Polson John Dowdall Theatre at Boetcher Park at Polson golf course off U.S. 93 406/883–9212 www.portpolsonplayers.com $7.*

River Bend Stage

CONCERTS | Every Summer Sunday from June through August at Bigfork's Everit L. Sliter Memorial Park, hear live music—from orchestral to salsa—performed by local musicians and regionally known bands at the River Bend Stage. *281 Bridge St., Bigfork riverbendconcerts-bigfork.com.*

Shopping

Bigfork's Electric Avenue is lined with galleries and eclectic gift shops, and is recognized for unparalleled dining and sweets.

Electric Avenue Gifts

GIFTS/SOUVENIRS | The owners call it the West's most whimsical store, and Electric Avenue Gifts doesn't disappoint. It carries unique Flathead cherry designs in everything from dishes to napkins, vintage and custom wood signs in Western themes, and a multitude of unique gifts. *490 Electric Ave., Bigfork 406/837–4994 www.electricavenuegifts.com.*

Eric Thorsen Fine Art Gallery

ART GALLERIES | While you peruse this huge gallery full of beautiful paintings, sculptures and carvings, you can also watch award-winning artist Eric Thorsen at work in his studio. A rare treat not to

Flathead Lake is the largest natural freshwater lake in Montana (Fort Peck Lake is bigger, but it's a man-made reservoir). It's slightly larger than Lake Tahoe.

be missed. ✉ *570 Electric Ave., Bigfork* ☎ *406/837–4366* 🌐 *www.ericthorsengallery.com* ⊗ *Closed Sun.*

Eva Gates Homemade Preserves

FOOD/CANDY | You can pick up a tiny jar of huckleberry jam or flavored honey at Eva Gates Homemade Preserves, or have one of the family-size jars of various treats shipped back home. You can also order and send gift boxes online. ✉ *456 Electric Ave., Bigfork* ☎ *406/837–4356, 800/682–4283* 🌐 *www.evagates.com.*

Sandpiper Art Gallery

ART GALLERIES | A nonprofit artist cooperative, Sandpiper Gallery shows the work of local and regional artists and holds workshops throughout the summer. Don't miss their annual art show on the county courthouse lawn the second Saturday in August. ✉ *306 Main St., Polson* ☎ *406/883–5956* 🌐 *www.sandpiperartgallery.com* ⊗ *Closed Sun.*

Activities

BOATING

Big Arm Boat Rentals

BOATING | From paddleboards to powerboats, Big Arm Boat Rentals has everything you need to visit Wildhorse Island and explore Flathead Lake. ✉ *Big Arm* ⊕ *From Polson, drive north on Hwy. 93 until you reach mile marker 73 at Big Arm* ☎ *406/260–5090* 🌐 *www.boatrentalsandrides.com.*

Dayton Yacht Harbor

BOATING | Here you can rent a sailboat, take sailing lessons, or moor your own sailboat near Wild Horse and Cromwell islands. ✉ *399 C St., Dayton* ☎ *406/849–5423.*

Two-hour Sail on Historic Sloops

BOATING | One of the most pleasant ways to see the lake is to take a two-hour sail on the historic *Questa* or the *Nor'Easter,* both 51-foot Q-class racing sloops built in the 1920s. They depart from Flathead Lake Lodge. ✉ *150 Flathead Lodge*

Rd., Bigfork ☎ *406/837–5569* 🌐 *www.flatheadlakesailing.com.*

CAMPING

Five lakeside parks are scattered around Flathead, offering quiet camping, boat launches, and good views. Bigfork's Wayfarers, Lakeside's West Shore, and Polson's Big Arm, Finley Point, and Yellow Bay parks are all owned by the state of Montana and run by Montana Fish, Wildlife & Parks.

Finley Point State Park Campground. With large, forested park on Flathead Lake and ample beachfront for swimming and paddling, Finley Point is the best of the five excellent state campgrounds on Flathead Lake. Some of the shaded campsites (which have fire pits) are right on the lake. It also boasts a good boat ramp and a small harbor, including for boat camping slips. ✉ *2869 S. Finley Point Rd.. Polson* ☎ *406/887–2715, 406/752–5501* 🌐 *www.fwp.mt.gov/finley-point* ⛺ *27 sites.*

Polson Motorcoach and RV Resort/ KOA. Perched above Flathead Lake with incredible views of the Mission and Swan mountains, this grassy spot is convenient to the lake and town, and hosts can direct you to fossil and arrowhead hunting. Not just for campers, this resort has a cottage complete with its own kitchenette and private hot tub. ✉ *200 Irving Flats Rd. Polson* ☎ *406/883–2333* 🌐 *www.polsonrvresort.com* ⛺ *60 sites.*

FISHING

Howe's Fishing Charters & Tours

FISHING | Flathead Lake is full of enormous lake trout, as well as perch and Lake Superior Whitefish, and Howe's (formerly AAble) can show you how to catch them any time of the year. They take individuals and groups of up to 15 people. In the spring, fall and winter, charters to other area lakes are also available. ✉ *Bigfork* ☎ *406/257–5214* 🌐 *www.howesfishing.com.*

Two River Gear and Outfitter

FISHING | Fly-fish with this local outfitter on local streams, rivers, and lakes. ✉ *603 Electric Ave., Bigfork* ☎ *406/837–3474* 🌐 *www.tworivergear.net.*

HIKING

★ Jewel Basin Hiking Area

HIKING/WALKING | **FAMILY** | **Jewel Basin Hiking Area** provides 35 miles of well-maintained trails among 27 trout-filled alpine lakes. You'll find the nearest phone and hearty to-go trail lunches at the Echo Lake Café at the junction of Highway 83 and Echo Lake Road. ✉ *Bigfork* ✣ *10 miles east of Bigfork via Hwy. 83 and Echo Lake Rd. to Jewel Basin Rd., No. 5392.*

Seeley-Swan Valley

HIKING/WALKING | The Seeley-Swan Valley southeast of Bigfork offers miles of hiking trails in the Mission and Swan mountains. Local favorites include Bond and Trinkus lakes; where Bond Creek falls, autumn huckleberries and cutthroat trout await the intrepid hiker. Visit the Swan Lake District Office in Bigfork for hiking maps and more information. ✉ *Swan Lake Ranger District, 200 Ranger Station Rd., Bigfork* ☎ *406/837–7500* 🌐 *www.fs.usda.gov/flathead.*

KAYAKING

Bigfork Whitewater Festival

KAYAKING | World-class kayaking on the Swan River's Wild Mile draws boaters and spectators to the white water during spring and summer runoff. The annual **Bigfork Whitewater Festival** celebrates the torrent every Memorial Day weekend with a water rodeo, races, and entertainment at local pubs and eateries. ✉ *Old Town Center, 451 Electric Ave., Bigfork* ☎ *406/837–5888* ✉ *bigforkwhitewaterfestival@gmail.com* 🌐 *www.bigforkwhitewaterfestival.com.*

RAFTING

Flathead Raft Co.

WHITE-WATER RAFTING | **FAMILY** | Flathead Raft Co. runs the Wild Buffalo Rapids on eight white-water miles of the lower Flathead River. From June through September, it provides wild rafting adventures, kayaking, and Native American interpretive trips between Kerr Dam and Buffalo Bridge, overnight trips, and tours of Wild Horse Island. The outfitter will design family floats suitable for any age. ✉ *50362 S. Hwy. 93, Polson* ✣ *Across from Super 1 Foods* ☎ *406/883–5838* 🌐 *www.flatheadraftco.com.*

SKIING

Blacktail Mountain Ski Area

SKIING/SNOWBOARDING | **FAMILY** | As you schuss the runs of **Blacktail Mountain Ski Area**, you'll glimpse Flathead Lake and surrounding peaks. This family-friendly mountain is known for inexpensive lift tickets, uncrowded, mostly intermediate slopes, a lovely log-accented lodge, and friendly staff. ✉ *3990 Blacktail Rd., Lakeside* ☎ *406/844–0999* 🌐 *www.blacktailmountain.com.*

Kalispell

20 miles northwest of Bigfork via Hwy. 35; 33 miles southwest of Glacier National Park via U.S. 2.

Main Street (U.S. 93) in busy downtown Kalispell is lined with galleries, jewelry stores, boutiques, and restaurants. This century-old city, the Flathead County seat, is a regional business and retail center for people from northwest Montana. An Andrew Carnegie library is now home to the Hockaday Museum of Art, and just a few blocks away, Kalispell's first school building has been turned into the Northwest Montana History Museum. Pick up visitor information at the historic Great Northern Depot.

GETTING HERE AND AROUND

Daily flights fly into Glacier International Airport in Kalispell. Amtrak arrives daily in Whitefish, which is 15 miles to the north on Highway 93. From Glacier National Park, U.S. Highway 2 West will lead right into the heart of Kalispell.

Sights

Conrad Mansion National Historic Site Museum

BUILDING | **FAMILY** | A town highlight is the Conrad Mansion National Historic Site Museum, a 26-room Norman-style mansion that was the home of Charles E. Conrad, who made a fortune in shipping and freighting on the Missouri River and founded Kalispell. Docents lead entertaining and informative guided tours, including a variety of special theme tours offered throughout the year. ✉ *330 Woodland Ave.* ☎ *406/755–2166* 🌐 *www.conradmansion.com* 🎟 *$20* 🕑 *Closed Sat.–Mon.*

Great Northern Depot

INFO CENTER | **FAMILY** | Inside the historic Great Northern Depot is visitor information from the Kalispell Chamber of Commerce and the Flathead Convention and Visitors Bureau. Outside is the lovely Depot Park, where live music, arts shows, a gazebo, picnicking, and a playground attract both locals and travelers. ✉ *15 Depot Park* ☎ *406/758–2800, 888/888–2308* 🌐 *www.kalispellchamber.com* 🎟 *Free* 🕑 *Closed weekends.*

Hockaday Museum of Art

MUSEUM | Housed in a renovated, turn-of-the-20th-century Carnegie library building, the Hockaday Museum of Art presents contemporary art exhibits focusing on Montana artists and the art and culture of Glacier National Park. ✉ *302 2nd Ave. E* ☎ *406/755–5268* 🌐 *www.hockadaymuseum.org* 🎟 *$5* 🕑 *Closed Sun. and Mon.*

Lone Pine State Park

NATIONAL/STATE PARK | At an elevation of 2,959 feet, this 186-acre park offers breathtaking views of Kalispell, Flathead Lake, and the Whitefish Mountain Range. Features include a self-guided nature trail, a gift shop and visitor center that has exhibits detailing the local wildlife and ecology, nature interpretive programs, picnic areas and shelters, horse trails, and a horseshoe pit. Be sure to bring your camera. ✉ *300 Lone Pine Rd.* ✥ *4 miles southwest of Kalispell on Foyes Lake Rd., then 1 mile east on Lone Pine Rd.* ☎ *406/755–2706* 🌐 *www.fwp.mt.gov/lone-pine* 🎫 *$8* ⏲ *Visitor center closed Mon. and Tues.*

Northwest Montana History Museum
MUSEUM | You can ring the old school bell at the Northwest Montana History Museum, housed in the Central School building that served as the educational backdrop for students of the Flathead Valley for nearly 100 years. The museum hosts galleries, activities, and displays about regional heritage and history, including local Native American culture. You'll also find a café, a museum store, conference rooms, and a reference library. ✉ *124 2nd Ave. E* ☎ *406/756–8381* 🌐 *www.nwmthistory.org* 🎫 *$5* ⏲ *Closed weekends.*

Woodland Park
CITY PARK | **FAMILY** | One of 28 city green spaces, Woodland Park has a playground, ball fields, rose gardens, and a picnic area. Geese, ducks, peacocks, and black swans flutter to the pond, which in winter opens for ice skating; there's a warming hut nearby. Open June–August, Woodland Water Park is an affordable and popular attraction with a pool, waterslides, and the "Lazy River" float. ✉ *705 2nd St. E* ✥ *At Conrad Dr. and Woodland Dr.* ☎ *406/758–7718* 🌐 *www.kalispell.com* 🎫 *Waterpark $6.*

Restaurants

Hop's Downtown Grill
$$ | **AMERICAN** | Craft beer and gourmet burgers are the thing at Hop's, a popular chef-owned eatery in the historic downtown area. Its menu boasts 100 craft beers, regional wines, and more than a dozen burgers, including at least one vegetarian option. **Known for:** burgers, which people rave about; a great selection of craft beers; can be busy around dinner time. $ *Average main: $18* ✉ *121 Main St.* ☎ *406/755–7687.*

The Knead Cafe
$$ | **CONTEMPORARY** | Come here for the best bread and soup in the valley. The café's baked goods, including fresh croissants, baguettes, and scones, will entice you in, but it's worth your while to stay for breakfast or lunch—the Reuben sandwiches are sublime, and any one of the salads makes a great lunch. **Known for:** perfectly cooked pastrami; plenty of gluten-free and vegetarian options; focus on responsibly sourced produce and farm-to-table cuisine. $ *Average main: $13* ✉ *21 5th St. E* ☎ *406/755–3883* ⏲ *Closed Sun. and Mon.*

Hotels

Hampton Inn Kalispell
$$$$ | **HOTEL** | This hotel 1 mile west of downtown features an indoor pool, fitness center, gift shop, and shuttle service. **Pros:** hot buffet breakfast included; swimming pool is open 24 hours; great room rates often available from end of September through April. **Cons:** pool is directly off lobby; located in a busy, high traffic area; no restaurant on-site. $ *Rooms from: $275* ✉ *1140 U.S. 2 W* ☎ *406/755–7900* 🌐 *www.hamptoninnkalispell.com* 🛏 *120 rooms* 🍽 *Free breakfast.*

Kalispell Grand Hotel
$$$ | **HOTEL** | The smell of freshly baked cookies greets travelers in the afternoon as soon as they walk into the Kalispell Grand. **Pros:** downtown location close to restaurants and shops; local artists showcase their works in the art gallery; homemade pound cake for the continental breakfast. **Cons:** although clean and updated, this older property may not appeal to everyone; rooms are a little on the small size; it's downtown, so light sleepers might notice street noise.

Rooms from: $200 ✉ *100 Main St.* ☎ *406/755–8100, 800/858–7422* 🌐 *www.kalispellgrand.com* *40 rooms* *Free breakfast.*

Nightlife

Moose's Saloon

BARS/PUBS | Cowboy boots and sneakers kick up the sawdust and peanut shells on the floor at the legendary Moose's Saloon, where tunes from the jukebox get the raucous crowd moving. You can order pizza or a hearty sandwich to go with your beer. Leave your mark by carving your name on one of the walls. ✉ *173 N. Main St.* ☎ *406/755–2337* 🌐 *www.moosessaloon.com.*

Performing Arts

Glacier Symphony, Orchestra and Chorale

CONCERTS | Voices of the mountains blend at concerts by the Glacier Symphony, Orchestra and Chorale, held in several venues around Whitefish and Kalispell. Conductor John Zoltek and his talented musicians hold a Spring Festival in April (Kalispell) and the week-long Festival Amadeus in August (Whitefish) only a short drive from the splendor of Glacier National Park. ✉ *69 N. Main St.* ☎ *406/257–3241, 406/407–7000 box office* 🌐 *www.glaciersymphony.org.*

Shopping

Noice Studio and Gallery

ART GALLERIES | Situated in a lovingly restored turn-of-the-20th-century building, Noice Studio and Gallery features ongoing exhibits of paintings, pastels, sculptures, fiber arts, and photography by Montana artists such as Rudy Autio, Russell Chatham, and Marshall Noice. ✉ *127 Main St.* ☎ *406/755–5321* 🌐 *www.facebook.com/NoiceStudioandGallery* ⏲ *Closed Sun. and Mon.*

Sportsman & Ski Haus

SPORTING GOODS | If you need outdoor equipment of any kind, this well-equipped sporting goods store probably has it. They can also tune your skis and bikes, and rent you either if you didn't bring your own. There's also a store in the Whitefish Mountain Mall off Highway 93. ✉ *145 Hutton Ranch Rd.* ☎ *406/755–6484 Kalispell store* 🌐 *www.sportsmanski-haus.com.*

Activities

CAMPING

Glacier Pines RV Park. A bit of forest in the city, this spacious campground set among pines has paved roads and no maximum size limit or time limit. There are no tent sites, but the grounds are open year-round, and there's a pool, play area, horseshoes, laundry facility, showers, and Wi-Fi. ✉ *1850 Hwy. 35 E, Kalispell* ☎ *406/752–2760, 800/533–4029* 🌐 *glacierpinesrvpark.com/* *75 sites with full hookups.*

HIKING

Montana Wilderness Association

HIKING/WALKING | Every year from May through October, the Montana Wilderness Association offers free Wilderness Walks booklets describing dozens of trails in the state. Join one of their free guided hikes, which vary from short wildflower walks to strenuous climbs, or one of their winter wilderness walks, guided snowshoe excursions through Montana's magnificent backcountry. ✉ *80 S. Warren St., Helena* ☎ *406/443–7350* 🌐 *www.wildmontana.org.*

TRAIL RIDING

High Country Trails

HORSEBACK RIDING | Hop on one of High Country Trails' trail horses and ride for a couple of hours or an entire day on the beautiful rolling hills and open meadows of this 800-acre ranch, located 6 miles southwest of Kalispell. Kids seven years and older are welcome. ✉ *2800 Foy's*

Lake Rd. ☎ *406/755–1283* 🌐 *www.horse-rentals.com.*

Whitefish

15 miles north of Kalispell via U.S. 93; 26 miles west of Glacier National Park via Hwy. 40 and U.S. 2.

A hub for golfing, lake recreation, hiking, mountain biking, and skiing, Whitefish sits at the base of Whitefish Mountain Resort. Nine lifts serve 3,000 acres of powder skiing and summer activities, as well as outstanding views (the mountain is closed from mid-April to mid-June and from late September to early December) into Glacier National Park and the Canadian Rockies. At Whitefish Lake, Native Americans once caught and dried whitefish. Euro-American settlers came a century ago to farm or join the timber or railroad industries; the sporty resort town now has 8,300 residents. Skiers descend Whitefish Mountain late fall through early spring, and summer attracts hikers, mountain bikers, and zipliners. The Danny On Trail leads to the mountain summit, which can also be accessed via the Glacier Chaser chairlift. Numerous other activities—such as summer tubing, an Aerial Adventure Park, a Summer Nature Center, art and music festivals, and nighttime stargazing events—keep the mountain busy throughout the warmer months. The nature center and a few gift shops and restaurants remain open mid-June–mid-September.

GETTING HERE AND AROUND

Amtrak's Empire Builder arrives daily right in downtown Whitefish, making this an economical choice for some travelers. The westbound train arrives in late afternoon, but the eastbound arrives in the early morning, making it difficult to check into hotels. Glacier International Airport has daily flights and is 15 miles away. Many hotels have shuttles back and forth. From Glacier National Park it's an easy 30-minute trip via U.S. Highway 2 and then U.S. Highway 40.

VISITOR INFORMATION

CONTACTS Whitefish Visitor Information Center. ✉ *505 E. 2nd St.* ☎ *877/862–3548* 🌐 *www.explorewhitefish.com.*

Sights

Stumptown Historical Society's Museum

MUSEUM | If you want to check out a cross section of American life, drop by the Whitefish train station at 6 am as a sleepy collection of farmers, cowboys, and skiers awaits the arrival of Amtrak's *Empire Builder*, en route from Seattle to Chicago. Inside the half-timber depot is the Stumptown Historical Society's Whitefish Museum. The focus here is the Great Northern Railway, the nation's first unsubsidized transcontinental railway that passed through Whitefish. On display are lanterns, old posters, and crockery, as well as reminders of local history, such as the books of author Dorothy M. Johnson and photos of the Whitefish football team from 1922 through 1954, plus some real fun (look for the fur-covered trout). You can pick up a walking-tour map of Whitefish's historic district here. ✉ *500 Depot St.* ☎ *406/862–0067* 🌐 *www.stumptownhistoricalsociety.org* ⏲ *Closed Sun.*

Restaurants

★ Buffalo Cafe & Nightly Grill

$$ | **AMERICAN** | This is the place for the classic small-town café experience. Locals and visitors happily blend in a casual, friendly atmosphere as they dig into well-prepared breakfasts, lunches, and dinners. **Known for:** all-day service of good ol' home cooking; heaps of warm and friendly service; locally made, artisan Sweet Peaks ice cream. [$] *Average main: $15* ✉ *514 3rd St. E* ☎ *406/862–2833* 🌐 *www.buffalocafewhitefish.com* ⏲ *No dinner Sun. and Mon.*

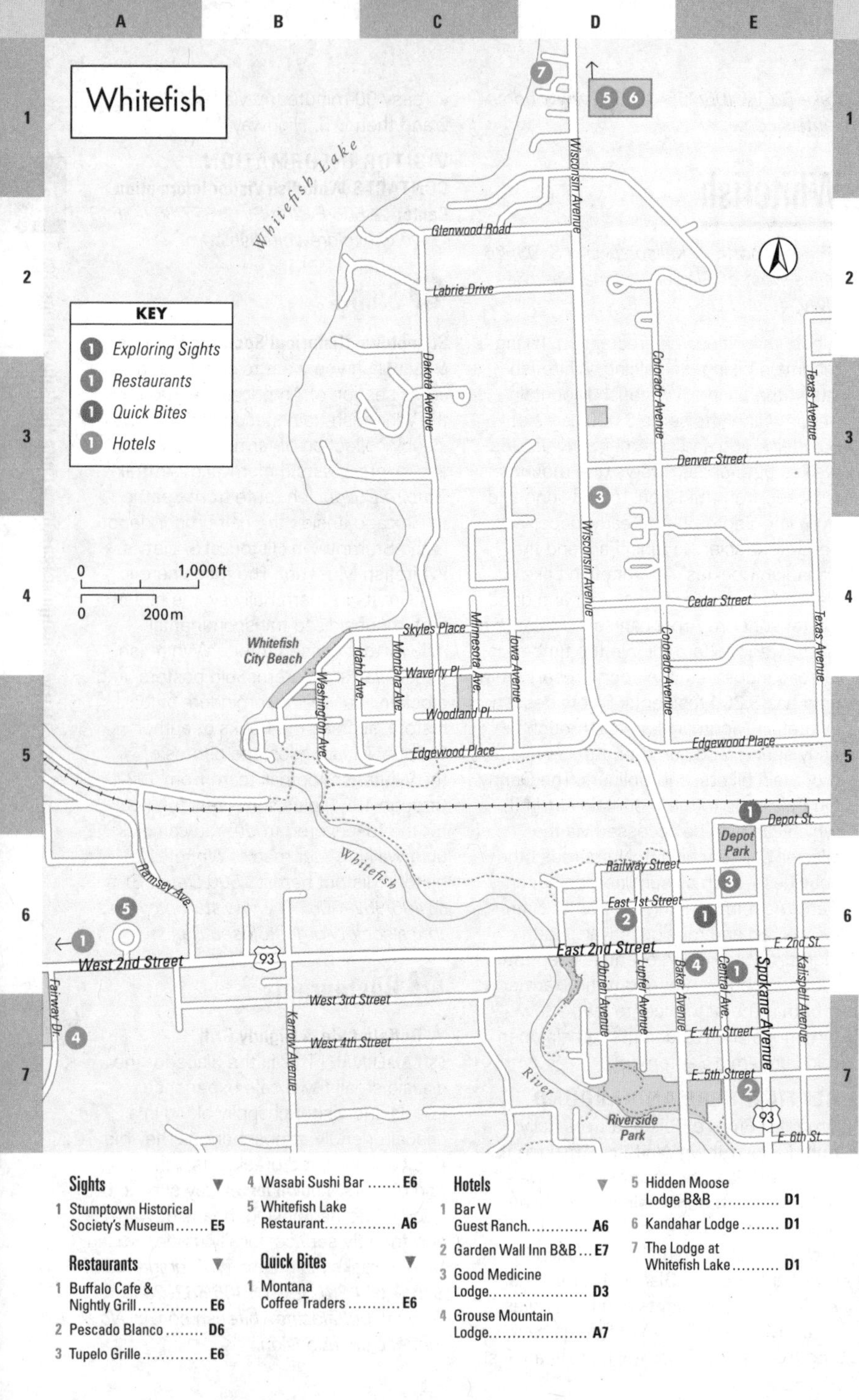

Whitefish
KEY
Exploring Sights
Restaurants
Quick Bites
Hotels
0 1,000 ft
0 200 m
A
B
C
D
E
1
2
3
4
5
6
7
Whitefish Lake
Glenwood Road
Labrie Drive
Wisconsin Avenue
Dakota Avenue
Colorado Avenue
Texas Avenue
Denver Street
Cedar Street
Skyles Place
Minnesota Ave.
Iowa Avenue
Whitefish City Beach
Idaho Ave.
Montana Ave.
Washington Ave.
Waverly Pl.
Woodland Pl.
Edgewood Place
Depot St.
Depot Park
Railway Street
East 1st Street
Whitefish
Ramsey Ave.
East 2nd Street
E. 2nd St.
West 2nd Street
93
West 3rd Street
West 4th Street
Karrow Avenue
Fairway Dr.
Obrien Avenue
Lupfer Avenue
Baker Avenue
Central Ave.
Spokane Avenue
Kalispell Avenue
E. 4th Street
E. 5th Street
E. 6th St.
River
Riverside Park
Sights
1 Stumptown Historical Society's Museum E5
Restaurants
1 Buffalo Cafe & Nightly Grill E6
2 Pescado Blanco D6
3 Tupelo Grille E6
4 Wasabi Sushi Bar E6
5 Whitefish Lake Restaurant A6
Quick Bites
1 Montana Coffee Traders E6
Hotels
1 Bar W Guest Ranch A6
2 Garden Wall Inn B&B ... E7
3 Good Medicine Lodge D3
4 Grouse Mountain Lodge A7
5 Hidden Moose Lodge B&B D1
6 Kandahar Lodge D1
7 The Lodge at Whitefish Lake D1

Pescado Blanco

$$ | **MEXICAN** | Mountain-Mexican fusion—fine Mexican cuisine with a Rocky Mountain flair—includes handmade tacos, enchiladas, fresh seafood, and a fresh salsa bar. In the summer, enjoy a cold beer or glass of wine on the patio with stunning mountain views. **Known for:** Grande Nachos that will bring you back again and again; friendly service in a relaxed and cozy setting; wild game twists on Mexican favorites. *Average main: $18 ✉ 235 1st St. ☎ 406/862–3290 🌐 www.pescadoblancorestaurant.com.*

Tupelo Grille

$$$ | **SOUTHERN** | In homage to the South, Louisiana native chef-owner Pat Carloss cooks up excellent dishes such as Low Country shrimp and grits, braised short ribs, Tupelo gumbo, and the tenderest bison filet you'll ever eat. Carloss rotates his well-chosen art collection in the dining room and further enlivens the atmosphere with piped-in New Orleans jazz, Dixieland, or zydeco music. **Known for:** one of the best restaurants in NW Montana; thoughtfully prepared Southern cuisine; busy in peak season, so make a reservation. *Average main: $30 ✉ 17 Central Ave. ☎ 406/862–6136 🌐 www.tupelogrille.com ⏲ No lunch.*

Wasabi Sushi Bar

$$$ | **ASIAN FUSION** | Not your typical Western ski-town eatery, Wasabi is the place for your sushi fix and Japanese cuisine. A nice selection of "fusion rolls" put new spins on old standbys. **Known for:** lavender-and-red walls bearing a huge fish mural; reservations needed during peak season; somewhat slow service. *Average main: $25 ✉ 419 E. 2nd St. ☎ 406/863–9283 🌐 www.wasabimt.com.*

Whitefish Lake Restaurant

$$$$ | **CONTEMPORARY** | In the historic clubhouse on the municipal golf course, dine on local favorites such as hand-cut steaks and prime rib, or fresh fish dishes such as baked halibut steak wrapped in herbs and phyllo dough. The Napoléon, made with eggplant, caramelized onions, roasted red peppers, and provolone, and topped with a spicy tomato sauce, makes a delicious vegetarian entrée. **Known for:** roasted duckling in blackberry brandy sauce; beautiful setting with fantastic views; classy Western ambience. *Average main: $32 ✉ 1200 U.S. 93 N ☎ 406/862–5285 🌐 www.whitefishlakerestaurant.com.*

Coffee and Quick Bites

Montana Coffee Traders

$ | **CAFÉ** | The Rocky Mountains might be a strange place for a coffee trader, but the folks at Montana Coffee Traders have been roasting their own beans south of Whitefish for decades. Fresh coffee, pastries, and homemade gelato are favorites at this popular downtown hangout. **Known for:** local farm-to-market pork bocadillo; organic, fair-trade, and socially responsible beans; can be crazy busy, but the staff works hard to smooth things out. *Average main: $4 ✉ 110 Central Ave. ☎ 406/862–7667 🌐 www.coffeetraders.com ⏲ No dinner.*

Hotels

Bar W Guest Ranch

$$$$ | **B&B/INN** | Just a short drive north of Whitefish, this working dude ranch, nestled between two pine-covered ridges at the base of Spencer Mountain, is a playground for horse people and outdoor-recreation enthusiasts. **Pros:** horse boarding provided, so you can bring your own to ride the 3,000-plus acres on state land; this is a great facility for business or family gatherings, with lots of activities and plenty of room; affordable daily B&B-only rates during the winter. **Cons:** children under seven not allowed on trail rides, though the ranch provides a miniature pony for them; there's a three-night minimum from June through August; summer rates are on the pricey side (but are all-inclusive). *Rooms from: $375*

⊠ 2875 Hwy. 93 W ☎ 406/863–9099, 866/828–2900 ⊕ www.thebarw.com ⇆ 10 rooms 🍴 Free breakfast.

Garden Wall Inn B&B
$$$$ | **B&B/INN** | This 1923, antiques-filled home has five spacious guest rooms with down duvets. **Pros:** gourmet breakfast is a three-course affair served on snow-white linens; afternoon complimentary beverages and hors d'oeuvres by the crackling fire; exceptional service with an attention to detail. **Cons:** the gardens are lovely but the house (and some of the rooms) are small; the front street can be busy and a little noisy; tends to book up fast, so plan ahead. $ *Rooms from: $215* ⊠ *504 Spokane Ave.* ☎ *406/862–3440, 888/530–1700* ⊕ *www.gardenwallinn.com* ⇆ *5 rooms* 🍴 *Free breakfast.*

Good Medicine Lodge
$$$$ | **B&B/INN** | Built of cedar timbers and decorated in a Western style, this lodge-style B&B is warm and inviting. **Pros:** Wi-Fi and many other amenities; handy services for skiers; one wheelchair-accessible room. **Cons:** no TV in most rooms; small property; small bathrooms. $ *Rooms from: $205* ⊠ *537 Wisconsin Ave.* ☎ *406/862–5488, 800/860–5488* ⊕ *www.goodmedicinelodge.com* ⇆ *9 rooms* 🍴 *Free breakfast.*

Grouse Mountain Lodge
$$$$ | **RESORT** | Always a Whitefish favorite, Grouse Mountain is consistently booked solid in July and August. **Pros:** Grouse Mountain provides shuttle service from the airport or Amtrak station, daily trips into town, and four trips each day to Whitefish Mountain Resort; they can also provide a rental car at the lodge for those who wish to travel to Glacier or the surrounding area; offers good ski-and-stay packages in the winter. **Cons:** must walk outside across parking lot to reach fitness room; hotel is too far from town to walk in for shopping or restaurants; some rooms and hallways are a little dark. $ *Rooms from: $225* ⊠ *2 Fairway Dr.* ☎ *844/868–7474* ⊕ *www.glacierparkcollection.com* ⇆ *145 rooms* 🍴 *No meals.*

★ **Hidden Moose Lodge B&B**
$$$$ | **B&B/INN** | At the foot of the road that climbs to Big Mountain, this two-story log lodge has a lively ski motif—a child's sled for a coffee table, an antique ski for a handrail. **Pros:** lodge is easy to find and away from hectic downtown traffic; atmosphere is very welcoming, and you may not want to leave; reasonably priced for outstanding accommodations. **Cons:** stairs could be difficult for some people with physical challenges, or who are stoved up after hitting the slopes for the first time; not close enough to town to walk for shopping or restaurants; strict cancellation policy means it is costly to cancel reservations within 30 days. $ *Rooms from: $239* ⊠ *1735 E. Lakeshore Dr.* ✣ *1.9 miles from downtown* ☎ *406/862–6516, 888/733–6667* ⊕ *www.hiddenmooselodge.com* ⇆ *14 rooms* 🍴 *Free breakfast.*

Kandahar Lodge
$$$$ | **HOTEL** | Located in the ski village, this hotel has the feel of a true mountain lodge: quiet and cozy, the massive lobby fireplace and the Snug Bar are attractive public spaces, while the wood-accented guest rooms feature tile-and-granite finishes, leather furniture, and down comforters on the beds. **Pros:** outstanding restaurant on-site serves the finest dinners on the mountain; wellness center spa is a plus, especially after that first day on the slope; ski-in, ski-out location is very convenient. **Cons:** even though it isn't ski season, they're closed to the public during some of the nicest times to be on the mountain; restaurant isn't open for breakfast or lunch, but they do provide a small continental breakfast; lots of stairs may make it difficult for people with physical limitations. $ *Rooms from: $250* ⊠ *3824 Big Mountain Rd.* ☎ *406/862–6247 café, 406/862–6098* ⊕ *www.kandaharlodge.com* ⊗ *Closed*

Apr., May, Oct., and Nov. 50 rooms Free breakfast.

The Lodge at Whitefish Lake
$$$$ | **RESORT** | On the edge of the lake, this luxury resort offers several accommodation options, including two lodges and a selection of luxury condo and home rentals nearby. **Pros:** Tesla charging station for your electric vehicle; lakefront location with stunning views; a walking path takes guests 1 mile into downtown. **Cons:** guests in roadside rooms have complained of highway noise and cramped quarters; pool area can get crowded and boisterous; no great room or large, comfy public space to relax in. *Rooms from: $350 1380 Wisconsin Ave. 406/863–4000, 877/887–4026 www.lodgeatwhitefishlake.com 145 rooms No meals.*

Nightlife

The Great Northern Bar and Grill
BARS/PUBS | A locals' hangout, particularly for the singles crowd, the Great Northern Bar and Grill rocks with local bands, open-mike nights, and the occasional sort-of-big-name gig. The stage is surrounded by signs from Whitefish enterprises that are now defunct. Hang out inside or head out to the patio to enjoy a brew and a pile of nachos on cool summer evenings. *27 Central Ave. 406/862–2816 www.greatnorthernbar.com.*

Performing Arts

O'Shaughnessy Cultural Arts Center
CONCERTS | Home of the Whitefish Theater Company, this intimate theater hosts a variety of year-round live performances and concerts, as well as classic and independent films. In August, the O'Shaughnessy hosts the Glacier Symphony's Festival Amadeus, a week-long classical music festival. *1 Central Ave. 406/862–5371.*

Shopping

Imagination Station
TOYS | **FAMILY** | The largest toy shop in northwest Montana, Imagination Station has myriad fun, educational, and creative toys and gifts in all price ranges. It also has shops in Kalispell and Missoula. *221 Central Ave. 406/862–5668 www.montanatoys.com.*

Sage and Cedar
SPA/BEAUTY | This shop sells homemade and organic lotions, soaps, massage products and perfumes inspired by Montana's natural legacy. There's also a store in Kalispell. *214 Central Ave. 406/862–9411 www.sageandcedar.com.*

Activities

CAMPING

Whitefish Lake State Park Campground. On Whitefish Lake in a shady grove of tall pines, this clean campground is very popular and fills early. It has a shallow bay for swimming, a boat launch, and views of the Whitefish Range. One downside is that trains rumble through at all hours. *1615 W. Lakeshore Dr., ½ mile from downtown on U.S. 93 N, then 1 mile north on State Park Rd. 406/862–3991 stateparks.mt.gov/whitefish-lake/ 25 sites*

DOGSLEDDING

Dog Sled Adventures
LOCAL SPORTS | The dogs are raring to run from early December to late March at Dog Sled Adventures, where friendly mushers gear the ride to passengers ranging from kids to senior citizens. Bundled up in a sled, you'll be whisked through Stillwater State Forest on a 1½-hour ride over a 12-mile trail. Reservations are necessary. *8400 U.S. 93 ✣ 20 miles north of Whitefish, 2 miles north of Olney 406/881–2275 www.dogsledadventuresmontana.com $150.*

Whitefish Mountain Resort is one of the top ski areas in Montana.

FISHING

Toss a fly on one of the region's trout streams or lakes and you might snag a Westslope cutthroat, rainbow trout, or grayling. In winter you can dangle a line through a sawed hole in the ice of Whitefish Lake.

Lakestream Fly Fishing Shop

FISHING | The best place for fishing gear in Whitefish is Lakestream Fly Fishing Shop. Guided trips to secluded private lakes, equipment, and fly-fishing gear are sold at the shop. Advice is free. ✉ *669 Spokane Ave* ☎ *406/862–1298* 🌐 *www.lakestream.com.*

Tally Lake Ranger District

FISHING | Stop here for recommendations on good fishing spots and for maps of the Flathead National Forest. ✉ *650 Wolfpack Way, Kalispell* ☎ *406/758–5204* 🌐 *www.fs.usda.gov/flathead.*

SKIING AND SNOWBOARDING

Whitefish Mountain Resort

SKIING/SNOWBOARDING | **FAMILY** | The Whitefish Mountain Resort on Big Mountain has been one of Montana's top ski areas since the 1930s. Eight miles from Whitefish, it's popular among train travelers from the Pacific Northwest and the upper Midwest. The Base Lodge houses a Kids Center, bar and cafe, shop, and office for lift tickets, rentals, and lockers. Chair 6 is directly off the upper-level exit. The snow season runs from early December through early April.

The mountain's most distinctive features are its widely spaced trees, which—when encased in snow—are known as snow ghosts. It's 3,000 skiable acres, plus out-of-bounds areas, are serviced by 11 chairlifts: three high-speed quads, two fixed-grip quads, and four triples. Two T-bars and a magic carpet round out the uphill transportation.

Whitefish Mountain offers a lot of terrain to explore and many different lines to discover among those widely spaced trees. The pleasure of exploration and discovery—such as finding a fresh cache of powder many days after a snowstorm—is perhaps the main reason to ski Whitefish Mountain. Easy discovery comes with the help of free tours by mountain ambassadors. They meet intermediate skiers near the bottom of the Big Mountain Express, at 10:30 am and 1:30 pm daily.

In general the pitch is in the intermediate to advanced-intermediate range; there's not a whole lot of super-steep or super-easy skiing, though recent improvements are correcting this. A sameness in pitch, however, doesn't mean a sameness in skiing. With trails falling away on all sides of the mountain, there is a tremendous variation in exposure and hence in snow texture; also take into consideration the number of trees to deal with and the views (the best being northeast toward Glacier National Park).

Five terrain parks provide aerial fun for the bravest freestylers, and Chair 3 on the front side provides access to four of them. The fifth, the Goat Haunt Skier/Boarder Cross Course, is accessed from Chair 7.

The only downside can be the weather. Foggy days are not uncommon; at those times you're thankful that those snow ghosts are around as points of reference. Sometimes, however, the fog is low enough that you can ski above it, as if you're skiing in heaven.

During the summer months the mountain comes alive with wildflowers and an abundance of activities provided by the resort. Ride the lift up the mountain and rent one of their mountain bikes to ride down. Go for a "walk in the treetops" from a boardwalk suspended in the trees and guided by expert naturalists. The zipline tour will carry you at 50 miles per hour to a height of more than 100 feet in the air. Children and adults alike will enjoy the thrill of the Alpine Slide as you race down the mountain on your own sled. ✉ *3808 Big Mountain Rd.* ☎ *406/862–2900, 877/754–3474, 406/862–1995 Equipment Rentals* 🌐 *www.skiwhitefish.com* ☞ *Full-day ticket $85; night skiing $26; snowboard or ski equipment rentals from $34 per day.*

BACKCOUNTRY SKIING AND SNOWBOARDING

Because of an unusually liberal policy regarding skiing out-of-bounds, backcountry powder skiing is possible from the top of Whitefish Mountain. For the most part, the ski patrol does not prevent riders from crossing ski-area boundary ropes, although if you do so and get into trouble, you're responsible for paying rescue costs. Those who choose to travel out-of-bounds run a high risk of getting lost: it's easy to ski too far down the wrong drainage, creating the prospect of a tiring and excruciating bushwhack back to the base.

Glacier Country Avalanche Center

SKIING/SNOWBOARDING | The backcountry avalanche danger varies with the winter snowpack, so it's best to check the local avalanche forecast with Glacier Country Avalanche Center and to carry transceivers, probe poles, shovels, and, most important, a knowledge of backcountry safety and first aid. Call the avalanche forecast hotline if you are planning to go out. ✉ *Flathead Avalanche Center, 10 Hungry Horse Dr.* ☎ *406/387–3887, 406/257–8402 avalanche forecast hotline* 🌐 *www.flatheadavalanche.org.*

FACILITIES

Overview: 2,300-foot vertical drop; 3,000 skiable acres; 12% beginner, 37% intermediate, 51% advanced; 3 high-speed quad chairs, 2 quad chairs, 4 triple chairs, 3 surface lifts; 4 terrain parks and a skier/boarder cross course; snow report ☎ *406/862–7669, 877/754–3474.*

LESSONS AND PROGRAMS

Ski and Snowboard School

SKIING/SNOWBOARDING | **FAMILY** | Group ski and snowboard lessons start at $89 for a half-day, including lower-mountain lift ticket; cross-country, telemark skiing, and adaptive lessons are also available. Specialty clinics such as racing, mogul, and freestyle techniques are also available, as are children's programs. ✉ *Whitefish* ☎ *406/862–2900* 🌐 *www.skiwhitefish.com.*

NORDIC SKIING

There are two machine-groomed track systems in the Whitefish area: both systems serve their purpose well enough, but don't expect inspiring views or a sense of wilderness seclusion. Visit the Glacier Nordic Club website for more information.

Big Mountain Trails

SKIING/SNOWBOARDING | The Big Mountain trails offer 15 miles of groomed trails. ✉ *3315 Big Mountain Rd.* ☎ *406/862–9498* 🌐 *www.glaciernordicclub.org.*

Glacier Nordic Club

SKIING/SNOWBOARDING | The well-groomed trails of the Glacier Nordic Touring Center meander around the rolling grounds of the Whitefish Lake Golf Course and are suitable for all levels, from children to serious fitness skiers. ✉ *1200 U.S. 93 W* ☎ *406/862–9498* 🌐 *www.glaciernordicclub.com.*

SNOWMOBILING

There are more than 200 groomed snowmobile trails in the Flathead region. Unless you are an experienced snowmobiler and expert at avalanche forecasting, you should take a guided trip.

Whitefish Marine

BOATING | This outfitter rents boats and water accessories in summer and leases snowmobiles and provides guided snowmobile tours in winter ✉ *5960 U.S. 93 S* ☎ *406/862–8594* 🌐 *www.whitefishmarine.com* 🎫 *From $250.*

Columbia Falls

8 miles east of Whitefish via U.S. 93 and Hwy. 40.

GETTING HERE AND AROUND

Glacier International Airport is 7 miles south via Highway 2. Amtrak in Whitefish is 7 miles to the west. Glacier National Park via U.S. Highway 2 is only 15 miles away.

Sights

Amazing Ventures Fun Center

AMUSEMENT PARK/WATER PARK | **FAMILY** | Get lost in the maze at the Amazing Ventures Fun Center, a circuitous outdoor route made of plywood walls and ladders, with viewing areas where parents can watch their kids (and give directions when necessary). Other attractions include Bankshot Basketball, go-karts, 18 holes of miniature golf, thriller bumper boats in a pond, and a picnic area. ✉ *10265 U.S. 2 E, Coram* ☎ *406/387–5902* 🌐 *www.amazingfuncenter.com* ⏲ *Closed Sept. 20–Memorial Day.*

Big Sky Waterpark

AMUSEMENT PARK/WATER PARK | **FAMILY** | A popular summertime spot, Montana's biggest water park has 10 waterslides and a giant whirlpool, as well as a miniature golf course, arcade games, bumper cars, a carousel, a climbing tower, barbecue grills, a picnic area, and food service. ✉ *7211 U.S. Hwy. 2 E* ✣ *at Hwy. 206* ☎ *406/892–5025* 🌐 *www.bigskywp.com* 🎫 *$28.*

House of Mystery–Montana Vortex

AMUSEMENT PARK/WATER PARK | **FAMILY** | You've found the power center of Montana at the House of Mystery–Montana Vortex, a wacky roadside attraction where the laws of physics don't apply and other mystifying phenomena prevail. ✉ *7800 U.S. 2 E* ☎ *406/892–1210* 🎫 *$12.*

North Fork Road

SCENIC DRIVE | Enter Glacier National Park through the back door by driving the

North Fork Road. It's a rutted, bumpy, dusty gravel road that's teeming with wildlife along the North Fork of the Flathead River. The 40 miles to the Polebridge entrance station passes through thick forests, some of which burned during fires of 2001 and 2003. As a result, many of these areas become seas of purple fireweed in early summer. You can opt out early and enter Glacier at the Camas Creek entrance gate and avoid rough roads. If you make it all the way to Polebridge, stop at the Mercantile for lunch or one of their famous huckleberry bear claws. ✉ *Columbia Falls* ✣ *From Nucleus Ave. drive north to the T, turn east and follow North Fork Rd. [Hwy. 486].*

Restaurants

The Back Room of the Nite Owl
$$ | **AMERICAN** | Locals wait in line for the fall-off-the-bone barbecue ribs, broasted chicken, and fry bread served with honey butter. The atmosphere is very casual, with a large main room, several smaller eating areas (great for families), and a spacious patio. *Average main: $15* ✉ *522 9th St. W* ☎ *406/892–3131* 🌐 *www.niteowlbackroom.com.*

Backslope Brewing
$$ | **AMERICAN** | Pair a great local beer with delicious casual fare at this local brewery, where there are always about eight different kinds of house beer on tap as well as kombucha, sparkling water, and nitro iced coffee. The premium burgers and sandwiches are exceptionally good, especially when accompanied by hand-cut garlic Parmesan fries. **Known for:** local brewery; creative menu; garlic Parmesan fries. *Average main: $13* ✉ *1107 9 St. W* ☎ *406/897–2850* 🌐 *backslopebrewing.com* ⏲ *Closed Sun. Closed nightly at 8 pm.*

Three Forks Grille
$$$ | **AMERICAN** | Italian-influenced mountain cuisine is prepared with care at the two-level Grille, which emphasizes local, sustainably produced ingredients. The regional focus extends to the artwork that adorns the walls; many pieces are by area artists. **Known for:** one of the only fine-dining spots in the area; offers vegetarian, gluten-free, and dairy-free choices; whitefish caught right in Flathead Lake. *Average main: $23* ✉ *729 Nucleus Ave.* ☎ *406/892–2900* 🌐 *threeforksgrille.com* ⏲ *No lunch Sun.*

Hotels

Cedar Creek Lodge
$$$$ | **HOTEL** | If you want the atmosphere of a mountain lodge with modern amenities and good connectivity, this property is ideal. **Pros:** mountain lodge atmosphere; modern amenities; great included extras. **Cons:** 18 miles from West Glacier; room price is high during peak season for location; inside a town, so room views are not great. *Rooms from: $350* ✉ *930 2nd Ave. W* ☎ *855/733–4542, 406/412–4660* 🌐 *www.glaciernationalparklodges.com/lodging/cedar-creek-lodge* *64 rooms* *Free breakfast.*

Meadow Lake Golf Resort
$$$$ | **RESORT** | **FAMILY** | As the name indicates, the links are front and center here. **Pros:** free shuttle service to Whitefish Mountain Resort; very accommodating for families; indoor and outdoor pools and two hot tubs. **Cons:** fine dining is limited in the Columbia Falls area; although centrally located between Whitefish Mountain Resort, Flathead Lake, or Glacier National Park, it's a fair distance to any of the places; the hotel is in the middle of a vacation home/condo association. *Rooms from: $360* ✉ *100 St. Andrew's Dr.* ☎ *800/321-4653, 406/892–8700* 🌐 *www.meadowlake.com* *264 rooms* *No meals.*

Nightlife

Blue Moon Nite Club, Casino & Grill
MUSIC CLUBS | Whether the owner's band is playing on the stage or cowboys are

serenading a sparse crowd of locals during karaoke, this place is a hoot. The wooden dance floor gets a good scuffing on Western dance and country-swing nights. Two stuffed grizzly bears rear up near the entrance, and other species decorate the large saloon as well. ✉ *6105 Hwy. 2 W* ☎ *406/892–3110* 🌐 *www.bluemoonmontana.com.*

Shopping

Huckleberry Patch Restaurant & Gift Shop
FOOD/CANDY | Huckleberry Patch Restaurant & Gift Shop has been the huckleberry headquarters of the state for more than 50 years, selling the purple wild berry native to the region. It has an excellent selection of jams, candies, coffee, fudge, barbecue sauce, and huckleberry-scented lotions. Don't miss their outstanding huckleberry pie or milkshakes. ✉ *8868 U.S. 2 E, Hungry Horse* ☎ *800/527–7340* 🌐 *www.huckleberrypatch.com.*

Activities

CAMPING

Columbia Falls RV Park. The in-town location, with tall trees to shelter against the breeze, is convenient to the Big Sky Waterpark, shopping, the city pool, and the Flathead River. Pull-through spaces are adequate for large RVs, and the tent area is grassy, with electricity for some sites. ✉ *1000 3rd Ave. E, on U.S. 2* ☎ *406/892–1122* 🌐 *www.columbiafalls-rvpark.com* *76 sites.*

Seeley Lake

120 miles south of Glacier National Park via U.S. 2, Hwy. 206, and Hwy. 83.

Bordered by campgrounds, hiking trails, and wildlife-viewing opportunities, this community of 1,659 centers on lovely Seeley Lake. Nearby is the Big Blackfoot River, a setting in *A River Runs Through It,* Norman McLean's reflection on family and fishing. Host to races and leisure outings, the Seeley Creek Nordic Ski Trails roll across hills and meadows. In winter, 350 miles of snowmobile trails rip through the woods. The major industry, logging, which began in 1892, is evident on some hillsides.

GETTING HERE AND AROUND

Missoula International is the nearest airport, 55 miles and an hour away via Montana Highway 200 and U.S. Highway 83. It is best to have a car, since few places provide a shuttle.

Sights

Clearwater Canoe Trail
SPORTS—SIGHT | Paddling on the 3½-miles along an isolated portion of the Clearwater River, you may see moose and will likely see songbirds, great blue herons, and belted kingfishers. The Seeley Lake Ranger Station has free maps and directions to the put-in for the two-hour paddle. ✉ *Seeley Lake* ✣ *3 miles north of Seeley on Hwy. 83* ☎ *406/677–2233* 🌐 *www.fs.usda.gov/lolo/* *Free.*

Morrell Falls
TRAIL | A 2½-mile hike (one-way) leads to the lovely cascades of Morrell Falls. It is actually a series of falls, with the longest about a 100-foot drop. This is a moderately difficult family hike, perfect for a picnic, and often used by bicyclists and horse riders. Maps and travel information are available at the Seeley Lake Ranger District office. **■ TIP→ Don't forget your bear spray.** ✉ *Seeley Lake* ✣ *From Hwy. 83, turn east on Morrell Creek Rd. and follow signs* ☎ *406/677–2233* 🌐 *www.fs.fed.us* *Free.*

Seeley Lake Museum and Visitors Center
INFO CENTER | Logging's colorful past is displayed in the big log barn at Seeley Lake Museum and Visitors Center, along with tools of the trade and visitor information. ✉ *2920 Hwy. 83 S* ✣ *At mile marker 13.5* ☎ *406/677–2990* 🌐 *www.*

seeleyhistory.org Free Closed Labor Day–Memorial Day.

Restaurants

Lindey's Steak House

$$$ | **STEAKHOUSE** | Locals will send you here to watch the sun set over the lake while dining on the only thing on the menu: steak. Select cuts, all 16-ounce portions, are served with potatoes, garlic bread, and pickled watermelon rind served family-style. *Average main: $27* *3129 Hwy. 83* *406/677–9229* *www.lindeysmontana.com* *No lunch.*

Hotels

Double Arrow Resort

$$$ | **RESORT** | The handsome log main lodge built in 1929 combines European grace and Western trimmings on a 200-acre spread. **Pros:** excellent location for a wedding or a family reunion; perfect combination of luxury and rustic and natural; wonderful customer-centered hospitality. **Cons:** closest airport is in Missoula, which is 55 miles from Double Arrow; it's 100 miles to Whitefish for those traveling by Amtrak; the town of Seeley Lake offers fewer cultural and culinary attractions than other communities. *Rooms from: $165* *301 Lodge Way* *Hwy. 83, milepost 12, 2 miles south of Seeley Lake* *406/677–2777* *www.doublearrowresort.com* *27 rooms* *Free breakfast.*

Rich Ranch

$$$$ | **RESORT** | At this small, personal, and beautiful guest ranch bordering the Bob Marshall Wilderness, all-inclusive packages are the rule. **Pros:** there is plenty to do even if you never leave the ranch; owners are very accommodating and helpful; great place to get far away from everything but nature. **Cons:** it's several hours to get to Glacier National Park; there's a three-day minimum and reasonably high daily rates, so it's not cheap; not suitable for those who want access to a variety of cultural and culinary experiences. *Rooms from: $375* *939 Cottonwood Lakes Rd.* *406/677–2317, 800/532–4350* *www.richranch.com* *9 cabins* *All-inclusive.*

Shopping

Deer Country Quilts

TEXTILES/SEWING | Find country fabrics in Deer Country Quilts, as well as thousands of bolts of flannels, batiks, and cotton in the store's lovely log lodge studio. Ask about receptions for quilters and the classes they offer all year long. *3166 Hwy. 83 N* *406/677–2730* *www.deercountryquilts.com.*

Grizzly Claw Trading Company

LOCAL SPECIALTIES | Beaver pelts, furs, blankets, and painted buffalo and elk hides hang from walls in the Grizzly Claw Trading Company. Other one-of-a-kind items also are available, including pottery, jewelry, clothing, wood carvings, and furniture. *3187 Hwy. 83* *406/677–0008* *www.grizzlyclawtrading.com.*

Activities

CROSS-COUNTRY SKIING

Seeley Creek Nordic Ski Trails

SKIING/SNOWBOARDING | **FAMILY** | You can romp in deep snows at the edge of town. Designed by Olympian Jon Elliot, this trail system is groomed for skate and classic skiing. Nearby are dogsled trails. The trail systems share a parking lot and covered picnic area, where you can join a campfire to warm your toes. *3583 Highway 83* *Forest Rd. 477; from Hwy. 83, turn east on Morrell Creek Rd., aka Cottonwood Lakes Rd., and drive 1 mile to trailhead* *406/677–2990* *www.seeleylakenordic.org.*

LLAMA TREKKING

Swan Mountain Llama Trekking

HIKING/WALKING | Lead your own llama on a day trip, overnight trek, or fishing expedition. The company even offers evening wine and cheese outings and yoga with llamas trips. Have no fear: llamas are smart and curious animals that can be handled by people of all ages. Located at Swan Valley Ranch between Big Fork and Seeley Lake just off Highway 83. ✉ *26356 Soup Creek Rd., Swan Lake* ☎ *406/387–4405* 🌐 *www.llamatreksmontana.com.*

Holland Lake

19 miles north of Seeley Lake via Hwy. 83.

Outdoorsy types come to this 400-acre lake for fishing, boating, swimming, hiking, trail riding, and camping in summer and ice fishing, cross-country skiing, snowshoeing, and snowmobiling in winter. To pursue any of the activities available in this remote setting, you must come equipped with your own canoe, motor launch, or snowmobile: your company will be kokanee salmon, rainbow trout, and bull trout, plus the handful of people who run Holland Lake Lodge. Maps for the numerous trails that depart from the lake area are available at the lodge or through the Forest Service office. Some routes climb the Swan Range into the Bob Marshall Wilderness.

GETTING HERE AND AROUND

Both Missoula International Airport and Glacier International Airport in Kalispell are approximately 85 miles away via U.S. Highway 83, otherwise known as the Seeley Swan Highway. A car is a must.

Sights

Holland Falls

TRAIL | The hike to Holland Falls is about 1½ mile from the lodge. The last bit is a steep climb, but it's well worth it for the view. ✉ *Holland Lake Rd., Condon* ✣ *From Hwy. 83, turn east on Forest Rd. 44 for 3 miles to Holland Lake Rd.* ☎ *406/837–7500* 🌐 *www.fs.fed.us* 🎟 *Free.*

Hotels

Holland Lake Lodge

$$$$ | **B&B/INN** | When the snow flies, this lodge is nearly buried, which makes for cozy fireside dining and relaxing. **Pros:** morning coffee (or afternoon cocktails) delivered to your room or cabin; you can't ask for a better place to relax, particularly during the shoulder seasons; the lake offers great paddling and fishing, so it's great the lodge rents kayaks. **Cons:** the 4 miles of unpaved road can be a bit rough and very congested during the summer; this is a heavily used area in July and August for packers and hikers heading into the backcountry; no TVs and shared bathrooms in the main lodge. 💲 *Rooms from: $300* ✉ *1947 Holland Lake Rd., Condon* ☎ *406/754–2282* 🌐 *www.hollandlakelodge.com* 🛏 *15 rooms* 🍽 *All-inclusive.*

Activities

CAMPING

Holland Lake Campground. Large trees provide lots of shade for campers near the lake. The spot is popular with outfitters who pack horses into the nearby Bob Marshall Wilderness. Food service is available nearby at Holland Lake Lodge. ✉ *200 Ranger Station Rd., Bigfork* ☎ *406/837–7503, 406/837–7500* 🌐 *www.fs.usda.gov/activity/flathead/recreation/camping-cabins* 🛏 *40 sites.*

Bob Marshall Wilderness Area

5 miles east of Hwy. 83 via Pyramid Pass Trail, Lion Creek Pass Trail, or Smith Creek Pass Trail.

The Bob Marshall, Scapegoat, and Great Bear wilderness areas encompass 1.5 million rugged, roadless, remote acres within the Flathead National Forest. Preservation pioneer, forester, and cofounder of the Wilderness Society, Bob Marshall pushed Congress in 1964 to create the wilderness area that bears his name. Since then, little has altered the landscape, which runs 60 miles along the Continental Divide. Access more than 1,000 miles of wilderness trails from near Seeley Lake at Pyramid Pass Trail and Holland Lake at Pyramid Pass, Condon's Lion Creek Pass, and Smith Creek Pass, where hikers are sure to meet outfitters and packhorses. An old airstrip at Shafer Meadows is used for float parties on the wild white-water Middle Fork of the Flathead.

GETTING HERE AND AROUND

The Bob Marshall Wilderness can be accessed from the west near Seeley Lake and Holland Lake via Highway 83, from the east near Choteau and Bynum via Highway 89, and from the northwest near Hungry Horse via Highway 2 and the East Reservoir Road. The latter is a long, winding gravel road that's impassable during the winter; a four-wheel-drive vehicle is a good idea. A complete list of trails, elevations, and backcountry campsites can be found in the book *Hiking Montana's Bob Marshall Wilderness* by Erik Molvar.

The Rich Ranch offers pack trips into the wilderness from its location near Seeley Lake. *See Hotels in Seeley Lake.*

Sights

Flathead National Forest

FOREST | Information on the Bob Marshall Wilderness is available through the Flathead National Forest website or office, which have maps, listings of outfitters and access points, and safety information about travel in bear country. ✉ *650 Wolfpack Way, Kalispell* ☎ *406/758–5208* 🌐 *www.fs.fed.us* 🎟 *Free* ⏲ *Closed weekends.*

Spotted Bear

FOREST | At the end of a long and often washboarded gravel road, Spotted Bear is a remote entrance into the Bob Marshall Wilderness. You'll find there a ranger station, outfitter's ranch, campground, swimming, and rafting a short distance down the South Fork of the Flathead River to the Hungry Horse Reservoir. ✉ *East Side Reservoir Rd. #38* ✣ *55 miles from Hungry Horse on either E. or W. Hungry Horse Reservoir Rd.* ☎ *406/387–3800* 🌐 *www.fs.usda.gov* 🎟 *Free.*

Hotels

★ Deep Canyon Guest Ranch

$$$$ | **ALL-INCLUSIVE** | A snug haven in a rugged landscape, this 1,200-acre ranch is surrounded by pines and aspens deep in Teton Canyon, an eastern gateway to the Bob Marshall Wilderness. **Pros:** true Montana experience; clean, rustic wood cabins; longtime Montana natives as hosts. **Cons:** nearest airport is 1½ hours away; no cell-phone service; pricey, multiday packages make it a big commitment. $ *Rooms from: $2360* ✉ *2055 Teton Canyon Rd., Choteau* ☎ *406/466–2044* 🌐 *www.deepcanyonguestranch.com* ⏲ *Closed late Nov.–Apr.* *8 rooms* 🍴 *Free breakfast.*

Activities

CAMPING

Spotted Bear Campground. Alongside the South Fork of the Flathead River, this remote campground offers flat sites shaded by tall pines. Grizzly bears frequent the area, so a clean camp is imperative. Trailheads lead into wilderness areas. ✉ *Forest Service Rd., 55 miles southeast of U.S. 2 at Hungry Horse* ☎ *406/387–3800 (winter), 406/758–5376 (summer)* 🌐 *www.fs.usda.gov/activity/flathead/recreation/camping-cabins* *13 sites.*

FISHING

Bob Marshall Wilderness Outfitters

FISHING | Week-long pack and float trips go deep into the backcountry for fly-fishing in the wilderness. This

Orvis-endorsed expedition is limited to 12 people per trip. ✉ *41088 Roberts Rd., Charlo* ✣ *55 miles from Hungry Horse on either E. or W. Hungry Horse Reservoir Rd. toward Spotted Bear Ranger Station* ☎ *406/644–7889* 🌐 *www.bobmarshallwildernessoutfitters.com.*

Montana Wilderness Lodge & Outfitters
FISHING | Lodge guides conduct seven-day wilderness float and fishing trips in the wilderness area from the end of June to mid-September. Fishing from the lodge is also a fruitful way to hook a bunch of wily cutthroats. All-inclusive family-friendly vacations are also available. ✉ *West Side Hungry Horse Reservoir Rd.* ✣ *55 miles east of Hungry Horse* ☎ *406/249–6501* 🌐 *www.wildmontana.com.*

HORSEBACK RIDING

Diamond R Guest Ranch
HORSEBACK RIDING | The outfitters offer trail rides and guided fishing, floating, and hiking trips (as well as combinations of these activities) in some of the wildest country you will ever experience. Lodging and meals on-site are available for $150/night. ✉ *East Side Hungry Horse Reservoir Rd.* ✣ *55 miles from Hungry Horse* ☎ *800/597–9465* 🌐 *www.diamondrranch.com.*

Missoula

A fertile valley hemmed in by mountains cradles Missoula, the cultural center of northwest Montana. The largest city in the vicinity (population 75,500) is the home of the University of Montana. In the aptly nicknamed Garden City, maple trees line the residential streets and the Clark Fork River meanders through the center of town; a 6-mile riverside trail passes the university en route to Hellgate Canyon. Missoula makes a good base for regional exploration by way of Interstate 90 east–west, U.S. 93 north–south, and numerous back roads.

In 1860 French trappers dubbed this trading settlement the Hell Gate when they discovered bones and bodies in the canyon after a bloody battle between Blackfeet and other Native Americans. Settlers did not arrive until more than 50 years after the Lewis and Clark expedition traveled through the area. Gold speculators, homesteaders, and the coming of the Northern Pacific Railroad in 1883 all helped establish the town.

Many of Missoula's most unique businesses are found on the so-called Hip Strip (primarily South Higgins Street, from the intersection of Brooks Street to the south end of the bridge). It's a great place to stroll, shop, sip, and eat, especially in the summer. In addition to numerous shops, there's a popular ice-cream store, a brewery, restaurants, and nightspots.

GETTING HERE AND AROUND

The recently expanded Missoula International Airport operates flights daily with several major airlines. Most hotels have shuttles to and from the airport. By car, it is 120 miles south of Kalispell via U.S. Highway 93, and 200 miles north of Bozeman via Interstate Highway 90. Greyhound provide bus service to Missoula, but exploring the region beyond Missoula requires a car.

Missoula is home to the Adventure Cycling Association (formerly Bike Centennial), so it's no surprise that the city has more bicycles than people. Exploring by bicycle is popular and easy: downtown and the university district are relatively flat and have bike paths and bike traffic lanes; many storefronts are adorned with bike racks. Within the center of the city, walking is a good option, too, particularly given that parking is at a premium and that the university itself is a car-free zone. There are numerous parks, and dozens of walking and biking paths wend through town.

VISITOR INFORMATION

CONTACTS Destination Missoula. ✉ *101 E. Main St.* ☎ *800/526–3465* 🌐 *www.destinationmissoula.org.*

Sights

A Carousel for Missoula

CAROUSEL | FAMILY | In 1995, after four years and more than 100,000 hours of volunteer work, this restored 1918 carousel took its first spin in downtown Caras Park. Kids hop in the saddles of hand-carved steeds and try to grab their very own brass ring. The carousel's horses and chariots are accompanied by tunes from the largest band organ in continuous use in the United States. The Dragon Hollow play area next to the carousel features a dragon, a castle, and many play structures. ✉ *101 Carousel Dr.* ☎ *406/549–8382* 🌐 *www.carouselformissoula.com* 🎫 *$3.*

Caras Park

CITY PARK | Downtown's favorite green space, the park has a walking path along the Clark Fork River and a summer pavilion that hosts live musical performances and other events. The annual calendar includes several brewfests, the River City Roots Festival (last weekend in August), and GermanFest (early September). In the summer, Downtown ToNight is a Thursday evening event that also features food, music, and what the Chamber of Commerce likes to call a "beverage garden." On Wednesday, Out to Lunch brings a band, food trucks, and vendors, and activities for the kids to help get everyone over Hump Day. ✉ *Front and Ryman Sts.* ☎ *406/543–4238* 🌐 *www.missouladowntown.com* 🎫 *Free.*

Council Grove State Park

HISTORIC SITE | History buffs appreciate this park's significance as the place where Isaac Stevens and the Pend d'Oreille and Flathead Kootenai Indians signed the Hell Gate Treaty in 1855 to relinquish their ancestral lands in exchange for the Flathead Reservation in the Mission Valley. The park occupies 187 primitive acres; it has interpretive signs, a picnic area, fishing access, and a hiking trail. ✉ *11249 Mullan Rd.* ✣ *To get here, travel west from downtown on Interstate 90, exit at Reserve Street, then drive 2 miles south on Reserve and 10 miles west on Mullan Rd.* ☎ *406/542–5500* 🌐 *www.stateparks.mt.gov* 🎫 *$6 per vehicle, $4 walk in, on bicycle, or by bus.*

Higgins Block

BUILDING | This Queen Anne–style commercial structure, a granite, copper-domed corner building with red polychromed brick, occupies a block in the heart of downtown. On the National Register of Historic Places, it's now home to a bank and several shops. ✉ *202 N. Higgins Ave.* 🌐 *www.missouladowntown.com* 🎫 *Free.*

Historical Museum at Fort Missoula

MUSEUM | Fort Missoula, at the western edge of town, was established in 1877 at the height of the U.S. Army's conflict with the Nez Perce, led by Chief Joseph. The museum's indoor and outdoor exhibits, including 13 historic structures relocated from nearby sites, depict and explain the early development of Missoula County. The black 25th Infantry of bicycle soldiers arrived in 1888 to test bicycles for military use; near-life-size photos depict the soldiers during an expedition to Yellowstone National Park's Mammoth Terraces. Uniforms and artifacts are also on display. They ultimately rode one-speed bicycles from Missoula to St. Louis. Guided tours are available by appointment. Sadly, there is very little material about the Native Americans who lived here before the fort was established. ✉ *Fort Missoula, 3400 Captain Rawn Way* ☎ *406/728–3476* 🌐 *www.fortmissoulamuseum.org* 🎫 *$4.*

Missoula Art Museum

MUSEUM | Each year two-dozen changing contemporary art exhibits join a permanent collection featuring works by

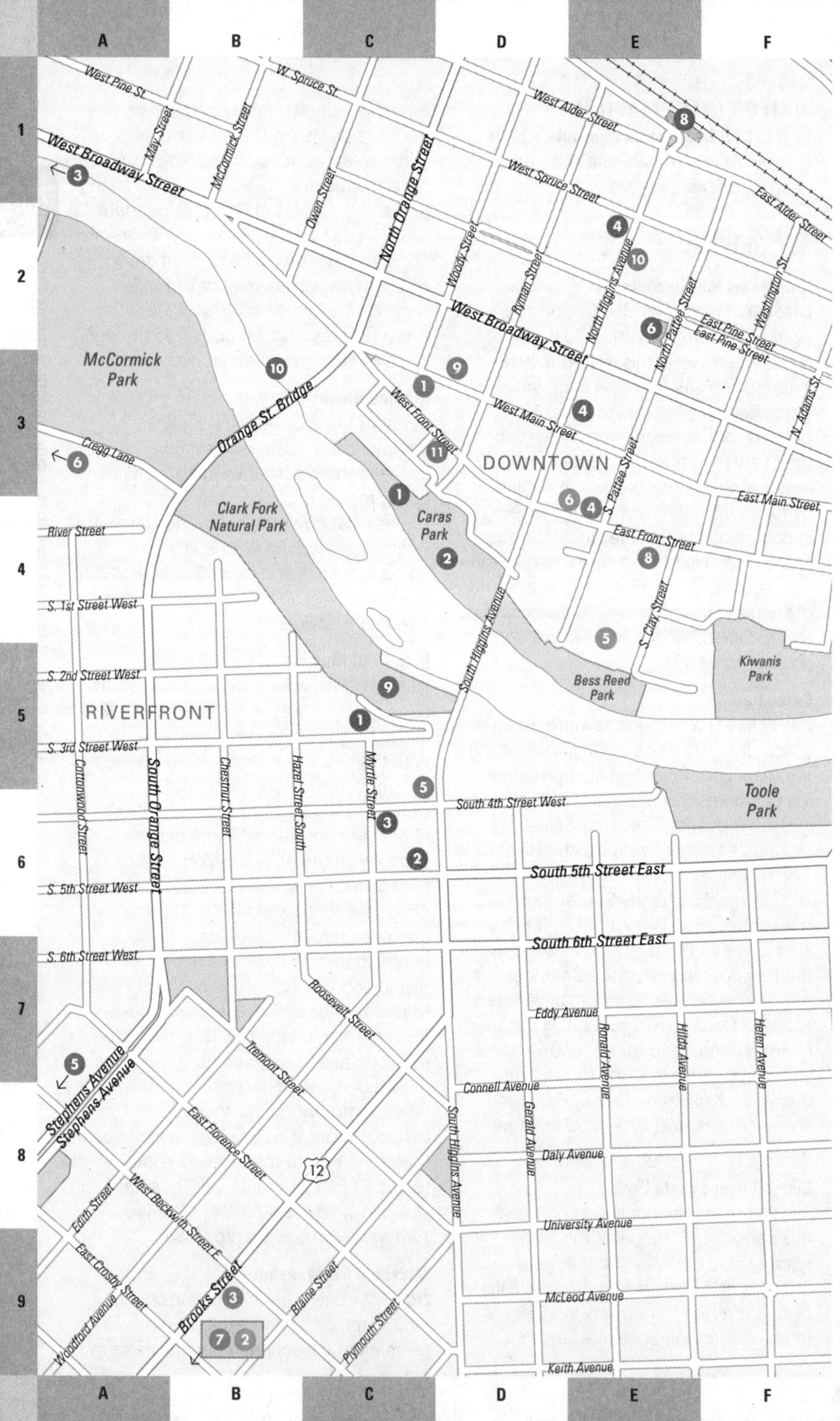

A
B
C
D
E
F
1
2
3
4
5
6
7
8
9
West Pine St.
W. Spruce St.
May Street
McCormick Street
West Broadway Street
Owen Street
North Orange Street
West Alder Street
West Spruce Street
East Alder Street
Woody Street
Ryman Street
North Higgins Avenue
North Pattee Street
Washington St.
East Pine Street
East Pine Street
N. Adams St.
West Broadway Street
McCormick Park
Orange St. Bridge
West Front Street
West Main Street
DOWNTOWN
Cregg Lane
Clark Fork Natural Park
Caras Park
S. Pattee Street
East Main Street
East Front Street
River Street
S. 1st Street West
South Higgins Avenue
S. Clay Street
S. 2nd Street West
Kiwanis Park
Bess Reed Park
RIVERFRONT
S. 3rd Street West
Cottonwood Street
South Orange Street
Chestnut Street
Hazel Street South
Myrtle Street
South 4th Street West
Toole Park
South 5th Street East
S. 5th Street West
South 6th Street East
S. 6th Street West
Roosevelt Street
Eddy Avenue
Ronald Avenue
Hilda Avenue
Helen Avenue
Tremont Street
Stephens Avenue
Stephens Avenue
Connell Avenue
East Florence Street
Gerald Avenue
South Higgins Avenue
Daly Avenue
12
Edith Street
West Beckwith Street E.
University Avenue
East Crosby Street
Brooks Street
Blaine Street
McLeod Avenue
Woodford Avenue Street
Plymouth Street
Keith Avenue

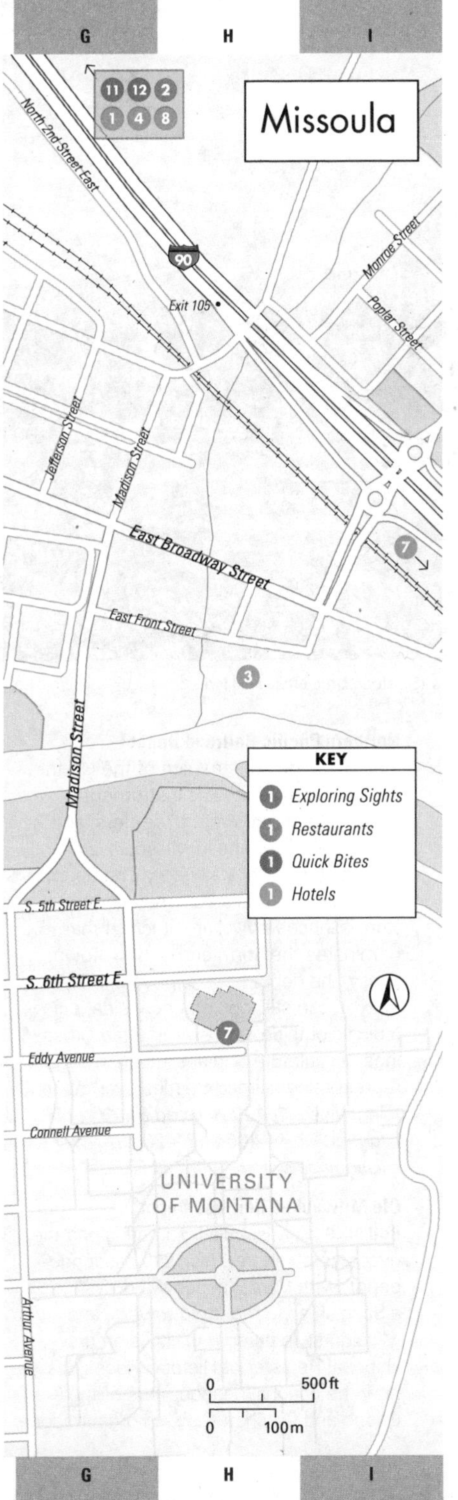

Sights

1. A Carousel for Missoula ... C3
2. Caras Park ... D4
3. Council Grove State Park ... A1
4. Higgins Block ... E3
5. Historical Museum at Fort Missoula ... A7
6. Missoula Art Museum ... E2
7. Montana Museum of Art and Culture at the University of Montana ... H7
8. Northern Pacific Railroad Depot ... E1
9. Old Milwaukee Railroad Depot ... C5
10. Riverfront Trail ... B3
11. Rocky Mountain Elk Foundation Wildlife Visitor Center ... G1
12. Smokejumper Visitor Center ... G1

Restaurants

1. Biga Pizza ... C3
2. Blue Canyon Kitchen and Tavern ... G1
3. Caffe Dolce ... B9
4. The Camino ... E4
5. Ciao Mambo ... C6
6. Edelweiss Bistro ... A3
7. Lolo Creek Steakhouse ... B9
8. Pearl Cafe ... E4
9. The Shack Cafe ... D3
10. Taco del Sol ... E2
11. Tamarack Missoula ... C3

Quick Bites

1. Bernice's Bakery ... C5
2. Big Dipper ... C6
3. Le Petit Outre ... C6
4. Worden's Market & Deli ... E2

Hotels

1. C'mon Inn Hotel & Suites ... G1
2. Gibson Mansion Bed and Breakfast ... B9
3. Goldsmith's Bed and Breakfast ... H4
4. Hilton Garden Inn Missoula ... G1
5. Holiday Inn Missoula Downtown ... E4
6. Residence Inn Missoula Downtown ... E4
7. The Resort at Paws Up ... I4
8. Wingate by Wyndham Missoula Airport ... G1

Fort Missoula, which was established in 1877, offers 13 historic structures to explore.

E.S. Paxson, Walter Hook, Rudy and Lela Autio, and modern-day Native American artists. The 1903 Carnegie Library building, reopened in summer 2006 after extensive remodeling that added handicapped accessibility, has much more gallery space and classrooms. ✉ *335 N. Pattee St.* ✣ *1 block from intersection with W. Broadway* ☎ *406/728–0447* 🌐 *www.missoulaartmuseum.org* 🎫 *Free* 🕓 *Closed Sun. and Mon.*

Montana Museum of Art and Culture at the University of Montana

MUSEUM | The university's art museum, divided into the Meloy and Paxson galleries, hosts traveling exhibitions and has a permanent collection of more than 10,000 works, with an emphasis on historic and contemporary art from the West. ✉ *Performing Arts and Radio/Television Center, University of Montana, Eddy Ave.* ☎ *406/243–2019* 🌐 *www.umt.edu/montanamuseum* 🎫 *Donations accepted.*

Northern Pacific Railroad Depot

BUILDING | The construction of the Northern Pacific Railroad was instrumental in opening up the West to settlers, and the arrival of the line in Missoula is a key point in the city's history. The depot, opened in 1901, is an example of the Renaissance Revival architecture that dominates the north end of downtown. Today, the depot houses private offices, but you can still look around inside, enjoy a picnic outside, and examine the Crossings, a sculpture of giant red enamel Xs representing railroad trestles over mountain ravines. ✉ *100 Railroad St. W., at N. Higgins Ave.* ☎ *406/543–4238* 🌐 *www.missouladowntown.com* 🎫 *Free.*

Old Milwaukee Railroad Depot

BUILDING | A Missoula landmark along the river's south shore, this 1910 passenger depot, with Romanesque windows, a Spanish-style roof, two towers, and Mission-style parapet walls, is on the National Register of Historic Places. It's now the national headquarters of the Boone and Crockett Club, an organization founded in 1887 by Theodore Roosevelt to establish conservation of wild habitats. Open to the public is a display of a world-record taxidermied elk, bighorn sheep, and other wildlife. ✉ *250 Station Dr., near Higgins Ave. Bridge* ☎ *406/542–1888* 🌐 *www.boone-crockett.org* 🎫 *Free.*

Riverfront Trail

TRAIL | The heart of Missoula is defined by the Clark Fork River, which cuts through Hellgate Canyon between Mount Sentinel and Mount Jumbo, passes by the university, and slices through downtown. A 6-mile-long riverside trail (as well as the connecting 2½-mile Kim Williams Trail) makes for easy, pleasant walks, with picnic spots and benches along the way where you can watch the river. Look down from Higgin's Bridge and watch the surfers, kayakers and paddleboarders lay on Brennan's Wave. Take note: the powerful currents of the Clark Fork are dangerous—they've taken many lives over the years. ✉ *Missoula.*

Rocky Mountain Elk Foundation Wildlife Visitor Center

NATURE PRESERVE | **FAMILY** | The visitor center features natural-history displays (including hands-on displays for kids), films, art, taxidermied animals, a world-record pair of elk antlers, and an outdoor nature trail. The foundation works to preserve wild lands for elk and other wildlife; since 1984 the nonprofit organization has saved almost 8 million acres from development. ✉ *5705 Grant Creek Rd., look for big bronze elk* ☎ *406/523–4500, 800/225–5355* 🌐 *www.rmef.org* 🎫 *Donations accepted.*

Smokejumper Visitor Center

INFO CENTER | A replica 1930s lookout tower, fire photos, videos, and murals explain wildland fire ecology and behavior, fire-fighting technique, and the nation's history of smoke jumping, which began here in 1942. Today it's the largest smoke-jumper base in the nation. From Memorial Day through Labor Day the center offers five tours daily, given by guides who provide firsthand accounts of jumping into blazing forests. ✉ *5765 W. Broadway, 6 miles west of town, next to airport* ☎ *406/329–4934* ✉ *smokejumpercenter@yahoo.com* 🎫 *Donations accepted.*

Restaurants

Biga Pizza

$$ | **PIZZA** | This intimate, downtown pizza place is popular for its unusually creative flavor combinations. Locals come for the Caramelized Goat, a piping-hot pie capped with caramelized onions, goat cheese, roasted garlic, mozzarella, and fresh herbs. **Known for:** local microbrews sold by the can or the six-pack; the dough is made the old-fashioned Italian way, and pizzas are cooked in a big brick oven; long lineups are the norm in summer. $ *Average main: $17* ✉ *241 W. Main St.* ☎ *406/728–2579* 🌐 *www.bigapizza.com* ⏲ *Closed Sun.*

Blue Canyon Kitchen and Tavern

$$$ | **CONTEMPORARY** | With its lodgelike dining room anchored by a floor-to-ceiling fireplace and exposed log beams, Blue Canyon pairs rustic yet elegant Montana ambience with excellent, hearty cuisine. Innovative, seasonally inspired dishes fill the menu. **Known for:** tasty elk meatballs with huckleberry sauce; unlike Lolo Creek Steakhouse, they take reservations; one of the best restaurants on the west end of town. $ *Average main: $22* ✉ *3720 N. Reserve St.* ☎ *406/451–2583* 🌐 *www.bluecanyonrestaurant.com* ⏲ *Closed Sun.*

★ Caffe Dolce

$$$ | **ITALIAN** | Located in the heart of an historic neighborhood (in the space formerly occupied by Red Bird), Cafe Dolce serves up well-crafted Italian dishes in an airy dining room painted with frescoes. The menu changes with the seasons because the focus is on fresh, local ingredients, including homemade horseradish and morel mushrooms from the surrounding mountains. **Known for:** friendly knowledgeable staff who can help pair wine and beer with food; a large well-manicured patio open in the summer; parking can be tricky and wait times long. *Average main: $27 500 Brooks St. 406/830–3055 www.caffedolce.com Closed Mon.*

The Camino

$$$ | MEXICAN | The best of four new restaurants in Missoula's downtown Residence Inn, which was recently constructed on the site of the old Missoula Mercantile, borrows from the culinary traditions of Oaxaca and the Yucatan to deliver outstanding Mexican cuisine and creative tequila-based cocktails. The menu is largely centered around shareable apps and taco plates. **Known for:** superb tacos on house-made corn tortillas made with several varietals from Mexico; a tequila and mezcal collection that would make George Clooney envious; supporting small-scale Oaxacan farmers. *Average main: $20 125 N. Pattee St. 406/317–1260 www.thecaminomissoula.com Closed Mon.*

Ciao Mambo

$$$ | ITALIAN | With offerings like penne alla vodka and linguini alla carbonara, Ciao Mambo is the place to come for pasta in Missoula. Start with fried fresh mozzarella balls or classic bruschetta. **Known for:** it's near the Kettlehouse or Gild if you are looking for a good microbrew; the tablecloths are paper and the crayons are free; decorated with wine-focused artwork by Leanne Laine. *Average main: $22 541 S. Higgins Ave. 406/543–0377 www.ciaomambo.com.*

Edelweiss Bistro

$ | GERMAN | One of a very few small, local breweries that is all about lagers rather than ales, the Bayern Brewery offers dozen craft beers in this German-style brewery's tasting room. The Edelweis Bistro upstairs serves good German staples, including excellent sausages and schnitzels. **Known for:** tasty locally brewed lagers; authentic German food; the brewery reuses all its bottles. *Average main: $10 1507 Montana St. 406/721–1482 www.bayernbrewery.com Closed Sun.*

Lolo Creek Steakhouse

$$$ | STEAKHOUSE | For an authentic taste of Montana, head to this hearty steak house in a rustic log structure 8 miles south of Missoula, in Lolo. The dining room has a hunting-lodge atmosphere, replete with taxidermied wildlife on the walls. **Known for:** high-quality rib-eye steaks cooked over a wood-fired grill; stop on your way home from Lolo Hot Springs, 30 minutes west of the restaurant; long wait times in the busy summer season. *Average main: $29 6600 U.S. 12 W, Lolo 12 miles south of Missoula 406/273–2622 www.lolocreeksteakhouse.com No lunch.*

Pearl Cafe

$$$ | MODERN FRENCH | Missoulians head to this cozy, French-inspired eatery for upscale fare in an elegant setting. With its exposed brick wall anchored by a charming fireplace and sconce lighting, Pearl Cafe is routinely voted Missoula's best and most romantic restaurant. **Known for:** authentic ambience that is both elegant and comfortable; really good European-inspired food; high prices. *Average main: $30 231 E. Front St. 406/541–0231 www.pearlcafe.us Closed Sun.*

The Shack Cafe

$$ | AMERICAN | Opened in 1949, this cozy café is a longtime Missoula favorite for any meal, especially breakfast. Hardly a shack, this elegant little eatery, in an old auto dealership, offers all kinds of American fare—from an array of salads and sandwiches to huckleberry pancakes and almost 20 omelets, including interesting options like apple, cheddar, nutmeg, and cinnamon; and veggie, cheddar, garlic, and crouton. **Known for:** an oak bar that arrived in Montana via steamship up the Missouri River a century ago; one of the best breakfast places in Missoula; get there early or prepare to wait in line. *Average main: $12* *222 W. Main St.* *406/549–9903* *www.theshackcafe.com.*

Taco del Sol

$ | **MEXICAN** | For a quick bite to eat, this local favorite offers a variety of tasty burritos and tacos inspired by similar shops in San Francisco's Mission District. Try the Mission Supreme with your choice of baked cod, pulled pork, or carne asada. **Known for:** great burritos and good value; quick, friendly service by employees who enjoy what they do; a community-oriented business that supports local groups and events. *Average main: $6* *422 N. Higgins Ave.* *406/240–3480* *www.tacodelsol.com.*

Tamarack Missoula

$$ | **AMERICAN** | Sip a Yard Sale Amber or the award-winning Hat Trick Hop IPA in this two-story establishment overlooking the river. The main-floor restaurant offers a casual atmosphere with good views. **Known for:** you can't go wrong with keg nachos topped with bison; if the kids get antsy, walk a few paces out back and let them whirl on the carousel; ample parking in the back lot beside the river. *Average main: $14* *231 W. Front St.* *406/830–3113* *www.tamarackbrewing.com.*

Coffee and Quick Bites

Bernice's Bakery

$ | **BAKERY** | Buttery croissants, cookies, cupcakes, scones, quiches, muffins, and other glorious baked treats abound at Missoula's best bakery, a longtime local favorite. Come in for coffee seven days a week from 6 am to 8 pm or for lunch from 11 am to 4 pm, when there's a small selection of soups, salads, and sandwiches, such as roast beef and Swiss, or hummus on whole wheat with feta and artichoke hearts. **Known for:** delicious cupcakes and big cakes for birthdays and anniversaries; quiet, comfy place to work or read a book; new menus posted online every morning. *Average main: $5* *190 S. 3rd W* *406/728–1358* *www.bernicesbakerymt.com* *No dinner.*

Big Dipper

$ | **FAST FOOD** | Shakes come in two sizes—regular or large—at Big Dipper, where folks line up for homemade ice cream in flavors like cardamom, green tea, huckleberry, maple walnut, and Mexican chocolate. In the summer, the line can extend around the block. **Known for:** exotic ice cream flavors; long lines; great place to meet the locals on the Hip Strip. *Average main: $5* *631 S. Higgins* *406/543–5722* *www.bigdippericecream.com.*

Le Petit Outre

$ | **BAKERY** | Loosely translated, the name means "The Little Outrageous," which is fitting since the croissants, scones, brioches, canneles, and other sweet baked treats here are outrageously good. It also serves the best coffee in town. **Known for:** great lattes, pastries, and baguettes; quiet place with lots of light to work or read; benches out front to drink your coffee and meet the locals. *Average main: $5* *129 S. 4th St. W* *406/543–3311* *www.lepetitoutre.com.*

Worden's Market & Deli

$ | **DELI** | Floorboards creak beneath your feet as you explore this old-fashioned market, opened in the 1880s as Missoula's first grocery store and spilling over with deli delicacies today. With 150 cheeses to choose from, the sandwich possibilities are endless; have them pile on Black Forest ham and horseradish for a creation that will get you down the trail. **Known for:** well-chosen variety of bang-for-your buck wines; this is the place to find a bottle of Belgian trippel or a keg of local microbrew; the walk-in humidor is Montana's best-kept secret. *Average main: $8* *451 N. Higgins*

Ave. ☎ *406/549–1293* 🌐 *www.wordens.com* ⊗ *No dinner.*

Hotels

C'mon Inn Hotel and Suites

$$$ | RESORT | FAMILY | Located at the bottom of Grant Creek, near the Snowbowl ski area, this family-favorite features a tree-filled courtyard with a pool, baby pool, five hot tubs, and a waterfall. **Pros:** easily accessible off the interstate; ideal location for those skiing at Snowbowl; pool and hot tubs make this a good choice for families. **Cons:** away from downtown's restaurants and entertainment; central pool area can make it seem like a water park; customer service can be inconsistent. $ *Rooms from: $179* ✉ *2775 Expo Pkwy. , off I–90* ☎ *406/543–4600, 888/989–5569 toll-free* 🌐 *www.cmoninn.com* *119 rooms* *Free breakfast.*

Gibson Mansion Bed and Breakfast

$$$$ | B&B/INN | From luxurious linens to customized breakfast times, including delivery of the first course right to your door, this elegant 1903 mansion offers an intimate retreat. **Pros:** open-kitchen policy and flexible breakfast schedule; spectacular bedding that is available for purchase; gracious innkeeper-owners on-site for round-the-clock hospitality. **Cons:** in a residential neighborhood south of historic hub; downtown boutiques and restaurants not within walking distance; a little pricey for the location. $ *Rooms from: $240* ✉ *823 39th St.* ☎ *406/251–1345* 🌐 *www.gibsonmansion.com* *4 rooms* *Free breakfast.*

Goldsmith's Bed and Breakfast

$$$ | B&B/INN | Built in 1911 for the first president of the University of Montana, this stately, prairie-style brick home sits on the bank of the Clark Fork River, at the end of a footbridge that leads to the campus. **Pros:** gorgeous river and mountain views; convenient walk to downtown shops and restaurants; you could fish or float on the river right out the front door. **Cons:** near the railroad, so expect frequent train whistles; main entrance is next to the honeymoon suite's private porch; books up far in advance for university events like graduation and football games. $ *Rooms from: $139* ✉ *809 E. Front St.* ☎ *406/728–1585, 866/666–9945* 🌐 *www.goldsmithsinn.com* *7 rooms* *Free breakfast.*

Hilton Garden Inn Missoula

$$$ | HOTEL | With a fully equipped business center near the lobby and spacious, Montana-theme rooms anchored by large desks and flat-screen TVs, this upscale facility is a business traveler's dream. **Pros:** convenient business amenities; the in-house Blue Canyon Kitchen & Tavern is very good; convenient shuttle to and from the airport. **Cons:** view from the grill overlooks the parking area; you have to walk outside to enter the restaurant and tavern; like a lot of hotels, sound from other rooms does travel. $ *Rooms from: $154* ✉ *3720 N. Reserve St.* ☎ *406/532–5300* 🌐 *www.hilton.com* *146 rooms* *No meals.*

Holiday Inn Missoula Downtown

$$$$ | HOTEL | The Missoula member of the Holiday Inn chain is a large, comfortable hotel with a lush atrium in the center and remodeled rooms, some with a lovely river view. **Pros:** great area for walks along the river; easy walk into town for shopping and dining; bar serve both terrific food and tasty mixed drinks. **Cons:** rooms overlooking the atrium can be noisy when the hotel is hosting large functions; as of January 2021, the restaurant is closed for renovations; parking can be a challenge when it's full. $ *Rooms from: $220* ✉ *200 S. Pattee St.* ☎ *406/721–8550, 877/865–6578 toll-free* 🌐 *www.ihg.com* *200 rooms* *No meals.*

Residence Inn Missoula Downtown

$$$$ | HOTEL | Constructed on the site of the Missoula Mercantile and incorporating its old heavy timbers, this new hotel is the perfect blend of modern and historical. **Pros:** very close to the Wilma Theater, the Top Hat, and the Clark Fork River Market; lobby decorated with historic photographs of Missoula and the work of local artists; four great bars and restaurants on the ground floor. **Cons:** downtown noise can be annoying for light sleepers; parking can be a challenge; pricey rates. *Rooms from: $250* *125 N. Pattee St.* *406/452–6252, 833/999–0418 reservations only* *www.marriott.com/hotels/travel/msori-residence-inn-missoula-downtown/* *175 rooms* *Free breakfast.*

The Resort at Paws Up
$$$$ | RESORT | FAMILY | This authentic cattle ranch of some 37,000 acres of forests and grasslands is the perfect place to try "glamping," though staying in one of the perma-tents at Paws Up is a long way from roughing it. **Pros:** one-of-a-kind upscale nature experience in Montana; true luxury accommodations and first-class service; earned a Dining-Wine Award of Excellence from Wine Spectator. **Cons:** prices are super steep; not as inclusive as you might like; can be difficult to figure out how everything works. *Rooms from: $2000* *40060 Paws Up Rd., Greenough* *406/244–5200, 877/588–6764* *www.pawsup.com* *58 rooms* *All-inclusive.*

Wingate by Wyndham Missoula Airport
$$$ | HOTEL | FAMILY | Oversize guest rooms and a 24-hour self-service business center here are designed with the business traveler in mind, but two waterslides and a splash pool please kids as well. **Pros:** great waterslides for the kids; designed with business travellers in mind; good free breakfast. **Cons:** no restaurants within walking distance; traffic into town at rush hour can be heavy; the surrounding area is pretty nondescript. *Rooms from: $159* *5252 Airway Blvd.* *406/541–8000, 866/832–8000* *www.wingatemissoula.com* *100 rooms* *Free breakfast.*

Nightlife

KettleHouse Brewing Co.
BREWPUBS/BEER GARDENS | A true microbrewery that has hit the big time without losing its micro-ness, the Kettlehouse Brewing Co. has two taprooms. The original Myrtle Street location is near the Hip Strip on the south side of the river, and it hasn't changed since opening in the early 2000s. Which is a good thing. Their most popular beers are Coldsmoke, a Scotch Ale, and the uber-hoppy Double Haul IPA. The new taproom is down the road in Bonner, where it's part of the new Kettlehouse Brewery & Amphitheatre. Try a chocolatey Brick and Mortar Imperial Belgian Porter, Olde Bongwater Hemp Porter, or Fresh Bongwater Hemp Pale Ale. There's no bar food other than peanuts, but you're welcome to bring in fare from local eateries. *602 Myrtle St.* *406/728–1660* *www.kettlehouse.com.*

Montgomery Distillery Tasting Room
BREWPUBS/BEER GARDENS | Sample high-quality, locally made gin, vodka, aquavit, and an award-winning single malt whiskey at the beautiful and now-famous distillery. Be warned, however, that there's a two-drink *maximum* per customer, which will make it difficult to choose from the long list of handcrafted cocktails. *Average main: $12* *129 W. Front St.* *406/926–1725* *www.montgomerydistillery.com.*

The Top Hat
MUSIC CLUBS | Missoula's most intimate live-music venue was remodeled to add a world-class sound system and a great restaurant to its popular bar. There are shows by popular performers almost every evening and programs for kids in late afternoon on the weekends. *134 W. Front St.* *406/728–9865* *www.logjampresents.com/top-hat-restaurant-bar/.*

Performing Arts

Big Sky Documentary Film Festival

FILM FESTIVALS | **FAMILY** | Missoula is home to several film festivals each year, but the biggest and best of them is the Big Sky Documentary Film Festival, the premier venue for nonfiction film in the American West. Over the course of a week in late February, 20,000 people watch more than 140 of the most compelling films from all over the world, dozens of them making their premieres. Most of the films are shown in the Wilma Theatre, a state-of-the-art venue with the character of a 1920s theater. For the locals, it is an annual ritual, and visitors, too, come from all over to spend a week watching films and hobnobbing with directors. This makes the cold month of February a perfect time to visit Missoula. ✉ *216 W. Main St., Studio 7* ☎ *406/541–3456* 🌐 *www.bigskyfilmfest.org.*

Kettlehouse Amphitheater

CONCERTS | Located on the banks of the legendary Blackfoot River 8 miles west of downtown, the Kettlehouse Amphitheater has helped put Missoula on the map as a mecca for live music. This 4,250-seat outdoor concert venue allows concertgoers to enjoy their favorite bands in a beautiful mountain setting. Recent shows include Nora Jones, Robert Plant, The Decemberists and Primus. ✉ *605 Coldsmoke Ave.* ☎ *406/830–4640* 🌐 *www.logjampresents.com.*

Missoula Children's Theatre

THEATER | **FAMILY** | At the Missoula Children's Theatre, year-round productions vary from Broadway musicals to community theater for and by children from 5 to 18 years old. From October to June you can see local talent and guest artists (usually professionals) perform family favorites, and in summer there's a theater camp where kids are the stars of the productions. ✉ *200 N. Adams* ☎ *406/728–1911 administrative office, 406/728–7529 box office* 🌐 *www.mctinc.org.*

Montana Book Festival

ARTS FESTIVALS | Western Montana, and Missoula in particular, is a writer's place. *A River Runs Through It,* by Norman Maclean, is perhaps the most well-known book set in the region, but William Kittredge, James Crumley, Richard Hugo, Rick Bass, Judy Blunt, and many others have also left their mark on Montana literature. In celebration of this history, the Montana Book Festival brings writers and readers together to pay tribute to the tradition of writing in and about the West. Previous literary personalities featured have included James Lee Burke, Jane Smiley, Charles D'Ambrosio, Gretel Ehrlich and David Quammen. If you relish the literature of the West, you'll visit in Montana in late September. ✉ *327 E. Broadway* ☎ *406/541–0860* 🌐 *www.montanabookfestival.com.*

Montana Repertory Theatre

THEATER | The University of Montana's College of the Arts and Media manages the Montana Repertory Theatre, the only full-season professional company in the state. The Rep provides the region with a steady diet of popular Broadway shows; recent showings include War of the Worlds, Room Service and On Golden Pond. ✉ *College of the Arts and Media, University of Montana, 32 Campus Dr., PARTV Bldg.* ☎ *406/243–6809* 🌐 *www.montanarep.org.*

Shopping

Butterfly Herbs

FOOD/CANDY | Take a break while touring downtown Missoula and have a cappuccino or chai shake at Butterfly Herbs, or try the Butterfly Ice Cream Coffee Soda—a cold drink with multiple layers of sweetness. The shop sells herbs and spices in bulk, candies, soaps, candles, china, and other odds and ends. ✉ *232 N. Higgins Ave.* ☎ *406/728–8780.*

Missoula Farmers' Market

OUTDOOR/FLEA/GREEN MARKETS | There are no less than three outdoor Saturday morning markets held downtown in the summer. The oldest and biggest is the Missoula Farmers' Market, which boasts 100 local vendors selling an amazing array of flowers, fresh fruits and vegetables, locally baked breads, and other handmade goods. It's held adjacent to the old train depot at the north end of Higgins Street every Saturday morning from mid-May to mid-October, as well as Tuesday evening from July through mid-September. You can even view what's available on the market's website before you go. You can also check out the Clark Fork River Market under the Higgins Street Bridge and Missoula People's Market on East Pine Street, not far from the farmers' market. ✉ *N. Higgins Ave. on Circle Sq. between Railroad and Alder Sts.* ☎ *406/526–3465* 🌐 *www.destinationmissoula.org/farmers-markets.*

Missoula People's Market

OUTDOOR/FLEA/GREEN MARKETS | The Missoula People's Market showcases more than 80 local artisans, featuring unique Montana arts and craft. Stop by to check out fine pottery, metalworks, fine woodworking, photography, leather work, clothing, jewelry, and functional and whimsical art—and the artists who created it. Open Saturday morning from mid-May to mid-October. ✉ *Pine St. between Higgins Ave. and Pattee St.* ☎ *406/526–3465* 🌐 *www.missoulapeoplesmarket.org.*

Monte Dolack Gallery

ART GALLERIES | Monte Dolack is something of a legend in western Montana and his nature-focused lithographs and watercolors, shown in galleries all over the world, have become iconic. Even if you're not in the buying mood, it's worth checking out his gallery on Front Street. ✉ *139 W. Front* ☎ *406/549–3248* 🌐 *www.dolack.com.*

Shakespeare & Company

BOOKS/STATIONERY | Works by Montana authors, a fine selection of the best books from anywhere, and gifts are found at this literary outlet, a linchpin in Missoula for more than 25 years. Readings, signings, and other literary events are scheduled year-round at this comfortable shop, where you're likely to rub elbows with an author browsing the shelves. ✉ *103 S. 3rd St. W* ☎ *406/549–9010* 🌐 *www.shakespeareandco.com.*

Activities

BICYCLING

Adventure Cycling

BICYCLING | The folks at Adventure Cycling in downtown Missoula have good suggestions for nearby bike routes and an extensive selection of regional and national bike maps for sale. And for avid cyclists, it's just a fun place to visit to chat with some of the most knowledgeable and passionate cyclists you'll ever meet, and who aren't afraid to boast (accurately) that they "research and produce the best cycling maps on the planet." ✉ *150 E. Pine St.* ☎ *406/721–1776, 800/755–2453* 🌐 *www.adventurecycling.org.*

Bicycle and Pedestrian Office

BICYCLING | That's right: Missoula is such a bike and hike friendly town that it has a Bicycle and Pedestrian plan with its own program and office. Nearly 62 miles of bike and pedestrian trails thread through Missoula, an interactive map of which can be found on the City of Missoula's website. There's even a downloadable MyCityBikes smartphone app for your convenience. Call the city's Bicycle and Pedestrian Office for more information. ✉ *435 Ryman St.* ☎ *406/552–6352 bike program manager* 🌐 *www.ci.missoula.mt.us/404/Bicycle-and-Pedestrian-Office.*

Open Road Bicycles & Nordic Equipment

BICYCLING | It may not look like much, but Open Road Bicycles & Nordic Equipment is a great place to buy or rent bikes and cross-country ski gear. They also have a good selection of clothing and accessories and a full-service repair shop that can do everything from wax your skis to overhaul your mountain bike. ✉ *517 S. Orange St.* ☎ *406/549–2453* 🌐 *www.orbicycleandnordic.com.*

CAMPING

Missoula KOA. This lovely campsite in the Montana-born KOA chain is easy to reach from I–90. It has a pool and two hot tubs, a game center, miniature golf, bike rentals, a playground, and a bonfire pit area. Nightly ice-cream socials and weekend activities during the summer make this more of a community than a campground. ✉ *3450 Tina Ave., I–90, Exit 101, 1½ miles south, right on England Blvd., Missoula* ☎ *406/549–0881, 800/562–5366* 🌐 *www.missoulakoa.com* *146 full hookups, 31 tent sites; 19 cabins.*

Yogi Bear's Jellystone Camp Resort. On the outskirts of town, this lively park is popular with families for the playground, miniature golf, swimming pools, and, a kid favorite, pictures with Yogi Bear. The friendly owners serve huckleberry ice cream nightly. Camping cabins, which sleep four comfortably, have air-conditioning, refrigerators, and microwaves. ✉ *9900 Jellystone Ave., I–90, Exit 96, ½ mile north of Missoula* ☎ *406/543–9400, 800/318–9644* 🌐 *www.jellystonemt.com* *110 full hookups, 7 tent sites, 6 cabins.*

FISHING

Blackfoot River Outfitters

FISHING | FAMILY | A family-run, Orvis-endorsed outfit that will happily take you out on any of the rivers in the area. Whether you are a beginner or an expert, or want to float or walk and wade, their guides will help you find the fish and figure out how to get the big ones on the end of your line. ✉ *275 N. Russell St.* ☎ *406/542–7411* 🌐 *www.blackfootriver.com.*

Grizzly Hackle

FISHING | Grizzly Hackle offers guided fly-fishing and outfitting for half-day float trips on the Bitterroot, Blackfoot, and Clark Fork rivers. Pick up supplies in the retail shop or sign up for a lesson. Their website offers regular fishing reports and good fishing advice on what to throw for the five major rivers in the area. ✉ *215 W. Front St.* ☎ *406/721–8996, 800/297–8996* 🌐 *www.grizzlyhackle.com.*

RAFTING

Montana River Guides

WHITE-WATER RAFTING | Raft and kayak adventures with Montana River Guides splash down the Blackfoot and Bitterroot rivers and the rowdy Alberton Gorge of the Clark Fork River. You can also let them teach you how to "riverboard," which is similar to rafting except you run the rapids prone on a 4-foot belly board with flippers on your feet. It's about the funnest way to experience a river firsthand. ✉ *138 Big Bend La., 35 mins west of Missoula on I–90, Exit 70 at Cyr, cross Cyr Bridge, turn left on Sawmill Gulch, and look for yellow rafts, Alberton* ☎ *406/722–7238 office, 406/240–8060 cell, 406/214–0245 cell* 🌐 *www.montanariverguides.com.*

SKIING

Montana Snowbowl

SKIING/SNOWBOARDING | This 950-acre ski area is just 12 miles northwest of Missoula and offers slopes for advanced skiers who relish steep, challenging runs and powdery views of nearby Rattlesnake Wilderness. Telemarkers and geländesprung alpine ski jumpers add a colorful element to the scene. New skiers aren't neglected: groomed beginner and intermediate runs make up more than half the trails. Services include a restaurant and Geländesprung Lodge in the base area. The Last Run Inn is famous for its food and fun, including great pizzas and signature Bloody Marys. ✉ *1700 Snow Bowl Rd., off Grant Creek*

Rd. ☎ *406/549–9777* 🌐 *www.montanasnowbowl.com.*

SWIMMING

Splash Montana

SWIMMING | Keep your kids happy and cool on a hot summer at Splash Montana. This water park boasts three, three-story waterslides, a zero-entry kiddie pool, a splash park, and a lazy river ride. They keep the Olympic-size pool cold for swimmers or triathletes who want to get some exercise. Everyone can enjoy a bite to eat at the Crazy Creek Cafe or the Fireline Grill. ✉ *3001 Bankcroft, in Playfair Park* ☎ *406/542–9283* 🌐 *www.ci.missoula.mt.us/169/Splash-Montana* 🎫 *$8.*

Stevensville

30 miles south of Missoula via U.S. 93.

Stevensville, population 1,809, sits on the site of the state's first non–Native American settlement, St. Mary's Mission, a restored treasure that dates back to 1841. Nearby Fort Owen is a partially restored 1850s trading post. The town itself is named for General Isaac Stevens, who was in charge of the Northwest Territory's military posts and Native American affairs. Today it's a mix of beautiful old homes and haphazard modern construction in a mountain valley. The Bitterroot River offers exceptional fishing for wild Westslope cutthroat, rainbow and brown trout, and there are excellent guides in Darby and Missoula to help you find the fish.

GETTING HERE AND AROUND

Stevensville is 30 miles south of Missoula via U.S. Highway 93. The road was widened in 2009 and is a relaxing, scenic drive.

VISITOR INFORMATION

CONTACTS Ravalli County Tourism. 🌐 *www.visitbitterrootvalley.com.*

Sights

Fort Owen

HISTORIC SITE | Major John Owen established Fort Owen as a trading post in 1850. The property also served as the headquarters of the Flathead Agency until 1860. It's worth a half hour to visit the museum to see the restored barracks, artifacts, and some of the fort's original furnishings. ✉ *94 Stevensville Cutoff Rd. E* ✥ *Off Hwy. 269, ½ mile east of U.S. 93 at Stevensville* ☎ *406/273–4253* 🌐 *stateparks.mt.gov* 🎫 *$8.*

Lee Metcalf National Wildlife Refuge

NATURE PRESERVE | **FAMILY** | The Lee Metcalf National Wildlife Refuge, on the edge of town, is nearly as pristine as it was before development encroached upon the wilds in this part of the state. Within its 2,800 acres reside 242 species of birds, 41 species of mammals, and 17 species of reptiles and amphibians. Bald eagles, osprey, deer, and muskrats are frequently seen along the preserve's 2 miles of nature trails and in the wildlife-viewing area. Fishing is permitted on the river and in Francois Slough. Archery season for deer and waterfowl hunting occur during their specific seasons in autumn. ✉ *4567 Wildfowl La.* ✥ *2 miles north of Stevensville* ☎ *406/777–5552* 🌐 *www.fws.gov* 🎫 *Free.*

St. Mary's Mission

HISTORIC SITE | St. Mary's Mission, established by Father Pierre DeSmet in 1841, was the first Catholic mission in the Northwest and the site of the first permanent non–Native American settlement in Montana. The site is run by a nonsectarian, nonprofit organization that encourages tour groups, school groups, and individuals to explore the home of Father Anthony Ravalli, an Italian priest recruited to the mission by Father DeSmet in 1845. Ravalli was also Montana's first physician and pharmacist. On the site are a photogenic chapel, a priest's quarters, a pharmacy, Father Ravalli's log house, and

You'll see more than wild turkeys at Lee Metcalf National Wildlife Refuge; over 240 bird species have been spotted in the area.

the cabin of Chief Victor, a Salish Indian who refused to sign the Hell Gate Treaty and move his people onto the Flathead Reservation. A burial plot has headstones bearing the names of both Native Americans and white settlers. ✉ *315 Charlos St.* ✥ *Off 4th St.; from Main St., turn west at 4th and drive 3 blocks* ☎ *406/777–5734* 🌐 *www.saintmarysmission.org* 🎫 *$7* ⏲ *Closed Sun. and Mon.*

Stevensville Museum

HISTORIC SITE | Historical artifacts in the Stevensville Museum include the belongings of early settlers, particularly the missionaries who came to convert the Native Americans of the West. Other exhibits provide an overview of the area's original cultures (Salish, Nez Perce, and Lemhi Shoshone), background on Lewis and Clark's two visits, and a look at later residents, from orchard farmers to today's cybercommuters. ✉ *517 Main St.* ☎ *406/777–1007* 🌐 *www.stevensvillemuseum.com* 🎫 *Donations accepted* ⏲ *Closed Mon.–Wed.*

Teller Wildlife Refuge

NATURE PRESERVE | A refreshing stop for wildlife viewing, this 1,300-acre wildlife conservation property is intended to inspire, educate, and demonstrate conservation in action. Situated along 3 miles of the Bitterroot River, about 8 miles north of Hamilton, the refuge is home to otters, beavers, spotted frogs, and salamanders, as well as pileated woodpeckers, birds of prey, waterfowl, whitetail deer, and many native plants. Although most of the refuge is off-limits to the public (except by appointment), any visitors can take a stroll on the 1.5-mile walking trail along the Bitterroot River. An education center conducts numerous conservation programs for the public. To get here, take Route 269 (Eastside Highway) to Quast Lane and follow the signs. ✉ *1288 Eastside Hwy., Corvallis* ☎ *406/961–3507* 🌐 *www.tellerwildlife.org.*

Traveler's Rest State Park

HISTORIC SITE | **FAMILY** | This park includes a Lewis and Clark camp on a floodplain overlooking Lolo Creek. The explorers stayed here from September 9 to 11, 1805, and again from June 30 to July 3, 1806. Archaeologists in 2002 found evidence of a latrine and a fire hearth, making this one of only a few locations with a physical record of the expedition's camp. Tepee rings suggest that Native Americans used the riverside location, too. Self-guided tours meander through cottonwoods and the historic campsite. Daily interpretive presentations and guided tours run during the summer. ✉ *6717 U.S.-12, Lolo ✣ South of Lolo, ¼ mile west of U.S. 93* ☎ *406/273–4253* 🌐 *www.travelersrest.org* 🎫 *Free.*

Restaurants

Frontier Cafe

$ | **CAFÉ** | For a bit of town gossip and great burgers, stop in this classic small-town café, a dressed-down spot where the locals love to hang out. On the weekends, enjoy the best breakfast buffet in the Bitterroot Valley. **Known for:** a go-to spot for a hearty breakfast; the kindest, friendliest staff you'll ever meet; get a trip to the salad bar for just $1. $ *Average main: $10* ✉ *3954 U.S. 93 N* ☎ *406/777–4228* 🌐 *www.frontiercafemt.com.*

Marie's Italian Restaurant

$$ | **ITALIAN** | This family-run sit-down restaurant is known for its gourmet Italian cuisine and fresh seafood. A good way to decide what you like best is to try the sampler, which includes handmade pasta stuffed with different fillings, spinach gnocchi, fettuccine Alfredo, shrimp, vegetables, and another side. **Known for:** delicious leftovers from the night before served for lunch; dinner sampler; good seafood for Montana. $ *Average main: $13* ✉ *4040 Hwy. 93 N* ☎ *406/777–3681.*

Hotels

Bitterroot River Bed and Breakfast

$$$ | **B&B/INN** | Views of the Bitterroot River give this inn a peaceful, country feel even though it's within walking distance of many of the shops and restaurants in downtown Stevensville. **Pros:** owners are longtime Montana residents who are happy to offer advice on activities; hearty hot breakfast with farm-fresh eggs included; on the edge of town, with great views of the Bitterroot River. **Cons:** no phones in the rooms for private conversation, but cell phones should work; some of the bedrooms are a little tight. $ *Rooms from: $160* ✉ *501 South Ave.* ☎ *406/777–5205* 🌐 *www.bitterrootriverbb.com* 🛏 *4 rooms* 🍽 *Free breakfast.*

Activities

CAMPING

Charles Waters Campground. Located in the historic area of Stevensville, this is an access point to the Selway-Bitterroot Wilderness. Trails, fishing, picnic spots, and a bicycle campsite are sheltered among trees, affording glimpses of the surrounding mountains. A fire-ecology interpretive trail explores regrowth after recent forest fires. ✉ *Hwy. 93, 2 miles west of U.S. 93 on County Rd. 22 (Bass Creek Rd.), then 1 mile northwest on Forest Rd. 1316* ☎ *406/777–7423, 406/821–3269* 🌐 *www.fs.usda.gov/activity/bitterroot/recreation/camping-cabins* 🛏 *22 sites.*

Hamilton

21 miles south of Stevensville via U.S. 93.

Home to retirees, gentleman ranchers, and the Ravalli County Museum, Hamilton (pop. 5,000) is a gateway to the Selway-Bitterroot Wilderness. It was established by 19th-century industrialist Marcus Daly to house employees at his 22,000-acre Bitterroot Stock Farm. There he raised thoroughbred racehorses, funding the venture with part of the fortune he made mining copper in Montana. His own home, the Daly Mansion, is open for tours. The Bitterroot River offers exceptional fishing for wild Westslope cutthroat, rainbow and brown trout, and there are excellent guides in Darby and Missoula to help you find the fish.

GETTING HERE AND AROUND

Hamilton is 50 miles south of Missoula via U.S. Highway 93. A car is essential, since few hotels have an airport shuttle and many of the places to see are far apart and off the beaten path.

VISITOR INFORMATION

CONTACTS Ravalli County Tourism. *www.visitbitterrootvalley.com.*

Sights

Daly Mansion

HOUSE | FAMILY | Over the last decade, copper king Marcus Daly's 24,000-square-foot, 56-room Daly Mansion, with 25 bedrooms, 15 baths, and five Italian marble fireplaces, has been meticulously restored to preserve its history and elegance. The showplace of Hamilton, this Georgian Revival–style house is open to the public, and tours run every two hours, starting at 11 am. There's also a printed walking guide available to the extensive grounds. A number of events and festivities are held at the mansion during the summer. *251 Eastside Hwy. 406/363–6004 dalymansion.org $15.*

Ravalli County Museum

MUSEUM | The Ravalli County Museum, in the former courthouse, contains exhibits on natural history, fly-fishing, Native Americans, Lewis and Clark, and other subjects related to the region. During the Saturday Series (most Saturdays 2 pm, $5), speakers share local history and lore. *205 Bedford St. 406/363–3338 www.ravallimuseum.org $3 Closed Sun.–Tues.*

Selway-Bitterroot National Forest

FOREST | Hamilton, like Stevensville and Darby, is on the doorstep of the 1.3-million-acre Selway-Bitterroot Wilderness Area and is not far from the Anaconda-Pintler Wilderness Area to the east. Hundreds of miles of trails wend through the forests, where visitors may encounter bears, elk, moose, deer, and bighorn sheep. There are also songbirds and birds of prey such as eagles and owls. *Bitterroot Naitonal Forest Office, 1801 N. 1st Ave. 406/363–7100 www.fs.usda.gov/bitterroot Free.*

Skalkaho Highway

SCENIC DRIVE | Three miles south of Hamilton, turn east onto Route 38, also known as the Skalkaho Highway, and you'll find yourself on a beautiful route leading into the Sapphire Mountains and on to Philipsburg and the Georgetown Lake area. This fair-weather road is best traveled in summer, since 20 miles of it are gravel. Mountain bikers tour here, and there are plenty of hiking trails through the 23,000-acre Skalkaho Wildlife Preserve. Note that trailers are not recommended. Forest Road 1352 into the preserve is closed October 15 to December 1, making that a fine time for nonmotorized travel. Only 10 miles of the Skalkaho Highway are plowed in winter, which means the area is excellent for cross-country skiing and snowshoeing. *Hamilton.*

Restaurants

Bitter Root Brewing

$ | CONTEMPORARY | Meet the brewmaster, sample a Bitterroot Bock or Single Hop Pale Ale and enjoy live music Thursday and Saturday. One of the oldest breweries in the state, Bitter Root Brewing brews 40 different styles of beer annually, and the kitchen churns out all your favorite brewpub staples, including their specialty, hand-dipped, Sawtooth Ale-battered fish-and-chips. **Known for:** a large variety of great microbrewed ales; it's pub on the inside, but a little industrial on the outside; the service can be a little skimpy when it's busy. *Average main: $12 ✉ 101 Marcus St. ✣ 1 block east of town center ☎ 406/363–7468 🌐 www.bitterrootbrewing.com.*

Naps Grill

$$ | CONTEMPORARY | This local favorite is known throughout the Bitteroot Valley as the place with the best burger in the region—and possibly the state. The locally owned family restaurant serves burgers, steaks, and sandwiches, all made with fresh ingredients and Bitterroot Valley beef. **Known for:** a two-patty, 24-oz. monster burger called the Belly Buster; reasonable prices and good value; long lines and a packed bar. *Average main: $15 ✉ 200 W. Main St. ☎ 406/363–0136 🌐 www.napsgrill.com.*

Hotels

Deer Crossing B&B

$$$ | HOTEL | On this homestead, two deluxe rooms, two luxury suites, and two cabins are set on 25 acres surrounded by pastureland, pines, the Sapphire Mountains and Como Peak. **Pros:** facilities for horses; family-friendly accommodation can host large groups; beautiful Montana mountain locale. **Cons:** carpet in the main lodge is a little dated; no Wi-Fi; a relatively long drive from town. *Rooms from: $145 ✉ 396 Hayes Creek Rd. ☎ 406/363–2232 🌐 www.deercrossingmontana.com 6 rooms Free breakfast.*

Performing Arts

Hamilton Players

THEATER | Comedies, dramas, musicals, Shakespeare in the Park, and many more performances are a sampling of the year-round schedule put on at the Hamilton Playhouse. Offerings have included "I Love You, You're Perfect, Now Change" and "Steel Magnolias." Tickets can be purchased by calling the box office. *✉ 100 Ricketts Rd. ☎ 406/375–9050.*

Hard Times Bluegrass Festival

FESTIVALS | FAMILY | The Hard Grass Bluegrass Festival draws musicians from around the West for three days in July. Ten bands from as far away as Kentucky will rip it up July 23–25. Youngsters under 18 can bring their acoustic-stringed instrument for the Kids Music Program. The outdoor event also includes arts-and-crafts vendors, pickers' workshops, and food stands. *✉ 424 Forest Hill Rd. ☎ 406/821–3777 🌐 www.hardtimesbluegrass.com.*

Shopping

Ponderosa Art Gallery

ART GALLERIES | Original Western art, including oils, watercolors, and prints, is available at the Ponderosa Art Gallery, which hosts special guest artists' shows. Artists include Bill Anton, Dan Gerhartz, Ray Sexton, Matt Smith, and many others. Open by appointment. *✉ 944 Springhill Rd. ☎ 406/375–1212 🌐 www.ponderosaartgallery.com.*

Activities

CAMPING

Blodgett Canyon Campground. From this undeveloped campsite along a canyon creek you have easy access to hiking and biking trails, fishing, and rock climbing. There's no garbage haul, so cleanliness depends on good camping etiquette. *✉ Blodgett Camp Rd., Blodgett Canyon, 5 miles northwest of Hamilton ☎ 406/363–7100 🌐 www.fs.usda.gov/activity/bitterroot/recreation/camping-cabins 6 sites.*

FISHING

If you are looking for a guided fishing experience, Blackfoot River Outfitters, based in Missoula (as well as other outfitters there), can bring you to some of their favorite trout-fishing spots on the Bitterroot River.

Darby

14 miles south of Hamilton via U.S. 93.

This town of 800, site of the U.S. Department of Agriculture's first Forest Service ranger station, is a destination for wilderness adventurers. If you're driving through the Bitterroot Valley, take a break here and have a meal or do some shopping. Riders who come into town for a local brew often tie their horses along the sidewalks.

VISITOR INFORMATION

CONTACTS Ravalli County Tourism. *www.visitbitterrootvalley.com.*

Sights

Darby Pioneer Memorial Museum

MUSEUM | One of the area's first hand-hewn-log homesteads, built in 1886, is now the Darby Pioneer Memorial Museum, a repository for pioneer artifacts, photographs, and memorabilia. There is even a photograph of the building, constructed near the mouth of Tin Cup Creek, in its original setting, before it was moved into town. *101 E. Tanner, On U.S. 93* *406/361–1214* *www.visitbitterrootvalley.com.*

Hotels

★ Triple Creek Ranch

$$$$ | **HOTEL** | Lavishly appointed log cabins sit amid 1.6 million acres of Montana's Bitterroot National Forest, providing a wonderful sense of heritage with log post beds, Western-theme quilts, spectacular photos, and world-class artworks, not to mention blissful isolation and excellent food. **Pros:** superb farm-to-table cuisine; romantic setting (no kids allowed); incredible workshops, from cooking to photography. **Cons:** no cell service (but Wi-Fi is available); not family-friendly; off-ranch activities pricey. *Rooms from: $1700* *5551 W. Fork Rd.* *406/821–4600* *www.triplecreekranch.com* *Closed mid-Mar.–mid-Apr. and mid-Nov.–mid-Dec.* *30 cabins* *All-inclusive.*

Shopping

Old West Gallery and Antiques

ANTIQUES/COLLECTIBLES | **FAMILY** | Old West Gallery and Antiques is a huge shop selling gifts, collectibles, Native American and Western art, and furniture. The kids are likely to be enamored of the Old West Candy Store inside, which features fudge and hand-dipped chocolates. The entire family will enjoy player piano and other music machines. *202 S. Main* *406/821–4076* *www.oldwestcandy.com/.*

Activities

CAMPING

Lake Como Lower Campground. This popular reservoir-side site among the tall pines fills up fast during July and August. There's also an upper campground with 11 sites available when there's no vacancy here. Note that a $2-per-day vehicle pass is required to park at the trailheads, boat launch, and beach access. *4 miles north of Darby on U.S. 93, then 4.8 miles west on Lake Como Rd. (County Rd. 82)* *406/821–3269, 406/821–3913* *www.fs.usda.gov/activity/bitterroot/recreation/camping-cabins* *11 sites.*

FISHING

Bitterroot Fly Company

FISHING | **FAMILY** | Bitterroot Fly Company, an Orvis-endorsed fly shop, is a few minutes away from the convergence of the east and west forks of the Bitterroot River, a revered native Westslope cutthroat trout fishery (as well as rainbows and browns). They sell rods, reels, clothing, and fishing supplies, and offer fly-tying clinics and guided float and wading trips on the Bitterroot, Bighole, Beaverhead, Madison, Clark Fork, Blackfoot, and Rock Creek rivers. *808 N. Main St. #2* *406/821–1624* *www.bitterrootfly-company.com.*

Chapter 7

GREAT FALLS, BILLINGS, AND THE MONTANA PLAINS

Updated by Jeff Gailus and Katie Jackson

Sights ★★★☆☆ | Restaurants ★★★☆☆ | Hotels ★★★☆☆ | Shopping ★★☆☆☆ | Nightlife ★★☆☆☆

WELCOME TO GREAT FALLS, BILLINGS, AND THE MONTANA PLAINS

TOP REASONS TO GO

★ **Charles M. Russell Wildlife Refuge:** Marvel at the eroded breaks, see elk bugling in the fall, and soak in the quiet beauty.

★ **Downtown Great Falls:** The solid Edwardian architecture and the quirky shops satisfy contemporary visitors.

★ **Billings Rimrocks:** One of the best spots in the West for Insta-worthy sunsets.

★ **Fort Peck Reservoir:** Rent a boat and sail across this sprawling lake in June or July.

★ **Big Springs Trout Hatchery:** Tote a picnic to this oasis outside Lewistown.

1 **Great Falls.** Home to the C.M. Russell Museum.

2 **Fort Benton.** Montana's oldest settlement.

3 **Lewistown.** Geographical center of the state.

4 **Big Snowy Mountains.** One of Montana's mountain ranges.

5 **Billings.** Montana's biggest city.

6 **Hardin.** County seat of Bighorn County.

7 **Little Bighorn Battlefield National Monument.** Site of Custer's Last Stand.

8 **Bighorn Canyon National Recreation Area.** 55 miles of lake set in a deep canyon.

9 **Miles City.** Hosts the famous Bucking Horse Sale.

10 **Fort Peck.** Montana's largest lake.

11 **Charles M. Russell National Wildlife Refuge.** The second-largest U.S. refuge.

12 **Medicine Lake National Wildlife Refuge.** A plains paradise for bird-watchers.

13 **Bowdoin National Wildlife Refuge.** Breeding ground for migratory birds.

14 **Havre.** Crown jewel of the Hi-Line.

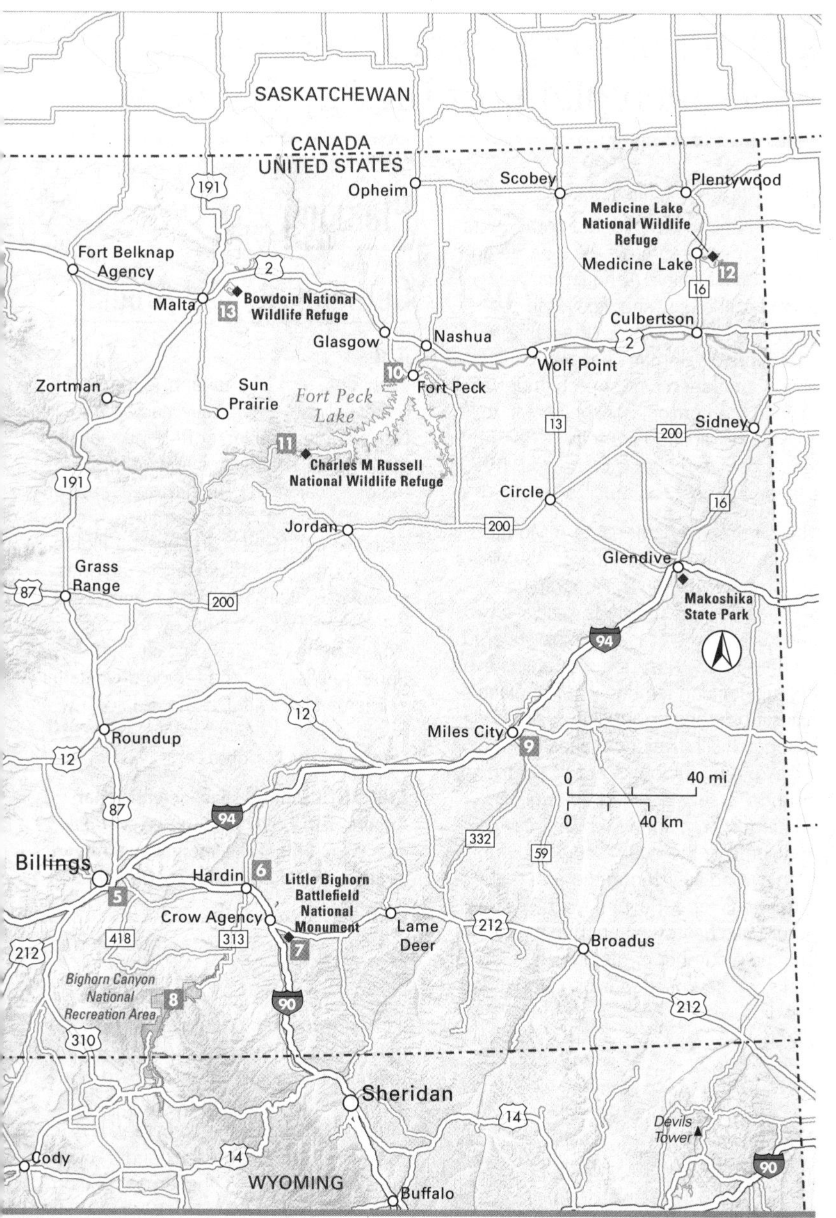
SASKATCHEWAN
CANADA
UNITED STATES
191
Opheim
Scobey
Plentywood
Medicine Lake National Wildlife Refuge
Medicine Lake
12
16
Fort Belknap Agency
2
Malta
Bowdoin National Wildlife Refuge
13
Glasgow
Nashua
Culbertson
2
Wolf Point
10
Fort Peck
Zortman
Sun Prairie
Fort Peck Lake
13
Sidney
200
11
Charles M Russell National Wildlife Refuge
191
Circle
16
Jordan
200
Glendive
Grass Range
87
200
Makoshika State Park
94
12
Miles City
9
Roundup
12
0
40 mi
0
40 km
87
94
332
59
Billings
6
Hardin
Little Bighorn Battlefield National Monument
5
Crow Agency
Lame Deer
212
418
313
7
Broadus
212
Bighorn Canyon National Recreation Area
8
90
212
310
Sheridan
14
Devils Tower
Cody
14
90
WYOMING
Buffalo

Space, lots of space, is the hallmark of eastern Montana's gently rolling plains. If you're looking to escape stifling crowds and urban sprawl, you'll take well to the wide-open plains of Big Sky Country.

The state as a whole averages seven people per square mile, but some of its prairies measure in reverse: one person per 7 square miles. Although largely devoid of the epic snow-covered peaks of the towering Rockies, the eastern two-thirds of Montana have an expansive beauty that seems to stretch endlessly beyond the horizon, beckoning you to bask in the isolated serenity of one of the least-populated places in the country—in a land of almost too much sky.

That's not to say that eastern Montana is flat and boring. In fact, the grassy plains are often broken up by geographical oddities such as badlands, glacial lakes, and ice caves. Occasional pine-covered foothills or snowcapped mountains even pop up, looking strangely out of place rising from the surrounding prairie. This topographical diversity makes the region a playground for lovers of the outdoors. Hiking, horseback riding, wrangling, boating, skiing, snowmobiling, caving, and some of the best fishing and hunting in the world are among the greatest attractions here. Beyond the blessings nature has bestowed upon the state are an ample number of historic sites, state parks, museums, and even paleontological digs.

Planning

Getting Here and Around

AIR

Within eastern Montana, frequent commercial flights—generally via Salt Lake City, Seattle, Denver, or Phoenix—are available only to Billings and Great Falls, the only major airports in this vast region. Cape Air offers flights to small towns like Glendive and Sidney, and charter flights can be arranged. Because the region is so isolated, flights here from anywhere in the country can be pricey—often more expensive than coast-to-coast flights. Some residents of the region drive as far as Bismarck, North Dakota; Rapid City, South Dakota; or Gillette, Wyoming, to catch departing flights.

AIRPORTS Billings Logan International Airport. ☎ *406/247–8609* 🌐 *www.flybillings.com.* **Great Falls International Airport.** ☎ *406/727–3404* 🌐 *www.flygtf.com.*

CAR

It is virtually impossible to travel around the Montana plains without a car. You can get by in Billings with Uber, Lyft, or a taxi service, but drivers are few and far between, and it will be expensive. One of the best things about driving here is the lack of traffic. Aside from a little bustle in Great Falls or Billings on weekdays in the late afternoon, gridlock and traffic jams are unheard of. The largest driving hazards will be slow-moving farming or ranching equipment, herds of grazing livestock that refuse to move off the highway, and deer bounding over ditches in the evening. Driving gets a little hairy in winter, but not because of the amount of snow that falls, which is generally very little. Whiteouts, when winds tearing across the plains whip up the tiniest bit of snow into ground blizzards, are the most common hazard. Large drifts and slick roads become more problematic at higher elevations.

TRAIN

Amtrak serves the isolated communities of the Hi-Line with its Empire Builder line, running three trains a week from Chicago to Seattle or Portland. The tracks run nearly parallel to U.S. 2 the entire length of the state. Trains stop in the towns of Glasgow, Malta, Havre, Wolf Point, and Cut Bank, among others.

Hotels

The strength of eastern Montana's hospitality doesn't lie in luxury resorts, bustling lodges, or crowded dude ranches, which are confined almost entirely to the western third of the state. The crown jewels of lodging on the plains are historic hotels and bed-and-breakfasts. Nearly every town with more than a few hundred residents has at least one of these properties, but no two are alike. From turreted Victorian mansions and rustic log ranch houses to Gothic manors and hulking sandstone inns with intricately carved facades, these lodgings have their own appeal and local flavor that set them apart from chain accommodations and commercial strip motels.

CAMPING

Many federal- and state-owned lands allow camping for little or no charge, and you can often set up camp wherever you like, so long as you don't light a fire. In the more developed towns and cities there is almost always a campground or two with more modern conveniences, such as hot showers and flush toilets. It's a testament to this treeless terrain that most commercial campgrounds advertise their shade before their other amenities.

Planning Your Time

Space, one of Montana's most abundant natural resources, can make traveling between major communities and attractions tedious. The drive from Great Falls to Billings, for instance, takes four hours. It's tempting to rush the drive to get from point A to point B, but that tactic can make you—and your traveling companions—batty with the vehicular version of cabin fever.

Break up long drives with side trips and random stops. Even if the trip could take only four or five hours, give yourself the entire day. Survey your route on a map before you set out and choose two or three possible stops along the way. Between Great Falls and Billings you might pause in the Big Snowy Mountains for a brisk hike. Break up the drive from Great Falls to Havre with an early dinner in Fort Benton, at the Union Grille in the Grand Union Hotel. Don't hesitate to stop in the random small town. You may not find much more than a gas station and a diner, but the locals will almost always offer friendly conversation and a few tall tales.

There is plenty to do in the two largest cities on the Montana plains. Lake Elmo State Park, ZooMontana, and Pictograph Cave State Monument are good stops in Billings, and the C. M. Russell Museum, Giant Springs State Park, and the Lewis and Clark National Historic Trail Interpretive Center are must-sees in Great Falls. Both cities make good base camps for further exploration: most of the region's attractions are day trips from these communities.

If you have the time, explore some of the state's smaller towns. These mini-municipalities have few obvious visitor attractions. You just have to do a little creative thinking in these remote villages. It may look a little primitive next to its big-city counterparts, but don't hesitate to pay a visit to the local museum. Remember outdoor recreation opportunities, too: for example, Miles City may look a little dull at first glance, but it's the perfect base from which to float down the Yellowstone River to Pirogue Island State Park or kick around on the rocky shorelines for agates and arrowheads.

Indeed, the great outdoors are probably why you're in Montana to begin with. If you are unaccustomed to so much space, the state's endless plains and wide-open skies may become wearisome after a while, but they can be every bit as beautiful as the mountain peaks that tower in the distance. Appreciate the empty countryside while you can, and stop on the side of the road in this strangely deserted landscape and marvel at the scale of the sky and the horizon. Once you're back home, you'll miss it.

Restaurants

Showy dress and jewelry matter little to most Montanans. A cowboy in dusty blue jeans, flannel shirt, and worn boots leaning against his rust-eaten Ford could be a millionaire rancher and stockbroker, and the ponytailed woman behind the counter of the ranch supply store might be the town mayor. Because of this, no matter where you go to eat—whether the food is extravagant or simple, the prices expensive or dirt-cheap—dress is casual. But despite the universal informality in dining, eastern Montana has a surprising number of upscale restaurants turning out sophisticated dishes. Good ethnic food, with the possible exception of Mexican and Native American cuisine, is scarce, however. Classic steak houses and local ma-and-pa eateries are ubiquitous.

Restaurant and hotel reviews have been shortened. For full information, visit Fodors.com.

HOTEL AND RESTAURANT PRICES

What it Costs			
$	$$	$$$	$$$$
HOTELS			
under $80	$80–$130	$131–$200	over $200

When to Go

Each season offers something different in Montana: summer brings warm, dry weather perfect for hiking, biking, and horseback riding; autumn yields throngs of wildlife for animal watchers, and anglers; winter used to mean plenty of snow for skiing, snowmobiling, and ice fishing; however, recent winters have been mild with less snowfall. Although summer is the busiest season here, many travelers are only passing through on their way farther west. The roads may be crowded, but the attractions, hotels, and restaurants are likely not. Winter can sometimes be just as busy as summer, as thousands of avid skiers rush through on their way to the slopes.

Great Falls

One of Great Falls' greatest assets is its sense of history. Here, along the banks of the Missouri where the plains meet the Rockies, explorers Meriwether Lewis and William Clark encountered one of the more daunting obstacles of their expedition: the thundering waterfalls that gave the city its name. The waterfalls have since been tamed by hydropower dams, but an interpretive center, guided boat trips, and paved trails that recall the passage of the two explorers in 1805 are impressive, and a slew of other museums and attractions celebrate other chapters in the city's history. From prehistoric buffalo jumps and famous Western artists to pioneering cowboys and the Missouri River fur trade, Great Falls has a storied past rich enough to make its people proud. And they are.

This is a beautiful city for a sightseeing drive. Maple and linden trees line the residential streets, the Missouri River slices through the center of town, and the Rockies sink their teeth into the western horizon. The Highwoods and Little Belts mountains frame the views to the north and east of town. Despite the curves of the river, most streets are straight and relatively easy to navigate, thanks largely to the flat terrain. However, with an Air Force base on the east side of town, a commercial airport on the west side, and only four bridges spanning the river in between, traffic can get heavy, especially in late afternoons and on weekends. Pedestrian paths are far less congested. A gorgeous 60-mile-long riverside trail system, ideal for walking and cycling, passes the city's largest green space, Gibson Park, and one of the largest cold-water springs in the world at Giant Springs State Park.

With 59,000 residents, Great Falls is no longer Montana's second-largest city, demoted in the 2000 census to third place, below the burgeoning mountain town of Missoula. But Great Falls is still the commercial and social hub for northern Montana and southern Alberta, with a bi-level mall, thriving downtown district, bustling civic center, and near-boundless opportunities for outdoor recreation.

GETTING HERE AND AROUND

Many roads lead to Great Falls, and drivers have several options for getting here, depending on whether scenery or speed is the goal. From points west, one of the prettiest routes is dropping down from Highway 2 just east of Browning to Highway 89. The winding road has great views of the Rockies, and the little town of Choteau is a perfect place to stop to stretch your legs. If efficiency is the aim, take Highway 2 east to I–15 at Shelby.

The street layout in Great Falls is a standard grid, with avenues running east–west and streets north–south. Several one-ways make it easier to get from one end of town to the other while avoiding the busy traffic on Central and 10th Avenue South. Great Falls Transit, the city bus system, runs six days a week. And Great Falls is a bicycle-friendly town.

VISITOR INFORMATION

CONTACTS Great Falls Visitor Information Center. ✉ *100 1st Ave. N* ☎ *406/761–4436* 🌐 *www.visitgreatfallsmontana.org.*

Sights

Great Falls has many stories to tell in its historic homes and businesses, including the beautiful brick buildings of the railroad era. There are more than 200 historic houses and small businesses along the east bank of the Missouri River. The structures reflect various architectural styles, including bungalow, prairie, colonial, Queen Anne, Victorian, and Second Empire.

Black Eagle Falls

BODY OF WATER | On the north side of the historic part of town is 40-foot-high, 500-foot-wide Black Eagle Falls, one of the places where the Missouri River takes a sharp dive on its 500-foot descent through town. A pedestrian bridge from the parking area leading to an island alongside the falls makes a nice place to watch birds or the water. The adjacent golf courses and baseball diamond give the area plenty of green space and a seminatural feel, although it's hard not to notice the concrete dam looming above. ✉ *Great Falls* ✣ *Intersection of U.S. 87 and 25th St. N.*

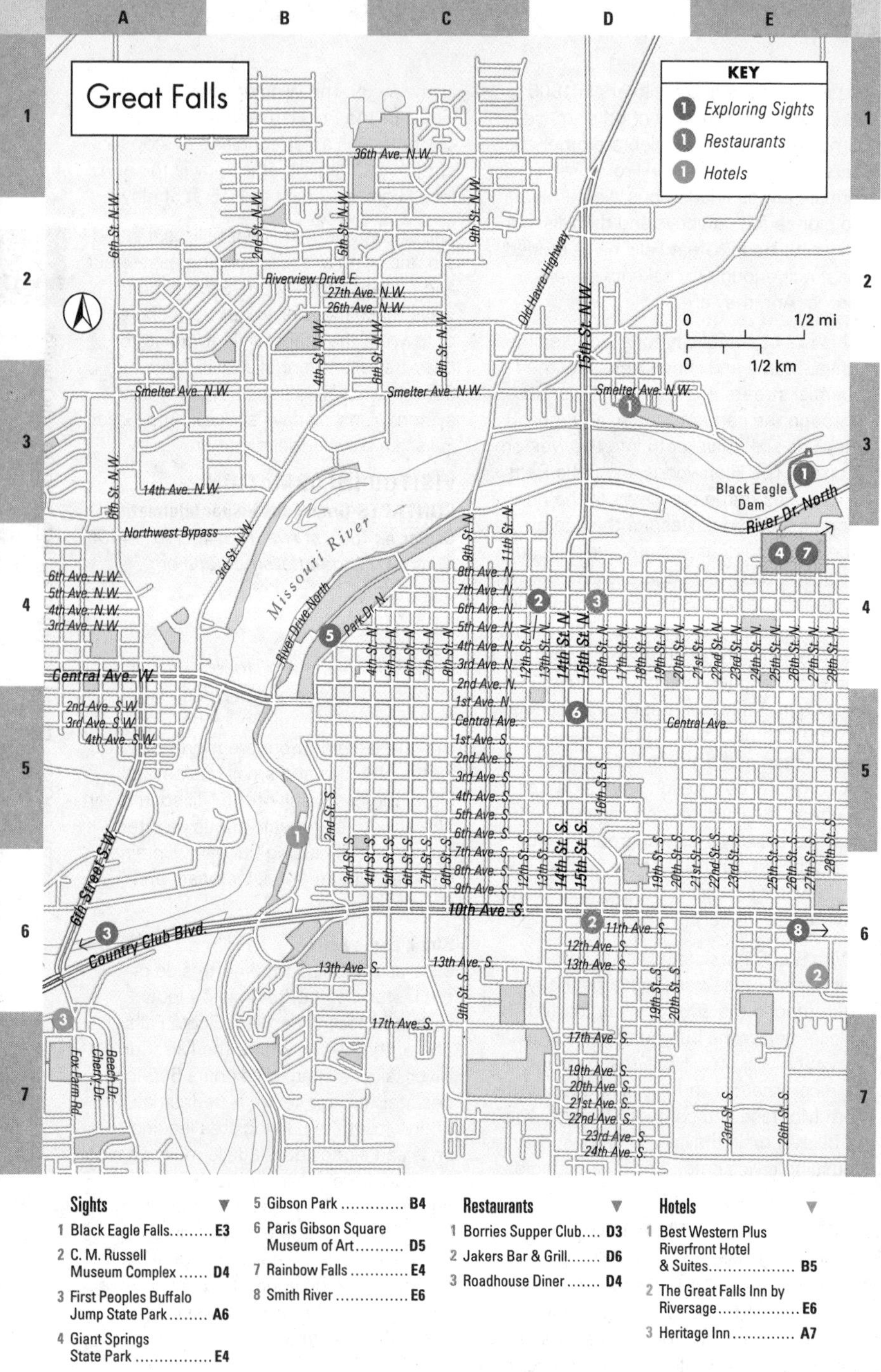

Sights

1 Black Eagle Falls......... **E3**

2 C. M. Russell Museum Complex...... **D4**

3 First Peoples Buffalo Jump State Park........ **A6**

4 Giant Springs State Park................ **E4**

5 Gibson Park............ **B4**

6 Paris Gibson Square Museum of Art.......... **D5**

7 Rainbow Falls........... **E4**

8 Smith River............... **E6**

Restaurants

1 Borries Supper Club.... **D3**

2 Jakers Bar & Grill....... **D6**

3 Roadhouse Diner....... **D4**

Hotels

1 Best Western Plus Riverfront Hotel & Suites................. **B5**

2 The Great Falls Inn by Riversage................ **E6**

3 Heritage Inn............ **A7**

★ C.M. Russell Museum Complex

MUSEUM | This 76,000-square-foot complex houses the largest collection of original art and personal objects of legendary cowboy artist Charlie Russell (1864–1926). Russell's more than 4,000 works of art—sculptures, watercolors, oil paintings—primarily portray the vanishing era of the Old West. His log studio and home, built at the turn of the 20th century, are adjacent to the main galleries. A highlight is the bison exhibit: more than 1,000 objects are used to tell the epic story of this Western icon, and you feel the floor tremble as you experience the sensation of being in the middle of a stampede. Also here are collections of paintings by other 19th-century and modern Western artists, interactive exhibits, and a research library. ✉ *400 13th St. N* ☎ *406/727–8787* 🌐 *www.cmrussell.org* 🎟 *$14* ⏲ *Closed Tues. and Wed.*

First Peoples Buffalo Jump State Park

NATIONAL/STATE PARK | For centuries Native Americans hunted bison by stampeding them off a cliff at this 2,000-acre park, which is sacred to the state's original residents. This is one of the largest and best-interpreted buffalo jumps in the United States. The mile-long cliff affords a spectacular view of the Rocky Mountains, the Missouri River, and the plains. An interpretive center focuses on the culture of the Plains Indians before white settlement. You can hike the 1.5-mile-long trail to the top of the hill where buffalo runners led herds over the cliff to their demise. ✉ *342 Ulm-Vaugh Rd.* ✣ *10 miles south of Great Falls on I–15 to Ulm exit, then 3½ miles northwest* ☎ *406/866–2217* 🌐 *fwp.mt.gov* 🎟 *$8 for out-of-state vehicles* ⏲ *Closed Mon. and Tues. in winter.*

Giant Springs State Park

NATIONAL/STATE PARK | **FAMILY** | The freshwater springs here feed a state fish hatchery that covers 400 acres of parkland. According to residents, the waters that flow from the springs form the shortest river in the world, the 200-foot-long Roe River (Oregonians hold that their D River is shorter, but most independent record keepers side with Montana on the issue). In addition to the hatchery, a visitor center, picnic grounds, a river drive, hiking and biking trails, and a playground are all on-site, and you can walk up the hill to Fish, Wildlife & Parks' regional headquarters, filled with educational displays featuring life-size mounts of area wildlife. You can also fish, attend educational programs, and take tours. Kids will enjoy feeding the hatchery's fish. ✉ *4803 Giant Springs Rd.* ☎ *406/727–1212* 🌐 *www.fwp.mt.gov* 🎟 *$8 for out-of-state vehicles.*

Gibson Park

NATIONAL/STATE PARK | **FAMILY** | This park, named for the insightful founder of Great Falls, is the crown jewel of the city's 400-acre park system. The most popular features are the duck pond and extensive flower gardens. There are also jogging paths, outdoor exercise equipment, basketball courts, horseshoe pits, restrooms, a playground, a band shell, and prime picnicking spots. Riverside Railyard Skate Park, reputed to be one of the best in the Northwest and one of the largest in the country, connects to Gibson Park via the walking path leading underneath the railroad overpass. The restored log cabin of Vinegar Jones, reportedly Great Falls' first permanent resident, is also on display in the park near the gardens. ✉ *Park Dr. N and 1st Ave. N* ☎ *406/771–1265* 🌐 *www.greatfallsmt.net* 🎟 *Free.*

Paris Gibson Square Museum of Art

MUSEUM | **FAMILY** | Contemporary artwork of the northwest United States makes up the bulk of the collection here. There is an educational resource room where kids and adults can try hands-on puzzles and projects, along with several exhibition halls and a photography collection. A perennial and butterfly garden on the south side of the building is a perfect spot for a summer picnic. ✉ *1400 1st Ave. N*

At 200 feet, locals claim that the Roe River, which was created from the springs in Giant Springs State Park, is the shortest river in the world.

☎ *406/727–8255* 🌐 *www.the-square.org* 🎫 *Free* 🕙 *Closed Sun.*

Rainbow Falls

BODY OF WATER | One of the waterfalls that gives the city its name, 50-foot-high Rainbow Falls is below Rainbow Dam, about 1½ mile east of Giant Springs State Park. An overlook has informational signs about the history of the area, as well as excellent views of the river. The surrounding land is mostly owned by ranchers, although there are some trails cut into the hills near the falls. ✉ *Giant Springs Rd.*

Smith River

BODY OF WATER | Flowing out of the Helena National Forest in the heart of Montana is the 60-mile Smith River. Like most other waterways in the state, it fluctuates with the seasons, ranging from a trickle in September to a raging torrent in June (thanks to the melting mountain snowpack). Although the river is popular for numerous activities, including camping on its banks, fishing, and swimming, the most prevalent activity on the Smith is floating. The only put-in spot is in White Sulpher Springs, about 2½ hours south of Great Falls. The only take-out spot is at Eden Bridge State Fishing Access, about 20 miles south of Great Falls. Floating is so popular, in fact, that Montana Fish, Wildlife & Parks limits the number of groups boating down the river and has a lottery system for floating permits. (It also prohibits dogs.) Despite the river's popularity, this is still Montana, and the sense of serene isolation that comes from the sight of towering mountains and open prairie will far outweigh any annoyance at seeing a few other boats during your journey. ✉ *Great Falls* ✥ *Between I–15 and U.S. 85* ☎ *406/454–5840* 🌐 *fwp.mt.gov.*

Restaurants

Borries Supper Club

$$$ | **ITALIAN** | Discerning diners flock to Black Eagle, a small community that borders the northeast edge of Great

Falls, for dinner at Borries. Regulars favor the steaks, fried chicken, lobster, and burgers, and the huge portions of spaghetti, ravioli, and rigatoni are legendary. **Known for:** amazing prime rib; long wine list; excellent service. *Average main: $30* *1800 Smelter Ave. NE, Black Eagle* *406/761–0300* *Closed Mon. No lunch.*

Jakers Bar & Grill

$$$ | **STEAKHOUSE** | The menu at this restaurant, part of a regional chain of steak houses, offers a large array of enticing appetizers, such as the rim-fire shrimp cocktail served with wasabi-infused cocktail sauce, creative salads, signature burgers, more elaborate dishes such as seafood linguini, almond-crusted halibut, and filet à la Jakers, a steak topped with crab, asparagus, and béarnaise sauce. Dress is casual, although the cherrywood interior adds a feeling of sophistication. **Known for:** five-star service; steak cooked to perfection; reservations needed on the weekends. *Average main: $30* *1500 10th Ave. S* *406/727–1033* *www.jakers.com.*

Roadhouse Diner

$$ | **BURGER** | While its burgers have been deemed "the best" in Great Falls and even in Montana, this diner's claim to fame came when it won the Food Network's *Guy's Grocery Games* in 2017. Each burger is made with grass-fed, sprout-finished Montana beef cut and ground on-site, every few hours. **Known for:** "Hell Fries" (topped with spicy cheese sauce, the "hottest south of Heaven"); house-made sauces like spiked ranch and roadie sauce; no substitutions. *Average main: $14* *613 15th St. N* *406/788–8839* *www.roadhousegf.com* *Closed Sun.–Tues.*

Hotels

Best Western Plus Riverfront Hotel & Suites

$$ | **HOTEL** | Overlooking the Missouri River just southwest of downtown and within easy walking distance of casual restaurants and watering holes, this clean, trendy property (formerly a LaQuinta) is a nice balance between bland franchise hotels and pricey upper-end lodging. **Pros:** River's Edge Trail is outside the door; well-kept grounds give the property a luxury resort feel; off the main thoroughfares but close to downtown and the 10th Avenue South retail district. **Cons:** can be difficult to find; few restaurants within walking distance; says it's pet-friendly but has a weight limit and cats are on a case-by-case basis. *Rooms from: $90* *600 River Dr. S* *406/761–2600* *www.bestwestern.com* *92 rooms* *Free breakfast.*

The Great Falls Inn by Riversage

$ | **HOTEL** | The fireplace is so cozy and the furniture in the common areas of this small (but well-appointed downtown hotel) is so comfortable you'll want to meet friends in the lobby. **Pros:** off the busy main drag of 10th Avenue South; comfortable, no-nonsense rooms; the Business King Rooms offer extra insulation. **Cons:** not easy to find; views of the back of the hospital; not close to shopping or restaurants. *Rooms from: $75* *1400 28th St. S* *406/453–6000, 800/454–6010* *www.riversageinns.com* *61 rooms* *Free breakfast.*

Heritage Inn

$$ | **HOTEL** | What used to be a cookie-cutter Best Western is now a locally owned and operated convention center hotel proud of its business center, indoor pool, solarium, dry sauna, exercise center, and king suites with jetted tubs, among other amenities. **Pros:** rates are very reasonable; 3 miles from the airport; restaurants, the Missouri River, and the AMC movie theater are within a mile. **Cons:** not the prettiest location; congested area, particularly during rush hour; can be loud if you have a poolside room. *Rooms from: $85* *1700 Fox Farm Rd.* *406/761–1900* *www.gfheritageinn.com* *230 rooms* *No meals.*

Shopping

Thanks to insightful city planners, Great Falls is blessed with a beautiful and extensive downtown shopping district full of the kind of old-fashioned stores—including galleries, toy stores, and clothiers—that in other parts of the country are rapidly giving way to chain stores and shopping malls. During the summer the downtown area comes alive with events such as the Great Falls Farmer's Market, held outside the Civic Center from June through September, and Alive at Five, which brings live music downtown one evening a week. Most of these businesses are in an area bounded by the Missouri River, 8th Street, 4th Avenue North, and 4th Avenue South.

Bighorn Outdoor Specialists
SPORTING GOODS | In downtown Great Falls, this outdoors specialty store carries everything from camping-stove fuel and freeze-dried food to ice-climbing equipment and kayaks. The store also rents canoes, kayaks, stand-up paddleboards, cross-country skis, skate skis, and snowshoes. ✉ *206 5th St. S* ☎ *406/453–2841* 🌐 *www.bighornoutdoorspecialists.com.*

Dragonfly Dry Goods
CLOTHING | Billing itself as Montana's largest specialty store, Dragonfly Dry Goods carries a huge selection of carefully curated women's clothing, boots, backpacks, blankets, tea towels, candles, earrings, magnets, and more. If you can't find something that you have to have here, you won't find it anywhere in Great Falls. ✉ *504 Central Ave.* ☎ *406/454–2263* 🌐 *www.dragonflyshopping.com.*

Activities

Unlike some of Montana's more westerly cities, Great Falls does not lie at the base of world-class ski runs or sheer cliffs for rock climbing. It is nevertheless popular with outdoor enthusiasts, largely because of its central location. Ski lodges and climbing trails are a short drive west, and stretching out north and south are Montana's famed blue-ribbon fishing streams. Not to be forgotten is the "Mighty Mo"—the Missouri River, a recreational playground that runs straight through the middle of the city.

BIKING AND HIKING

River's Edge Trail
HIKING/WALKING | With nearly 60 miles of paved and single-track trail, the **River's Edge Trail** follows the Missouri River through the city on both banks; four bridges connect the trail's two branches. The trail, which attracts bikers, joggers, and strollers, passes Gibson Park, the West Gate Mall, Giant Springs State Park, and several waterfalls and dams. In addition, there are 18 pieces of public art located along the trail. More primitive and challenging trails extend downstream of Rainbow Dam. ✉ *Great Falls* ☎ *406/788–3313* 🌐 *www.thetrail.org.*

BIKE RENTALS

Knicker Biker
BICYCLING | Rent a recreational bike or a performance bike for the day three blocks from the River's Edge Trail near Gibson Park. They have one of the best selections of bikes and bicycle accessories in town. ✉ *1525 10th Ave S., Suite 2* ☎ *406/454–2912* 🌐 *www.knickerbiker.com.*

CAMPING

Great Falls KOA. Regular evening entertainment at this campsite on the south edge of town includes bluegrass music, country humor, and a little cowboy poetry. Facilities are kid-friendly, with a small petting zoo, playground, horseshoe pits, basketball hoops, and a sand volleyball court. The site is near three golf courses, and has a large outdoor water park, a hot tub and sauna, spacious tent sites, and even rental cottages and a glamping tent. ✉ *1500 51st St. S* ☎ *406/727–3191* 🌐 *www.koa.com* *220 sites.*

BOATING AND FISHING

Craig Madsen's Montana River Outfitters
TOUR—SPORTS | Facing the river on the north side of town, this company is known for its guided trips along the river by canoe, raft, or kayak. You can also get outfitted for a float trip with a wide selection of rental equipment. ✉ *923 10th Ave. N* ☎ *406/761–1677* 🌐 *www.montanariveroutfitters.com*.

Fort Benton

40 miles northeast of Great Falls via U.S. 87.

The gateway to the Upper Missouri River, this town of 1,464 people has a rich and rugged past that's captured in a complex of excellent museums and an interpretive center all covered by a $15 admission fee. Lewis and Clark first camped at this site less than an hour downriver from Great Falls in 1805. As a quick and easy way to move people, the Missouri River was the lifeblood of 19th-century Fort Benton. The first steamboat arrived here from St. Louis in 1859, and the city once claimed distinction as the farthest inland port in the world. Throughout the 1860s gold taken from mines across Montana was shipped downriver via Fort Benton; in 1866 alone, the town shipped 2½ tons of gold dust. The river still moves people today, not to seek their fortune in the goldfields but to paddle its placid waters amid the peaceful, serene, and beautiful countryside.

GETTING HERE AND AROUND

Highway 87, also known as the Havre Highway, travels from Great Falls to Havre, and is the most logical route to Fort Benton from either direction. The fact that there are no major hills or sharp turns along the way encourages speed; be on the lookout for reckless motorists.

Fort Benton is set up in a grid, with most of the travel-related sights situated near the river between Main Street and River Street. It's an easy town to walk or bicycle.

Sights

Missouri Breaks Interpretive Center
INFO CENTER | The Missouri Breaks Interpretive Center puts the fabled Missouri Breaks in perspective, and offers a virtual glimpse of the river to those not floating down the Mighty Mo and maps for those who do. The front of the building, on Fort Benton's historic levee, looks like the stunning White Cliffs of the Missouri; the rear resembles the deck of a paddle-wheel steamer. Inside, photos and films of the river and its wildlife, interactive exhibits, and history lessons await. Don't miss the rifle surrendered by Chief Joseph of the Nez Perce. ✉ *701 7th St.* ☎ *406/622–4000* 🌐 *www.fortbentonmuseums.com* 🎟 *$15 (for all Fort Benton museums)* ⏲ *Oct.–May 23 by appointment only (call to book).*

Museum of the Northern Great Plains
MUSEUM | Montana's official agriculture museum, the Museum of the Northern Great Plains tells the story of three generations of farmers from 1908 until 1980. The 30,000 square feet of exhibition space hold a village of businesses from the homestead era and a library. On display are the Hornaday-Smithsonian Bison, specimens taken from the Montana plains when it seemed likely that the species faced extinction. In 1886 the six buffalo were stuffed, then exhibited in the Smithsonian for more than 70 years before being returned to their native state. ✉ *1205 20th St.* ☎ *406/622–5316* 🌐 *www.fortbentonmuseums.com* 🎟 *$15 (for all Fort Benton museums)* ⏲ *Closed Oct.–May 21.*

★ **Museum of the Upper Missouri**
MUSEUM | Covering the era from 1800 to 1900, the Museum of the Upper Missouri highlights the importance of Fort Benton and the role it played as a trading post, military fort, and the head

of steamboat navigation. In the summer there are daily guided tours at the adjacent Old Fort Benton, considered the birthplace of Montana; its 1846 blockhouse is the oldest standing structure in the state. ✉ *Old Fort Park, 20th St.* ☎ *406/622–5316* 🌐 *www.fortbentonmuseums.com* 🎫 *$15 (for all Fort Benton museums)* 🕒 *Closed Oct.–May 21.*

Upper Missouri National Wild and Scenic River

BODY OF WATER | In 1805–06 Lewis and Clark explored the upper Missouri River and camped on its banks. Today the stretch designated the Upper Missouri National Wild and Scenic River runs 149 miles downriver from Fort Benton. Highlights include the scenic White Cliffs area, Citadel Rock, Hole in the Wall, Lewis and Clark Camp at Slaughter River, abandoned homesteads, and abundant wildlife. Commercial boat tours, shuttle service, and boat rentals—including rowboats, powerboats, and canoes—are available in Fort Benton and Virgelle. Be aware of seasonal restrictions that prohibit motorized boats and limit campsites on the river. ✉ *Missouri Breaks Interpretive Center, 701 7th St.* ☎ *406/622–4000* 🎫 *Free.*

Restaurants

Union Grille

$$$$ | **AMERICAN** | The Union Grille's constantly changing seasonal menu features Montana regional cuisine and fare from afar, such as Pacific troll salmon, tagliatelle pasta with sautéed tiger prawns, and grilled pork tenderloin. The varied wine list is populated predominantly by choices from California and Oregon vineyards and offers a number of exceptional beer choices from Montana microbreweries. **Known for:** lovely dining room setting with period furniture; superb prime rib; Missouri River views. 💲 *Average main: $32* ✉ *1 Grand Union Sq.* ☎ *406/622–1882* 🌐 *www.grandunionhotel.com* 🕒 *Closed Tues. Closed Mon. Sept.–May. No lunch.*

Hotels

★ **Grand Union Hotel**

$$ | **HOTEL** | Possibly the oldest hotel in Montana, the Grand Union was built on the bank of the Missouri in 1882 to serve steamboat and stage travelers. **Pros:** the hotel has a colorful history; easy walking around town; friendly atmosphere. **Cons:** hard to get a room at the last minute; no lunch at the Union Grille; detractors say it's overpriced. 💲 *Rooms from: $130* ✉ *1 Grand Union Sq.* ☎ *406/622–1882* 🌐 *www.grandunionhotel.com* 🛏 *26 rooms* 🍽 *Free breakfast.*

Activities

Although sparsely inhabited, this calm stretch of the Mighty Mo is becoming more and more popular with visitors. There's no shortage of outfitters and guides offering their services at competitive prices.

Missouri River Outfitters

TOUR—SPORTS | Owner Nicolle Fugere has been a guide on this river for more than a decade, and most of her team of guides grew up in the area. Guided trips range from one to six days. Or simply take advantage of their rental and shuttle service. Missouri River Outfitters rents canoes and kayaks. ✉ *Fort Benton* ☎ *406/622–3295, 866/282–3295* 🌐 *www.mroutfitters.com.*

Lewistown

90 miles southeast of Fort Benton via Hwys. 80 and 81.

Started as a small trading post in the shadow of the low-lying Moccasin and Judith mountains, Lewistown has evolved into a pleasant town of nearly 6,000 residents. Several locations are listed on the National Register of Historic Places, including the Silk Stocking and Central Business districts, Courthouse Square, Judith Place, and Stone Quarry. Every September the town hosts the **Chockecherry Festival,** which draws thousands of visitors and dozens of vendors from around the state. The highlight of the event is the chokecherry pit-spitting contest.

GETTING HERE AND AROUND

Lewistown is in the geographic center of the state, but there's no easy way to arrive here. Two-lane state roads are the only option, and the most popular route is Highway 87/200 running from Great Falls to Billings. Like most small towns in these parts, Lewistown is easy to navigate. Highway 87/200 becomes Main Street.

VISITOR INFORMATION

CONTACTS Lewistown Area Chamber of Commerce. ✉ *408 N.E. Main St.* ☎ *406/535–5436* 🌐 *www.lewistown-chamber.com.*

Sights

American Prairie Reserve

MUSEUM | FAMILY | The American Prairie Foundation is creating the largest nature reserve in the contiguous United States by restoring prairie ecosystems, replete with bison, pronghorn antelope, and sage grouse. The APR, as it's commonly referred to, also provides an excellent destination for visitors to the area. You can visit their vast properties north and south of the Missouri River, where modest, high-quality accommodations include cabins, yurts, and tent and RV camping. **Bison Camp** on the Sun Prairie Unit, where the APR bison herd lives, is 50 miles south of Malta on the way to Fort Peck Reservoir. Head south on Short Oil Road and read the signs to guide your way. The **Antelope Creek Campground** at Mars Vista is 70 miles southwest of Malta (and 65 miles northeast of Lewiston) on Highway 191, and offers RV sites, tent platforms, and rental cabins. It offers stunning views, hiking, an interpretive nature trail and easy access to the south end of the Charles M. Russel Wildlife Refuge Auto Trail and the Slippery Ann Wildlife Viewing Area. The **PN Property** is on the south side of the Missouri River 60 miles north of Lewiston. The **Lewis and Clark Hut** is a large, clean cabin that can sleep eight, and a set of state-of-the-art 30-foot yurts can sleep up to nine people. If you're traveling light, Lewis and Clark Trail Adventures can provide meals, sleeping bags, and guided trip options. Reservations can be made starting February 15; book early, because they fill up quickly. Starting in summer 2021, you can visit APR's new **American Prairie Reserve National Discovery Center** in Lewiston. ✉ *American Prairie Reserve National Discovery Center, 302 W. Main* ☎ *877/273–1123* 🌐 *www.americanprairie.org* 🎫 *Free.*

Big Springs Trout Hatchery

FISH HATCHERY | FAMILY | At the head of one of the purest cold-water springs in the world is the Big Springs Trout Hatchery. The state's largest cold-water production station nurtures several species of trout and kokanee salmon. The show pond, where you can view oddities such as albino rainbow trout and perhaps even fish weighing a monstrous 15 pounds, is a popular attraction, but the hatchery grounds are a sight in and of themselves and a wonderful spot to enjoy a picnic under giant willow and cottonwood trees. You can see the place where Big Spring Creek spurts from the earth, and the native wildlife—including white-tailed deer, beavers, wood ducks, and belted kingfishers—makes frequent appearances. ✉ *2035 Fish Hatchery Rd.* ✣ *Hwy. 466, 7 miles southeast of Lewistown* ☎ *406/538–5588* 🎫 *Free* ⏲ *Closed weekends.*

Central Montana Museum

MUSEUM | Pioneer relics, blacksmith and cowboy tools, guns, and Native American artifacts are displayed at the Central Montana Museum. The most popular new exhibit is a full-scale replica of a Torosaurus skull found just 65 miles away. Guided tours are available in the summer from Memorial Day through Labor Day. ✉ *408 N.E. Main St.* ☎ *406/535–3642* 🌐 *centralmtmuseum.weebly.com* 🎫 *Free* 🕒 *Closed Labor Day–Memorial Day.*

Charlie Russell Chew-Choo

SCENIC DRIVE | **FAMILY** | Discover the vistas that inspired Western artist Charles M. Russell on the Charlie Russell Chew-Choo, a vintage 1950s-era train that travels on the old Milwaukee Road tracks through some of the most beautiful and remote landscapes in the state. The tour, which departs from Kingston, about 10 miles northwest of Lewistown, covers 56 miles and lasts 3½ hours. It includes a prime-rib dinner and a cash bar as well as live entertainment and maybe even a holdup. On weekends before Christmas the Chew-Choo transforms into a prairie Polar Express, and there are special Halloween and New Year's Eve runs. ✉ *408 N.E. Main St.* ✣ *U.S. 191 north 2 miles, then Hanover Rd. west for 7½ miles* ☎ *406/535–5436* 🌐 *www.montanadinnertrain.com* 🎫 *$100.*

Judith River

BODY OF WATER | The tame, deserted Judith flows more than 60 miles from the Lewis and Clark National Forest through arid plains and sandy mesas before emptying into the Missouri. The scenery is stunning, but the variably low water levels and stifling hot summer sun are not conducive to float trips. This is, however, excellent fossil-hunting ground, and the **Judith River Dinosaur Institute** sponsors frequent digs here. Most of the land surrounding the river is private, though, so check before you start wandering the banks looking for bones. As always, remember to leave fossils where you find them, and report anything significant to the Dinosaur Institute. ✉ *Lewistown* ✣ *North of Hwy. 200* ☎ *406/696–5842 Judith River Dinosaur Institute.*

Lewistown Art Center

MUSEUM | The regional Lewistown Art Center showcases artwork by local talent and hosts community art classes. ✉ *323 W. Main St.* ☎ *406/535–8278* 🌐 *www.lewistownartcenter.net* 🎫 *Free* 🕒 *Closed Sun. and Mon.*

Restaurants

Central Feed Grilling Co.

$$$ | **AMERICAN** | Housed in the historic (1916) former Central Feed building, until recently this family-owned brewery was where farmers and ranchers came to buy grain and seed. Today it serves typical brewpub fare, but with a slightly elevated twist. **Known for:** exotic (for Central Montana) appetizers like salmon ceviche and ahi tuna; Grains of Montana brioche burger buns; great outdoor deck with views of Big Spring Creek. 💲 *Average main: $20* ✉ *220 E. Main St., Suite 1* ☎ *406/535–2337* 🌐 *www.cfgrillco.com.*

Hotels

Yogo Inn

$$ | **HOTEL** | This sprawling brick hotel on the east side of Lewistown takes its name from the Yogo sapphires mined nearby. **Pros:** borders the new rails-to-trails walking path; indoor pool; good on-site restaurant. **Cons:** noise is an issue when it's busy; has an "old hotel" smell. 💲 *Rooms from: $110* ✉ *211 E. Main St.* ☎ *406/535–8721* 🌐 *www.yogoinn.com* 🛏 *123 rooms* 🍽 *No meals.*

Activities

Lewistown has access to water—and plenty of it. From natural springs to alpine lakes to crystal-clear creeks fed by melting snow, there are all kinds of ways to get wet in town, or within a few short miles. Big Spring Creek flows right through downtown, and even underneath several establishments on Main Street.

Ackley Lake State Park

PARK—SPORTS-OUTDOORS | **FAMILY** | **Ackley Lake State Park** has two boat ramps, a seasonal boat dock, great fishing for rainbow trout, and a 23-site campground with vault toilets. It's to the north of the Little Belt Mountains, about 26 miles southwest of Lewistown. ✉ *Lewistown* ✥ *U.S. 87 to Hwy. 400, then 7 miles southwest* ☎ *406/454–5840* 🌐 *fwp.mt.gov/stateparks/ackley-lake-state-park.*

Gigantic Warm Springs

SWIMMING | In a clearing roughly 15 miles outside Lewistown you can swim on a family farm in a small spring-fed lake (but supposedly the largest natural warm spring in the world) that keeps a constant temperature of 68°F. It's only open in the summer. ✉ *749 Warm Spring La.* ☎ *406/538–9825* 🎫 *$4 to swim.*

Lewistown Municipal Swimming Pool

SWIMMING | From June through August one of the most popular places in Frank Day City Park is the town's Olympic-size pool with two large slides, a wading pool for kids and a splash pad. For a more relaxing experience, stroll the park's beautiful labyrinth garden planted in annuals and perennials. ✉ *210 6th Ave. S* ☎ *406/535–4503* 🎫 *$4.*

Big Snowy Mountains

30 miles south of Lewistown via Red Hill Rd.

South of Montana's geographical center an island of rocky peaks rises more than 3,000 feet from the sea of windswept prairie, beckoning scenery lovers and hard-core adventurers alike. A combination of pine and fir forests and barren tundra, much of the Big Snowy Mountains area is undeveloped. More than 90% of its 106,776 acres are designated federal wilderness study area—there are no homes, no commercial services, no industry, and very few roads. The result is almost total solitude for anyone who treks into the Big Snowies to explore their rocky pinnacles, icy caves, and tranquil forests. The best road accesses are Red Hill Road about 30 miles south of Lewistown and Niel Creek east of the small town of Judith Gap.

GETTING HERE AND AROUND

The Big Snowies are close to Lewistown and easy to access via county roads. Once up there, most of them turn into fairly decent gravel roads. On the west side, head west on Highway 87/200 to Eddie's Corner and drop down to Judith Gap. To reach points east, take Highway 238 all the way past Big Spring Creek where it turns into Red Hill Road.

VISITOR INFORMATION

CONTACTS Musselshell Ranger Station. ✉ *809 2nd St. NW, Harlowton* ☎ *406/632–4391* 🌐 *www.fs.usda.gov/lcnf.*

Sights

Big Snowy

MOUNTAIN—SIGHT | The second-highest point in the Big Snowies is Big Snowy, also called Old Baldy. Just 41 feet shorter than Greathouse Peak, the 8,640-foot-high mountain makes an enjoyable climb. A designated path, Maynard Ridge Trail, follows an old jeep road almost to the summit. The peak is a barren plateau with a small rocky outcropping marking the highest point. ✉ *Red Hill Rd.* ☎ *406/566–2292.*

Crystal Lake

MOUNTAIN—SIGHT | In the higher reaches of the mountains is pristine Crystal Lake. There's excellent hiking along interpretive and wildflower trails as well as camping, fossil hunting, and ice-cave exploration. The ice cave is a 5-mile hike from the 28-site campground; June is the best time to see the 30-foot ice pillars formed over the winter. There's a cabin 6 miles from the gate for snowmobilers, cross-country skiers, and snowshoers, but it's closed when the snow is too deep to navigate (which is most of the winter). Motorized boats are not allowed on the lake. ✉ *Crystal Lake Rd.* ☎ *406/566–2292* 🎫 *Free.*

Greathouse Peak

MOUNTAIN—SIGHT | At 8,681 feet, Greathouse Peak is the tallest mountain in the Big Snowies. Vehicles are permitted on Forest Service roads that reach partially to the peak, but the simplest way up is to hike the 6 miles of unmarked trails that zigzag up the slope from Halfmoon Canyon. The main trail, which is only mildly strenuous, doesn't quite make it to the top; to reach the summit, you'll need to hike a few yards off the main path. You'll know you've reached the highest point when you see the two stone cairns. The Judith Ranger Station in Stanford is your best source for Snowies information. ✥ *Pack Trail* ☎ *406/566–2292.*

Halfbreed Lake National Wildlife Refuge

NATURE PRESERVE | Any combination of U.S. 12, U.S. 191, U.S. 87, and I–90 will make a quick route to Billings. However, if you have the time, try getting off the main roads. The square of beautiful country between these four highways is the location of Halfbreed Lake National Wildlife Refuge, part of the Charles M. Russell National Wildlife Refuge. The several thousand acres of Halfbreed encompass a seasonally wet lake and wetlands, creeks, and grassy plains. Wildlife includes grouse, waterfowl, grasslands birds, deer, and antelope. This is a favorite spot for birders. ✉ *Molt-Rapelje Rd.* ☎ *406/538–8706.*

Upper Musselshell Museum

MUSEUM | A pair of 1909 sandstone buildings in the town of Harlowton, 25 miles southwest of the mountains, house the Upper Musselshell Museum. The collection primarily contains artifacts of the people who lived in, worked, and developed the land around the Upper Musselshell River. There are also fossils of bison and dinosaurs (including a full-size reproduction of "Ava," from the recently discovered species Avaceratops) in the two buildings in Harlowtown's small but picturesque commercial district. ✉ *11 and 36 S. Central St., Harlowton* ☎ *406/632–5519* 🌐 *www.harlowton-museum.org* 🎫 *$5* ⏲ *Closed Sun.*

Hotels

Corral Motel

$ | **HOTEL** | Three family units, some with two bedrooms, and three full kitchenette units are what travelers find at this vintage roadside motel marked by a neon sign. **Pros:** perfect base camp for three different mountain ranges; dog-friendly; very affordable. **Cons:** traffic noise from U.S. 191; nothing fancy; feels like a trucker's motor inn. 💲 *Rooms from: $63* ✉ *U.S. 12 and U.S. 191 E, Harlowton* ☎ *406/632–4331* 🛏 *18 rooms* 🍽 *No meals.*

Shopping

Country Junction

GIFTS/SOUVENIRS | This Main Street mainstay smells like the tempting candles it sells and is worth checking out even if it's just to sample fancy goat milk lotions. It also sells cute tea towels, funny signs, MT apparel, and gifts galore for the folks back home. ✉ *209 W. Main St., Lewistown* ☎ *406/535–8402* 🌐 *www.countryjunctionmt.com* ⏲ *Closed Sun.*

Activities

In the evergreen forests and rocky slopes of the Big Snowies and the Judith and Little Belt mountains you can pursue numerous outdoor activities, including fishing, hiking, rock climbing, snowmobiling, and cross-country skiing. The utter isolation of the region enhances the experience, but be sure to get supplied in the larger communities of Lewistown, Great Falls, or Billings before making the trek out to the mountains.

CAMPING

Crystal Lake Campground. Tucked inside the lip of the crater that contains the often turquoise waters of Crystal Lake, this primitive Forest Service campground may be one of the most dramatic (and cold) places to pitch a tent in the state. There are year-round ice caves nearby, and snow can fly just about any month of the year. There's plenty of space separating the campsites. ✉ *Crystal Lake Rd., 22 miles west of U.S. 87* ☎ *406/566–2292* 🌐 *www.fs.usda.gov/activity/hlcnf/recreation/camping-cabins* *28 sites.*

Billings

A bastion of civilization on an otherwise empty prairie, Billings is a classic Western city, full of the kind of history that shaped the frontier. The Minnesota and Montana Land and Improvement Company founded the town simply to serve as a shipping point along the Northwestern Railroad. In the spring of 1882 the settlement consisted of three buildings—a home, a hotel, and a general store—but before six months passed 5,000 city lots had been sold and more than 200 homes and businesses had been erected. The city's immediate and consistent growth earned Billings the nickname "the Magic City." Its location earned it its other nickname, "Montana's Trailhead."

In 2007 the population for the city proper hit the 100,000 mark, making it not only the largest city in Montana, but the largest for 500 miles in any direction. Today, it's home to nearly 110,000 people, and it's still the state's largest city by a long shot. Since the 1951 discovery of an oil field that stretches across Montana and the Dakotas into Canada, refining and energy production have played a key role in keeping Billings vibrant and productive.

GETTING HERE AND AROUND

Several exits access Billings from I–90. Livingston lies 116 miles to the west and Miles City 145 miles to the east along the same highway. Great Falls, 219 miles northwest, is reached by following I–90 to U.S. 287, then I–15, or by taking U.S. 87 via Lewistown. A number of airlines serve Logan International Airport.

Although city planners in its first century did a fine job of laying out the constantly growing community of Billings, most growth in recent years, both residential and commercial, has been in what is commonly called the West End. The primary residential districts are on the northern and western sides, the industrial parks are on the city's southern and eastern perimeters, and a historic downtown district is a bit east of center. Major avenues ease the flow of traffic between the sectors, and downtown streets, which are primarily one-way, are logically numbered. Although most of the newer hotels and motels are in the western part of the city, the majority of tourist sights and better restaurants are downtown. Therefore, expect to do far more driving than walking to reach your destination. Locals complain mightily about rush-hour traffic, but gridlock is unheard of, and those from bigger metropolitan areas will wonder what the gripe is.

VISITOR INFORMATION

CONTACTS Billings Area Visitor Center and Cattle Drive Monument. ✉ *815 S. 27th St.* ☎ *406/245–4111* 🌐 *www.visitbillings.com.*

Sights

Alberta Bair Theater

BUILDING | In the 1930s, 20th Century Fox built this art deco movie theater on land homesteaded by a successful sheep-ranching family. Saved from the wrecking ball by community groups in

A
B
C
D
E
F
1
2
3
4
5
6
7
8
9
Billings
Billings Logan International Airport
3
Rimrock Road
Poly Drive
Colton Boulevard
Parkhill Drive
Grand Avenue
Lewis Avenue
Broadwater Avenue
Central Avenue
Monad Road
King Avenue West
Midland Road
Laurel Road
Gabel Road
Gabel Rd
South Frontage Road
Shiloh Road
Zimmerman Trail
32nd Street W.
32nd Street West
24th Street West
19th Street West
17th Street West
16th Street West
15th Street West
14th Street West
13th Street West
8th Street West
South Billings Blvd.
S. Billings Blvd.
Wise Lane
302
90
Canyon Creek
Yellowstone River
0
1/2 mi
0
1/2 km
KEY
Exploring Sights
Restaurants
Quick Bites
Hotels

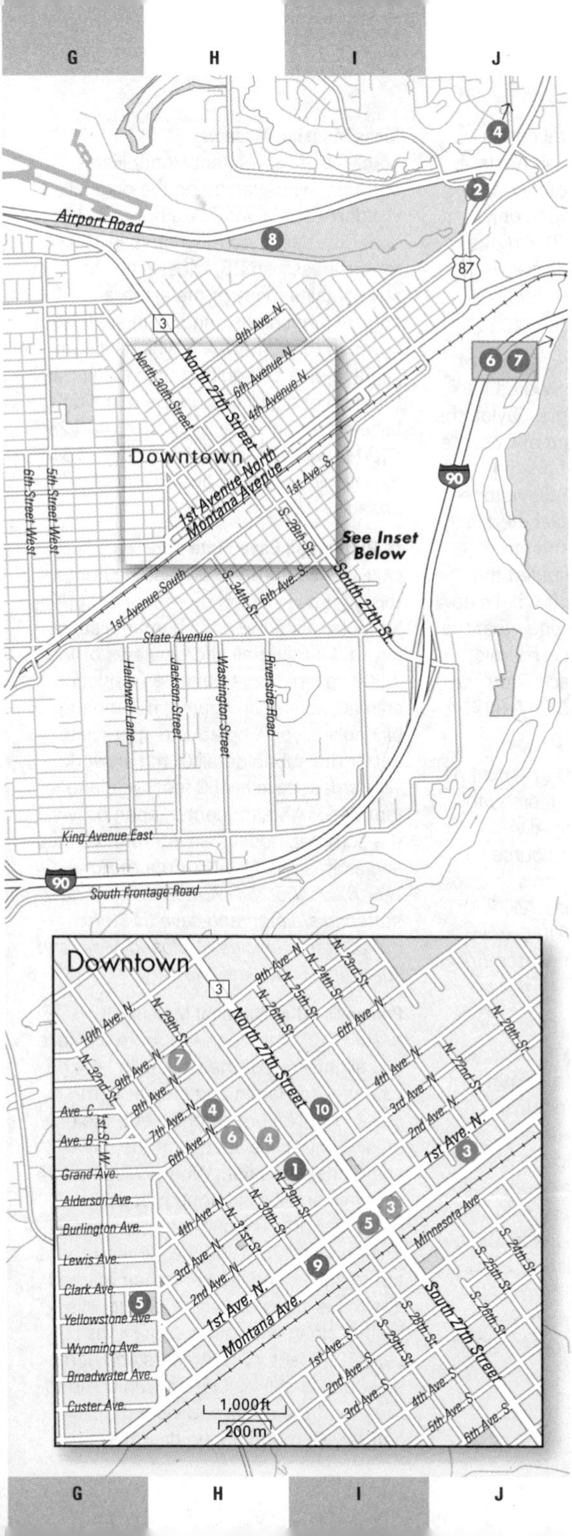

Sights

1 Alberta Bair Theater I8
2 Boothill Cemetery....................J1
3 Geyser Park B8
4 Lake Elmo State Park.................J1
5 Moss Mansion Museum.......... G8
6 Pictograph Cave State Park.......J2
7 Pompey's Pillar National Monument................J2
8 Swords Rimrock Park............. H2
9 Western Heritage Center.......... I8
10 Yellowstone Art Museum.......... I7
11 Yellowstone County Museum F1
12 ZooMontana A8

Restaurants

1 Bistecca at the Granary E2
2 Bistro Enzo C3
3 Ciao Mambo.........................J7
4 Juliano's Restaurant.............. H7
5 Walkers............................. I8

Quick Bites

1 Black Dog Coffeehouse D3

Hotels

1 Best Western Plus Kelly Inn & Suites...................F5
2 Big Horn Resort, Ascend Hotel Collection.......... B7
3 DoubleTree by Hilton Hotel Billings.............................. I8
4 Dude Rancher Lodge.............. H7
5 Hilton Garden Inn Billings......... D6
6 The Josephine Bed and Breakfast................ H7
7 Riversage Billings Inn............. H7
8 Springhill Suites by Marriott Billings.....................E6

the 1980s, it is now a cultural center for the region. The Alberta Bair hosts a variety of national and international companies each year. It is open only during performances. ✉ *2801 3rd Ave. N* ☎ *406/256–6052* 🌐 *www.albertabairtheater.org* ⏲ *Closed Fri.–Sun.*

Boothill Cemetery

CEMETERY | Atop the Rimrocks, north of downtown and adjacent to Swords Park, lie the graves of H.M. Muggins Taylor, the army scout who carried word of Custer's defeat through 180 miles of hostile territory; Western explorer Yellowstone Kelly; and several outlaws executed in territorial days. A sign tells the story of Crow warriors who blindfolded their horses before riding them off what's now known as Sacrifice Cliff in hopes that the gods would end a smallpox epidemic. ✉ *Billings* ✣ *East end of Black Otter Trail, parallel to Airport Rd.* ☎ *406/657–8371.*

Geyser Park

AMUSEMENT PARK/WATER PARK | **FAMILY** | A favorite diversion for area visitors with children, Geyser Park has an ADA-compliant 18-hole miniature golf course with waterfalls and geyser pools. It also has an arcade and laser maze. ✉ *7250 Entryway Dr.* ☎ *406/254–2510* 🌐 *www.geyserpark.net* ⏲ *Closed in winter; hrs vary by season.*

Lake Elmo State Park

NATIONAL/STATE PARK | **FAMILY** | Surrounding a 64-acre reservoir in the Billings Heights area, this park is a popular spot for hiking, swimming, fishing, and nonmotorized boating. Although it's not far from downtown, the park is still wild enough to seem miles away from civilization. The regional on-site headquarters for Montana Fish, Wildlife & Parks is a source of recreational information and museum-quality wildlife displays. ✉ *2400 Lake Elmo Dr.* ☎ *406/247–2940* 🌐 *www.fwp.mt.gov* 🎟 *$8 for out-of-state vehicles.*

Moss Mansion Museum

HOUSE | Dutch architect Henry Hardenbergh, who worked on the original Waldorf-Astoria and Plaza hotels in New York City, designed this house in 1903 for businessman P.B. Moss. The mansion still contains many of the elaborate original furnishings, ranging in style from Moorish to art nouveau, which visitors can see on a self-guided tour. Don't miss the gem of a gift shop in the mansion's basement. ✉ *914 Division St.* ☎ *406/256–5100* 🌐 *www.mossmansion.com* 🎟 *$15* ⏲ *Days and hrs vary by season so call ahead.*

★ Pictograph Cave State Park

CAVE | Once home to prehistoric hunters, this spot has yielded more than 30,000 artifacts related to early human history. A paved 3/4-mile trail affords views of the 2,200-year-old cave paintings depicting animal and human figures; if you bring binoculars, you'll be able to appreciate better the subtle detail of the artwork. The largest cave is 160 feet wide and 45 feet deep. A visitor center, open daily in the summer, houses an interpretive area and a gift shop. ✉ *3401 Coburn Rd.* ✣ *Off U.S. 87* ☎ *406/254–7342* 🌐 *fwp.mt.gov/stateparks/pictograph-cave* 🎟 *$8 for out-of-state vehicles* ⏲ *Closed Mon. and Tues. late Sept.–late May.*

Pompey's Pillar National Monument

NATURE SITE | Although the route will take you slightly out of the way, take I–94 on your way to Hardin and stop at Pompey's Pillar National Monument, the only on-site physical evidence of the Lewis and Clark expedition. When William Clark saw this small sandstone mesa rising out of the prairie along the Yellowstone River on July 25, 1806, he climbed to the top to survey the area and then marked it with his signature and the date. His graffiti, along with other engravings by early-19th-century fur traders and homesteaders, is still visible. You can climb to the top of the mesa and view the signature year-round during daylight hours.

Replicas of the canoes used by Lewis and Clark are on display at Pompey's Pillar National Monument, which has the only remaining phyiscal evidence of the expedition (William Clark's graffitti signature).

To get to Hardin, continue east on I–94 for a few miles and then head south on Highway 47. ✉ *Billings* ✣ *I–94, 25 miles east of Billings* ☎ *406/875–2400* 🌐 *www.pompeyspillar.org.*

Swords Rimrock Park

TRAIL | This trail system on the northern edge of Billings is a pleasant mix of paved urban paths and rugged dirt tracks, where elderly locals out for a Sunday stroll are just as content as extreme mountain bikers. Several individual trails make up the Rimrock system, which starts at Boothill Cemetery and winds past the airport up into the rocky formations that surround the city and give the trail its name. Expect fantastic views of the open plains and five distinct mountain ranges in some places, and the roar of jet engines and the sight of oil-refinery smokestacks in others. ✉ *Billings* ✣ *Airport Rd.* ☎ *406/245–4111* 🌐 *www.billingsparks.org.*

Western Heritage Center

MUSEUM | **FAMILY** | The permanent exhibits here include oral histories, artifacts, and kid-friendly interactive displays tracing the lives of Native Americans, ranchers, homesteaders, immigrants, and railroad workers who lived in the area from 1880 onward. Native American interpretive programs also are offered. The impressive castlelike building that houses the center is almost as interesting as the exhibits. ✉ *2822 Montana Ave.* ☎ *406/256–6809* 🌐 *www.ywhc.org* 🎫 *$5* ⏲ *Closed Sun. and Mon.*

Yellowstone Art Museum

MUSEUM | One of the premier art museums in a four-state region, "YAM" displays Western and contemporary art by nationally and internationally known artists. The permanent collection numbers more than 4,000 works, including pieces by Charles M. Russell and cowboy author and illustrator Will James. (It has the largest collection of art by James in the country.) Beyond the Palette, the attractive museum café, Raven's Café d'Art, ($), serves lunch Tuesday through Friday. ✉ *401 N. 27th St.* ☎ *406/256–6804* 🌐 *www.artmuseum.org* 🎫 *$15* ⏲ *Closed Mon.*

Yellowstone County Museum

MUSEUM | Once frequented by the likes of Teddy Roosevelt and Buffalo Bill Cody, today this log cabin, standing near the exit of Logan Airport, houses a Montana frontier history museum filled with more than 25,000 objects. Check out the chuck wagon, Native American artifacts, wildlife taxidermy, and a Lewis and Clark fur-trading post. A veranda affords unparalleled views of the Bighorn, Pryor, and Beartooth mountains. ✉ *1950 Terminal Circle* ☎ *406/256–6811* 🌐 *www.ycmhistory.org* 🎫 *Free* ⏲ *Closed Sun. and Mon.*

ZooMontana

ZOO | **FAMILY** | Ranging over 70 acres of zoological park and botanical gardens, ZooMontana has inhabitants evenly divided between those native to the region, such as grizzlies, gray wolves, and bighorn sheep, and the exotic, including Amur tigers, red pandas, and a Laughing Kookabura. Its most recent addition is a sloth named Winston. There's a farm and ranch area, complete with a petting zoo. Because there are few zoos in the region, it can be extremely busy here in summer. ✉ *2100 S. Shiloh Rd.* ☎ *406/652–8100* 🌐 *www.zoomontana.org* 🎫 *$11.*

Restaurants

Bistecca at the Granary

$$$ | **MODERN AMERICAN** | A restored flour mill houses this restaurant, which prides itself on serving locally raised and processed proteins. Steaks, chicken, and pasta are mainstays, but the seafood selection is also noteworthy. **Known for:** locally famous nachos; taproom with two dozen beers on tap; attentive staff, even when busy. [$] *Average main: $28* ✉ *1500 Poly Dr.* ☎ *406/259–3488* 🌐 *www.bisteccagranary.com* ⏲ *Closed Sun.*

Bistro Enzo

$$$ | **MODERN AMERICAN** | People come to this attractive chalet-style building for European, pan-Asian, and American specialties such as quinoa tajine, veal picatta, coconut prawns in Thai curry sauce, and wood-fired pizzas. **Known for:** being Billings' best date night spot; an entrée-worthy ahi tuna tartare; a long, but well-curated, wine list. [$] *Average main: $30* ✉ *1502 Rehberg La.* ✣ *At Grand Ave.* ☎ *406/651–0999* 🌐 *www.bistroenzobillings.com.*

Ciao Mambo

$$ | **ITALIAN** | For hand-tossed pizza and homemade pastas in Billings, it doesn't get any more authentic than at Ciao Mambo. This Montana chain, which also has locations in Whitefish and Missoula specializes in "immigrant-style Italian cuisine." For your antipasti course, try their famous tootsie rolls: egg wrappers stuffed with fresh ricotta cheese, mozzarella, and pesto. **Known for:** being a great date night spot; having a decent "Bambino Menu" for the kids; its open kitchen so you can watch your dinner being prepared. [$] *Average main: $17* ✉ *2301 Montana Ave.* ☎ *406/325–5100* 🌐 *www.ciaomambo.com.*

★ Juliano's Restaurant

$$$$ | **MODERN AMERICAN** | Award-winning Hawaiian-born chef Carl Kurokawa's menu changes monthly, but you can count on fresh fish, often flown in the day before from Hawaii. Other offerings might include proscuitto-wrapped chicken marsala, and London broil made with local beef. **Known for:** patio with a lovely garden view; offering a true culinary experience; romantic atmosphere; great for date night. [$] *Average main: $34* ✉ *2912 7th Ave. N* ☎ *406/248–6400* 🌐 *www.julianosrestaurant.com* ⏲ *Closed Sun. and Mon. No lunch Sat.*

Walkers

$$$ | **AMERICAN** | Situated downtown near the Alberta Bair Theater, this prime people-watching restaurant has a loyal dinner following, understandable considering its casual yet elegant decor, pleasant, attentive service, and such entrées as buttermilk fried chicken, Alaska king salmon, apple-brined pork shank, and made-from-scratch pastas. Walkers also has an upscale bar scene, attracted, in part, by a tempting selection of craft cocktails served by bartenders so hip they look like they belong in Brooklyn. **Known for:** one of the only restaurants in town with a community table; its spicy pork fat–fried cauliflower starter; the bacon jam served on its signature burger. *Average main: $28 2700 1st Ave. N 406/245–9291 www.walkersgrill.com No lunch.*

 Coffee and Quick Bites

Black Dog Coffeehouse

$ | **CAFÉ** | This locally owned café is one of the only cafés in the state that allows dogs—all well-behaved dogs inside. The staff is friendly, the dogs are even friendlier, and the coffee, which is brewed in town at Stumptown Roasters, is superb. **Known for:** fast Wi-Fi and lots of outlets; beautiful latte art; the cute boutique next door (same owner). *Average main: $5 1528 24th St W 406/534–8822 www.blackdogcoffeehouse.com.*

Best Western Plus Kelly Inn & Suites

$$ | **HOTEL** | A Cracker Barrel next door and proximity to I–90 make this chain hotel by Best Western a good stop for last-minute or late arrivals. **Pros:** easy access off Interstate 90; larger rooms and closets; free cookies in the lobby in the evening. **Cons:** if you don't have a car you're stranded on the Frontage Road/no-man's land; can be noisy due to location; detractors cite hard beds. *Rooms from: $91 5610 S. Frontage Rd. 406/248–9800 www.bestwestern.com 80 rooms Free breakfast.*

Big Horn Resort, Ascend Hotel Collection

$$ | **HOTEL** | **FAMILY** | If you've brought the kids along, this is the choice, hands down, for one clear reason: a 35,000-square-foot indoor water park ($10 per person per day for in-house guests) with two three-story slides, four minislides, a wave pool, and a 20-person hot tub for the older set. **Pros:** free 24/7 access to Fuel Fitness Center (not on-site); Montana's Rib & Chop House is right next door; has three different types of suites. **Cons:** far from downtown and shopping; between handling reservations and selling water park tickets front desk staff are too busy for speedy service; water park is open to the public so it can get crowded. *Rooms from: $90 1801 Majestic La. 406/839–9300 www.choicehotels.com 109 rooms Free breakfast.*

DoubleTree by Hilton Hotel Billings

$$$ | **HOTEL** | With 23 stories, this property is one of the few high-rises in Billings, making it a handy orientation point. **Pros:** a $16.5 million renovation completed in 2008; lobby coffee shop; complimentary gym and airport shuttle. **Cons:** some complain of noise from trains passing a couple of blocks away; front desk staff gets mixed reviews; not pet-friendly. *Rooms from: $160 27 N. 27th St. 406/252–7400 doubletree3.hilton.com 289 rooms No meals.*

Dude Rancher Lodge

$ | **HOTEL** | Featured on *Hotel Impossible* in 2012, this downtown institution has come a long way from the dump it once was. **Pros:** within easy walking distance of attractions and restaurants; some baths have jetted tubs; guests can have any breakfast on the menu for $5. **Cons:** rooms and baths are on the small side; you'll love or hate the brightly colored bathroom vanities; could use a deep cleaning and new furniture. *Rooms from: $70 415 N. 29th St. 406/259–5561 www.duderancherlodge.com 56 rooms No meals.*

Hilton Garden Inn Billings

$$ | **HOTEL** | A double-sided fireplace serves as the lobby focal point for this West End property. **Pros:** pleasant front desk staff; comfortable conversation areas in lobby; close to lots of shopping. **Cons:** duvets are not the bedding of choice for some; situated in a busy (rather than attractive) part of town; detractors cite slow Wi-Fi. *Rooms from: $120 2465 Grand Rd. 406/655–8800 hiltongardeninn3.hilton.com 128 rooms No meals.*

The Josephine Bed and Breakfast

$$ | **B&B/INN** | Within walking distance of downtown, this lovely home, built in 1912, offers five theme guest rooms, including the Garden Room, with its floral fabrics, and the Captain's Room, complete with a mahogany four-poster bed and a claw-foot tub. **Pros:** like staying in a favorite aunt's house; can arrange for guest passes to the local YMCA; nice selection of antiques and old photographs. **Cons:** booking preference given to long-term guests; not a good environment for young kids; could use some updating. *Rooms from: $115 514 N. 29th St. 406/248–5898 www.thejosephine.com 5 rooms Free breakfast.*

Riversage Billings Inn

$$ | **HOTEL** | Bright white walls stand out against curtains and upholstery in vibrant green tones at this hotel with some of the most pleasant staff in town. **Pros:** prime location for folks visiting Billings's impressive medical facilities; pet-friendly; easy access to the airport up the hill. **Cons:** unless you have business in the medical district, this hotel is out of the way; wide disparity in the size and furnishings of the rooms; rooms are slightly dated. *Rooms from: $90 880 N. 29th St. 406/252–6800 www.riversage-inns.com 59 rooms Free breakfast.*

Springhill Suites by Marriott Billings

$$ | **HOTEL** | Among the newish properties in the West End, this all-suite hotel with an indoor pool and hot tub has a lot going for it. **Pros:** excellent value; fitness center; several restaurants nearby. **Cons:** situated just off a busy street; far from airport; pool and hot tub are often in need of repairs. *Rooms from: $125 1818 King Ave. W 406/652–9313 79 suites Free breakfast.*

 Nightlife

Downtown Billings is most famous for its walkable **Brew Trail** (*www.visitbillings.com/billings-brew-trail*), consisting of six breweries, a distillery, and a cider house. If you want to do the 1.5-mile trip on your own, it consists of the following establishments: **Thirsty Street at the Garage** (*2123 1st Ave. N #B www.thirstystreet.com/thirsty-street-at-the-garage*); **Last Chance Pub & Cider Mill** (*2305 Montana Ave. www.lastchancecider.com*); **Asylum Distillery** (*2223 Montana Ave. asylumdistilleryinc.com*); **Überbrew** (*2305 Montana Ave. uberbrew.beer/taproom/*); **Carter's Brewing** (*2526 Montana Ave. www.facebook.com/cartersbrewery/*); **Angry Hank's** (*20 N. 30th St. angryhanks.com*); **Thirsty Street Brewing Co., Tap Room & Bottle Shop** (*3008 1st Ave. N www.thirstystreet.com/thirsty-street-first*); and **Montana Brewing Co.** (*113 N. 28th St. montana-brewing-co.business.site*). You can find a handy map on the Billings Visitor Bureau's website.

Bar MT

BARS/PUBS | The passenger trains are gone, but Billings's 19th-century depot has a new life as Bar MT, which bills itself as a beer depot and wine bar. It may only be open until 10 pm, but that doesn't stop the discerning patrons who come for the big selection of beverages (28 beers on tap) and lively atmosphere. *2314 Montana Ave. 406/534–1810 www.thebarmt.com.*

Guest Ranches on the Plains

Most eastern Montana ranchers are busy enough with making a living that their concession to visitors is a two-fingered wave through the windshield. But a few ranches, most in the mountains south of Billings, cater to guests, who take part in calving and branding, trailing cows to summer pasture, fixing fence, and other staples of ranch life.

Dryhead Ranch (☎ *307/548–6688*) is headquartered in Lovell but sprawls up the arid east slopes of the Pryor Mountains in Montana. A dozen horse-loving guests a week visit from April through November, helping Iris Basset and her family run their thousand head of cattle and dozens of horses. "They come for as much horseback riding as we can give them, and we can wear them out in four or five days," says Basset.

Nestled in the Clarks Fork Valley to the west, **Lonesome Spur Ranch** (☎ *406/662–3460*) also caters to horsey guests, more than half of whom hail from overseas. This is where Nicholas Evans, author of *The Horse Whisperer*, lived as he researched the best-selling novel, and a week at the ranch revolves around saddle horns and bridle bits and includes a trip to see the Pryor Mountains' wild-horse herd.

Just to the west, in the shadow of the Beartooth Mountains, the **Lazy E-L Ranch** (☎ *406/328–6858*) is similarly devoted to horses and includes ranch work. Guests are treated like family, not guests.

Don't expect wine tastings or hot-towel spas at these working ranches, but if you want to spend a week in the saddle experiencing authentic Western landscapes from the back of a horse, these ranches are worth a look. Rates range from $1,500 to $1,800 per week per adult, and some ranches allow groups to book the entire facility.

Tiny's Tavern
BARS/PUBS | This corner bar—dubbed a "local treasure" by many in and out of town—is famous for its Cajun-style chicken wings. The owners, who founded Tiny's in 1983 and consider themselves to be the dwarves Doc, Grumpy, and Dopey, have a refreshing sense of humor. They advertise their pizza as "voted the best" in town. They did the voting. Enjoy covered patio seating when it's warm outside and the sports bar when the big game is on. ✉ *323 N. 24th St.* ✣ *Corner of 3rd Ave.* ☎ *406/259–0828* 🌐 *www.tinystavern.com.*

Performing Arts

Alberta Bair Theater
THEATER | The historic Alberta Bair Theater presents music, theater, dance, and other cultural events. ✉ *2801 3rd Ave. N* ☎ *406/256–6052* 🌐 *www.albertabairtheater.org.*

Billings Art Walks
ART GALLERIES—ARTS | Upward of 20 downtown galleries host free receptions with food, beverages, and live music during Billings Art Walks held on the first Friday of even-numbered months (February, April, June, etc.). Maps are available at participating galleries. ✉ *2815 2nd Ave. N* ☎ *406/690–1662* 🌐 *www.artwalkbillings.com* 🎟 *Free.*

NOVA Center For The Performing Arts
THEATER | Venture Theatre and Rimrock Opera Company come together to bring productions, ranging from works for young people to cutting-edge dramas, to its small stage on select weekends. Though the actors aren't professional (yet), you wouldn't know it. ✉ *2317 Montana Ave.* ☎ *406/591–9535* 🌐 *www.novabillings.org.*

Shopping

Al's Bootery
SHOES/LUGGAGE/LEATHER GOODS | Al's Bootery corrals your toes into no-nonsense work boots, moccasins, and fancy cowboy boots with prices to suit the ranch hand's wallet as well as the millionaire ranch owner's. ✉ *1820 1st Ave. N* ☎ *406/245–4827* 🌐 *www.alsbootery.com* ⏲ *Closed Sun.*

Harry Koyama Fine Art
ART GALLERIES | Impressionist images by the award-winning Montanan artist Harry Koyama are on view at Harry Koyama Fine Art. Subjects include horses, wildlife, Native Americans, and landscapes. ✉ *2509 Montana Ave.* ☎ *406/259–2261* 🌐 *www.harrykoyama.com.*

Meadowlark Gallery
ART GALLERIES | From paintings and etchings to sculpture and vintage rifles, the Meadowlark Gallery showcases all kinds of Western artwork. It's housed in an old barn, and viewings are by appointment only. ✉ *9460 U.S.-212, Joliet* ☎ *406/962–3575* 🌐 *www.meadowlarkgallery.com.*

Rand's Custom Hats
LOCAL SPECIALTIES | Rand's Custom Hats creates cowboy hats for working cowboys and movie stars, and will custom-fit a felt fur hat. Prices range from $300 to $2,000. ✉ *2205 1st Ave. N* ☎ *800/346–9815* 🌐 *www.randhats.com* ⏲ *Closed weekends.*

Scheels
SPORTING GOODS | **FAMILY** | It's easy to spot this behemoth of a sporting goods store against Billings' horizon. In fact, Scheels is so big it has a Ferris wheel inside. You can also bowl, admire the exotic fish in the floor-to-ceiling aquariums, have lunch, or simply shop while the kids play in the jungle gym. Scheels is two very impressive stories of apparel, fishing gear, firearms, home goods, ski equipment, bikes, Montana-theme gifts, and just about everything you need to enjoy the local outdoors. ✉ *1121 Shiloh Crossing Blvd.* ☎ *406/656–9220* 🌐 *www.scheels.com.*

Toucan Gallery
ART GALLERIES | Contemporary artists are represented at the downtown Toucan Gallery. On display are paintings, sculptures, ceramics, fabric art, glass pieces, jewelry, and artisan-made gifts. ✉ *2505 Montana Ave.* ☎ *406/252–0122* 🌐 *www.toucanarts.com.*

Activities

The Rimrocks are easily the dominant feature of Billings. These 400-foot sandstone rock walls provide a scenic backdrop for numerous recreational pursuits. One of the most popular is mountain biking; suitable terrain for beginners, experienced thrill seekers, and everyone in between can be found within a short driving distance. The Yellowstone River flows through town; best access points are East Bridge on the east side of Billings and South Hills southeast of town off Blue Creek Road.

MOUNTAIN BIKING

The Bike Shop
BICYCLING | Founded by a local family in the 1970s, this shop was sold to another Billings native in 2016. It still sells and services mountain and road bikes. ✉ *1934 Grand Ave.* ☎ *406/652–1202* 🌐 *www.billingsbikeshop.com.*

The Spoke Shop

BICYCLING | Head to this local institution since 1973 for road bikes, mountain bikes, and equipment. They sell specialized and trek bikes but can repair just about any brand. ✉ *1910 Broadwater Ave.* ☎ *406/656–8342.*

Hardin

50 miles east of Billings via I–90.

Although its roots are firmly planted in cattle ranching, Hardin makes a significant portion of its living as a visitor gateway to the Little Bighorn Battlefield National Monument just a few miles to the south. With 3,833 residents, Hardin is among the largest communities in southeast Montana. Due to its proximity to the Crow Reservation, more than half of its residents are Native Americans. During the third week in August, a stretch of land along the Bighorn River about 15 minutes south of Hardin becomes the "tepee capital of the world" during the Crow Fair and Rodeo, the official fair of the Crow tribe. The festival focuses on traditional dances, activities, and sports tournaments.

GETTING HERE AND AROUND

It's difficult to get lost in the small town of Hardin. Arriving from the south on Interstate 90, exiting at Old U.S. 87 will get you to the Bighorn County Historical Museum and its visitor information center. Restaurants, hotels and campgrounds are easily accessed via Route 47 and North Central Avenue, and the downtown center is found on 3rd Street.

Sights

Arapooish Fishing Access Site

BODY OF WATER | The Arapooish Fishing Access Site, 2½ miles northeast of Hardin, is a favorite spot among locals, who pack the family up, set up in a shaded picnic area, cast a line into the Bighorn River, and have a cookout. It's also a prime bird-watching venue. ✉ *Hardin* ✣ *½ mile north of Hardin on Hwy. 47, then 2 miles east on undesignated county road (signage will direct you to the site)* ☎ *406/247–2940* 🌐 *www.fwp.mt.gov* 🎫 *Free.*

Bighorn County Historical Museum and Visitor Information Center

HISTORIC SITE | Focusing on Native American and early homestead settlement, the 35-acre Bighorn County Historical Museum and Visitor Information Center complex comprises 24 historic buildings that have been relocated to the site. The buildings are open May 1–October 1, and interpretive exhibits in the museum explore the region's Native American and pioneer history. Friendly staff and volunteers help bring life to the museum. ✉ *1163 3rd St. E* ✣ *I–90, Exit 497* ☎ *406/665–1671* 🌐 *www.bighorncountymuseum.org* 🎫 *$6* ⏲ *Closed weekends Labor Day–Memorial Day.*

Restaurants

3 Brother's Bistro

$$ | **AMERICAN** | Once an ice-cream parlor, today 3 Brother's Bistro, named for chef Greg Smith's three sons, is Hardin's finest dining establishment. That said, it's still a casual place that serves mostly pizza, barbecue, and beer. **Known for:** the smell of meat smoking; the tri-tip cheesesteak; a passionate chef who stops by your table to say hi. 💲 *Average main: $13* ✉ *316 N. Center Ave.* ☎ *406/545–5133* 🌐 *3brothersbistro.com* ⏲ *Closed Sun. and Mon. No lunch Sat.*

Activities

CAMPING

Grandview Campground. Cable TV, ice-cream socials, and a game room with Nintendo Wii are some of the extras at this full-service campground. On the edge of town, in the narrow corridor between downtown Hardin and I–90, it is near the Hardin Community Activity Center, giving you access to an Olympic-size indoor pool and fitness facilities (fee). The owner is a font of knowledge and takes great pride in the community. The Grandview is open year-round, but only a few full hookup sites are available in winter. ✉ *1002 N. Mitchell* ☎ *406/671-0121* 🌐 *www.grandviewcamp.com* *59 sites.*

Little Bighorn Battlefield National Monument

15 miles south of Hardin via I–90.

When the smoke cleared on June 25, 1876, neither Lieutenant Colonel George Armstrong Custer (1839–76) nor the 200 soldiers, scouts, and civilians were alive to tell the story of their part of the battle against several thousand Lakota-Sioux and Northern Cheyenne warriors inspired by Sitting Bull (circa 1831–90) and Crazy Horse (1842–77). It was a Pyrrhic victory for the tribes; the loss pushed the U.S. government to redouble its efforts to remove them to the Great Sioux Reservation in Dakota Territory. Now the Little Bighorn Battlefield, on the Crow Reservation, memorializes the warriors and the men of the Seventh Cavalry who took part in the conflict, with monuments and an interpretive center. In 2020, plans to build a new visitor center, with the help of a $4.5 million grant, were announced. For now, the site, made up of broken river bluffs and river bottoms along the Little Bighorn River, remains largely undeveloped. Note that there are rattlesnakes around the area. During the summer visiting season, daytime temperatures hover in the 80°F–90°F range. Bring clothing that is comfortable in hot weather, as well as sunscreen and water, both of which will make your outdoor experience here safer and more enjoyable.

GETTING HERE AND AROUND

The national monument is 15 miles south of Hardin, off Interstate 90, Exit 510, and Highway 212. The site is 3 miles south of Crow Agency, Montana.

Sights

Little Bighorn Battlefield National Monument

MEMORIAL | The interpretive exhibits at the **Little Bighorn Battlefield Visitor Center** explain the events that led to and resulted from the battle, as well as the deeper issues regarding the historical conflict between white and Native American culture. Talks by park rangers contain surprises for even the most avid history buff.

The old stone superintendent's house is now the **White Swan Memorial Library**, which has one of the most extensive collections of research material on the Battle of the Little Bighorn. You can view the material by appointment only; contact the visitor center for more information.

Among those interred at **Custer National Cemetery**, near the visitor center, are Custer's second-in-command, Marcus Reno; some of Custer's Native American scouts; and many soldiers from more modern wars, from World Wars I and II to Korea and Vietnam. Note that you can visit the cemetery without paying the park entrance fee.

For more than 120 years the only memorial to those killed in the battle was the towering obelisk of the **7th Cavalry Monument** at the top of Last Stand Hill. Although the hill isn't particularly high, it affords a good overall view of the battlefield site.

Until the **Indian Memorial** was unveiled in 2003, the battlefield's only monument paid tribute to the immediate losers. Although they are meant to honor Native Americans who died on both sides (Custer had a few Crow and Arikara scouts), the three bronze riders of this

Past and Future on the Plains

It's no wonder that in the 1870s the Lakota Sioux, Northern Cheyenne, and Arapahoe hid out in southeastern Montana; 130 years later, this region may still be the last best place to hide in the Lower 48. Most of the Montana plains didn't see white settlers until the 19th century was well along, and in some places nearly over. As a result, Montana's plains have an extremely brief documented history—perhaps that's why locals hang on dearly to remnants of the past. Even tiny settlements and cow towns have museums, which are essential community fixtures. Although often modest, such places are important for preserving the heritage of one of America's last frontiers. Among the finest are the C.M. Russell Museum Complex in Great Falls and Fort Benton's Museum of the Northern Great Plains.

It was in southeast Montana that Native Americans marked an epic and pivotal victory against the U.S. Army on the banks of the Little Bighorn. Here, a cavalry leader who may well have become president instead met defeat. The dramatic death of Lieutenant Colonel George Armstrong Custer redoubled the federal government's resolve to eradicate Native Americans; the policy of genocide endured until the massacre at Wounded Knee, in South Dakota, 14 years later.

Woven through the conflicts between whites and Native Americans is the ageless story of humanity's struggle with nature. This is a rough and often unforgiving land, where too much rain and too much drought often defeated even the most dedicated settler. The government responded by building giant dams and laying asphalt ribbons. In large measure, they succeeded. Even where the horizon remains unbroken by power lines, residents have been brought into the mainstream by the Internet, satellite TV, and GPS navigation.

memorial represent the united forces of the Lakota Sioux, Northern Cheyenne, and Arapahoe, who defeated the government troops. The stone opening off to the side forms a "spirit gate" welcoming the dead riders.

Scattered around the battlefield are short white **markers** indicating the places where soldiers died. Although the markers may look like graves, the actual bodies are interred elsewhere, including that of Custer, whose remains rest at the military academy at West Point. One marker belongs to Custer's younger brother, Thomas, one of the most decorated soldiers of the Civil War. Nineteen red markers represent Native American warriors, in part because no one knows exactly where they fell: the Native American survivors buried their dead immediately after the battle in traditional fashion.

After Custer's defeat, two of his officers held their ground against the Native American forces at **Reno-Benteen Battlefield.** The seven companies lost only 53 men during the two-day siege; more soldiers might have shared Custer's fate had not the advance of several thousand fresh troops caused the Native Americans to break camp and flee the region. ✉ *Battlefield Rd., Busby* ✣ *U.S. 212, 25 miles east of Crow Agency* ☎ *406/638–3204* 🌐 *www.nps.gov/libi* 🎫 *$25 per vehicle.*

St. Xavier Mission

RELIGIOUS SITE | North of Bighorn Canyon is the tiny settlement where Father

Both sides are remembered at Little Bighorn Battlefield, the most decisive defeat of U.S. forces during the Great Sioux War of 1876, when General George Armstrong Custer and most of his men were killed.

Prando, a Jesuit missionary, founded the St. Xavier Mission in 1887. This was the first mission to the Crow tribe and, as such, offered the people their first primary school. Although the town is barely inhabited, the church and school are still in use and may be visited. The school, called Pretty Eagle School, provides a free K–8 education for 160 students, 98% of whom are Crow. ✉ *Mission Ave.* ☎ *406/784–4500.*

Restaurants

Custer Battlefield Trading Post and Cafe
$$ | **SOUTHWESTERN** | With its stock of T-shirts, inexpensive jewelry, Indian fry bread mix, and dream catchers, the trading post is touristy, but the small attached restaurant is quite good—as evidenced by the locals who regularly congregate here. Steak is the dish of choice, and there are no fewer than three ways to get it on a sandwich. **Known for:** homemade Ghirardelli brownies; 100% buffalo burger; beautiful local beadwork and artwork on the walls. $ *Average main: $12* ✉ *347 U.S. 212* ✣ *Exit 510* ☎ *406/638–2270* 🌐 *www.laststand.com.*

Bighorn Canyon National Recreation Area

40 miles southwest of Little Bighorn Battlefield National Monument via I–90 and Hwy. 313.

Centered on a 60-mile-long lake, this park stretches between the Pryor and Bighorn mountains, well into Wyoming. Really just a wide spot on the Bighorn River, the lake fills much of Bighorn Canyon, whose steep walls, carved by geological upheaval and the force of wind and water, are too rugged for casual access.

GETTING HERE AND AROUND

Most people visit the park by boat, which is the only way within the park to get directly from the northern unit, in Montana, to the southern unit, much of which is in Wyoming. Most of the major sights are accessible by boat, but you can also reach them by driving north from Wyoming on Highway 37. If you're visiting from Wyoming, Lovell makes a good base for exploring the area. Check locally about useable boat ramps; fluctuating lake levels can leave the upper 15 miles mostly dry.

Sights

Bighorn Canyon National Recreation Area
NATIONAL/STATE PARK | To learn about this 120,000-acre national park wilderness that was established in 1966 following the creation of Yellowtail Dam, visit the South District's **Cal Taggart Visitor Center** in Lovell, where you can view geological and historical exhibits on the area, as well as a film about the canyon. Two shorter movies, one on the Pryor Mountain wild horses and the other about Medicine Wheel National Historic Landmark (east of Lovell), are shown on request, and there's a small gift and bookshop. The park's South District is reached by heading north on Highway 37 east of Lovell and encompasses Horseshoe Bend Marina, Devil Canyon Overlook, 12 hiking trails (in both Wyoming and southern Montana), four historic ranches that you can tour on your own, and three campgrounds. The park's North District is 120 miles north, in Fort Smith, Montana. Note that part of the park near Lovell is adjacent to Yellowtail Wildlife Management Area at the southern end of Bighorn Lake. More than 155 species of birds—including white pelicans, pheasants, bald eagles, and great blue herons—inhabit the 19,424-acre refuge, as do numerous other animal species, including red fox, mule deer, and cottontail rabbits. ✉ *20 U.S. 14A, Lovell* ☎ *307/548–5406* 🌐 *www.nps.gov/bica* 🎫 *Free.*

Chief Plenty Coups State Park
NATIVE SITE | **FAMILY** | Although many Plains Indian tribes opposed the intrusion of whites into their lands, the Crow did not. Hoping that U.S. troops would keep the rival Cheyenne and Lakota off their lands, the Crow allied themselves with the U.S. government. Ultimately, the army protected Crow territory from the other tribes—but only so it could be settled by whites. Despite the betrayal, the last traditional chief of the Crow, Plenty Coups, strongly encouraged his people to adopt modern ways and cooperate with the U.S. government. At his request, his home and general store in the town of Pryor were preserved as a state park after his death. Note the blending of modern and traditional ways, such as the room of honor in the rear of his log home, meant to parallel the place of honor along the back wall of a tepee. Parks Passports are not valid here. ✉ *1 Edgar/Pryor Rd., Pryor* ✥ *1 mile west of Pryor on county road* ☎ *406/252–1289* 🌐 *stateparks.mt.gov* 🎫 *$8 for out of state vehicles* ⏲ *Closed Mon. and Tues. during winter.*

Crooked Creek Ranger Station
INFO CENTER | The Crooked Creek Ranger Station, past the south entrance of the park in Wyoming, is staffed during the summer and offers information as well as a restroom. ✉ *Bighorn Canyon National Recreation Area* ✥ *Hwy. 37* ☎ *307/548–7326* 🌐 *www.nps.gov/bica/* 🎫 *Free* ⏲ *Closed Sept.–May.*

Devil's Canyon Overlook
NATURE SITE | Devil's Canyon Overlook, a few miles north of the Wyoming border, affords breathtaking views of the point where narrow Devil's Canyon joins sheer-walled Bighorn Canyon. The overlook itself is on a cliff 1,000 feet above the lake. Look for fossils in the colorful rock layers of the canyon walls. ✉ *Bighorn Canyon National Recreation Area* ✥ *Hwy. 37* 🌐 *www.nps.gov/bica/* 🎫 *Free.*

Hillsboro Dude Ranch
HISTORIC SITE | The old Hillsboro Dude Ranch complex is probably the best known and easiest to reach of the four ranch ruins within the recreation area.

Pryor Mountain Wild Horse Range is the habitat of a large herd of wild mustangs, among the last undomesticated descendants of the horses brought by the Spanish in the 16th century.

There are old log cabins, cellars, chicken coops, and other buildings that belonged to Grosvener W. Barry, one of the area's more colorful characters in the early 20th century. He attempted three gold-mining ventures, all of which failed, before opening a dude ranch here. ✉ *Bighorn Canyon National Recreation Area* ⊕ *Hwy. 37* 🎫 *Free.*

★ Pryor Mountain Wild Horse Range

NATURE PRESERVE | When Spanish explorers introduced horses to the Americas, some of the animals inevitably escaped and roamed wild across the land. You can see some of the last members of these breeds in the Pryor Mountain Wild Horse Range, the first such nationally designated refuge. Approximately 120 horses, generally broken into small family groupings, roam these arid slopes with bighorn sheep, elk, deer, and mountain lions. Coat variations such as grulla, blue roan, dun, and sabino indicate Spanish lineage, as do markings such as dorsal stripes, zebra stripes on the legs, and a stripe on the withers. The best way to view the herds is simply to drive along Highway 37 and look out your window. ✉ *Bighorn Canyon National Recreation Area* ⊕ *Hwy. 37* ☎ *406/896–5013* 🌐 *www.kbrhorse.net/wclo/blmdak01.html* 🎫 *Free.*

Yellowtail Dam Visitor Center

INFO CENTER | The Yellowtail Dam Visitor Center in the northern unit features exhibits focusing on the life of Crow Chief Robert Yellowtail, the Crow people, the history of the Bighorn River, the dam's construction, and the wildlife in the area, including the wild mustangs that roam the high grasslands of the Pryor Mountains above the canyon. ✉ *Fort Smith* ⊕ *Hwy. 313* ☎ *406/666–3218* 🎫 *Free* ⏲ *Closed after Labor Day–Memorial Day.*

Activities

The Lewis and Clark expedition, and later, fur traders avoided the Bighorn River at all costs, for the narrow channel, high canyon walls, and sharp rocks were treacherous. With the construction of the

Yellowtail Dam in the 1960s, however, the water levels in the canyon rose above most rocky obstacles and created new access points along the shore of the now-tamed river. The fishing here—for smallmouth bass, rainbow and brown trout, walleye, yellow perch, and more—is excellent above the dam. Below the dam, the cold, clear water exiting the hydropower facility has created a world-class trout fishery. Many visitors never wet a line, opting instead to simply rest on the water and enjoy the calm winds and pleasant views.

Fluctuating reservoir levels, caused by extended drought and light mountain snowpack, can periodically shut down the lake's marinas and boat launches. Because canyon walls create sharp turns and bottlenecks in the lake, there are some boating speed limits. All the marinas on Bighorn Lake operate during the peak summer season and are closed in the fall, winter, and early spring.

BOATING

Barry's Landing

BOATING | One of the most popular boat launches in the southern unit is **Barry's Landing**. There isn't much here—not even electricity—but the scenic campground, shaded picnic area, and central location are big draws. ✉ *Bighorn Canyon National Recreation Area* ✣ *Hwy. 37* ☎ *406/666–2412.*

Horseshoe Bend Marina

BOATING | Many boats in the southern unit are based at **Horseshoe Bend Marina**, which has boat rentals, a beach, a small general store, a modest restaurant, and the largest campground in the park. A nearby buildup of silt from the Shoshone and Bighorn rivers has made boat launching here a tricky business. ✉ *Hwy. 37* ☎ *307/548–7230* 🌐 *www.nps.gov.*

Ok-A-Beh Marina

BOATING | Boats can be docked or rented in the northern unit of the park at **Ok-A-Beh Marina**. The facilities here aren't luxurious, but you'll find a basic eatery, fuel, a few groceries, tackle, a swimming area, and reasonable rates. ✉ *Bighorn Canyon National Recreation Area* ✣ *Off Hwy. 313, on north end of lake* ☎ *406/623–9281.*

CAMPING

Black Canyon Campground. This campground, about 5 miles south of the Ok-A-Beh Marina up the tight Black Canyon Creek, is accessible only by boat, and only during high water. It's very primitive, but the isolation is unmatched. ✉ *Black Canyon Creek* ☎ *406/666–3218* 🌐 *www.nps.gov/bica* ⛺ *17 sites.*

Horseshoe Bend Campground. The proximity to the marina in the southern unit makes this, the largest campground in the park, especially popular, although never very busy. It's open all year, but most services are unavailable in winter. ✉ *Hwy. 37* ☎ *307/548–7230* 🌐 *www.nps.gov/bica* ⛺ *48 sites.*

Medicine Creek Campground. Just 2.8 miles north of Barry's Landing, this isolated site offers a good central location without the summer bustle of some other camping spots. You can boat or hike in. ✉ *Black Canyon Creek* ☎ *307666–3218* 🌐 *www.nps.gov/bica* ⛺ *5 sites.*

Miles City

160 miles northeast of Bighorn Canyon National Recreation Area via Hwy. 313 and I–94.

History buffs enjoy the ranch town of Miles City (population 8,264) at the confluence of the cottonwood-lined Tongue and Yellowstone rivers. The federal Fort Laramie Treaty of 1868 stated that this land would be "Indian country as long as the grass is green and the sky is blue." The government reneged on its promise only six years later, when gold was found in the Black Hills of South Dakota to the southeast. White settlers streamed into the area, setting in motion events that led to the Battle of the Little Bighorn. After the battle the army built a new post less than 2 miles from where Miles City would be founded. In time the ranchers took over, and in 1884 the last of the great herds of bison was slaughtered near here to make room for cattle. Ranching has been a way of life ever since.

The third weekend in May, Miles City holds its famed **Bucking Horse Sale** (🌐 *www.buckinghorsesale.com*) at the Eastern Montana Fairgounds, a lively three-day event with a rodeo, a concert, and a giant block party. Rodeo-stock contractors come from all over the country to buy the spirited horses sold here. Faded Wranglers and cowboy boots are proudly displayed downtown, along with open containers and a sort of rowdy civic pride.

GETTING HERE AND AROUND

Hugging the north side of Interstate 94, Miles City is easily traversed via the I–94 Business Loop, which takes motorists through the heart of the town. Alternatively, travelers may take Route 59 from I–94 past Miles Community College, then left on Main Street to the downtown area. To reach Pirogue Island State Park, follow Valley Drive East northeast from downtown.

Sights

Custer National Forest, Sioux Ranger District

FOREST | The name of these expansive federal lands is misleading: it should really be "Custer National Forests." Composed of dozens of discrete tracts dotting the landscape from Red Lodge (60 miles southwest of Billings, near Yellowstone National Park) all the way into South Dakota, Custer National Forest is one of the most ecologically diverse federally managed lands. The units in southeast Montana are called the Ekalaka Hills, and like their nearby neighbors in South Dakota, these pine-covered bluffs and mesas are often referred to as "an island of green in a sea of prairie," for good reason. Visible from miles away, the tiny forested ridges appear like mountains in the middle of the grassy plains. Drive any of the four-wheeler roads off Highway 212 between Ashland and Broadus and climb to a timbered ridge. Get out and hike to a vista, where you can breathe the scent of sagebrush from what appears to be a great height, but is only a couple of hundred feet above the prevailing landscape. Deer, turkey and elk inhabit the woods, and herds of pronghorn (the fastest land mammal in North America) roam the plains. Many species of raptors are known to nest here, too. The area is completely undeveloped and offers few services. ✉ *Miles City* ✣ *11 miles southeast of Ekalaka on Hwy. 323, 6 miles east of Ashland on U.S. Hwy. 212* ☎ *605/797–4432* 🌐 *www.fs.usda.gov/main/custer*.

Makoshika State Park

NATIONAL/STATE PARK | **FAMILY** | The largest state park in Montana is filled with badlands and prehistoric dinosaur fossils. At the entrance to the park is a recently expanded visitor information center, which supplies information on the park's history and geology and has an impressive museum full of dinosaur bones and skulls. During the summer, take a paleo-hike with an interpreter on Saturday to look for and learn about the fossils that litter the badlands landscape. You'll also get to visit the paleolab and handle fossils that have been found here over the years. Special events, including Montana Shakespeare in the Park and the famous Buzzard Day Festival (second Saturday in June) only add to its value as a destination. There's a nice campground, too, and an archery range and disc golf course. For those who want to spend the night without having to camp on your way to Medicine Lake, there are a few chain hotels across the highway in

Eerie, naturally wind-carved sandstone pillars dominate the landscape of Medicine Rocks State Park, which still looks pretty much the way it did during ancient times.

Glendive, including a Holiday Inn Express and La Quinta Inn & Suites that get good reviews from travelers. ✉ *Makoshika State Park* ✣ *2 miles southeast of Glendive, 77 miles northeast of Miles City via I–94* ☎ *406/377–6256* ⊕ *fwp.mt.gov/makoshika.*

Medicine Rocks State Park

NATURE SITE | FAMILY | Over millenia, wind and water carved holes in the sandstone pillars north of Ekalaka, creating an eerie and barren landscape. Embracing the terrain's mystery, Native Americans used the site for rituals to conjure spirits centuries ago. Teddy Roosevelt was struck by the area's unique beauty when he visited in the late 19th century, calling it "as fantastically beautiful a place as I have ever seen." In 1957 the area was designated Medicine Rocks State Park. The 320-acre park is largely undeveloped: aside from a few picnic tables, a short hiking trail, and a handful of unmarked campsites, the land is exactly how it was when Native Americans first performed their ceremonies here. ✉ *1141 Hwy. 7* ✣ *Hwy. 7 north of Miles City between Baker and Ekalaka* ☎ *406/377–6256* ✉ *cdantic@mt.gov* ⊕ *www.fwp.mt.gov/medicine-rocks* 🎫 *Free.*

Pirogue Island State Park

NATIONAL/STATE PARK | Pirogue Island State Park, a 269-acre chunk of land in the middle of the Yellowstone River, is completely undeveloped; the only way to access the park is by floating down the river or (carefully) fording in times of low water. The old cottonwood trees are excellent habitat for waterfowl, raptors, and deer, and the geology of the island makes it prime agate-hunting ground. ✉ *Miles City* ✣ *1 mile north of Miles City on Hwy. 59, 2 miles east on Kinsey Rd., then 2 miles south on county road* ☎ *406/377-6256* ⊕ *stateparks.mt.gov* 🎫 *Free.*

Range Riders Museum

MUSEUM | The Range Riders Museum, built on the site of the 1877 Fort Keogh cantonment, is jammed to the rafters with saddles, chaps, spurs, guns, arrowheads, and other frontier artifacts. Some of the 12 museum buildings of this complex were once part of the fort, which was abandoned in 1924 after being used as a remount station during World War I. The volunteers and staff love to talk about local history and are great sources for information about modern amenities, too. ✉ *W. Main St., 435 W. I–94 Business Loop* ✣ *Across Tongue River Bridge on west end of Main St., Exit 135 off I–94* ☎ *406/232–6146* 🌐 *www.rangeridersmuseum.com* 🎫 *$8* ⏲ *Closed Nov.–Mar.*

WaterWorks Art Museum
MUSEUM | **FAMILY** | Although the holding tanks of a 100-year-old water-treatment plant might not seem like the best location for fine art, the 10,000-square-foot WaterWorks Art Museum is actually very attractive. Overlooking the Yellowstone River, this permanent exhibit reflects the town's Western heritage and features both regional and national exhibits and features. The museum store features a variety of original artworks, reproductions, ceramics, and a good selection of Western history books. ✉ *85 Water Plant Rd.* ☎ *406/234–0635* ✍ *ccartc@midrivers.com* 🌐 *www.wtrworks.org* 🎫 *Free* ⏲ *Closed Sun. and Mon.*

Restaurants

Trail's Inn Tap Haus and Mama Stella's Pizza
$ | **PIZZA** | The historic bar serves excellent pizza and offers the best selection of draught beer and top-shelf whiskey in eastern Montana. Play pool or darts while quaffing one of 40 beers on tap and enjoying a slice or three from one of Mama Stella's locally famous pizzas. **Known for:** great pizza; wide selection of draught beer; breakfast pizza with eggs, gravy, and bacon. 💲 *Average main: $10* ✉ *607 Main St.* ☎ *406/234–2922.*

Best Western War Bonnet Inn
$$ | **HOTEL** | The two-room family suites and complimentary hot breakfast make this chain hotel stand out. **Pros:** easy access off Interstate 90, and fairly easy walk or short drive to the vehicle-friendly cafés and gas stations off the highway; serviceable rooms; decent breakfast. **Cons:** restaurant across the street is dated and even a little dingy; stay here for a quick overnight, not for the amenities; truck traffic can be distracting. 💲 *Rooms from: $95* ✉ *1015 S. Haynes Ave.* ☎ *406/234–4560* 🌐 *www.bestwestern.com* ➪ *54 rooms* 🍴 *Free breakfast.*

Miles City Saddlery
SHOES/LUGGAGE/LEATHER GOODS | The craftspeople at Miles City Saddlery, in business since 1909, design custom saddles of legendary quality. They also craft saddlebags, holsters, and other leather goods. Even if you're not buying, this is worth a stop. ✉ *808 Main St.* ☎ *406/232–2512* 🌐 *www.milescitysaddlery.com* ⏲ *Closed Sun.*

CAMPING

Makoshika State Park Campground. This small campground doesn't offer much in the way of amenities, but the views of the surrounding sheer cliffs and stone bluffs are incredible. There's a Frisbee-golf course nearby. Some facilities are at the nearby visitor center. ✉ *Makoshika State Park Rd.* ☎ *406/377–6256* 🌐 *stateparks.mt.gov* ➪ *22 sites.*

Medicine Rocks Campground. Although these campsites are primitive—they aren't even marked—the weathered rocks here make an incredible backdrop for a night sleeping under the stars. ✉ *Off Hwy. 7, north of Miles City between Baker and Ekalaka* ☎ *406/234–0900* 🌐 *stateparks.mt.gov* ➪ *12 tent sites, 12 RV sites.*

Fort Peck

147 miles northwest of Makoshika State Park via Hwy. 200 S, Hwy. 13, U.S. 2, and Hwy. 117.

Fort Peck itself is mostly a quiet retirement town, with 240 residents; at night the lights of ranch houses are few and far between. It owes its existence to massive Fort Peck Dam, built on the Missouri River during the Great Depression. One of President Franklin Roosevelt's earliest and largest New Deal projects, the Fort Peck Dam, provided a source of water and jobs. Now the 6-mile-long dam holds back sprawling Fort Peck Reservoir and wows visitors with the sheer scale of the earthen works. Fort Peck is a great base from which to take advantage of this world-class fishery, especially for walleye, northern pike, and smallmouth bass, or you can camp and hike the remote Missouri River Breaks on either side of the lake.

GETTING HERE AND AROUND

Get to Fort Peck townsite from Nashua—turn south off U.S. 2 onto Route 117 and drive 12 miles south. From Glasgow, drive 19 miles on Highway 24. And from Circle, drive Highway 24 north for about 65 miles. Fort Peck Reservoir boasts more shoreline than the coast of California and has the fewest public access points of any big reservoir and recreation area in America. That means you have to carefully plan your route if you want to get anywhere near the water up-lake from the dam, and you have to watch the weather when you go; if it rains, the region's infamous gumbo can bog you down. Managed access points on the northern shore include Duck Creek Bay, just west of the marina; The Pines, a remote cluster of private cabins about 20 miles up-lake from the dam; Bone Trail, a remote fishing access site and campground about halfway up the lake; and Fourchette Bay, another boat ramp and campground south of Malta. On the south shore of the lake the best access is at Hell Creek State Park north of Jordan, reachable by a well-maintained gravel road. Fort Peck Reservoir's Big Dry Arm, which juts due south from the dam, hosts Rock Creek Marina.

Sights

Fort Peck Interpretive Center

INFO CENTER | FAMILY | The 18,000-square-foot Fort Peck Interpretive Center features interpretive displays recounting the history and significance of the dam's construction, wildlife of the lower river and Missouri River Breaks. You'll find one of the most striking life-size dinosaur displays in the West, a reproduction of Peck's Rex, a tyrannosaurus Rex unearthed near Fort Peck, as well as other local dinosaur discoveries. The center also features the largest aquariums in Montana, filled with the native and introduced fish species of Fort Peck Reservoir and the Missouri River. Guided tours of the dam and its power plants are available April through October. ✉ *Lower Yellowstone Rd.* ☎ *406/526–3493* 🌐 *www.fws.gov* 🎫 *Free.*

Fort Peck Reservation

NATIVE SITE | The drive from Makoshika State Park to Fort Peck will take you along the Hi-Line, otherwise known as U.S. 2. Drive Highway 200 to Circle, then north on Highway 13, one of Montana's designated Scenic Backcountry Byways, or drive north through the wide, fertile Yellowstone River valley on Highway 16 to Sidney, then Culbertson, where you'll catch U.S. Highway 2. Either way, you'll travel through the Fort Peck Reservation. Like most of eastern Montana, much of the land here is beautifully austere; at nearly 2 million acres, the reservation is home to only 9,400 tribal members. However, the reservation does have a bustling industrial center, a community college, and an interesting tribal cultural center and museum in Poplar. ✣ *U.S. 2, 75 miles northeast of Fort Peck*

☎ 406/768–2300 ⊕ *www.fortpecktribes.org.*

Fort Peck Summer Theatre

ARTS VENUE | FAMILY | At the peak of dam construction, nearly 11,000 workers lived in Fort Peck; together with their families, they made up a thriving population center of 50,000. To help keep the populace entertained, the Army Corps of Engineers built a movie house in 1934. It was supposed to be a temporary structure, but instead it eventually became the Fort Peck Summer Theatre. The chalet-style building is a venue for live entertainment on weekend nights in summer. ✉ *Theatre Box Office, 201 Missouri Ave.* ☎ *406/228–9216* ✍ *fptheatre@nemont.net* ⊕ *www.fortpecktheatre.org* 🎫 *$18.*

Hotels

Cottonwood Inn and Suites

$$ | HOTEL | Located just 19 miles from Fort Peck, you'll find all the comforts you'd expect from a modern chain hotel. **Pros:** only a 20-minute drive to some of the best fishing in North America; fitness center, indoor pool, and hot tub; small RV park that allows campers to use hotel amenities. **Cons:** heaters in room are a tad noisy; the west wing is a separate building, so it's a cold walk to the pool and restaurant in winter; some rooms are a little small. $ *Rooms from: $105* ✉ *54250 U.S. Hwy. 2, Glasgow* ✣ *18 miles northwest of Fort Peck Lake* ☎ *800/321–8213, 406/228–8213* ⊕ *www.cottonwoodinn.net* ⇨ *168 rooms* 🍽 *No meals.*

Activities

CAMPING

Downstream Campground. Known locally as Kiwanis Park, this large wooded campground sits just below Fort Peck Dam on the shores of the Missouri River. If Kiwanis is full—and it's popular with Hi-Liners on holiday weekends—then drive past Fort Peck Marina to West End Campground. ✉ *Hwy. 24 N* ☎ *406/526–3224, 406/526–3593* ⊕ *stateparks.mt.gov* ⇨ *71 partial hookup sites, 3 tent sites.*

FISHING

Stretching 134 miles along the border between the Big Open and the Hi-Line (U.S. 2), Fort Peck Reservoir is a prime outdoor-adventure destination. Fishing is especially popular here, with walleye being the lake's best-known and hotly pursued fish. Other species include northern pike, lake trout, smallmouth bass, and Chinook salmon. Outfitters are hard to come by, so be sure to get most of your supplies before you arrive.

The lake is the venue for the annual **Governor's Cup Walleye Tournament** (⊕ *www.mtgovcup.com*) held on the second weekend in July.

Fort Peck Dredge Cuts

FISHING | FAMILY | Also known as the Fort Peck Trout Pond, this is a state fishing access site just below Fort Peck Dam off the Missouri River. It has a boat launch and family-friendly swimming beaches. ✉ *Fort Peck* ✣ *Hwy. 117* ☎ *406/228–3700.*

Rock Creek Marina

FISHING | The marina offers cabins, a modern campground, marina facilities, and a boat launch on the remote Big Dry Arm of the lake. Fort Peck Marina, on the west side of Fort Peck Dam, is probably the most accessible concession on the big lake. The store has basic and walleye-specific fishing tackle, basic groceries, bait, boat gas, and a boat-repair facility. The associated bar has beverages to go or for on-site consumption, and a simple restaurant. ✉ *652 S. Rock Creek Rd.* ☎ *406/485–2560* ⊕ *www.rockcreekmarina.com.*

Scott Collinsworth

FISHING | Whether it's big spring walleye or giant lake trout and Chinook salmon in late summer, Scott Collinsworth, who owns Fort Peck Marina, is the guide who can help you catch a fish of a lifetime. He can accommodate individuals and small groups. ✉ *Fort Peck Marina, 15 S.W. Marina Rd.* ☎ *406/526–3442* ✉ *ftpeck-marina1@gmail.com.*

Charles M. Russell National Wildlife Refuge

1 mile south of Fort Peck via Missouri Ave.

Locals call it the CMR, and it's a stunning place to visit in the summer, when the weather is stable (and sometimes really hot). It's teeming with birds and wildlife, and the remote nature of the Breaks makes the endless prairies, deep canyons, and remote timbered ridges great places for day hiking and back-country exploration. Bring good boots, sunscreen, and insect repellent. You are unlikely to see other people besides local ranchers out checking fences and cattle. At the center of it all is Fort Peck Lake, a world-class fishery, where big specimens of many species are catchable right from shore. Keep in mind that much of the CMR is remote and the weather can change quickly, so plan ahead and keep your gas tank topped up.

Approximately 4 miles north of the Charles M. Russell National Wildlife Refuge (and 50 miles south of Malta) is the **Buffalo Camp** for the American Prairie Reserve, which is in close proximity to a large prairie dog town. *For more information about the reserve, see the listing in Lewiston.*

GETTING HERE AND AROUND

This is four-wheel-drive country, and if you travel off paved or gravel roads, pack enough food to stay for at least three days longer than you planned. That's because once the dirt roads get wet with rain or snow, they become as greasy as Crisco and often become impassable. Bring extra fuel, because gas stations are as distant as Malta and Glasgow to the north and Grassrange to the south.

Sights

Charles M. Russell National Wildlife Refuge

NATURE PRESERVE | Bordering the shores of Fort Peck Lake—and extending west more than 100 miles to U.S. 191—is the massive Charles M. Russell National Wildlife Refuge, a 1.1-million-acre preserve teeming with more than 200 species of birds, including bald eagles and game birds; 45 different mammals, including elk, bighorn sheep, antelope, prairie dogs, and deer; and a variety of fish and reptiles. But this is also a refuge for history: each year scientists from around the country march into the preserve, and each year they find something new, whether it's dinosaur bones, buffalo jumps, tepee rings, or an old homesteader's shack. The refuge, one of the largest under the U.S. Fish & Wildlife Service's management, is open for hiking, horseback riding, fishing, boating, and other activities. Several access roads run through the area; most of these are unpaved, aside from U.S. 191, which runs north–south through the western edge of the refuge. ✉ *Charles M. Russell National Wildlife Refuge* ☎ *406/538–8706* ✉ *cmr@fws.gov* 🌐 *www.fws.gov/refuge/charles_m_russell/* *Free.*

Charles M. Russell Wildlife Refuge Auto Tour Route

SCENIC DRIVE | Located along Highway 191, 55 miles southwest of Malta, this 20-mile all-weather gravel road allows visitors an up-close and personal view of the inner workings of the refuge. Interpretive stops along the way provide information on the wildlife, geology, and history of this unique landscape. Keep your eyes out for a rare sighting of an endangered black-footed ferret, as this part of the refuge protects one of the largest free-ranging populations in the world. Stop at the Slippery Ann Wildlife Viewing Area to look for elk and deer;

The Charles M. Russell National Wildlife Refuge is large and remote, known for both its large number of resident birds and also its significant populations of Rocky Mountain elk and bighorn sheep.

early mornings and evenings are best. Expect to spend three or more hours on the drive. ✉ *Malta* ✣ *Drive south from Malta (or north from Lewiston) on H191. Look for sign a few miles north of river and turn east onto road* ☎ *406/538–8706* 🌐 *www.fws.gov/refuge/Charles_M_Russell/visit/visitor_activities.html.*

Charles M. Russell Wildlife Refuge Field Stations

INFO CENTER | There are three staffed field stations in the refuge: the **Sand Creek Wildlife Station,** the **Jordan Wildlife Station,** and the **Fort Peck Wildlife Station.** Although they have no public facilities, they are conveniently scattered around the park, and are good sources of information, including maps, road conditions, and points of interest. If they're in, the rangers will help you with directions or problems. ✉ *U.S. 91, Hwy. 200, and Hwy. 24* ☎ *406/538–8706* 🌐 *https://www.fws.gov/refuge/charles_m_russell/.*

Slippery Ann Wildlife Viewing Area

NATURE PRESERVE | **FAMILY** | In the fall, hundreds of elk congregate in morning and evening at the Slippery Ann Wildlife Viewing Area. During the autumn mating season the bulls bugle and spar with their antlers while herds of cows come to watch and be courted. Be sure to bring binoculars and zoom lenses for your camera, because you must keep your distance from these massive animals. ✉ *U.S. 191* ☎ *406/538–8706* ✉ *cmr@fws.gov* 🌐 *www.fws.gov/refuge/Charles_M_Russell/visit/visitor_activities/elk_viewing.html.*

UL Bend National Wildlife Refuge

NATURE PRESERVE | **FAMILY** | A refuge within a refuge, the UL Bend National Wildlife Refuge consists of more than 20,000 acres of wilderness entirely within the boundaries of the Charles M. Russell National Wildlife Refuge. Its primary mission at the moment is to rescue one of the nation's most endangered animals:

the black-footed ferret. The ferrets depend on the high concentration of prairie dog towns for food. There are also plenty of grouse and burrowing owls, who use abandoned prairie-dog tunnels for homes. ✉ *UL Bend National Wildlife Refuge Rd.* ☎ *406/538–8706* 🌐 *www.fws.gov/refuge/charles_m_russell/* 🎫 *Free.*

Activities

CAMPING

Buffalo Camp. The American Prairie Reserve's campground is 4 miles north of the reserve for those wishing to pitch a tent or park their RV for the night. The campground has vault toilets for tent campers; some electricity hookups are available, but access is on approximately 5 miles of unimproved gravel roads. Nearby is the American Prairie Reserve's bison herd, a large prairie dog town, and the Prairie Union School. The cost is $10 per night without electricity, $15 with electricity, and you must reserve your site online in advance on the American Prairie Reserve's website. (Only nonpotable water is available on-site, so be sure to bring sufficient drinking water or a purifier.) ✉ *Off U.S. 191, 4 miles north of Charles M. Russell National Wildlife Refuge* ☎ *877/273–1123* 🌐 *americanprairie.org* *6 tent sites, 7 RV sites.*

Medicine Lake National Wildlife Refuge Complex

230 miles northeast of Charles M. Russell National Wildlife Refuge via Larb Creek Rd. and U.S. 2.

Established in 1935, this refuge sandwiched between U.S. 2 and the Canadian border encompasses more than 30,000 acres of wetlands that provide habitat for dozens of mammal species, including beavers, muskrats, and bobcats, and a variety of shorebirds and upland birds. For travelers who aren't hardcore birders or hunters, the main allure will be the paved Auto Tour Route through the park, open during the day.

GETTING HERE AND AROUND

State Highway 16, which heads north to one of the few 24-hour ports on the Canadian border, cuts right through the refuge. Medicine Lake's main roads are well maintained, but the secondary roads are rutted and slippery in wet weather.

Sights

Medicine Lake National Wildlife Refuge Complex

NATURE PRESERVE | **FAMILY** | Medicine Lake hosts one of the largest concentrations of American white pelicans in the nation, a colony of thousands of birds that has occupied Big Island and Bridgeman Point for almost 100 years. There are few facilities available, but that's the point. The refuge has a relatively high visitation from hard-core birders who view migrating waterbirds in the spring and hunters who pursue upland game birds and waterfowl in the fall. Other than those seasons, you'll have the refuge to yourself. Bring good boots and long pants and hike into remote ponds and prairie potholes that hold an unbelievable amount of wildlife. Winding through the central unit of the refuge is the Auto Tour Route, an excellent way to get a peek at the animals that call this pristine park home. Most of the route is open only during daylight hours. Birders often congregate in the Grouse Observation Blind, 2¼ miles east of the refuge headquarters, to watch sharp-tailed grouse do their mating dance. The covered area is also good for watching other wildlife, including white-tailed deer and pronghorn antelope. ✉ *223 N. Shore Rd.* ☎ *406/789–2305* 🌐 *www.fws.gov/refuges/* 🎫 *Free.*

Bowdoin National Wildlife Refuge

200 miles west of Medicine Lake National Wildlife Refuge via U.S. 2.

An oxbow of the Missouri River before the last ice age, Bowdoin National Wildlife Refuge is a massive series of lakes and wetlands just off U.S. 2 a few miles east of Malta. The 15,000-acre preserve shelters numerous birds and mammals. Aside from typical prairie animals and field songbirds, there are sizeable populations of pelicans, gulls, and herons. Several protected species also live here, including the piping plover, black-footed ferret, bald eagle, and peregrine falcon. The Bowdoin Wildlife Refuge Headquarters, at the main entrance, provides information on refuge conditions, species lists, a variety of mounted birds and mammals, and instructions for the Bowdoin Refuge Auto Tour Route.

GETTING HERE AND AROUND

The best all-weather road to the refuge turns off the highway just 3 miles east of Malta. Turn onto Old Highway 2 at the brown-and-white refuge sign and drive the well-maintained gravel road to the two stone pillars marking the entrance to the refuge and its headquarters complex. Two-wheel-drive sedans can navigate most roads, but a higher-clearance four-wheel drive is a better option.

Sights

Bowdoin National Wildlife Refuge Self-Guided Auto Tour

NATURE PRESERVE | FAMILY | One of the best ways to experience the refuge is to take the 15-mile, 1½-hour self-guided auto tour around Lake Bowdoin. The one-way gravel road will expose you to a wide array of bird species and habitat types, and there are 11 signed stops along the way. The auto tour guide, available for download on the refuge's website, provides all the history and nature knowledge you'll need to get the most out of your experience. Depending on the time of year, you can expect to see a colony of gulls on Long Island and pelicans, cormorants, and blue herons on Pelican Islands. As always, spring and fall and early morning and evening will offer you the best opportunity to see wildlife. Don't forget your binoculars and camera. ✉ *194 Bowdoin Auto Tour Rd., Malta* ☎ *406/654–2863* 🌐 *www.fws.gov/refuges/* 🎟 *Free.*

Bowdoin Wildlife Refuge Headquarters

INFO CENTER | The Bowdoin Wildlife Refuge Headquarters, at the main entrance to Bowdoin, provides information on refuge conditions, species lists, a variety of mounted birds and mammals, and instructions for the auto tour. ✉ *194 Bowdoin Auto Tour Rd.* ☎ *406/654–2863 Bowdoin Refuge Auto Tour Rte.* 🌐 *bowdoin.fws.gov.*

Great Plains Dinosaur Museum and Field Station

MUSEUM | Surprisingly sophisticated given the location, this great little museum is right next door to the Phillips County Historical Museum. The station houses some of Montana's finest fossils and includes a fossil preparation laboratory that visitors can view. Specimens on display include Roberta, a well-preserved Brachylophosaur, and Leonardo, which has been celebrated as the best-preserved dinosaur fossil ever discovered. Both specimens were unearthed near Malta. Other gems include rotating exhibits of fossil collections and a great kids' education program. The station includes a gift shop. Amateur dino hounds can sign up here for a guided dig. ✉ *405 N. 1st Ave. E, Malta* ☎ *406/654–5300* ✉ *dinosaur@itstriangle.com* 🌐 *www.greatplainsdinosaurs.org* 🎟 *$5* ⏲ *Closed Sun. and Mon.*

Phillips County Historical Museum

MUSEUM | This museum, and the Dinosaur Field Station next door, is an official repository for fossils found in the Judith River basin. The highlight of the dinosaur display is a reconstructed albertosaur skeleton, which towers above the rest of the collection. There are also exhibits on outlaws who spent time here: Butch Cassidy, the Sundance Kid, Kid Curry, the Tall Texan, and other members of the Wild Bunch gang. Ask about tours of the H.G. Robinson House and gardens next door. The house, ordered from a Sears & Roebuck catalog and erected in 1900, is an example of frontier simplicity. *431 U.S. 2, Malta 406/654–1037 www.phillipscountymuseum.org $5 Closed Sun.*

Hotels

Maltana Hotel
$ | **HOTEL** | Easy to find, this recently remodeled downtown hotel is within walking distance of Malta's Amtrak station and a few blocks from the junction of U.S. 2 and 191. **Pros:** well-tended small hotel with great service and comfortable rooms; within walking distance to town center; reasonable price offers good value. **Cons:** hot in the summer and a little breezy in the winter; bring your own soap and shampoo; a little dated by big city standards. *Rooms from: $75 138 1st Ave. E, Malta 406/654–2610 arlys@maltanamotel.com 19 rooms No meals.*

Havre

103 miles west of Bowdoin National Wildlife Refuge via U.S. 2.

Mainly a place to stay when visiting Fort Assinniboine, the town of Havre (population 9,791) is the trading center for a wide area of extreme north-central Montana and southern Alberta and Saskatchewan. It lies in the Milk River valley in the shadow of the Bears Paw Mountains, and in a preserve south of town you can fish, picnic, or just enjoy the view.

GETTING HERE AND AROUND

Havre is in many ways the buckle of the Hi-Line belt that runs across northern Montana. It has by far the most amenities of any community and lies at a crossroads between the Canadian cities of Swiftcurrent and Lethbridge and Great Falls to the south. The highway is the main travel route, but Amtrak also stops here, and because this is the crew-changing point, train travelers are afforded a few minutes to stretch their legs. If you have a day, there are some appealing destinations here, from the bustling downtown to its wonderful museums and historical centers.

Sights

Beaver Creek Park
NATIONAL/STATE PARK | Set in the ancient Bears Paw Mountains, about 10 miles south of town, is the 10,000-acre Beaver Creek Park, the largest county park in the country. It's a favorite spot for locals, who come here to fish in the two lakes and winding Beaver Creek, camp, picnic, and enjoy the grassy foothills and timbered ridges of this island mountain range surrounded by dryland wheat fields. *17863 Beaver Creek Rd. 406/395–4565 www.bcpark.org $10.*

Fort Assinniboine
HISTORIC SITE | Once the largest military reservation west of the Mississippi, Fort Assinniboine was established in 1879 in the aftermath of the Battle of the Little Bighorn. At its peak, the fort had more than 100 brick and stone buildings and nearly 500 men. The soldiers stationed here brought along their families, who lived on the post. As a result, the Victorian-era fort became a cultural center as well as a military one, hosting plays and dances along with parades and training exercises. The fort is now a museum, and many of the imposing buildings still stand, although they appear eerily deserted. In fact, a few are storage or administrative facilities for the Northern

Research Agricultural Center. Others are open to public tours, which begin at the H. Earl Clack Memorial Museum. *Holiday Village Mall, 1753 U.S. Hwy. 2 W* *406/265–4383* *l.taplin@bresnan.net* *www.fortassinniboine.org* *$6.*

Havre Beneath the Streets

HISTORIC SITE | A tour of Havre Beneath the Streets takes you to a bordello, an opium den, a bakery, and other stops in an underground business center dating from the early days of the frontier—the equivalent of a modern underground mall. The subterranean businesses were mainly built and operated by the town's Asian population, drawn to the area by the Great Northern Railroad and its attendant business opportunities. Reservations for tours are recommended. *120 3rd Ave.* *406/265–8888* *hbtsrr@havremt.net* *www.havrechamber.com* *$17.*

H. Earl Clack Memorial Museum

MUSEUM | Displays at the H. Earl Clack Memorial Museum include murals, artifacts, dioramas, and military exhibits that explore the lives of Plains Indians and Havre's early settlers and ranchers. The museum arranges tours of Fort Assinniboine and the Wahkpa Chu'gn Archaeological Site, a major buffalo jump. *1753 U.S. Hwy. 2 W* *406/265–4000* *ClackMuseum@co.hill.mt.us* *www.hearlclackmuseum.com* *Free.*

Restaurants

Lunch Box

$ | AMERICAN | There are daily soup and sandwich specials at this family-style deli, where the bread is all homemade. The menu lists a lot of healthful choices, as well as salads, nachos, and baked potatoes. **Known for:** two homemade soups are available daily; over 70 different sandwich choices; good lattes and espresso. *Average main: $5* *213 3rd Ave.* *406/265–6588* *Closed Sun.*

Hotels

Best Western Great Northern Inn

$$ | HOTEL | A clock tower, colorful flags, and off-white stones and bricks decorate the proud exterior of this spacious hotel that offers one of the best breakfasts on the Hi-Line. **Pros:** great hot breakfast in the morning and comfortable rooms; good beds and spacious bathrooms; the best option in town and close to the city center. **Cons:** parking can be tight; the rail yard behind the hotel can get noisy; Internet speed occasionally slows to a crawl. *Rooms from: $110* *1345 1st St.* *406/265–4200* *www.bestwestern.com* *75 rooms* *Free breakfast.*

Chapter 8

GRAND TETON NATIONAL PARK

Updated by
Andrew Collins

Camping	Hotels	Activities	Scenery	Crowds
★★★★★	★★★★★	★★★★☆	★★★★★	★★★★☆

WELCOME TO GRAND TETON NATIONAL PARK

TOP REASONS TO GO

★ **Heavenward hikes:** Trek where grizzled frontiersmen roamed. Jackson Hole got its name from mountain man Davey Jackson; now there are hundreds of trails for you to explore.

★ **Wildlife big and small:** Keep an eye out for little fellows like short-tailed weasels and beaver, as well as bison, elk, moose, wolves, and both black and grizzly bears.

★ **Waves to make:** Float the Snake River or take a canoe, kayak, or stand-up paddleboard onto Jackson Lake or Jenny Lake.

★ **Homesteader history:** Visit the 1890s barns and ranch buildings of Mormon Row or Menor's Ferry.

★ **Cycling paradise:** Safely pedal your way to and through Grand Teton on miles of pathways and rural roads.

★ **Trout trophies:** Grab your rod and slither over to the Snake River, where cutthroat trout are an angler's delight.

1 **Moose.** Anchoring the southern end of the park, Moose is home to the Craig Thomas Discovery and Visitor Center, Dornan's lodgings and other services, the Menor's Ferry and Mormon Row historic districts, and Laurance S. Rockefeller Preserve. Grand Teton's nearest section to Jackson and Jackson Hole Ski Resort is laced with bike paths and both gentle and rigorous hiking trails, with mountain peaks looming on the west side and sagebrush-covered open range to the east, across the Snake River and around Antelope Flats.

2 **Jenny Lake.** The Teton Range reflects in this small (1,191-acre) but spectacular lake in the middle of the park that has visitor services on its developed east shore and pristine trails on its west shore—you can take a boat ride across the lake or hike entirely around it.

3 **Jackson Lake.** Most adventures in the northern end of the park revolve around this large alpine lake, which offers several lodging and dining options as well as marinas where you can launch or rent boats. The Snake River passes through the north end of the lake and back out to the south through Jackson Lake Dam around Oxbow Bend, a famously scenic spot for watching wildlife.

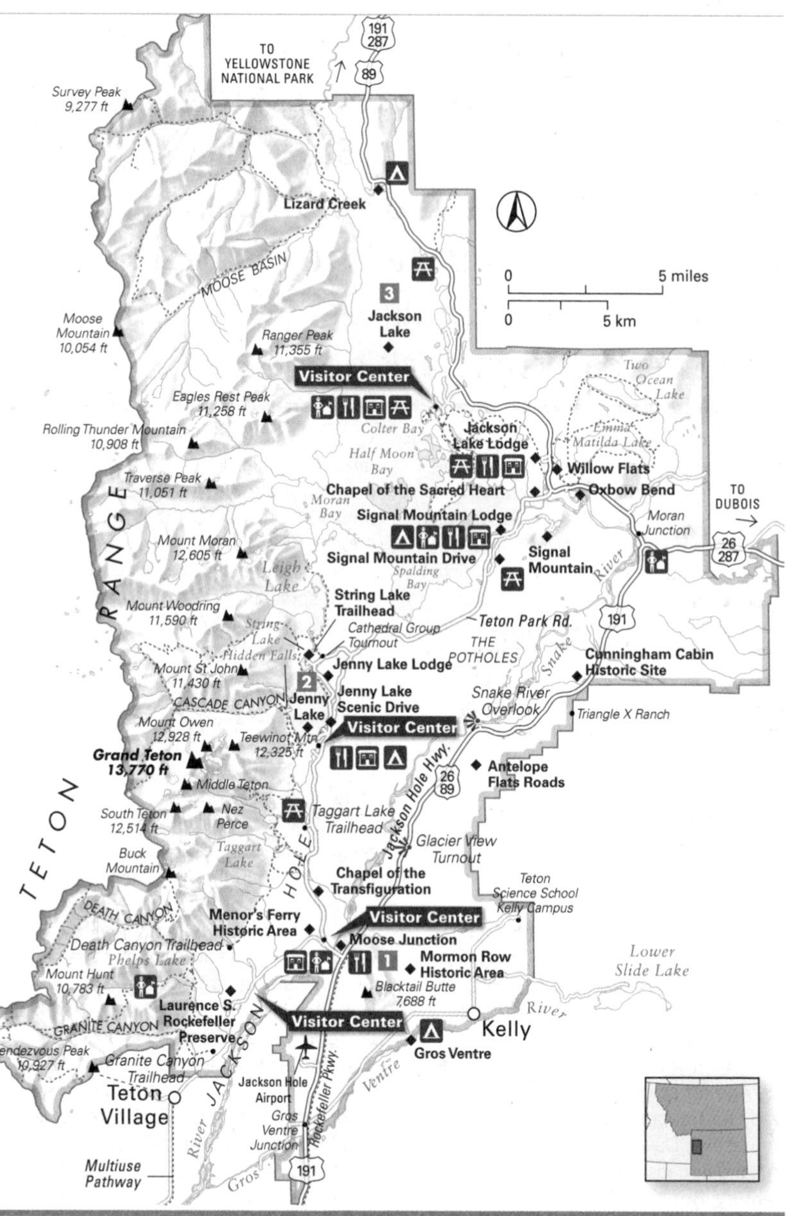
TO YELLOWSTONE NATIONAL PARK
191
287
89
Survey Peak 9,277 ft
Lizard Creek
MOOSE BASIN
3
Jackson Lake
Moose Mountain 10,054 ft
Ranger Peak 11,355 ft
0
5 miles
0
5 km
Visitor Center
Eagles Rest Peak 11,258 ft
Rolling Thunder Mountain 10,908 ft
Colter Bay
Jackson Lake Lodge
Two Ocean Lake
Emma Matilda Lake
Half Moon Bay
Willow Flats
Traverse Peak 11,051 ft
Chapel of the Sacred Heart
Oxbow Bend
TO DUBOIS
Moran Bay
Signal Mountain Lodge
Moran Junction
26
287
Mount Moran 12,605 ft
Signal Mountain Drive
Signal Mountain
River
Leigh Lake
Spalding Bay
RANGE
String Lake Trailhead
Mount Woodring 11,590 ft
Teton Park Rd.
191
String Lake
Cathedral Group Turnout
THE POTHOLES
Hidden Falls
Jenny Lake Lodge
Cunningham Cabin Historic Site
Snake
Mount St John 11,430 ft
2
Jenny Lake
Jenny Lake Scenic Drive
Snake River Overlook
CASCADE CANYON
Triangle X Ranch
Visitor Center
Mount Owen 12,928 ft
Teewinot Mtn 12,325 ft
Grand Teton 13,770 ft
Jackson Hole Hwy.
26
89
Antelope Flats Roads
Middle Teton
TETON
South Teton 12,514 ft
Nez Perce
Taggart Lake Trailhead
Glacier View Turnout
Buck Mountain
Taggart Lake
HOLE
Chapel of the Transfiguration
Teton Science School Kelly Campus
DEATH CANYON
Menor's Ferry Historic Area
Visitor Center
Death Canyon Trailhead
Moose Junction
Phelps Lake
1
Mormon Row Historic Area
Lower Slide Lake
Mount Hunt 10,783 ft
Blacktail Butte 7,688 ft
Laurence S. Rockefeller Preserve
River
GRANITE CANYON
Visitor Center
Kelly
JACKSON
Gros Ventre
Rendezvous Peak 10,927 ft
Granite Canyon Trailhead
Ventre
Rockefeller Pkwy.
Teton Village
Jackson Hole Airport
Gros Ventre Junction
River
Multiuse Pathway
Gros
191

The Teton Range—dominated by the 13,770-foot Grand Teton—rises more than a mile above Jackson Hole's valley floor, with unimpeded views of its magnificent, jagged, snowcapped peaks. Mountain glaciers creep down 12,605-foot Mt. Moran, and large and small piedmont lakes gleam along the range's base. Many of the West's animals—elk, bears, bald eagles—call this park home.

First-time visitors to Grand Teton sometimes underestimate all there is to see and do here, visiting the park briefly as a detour from either its northern neighbor, Yellowstone National Park—which is seven times larger—or its southern neighbor, Jackson, a swanky year-round resort town famous for skiing and snowboarding in winter and a host of activities in summer. But it's well worth budgeting at least two or three days to fully grasp the wonder of Grand Teton National Park. With a mix of bustling recreation areas and utterly secluded wilderness, this 485-square-mile park appeals equally to active adventurers and contemplative serenity seekers.

The region's harsh winters and challenging terrain helped keep it free of permanent development until relatively recently. Nomadic indigenous groups traversed the area's meadows and streams from the end of the Pleistocene Ice Age for some 11,000 years, and early fur trappers—including the valley's namesake, Davey Jackson—began making inroads throughout the early 19th century. But the region's first year-round ranching settlements in what would become the town of Jackson didn't occur until 1894. It wasn't long before wealthy "dudes" from the eastern United States began paying gobs of money to stay at these sprawling, scenic compounds, and thus was born the concept of the modern "dude ranch."

Jackson Hole and the Tetons began to develop at breakneck speed by the 1920s, drawing the interest of conservationists, too, including industrialist John D. Rockefeller, who toured the region in 1926 with the Superintendent of nearby Yellowstone National Park, Horace Albright. Although many locals recoiled at the thought of federal intervention, Rockefeller and other preservationists led a successful campaign for congress to establish Grand Teton National Park in 1929. Over the next 20 years, Franklin D. Roosevelt set aside additional land through the establishment of Jackson Hole National Monument, and Rockefeller donated another 35,000 acres of land that he'd steadily amassed to the federal government. All of these holdings were combined into the current Grand Teton

AVERAGE HIGH/LOW TEMPERATURES					
JAN.	FEB.	MAR.	APR.	MAY	JUNE
28/5	33/8	43/17	53/24	63/31	74/37
JULY	AUG.	SEPT.	OCT.	NOV.	DEC.
82/41	81/39	71/31	59/23	40/16	28/6

National Park in 1950. Throughout the park's evolution, Rockefeller also helped to spur its commercial and recreational development by establishing Jenny Lake and Jackson Lake lodges, along with smaller compounds of cabins and campgrounds throughout the park. And in 2001, his son donated the family's last piece of land in the area, 1,106-acre Laurance S. Rockefeller Preserve.

Although it receives the most recognition for its hulking mountain peaks, this is as much a park of scenic bodies of water and sweeping wildlife-rich meadows as it is an alpine destination. Boating, fishing, and lakeside camping are every bit as popular as hiking and climbing in the peaks, and photographers flock here from all over the world for the chance to see rare birds, lumbering moose and elk, and formidable wolves and black and grizzly bears. Some of the best terrain in the park can be accessed from well-maintained park roads and relatively short trails, but opportunities for rugged treks through miles of pristine back-country also abound. Grand Teton offers splendid activities for a range of abilities and interests.

Planning

When to Go

In July and August all the roads, trails, and visitor centers are open, and the Snake River's float season is in full swing. You can expect smaller crowds and often lower rates in spring and fall, but some services and roads are limited. Grand Teton Lodge Company, the park's major concessionaire, winds down its activities in late September, and most of Teton Park Road closes from November through April (U.S. 26/191/89 stays open all winter). In spring and fall, Teton Park Road is open to pedestrians, cyclists, and in-line skaters; in winter, it's transformed into a cross-country ski trail.

The towns south of the park rev up in winter. Teton Village and Jackson both buzz with the energy of Snow King Resort and Jackson Hole Mountain Resort. Prices rise for the peak winter season.

FESTIVALS AND EVENTS

ElkFest. Begun in 1967, this popular two-day festival is held the third weekend in May. Its centerpiece is the Elk Antler Auction, when thousands of pounds of naturally shed antlers are sold to the highest bidder. Get a taste of the High Noon Chili Cookoff, and enjoy the spectacle of khaki-clad lads hauling around massive racks. 🌐 *www.elkfest.org.*

Fall Arts Festival. More than 50 events celebrate art, music, food, and wine throughout Jackson Hole during this 11-day annual festival in mid-September. 🌐 *www.jacksonholechamber.com.*

Grand Teton Music Festival. Since 1962, these summer symphony concerts have been wowing audiences in the world-renowned Walk Festival Hall in Teton Village. The festival presents full orchestra concerts as smaller ensembles. 🌐 *www.gtmf.org.*

Grand Teton in One Day

Pack a picnic lunch and make your way to **Craig Thomas Discovery and Visitor Center** for a 9 am, two-hour, guided Snake River scenic float trip (book with one of the half-dozen outfitters that offer the trip). When you're back on dry ground, drive north on Teton Park Road, stopping at scenic turnouts—don't miss Teton Glacier—until you reach the Jenny Lake ranger station. Take the 20-minute boat ride to the **west shore boat dock** for a short but breathtaking hike to **Hidden Falls** and **Inspiration Point.** Return to your car by mid-afternoon, and follow Teton Park Road, detouring on Signal Mountain Road to the summit, where you can catch an elevated view of the Tetons.

Return to Teton Park Road and continue north, turning east at Jackson Lake Junction to **Oxbow Bend** or north to **Willow Flats,** both excellent spots for wildlife viewing before you backtrack to **Jackson Lake Lodge** for dinner and an evening watching the sun set over the Tetons. Or if you'd like to get back on the water, drive to **Colter Bay Village Marina,** where you can board a 1½-hour sunset cruise across Jackson Lake to Elk Island. You can reverse this route if you're heading south from Yellowstone: start the day with a breakfast cruise from Colter Bay and end it with a sunset float down the Snake River.

Getting Here and Around

AIR

Five major airlines offer service to Jackson Hole Airport (JAC), the only commercial airport inside a national park (it was established before the park opened).

CAR

Jackson Hole's main highway (U.S. 89/191) runs the length of the park, from Jackson to Yellowstone National Park's south entrance. This highway also joins with U.S. 26 south of Moran Junction and U.S. 287 north of Moran Junction. This road is open all year from Jackson to Moran Junction and north to Flagg Ranch, 2 miles south of Yellowstone. From Jackson, it's about 20 minutes to the park's southern (Moose) entrance. Coming from the north, it's about a 10-minute drive to the park's northern boundary.

Two scenic back-road entrances to Grand Teton are closed by snow from November through mid-May and can be heavily rutted through June. Moose-Wilson Road (Hwy. 390) starts at Highway 22 in Wilson and travels 7 miles north past Teton Village to the Granite Canyon entrance station. Of the 9 miles from here to Moose, 1½ are gravel and can be a little bumpy; high-clearance vehicles are best, but you can manage this route with a regular passenger car if you take it slow. This route is closed to large trucks, trailers, and RVs. Even rougher is 60-mile Grassy Lake Road, which heads east from Highway 32 in Ashton, Idaho, through Targhee National Forest. It connects with the John D. Rockefeller, Jr. Memorial Parkway span of U.S. 89/191/287, between Grand Teton and Yellowstone.

Inspiration

A Field Guide to Yellowstone and Grand Teton National Parks, by Kurt F. Johnson, provides a comprehensive compilation of the flora and fauna of the greater

Yellowstone area, including more than 1,200 color photographs.

Robert W. Righter's *Peaks, Politics, and Passion: Grand Teton National Park Comes of Age* gives the fascinating back-story behind the park's evolution since its establishment in 1950.

In Rising from the Plains, Pulitzer Prize–winning author John McPhee examines the geology of the Rocky Mountains and Wyoming through the personal history of a geologist and his family.

Windows into the Earth: The Geologic Story of Yellowstone and Grand Teton National Parks, by Robert B. Smith and Lee J. Siegel, is the best book on the market for nonspecialists hoping to grasp Teton and Yellowstone geology.

Park Essentials

ACCESSIBILITY

The frontcountry portions of Grand Teton are largely accessible to people using wheelchairs. There's designated parking at most sites, and some interpretive trails and campgrounds are easily accessible. There are accessible restrooms at visitor centers. The visitor centers also distribute an *Accessibility* brochure, which you can download from the park website.

PARK FEES AND PERMITS

Park entrance costs $35 for autos; $30 for motorcycles; and $20 per person on foot or bicycle, good for seven days in Grand Teton. The winter day-use fee is $15.

PARK HOURS

The park is open 24/7 year-round. It's in the Mountain time zone.

CELL PHONE RECEPTION

Cell phones work in most developed areas and occasionally on trails, especially at higher elevations in the park's frontcountry.

Hotels

For a park its size, Grand Teton has a tremendous variety of lodging options, from simple campgrounds, cabins, and standard motel rooms to fancier (and quite pricey) suites in historic lodges. Nearby Jackson has plenty of additional options, but rates can be steep for what you get in this upscale resort town, especially in summer and during winter ski season—if visiting during these busy times, try to book several weeks in advance in Jackson, and several months ahead for lodgings in the park. *Hotel reviews have been shortened. For full information, visit Fodors.com.*

Restaurants

Though the park itself has some decent, and in some cases quite good, restaurants, nearby Jackson is one of the top small towns in the Rockies when it comes to creative cooking—restaurants in both the park and Jackson are especially strong on local game, fowl, and fish dishes, and it's easier and easier to find tasty, often seasonal, vegetarian fare, too. Steaks are usually cut from grass-fed Wyoming or Montana beef, but you'll also find buffalo and elk on many menus. Rocky Mountain trout and Pacific salmon are also common. Down-home comfort fare and hearty all-American breakfasts are the norm at most casual eateries, although a handful of excellent international restaurants, mostly specializing in Asian and Latin American cooking, are now getting notice around Jackson Hole, as are craft breweries, artisan bakeries and coffeehouses, and wine bars. Casual is the word for most dining within and outside the park, the exception being where jackets and ties for men are appreciated. *Restaurant reviews have been shortened. For full information, visit Fodors.com.*

What It Costs

$	$$	$$$	$$$$
RESTAURANTS			
under $16	$16–$22	$22–$30	over $30
HOTELS			
under $150	$151–$225	$226–$300	over $300

Tours

Grand Teton Lodge Company Bus Tours
BUS TOURS | FAMILY | Half-day tours depart from Jackson Lake Lodge and include visits to scenic viewpoints, visitor centers, and other park sites. Guides provide information about park geology, history, wildlife, and ecosystems. Full-day tours continue into Yellowstone. ✉ *Grand Teton National Park* ☎ *307/543–3100* 🌐 *www.gtlc.com* 🎟 *From $90.*

Jackson Hole Wildlife Safaris
GUIDED TOURS | Run by a staff of world-class photographers, this Jackson company offers half-, full-, and multiday tours in summer and winter that bring guests to some of the best places in Grand Teton to view elk, bison, big-horn sheep, coyotes, foxes, and other wildlife that thrives in the park. Tours to Yellowstone are offered, too. ✉ *Jackson* ☎ *307/690–6402* 🌐 *www.jacksonholewildlifesafaris.com* 🎟 *Tours from $275.*

★ **Jackson Lake Cruises**
BOAT TOURS | FAMILY | Grand Teton Lodge Company runs 1½-hour Jackson Lake cruises from Colter Bay Village Marina throughout the day, as well as breakfast, lunch, and dinner cruises. Guides explain how forest fires and glaciers have shaped the Grand Teton landscape. ✉ *Grand Teton National Park* ☎ *307/543–3100* 🌐 *www.gtlc.com* 🎟 *From $40.*

Teton Science School
SPECIAL-INTEREST | FAMILY | The school conducts guided wildlife expeditions in Grand Teton, Yellowstone, and surrounding forests—participants see and learn about wolves, bears, bighorn sheep, and other animals. Full-day and half-day excursions are offered, as well as custom trips. The bear and wolf expedition is a thrilling three-day, two-night field adventure during spring and fall. ✉ *700 Coyote Canyon Rd., Jackson* ☎ *307/733–1313* 🌐 *www.tetonscience.org* 🎟 *Tours from $165.*

★ **Teton Wagon Train and Horse Adventures**
ADVENTURE TOURS | FAMILY | Unforgettable four- and seven-day covered wagon rides and horseback trips follow Grassy Lake Road on the "back side" of the Tetons. You can combine the trip with a river trip and a tour of Yellowstone and Grand Teton. ✉ *Jackson* ☎ *307/734–6101, 888/734–6101* 🌐 *www.tetonwagontrain.com* 🎟 *From $1,095.*

Visitor Information

CONTACTS Grand Teton National Park. ☎ *307/739–3300* 🌐 *www.nps.gov/grte.* **Jackson Hole and Greater Yellowstone Visitor Center.** ✉ *532 N. Cache St., Jackson* ☎ *307/733–3316* 🌐 *www.fws.gov.*

Moose

13 miles north of Jackson, 65 miles south of Yellowstone's Grant Village.

Most visitors to Grand Teton spend a good bit of time, and often begin their adventures, in and around Moose, which is the hub for exploring the southern end of the park (nearest to Jackson). The striking, contemporary Craig Thomas and Laurance S. Rockefeller Preserve visitor centers are excellent places to learn about the park's natural history and conservation efforts, and there's easy and more challenging hiking near both. Also near Moose is Dornan's service complex, with dining, lodging, gas, and a market.

Sights

HISTORIC SITES

Chapel of the Transfiguration

RELIGIOUS SITE | This tiny chapel built in 1925 on land donated by Maud Noble is still a functioning Episcopal church. Couples come here to exchange vows with the Tetons as a backdrop, and tourists snap photos of the small church with its awe-inspiring view. ✉ *End of Menors Ferry Rd., ½ mile off Teton Park Rd., Moose* ☎ *307/733–2603* 🌐 *www.stjohns-jackson.org/chapel-of-the-transfiguration* ⏲ *Closed Sept.–late May.*

Menor's Ferry Historic Area

HISTORIC SITE | **FAMILY** | Down a path from the Chapel of the Transfiguration, the ferry on display here is not the original, but it's an accurate re-creation of the double-pontoon craft built by Bill Menor in 1894. That was how people crossed the Snake River before bridges were installed. While the replica ferry is no longer in operation, it's fun to see. In the cluster of turn-of-the-20th-century buildings there are displays on historical transportation methods. Pick up a pamphlet for a self-guided tour. ✉ *End of Menors Ferry Rd.* ✣ *¼ mile off Teton Park Rd.*

Mormon Row Historic Area

HISTORIC SITE | Settled by homesteaders between 1896 and 1907, this area received its name because many of them were members of the Church of Jesus Christ of Latter-day Saints, also known as Mormons. The remaining barns, homes, and outbuildings are representative of early homesteading in the West. You can wander around, hike the row, and take photographs. The century-old T.A. Moulton Barn is said to be the most-photographed barn in the state. ✉ *Grand Teton National Park* ✣ *Off Antelope Flats Rd., 2 miles north of Moose Junction.*

Murie Ranch

HISTORIC SITE | **FAMILY** | Set on a former 1930s dude ranch, this complex of historic log buildings is sometimes credited as being the home of America's conservation movement—the work of its former owners, the Muries, led to passage of the 1964 Wilderness Act. You can hike the grounds and view interpretive signs on an easy 1-mile round-trip stroll from the nearby Craig Thomas Discovery and Visitor Center. Part of the property is used as a satellite campus of the superb Teton Science School, which offers conservation and educational programs about the park. ✉ *Moose* ✣ *Trailhead: Craig Thomas Discovery and Visitor Center.*

SCENIC DRIVES

Antelope Flats Road

SCENIC DRIVE | Off U.S. 191/26/89, about 2 miles north of Moose Junction, this narrow road wanders eastward over sagebrush flats, intersecting with the gravel lane to the Mormon Row Historic District. Less than 2 miles past here is a three-way intersection where you can turn right to loop around past the tiny hamlet of Kelly and Gros Ventre campground and rejoin the main highway at Gros Ventre Junction. Keep an eye out for abundant and swift pronghorn, along with bison, foxes, raptors, and more than a few cyclists. ✉ *Grand Teton National Park* ⏲ *Closed winter.*

SCENIC STOPS

Laurance S. Rockefeller Preserve

NATURE PRESERVE | **FAMILY** | This immense 1,106-acre preserve devoted to conversation includes miles of trails. You can access it via the Valley Trail, 1¾ miles north of the Granite Canyon trailhead and ½ mile south of the Death Canyon turnoff. Hikers can admire the Phelps Lake shoreline from a loop trail beginning at the preserve's sleek, contemporary interpretive center, or climb a ridgeline with beautiful views of aspens, wildflowers, and regional birds. ✉ *Off Moose-Wilson Rd.*

Plants and Wildlife in Grand Teton

Grand Teton's short growing season and arid climate create a complex ecosystem and hardy plant species. The dominant elements are big sagebrush—which gives the valley its gray-green cast—lodgepole pine trees, quaking aspen, and ground-covering wildflowers such as bluish-purple lupine.

Short Growing Season

In spring and early summer you will see the vibrant yellow arrowleaf balsamroot and low larkspur. Jackson Hole's short growing season gives rise to spectacular if short-lived displays of wildflowers, best seen between mid-June and early July. The changing of the aspen, willow, black hawthorn, and cottonwood leaves in early fall can be equally dazzling.

Oft and Rarely Seen Wildlife

On almost any trip to Grand Teton, you'll likely see bison, pronghorn antelope, and moose. More rarely you will see a black or grizzly bear, a fox, or a wolf. Watch for elk along the forest edge, and, in the summer, on Teton Park Road. Oxbow Bend and Willow Flats are good places to look for moose, beaver, muskrats, and otter in twilight hours any time of year. Pronghorn and bison appear in summer along the highway and Antelope Flats Road.

Smaller Animals

The park's smaller animals—yellow-bellied marmots, pikas, and Uinta ground squirrels, as well as a variety of birds and waterfowl—are commonly seen along park trails and waterways. Seek out water sources—the Snake River, the glacial lakes, and marshy areas—to see birds such as bald eagles, ospreys, Northern harriers, American kestrels, great blue herons, ducks, and trumpeter swans. Your best chance to see wildlife is at dawn or dusk.

TRAILS

Death Canyon Trail

TRAIL | This 7.9-mile round-trip trail to the junction with Static Peak Trail climbs some 2,100 feet, with lots of hills to traverse, a great view of Phelps Lake, and a final 1,061-foot climb up to a patrol cabin into this verdant glacial canyon. Give yourself about six hours to manage this rugged adventure. *Difficult.* ✉ *Grand Teton National Park* ✥ *Trailhead: end of Whitegrass Ranch Rd., off Moose-Wilson Rd.*

Lake Creek–Woodland Trail Loop

TRAIL | This relaxing, mostly level ramble alongside Lake Creek leads through a verdant forest to the southern shore of Phelps Lake, where you're rewarded with grand views up into Death Canyon. *Easy.* ✉ *Moose* ✥ *Trailhead: Laurence S. Rockefeller Preserve Center.*

★ Phelps Lake Overlook and Loop Trail

TRAIL | The quickest way to view this stunning lake, this 2-mile round-trip Phelps Lake Overlook Trail takes you from the Death Canyon trailhead up conifer- and aspen-lined glacial moraine to a view that's accessible only on foot. Expect abundant bird life: Western tanagers, northern flickers, and ruby-crowned kinglets thrive in the bordering woods, and hummingbirds feed on scarlet gilia beneath the overlook. From here, if you're up for a longer, enjoyable adventure, continue along the steep trail down to the north shore of the lake, where you can pick up the Phelps Loop Trail and follow it around the lake or all the way to Rockefeller Preserve. Hiking just to the overlook and back takes just over an hour, but allow four to five hours if continuing on to the Phelps Loop Trail. *Moderate–Difficult.* ✉ *Grand Teton National Park* ✣ *Trailhead: End of Whitegrass Ranch Rd., off Moose-Wilson Rd.*

Taggart Lake Trail

TRAIL | Hike 1½ miles from the trailhead to the lake and then, optionally, you can extend your trek by continuing on a 4-mile route around the lake where the terrain becomes steeper near Beaver Creek, or making the 5-mile loop trail around Bradley Lake, just to the north. There are views of Avalanche Canyon and areas where you might see moose. Allow an hour to get to the lake and back and another two to three hours to make it around one or both lakes. *Moderate.* ✉ *Grand Teton National Park* ✣ *Trailhead: Teton Park Rd., 4.8 miles south of Jenny Lake Visitor Center.*

VISITOR CENTERS

Craig Thomas Discovery and Visitor Center

INFO CENTER | This strikingly designed contemporary building contains interactive and interpretive exhibits dedicated to themes of preservation, mountaineering, and local wildlife. There's also a 3D map of the park and streaming video along a footpath showing the area's intricate natural features. Dozens of Native American artifacts from the David T. Vernon Collection are housed here. A plush, 155-seat theater shows a nature documentary every half hour. ✉ *Teton Park Rd., Moose* ☎ *307/739–3399* 🌐 *www.nps.gov/grte* ⏲ *Closed Nov.–late Mar.*

★ **Laurance S. Rockefeller Preserve Center**

INFO CENTER | **FAMILY** | This contemporary structure feels more like an art gallery than an interpretive facility. The elegant, eco-friendly building is more than just eye candy—you can experience the sounds of the park in a cylindrical audio chamber, and laminated maps in the reading room are great for trip planning. Rangers here promote "contemplative hiking" and are well informed about the many birds around the center's trailheads. It's best to get here in the early morning or late evening because the small parking area fills quickly. A ranger leads a hike to the lake every morning. ✉ *End of LSR Preserve Entrance Rd.* ☎ *307/739–3300* 🌐 *www.nps.gov/grte* ⏲ *Closed late Sept.–May.*

Restaurants

Dornan's Pizza & Pasta Company

$$ | **PIZZA** | Simple but hearty pizzas and pastas are the draw here, but you'll also find generous margaritas, a diverse wine list, and occasional live music. Place your order at the front counter, then head to a table inside, on the side deck, or upstairs on the roof, which has stunning mountain views. **Known for:** well-priced food; great wine shop next door (and no corkage fee); spectacular mountain views. $ *Average main: $17* ✉ *12170 Dornan's Rd.* ☎ *307/733–2415* 🌐 *www.dornans.com.*

Hotels

★ **Dornan's Spur Ranch Cabins**

$$$ | **RENTAL** | **FAMILY** | The lodging component of Dornan's shopping, dining, and recreation development in Moose, at the south end of the park, offers one- and two-bedroom cabins with fully stocked kitchens and great views of meadows, the peaks of the Tetons, or the Snake River. **Pros:** simple, clean cabins with good Wi-Fi; great for families; you may see wildlife out your window. **Cons:** not much privacy; rustic interiors not for everyone; no pets. $ *Rooms from: $275* ✉ *12170 Dornan's Rd., Moose* ☎ *307/733–2415* 🌐 *www.dornans.com* ⏲ *Closed Nov. and Apr.* 🛏 *12 cabins* 🍽 *No meals.*

Jenny Lake

7 miles north of Moose, 12 miles southwest of Jackson Lake Junction.

Framed to the west by Teton's magnificent peaks, Jenny Lake is one of the most picturesque—and indeed photographed—bodies of water in the Rockies. It's also the main developed area in the park's mid-section, home to a luxurious and historic lodge as well as a visitor center and ranger station, and a very popular campground. From the lake's eastern shore, you can access miles of hiking trails into the mountains across the lake, either by taking the short boat ride to the western shore or hiking there via the trail that encircles the lake. Trails also lead nearby to similarly stunning but undeveloped Leigh Lake, which is popular for paddle-sports enthusiasts and hikers.

Sights

PICNIC AREAS

Jenny Lake

LOCAL INTEREST | Shaded and pine-scented, this picnic site adjacent to the Jenny Lake shuttle boat dock is a good place to have lunch before catching a shuttle boat across the lake for some hiking. ✉ *Grand Teton National Park* ✣ *Near Jenny Lake Visitor Center.*

SCENIC DRIVES

★ Jenny Lake Scenic Drive

SCENIC DRIVE | This 4-mile, one-way loop provides the park's best roadside close-ups of the Tetons and the eastern shore of Jenny Lake as it winds south through groves of lodgepole pine and open meadows. Roughly 1½ miles off Teton Park Road, the Cathedral Group Turnout faces 13,770-foot Grand Teton (the range's highest peak), flanked by 12,928-foot Mt. Owen and 12,325-foot Mt. Teewinot. ✉ *Jenny Lake.*

TRAILS

★ Cascade Canyon–Hidden Falls–Inspiration Point Trail

TRAIL | **FAMILY** | Take Jenny Lake Boating's 20-minute boat ride or the 2¼-mile (each way) Jenny Loop Trail around the south side of the lake from the Jenny Lake Visitor Center to the start of a gentle, ½-mile climb to 200-foot Hidden Falls, the park's most popular (though crowded) hiking destination. Listen for the distinctive bleating of the rabbitlike pikas among the glacial boulders and pines. The trail continues half a mile to Inspiration Point over a moderately steep, rocky path with sweeping lake views. From here, continue west another 1½ miles into the heart of Cascade Canyon, with its dramatic views through the mountains and out toward Petersen Glacier. With the 10-minute boat shuttle ($18 round-trip), plan on a couple of hours to experience this trail—add another two hours if you hike the whole way, which is your only option from October through mid-May, when the shuttle doesn't run. *Easy–Moderate.* ✉ *Grand Teton National Park* ✣ *Trailhead: Jenny Lake Visitor Center* 🌐 *www.jennylakeboating.com.*

Jenny Lake Loop Trail

TRAIL | **FAMILY** | You can walk to Hidden Falls from Jenny Lake Visitor Center by following the mostly level trail around the south shore of the lake to Cascade Canyon Trail. Jenny Lake Trail continues around the lake for a total of 6½ miles. It's an easily managed though somewhat long trail hike if you circumnavigate the whole lake—allow three hours, not counting any forays into Cascade Canyon on the west side of the lake. You'll walk through a lodgepole-pine forest, have expansive views of the lake and the land to the east, and hug the shoulder of the massive Teton range itself. Along the way you may see elk, foxes, pikas, golden-mantled ground squirrels, and a variety of ducks and water birds. *Moderate.* ✉ *Grand Teton National Park* ✣ *Trailhead: Jenny Lake Visitor Center.*

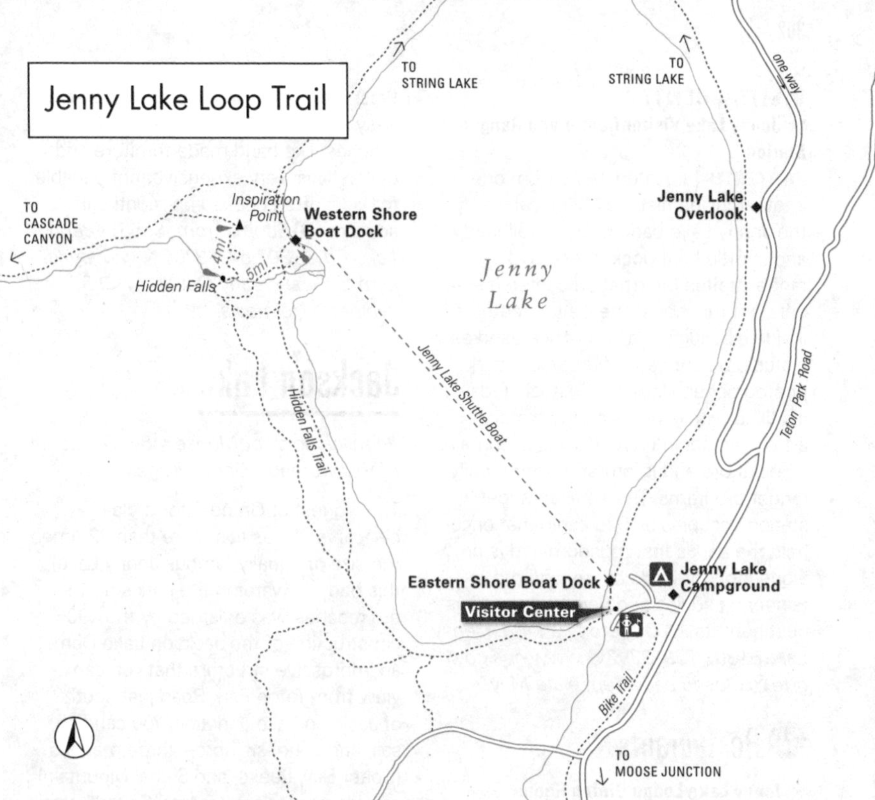

★ **Leigh Lake Trail**

TRAIL | This flat trail follows String Lake's northeastern shore to Leigh Lake's southern shore, covering 2 miles in a round-trip of about an hour. You can extend your hike into a moderate 7½-mile, four-hour round-trip by following the forested east shore of Leigh Lake to tiny but pretty Bearpaw Lake. Along the way you'll have views of Mt. Moran across the lake, and you may be lucky enough to spot a moose or a bear. Another option from Leigh Lake's southern shore is the 13-mile round-trip hike into Paintbrush Canyon to Holly Lake. *Moderate.* ✉ *Grand Teton National Park* ✣ *Trailhead: String Lake Picnic Area.*

String Lake Trail

TRAIL | The 3½-mile loop around String Lake lies in the shadows of 11,144-foot Rockchuck Peak and 11,430-foot Mt. Saint John. This is also a good place to see moose and elk, hear songbirds, and view wildflowers. The hike, which takes about three hours, is a bit less crowded than others in the vicinity. *Easy–Moderate.* ✉ *Grand Teton National Park* ✣ *Trailhead: off Jenny Lake Rd.*

Surprise and Amphitheater Lake Trails

TRAIL | A little more than 10 miles round-trip, this rigorous all-day hike starts at Lupine Meadows and switches back through steep pines and flowered meadows to Surprise Lake and the regal Amphitheater Lake, tucked away in an expansive rock basin. The trail weaves out for views of the sprawling valley, while Disappointment Peak looms above. Get to the trail early and allow six to eight hours to tackle the 3,000-foot gain. *Difficult.* ✉ *Jenny Lake* ✣ *Trailhead: Lupine Meadows Trailhead.*

VISITOR CENTER

★ Jenny Lake Visitor Center and Ranger Station

INFO CENTER | Located steps from one another inside historic 1920s cabins by the Jenny Lake parking area, trailhead, and shuttle boat dock, these two ranger-staffed information centers serve different functions. The visitor center is inside a building that was once used as a studio by the park's first official park photographer, Harrison Crandall. Today it's filled with exhibits on the history of art and artists in the park. It also contains a bookstore and information about daily ranger programs. The smaller ranger station occupies a 1925 cabin that once held the park's first museum and is now a one-stop for backcountry and mountaineering advice and permits as well as boat permits. ✉ *Off Teton Park Rd., Jenny Lake* ☎ *307/739–3392* 🌐 *www.nps.gov/grte* ⏲ *Closed early Sept.–late May.*

★ Jenny Lake Lodge Dining Room

$$$$ | **MODERN AMERICAN** | Elegant yet rustic, Grand Teton's finest dining space is highly ambitious for a national park restaurant. For dinner, the prix-fixe, five-course menu features locally sourced ingredients and an inventive, thoughtfully assembled wine list. **Known for:** jackets encouraged for men and reservations a must; regional meats and fish, like bison, bass, and duck; lovely mountain views. $ *Average main: $98* ✉ *Jenny Lake Rd.* ☎ *307/543–3100* 🌐 *www.gtlc.com* ⏲ *Closed early Oct.–May.*

★ Jenny Lake Lodge

$$$$ | **RESORT** | This 1920s lodge resort, the most expensive and arguably the most elegant in any national park, is nestled off the scenic Jenny Lake Loop Road and bordering a wildflower meadow. **Pros:** ultracushy digs in a pristine setting; easy stroll from Jenny Lake trails; homey touches, like hand-made furniture and quilts. **Cons:** very expensive; not suitable for kids; often booked up months in advance. $ *Rooms from: $555* ✉ *Jenny Lake Rd.* ☎ *307/543–3100* 🌐 *www.gtlc.com* ⏲ *Closed early Oct.–May* 🛏 *37 cabins* 🍽 *No meals.*

Jackson Lake

24 miles north of Moose, 45 miles south of Yellowstone's Grant Village.

The biggest of Grand Teton's glacier-carved lakes (it's more than 22 times the size of equally famous Jenny Lake), this body of water in the park's northern reaches was enlarged by the 1906 construction of the Jackson Lake Dam, an impressive structure that you can view from Teton Park Road just south of Jackson Lake Junction. You can fish, sail, and water-ski here—three marinas (Colter Bay, Leeks, and Signal Mountain) provide access for boaters. Several picnic areas, campgrounds, and lodges overlook the lake, and vista points like Oxbow Bend, the summit of Signal Mountain, and Willow Flats are excellent places to take in the park's geological and wildlife scenery.

HISTORIC SITES

Cunningham Cabin Historic Site

HISTORIC SITE | At the end of a gravel spur road, an easy ¾-mile trail runs through sagebrush around Pierce Cunningham's low-slung 1888 log-cabin homestead. Although you can peer inside, the building has no furnishings or displays. Watch for badgers, coyotes, and Uinta ground squirrels in the area. ✉ *Antelope Flats* ✥ *½ mile off U.S. 26/89/191, 5 miles south of Moran Junction.*

PICNIC AREAS

★ Colter Bay

LOCAL INTEREST | This big picnic area, spectacularly located right on the beach at Jackson Lake, gets crowded in July and August but is lovely nonetheless. It's close to flush toilets and stores. ✉ *Grand Teton National Park* ✣ *Just north of Colter Bay Visitor Center.*

SCENIC DRIVES

Signal Mountain Summit

SCENIC DRIVE | **FAMILY** | This popular 4-mile drive climbs 700 feet along a winding forest road that offers glimpses of Jackson Lake and Mt. Moran. At the top, park and follow the well-marked path to one of the park's best panoramas. From 7,593 feet above sea level your gaze can sweep over all of Jackson Hole and the 40-mile Teton Range. The views are particularly dramatic at sunset. The road is not appropriate for long trailers and is closed in winter. ✉ *Off Teton Park Rd.* ⏲ *Closed Nov.–May.*

SCENIC STOPS

Chapel of the Sacred Heart

RELIGIOUS SITE | This small log Catholic chapel sits in the pine forest with a view of Jackson Lake. It's open only for services, but you can enjoy the view anytime, and the grounds are nice for a picnic. ✉ *Grand Teton National Park* ✣ *Off Teton Park Rd., ¼ mile east of Signal Mountain Lodge* ☎ 🌐 *www.olmcatholic.org* ⏲ *Closed Oct.–June.*

★ Oxbow Bend

VIEWPOINT | This peaceful spot overlooks a quiet backwater left by the Snake River when it cut a new southern channel. White pelicans stop here on their spring migration (many stay on through summer), sandhill cranes and trumpeter swans visit frequently, osprey nest nearby, and great blue herons nest amid the cottonwoods along the river. Use binoculars to search for bald eagles, moose, beaver, and otter. The Oxbow is known for the reflection of Mt. Moran that marks its calm waters in early morning. ✉ *Grand Teton National Park* ✣ *U.S. 89/191/287, 2½ miles east of Jackson Lake Junction.*

Willow Flats

NATURE PRESERVE | You'll often see moose grazing in this marshy area, in part because of its flourishing willow bushes, where moose both eat and hide. Elk also graze here, and you'll occasionally see grizzly bears and wolves pursue their calves at the start of summer. This is also a good place to see birds and waterfowl, and the short Lunch Tree Hill Trail heads from the overlook parking area past beaver ponds to some vibrant bird-watching terrain. ✉ *Grand Teton National Park* ✣ *U.S. 89/191/287, 1 mile north of Jackson Lake Junction.*

TRAILS

★ Colter Bay Lakeshore Trail

TRAIL | **FAMILY** | This easy, wonderfully picturesque 1¾-mile round-trip excursion treats you to views of Jackson Lake and the Tetons. As you follow the level trail along the rocky shore and forest's edge, you may see moose and bald eagles. Allow two hours to complete the walk. *Easy.* ✉ *Grand Teton National Park* ✣ *Trailhead: on the beach just north of Colter Bay Visitor Center.*

Grand View Point Trail

TRAIL | Give yourself about four hours, which allows time for relaxing and soaking up dramatic views of back toward Jackson Lake and the Teton Range, to complete this moderately challenging 5.6-mile round-trip trek that starts at Jackson Lake Lodge. The trail curves around tiny Christian Pond and along the western shore of the much larger Emma Matilda Lake before climbing nearly 1,000 feet in elevation to this lovely viewpoint. ✉ *Moran* ✣ *Trailhead: Jackson Lake Lodge.*

VISITOR CENTERS

Colter Bay Visitor Center

INFO CENTER | At this useful center near the shore of Jackson Lake, a small display shows off items from the park's collection of Native American artifacts. (Hundreds more are being conserved and stored for future displays.) In summer, rangers lead daily hikes from here. Nightly ranger talks on various topics are also offered. ✉ *Colter Bay Marina Rd., Colter Bay* ☎ *307/739–3594* 🌐 *www.nps.gov/grte* ⏲ *Closed early Oct.–mid-May.*

Flagg Ranch Information Station

INFO CENTER | This small seasonal visitor center with exhibits on John D. Rockefeller and the region's natural history is the first place you'll come to if driving south from Yellowstone. It's in the same village as Headwaters Lodge, along with a convenience store, restaurant, and gas station. ✉ *100 Grassy Lakes Rd., Moran* ✣ *20 miles north of Jackson Lake Lodge* ☎ *307/543–2372* 🌐 *www.nps.gov/grte* ⏲ *Closed early Sept.–early June.*

Cafe Court Pizzeria

$ | AMERICAN | FAMILY | Quick and cheap is the name of the game at this no-frills cafeteria at Colter Bay Village. The menu features pizzas, salads, and toasted subs. **Known for:** big, simple meals to eat in or take out; pizza offered by the slice or whole pie; closes later than many other options. 💲 *Average main: $11* ✉ *Colter Bay Village Rd.* ☎ *307/543–2811* 🌐 *www.gtlc.com* ⏲ *Closed late Sept.–late May.*

Jackson Lake Lodge Mural Room

$$$$ | AMERICAN | One of the park's most picturesque restaurants gets its name from a 700-square-foot mural painted by the Western artist Carl Roters that details a Wyoming mountain man rendezvous. The menu showcases lavishly presented American fare, such as chilled prawns with a bloody Mary vinaigrette, seared King salmon with toasted-almond couscous, and grilled elk rib eye with a cherry compote. **Known for:** sumptuous mountain views; upscale lunches, dinners, and buffet breakfasts; regional favorites like bison, elk, and trout. 💲 *Average main: $35* ✉ *100 Jackson Lake Lodge Rd.* ☎ *307/543–2811* 🌐 *www.gtlc.com* ⏲ *Closed early Oct.–mid-May.*

★ Peaks Restaurant

$$$ | MODERN AMERICAN | At Signal Mountain Lodge, this casual Western-style bistro offers up delectable fish and meat dishes, as well as views of Jackson Lake and the Tetons. The Trapper Grill next door also serves lunch, the adjacent Deadman's Bar is a fun spot for nachos and huckleberry margaritas, and about 10 miles north, the same concessionaire operates the popular Leek's Pizzeria, overlooking the marina of the same name. **Known for:** menu focuses on seasonal, regional ingredients; among the park's more reasonably priced restaurants; nice lake views. 💲 *Average main: $27* ✉ *Signal Mountain Lodge Rd.* ☎ *307/543–2831* 🌐 *www.signalmountainlodge.com* ⏲ *Closed mid-Oct.–mid-May.*

Pioneer Grill at Jackson Lake Lodge

$$ | AMERICAN | With an old-fashioned soda fountain, friendly service, and seats along a winding counter, this eatery recalls a 1950s-era luncheonette. Tuck into Cobb salads, apple-cheddar burgers, banana splits, and other classic American fare. **Known for:** quick, reasonably priced food; seating is along a 200-foot-long counter; huckleberry pancakes and milkshakes. 💲 *Average main: $17* ✉ *100 Jackson Lake Lodge Rd.* ☎ *307/543–2811* 🌐 *www.gtlc.com* ⏲ *Closed early Oct.–mid-May.*

Ranch House at Colter Bay Village

$$ | AMERICAN | The casual Ranch House offers friendly service and moderate prices, making it a good choice for travelers on a budget or families who can't take another cafeteria meal. Western-style meals—pulled pork sandwiches, smoked spare ribs, rotisserie chicken—dominate the menu. **Known for:** traditional barbecue fare; hearty pasta dishes; gluten-free, vegetarian, and vegan. *Average main: $20 Colter Bay Village Rd., Colter Bay 307/543–2811 www.gtlc.com Closed late Sept.–late May.*

Hotels

Colter Bay Village

$$$ | **HOTEL** | **FAMILY** | A stroll from Jackson Lake, this cluster of Western-style one- and two-room cabins is close to trails, dining options, a visitor center, and plenty of other activities. **Pros:** good value; many nearby facilities; close to lake and hiking trails. **Cons:** not much privacy; no TVs or phones, and unreliable Wi-Fi; rustic feel won't appeal to everyone. *Rooms from: $200 Colter Bay Village Rd., Colter Bay 307/543–3100 www.gtlc.com Closed late Sept.–late May 232 cabins No meals.*

Headwaters Lodge & Cabins at Flagg Ranch

$$$ | **HOTEL** | Set along the scenic connecting road between the north boundary of Grand Teton and the South Entrance of Yellowstone, this secluded compound offers both upscale cabins with patios, handcrafted furniture, and private baths, and less-expensive rustic camping cabins that share a common bathhouse with the campground and RV park. **Pros:** good base between Grand Teton and Yellowstone; tranquil setting; mix of upscale and budget accommodations. **Cons:** no Wi-Fi; limited dining options; remote location. *Rooms from: $248 100 Grassy Lake Rd., Moran 307/543–2861 www.gtlc.com Closed Oct.–May 92 rooms No meals.*

★ **Jackson Lake Lodge**

$$$$ | **HOTEL** | This sprawling resort with its distinctive mid-century modern features was designed by renowned architect Gilbert Stanley Underwood and stands on a bluff with spectacular views across Jackson Lake to the Tetons. **Pros:** in center of Grand Teton; heated outdoor pool; great restaurants. **Cons:** some rooms don't have great views; very pricey; spotty Wi-Fi. *Rooms from: $346 100 Jackson Lake Lodge Rd. 307/543–3100 www.gtlc.com Closed early Oct.–mid-May 385 rooms No meals.*

★ **Signal Mountain Lodge**

$$$ | **HOTEL** | The main building of this lodge on Jackson Lake's southern shoreline has a cozy lounge and a grand pine deck overlooking the lake; stay in a traditional lodge room or a rustic cabin, some with sleek kitchens. **Pros:** excellent restaurants and bar; great lakefront location; some rooms have fireplaces. **Cons:** rustic, simple decor; not all rooms have water views; lakefront rooms are expensive. *Rooms from: $287 Signal Mountain Lodge Rd. 307/543–2831 www.signalmountainlodge.com Closed mid-Oct.–mid-May 79 rooms No meals.*

Activities

BIKING

Since the first paved pathways were completed in Jackson Hole in 1996, the valley has become a cyclist's paradise. Almost 60 miles of paved pathways thread through Jackson Hole, with more in the works. Those on two wheels can access Grand Teton on a path that begins at the north end of town and travels 21 miles to South Jenny Lake Junction. A bike lane permits two-way bike traffic along the one-way Jenny Lake Loop Road, a one-hour ride. The River Road, 4 miles north of Moose, is an easy four-hour mountain-bike ride along a ridge above the Snake River on a gravel road. Bicycles are not allowed on trails or in the backcountry.

Hoback Sports

BICYCLING | FAMILY | Get your own bike tuned up or rent one: road, mountain, hybrid, kids', and trailers. The shop also sells bikes, clothing, and mountain sporting accessories, as well as ski rentals and other winter-sports equipment. ✉ *520 W. Broadway, Suite 3, Jackson* ☎ *307/733–5335* 🌐 *www.hobacksports.com.*

Teton Mountain Bike Tours

BICYCLING | Mountain bikers of all skill levels can take this company's guided half-, full-, or multiday tours into Grand Teton and Yellowstone national parks, as well as winter tours of Jackson Hole on snow bikes with fat, studded tires. The outfit also rents bikes. ✉ *545 N. Cache St., Jackson* ☎ *307/733–0712* 🌐 *www.tetonmtbike.com* 🎫 *Tours from $80.*

BIRD-WATCHING

With more than 300 species of birds, the Tetons make excellent bird-watching country. Here you might spot both the calliope hummingbird (the smallest North American hummingbird) and the trumpeter swan (the world's largest waterfowl). Birds of prey circle around Antelope Flats Road—the surrounding fields are good hunting turf for red-tailed hawks and prairie falcons, and Oxbow Bend, which draws white pelicans during their spring northerly migration along with bald eagles and great blue herons. At Taggart Lake and Phelps Lake you might see woodpeckers, bluebirds, and hummingbirds. Look for songbirds, such as pine and evening grosbeaks and Cassin's finches, in surrounding open pine and aspen forests.

BOATING

Water sports in Grand Teton are diverse. You can float the Snake River, which runs high and fast early in the season (May and June) and more slowly in late summer. Canoes, kayaks, and stand-up paddleboards (SUPs) dominate the smaller lakes and share the water with motorboats on large Jackson Lake and smaller Jenny Lake (which has an engine limit of 10 horsepower). You can launch your boat at Colter Bay, Leek's Marina, Signal Mountain, and Spalding Bay on Jackson Lake and at the launch on the south shore of Jenny Lake, just off Lupine Meadows Road.

Before launching on any of the state's waters, including those in the park, you must purchase a seasonal permit ($40 for motorized boats, $12 for nonmotorized, including SUPs), available year-round at Craig Thomas and Colter Bay visitor centers, where you can also check with rangers about current conditions. You also must go through an AIS (Aquatic Invasive Species) inspection, which costs $30 for motorized boats and $15 for nonmotorized; the nearest inspection sites are at the Moose and Moran park entrance stations.

Additionally, many guided float trips are offered on calm-water sections of the Snake; outfitters pick you up at the float-trip parking area near Craig Thomas Discovery and Visitor Center for a 15-minute drive to upriver launch sites. Ponchos and life preservers are provided. Early morning and evening floats are your best bets for wildlife viewing. Be sure to carry a jacket or sweater. Float season runs from mid-April to mid-October.

★ Barker-Ewing Scenic Float Trips

BOATING | FAMILY | Float along a peaceful 10-mile stretch of the Snake River within the park and look for wildlife as knowledgeable guides talk about area history, geology, plants, and animals. Private custom trips can also be arranged. ✉ *Moose* ☎ *307/733–1800, 800/365–1800* 🌐 *www.barkerewing.com* 🎫 *From $80.*

★ Colter Bay Village Marina

BOATING | FAMILY | You can rent motorboats, kayaks, and canoes at Colter Bay from Grand Teton Lodge Company. Guided fishing trips are also available. ✉ *Colter Bay Village Rd.* ✣ *Off U.S. 89/191/287* ☎ *307/543–3100* 🌐 *www.gtlc.com.*

Dave Hansen Whitewater & Scenic Trips
WHITE-WATER RAFTING | Going strong since 1967, this highly respected outfit offers both rip-roaring white-water trips down class II–III Snake River rapids and more relaxing floats on calmer stretches. ✉ *Jackson* ☎ *307/733–6295* 🌐 *www.davehansenwhitewater.com* ☞ *From $87.*

Leek's Marina
BOATING | At this Signal Mountain Lodge–operated marina on the northern end of Jackson Lake, there are boat rentals, nightly buoys, an excellent pizza restaurant, and parking for boat trailers and other vehicles for up to three nights. ✉ *U.S. 89/191/287, 6 miles north of Jackson Lake Junction* ☎ *307/543–2831* 🌐 *www.signalmountainlodge.com.*

★ **National Park Float Trips**
BOATING | **FAMILY** | The knowledgeable and charismatic Triangle X guides will row you down 10 miles of the Snake River through pristine riparian habitat in Grand Teton National Park. For the best wildlife viewing, book a dawn or evening dinner float. ✉ *Moose* ☎ *307/733–5500* 🌐 *nationalparkfloattrips.com* 🎫 *From $82.*

★ **Rendezvous River Sports**
BOATING | **FAMILY** | However you'd like to hit the water, the river rats at Rendezvous are here to help. They offer instruction for stand-up paddleboarding and kayaking, as well as guided trips on area rivers and lakes. Or you could choose a backcountry adventure in the national parks. The shop rents kayaks, canoes, rafts, and paddleboards. ✉ *945 W. Broadway, Jackson* ☎ *307/733–2471* 🌐 *www.jacksonholekayak.com* 🎫 *From $205.*

Signal Mountain Lodge Marina
BOATING | This Jackson Lake marina rents pontoon boats, deck cruisers, motorboats, kayaks, and canoes by the hour or all day. ✉ *Signal Mountain Lodge Rd.* ☎ *307/543–2831* 🌐 *www.signalmountainlodge.com.*

CAMPING

You'll find a variety of campgrounds, from small areas where only tents are allowed (starting from $11 nightly) to full RV parks with all services (from $64 nightly for full hookups). If you have a sleeping bag but no tent, you can take advantage of the tent cabins at Colter Bay and Headwaters Campground at Flagg Ranch. Standard campsites include a place to pitch your tent or park your trailer/camper, a fire pit for cooking, and a picnic table. All developed campgrounds have toilets and water; plan to bring your own firewood. Check in at National Park Service campsites as early as possible—sites are assigned on a first-come, first-served basis.

Colter Bay Campground and RV Park. Big, busy, noisy, and filled by noon, this centrally located campground has tent and trailer or RV sites. ☎ *307/543–2811 for tent campground, 307/543–3100 for RV Park.*

Gros Ventre. The park's second biggest campground is set in an open, grassy area on the bank of the Gros Ventre River, away from the mountains but not far from the village of Kelly, on the park's southeastern edge. ☎ *307/734–4431.*

Headwaters Campground at Flagg Ranch. In a shady pine grove overlooking the headwaters of the Snake River, these sites set just north of the park border along John D. Rockefeller, Jr. Memorial Parkway provide a great base for exploring Grand Teton or Yellowstone. The showers and laundry facilities are a bonus, and camper cabins are available. ☎ *307/543–2861.*

Jenny Lake. Wooded sites and Teton views make this tent-only spot the most desirable campground in the park, and it fills early. ☎ *307/543–3390.*

Lizard Creek. Views of Jackson Lake's north end, wooded sites, and the relative isolation of this campground make it a relaxing choice. ☎ *307/543–2831.*

Signal Mountain. This campground in a hilly setting on Jackson Lake has boat access to the lake. ☎ *307/543–2831.*

You can reserve a backcountry campsite between early January and mid-May for a $45 nonrefundable fee using the online reservation system. Two-thirds of all sites are set aside for in-person, walk-in permits, so you can also take a chance on securing a site when you arrive. Obtain walk-in permits, which cost $35, from Craig Thomas Visitor and Discovery Center or Jenny Lake Ranger Station, where you can also pick up a park-required bear-proof food storage canister (these are lent out for free). The Jackson Hole Mountain Resort aerial tram provides quick access to the park's backcountry, which can also be reached on foot from various trailheads. 🌐 *www.nps.gov/grte/planyourvisit/bcres.htm.*

CLIMBING

The Teton Range has some of the nation's most diverse mountaineering. Excellent rock, snow, and ice routes abound. Unless you're already a pro, it's recommended that you take a course from one of the park's concessionaire climbing schools before tackling the tough terrain. Practice your moves at Teton Boulder Park, a free outdoor artificial climbing wall in Phil Baux Park at the base of Snow King Mountain.

Exum Mountain Guides

CLIMBING/MOUNTAINEERING | FAMILY | The climbing experiences offered by the oldest guide service in North America include one-day mountain climbs, shorter and easier adventures geared toward beginners, weeklong clinics culminating in a two-day ascent of the Grand Teton, and backcountry adventures on skis and snowboards. ✉ *Grand Teton National Park* ☎ *307/733–2297* 🌐 *www.exumguides.com* 🎟 *From $180.*

EDUCATIONAL PROGRAMS

Check visitor centers and the park newspaper for locations and times of the park's many ranger programs.

Campfire Programs

TOUR—SIGHT | FAMILY | In summer, park rangers give free slide-show presentations, usually at Colter Bay. ✉ *Grand Teton National Park* 🌐 *www.nps.gov/grte.*

Junior Ranger Program

TOUR—SIGHT | FAMILY | Children and even adults can earn a Junior Ranger badge or patch by picking up a Junior Ranger booklet at any park visitor center. ✉ *Grand Teton National Park* 🌐 *www.nps.gov/grte.*

Nature Explorer's Backpack Program

INFO CENTER | FAMILY | Rangers at the Laurance S. Rockefeller Preserve Center lend a nature journal and a backpack full of activities to children ages 6 –12 before sending them out along the trails at the Rockefeller Preserve. ✉ *Grand Teton National Park* ☎ *307/739–3654.*

FISHING

Rainbow, brook, lake, and native cutthroat trout inhabit the park's waters. The Snake's 75 miles of river and tributary are world-renowned for their fishing. To fish in the park, you need a Wyoming fishing license, which you can purchase from the state game and fish department or at Colter Bay Village Marina, Dornan's, Signal Mountain Lodge, and area sporting-goods stores. A day permit for nonresidents costs $14, and an annual permit costs $102 plus $12.50 for a conservation stamp.

Grand Teton Lodge Company Fishing Trips

FISHING | The park's major concessionaire operates guided fishing trips on Jackson Lake and guided fly-fishing trips on the Snake River. ✉ *Grand Teton National Park* ☎ *307/543–3100* 🌐 *www.gtlc.com* 🎟 *From $115.*

Signal Mountain Lodge

FISHING | Hourly and half-day Jackson Lake guided fishing trips depart from the marina at Signal Mountain Lodge, weather permitting. The rates include equipment and tackle. ✉ *Signal Mountain Rd.* ☎ *307/543–2831* 🌐 *www.signalmountainlodge.com* 🎫 *From $139.*

HIKING

To fully appreciate the grandeur of the park's soaring mountains and pristine lakes, it's best to try at least one or two trails that venture well beyond the parking areas. Of Grand Teton's more than 250 miles of maintained trails, the most popular are those around Jenny Lake, the Leigh and String lakes area, and Taggart Lake Trail, with views of Avalanche Canyon.

Frontcountry or backcountry you may see all kinds of wildlife—keep your distance, at least 25 yards from bison, elk, and moose, and 100 yards from bears and wolves. Pets are not permitted on trails or in the backcountry. Many of the park's most popular trails traverse rugged, challenging terrain. If you're inexperienced, start with an easier trek. Grand Teton has several short hikes, some of them paved, in the vicinity of developed areas, such as historic sites and park visitor centers, where you can also obtain advice and good trail maps.

The Hole Hiking Experience

HIKING/WALKING | For more than three decades, guides have led hikes and wildlife tours for all ages and ability levels in the Greater Yellowstone Ecosystem. The trips have an interpretive focus,with information about the history, geology, and ecology of the area. Many excursions incorporate yoga or have a holistic bent. In winter, cross-country ski and snowshoe tours in are offered in the park. ✉ *Jackson* ☎ *307/690–4453* 🌐 *www.holehike.com* ☞ *From $150.*

HORSEBACK RIDING

You can arrange a guided horseback tour at Colter Bay Village and Jackson Lake Lodge corrals or with private outfitters. Most offer rides from an hour or two up to all-day excursions. If you want to spend even more time riding in Grand Teton and the surrounding mountains, consider a stay at a dude ranch, such as Triangle X, on the east side of the park. Most shorter rides are appropriate for novice riders. More experienced riders will enjoy the longer journeys where the terrain gets steeper and you may wind through deep forests.

Grand Teton Lodge Company Horseback Rides

HORSEBACK RIDING | **FAMILY** | Rides start at Jackson Lake Lodge, Colter Bay Village, Headwaters Lodge, and Jenny Lake Lodge corrals. One- and two-hour trips are available, and beginners are welcome, with pony rides for small children. ✉ *Grand Teton National Park* ☎ *307/543–3100* 🌐 *www.gtlc.com* ☞ *From $50.*

Triangle X Ranch

HORSEBACK RIDING | **FAMILY** | This classic dude ranch just south of Moran Junction on the eastern edge of the park offers day horseback trips as well as multiday experiences that include comfy cabin accommodations, meals, rides, and lots of other fun activities. ✉ *2 Triangle X Ranch Rd., Moose* ☎ *307/733–2183* 🌐 *www.trianglex.com.*

WINTER ACTIVITES

Grand Teton has some of North America's finest and most varied cross-country skiing and snowshoeing. Try the gentle 3-mile Swan Lake–Heron Pond Loop near Colter Bay, the mostly level 10-mile Jenny Lake Trail, or the moderate 4-mile Taggart Lake–Beaver Creek Loop and 5-mile Phelps Lake Overlook Trail. Teton Park Road is groomed for classic and skate-skiing from early January to mid-March, and rangers sometimes give guided snowshoe walks from Craig Thomas Discovery and Visitor Center. The Flagg Ranch Information Station is closed in winter, but ski and snowshoe trails are open and marked with flagging tape, and the convenience store has maps.

Nearby Towns

The major gateway to Grand Teton National Park is the famously beautiful and beautiful-peopled town of **Jackson,** along with its neighbors **Teton Village**—popular among skiers and snowboarders from all over the world as the home of Jackson Hole Mountain Resort—and the small, unincorporated community of **Wilson.** These three communities form a triangle surrounded by greater Jackson Hole, with Teton Village at the northern tip and sharing a border with the south end of the national park, and Jackson and Wilson forming the two southern points. For a small town, Jackson has an extensive array of hotels and inns, restaurants and bars, and galleries and shops. Steadily growing Wilson has a handful of additional options, while Teton Village has hundreds of hotel rooms and condos, plus several restaurants, but it's really a self-contained resort community that while close to the park doesn't have the inviting small-town character that you'll find in Jackson. What all three of these communities share is a high cost of living and visiting—hotel rates, in particular, can be very high during winter's peak ski season and also quite high in summer and—increasingly—right through October.

If you're willing to stay an hour or more from Grand Teton's southern entrance, there are some smaller towns on the region's outskirts that offer more wallet-friendly lodging options, if fewer restaurants and attractions. On the "back side of the Tetons," as eastern Idaho is known, easygoing and rural **Driggs** is the western gateway to Grand Teton—it's about an hour's drive from Moose—and Yellowstone. **Dubois,** about 85 miles east of Jackson, has a smattering of hotel options, and you can usually still get a room for the night here during the peak summer travel period without making a reservation weeks or months in advance. About an hour south of Jackson, **Pinedale** is another small Wyoming town with a handful of lodging options, restaurants, and attractions.

Chapter 9

JACKSON AND THE WIND RIVER RANGE

Updated by Andy Austin

Sights	Restaurants	Hotels	Shopping	Nightlife
★★★☆☆	★★★☆☆	★★★☆☆	★★☆☆☆	★★☆☆☆

WELCOME TO JACKSON AND THE WIND RIVER RANGE

TOP REASONS TO GO

★ **The Grand Teton range and sweeping Snake River:** They're simply breathtaking.

★ **Wildlife:** Moose, bald eagles, elk, grizzlies, mountain lions ... This is home turf for an abundance of awe-inspiring wild animals.

★ **Restaurants:** Some of the best food in the region, not just Western fare, is available here.

★ **People:** Jacksonites are friendly and happy to share their knowledge of the area and the city with visitors.

1 **Jackson.** The town of Jackson is the main community in the so-called "Jackson Hole," which is surrounded by the Grand Tetons and the Gros Ventre Mountains.

2 **Teton Village.** At the base of the Tetons, this east-side ski resort village has the area's most noticeable ski access.

3 **Wilson.** Sitting at the base of the Teton Pass, Wilson is a small town between Jackson and Teton Village.

4 **Alta.** Better known as the backside of the Grand Tetons, Alta is home to Grand Targhee Resort.

5 **Pinedale.** Pinedale lies 77 miles southeast of Jackson, just south of the Wind River Range.

6 **Atlantic City.** Also known as "South Pass," Atlantic City is a ghost town 86 miles southeast of Pinedale on the way around Wind River Range to Lander.

7 **Lander.** Located east of the Wind River Range is the small town of Lander.

8 **Dubois.** A small town 55 miles east of Grand Teton National Park and 74 miles west of Lander.

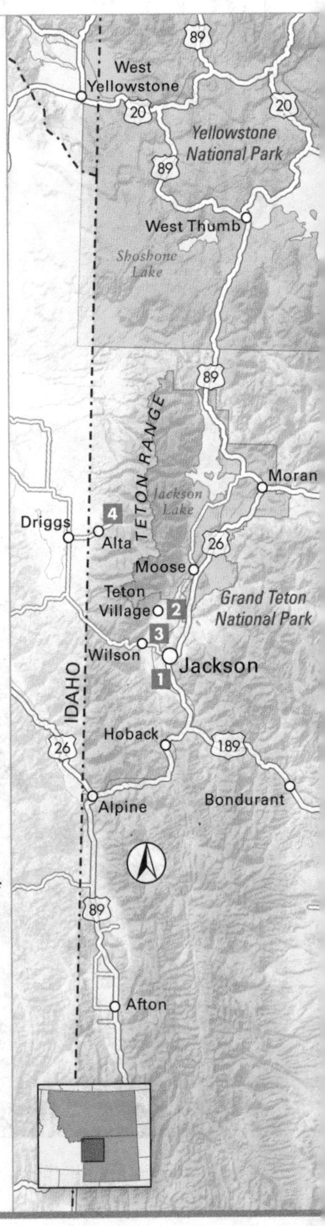

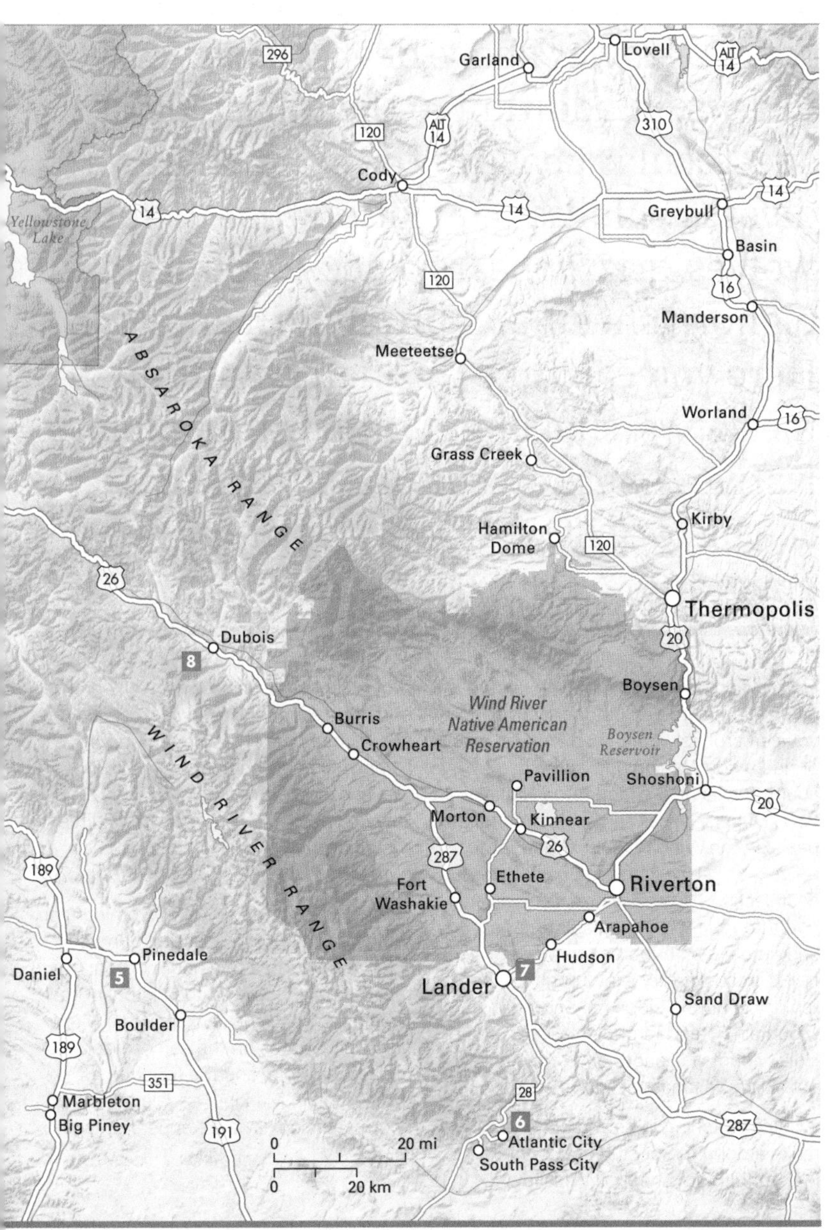
296
Garland
Lovell
ALT 14
120
ALT 14
310
Cody
14
14
14
Greybull
Yellowstone Lake
Basin
120
16
Manderson
ABSAROKA RANGE
Meeteetse
Worland
16
Grass Creek
Kirby
Hamilton Dome
120
26
Thermopolis
20
Dubois
8
Boysen
Wind River Native American Reservation
Burris
Crowheart
Boysen Reservoir
WIND RIVER RANGE
Pavillion
Shoshoni
20
Morton
Kinnear
26
287
189
Ethete
Riverton
Fort Washakie
Arapahoe
Pinedale
Daniel
5
Hudson
7
Lander
Sand Draw
Boulder
189
351
28
Marbleton
Big Piney
6
287
191
0
20 mi
Atlantic City
South Pass City
0
20 km

Northwest Wyoming is mountain country, where high peaks—some of which remain snowcapped year-round—tower above deep, glacier-carved valleys. In addition to the tallest, most spectacular peaks in the state, there's a diverse wildlife population that includes wolves, grizzly bears, Rocky Mountain bighorn sheep, and pronghorn antelope. Here you can hike through mountain meadows, challenge white water, explore Native American culture, and trace the history of westbound 19th-century emigrants.

From skiing, to hiking, kayaking, and paragliding, name an outdoor activity and you can probably do it here. You can hike or ride a horse along one of the back-country trails near Grand Teton National Park, Dubois, or Lander; scale mountain peaks in the Wind River or Grand Teton ranges; or fish or float the Snake River near Jackson. Come winter, take a sleigh ride through the National Elk Refuge; snowmobile on hundreds of miles of trails; cross-country ski throughout the region; or hit the slopes at Snow King Mountain, Grand Targhee, or Jackson Hole Mountain Resort, one of the greatest skiing destinations in the country.

Wildlife watching in northwest Wyoming ranks among the best in the country: look for bighorn sheep at Whiskey Mountain near Dubois; bison, elk, pronghorn, and even wolves in Jackson Hole; and moose near Pinedale or north of Dubois. One of the best ways to admire the landscape—mountain flowers, alpine lakes, and wildlife ranging from fat little pikas to grizzly bears—is to pursue an outdoor activity.

There's more to northwest Wyoming than the great outdoors. A handful of museums, well worth a few hours of your trip, offer a window on the history of the American West. The Jackson Hole Museum concentrates on the early settlement of Jackson Hole, and the Museum of the Mountain Man in Pinedale takes an informative look at the trapper heritage.

Planning

Getting Here and Around

You will need a car to tour northwest Wyoming; to reach the really spectacular backcountry, a four-wheel-drive vehicle is best. Major routes through the area are U.S. 191, which runs north–south through Jackson, on the western edge of the state, and U.S. 26/287, which runs east of Grand Teton National Park (also on the western edge of the state, within the Jackson Hole valley) toward Dubois. Much of the driving you do here will take you through the mountains, including the Absaroka and Wind River ranges that dominate the region.

AIR

American, Delta, SkyWest, Frontier, and United Airlines/United Express provide multiple flights to Jackson daily, with connections in Denver and Salt Lake City. Scheduled jet service increases during the summer and ski season, with non-stop service to Chicago, Atlanta, Dallas, Houston, Los Angeles, Minneapolis, Newark, New York–JFK, San Francisco, and Seattle. United and Great Lakes Airlines fly between Denver and Riverton.

The major airports in the region are Jackson Hole Airport, about 10 miles north of Jackson in Grand Teton National Park and nearly 50 miles south of Yellowstone National Park, and Riverton Regional Airport in Riverton, which is 30 miles northeast of Lander and about 76 miles southeast of Dubois.

Many lodgings have free shuttle-bus service to and from Jackson Hole Airport. Alltrans is the primary shuttle serving the Jackson Hole Airport, in addition to several taxi companies. If you're coming into the area from the Salt Lake City airport, you can travel to Jackson and back on a Mountain States Express shuttle for about $150 round-trip—even less from the airport in Pocatello or Idaho Falls.

AIRPORTS Jackson Hole Airport. ✉ *Grand Teton National Park, 1250 E. Airport Rd., Jackson* ⊕ *8 miles from Jackson Town Square* ☎ *307/733–7682 for reservations only* 🌐 *www.jacksonholeairport.com.* **Riverton Regional Airport.** ✉ *Fremont County, 4800 Airport Rd., Riverton* ⊕ *Approximately 3 miles NW of Riverton city* ☎ *307/856–1307 for reservation sales only* 🌐 *www.flyriverton.com.*

AIRPORT TRANSFERS Alltrans. ✉ *4125 S. Hwy. 89 , #6, Jackson* ☎ *307/733–3135 for local reservations only, 800/443–6133 for international reservation sales* 🌐 *www.jacksonholealltrans.com.* **Mountain States Express.** ✉ *1680 Martin La., Jackson* ⊕ *Approximately 0.7 miles from Jackson Whole Grocer & Cafe* ☎ *307/733–4629 for reservations only* 🌐 *www.mountainstatesexpress.com.* **Teton Mountain Taxi.** ☎ *307/699–7969* 🌐 *jacksonholecab.com.*

BUS

During the ski season, START buses shuttle people between Jackson and the Jackson Hole Mountain Resort as well as Star Valley to the south. The fare is free around town, $3 one-way to Teton Village, and $1 along the Teton Village Road. Buses operate from 6 am to 11 pm. In summer, START buses operate from 5:45 am to 10:30 pm. They stop at more than 45 locations in Jackson. People with mobility-related disabilities must make reservations 48 hours in advance for START buses. The Targhee Express runs between Jackson and the Grand Targhee Ski and Summer Resort, with pickups at various lodging properties in Jackson and Teton Village. The cost is $54 per day, or you can buy a combination shuttle/Grand Targhee lift ticket for $99. Advance reservations are required.

CONTACTS START. ☏ *307/733–4521* 🌐 *www.startbus.com.* **Targhee Express.** ☏ *307/734–9754, 800/443–6133* 🌐 *www.grandtarghee.com.*

CAR

If you didn't drive to Wyoming, rent a car once you arrive. The airports have major car-rental agencies, which offer four-wheel-drive vehicles and ski racks.

Northwest Wyoming is well away from the interstates, so drivers make their way here on two-lane highways that are long on miles and scenery. To get to Jackson from I–80, take U.S. 191/189 north from Rock Springs for about 177 miles. From I–90, drive west from Sheridan on U.S. 14 or Alternate U.S. 14 to Cody. U.S. 14 continues west to Yellowstone National Park, and in summer, you can also hook up with U.S. 191, which leads south to Jackson. Yellowstone National Park is closed to cars in winter.

Be extremely cautious when driving in winter; game crossings, whiteouts, and ice on the roads are not uncommon. Contact the Wyoming Department of Transportation for road and travel reports. For emergency situations, dial 911 or contact the Wyoming Highway Patrol.

CONTACTS Grand Teton Park Road Conditions. ☏ *307/739–3682* 🌐 *www.wyoroad.info.*

Planning Your Time

Any tour of northwest Wyoming should include a day or two, at minimum, in Jackson Hole, where you can explore Grand Teton National Park *(Chapter 8)*. Also in Jackson Hole is the small but bustling town of Jackson, with its one-of-a-kind town square entered through elk-antler arches and a stagecoach that gives rides throughout the day in summer. In winter, action is concentrated at nearby Teton Village, where you'll find unparalleled winter sports offerings at the Jackson Hole Mountain Resort. You're likely to share the slopes with Olympic champion skiers and snowboarders.

If you can extend your stay, travel east over Togwotee Pass to little Dubois, where you can stay at a guest ranch, ride horses in the Bridger-Teton National Forest, learn about local history at the Wind River Historical Center, and glimpse the region's wildlife at the National Bighorn Sheep Interpretive Center. After Dubois and environs, head south onto the Wind River Indian Reservation to find exceptional shops filled with arts and crafts locally made by Northern Arapaho and Eastern Shoshone tribal members.

Spend some time in Lander and explore the Wind River Mountains before heading south (in summer only) and then west to South Pass City State Historic Site, near Atlantic City. From here, follow the emigrant trail corridor west and then northwest to Pinedale and its excellent Museum of the Mountain Man.

Hotels

No other part of Wyoming has such a variety of lodging properties that appeal to all budgets. Lodging options in the area include elegant and expensive properties such as the Amangani and Four Seasons resorts in Jackson Hole, guest ranches in the Dubois and Jackson areas, historic inns, simple cabins, and dozens of chain motels.

It's a good idea to reserve well ahead for lodging in the town of Jackson in July and August. You should also reserve lodgings at Teton Village well in advance for skiing at Jackson Hole Mountain Resort.

Restaurants

Northwest Wyoming has many restaurants. Anyplace you go, you'll find basic Western fare such as steaks, chicken,

Camping in Northwest Wyoming

There are numerous campgrounds within Grand Teton National Park and Bridger-Teton, Shoshone, and Caribou-Targhee national forests. (Caribou-Targhee National Forest borders Grand Teton National Park on the west; most of the forest lies within Idaho.) Few of these campgrounds accept reservations. Campgrounds in the national forests tend to fill up more slowly than those in Grand Teton.

Reservations can be made for a small number of national-forest campgrounds near Jackson through U.S. Forest Service Recreation Reservations.

CONTACTS Bridger-Teton National Forest. ☎ *307/739–5500* 🌐 *fs.usda.gov/btnf.* **Caribou-Targhee National Forest.** ☎ *208/524–5900* 🌐 *fs.usda.gov/ctnf.* **Grand Teton National Park.** ☎ *307/739–3399* 🌐 *www.nps.gov/grte.* **U.S. Forest Service Recreation Reservations.** ☎ *877/444–6777 toll-free, 606/515–6777 international* 🌐 *www.recreation.gov.*

and burgers; in Jackson there's a wider selection, with menus listing everything from Mexican and Thai dishes to trout, buffalo, and elk. There are also a few fine-dining establishments in the region.

Restaurant and hotel reviews have been shortened. For full information, visit Fodors.com.

HOTEL AND RESTAURANT PRICES

What it Costs

$	$$	$$$	$$$$
RESTAURANTS			
under $10	$10–$18	$19–$30	over $30
HOTELS			
under $80	$80–$130	$131–$200	over $200

When to Go

Most people visit northwest Wyoming in summer, although winter draws skiing enthusiasts (the ski season generally lasts Thanksgiving through the first weekend of April). The months between Memorial Day and Labor Day are the busiest, with all attractions operating at peak capacity. If you don't mind a few limitations on what you can do and where you can stay and eat, the best times to visit the region are in late spring (May) and early fall (September and October). Not only will you find fewer people on the roads and at the sights, but you also will have some of the best weather (although springtime can be wet, and it can and does snow here every month of the year). In general, spring is the best time to see wildlife, particularly young animals. Fall brings a rich blaze of colors, painting the aspen and cottonwood trees with a palette of red, gold, and orange. The days are warm, reaching into the 60s and 70s, and the nights dip toward freezing in fall. There are also fewer thunderstorms than in midsummer, plus fewer mosquitoes and biting flies.

Jackson

Most visitors to northwest Wyoming come to Jackson, which remains a small but booming Western town that's "howdy" in the daytime and hopping in the evening. For active types, it's a good place to stock up on supplies before heading for outdoor adventures in Grand Teton National Park, Yellowstone, and the surrounding Jackson Hole area. It's also a great place to kick back and rest your feet while taking in the wealth of galleries, Western-wear shops, varied cuisines, a $35-million arts center, and active nightlife centering on bars and music.

Unfortunately, Jackson's cachet and popularity have put it at risk. On busy summer days, traffic sometimes slows to a crawl on the highway that doglegs through downtown. Proposals for new motels and condominiums sprout like the purple asters in the spring as developers vie for a share of the upscale vacation market. Old-timers suggest that the town—in fact, the entire Jackson Hole—has already lost some of its dusty charm from when horses stood at hitching rails around Town Square. However, with national parks and forests and state lands occupying most of the real estate in the county, only 3%–4% of it is unprotected ground on which to build. These limitations, along with the cautious approach of locals, may yet keep Jackson a delight to visit.

GETTING HERE AND AROUND

Coming from Yellowstone or Grand Teton national parks, you enter Jackson from the north on U.S. 89/191, passing the sagebrush flats of the National Elk Refuge. West of town, Highway 22 comes in from Idaho, over 8,431-foot Teton Pass; those entering Jackson from the "back side" of the Tetons should expect snowy conditions as late as June. Reach Jackson from the south via U.S. 191 from Pinedale or U.S. 89 from the Star Valley. The two routes merge 13 miles south of town at Hoback Junction. Driving in Jackson can be frustrating, particularly in the pedestrian-heavy and traffic-clogged downtown area, where parking is a challenge. Best to hoof it, ride the free and frequent START buses, or rent a bike from a local outfitter—a fleet cyclist can cross town end-to-end in 15 minutes.

HOTEL RESERVATIONS

Jackson Hole Central Reservations
You can make reservations for most lodgings in Jackson through Jackson Hole Central Reservations. ☎ *888/838–6606* 🌐 *www.jacksonholewy.com.*

Jackson Hole Resort Lodging
Properties managed by Jackson Hole Resort Lodging include rooms, condominiums, and vacation homes at Teton Village, Teton Pines, and the Aspens. ☎ *800/443–8613* 🌐 *www.jhrl.com.*

Mountain Property Management
Mountain Property Management offers condominium, cabin, and luxury-home rentals throughout Jackson Hole. ☎ *800/992–9948* 🌐 *www.mpmjh.com.*

VISITOR INFORMATION

CONTACTS Jackson Hole Chamber of Commerce. ✉ *532 N. Cache St.* ☎ *307/733–3316, 307/733–3316* 🌐 *www.jacksonhole-chamber.com.*

Sights

Granite Hot Springs
HOT SPRINGS | FAMILY | Soothing thermal baths in pristine outback country await in the heart of the Bridger-Teton National Forest, just a short drive south of Jackson. Concerted local and federal efforts have preserved the wild lands in this hunter's and fisherman's paradise where ranches dot the Teton Valley floor. The Snake River turns west and the contours sheer into steep vertical faces. By Hoback Junction there's white-water excitement. The drive south along U.S. 191 provides good views of the river's bends and turns and the life-jacketed

rafters and kayakers who float through the Hoback canyon. At Hoback Junction, about 11 miles south of Jackson, head east (toward Pinedale) on U.S. Highway 189/191 and follow the Hoback River east through its beautiful canyon. A tributary canyon 10 miles east of the junction is followed by a well-maintained and marked gravel road to Granite Hot Springs, in the Bridger-Teton National Forest. Drive 9 miles off U.S. 189/191 (northeast) on Granite Creek Road to reach the hot springs. People also come for the shady, creek-side campground and moderate hikes up Granite Canyon to passes with panoramic views. You'll want to drive with some caution, as there are elevated turns, the possibility of a felled tree, and wandering livestock that can own the road ahead on blind curves. In winter, the road is not plowed, and access is possible only by snowmobile, dogsled, skis, or fat bike from the highway. The 93°F to 112°F thermal bath at the end of the road is pure physical therapy, but it's closed from November through mid-December. ✉ *Granite Creek Rd.* ✣ *Granite Hot Springs Pool is at end of Granite Creek Rd., south of Jackson, WY off Hwy. 189* ☎ *307/690–6323* 🌐 *www.fs.usda.gov/btnf* 🎟 *$8* ⏲ *Closed Nov.–mid-Dec. snow dependent. Check website for up-to-date information. In winter months the hot springs are accessible only via snowmobile, dog sled, skis, and fat bike.*

★ Jackson Hole Historical Society & Museum

MUSEUM | **FAMILY** | At this excellent museum you can learn about historic homesteaders, dude ranches, and hunters, as well as Jackson's all-female town government of yore—a woman sheriff of that era claimed to have killed three men before hanging up her spurs. Native American, ranching, and cowboy artifacts are on display, some of them at the summer-only second location at 105 North Glenwood Street.

At this excellent museum you can learn about historic homesteaders, dude ranches, and hunters, as well as Jackson's all-female town government of yore—a woman sheriff of that era claimed to have killed three men before hanging up her spurs. Native American, ranching, and cowboy artifacts are on display, some of them at the summer-only second location at 105 North Glenwood Street. ✉ *225 N. Cache St.* ☎ *307/733–2414* 🌐 *www.jacksonholehistory.org* 🎟 *$10* ⏲ *Closed Nov.–mid-Dec.*

Jackson Town Square

HISTORIC SITE | **FAMILY** | You can spend an entire day wandering around Jackson's always-bustling Town Square, crisscrossed with walking paths and bedecked with arches woven from thousands of naturally shed elk antlers. Shops and restaurants surround the square, and there's often entertainment going on in the square itself, including a melodramatic "shoot-out" six nights per week in summer on the northeastern corner. At the southwestern corner you can board a stagecoach for a ride around the area. ✉ *Cache St. and Broadway.*

National Elk Refuge

NATURE PRESERVE | **FAMILY** | Wildlife abounds on this 25,000-acre refuge. From late November to March, more than 7,000 elk, many with enormous antler racks, winter here. Elk can be observed from various pull-outs along U.S. 191 or by slowly driving your car on the refuge's winding, unpaved roads. Other animals that make their home here include buffalo, bighorn sheep, and coyotes, as well as trumpeter swans and other waterfowl. In summer, the refuge is light on big game, but you can tour a historic homestead from June to September. From mid-December to early April, sleigh rides operated by Double H Bar (🌐 *nersleighrides.com*) depart several times a day from the Jackson Hole and Greater Yellowstone Visitor Center.

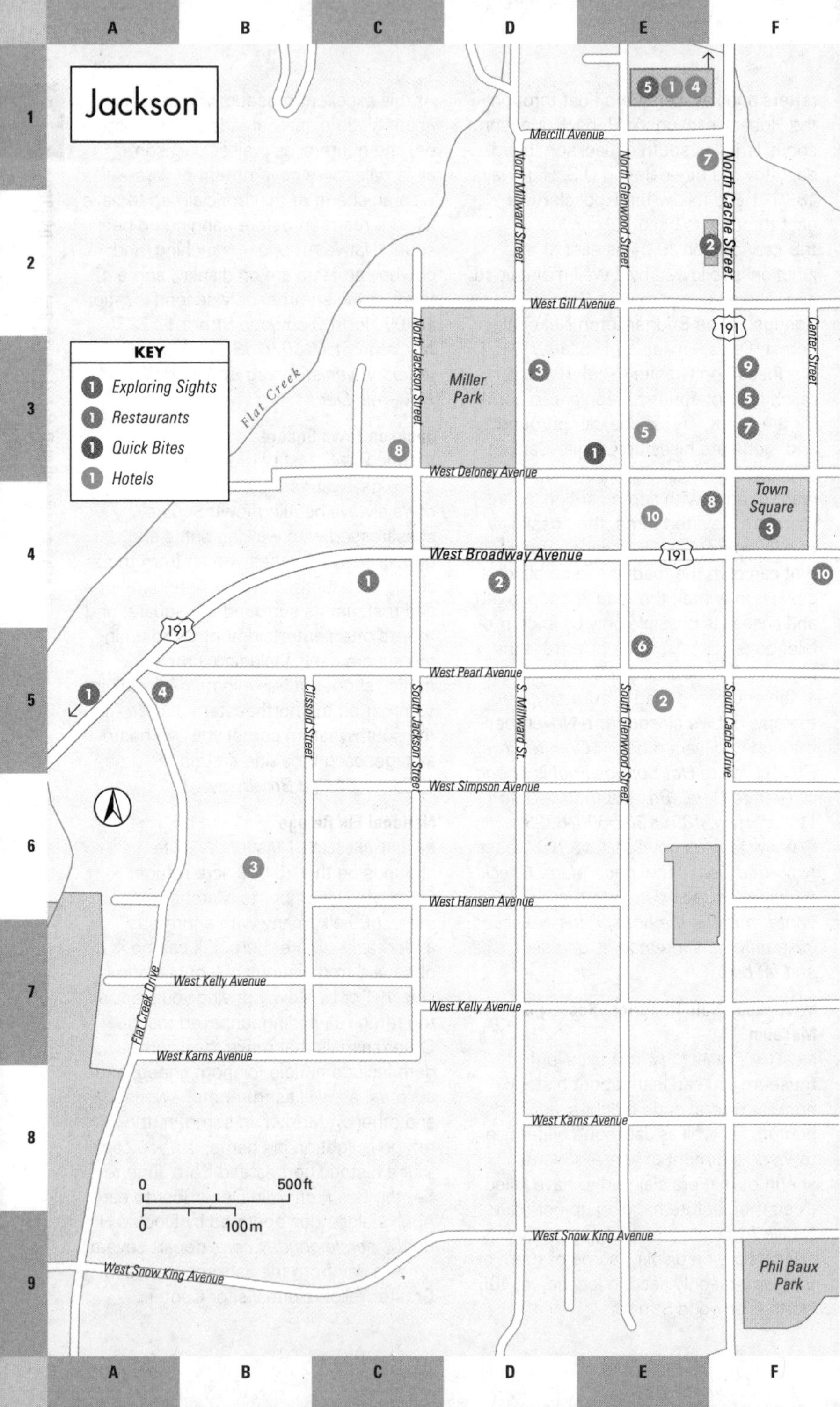

A
B
C
D
E
F
1
2
3
4
5
6
7
8
9
Jackson
KEY
Exploring Sights
Restaurants
Quick Bites
Hotels
Mercill Avenue
North Millward Street
North Glenwood Street
North Cache Street
West Gill Avenue
191
Center Street
North Jackson Street
Miller Park
Flat Creek
West Deloney Avenue
Town Square
West Broadway Avenue
West Pearl Avenue
Clissold Street
South Jackson Street
S. Millward St.
South Glenwood Street
South Cache Drive
West Simpson Avenue
West Hansen Avenue
West Kelly Avenue
Flat Creek Drive
West Karns Avenue
0
500ft
0
100m
West Snow King Avenue
Phil Baux Park

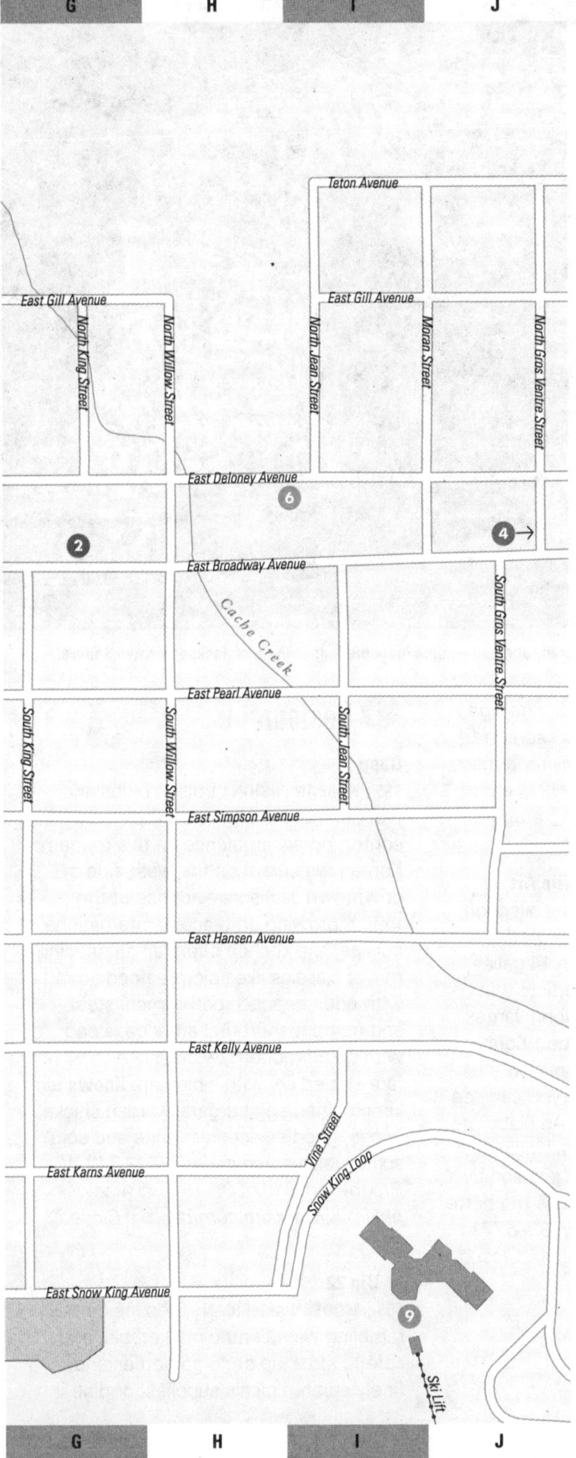

Sights

1 Granite Hot Springs A5
2 Jackson Hole Historical Society & Museum F2
3 Jackson Town Square F4
4 National Elk Refuge J4
5 National Museum of Wildlife Art E1

Restaurants

1 Bapp................................. C4
2 Bin22 .... D4
3 The Blue Lion...................... D3
4 Bubba's Bar-B-Que Restaurant.......................... A5
5 The Bunnery Bakery & Restaurant.......................... F3
6 Gather............................... E5
7 Hand Fire Pizza.................... F3
8 Local Restaurant & Bar........... F4
9 The Merry Piglets Mexican Grill....................... F3
10 Snake River Grill F4

Quick Bites

1 Cultivate Cafe E3
2 Persephone Bakery G4

Hotels

1 Amangani........................... E1
2 Antler Inn E5
3 Cowboy Village Resort........... B6
4 Elk Refuge Inn...................... E1
5 Hotel Jackson...................... E3
6 Huff House Inn & Cabins I4
7 The Lexington at Jackson Hole ... E1
8 Parkway Inn......................... C3
9 Snow King Mountain Resort I9
10 The Wort Hotel..................... E4

Four large arches made from naturally shed elk antlers mark the four corners of Jackson's Town Square.

✉ E. Broadway at National Elk Refuge Rd. ✥ Head north out of Jackson on E. Broadway until you reach visitor center on your right ☎ 307/733–9212 🌐 www.fws.gov/refuge/national_elk_refuge 🎫 Sleigh rides $27.

★ National Museum of Wildlife Art

MUSEUM | See an impressive collection of wildlife art—most of it devoted to North American species—in 14 galleries displaying the work of artists that include Georgia O'Keeffe, John James Audubon, John Clymer, Robert Kuhn, and Carl Rungius. A deck looks out on the National Elk Refuge, where you can see wildlife in a natural habitat. An elaborate ¾-mile outdoor sculpture trail includes a monumental herd of bronze bison by Richard Loffler trudging across the butte. *✉ 2820 Rungius Rd. ☎ 307/733–5771 🌐 www.wildlifeart.org 🎫 $15 ⏲ Closed Sun. and Mon.*

Restaurants

Bapp

$$$ | KOREAN FUSION | Edison bulbs and wooden booths impart a simple but contemporary ambience on this modern Korean restaurant on the west side of downtown Jackson, evidence of the town's growing embrace of international cuisine. The kitchen offers up an enticing mix of classics like spicy seafood soup with udon noodles, pork-kimchi stew, and fragrant short-rib barbecue, along with some modern twists, such as rare-seared ahi with bibimbap. **Known for:** kimchi–fried egg burgers; Korean chicken wings; good selection of wine and soju spirits. *💲 Average main: $20 ✉ 340 W. Broadway ☎ 307/201–1818 🌐 www.hnkim226.wixsite.com/bapp ⏲ Closed Sun.*

★ Bin 22

$$$ | MODERN AMERICAN | Step inside this rambling wine-centric market, bar, and café to stock up on to-go bottles and finely curated picnic supplies, or dine in.

The menu tends toward shareable small plates that pair well with the interesting vinos—consider a selection of imported salumi and cheeses, or Spanish- and Italian-inspired platters of patatas bravas with roasted-garlic aioli, steamed clams with chorizo, and roasted bone marrow over saffron gnocchi. **Known for:** impressive list of hard-to-find wines and liquor; artisan ice-cream sandwiches; deck seating with heat lamps. $ *Average main: $22* ✉ *200 W. Broadway* ☎ *307/739–9463* 🌐 *www.bin22jacksonhole.com.*

The Blue Lion

$$$ | **EUROPEAN** | For 30 years, consistently excellent, distinctive fare has been the rule at this white-and-blue clapboard house two blocks from Town Square. The sophisticated offerings range from Dijon-mustard-rubbed rack of lamb to grilled elk with port wine sauce to fresh fish dishes, including rainbow trout. **Known for:** incredible nightly specials; live music most nights; house-made desserts, including great tiramisu. $ *Average main: $28* ✉ *160 N. Millward St.* ☎ *307/733–3912* 🌐 *www.bluelionrestaurant.com.*

Bubba's Bar-B-Que Restaurant

$$ | **BARBECUE** | Succulent baby back ribs and mouthwatering spareribs are the specialties at this busy barbecue joint, which evokes the Old West with its wooden booths, Western paintings, and antique signs. Sandwiches and a huge salad bar with plenty of nonmeat choices are also available. **Known for:** longest running barbeque in Jackson, serving it up for more than 40 years; all coffee served at Bubbas is roasted in-house; massive portions to make sure you won't leave hungry. $ *Average main: $12* ✉ *100 Flat Creek Dr.* ☎ *307/733–2288* 🌐 *www.bubbasjh.com.*

The Bunnery Bakery & Restaurant

$$ | **AMERICAN** | Lunch is served year-round and dinner is served in summer, but it's the breakfasts and home-baked pastries that are irresistible here. It's elbow to elbow inside, so you may have to wait to be seated on busy mornings, but any inconvenience is well worth it. **Known for:** incredible baked treats like muffins and danishes; OSM Oatmeal Pancakes with oats, sunflower seeds, and millet; house-made granola. $ *Average main: $11* ✉ *Hole-in-the-Wall Mall, 130 N. Cache St.* ☎ *307/733–5474* 🌐 *www.bunnery.com.*

★ **Gather**

$$$ | **MODERN AMERICAN** | This stylish purveyor of locavore-driven modern American cuisine impresses with its deftly plated food, knowledgeable service, and light-filled dining room with a curved wall of windows and pale-green banquette seating. The menu changes seasonally but might feature Snake River Farms wagyu tartar with beet mustard and a bacon-fried egg, followed by red wine–marinated local bison or elk Bolognese. **Known for:** inventive craft cocktails; local game and produce; see-and-be-seen crowd. $ *Average main: $27* ✉ *72 S. Glenwood St.* ☎ *307/264–1820* 🌐 *www.gatherjh.com* ⏲ *No lunch.*

★ **Hand Fire Pizza**

$$ | **PIZZA** | Set in downtown Jackon's dramatic, imaginatively retrofitted art deco cinema building, this modern high-energy pizza place has mezzanine and ground-level tables that look directly toward an open kitchen with two massive wood-fired ovens. The flavorful pies and salads abound with mostly organic, often local ingredients: slow-roasted pork shoulder, pickled jalapeños, heirloom tomatoes, house-made burrata, and the like. **Known for:** the Chew-Baca pie with herbed ricotta, bacon, caramelized onions, and local honey; Tuesday-night fundraisers that support local charities; stunning interior. $ *Average main: $18* ✉ *120 N. Cache St.* ☎ *307/733–7199* 🌐 *www.handfirepizza.com* ⏲ *No lunch Mon.–Thurs.*

★ **Local Restaurant & Bar**

$$$$ | **AMERICAN** | This contemporary American steak house is located right on Jackson's historic town square and

serves locally ranched beef, bison, and elk. Come for a fine-dining quality meal, but without the stuffy atmosphere. **Known for:** the best steaks in town; one of the largest and highest-quality whiskey selections in the area; a plethora of delicious side options. *Average main: $37 55 N. Cache St. 307/201–1717 localjh.com Closed Sun.*

The Merry Piglets Mexican Grill

$$ | **MEXICAN** | **FAMILY** | No pork is served here (hence the name). But otherwise, you'll get more-than-generous portions of Mexican fare, over a mesquite grill if you like, with a range of homemade sauces from mild to spicy. **Known for:** margaritas made with fresh ingredients; nine kinds of tacos with options for all dietary restrictions; chips and salsa are made fresh from scratch every day. *Average main: $14 160 N. Cache Dr. Near Teton Theatre 307/733–2966 www.merrypiglets.com.*

Snake River Grill

$$$$ | **MODERN AMERICAN** | One of Jackson's mainstays for special-occasion dining, this sophisticated restaurant serves creatively prepared dishes using meats and fish loved across the West. The menu changes regularly, reflecting what's available in the market, and the extensive wine list has garnered countless awards. **Known for:** log cabin–chic interior; cast-iron-seared elk steak; lavish desserts. *Average main: $38 84 E. Broadway Ave. 307/733–0557 www.snakerivergrill.com Closed Mon. and Tues. in Apr. and Nov. No lunch.*

Coffee and Quick Bites

Cultivate Cafe

$$ | **CAFÉ** | **FAMILY** | A great option for organic breakfasts, fresh smoothies, and well-crafted coffees before setting out for a day of hiking and exploring, this popular café set inside downtown's oldest building has an Old West saloon vibe. Open-face breakfast sandwiches and waffles topped with house jam and matcha-coconut cream are among the morning specialties, while veggie-bowls and local grass-fed burgers star at lunch. **Known for:** lots of kid-friendly options; vegan and veggie fare; honey-cinnamon-vanilla lattes. *Average main: $11 135 W. Deloney Ave. 307/200–9631 www.cultivate-cafe.com Closed Mon. No dinner.*

★ **Persephone Bakery**

$ | **BAKERY** | The best seating at this rustic-contemporary bakery café a short stroll east of Jackson Town Square is on the spacious shaded deck overlooking lively Broadway Avenue. Choose from an extensive menu of eclectic breakfast and lunch fare, including shakshuka feta and poached eggs, bread pudding French toast with grapefruit-cranberry compote, and mortadella sandwiches with locally made sauerkraut and melted fontina. **Known for:** fresh-baked artisan breads and pastries; espresso drinks with house-made marshmallows; brunch cocktails. *Average main: $10 145 E. Broadway Ave. 307/200–6708 www.persephonebakery.com No dinner.*

Hotels

Amangani

$$$$ | **RESORT** | This exclusive resort built of sandstone and redwood blends into the landscape of Gros Ventre Butte, affording beautiful views of the Snake River Range from its cliff-top location. **Pros:** extremely luxurious; impeccable service; extensive amenities. **Cons:** high prices, but rates vary widely with the seasons; though the views are wonderful, few rooms can see the Tetons; small gym and spa. *Rooms from: $1295 1535 N.E. Butte Rd. 307/734–7333 www.aman.com 40 suites No meals.*

Antler Inn

$$$$ | **HOTEL** | **FAMILY** | No motel in Jackson has a better location than this old-school

lodging, a block south of Town Square. **Pros:** restaurants nearby; family-run; good prices in the off-season. **Cons:** frequently booked-up in summer; dated interiors; motel vibe won't appeal to all visitors. *Rooms from: $220 ✉ 43 W. Pearl St. ☎ 307/733–2535 🌐 www.townsquare-inns.com 106 rooms 🍽 No meals.*

Cowboy Village Resort

$$$ | **HOTEL** | This friendly, well-maintained establishment—with freestanding log cabins with kitchenettes, covered decks, and barbecue grills—is one of the better values in Jackson. **Pros:** bus shuttle to ski areas; several restaurants within walking distance; indoor pool and hot tub. **Cons:** crowded in summer; no restaurant on-site; decor is pleasant but unfancy. *Rooms from: $149 ✉ 120 S. Flat Creek Dr. ☎ 307/733–3121, 800/483–8667 🌐 www.townsquareinns.com 82 rooms 🍽 Free breakfast.*

Elk Refuge Inn

$$$$ | **HOTEL** | This simple, two-story motel with clean, warmly furnished rooms stands out for great reason: it's set along a minimally developed stretch of U.S. 26/89/191 that overlooks Flat Creek and the National Elk Refuge. **Pros:** rooms have views of elk refuge; reasonable rates; short drive from Jackson dining and shopping. **Cons:** not within walking distance of town; rates soar in summer; parking lot partially obscures views. *Rooms from: $211 ✉ 1755 U.S. 26/89/191 ☎ 307/200–0981 🌐 www.elkrefugeinn.net 24 rooms 🍽 No meals.*

★ **Hotel Jackson**

$$$$ | **HOTEL** | This swank, LEED-certified hotel built of iron, repurposed barn wood, and natural stone on the site of a Victorian hotel of the same name feels at once ruggedly Western and pleasingly cosmopolitan, its guest rooms and common spaces filled with artful, comforting touches. **Pros:** opulent rooms and design; steps from Jackson Square; superb service. **Cons:** steep rates; not a great choice for families; in a busy part of town. *Rooms from: $629 ✉ 120 N. Glenwood St. ☎ 307/733–2200 🌐 www.hoteljackson.com 55 rooms 🍽 No meals.*

Huff House Inn & Cabins

$$$$ | **B&B/INN** | With a mix of smartly furnished rooms and suites in cabins, a historic inn, and a newer building whose rooms have views of Snow King Mountain, this cozy and cushy inn abounds with inviting touches: soft robes, tasteful furnishings, and in some cases, gas fireplaces. **Pros:** easy stroll from town square; friendly staff; enchanting garden patio with fire pit and hot tub. **Cons:** pricey during summer months; no pets; often books up months in advance. *Rooms from: $319 ✉ 240 E. Deloney Ave. ☎ 307/733–7141 🌐 www.huffhouse-jh.com 25 rooms 🍽 Free breakfast.*

The Lexington at Jackson Hole

$$$$ | **HOTEL** | Within walking distance of Town Square, this lodging features modern furnishings and lots of light. **Pros:** walking distance to downtown hot spots; small pool and Jacuzzi; friendly and helpful staff. **Cons:** limited views; must drive to mountains; hotel-motel vibe instead of lodge feel. *Rooms from: $299 ✉ 285 N. Cache St. ☎ 307/733–2648 🌐 www.lexingtonhoteljacksonhole.com 89 rooms 🍽 Free breakfast.*

Parkway Inn

$$$$ | **B&B/INN** | From the moment you enter its ground-floor "salon," this hotel soothes the soul with vintage furniture and black-and-white photographs showing the rise of east Jackson. **Pros:** within walking distance of many restaurants; quiet setting; boutique atmosphere. **Cons:** not a full-service hotel; no restaurant; some guests noted dated furnishings. *Rooms from: $289 ✉ 125 N. Jackson St. ☎ 307/733–3143 🌐 www.parkwayinn.com 49 rooms 🍽 Free breakfast.*

Snow King Mountain Resort

$$$$ | **HOTEL** | **FAMILY** | At the base of Snow King Mountain ski area and eight blocks

from Town Square, this mid-rise resort with conventional rooms and condo rentals has a modern Western look, a popular restaurant, a cycling and ski shop, and outdoor fire pits near the beautiful pool. **Pros:** central yet away from the bustle of downtown; ski-in, ski-out; lots of amenities. **Cons:** often booked up with large groups; pricey during peak times; daily resort fee. *Rooms from: $265* ✉ *400 E. Snow King Ave.* ☎ *307/733–5200* 🌐 *www.snowking.com* *201 rooms* *No meals.*

★ The Wort Hotel

$$$$ | **HOTEL** | Built in 1941, this Tudor-style grande dame with a fascinating interior of priceless Western paintings and artifacts is just a block from Town Square and feels as though it's been around as long as the Tetons, but its inviting rooms feel up-to-date and feature woodsy, Western-style furnishings made locally. **Pros:** charming old building with lots of history; steps from local shopping and dining; specialty suites with one-of-a-kind designs. **Cons:** limited views; quite pricey in winter and summer; busy location. *Rooms from: $449* ✉ *50 N. Glenwood St.* ☎ *307/733–2190* 🌐 *www.worthotel.com* *55 rooms* *No meals.*

Nightlife

There's never a shortage of live music in Jackson, where local performers play country, rock, and folk. Some of the most popular bars are on Town Square.

Million Dollar Cowboy Bar

BARS/PUBS | Bring your boots and saddle up to the bar—yes, the bar stools are really saddles—or try your timing at the Western two-step to the frequent live music. ✉ *25 N. Cache St.* ☎ *307/733–2207* 🌐 *www.milliondollarcowboybar.com.*

The Rose

BARS/PUBS | A trendy go-to for après-ski and posthike relaxation and socializing, this dapper lounge with bordello-inspired chandeliers, brocade wallpaper, and red-leather booths pours interesting cocktails with artisan spirits. Light bar snacks are served, too. ✉ *50 W. Broadway Ave.* ☎ *307/733–1500* 🌐 *www.therosejh.com.*

Snake River Brewing

BARS/PUBS | Locals head to happy hour at Snake River Brewing for cold pints and pub fare. Avoid the loud chatter levels by nabbing a sought-after seat on the picnic-table patio. ✉ *265 S. Millward St.* ☎ *307/739–2337* 🌐 *www.snakeriverbrewing.com.*

★ Stillwest Brewery

BARS/PUBS | Several blocks south of downtown in the shadows of Snow King Mountain ski area, this spacious, modern brewery and taproom has a big covered deck overlooking the scenery. Stop by for a pint of mocha-vanilla oatmeal stout or the heady Belgian-style Trippel. There's pretty tasty gastropub fare served, too. ✉ *45 E. Snow King Ave.* ☎ *307/201–5955* 🌐 *www.stillwestbreweryandgrill.com.*

Performing Arts

Center for the Arts

ARTS CENTERS | **FAMILY** | Jackson's $35 million center is dedicated to supporting the fine and performing arts, including theater, film, and dance. It also hosts lectures on global issues, rotating exhibits, and showcases of star talent from Hollywood to Broadway. Classes for adults are included in the center's mission. ✉ *240 S. Glenwood* ☎ *307/734–8956* 🌐 *www.jhcenterforthearts.org.*

Jackson Hole Fall Arts Festival

ARTS FESTIVALS | **FAMILY** | Art galleries reserve their best exhibits for a 10-day extravaganza encompassing the first two weekends of September. Nationally known artists who work in a variety of mediums are showcased in the galleries, during a quickdraw competition and in a large auction. Other events highlight

The venerable Million Dollar Cowboy Bar has been pulling in crowds for drinks and country music since 1937.

food, poetry, jewelry, and dance. ✉ *Jackson* ☎ *307/733–3316.*

Jackson Hole Playhouse

THEATER | You can attend live theater from June through the end of September at the Jackson Hole Playhouse, the oldest building in town. The best seats are a hot commodity, but procrastinators can usually buy last-minute tickets. Eat dinner at 6:30 in the gaudy, Western-style saloon, and take in the show in the playhouse's theater at 8. Performances also take place from late November through New Year's Eve. ✉ *145 W. Deloney Ave.* ☎ *307/733–6994* 🌐 *www.jacksonhole-playhouse.com.*

Off-Square Theatre

ARTS FESTIVALS | For those seeking a contemporary theater experience, Off-Square Theatre is a space for children and adults where theater professionals and nonprofessionals strut their stuff and sometimes go outside the box. It's one of the leading theater companies in the region. ✉ *Center for the Arts, 240 S. Glenwood* ☎ *307/733–3021* 🌐 *www.offsquare.org.*

Shopping

Jackson's peaceful Town Square is surrounded by storefronts with a mixture of specialty and outdoor shops—most of them small scale—with moderate to expensive prices. Catty-corner to the square, at the northwest corner of Cache and Deloney, is a small cluster of fine shops in Gaslight Alley.

BOOKS

Valley Bookstore

BOOKS/STATIONERY | One of Gaslight Alley's best shops is Valley Bookstore. It ranks among the top bookstores in the region, with a big selection of local history, guidebooks on flora and fauna, and fiction by Wyoming and area authors. Knowledgeable staff can answer any question. ✉ *125 N. Cache St.* ☎ *307/733–4533* 🌐 *www.valleybookstore.com.*

CLOTHING

Hide Out Leathers

CLOTHING | Men's and women's clothing and accessories are the main finds here, including cowboy hats, belts, and deerskin jackets. Regionally made handbags and bison briefcases are other popular purchases. ✉ *40 Center St.* ✣ *Across Cowboy St.* ☎ *307/733–2422* 🌐 *www.hideoutleathers.com.*

CRAFT AND ART GALLERIES

Jackson is becoming an art destination. Its 30-plus art galleries serve a range of tastes, from contemporary to traditional, representational to abstract.

Images of Nature Gallery

ART GALLERIES | Fine nature photography by world-renowned photographer Tom Mangelsen from around the globe is displayed and sold at his Images of Nature Gallery. ✉ *170 N. Cache St.* ☎ *307/733–9752* 🌐 *www.mangelsen.com.*

★ MADE

CRAFTS | The whimsical, one-of-a-kind wares of more than 350 artisans, many of them from the surrounding region, are displayed in this cool and colorful little shop and gallery. ✉ *125 N. Cache St.* ☎ *307/690–7957* 🌐 *www.madejacksonhole.com.*

Tayloe Piggott Gallery

ART GALLERIES | Jackson's hot spot for contemporary work abandons wildlife and landscape art in favor of hip and often playful painting, sculpture, and one-of-a-kind jewelry. It's a bit of SoHo nestled in the Rockies. ✉ *62 S. Glenwood St.* ☎ *307/733–0555* 🌐 *www.tayloepiggottgallery.com* ⏲ *Closed Sun.*

Trailside Galleries

ART GALLERIES | Trailside Galleries sells representational Western works by some of the biggest names, including members of the prestigious Cowboy Artists of America and Oil Painters of America. ✉ *130 E. Broadway* ☎ *307/733–3186* 🌐 *www.trailsidegalleries.com* ⏲ *Closed Sun. and Mon.*

Wilcox Gallery

ART GALLERIES | Life-size bronzes greet visitors at Wilcox Gallery, which showcases wildlife and landscape paintings, sculpture, pottery, and other works by contemporary artists. Owner Jim Wilcox has won the highest honors at Prix de West several times for his breathtaking landscapes. ✉ *1975 N. U.S. 89* ☎ *307/733–6450* 🌐 *www.wilcoxgallery.com* ⏲ *Closed Sun.*

Wild by Nature Gallery

ART GALLERIES | At Wild by Nature Gallery, 95% of the fine-art photographs are of local wildlife and landscapes by Henry W. Holdsworth; there's also a selection of books and note cards. ✉ *95 W. Deloney Ave.* ☎ *307/733–8877* 🌐 *www.wildbynatureshop.com.*

FOOD

Jackson Whole Grocer

FOOD/CANDY | Jackson Whole Grocer is a full-service grocer that also sells wine and beer, as well as organic and health food products. ✉ *974 W. Broadway* ☎ *307/733–0450.*

SPORTING GOODS

JD High Country Outfitters

SPORTING GOODS | Stocked with the best in outdoor equipment for winter and summer, the shop carries everything from backpacks to skis and hunting rifles, as well as clothing and other supplies. Fishing gear can be rented. ✉ *50 E. Broadway Ave.* ☎ *307/733–3270* 🌐 *www.jdhcoutfitters.com.*

Skinny Skis

SPORTING GOODS | Skinny Skis offers everything a cross-country skier or runner might need, plus a nice selection of mountain-town clothing. ✉ *65 W. Deloney Ave.* ☎ *307/733–6094* 🌐 *www.skinnyskis.com.*

Teton Mountaineering

SPORTING GOODS | A favorite last stop for climbers, Teton Mountaineering specializes in Nordic-skiing, climbing, and hiking equipment and clothing. ✉ *170 N. Cache*

St. ☎ *307/733–3595* 🌐 *www.tetonmtn.com.*

Westbank Anglers
SPORTING GOODS | Westbank Anglers can provide all the equipment necessary for fly-fishing. They also offer guided fishing trips on the legendary Snake River. ✉ *3670 N. Moose–Wilson Rd.* ☎ *307/733–6483* 🌐 *www.westbank.com.*

Activities

BIKING

Hoback Sports
BICYCLING | You can rent a mountain bike to explore on your own or take a tour at Hoback Sports. General tours are geared to intermediate and advanced riders, but Hoback can also custom-design a tour to suit your abilities and interests. The store also sells bike, ski, skate, and snowboard apparel and equipment. ✉ *520 W. Broadway* ☎ *307/733–5335* 🌐 *www.hobacksports.com.*

Lower Slide Lake
BICYCLING | Upper and Lower Slide Lakes were formed by a massive landslide in 1925 that created a natural dam. The road up is a popular one among cyclists, but the lake also offers great fishing, camping, and hiking. ✉ *Jackson* ✢ *From Jackson, head north on US191 toward Grand Teton National Park. Turn right onto Gros Ventre Rd. and follow to lake.*

Spring Gulch Road
BICYCLING | Cyclists ride the Spring Gulch Road, part pavement, part dirt, off Route 22, along the base of Gros Ventre Butte, rejoining U.S. 26/89/191 near the Gros Ventre River. ✉ *Jackson.*

Teton Mountain Bike Tours
BICYCLING | Mountain bikers of all skill levels can take guided half-, full-, or multiday tours with Teton Mountain Bike Tours into both Grand Teton and Yellowstone national parks, as well as to the Bridger-Teton and Caribou-Targhee national forests and throughout Jackson Hole. In winter, tours and rentals continue over snow with fat bikes. ✉ *545 N. Cache* ☎ *307/733–0712* 🌐 *www.tetonmtbike.com.*

CANOEING, KAYAKING, AND RAFTING

South of Jackson, where the Hoback joins the Snake River and the canyon walls become steep, there are lively white-water sections. But the upper Snake, whose rating is Class I and II, is a river for those who value scenery over white-water thrills. For the most part, floating rather than taking on rapids is the theme of running the Snake. As such, it's a good choice for families with children. What makes the trip special is the Teton Range, looming as high as 8,000 feet above the river. This float trip can also be combined with two or more days of kayaking on Jackson Lake. Raft trips take place between June and September. Experienced paddlers run the Hoback, too.

The Snake River's western Idaho portion has earned a strange footnote in history. It's the river that Evel Knievel tried (and failed miserably) to jump over on a rocket-powered motorcycle in the mid-1970s.

Barker-Ewing Scenic Float Trips
CANOEING/ROWING/SKULLING | If you take a float trip with Barker-Ewing Scenic Float Trips, you will travel the peaceful parts of the Snake River looking for wildlife as knowledgeable guides talk about area history, plants, and animals. ✉ *Moose* ☎ *307/733–1800* 🌐 *www.barkerewing.com.*

Rendezvous River Sports
CANOEING/ROWING/SKULLING | Rendezvous River Sports is the premiere paddle-sports outfitter in the region, offering expert instruction so you can test yourself on western Wyoming's ancient rivers and lakes. The company also schedules more relaxed and scenic trips, including guided tours of Slide, Lewis, and Yellowstone lakes, and rapid-shooting rides on the Hoback River down Granite Creek

to the Snake River while you marvel at south Jackson's majestic canyons. Raft, canoe, and stand-up paddleboard rentals are also available. ✉ *945 W. Broadway* ☎ *307/733–2471* 🌐 *www.jacksonholekayak.com.*

DOGSLEDDING

Jackson Hole Iditarod Sled Dog Tours

LOCAL SPORTS | Veteran Iditarod racer Frank Teasley leads half-day introductory dogsledding trips and full-day trips to Granite Hot Springs. It's a great way to see wintering native wildlife such as moose, elk, bighorn sheep, deer, and bald eagles in the Bridger-Teton National Forest. Sled trips are offered only in season, which can begin as early as November and run as late as April. ✉ *11 Granite Creek Rd.* ☎ *307/733–7388* 🌐 *www.jhsleddog.com.*

HIKING

Bridger-Teton National Forest (☎ *307/739–5500* 🌐 *www.fs.usda.gov/btnf*) covers hundreds of thousands of acres of western Wyoming and shelters abundant wildlife. Permits for backcountry use of the forest are necessary only for groups and commercial operators such as outfitters. Contact the forest office for more information.

The Hole Hiking Experience

HIKING/WALKING | Guides at the Hole Hiking Experience will take you to mountain meadows or to the tops of the peaks on half- or full-day tours. Some outings are suitable for the very experienced, others for any well-conditioned adult, and still others for families. ✉ *Jackson* ☎ *307/690–4453* 🌐 *www.holehike.com.*

Jackson Hole Mountain Guides

HIKING/WALKING | You can take part in wilderness camping, climbing, and exploration of alpine areas with experienced guides on day trips, on overnight excursions, or as part of regular classes offered by Jackson Hole Mountain Guides. In winter, guides lead avalanche education courses, backcountry skiing, ski mountaineering, and ice-climbing trips. ✉ *1325 S. Hwy. 89* ☎ *307/733–4979* 🌐 *www.jhmg.com.*

MULTISPORT OUTFITTERS

★ Austin Adventures

ADVENTURE TOURS | **FAMILY** | The world-renowned adventure travel company offers all-inclusive, multisport packages departing and ending in Jackson. The six-day, five-night tours including cycling in Grand Teton, hiking in Yellowstone, kayaking on Jackson Lake, and rafting the Snake River as well as eating at the finest restaurants Jackson has to offer. ☎ *800/575–1540* 🌐 *www.austinadventures.com.*

SKIING

Snow King Mountain

SKIING/SNOWBOARDING | **FAMILY** | Snow King Resort, at the western edge of Jackson, has 400 acres of ski runs for daytime use and 110 acres suitable for night skiing, plus an extensive snowmaking system on Snow King Mountain. You'll also find a snow-tubing park. In summer there's a 2,500-foot alpine slide, and miles of biking and hiking paths go all the way to the mountaintop. For $20, you can also ride the scenic chairlift to the top and back. Or stop off at the summit, which is 7,808 feet above sea level, for a picnic, and feast on the stunning 50-mile view of Jackson Hole. From up here, on a clear day, you can see over the neighboring buttes and count the clouds passing around the Tetons. ✉ *400 E. Snow King Ave.* ☎ *307/733–5200* 🌐 *www.snowkingmountain.com.*

SLEIGH RIDES

Jackson Hole & Greater Yellowstone Visitor Center

SNOW SPORTS | **FAMILY** | This inter-agency visitor center is operated by Bridger-Teton National Forest, Grand Teton Association, Grand Teton National Park, National Elk Refuge, Jackson Hole Chamber of Commerce, and Wyoming Game & Fish. Sleigh rides into the National Elk Refuge last about 45 minutes and depart from in front of the Jackson Hole & Greater

Yellowstone Visitor Center daily in winter, 10 to 4, about every 20 minutes. ✉ *532 N. Cache Dr.* ☎ *307/733–3316* 🌐 *www.jacksonholechamber.com* 🎫 *$27.*

Spring Creek Ranch
SNOW SPORTS | FAMILY | Dinner sleigh rides are available through Spring Creek Ranch, with dinner at its Granary restaurant. ✉ *1800 Spirit Dance Rd.* ☎ *307/733–8833* 🌐 *www.springcreekranch.com* 🎫 *$64.*

Teton Village and Jackson Hole Mountain Resort

11 miles northwest of Jackson via Hwy. 22 and Teton Village Rd.

Teton Village resounds with the clomping of ski boots in winter and the sounds of violins, horns, and other instruments at the Grand Teton Music Festival in summer. The village mostly consists of the restaurants, lodging properties, and shops built to serve the skiers who flock to Jackson Hole Mountain Resort. Considered one of the best country's best resorts, Jackson has some of the most challenging runs in the United States and is where serious skiers go to test their might (and earn bragging rights). But don't let that intimidate you if you're a beginner; Jackson Hole offers plenty of green and blue runs to get your turns in. In summer, folks come here to hike, ride the tram, and attend high-caliber concerts. Because "the Vill" is small, with winding and sometimes unnamed streets, street addresses are often superfluous.

GETTING HERE AND AROUND

From Jackson, follow Highway 22 west for 6 miles, then head 7 miles north past resorts and trophy homes on Highway 390, commonly known as Teton Village Road. The city's START buses make the trip hourly for $3. Streets in the village are winding and far apart, and sometimes turn abruptly into parking lots—this is an area primarily designed for pedestrians. From Grand Teton National Park, scenic but mostly gravel Moose–Wilson Road is a direct route to Teton Village from the park entrance station at Moose. Be prepared to marvel at moose- and elk-sightings while simultaneously cursing your shocks.

VISITOR INFORMATION

CONTACTS Jackson Hole Mountain Resort. ✉ *3395 Cody La., Teton Village* ☎ *307/733–2292* 🌐 *www.jacksonhole.com.*

Sights

Aerial Tram
TRANSPORTATION SITE (AIRPORT/BUS/FERRY/TRAIN) | FAMILY | As it travels to the summit of Rendezvous Mountain, the Aerial Tramway has always afforded spectacular panoramas of Jackson Hole. There are several hiking trails at the top of the mountain. A newer, sleeker tram was unveiled to much fanfare in 2008, and the updated "Big Red Box" remains a popular attraction even outside of ski season. Tram rides are first-come, first-served and run every 20 minutes; fees are usually discounted online. Sightseeing tickets are available in winter to nonskiers as well. ✉ *Teton Village, Teton Village* ☎ *307/733–2292, 800/333–7766* 🌐 *www.jacksonhole.com* 🎫 *$32* ⊙ *Closed Oct.–early May.*

Restaurants

Bar Enoteca
$$$ | WINE BAR | This stylishly hip wine bar inside Hotel Terra offers a lower-keyed sipping and dining alternative to full-service Il Villagio Osteria and is great for happy hour or a late dinner after skiing or exploring nearby Grand Teton National Park. The small-plates menu focuses on raw-bar items like sea bass ceviche and yellowtail hamachi along with pork

You don't need to be a skiier to enjoy a ride to the top of Rendezvous Mountain on the Aerial Tram.

buns, salads, and crostini with creative toppings. **Known for:** chic postindustrial design; tasty breakfasts; well-chosen wine list. *Average main: $21 ✉ 3335 W. Village Dr., Teton Village ☎ 307/739–4225 🌐 www.enotecajacksonhole.com ⏲ No lunch.*

Il Villaggio Osteria

$$$ | MODERN ITALIAN | Underneath rustic barnwood timbers and columns or on an open-air patio, diners enjoy the flavors of Italy fused with fresh, inventive touches. Try the bone-marrow bruschetta, house-pulled mozzarella figs stuffed with blue cheese, or a generous slice of gooey lasagna. **Known for:** artisan pizza and pasta; hand-crafted cocktails; warm and cozy atmosphere. *Average main: $27 ✉ 3335 W. Village Dr., Teton Village ☎ 307/739–4100 🌐 www.jhosteria.com ⏲ No lunch.*

Mangy Moose

$$$ | AMERICAN | Folks pour in off the ski slopes for a lot of food and talk at this two-level restaurant with a bar and an outdoor deck. If you can endure the noise, you'll enjoy decent Alaskan halibut, buffalo meat loaf, and fish and pasta dishes. *Average main: $25 ✉ 3295 Village Dr., Teton Village ☎ 307/733–4913 🌐 www.mangymoose.net ⏲ Closed Apr.–mid-May and Nov.*

★ Teton Thai

$$$ | THAI | By the Ranch Lot at the base of Jackson Hole Mountain Resort, this casually smart Thai-owned restaurant serves some of the most authentic, if a bit pricey, Asian fare in the region. The pad Thai and *tom yum gai* soup are among the specialties, and there's a full bar. **Known for:** hefty portions; can be quite spicy, as requested; coconut sticky rice with ice cream. *Average main: $24 ✉ 7342 Granite Loop Rd., Teton Village ☎ 307/733–0022 🌐 www.tetonthai.com ⏲ Closed Sun.*

Hotels

In the winter ski season it can be cheaper to stay in Jackson, about 20 minutes away; in summer it's generally cheaper to stay at Teton Village.

Alpenhof Lodge
$$$$ | HOTEL | With more atmosphere than anywhere else in Teton Village, this Austrian-style hotel sits next to the tram in the heart of Jackson Hole Mountain Resort. **Pros:** quaint feel; great location near slopes; pet-friendly. **Cons:** some rooms are small; dated fixtures and flooring; Austrian-style interiors don't appeal to all travelers. *Rooms from: $219* *3255 W. Village Dr., Teton Village* *307/733–3242, 800/732–3244* *www.alpenhoflodge.com* *Hotel closed early Apr.–mid-May; restaurants closed mid-Oct.–Thanksgiving* *42 rooms* *Free breakfast.*

Four Seasons Resort and Residencies Jackson Hole
$$$$ | RESORT | FAMILY | World-class service, museum-quality artwork, and a lot of family entertainment set the Four Seasons apart. **Pros:** celebrity chef Michael Mina restaurant; tranquil spa; extravagant bathrooms with jetted tubs. **Cons:** pricey, even by resort town standards; expect mountain noise like ski-slope groomers; Some guests have noted a decline in service quality over the years. *Rooms from: $1750* *7680 Granite Loop Rd., Teton Village* *307/732–5000* *www.fourseasons.com* *156 rooms* *No meals.*

★ Hotel Terra Jackson Hole
$$$$ | RESORT | The opulent Hotel Terra takes green hospitality to the next level, but it's also luxe to the core, with a hip, urban feel and all the amenities the price tag suggests. **Pros:** gracious service; great dining and bar options; organic full-service spa. **Cons:** not for budget-conscious; in a crowded corner of Teton Village; a (short) walk to ski slopes. *Rooms from: $384* *3335 W. Village Dr., Grand Teton National Park* *307/739–4100* *www.hotelterrajacksonhole.com* *132 rooms* *No meals.*

★ R Lazy S Ranch
$$$$ | RESORT | FAMILY | With the spectacle of the Tetons in the background, this classic, family-friendly dude ranch at the southern border of the national park offers a bounty of activities, with horseback riding and instruction the main attraction, and a secondary emphasis on fishing in the property's private waters. **Pros:** all-inclusive, and with great food; very popular with kids (7 and older); beautiful setting. **Cons:** no TV; 20-minute drive from Jackson; week minimum stay. *Rooms from: $588* *7800 Moose-Wilson Rd., Teton Village* *307/733–2655* *www.rlazys.com* *Closed Oct.–mid-June* *14 cabins* *All-inclusive.*

Snake River Lodge & Spa
$$$$ | HOTEL | Anchored by an expansive four-level spa, Snake River combines the best elements of a genteel resort and a large lodge that feels both high-end and folksy. **Pros:** cool public spaces; vast spa menu; great mountainside location. **Cons:** labyrinthine hallways; most rooms have no real view; like many area lodges, charges a resort fee. *Rooms from: $359* *7710 Granite Loop Rd., Teton Village* *307/732–6000, 855/342–4712* *www.snakeriverlodge.com* *Closed Oct.–mid-Nov. and Apr.–mid-May* *146 rooms* *No meals.*

Performing Arts

Grand Teton Music Festival
FESTIVALS | In summer the symphony orchestra performances of the Grand Teton Music Festival are held five nights per week at Walk Festival Hall in Teton Village. A winter series holds less frequent concerts. Tickets are $35–$65 for adults, with many free events throughout the year. *3330 Cody La., Teton Village* *307/733–3050* *www.gtmf.org.*

Bear Safety

The northern Rockies are bear country—grizzlies and black bears are a presence throughout the region. Seeing one across a valley, through a pair of binoculars, is fun, but meeting one at closer range isn't. There have been few fatal encounters, but almost every summer there are incidents involving bears.

Practical Precautions

Avoid sudden encounters. Whenever possible, travel in open country, during daylight hours, and in groups. Make noise—talking or singing is preferable to carrying "bear bells"—and leave your dog at home. Most attacks occur when a bear is surprised at close quarters or feels threatened.

Stay alert. Look for signs of bears, such as fresh tracks, scat, matted vegetation, or partially consumed carcasses.

Choose your tent site carefully. Pitch the tent away from trails, streams with spawning trout, and berry patches. Avoid areas that have a rotten smell or where scavengers have gathered; these may indicate the presence of a nearby bear cache, and bears aggressively defend their food.

Keep food away from campsites. Cook meals at least 100 yards from tents, and store food and other items that give off odors (including personal products such as soap, shampoo, lotions, and even toothpaste) away from campsites. Hang food at least 10 feet high between trees where possible, or store your food in bear-resistant food containers. Avoid strong-smelling foods, and clean up after cooking and eating. Store garbage in airtight containers, or burn it and pack up the remains.

If You Encounter a Bear

Identify yourself. Talk to the bear in a firm, low voice, to identify yourself as a human. Don't yell. And don't run. Running will trigger a bear's predatory instincts, and a bear can easily outrun you. Back away slowly, and give the bear an escape route. Don't ever get between a mother and her cubs.

Bigger is better. Bears are less likely to attack a larger target. Therefore, increase your apparent size. Raise your arms above your head to appear larger, and wave them slowly, to better identify yourself as a human. With two or more people, it helps to stand side by side. In a forested area it may be appropriate to climb a tree, but remember that black bears and young grizzlies are agile tree climbers.

As a last resort, play dead. If a bear charges and makes contact with you, fall to the ground, lie flat on your stomach or curl into a ball, hands behind your neck, and remain passive. If you are wearing a pack, leave it on. Once a bear no longer feels threatened, it will usually end its attack. Wait for the bear to leave before you move. The exception to this rule is when a bear displays predatory behavior. Instead of simply charging, a bear hunting for prey will show intense interest while approaching at a walk or run, and it may circle, as if stalking you. But remember that such circumstances are exceedingly rare and most often involve black bears, which are much smaller and less aggressive than grizzlies (and can be driven off more easily).

Activities

GOLF

Jackson Hole Golf and Tennis Club

GOLF | This 18-hole course redesigned by Robert Trent Jones has views of the Teton Range and an eco-friendly and elegant clubhouse. One of Wyoming's top courses, it's very close to the national park. ✉ *5000 Spring Gulch Rd., Teton Village* ☎ *307/733–3111* 🌐 *www.jhgtc.com* 🎫 *From $65* ⛳ *18 holes, 7409 yards, par 72.*

Teton Pines Golf Club

GOLF | The 18-hole Teton Pines Golf Club lies south of the Jackson Hole Mountain Resort on Moose-Wilson Road. Former Vice President Dick Cheney owns a home here. Current green fees run $65 to $160, depending on the season and whether you are a guest at the resort. ✉ *3450 N. Clubhouse Dr., Wilson, Teton Village* ☎ *307/733–1005, 800/238–2223* 🌐 *www.tetonpines.com.*

SKIING

Few areas in North America can compete with Jackson Hole when it comes to the breadth, beauty, and variety of backcountry opportunities. For touring skiers, one of the easier areas (because of flatter routes) is along the base of the Tetons toward Jenny and Jackson lakes. Telemark skiers (or even skiers on alpine gear) can find numerous downhill routes by skiing in from Teton Pass, snow stability permitting. A guide isn't required for tours to the national-park lakes, but might be helpful for those unfamiliar with the lay of the land; trails and trail markers set in summer can become obscured by winter snows. When you are touring elsewhere, a guide familiar with the area and avalanche danger is a virtual necessity. The Tetons are big country, and the risks are commensurately large as well. There's downhill skiing as well at Jackson Mountain Resort.

The mountain has a 4,139-foot vertical drop, and there are 2,500 skiable acres (10% beginner, 40% intermediate, 50% expert). To get up the mountain, you'll find 1 tram, 1 gondola, 6 quad chairs, 2 triple chairs, 1 double chair, and 1 magic carpet.

Lift tickets average out to be $160. You can save about 10% to 20% if you buy a 5- to 15-day ticket.

Any equipment you need to ski can be rented in Jackson or in Teton Village.

BACKCOUNTRY GUIDES

Jackson Hole Mountain Guides

SKIING/SNOWBOARDING | Jackson Hole Mountain Guides leads half-day and full-day backcountry tours into Grand Teton National Park and Teton Pass for strong intermediate to advanced skiers. ✉ *1325 S. Hwy. 89, Suite 104, Jackson* ☎ *307/733–4979* 🌐 *www.jhmg.com.*

HELI-SKIING

In general, heli-skiing is best done when there has been relatively little recent snowfall. For two or three days after a storm, good powder skiing can usually be found within the ski area.

High Mountain Heli-Skiing

SKIING/SNOWBOARDING | Daily trips can be arranged through High Mountain Heli-Skiing. ✉ *Jackson Hole Mountain Resort base area, 1 W. Johnny Counts Rd, Teton Village* ☎ *307/733–3274* 🌐 *www.heliski-jackson.com.*

LESSONS AND PROGRAMS

Jackson Hole Mountain Sports School

SKIING/SNOWBOARDING | Group lessons at the Jackson Hole Mountain Sports School start at $375. There are extensive children's programs, including lessons for kids three and older, and day care is available for children starting at six months old. Nordic-skiing lessons are possible; call for pricing and availability. ✉ *Teton Village* ☎ *307/733–2292.*

Jackson Hole Ski Camps
SKIING/SNOWBOARDING | For expert skiers, the Jackson Hole Ski Camps, headed by such skiers as Tommy Moe, the 1994 Olympic gold medalist, and top snowboarders like Julie Zell and Stephen Koch, run for four or five days, teaching everything from big-mountain free-skiing to racing techniques. Rates start at $1,000 per person, not including lift tickets. ✉ *Teton Village* ☎ *307/739–2797* 🌐 *jacksonhole.com/ski-tommy-moe.*

RENTALS

Equipment can be rented at ski shops in Jackson and Teton Village.

Jackson Hole Sports
SKIING/SNOWBOARDING | Jackson Hole Sports, in the Bridger Center at the ski area, offers ski- and snowboard-rental packages starting at $41 a day. Booking online saves you 20%. ✉ *7720 Granite Loop Rd., Teton Village* ☎ *307/739–2649* 🌐 *www.jacksonhole.com/ski-and-snowboard-rentals.html.*

TRACK SKIING

Teton Pines Nordic Center. (✉ *Teton Village* ☎ *307/733–1500* 🌐 *www.tetonpinesnordiccenter.com*) is 4 miles south of the resort base along Wyoming 390. The scenic 17 km (10½ miles) of expertly groomed track is relatively flat, meandering along the terrain that's an exclusive golf course in summers. Day passes cost $17. Rentals and lessons are available.

DOWNHILL SKIING AND SNOWBOARDING

★ **Jackson Hole Mountain Resort**
SKIING/SNOWBOARDING | A place to appreciate both as a skier and as a voyeur, Jackson Hole Mountain Resort is truly one of the great skiing experiences in the United States. There are literally thousands of ways to get from top to bottom, and not all of them are hellishly steep, despite Jackson's reputation. First-rate racers such as Olympic champion skier Tommy Moe and snowboarders Julie Zell, Bryan Iguchi, and Rob Kingwill regularly train here. As Kingwill has put it, "Nothing really compares to Jackson Hole ... This place has the most consistently steep terrain. You can spend years and years here and never cross your trail."

On the resort map, 117 squiggly lines designate named trails, but this doesn't even begin to suggest the thousands of different skiable routes. The resort claims 2,500 skiable acres, a figure that seems unduly conservative. And although Jackson is best known for its advanced to extreme skiing, it is also a place where intermediates can go exploring and have the time of their lives. There are few green-coded beginner slopes, so lessons are recommended for novices to advance their skills and make the most of their time here.

⚠ **High snowfall some winters can lead to extreme avalanche danger in spite of efforts by the Ski Patrol to make the area as safe as possible.** The resort has an open-gate backcountry policy, but venturing from patrolled territory isn't recommended except for experts. Before departing from known trails and routes, check with the Ski Patrol for conditions. Ski with a friend, and always carry avalanche equipment such as a beacon, probe, and shovel. Ski passes average $160 at the ticket window, but discounts can be found online and when purchasing multiple days. ✉ *3395 Cody La., Teton Village* ☎ *307/733–2292* 🌐 *www.jacksonhole.com.*

Wilson

6 miles south of Teton Village on Teton Village Rd.; 4 miles west of Jackson on Hwy. 22.

If you want to avoid the hustle and bustle of Jackson, Wilson makes a good alternative base for exploring Grand Teton National Park or skiing at Jackson Hole Mountain Resort. This small town takes its name from Nick Wilson, one of the first homesteaders in the area, a man who spent part of his childhood living with the Shoshone people.

GETTING HERE AND AROUND

It's hard to get lost in Wilson, as 90% of it is clustered along a few blocks of Highway 22, a short drive west of Jackson. Travelers from the east will find the town right at the foot of the pass. Since summer bike traffic can be high on Highway 22, both drivers and cyclists should use caution.

Restaurants

★ Bar J Chuckwagon

$$$$ | BARBECUE | FAMILY | This may be the best value in Jackson Hole: you get a complete ranch-style meal plus a rollicking Western show. Served on a tin plate, the food is barbecue beef, chicken, pork ribs, or rib-eye steak with potatoes, beans, biscuits, applesauce, and spice cake, along with lemonade or coffee. **Known for:** some of the best Western music and grub around; reservations recommended; local staple for decades. *Average main: $31 4200 W. Bar J Chuckwagon Off Moose-Wilson Rd., 1 mile north of Hwy. 22 307/733–3370 www.barjchuckwagon.com Closed Oct.–late May.*

★ Nora's Fish Creek Inn

$ | AMERICAN | Nora's is one of those inimitable Western places that have earned their keep as local treasures among their many loyal customers. Look for the giant trout on the roof outside. **Known for:** familiar breakfast items; famous banana bread French toast; reasonable prices. *Average main: $10 5600 Hwy. 22 6 miles outside Jackson at base of pass 307/733–8288 www.norasfishcreekinn.com Closed Nov. and Apr. No lunch weekends.*

Streetfood at the Stagecoach

$$ | ECLECTIC | A happy option for fans of international food and good beer, this festive miniature food hall at Wilson's famously rollicking Stagecoach bar offers well-prepared Mexican, Asian, and American comfort foods. There's a large deck and an expansive lawn with picnic tables for alfresco dining during the warmer months, or you can dine in the lively bar. **Known for:** huge outdoor dining area; good selection of craft beers; Mexican street-food-style tacos. *Average main: $12 5755 Hwy. 22 307/200–6633 www.streetfoodjh.com.*

Hotels

★ Bentwood Inn

$$$$ | B&B/INN | This log lodge–style bed-and-breakfast creates a warm and welcoming invitation for a romantic retreat or family getaway. **Pros:** commitment to green practices and local, organic food sources; every room has a fireplace and porch/patio; high-end amenities. **Cons:** no pool or Jacuzzi; must have a car as it's 5 miles from Jackson and 5 miles from Teton Village; with only five rooms it is hard to get a room in peak season. *Rooms from: $489 4250 Raven Haven Rd. 307/739–1411 www.bentwoodinn.com 5 rooms Free breakfast.*

Jackson Hole Hideout

$$$ | B&B/INN | On a steep hillside and surrounded by trees, this lodgepole-pine B&B is a real retreat. **Pros:** scenic locale; good breakfast; knowledgeable hosts. **Cons:** small climb to the inn; must drive to town; no kids under five. *Rooms from: $280 6175 Heck of a Hill Rd. 307/733–3233 www.jacksonholehideout.com 6 rooms Free breakfast.*

★ The Wildflower Lodge At Jackson Hole

$$$$ | B&B/INN | You'll enjoy gourmet breakfasts and an afternoon beverage and snack at this luxurious country inn that's surrounded by 3 acres of aspen and pine trees frequented by moose, deer, and other wildlife. **Pros:** excellent views; frequent wildlife sightings;

convenient to Teton Village and southwest side of Grand Teton National Park. **Cons:** books up far in advance; not pet-friendly; 12 miles from Jackson. *Rooms from: $360* *3725 Shooting Star La., Jackson* *307/222–4400* *www.jhwildflowerlodge.com* *6 rooms* *Free breakfast.*

Nightlife

Stagecoach Bar

BARS/PUBS | The Stagecoach Bar fills to bursting when local bands play. Disco Night is on Thursday and attracts a packed house of swing dancers. "The Coach" is a good place to enjoy a drink and conversation at other times, and there's an adjacent Mexican café and kitchen where you can grab a quick bite. *5575 W. Hwy. 22* *307/733–4407* *stagecoachbar.net.*

Shopping

Hungry Jack's General Store

CONVENIENCE/GENERAL STORES | This old-fashioned general store is a local institution with a little bit of everything—with boots, bananas and boxers all in the same aisle, and a good selection of local beer and other products. *5655 W. Hwy. 22* *307/733–3561* *www.hungryjackswilson.com.*

Alta

27 miles northwest of Wilson via Hwy. 22 to Hwy. 33 (in Idaho) to Alta cutoff (back to Wyoming).

Alta is the site of the Grand Targhee Ski and Summer Resort, famed for its deep powder and family atmosphere. The slopes never feel crowded, but to experience complete solitude, try a day of Sno-Cat skiing in untracked powder.

GETTING HERE AND AROUND

The Targhee Express. (*307/733–9754, 800/443–6133* *www.jacksonholealltrans.com*) will bring you from Jackson to Alta by appointment for $46. By car, head 20 miles west from Jackson on Highway 22, over the Teton Pass and onto Idaho's Highway 33. From Victor, Idaho, it's another 8 miles north to Ski Hill Road in Driggs; follow that 5 miles west to Alta and Grand Targhee, then park and navigate the tiny ski town's few streets on foot.

Hotels

Grand Targhee Ski and Summer Resort

$$$ | **RESORT** | **FAMILY** | Lodging at this hidden gem ski resort on the west side of the Tetons has a handsome, natural-wood look and the atmosphere of an alpine village. **Pros:** a cozy and laid-back alternative to the glitz of Jackson Hole; excellent lift access; heated outdoor pool and hot tub. **Cons:** Wi-Fi can be spotty; fewer après options than in Jackson Hole; dining options are limited. *Rooms from: $175* *3300 E. Ski Hill Rd.* *307/353–2300* *www.grandtarghee.com* *128 rooms* *Free breakfast.*

Activities

Grand Targhee Ski and Summer Resort

SKIING/SNOWBOARDING | **FAMILY** | An average of 500 inches of powdery "white gold" attracts skiers to Grand Targhee Ski and Summer Resort, with 3,000 acres, 1,000 of which are dedicated to powder Sno-Cat skiing and 15 km (9 miles) to cross-country trails. Boarders have two trick terrain parks and lots of freestyle areas with rails and mailboxes to tear it up. There are four lifts and one rope tow, and the vertical drop is 2,419 feet. Lift tickets are about $100 per day; Nordic trail permits are $15. Classes by expert instructors are also available. Lifts operate 9–4 daily. *3300 E. Ski Hill Rd.* *307/353–2300* *www.grandtarghee.com.*

Grand Targhee, on the west side of the Tetons, is the less-visited hidden gem in Wyoming's premier ski country.

Pinedale

77 miles southeast of Jackson on Hwy. 191.

A southern gateway to Jackson Hole and the Wind River Range, Pinedale has much to offer on its own, for the spirit of the mountain man lives on here. Fur trappers found the icy streams of the Green River watershed to be among the best places to capture beaver. In the mid-1800s they gathered on the river near what is now Pinedale for seven annual rendezvous. Now the Museum of the Mountain Man preserves their heritage, and modern-day buckskinners continue to meet in the area each summer.

GETTING HERE AND AROUND

U.S. 191 reaches Pinedale from Jackson to the northwest and Farson and the South Pass area to the south. In town, the highway becomes the main thoroughfare of Pine Street. You can park on the street for free and do downtown on foot, but you'll need wheels to head northwest of town on Fremont Road, a paved route accessing Half Moon Lake, Fremont Lake, and the breathtaking Skyline Drive scenic route through the Winds.

VISITOR INFORMATION

CONTACTS Pinedale Chamber of Commerce. ✉ *19 E. Pine S* ☎ *307/367–2242* 🌐 *www.sublettechamber.com.*

Sights

To the east are millions of acres of Bridger-Teton National Forest, much of it off-limits to all but foot and horse traffic. The peaks reach higher than 13,000 feet, and the area is liberally sprinkled with more than a thousand high-mountain lakes where fishing is generally excellent.

Bridger-Teton National Forest, Pinedale Ranger District

INFO CENTER | Contact the Bridger-Teton National Forest, Pinedale Ranger District for more information. Although outdoor activities still beckon in the forest, an oil and gas boom in the area keeps motel

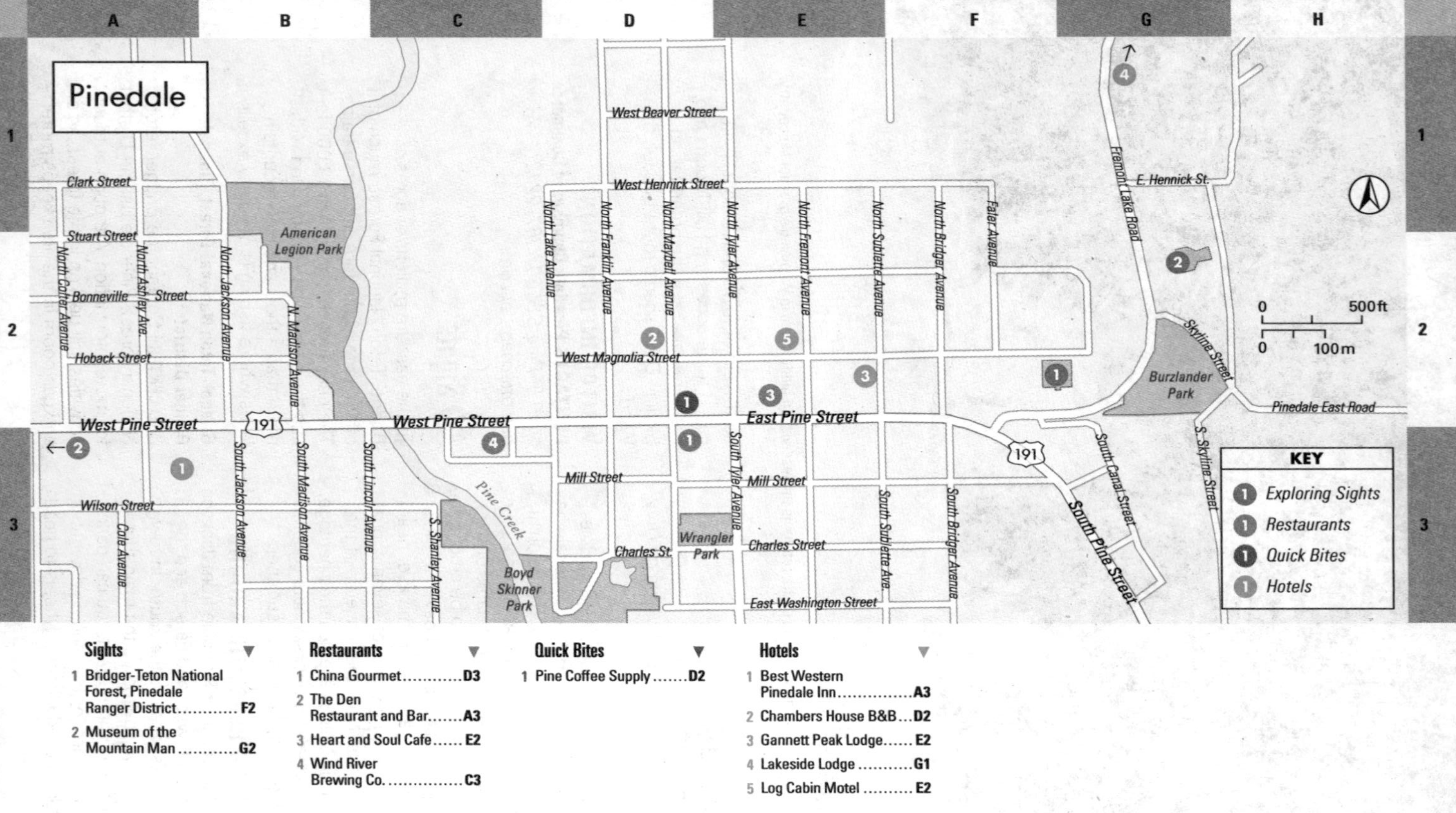

Sights

1 Bridger-Teton National Forest, Pinedale Ranger District............ F2
2 Museum of the Mountain Man G2

Restaurants

1 China Gourmet............D3
2 The Den Restaurant and Bar.......A3
3 Heart and Soul Cafe...... E2
4 Wind River Brewing Co. C3

Quick Bites

1 Pine Coffee Supply D2

Hotels

1 Best Western Pinedale Inn...............A3
2 Chambers House B&B...D2
3 Gannett Peak Lodge...... E2
4 Lakeside Lodge G1
5 Log Cabin Motel E2

rooms full year-round and restaurants often busy. ✉ *29 E. Fremont Lake Rd.* ☎ *307/367–4326* 🌐 *www.fs.fed.us.*

Museum of the Mountain Man

MUSEUM | FAMILY | Fur trappers were the first non-Native Americans to live in these parts year-round, arriving in the early 19th century when the area was the center of the Rocky Mountain fur trade. The museum celebrates that trapper history, with guns, traps, clothing, and beaver pelts from that time period. In the early summer the museum features living-history demonstrations, children's events, and lectures. In July it hosts reenactment of the Green River Rendezvous, when mountain men, Native Americans, and others got together to barter and socialize. ✉ *700 E. Hennick St.* ☎ *307/367–4101* 🌐 *www.museumofthemountainman.com* 🎟 *$10* ⏲ *Closed Nov.–May (except by advance appointment).*

Restaurants

China Gourmet

$$ | CHINESE | FAMILY | Serving full-fare, authentic Cantonese-style Chinese food, this might be the only joint in America where you'll find a Budweiser sign over the door, Asian decor on the walls, large-screen TVs playing all the big games, and ketchup on a table beside a bowl of egg-drop soup. It's good for families with picky eaters, as the menu carries more than 100 items—from lo mein and mu shu shrimp to hamburgers, pork chops, and fried chicken. **Known for:** something for everyone; fast service; great value for the money. 💲 *Average main: $13* ✉ *44 W. Pine St.* ☎ *307/367–4788* ⏲ *Closed Sun.*

The Den Restaurant and Bar

$$$ | STEAKHOUSE | FAMILY | A favorite of locals, the Den serves up traditional steak-house favorites and more. All beef is choice grade and has a minimum 28 days of dry aging before being served. **Known for:** a traditional German schnitzel complete with spaetzle; jalapeño poppers wrapped in bacon and dipped in homemade jalapeño huckleberry jam; burgers made with a house blend of brisket and chuck roast. 💲 *Average main: $21* ✉ *Daniel Junction, 191 11072 U.S.-191* ☎ *307/859–8469* 🌐 *www.thedaniel-junction.com.*

Heart and Soul Cafe

$ | AMERICAN | FAMILY | This fun, diner-inspired café with checkered floors and colorful booths serves up a hearty country-style breakfast all day and an assortment of burgers, sandwiches, and salads for lunch. There's also a full espresso bar and ice-cream selections. **Known for:** incredible pancakes; outdoor patio; homemade pizzas on Thursday, Friday, and Saturday night. 💲 *Average main: $10* ✉ *27 E. Pine St.* ☎ *307/367–4415.*

Wind River Brewing Co.

$$ | AMERICAN | FAMILY | This microbrewery and grill serves award-winning grog and high-quality pub grub, from steaks and sandwiches to daily specials. **Known for:** good burgers and house-made sides; rotating seasonal brews made from mountain waters; great patio with views of town and the mountains. 💲 *Average main: $14* ✉ *402 W. Pine St.* ☎ *307/367–2337* 🌐 *www.windriverbrewingco.com.*

Coffee and Quick Bites

★ **Pine Coffee Supply**

$ | CAFÉ | Wyoming's best coffeehouse resides in Pinedale but it looks like it belongs in Austin, Texas. That's because the owner, Cody Hamilton, moved from Wyoming to Austin for nine years before taking the inspiration back to Pinedale to open his dream shop. **Known for:** ethically sourced coffee; direct trade chocolate bars from Colombia; beautifully branded mugs and coffee-making tools for sale. 💲 *Average main: $5* ✉ *47 W. Pine St.* ☎ *307/367–4343* 🌐 *www.pinecoffeesupply.com* ⏲ *Closed Sun.*

North of Pinedale, Island Lake, in the vast Bridger-Teton National Forest, is reachable after a 10-mile hike and a popular campsite.

Hotels

Best Western Pinedale Inn
$$ | **HOTEL** | On the north side of town, this motel is within five blocks of downtown shopping and restaurants. **Pros:** swimming pool; continental breakfast included; good location. **Cons:** check cancellation policy (reportedly locked by computer); prices not always best around; no hotel bar. $ *Rooms from: $81* ✉ *864 W. Pine St.* ☎ *307/367–6869, 800/780–7834 reservations* ⊕ *www.bestwestern.com* *84 rooms* *Free breakfast.*

Chambers House B&B
$$$ | **B&B/INN** | Huge pine trees surround this 1933 log home filled with the owner's family antiques. **Pros:** charming old house; solid breakfast; satellite TV and Wi-Fi throughout. **Cons:** limited reading materials and games; two rooms share one bath; a little spendier compared to other options in town. $ *Rooms from: $165* ✉ *111 W. Magnolia St.* ☎ *307/367–2168* ⊕ *www.chambershouse.com* *7 rooms* *Free breakfast.*

Gannet Peak Lodge
$$ | **HOTEL** | **FAMILY** | Originally used as barracks for the Civilian Conservation Corps when they were building South Pass, the cabins at Gannet Peak Lodge are now a haven for budget-minded travelers. **Pros:** friendly, helpful staff; walking distance from downtown shops and dining options; modern touches and vibrant rooms. **Cons:** no air-conditioning; no breakfast included; more rooms than parking (street parking available). $ *Rooms from: $95* ✉ *46 N. Sublette Ave.* ☎ *307/231–5755* ⊕ *gannettpeaklodge.com* *Closed Nov.–Apr.* *19 rooms* *No meals.*

Lakeside Lodge
$$ | **RESORT** | Modern cabins at this year-round lakeside resort have gas fireplaces, satellite TV and Wi-Fi, comfortable beds, full baths, and a kitchen or kitchenette, as well as access to a full range of

The Allures of the Wind River Range

History: From ancient Native American settlements to early pioneer trails, towns, and red rock canyons and mountains ... nearly anywhere you look out here, man and nature have left their indelible marks.

Space: The drive westward and from the southeast never fails to enchant newcomers with one of America's least-populated frontiers.

Sights: As you approach Dubois from the flatlands of Riverton and enter the ascending Wind River Range, keep an eye peeled for mule deer and robust wildlife.

Sounds: Park the car at any scenic overlook, or camp out at the right time of year, and you'll understand why "The Wind River" area resounds with timeless music.

Colors: Yellowed, tawny prairies in late summer and early fall; ochre-stained geology around Dubois; and lazy sunsets that paint the skies indigo and red cast a spell on unhurried visitors.

activities and a good restaurant in the main lodge building. **Pros:** great views; on-site restaurant is one of the best in town; access to mountain and lake just steps away. **Cons:** far from dining and shops in Pinedale; no a/c; sells out quickly in summer. *Rooms from:* *99 Forest Service Rd.* *10 miles northeast of Pinedale; take Fremont Lake Rd. north out of Pinedale; turnoff for Half Moon Lake is about 8 miles from town along narrow, winding gravel road* *307/367–2221* *www.lakesidelodge.com* *18 cabins* *No meals.*

★ Log Cabin Motel

$$ | **HOTEL** | **FAMILY** | Pinedale's first lodging opened in 1929 as seven cabins and a washhouse; a major remodel was completed in 2021 to bring it up to speed. **Pros:** hands-on owners who treat guests like family; completely green operation from cleaning products to the bedding; full kitchen in every cabin. **Cons:** no pool or hot tub; no air-conditioning; small bathrooms. *Rooms from: $119* *49 E. Magnolia St.* *307/367–4579* *www.thelogcabinmotel.com* *13 cabins* *No meals.*

Shopping

Cowboy Shop

CLOTHING | From silk scarves to big shiny buckles, if cowboys wear it, here's the place to get it. Western-style clothing includes hats, boots, and leather goods. This is also a good spot for housewares and souvenirs. *129 W. Pine St.* *307/367–4300* *www.cowboyshop.com* *Closed Sun.*

Activities

Bridger-Teton National Forest, Pinedale Ranger District

CAMPING—SPORTS-OUTDOORS | Encompassing parts of the Wind River Range, the Bridger-Teton National Forest, Pinedale Ranger District holds hundreds of thousands of acres to explore. The fishing is good in the numerous mountain lakes, and you can also hike, horseback ride, snowmobile, camp, and picnic here. *Forest office, 29 E. Fremont Lake Rd.* *307/367–4326* *www.fs.fed.us.*

Atlantic City

81 miles southeast of Pinedale via U.S. 191 to Farson, then Hwy. 28.

As you drive south of Pinedale along U.S. 191, the mountains of the Wind River Range seem to fade to a low point. This is the area through which some 500,000 emigrants traveled over the Oregon, Mormon, and California trails between 1843 and 1870. A near ghost town amid the real ghost towns of Miner's Delight and South Pass City, this bygone gold rush–era settlement still has a few residents, a couple of tourist-oriented businesses, dirt streets, late-19th-century buildings, and a whole lot of character. Formed in 1868 when gold rushers flocked to the area seeking their fortunes and known for its red-light district, Atlantic City was where Wyoming Territory's first brewery opened in the late 1860s. Once the gold boom went bust less than a decade later, however, residents deserted the town. Atlantic City had a few more smaller rushes over the years, but none ever matched its early days.

GETTING HERE AND AROUND

From Highway 28 look for green sign "Atlantic City" and take wide dirt road for about 4 miles. More than likely, you'll need four-wheel drive in snow season. Both Atlantic City and South Pass City are literally one-road towns, so getting around is a snap. Park in front of one of the local businesses, and then hit the town on foot.

Sights

★ South Pass City State Historic Site

HISTORIC SITE | FAMILY | South Pass City, 2 miles west of Atlantic City, was established in 1867 after gold was discovered in a creek called Sweetwater in 1842. In its heyday, by various accounts, before the gold thinned out in the 1870s, there were between 1,500 and 4,000 residents. After Sioux and Cheyenne raids, over settlers hunting indigenous game herds and miners poisoning their drinking water, the town still boomed until going bust and dropping to double digits by 1872. Its well-preserved remains are now the South Pass City State Historic Site. You can tour many of the original surviving buildings that have been restored, and you can even try your hand at gold panning. With artifacts and photographs of the town at its peak, the small museum here gives an overview of the South Pass gold district.

South Pass City has another claim to fame. Julia Bright and Esther Hobart Morris are two of the women from the community who firmly believed that women should have the right to vote. It is suspected that they encouraged Bright's husband, Representative William Bright, to introduce a bill for women's suffrage in the Wyoming Territorial Legislature. He did so, the bill was ratified, and South Pass went down in history as the birthplace of women's suffrage in Wyoming. In 1870 Morris became the first female justice of the peace in the nation, serving South Pass City. ✉ *125 S. Pass Main St., South Pass City* ✣ *South Pass City Rd., off Hwy. 28* ☎ *307/332–3684* 🌐 *www.southpasscity.com* 🎫 *$5* ⏲ *Closed Oct.–mid-May.*

Restaurants

Atlantic City Mercantile

$$$ | AMERICAN | The town's oldest saloon, known as the "Merc," serves refreshments in a room that has seen its share of gold miners, perhaps an outlaw or two, and certainly some ruffians. When you step through the doors of this 1893 building with tin ceilings, a massive back bar, and an assortment of mismatched oak tables and chairs, you may feel as though you've walked directly into an episode of *Gunsmoke*. At times a honky-tonk piano player is on hand. **Known for:** an atmosphere to make you feel right at home; fast and friendly service; simple, but done-right menu. *Average main: $24* *100 E. Main St.* *307/332–5143.*

Miner's Grub Stake

$$$ | **AMERICAN** | Drop in for pancakes, French toast, omelets, and coffee for breakfast; or a buffalo burger, tuna salad, or Reuben sandwich for lunch. You can also warm your bones with beef vegetable soup, chili, and hot cider before stocking up on paper goods, groceries, sunscreen, soft drinks, two-cycle motor oil, pet food, and other supplies. **Known for:** a Western-movie feel; the best (and some of the only) food for miles; fresh and fast food to get you back on the road after your visit. *Average main: $24* *150 W. Main St.* *307/332–0915* *minersgrubstakedredge.com* *Closed Nov. and Mon.*

Hotels

Miner's Delight Inn & B&B

$$$ | **B&B/INN** | Live like the prospectors did in the olden days and stay in one of the authentic, rustic cabins, each with a small washstand (with a bowl and a pitcher of water), and it's a short walk to the main house's bathroom and shower, where the rooms have baths. **Pros:** true West ghost town charm; gracious hosts; late-night saloon and fireplace. **Cons:** remote location; no Internet/TV; some rooms share bath. *Rooms from: $155* *290 Atlantic City Rd.* *307/332–0248* *www.minersdelightinn.com* *8 rooms* *Free breakfast.*

Shopping

Atlantic City Mercantile

LOCAL SPECIALTIES | **FAMILY** | South Pass Mercantile sells Wyoming-made products ranging from clothing to the largest selection of books in the area by regional authors, plus gold mining and prospecting supplies. *100 Main St.* *307/332–5143.*

Lander

About 31 miles northeast of Atlantic City via Hwy. 28/U.S. 287.

At the southwestern edge of the Wind River Indian Reservation and in the heart of country held dear by Chief Washakie (circa 1804–1900), one of the greatest chiefs of the Shoshone tribe, and his people, Lander has always had a strong tie to the Native American community. East of the Wind River Range, Lander makes a good base for pursuing mountain sports and activities ranging from backcountry hiking to horse-packing trips.

GETTING HERE AND AROUND

Lander stretches out along U.S. 287 (Main Street, in town) with a few blocks of pedestrian-friendly downtown and a handful of other restaurants, shops, and attractions best reached by car on the north edge of the city. The **Wind River Transportation Authority** (*800/439–7118* *www.wrtabuslines.com*) runs weekday buses between and around Lander, Riverton, and Fort Washakie for a $1 fare. You can also call about shuttles from Jackson to Lander, which run on a somewhat arbitrary schedule throughout the year. Coming from Jackson or Pinedale involves going over South Pass, which may have snow into early summer.

VISITOR INFORMATION

CONTACTS Lander Chamber of Commerce. *160 N. 1st St.* *307/332–3892, 307/332–3893* *www.landerchamber.org.*

Sights

Sinks Canyon State Park

NATIONAL/STATE PARK | At Sinks Canyon State Park, the Popo Agie (pronounced "puh *po* sha," meaning "Tall Grass River" to the Crow Indians) flows into a limestone cavern. The crashing water "sinks" into fissures only to resurface ½ mile downstream in the "rise," where it reemerges and huge fish (mainly rainbow and brown trout) swim in the calm pool. Wildflowers, Rocky Mountain bighorn sheep, black bears, golden eagles, moose, mule deer, marmots, and other wildlife wander the grounds. The park is ideal for hiking, camping, and picnicking. No fishing is allowed, but visitors can toss fish food to the trout from the observation deck. ⊠ *3079 Sinks Canyon Rd.* ✣ *6 miles south of Lander on Hwy. 131* ☎ *307/332–3077* ⊕ *www.sinkscanyonstatepark.org.*

Restaurants

★ Cowfish

$$$ | **ECLECTIC** | At this funky restaurant you can dine on a cozy, outdoor patio and select from sandwiches and haute cuisine from both land and water. For starters try pot stickers and seared ahi tuna. **Known for:** incredible cocktails made with Wyoming-distilled spirits; innovative menu; house-made pasta dishes. [$] *Average main: $25* ⊠ *148 Main St.* ☎ *307/332–8227* ⊕ *www.cowfishlander.com.*

Gannett Grill

$ | **AMERICAN** | **FAMILY** | This crowded, noisy place serves large sandwiches, never-frozen half-pound hamburgers, and hand-tossed New York–style pizzas. In spring and summer you can sit on the garden deck while the kids play in the yard. **Known for:** a favorite of cowboys and climbers alike; affordable, hearty meals; cold beer from Lander Brewing. [$] *Average main: $10* ⊠ *126 Main St.* ☎ *307/332–8228* ⊕ *www.landerbar.com.*

The Middle Fork

$$ | **AMERICAN** | **FAMILY** | With almost everything locally sourced, from the food ingredients to the coffee, the Middle Fork serves up breakfast classics and lunch sandwiches with style. This trendy café is located in the historic 1918 Coolidge building and has a great selection of local beers, mimosas, and a Bloody Mary to start your morning right. **Known for:** all coffee from Speed Goat Roasting; made-to-order beignets; great vegetarian options. [$] *Average main: $11* ⊠ *351 Main St.* ☎ *307/335–5035* ⊕ *www.themiddleforklander.com* ⊙ *No dinner.*

Mulino Italian Bistro

$$$ | **ITALIAN** | Opened in 2019, Mulino aimed to fill a need for casual fine dining in Lander. With an extensive menu of fresh salads, authentic Italian food, house-made pasta, and a creative seasonal menu, it is the ultimate local date-night spot. **Known for:** 35 wines from around the world; all pasta made in-house; specialty cocktails made with Wyoming spirits. [$] *Average main: $20* ⊠ *129 Main St.* ☎ *307/438–4016* ⊕ *mulinolander.com* ⊙ *Closed Sun. and Mon. No lunch.*

★ Svilars' Bar & Dining Room

$$$ | **STEAKHOUSE** | This small, dark, family-owned restaurant with vinyl booths has what many locals say are the best steaks in all of Wyoming. A meal here usually begins with *sarma* (cabbage rolls) and other appetizers. **Known for:** some of the best steaks in Wyoming; generous portions; Wyoming hospitality. [$] *Average main: $25* ⊠ *173 S. Main St., Hudson* ✣ *10 miles east of Lander* ☎ *307/332–4516* ⊙ *Closed Sun. No lunch.*

Coffee and Quick Bites

★ Lander Bake Shop

$ | **BAKERY** | A local institution, this bakery is the perfect place to grab a cup of coffee and quick breakfast to go or hang out for hours sampling all the local delicacies. Sandwiches, soups, scratch-made bagels, muffins, cupcakes, cinnamon rolls, and so much more will keep you coming back every morning of your stay in Lander. **Known for:** Gertie cake, an incredible coffee cake passed down from Grandma Gertrude; rotating menu of sandwiches and homemade soups; full espresso bar made with Jackson Hole Roasters Coffee. *Average main: $8* *259 Main St.* *307/438–4305* *www.landerbakeshop.com* *No dinner.*

Hotels

The Inn at Lander

$$ | **HOTEL** | This two-story Travelodge by Wyndham motel sits on a hill overlooking Lander and is within walking distance of restaurants and discount-store shopping. **Pros:** good-size, clean rooms; close to downtown; bar/café. **Cons:** close to highway; can get crowded during conferences; no indoor pool. *Rooms from: $102* *260 Grandview Dr.* *At U.S. 287/789* *307/332–2847* *www.innatlander.com* *100 rooms* *Free breakfast.*

★ The Mill House

$$ | **HOTEL** | **FAMILY** | The Lander flour mill was built in 1888 and remained in operation in 1950, becoming a local institution and one of the first buildings you see upon entering the town. **Pros:** steps away from incredible dining and shopping options; common space with full kitchen and dining room; well laid-out rooms with incredible touches. **Cons:** no breakfast included; no pool or hot tub; with only four suites, it is hard to get a room in peak season. *Rooms from: $130* *125 Main St.* *307/349–4765* *millhouselander.com* *4 suites* *No meals.*

Nightlife

Lander Bar & Grill

MUSIC CLUBS | On weekends the Lander Bar & Grill gets crowded with people who come to dance and listen to live country bands. *126 Main St.* *307/332–7009* *www.landerbar.com.*

Performing Arts

Native American Cultural Program

ARTS CENTERS | **FAMILY** | June through August the Native American Cultural Program has dance exhibitions in nearby Riverton City Park most Thursday evenings. *Lander* *307/856–4801.*

Yellow Calf Memorial Powwow

CULTURAL FESTIVALS | Native American traditional dancing is part of the Yellow Calf Memorial Powwow, usually held in early June in Ethete to honor Chief Yellow Calf, the last chief of the Arapaho tribe, 16 miles north of Lander on the Wind River Indian Reservation. For information on area cultural events, such as the Shoshone tribe's Chokecherry Festival in Lander's City Park (3rd and Fremont streets) in late August, call 307/332–5542. You can also find a calendar of Wind River cultural activities under the "Events" tab on the website. *Blue Sky Hall, 506 Ethete Rd* *307/332–6120* *www.windriver.org.*

Activities

National Outdoor Leadership School

CAMPING—SPORTS-OUTDOORS | For more than 35 years, adventurers and students have been exploring the remote Wind River Range to learn all aspects of mountaineering—from low-impact camping and horse packing to rock climbing and fly-fishing—by taking a course from the **National Outdoor Leadership School**. *284 Lincoln St.* *800/710–6657* *www.nols.edu.*

CAMPING

Sleeping Bear RV Park. Next to a golf course, this campground and RV park has lots of grass and shade trees. You can enjoy various activities here, including basketball, horseshoes, volleyball, and a couple of old-school arcade games. There's often evening entertainment in the form of campfires and storytelling. ✉ *715 E. Main St., Lander* ☎ *307/332–5159* 🌐 *www.sleepingbearrvpark.com* ⛺ *50 sites (30 with full hookups).*

FISHING

Shoshone and Arapaho Tribes

FISHING | There's great fishing on the Wind River Indian Reservation, but you must first obtain a tribal license; contact **Shoshone and Arapaho Tribes** for more information. ✉ *Fish and Game Dept., 1 Wood Ave., Fort Washakie* ☎ *307/332–7207* 🌐 *www.windriverfishandgame.com.*

Sweetwater Fishing Expeditions

FISHING | At **Sweetwater Fishing Expeditions**, George Hunker, a former Orvis guide of the year, and his crew lead small guided horseback and backpacking camping trips into the Wind River Mountains as well as day trips along smaller streams. ✉ *2939 Sinks Canyon Rd.* ☎ *307/332–3986* 🌐 *www.sweetwaterfishing.com.*

HORSEBACK RIDING

Allen's Diamond Four Ranch

FISHING | **FAMILY** | **Allen's Diamond Four Ranch**, the highest-altitude dude ranch in Wyoming, arranges mountain horse-pack trips, big-game hunts, and guided fishing and other horseback excursions. Some trips originate at the ranch, where you stay in cabins and take day rides; others are overnight backcountry adventures. Children must be seven or eight years old to go on extended pack trips. Also available are drop-camp services. No pets are allowed. Call or check the website for directions. ✉ *Lander* ✣ *Off U.S. 287, 35 miles northwest of Lander* ☎ *307/332–2995* 🌐 *www.diamond4ranch.com.*

Dubois

86 miles east of Jackson via U.S. 26, U.S. 287, and U.S. 89/191.

The mountains around Dubois attracted explorers as early as 1811, when members of the Wilson Price Hunt party crossed through the region en route to Fort Astoria in Oregon. These high peaks still attract folks who like to hike, climb, ride horses, camp, and experience wilderness. The largest concentration of free-ranging bighorn sheep in the country—more than 1,400—lives here, roaming the high country in summer and wintering just above town on Whiskey Mountain.

South and east of Grand Teton and Yellowstone, Dubois is the least well-known of the gateway communities to the parks, but this town of 1,000 provides all the services a visitor in Jackson or Cody might need. You can still get a room during the peak summer season without making a reservation months in advance, although it's a good idea to call a week or so before you arrive.

GETTING HERE AND AROUND

Leave Grand Teton National Park headed east on Highway 26/287 to reach Dubois, heading over the 9,658-foot Togwotee Pass. The drive can be a real bear in the winter, when Togwotee sees as much as an astounding 25 feet of snow. The highway becomes Ramshorn Avenue in Dubois, the town's main drag, and then continues 75 miles southeast to Lander. A lot of Dubois's best lodging is on dude ranches way outside of town, but you can walk anywhere with ease inside the city limits.

VISITOR INFORMATION

CONTACTS Dubois Chamber of Commerce. ✉ *20 Stalnaker St.* ☎ *307/455–2556* 🌐 *www.duboiswyomingchamber.org.*

Sights

Brooks Lake Recreation Area

BODY OF WATER | About 20 miles west of Dubois, easy to moderate hiking trails lead around Brooks Lake, across alpine meadows, and through pine forest to high mountain points with expansive views of Brooks Lake Mountain and the Pinnacles. You can picnic or (in summer) hard-side camp here, and boat, fish, or swim on the lake. *Dubois + 20 miles west of Dubois on U.S. 26/287, then 7 miles northeast on gravel road 307/527–6241 fs.usda.gov Free; camping $10 per night.*

Dubois Rodeo

SPORTS—SIGHT | FAMILY | Every summer Friday night at 8, cowboys at the Dubois Rodeo kick up a ruckus in the downtown Clarence Allison Memorial Arena, one of the West's best rodeos. *Clarence Allison Memorial Arena , 5639 US-26 rodeosusa.com/rodeos/dubois-friday-night-rodeos/ $10.*

National Bighorn Sheep Center

NATURE PRESERVE | FAMILY | The local variety is known as the Rocky Mountain bighorn, but you can learn about all kinds of bighorn sheep at this nonprofit conservation center and wildlife museum about an hour east of Grand Teton National Park. Expect dioramas with full-scale taxidermy mounts that recreate bighorn habitat, as well as interactive exhibits about wildlife management and special adaptations of wild sheep. Reserve ahead for winter wildlife-viewing tours ($100) to Whiskey Mountain. *10 Bighorn La. 307/455–3429 www.bighorn.org $6 Closed Apr. and May and Sun. and Mon. in late Dec.–Mar.*

★ National Museum of Military Vehicless

MUSEUM | FAMILY | The world's largest private collection of military vehicles is housed in this 140,000-square-foot museum, which opened in August 2020 with more than 400 vehicles from 1897 to the present, including every vehicle type used in WWII (including tanks). Along with the vehicles, the museum also houses more than 200 historically significant firearms, including the musket that fired the "shot heard around the world" during the battle at Bunker Hill. *6419 U.S. 29 307/455–3802 www.nmmv.org $15 Closed Mon. and Tues.*

Wind River Historical Center

MUSEUM | FAMILY | Displays here focus on Wind River tie hacks (workers who cut ties for railroads), local geology, and the archaeology of the Mountain Shoshone. Outbuildings include the town's first schoolhouse, a saddle shop, a homestead house, and a bunkhouse. The center periodically offers tours in summer to see the nearby petroglyphs. Call at least a week ahead to set up a trip. *909 W. Ramshorn St. 307/856–0706 fremontcountymuseums.com Free; petroglyph tours from $50 Closed Sun.*

Restaurants

Cowboy Café

$$ | AMERICAN | Among the homemade, blue-ribbon dishes served at this small restaurant in downtown Dubois are sandwiches, steaks, buffalo burgers, chicken, pork, baby back ribs, and fish. For dessert the peach caramel crisp and chocolate bourbon pecan pie are not soon forgotten. **Known for:** buffalo or elk omelets to get a taste of the west; 12-hour slow-cooked baby back ribs; great variety of beers. *Average main: $14 115 E. Ramshorn Ave. 307/455–2595 www.cowboycafewyo.com.*

★ The Lone Buffalo Steakhouse

$$$ | STEAKHOUSE | More than a traditional steak house, The Lone Buffalo offers diners a treat for the palate with fresh fish, delectable appetizers, house-made pasta dishes, and, of course, perfectly cooked steaks. Not feeling like splurging?

Known for: rotating seafood specials based on what is fresh; 28-oz. bone-in buffalo rib eye for two (or one if you're extra hungry); perfect French onion soup. *Average main: $22 ✉ 120 E. Rams Horn ☎ 307/455–4222 ⏲ Closed Mon. No lunch.*

Hotels

★ Brooks Lake Lodge

$$$$ | **RESORT** | Guest ranch in the summer, ski and snowmobile hub by winter, historic mountain lodge on Brooks Lake combines great scenery with service and amenities, including all meals, which are served in the lodge dining room. **Pros:** warm, hospitable staff; diverse menu; year-round activities. **Cons:** no TV/phone; accessible only by snowmobile or snowcoach in winter; isolated location. *Rooms from: $1200 ✉ 458 Brooks Lake Rd. ✥ 23 miles west of Dubois ☎ 866/213–4022 🌐 www.brookslake.com 15 rooms All-inclusive.*

Longhorn RV & Motel

$$ | **HOTEL** | Remodeled in 2007, this family-owned lodging has cabins and a small camping area/RV park in a cottonwood grove. **Pros:** good shade and trees; long pull-throughs; beautiful views. **Cons:** a drive from town; Wi-Fi signal varies; some guests complained of thin walls. *Rooms from: $110 ✉ 5810 U.S. 26 ☎ 307/455–2337 🌐 www.thelonghorn-ranch.com 24 rooms No meals.*

Shopping

★ Absaroka Western Designs-Tannery

HOUSEHOLD ITEMS/FURNITURE | From leather couches to handmade lamps, painted hides, and lodgepole-pine and aspen furniture, you can furnish your home with the Western-style items sold at Absaroka Western Designs-Tannery. *✉ 1414 Warm Springs Dr. ☎ 307/455–2440.*

Activities

CROSS-COUNTRY SKIING

Among the best places for cross-country skiing is **Togwotee Pass,** east of Jackson and north of Dubois on U.S. 26/287, in the Bridger-Teton and Shoshone national forests.

MOUNTAIN CLIMBING

Much of the appeal of the Wind River Range, which you can access from the west near Pinedale, or the east near Lander and Dubois, is the (relatively difficult) access to major peaks, the most significant of which is Gannett Peak, at 13,804 feet the highest mountain in Wyoming. The trip to the base of Gannett Peak can take two days, with considerable ups and downs and stream crossings that can be dangerous in late spring and early summer. The reward for such effort, however, is seclusion: climbing Gannett Peak might not be as dramatic as climbing the Grand Teton to the west, but you won't have to face the national-park crowds at the beginning or end of the climb. Wind River is a world of granite and glaciers, the latter (though small) being among the last active glaciers in the U.S. Rockies. Other worthy climbs in the Wind River Range are Gannett's neighbors Mount Sacajawea and Fremont Peak.

Chapter 10

CODY, SHERIDAN, AND NORTHERN WYOMING

Updated by Andy Austin, Andrew Collins, and Seth Tupper

Sights ★★★☆☆

Restaurants ★★★☆☆

Hotels ★★★☆☆

Shopping ★★☆☆☆

Nightlife ★★☆☆☆

WELCOME TO CODY, SHERIDAN, AND NORTHERN WYOMING

TOP REASONS TO GO

★ **Cody:** Experience Cody's endearing Western style and incomparable museums.

★ **Thermopolis:** Soak in 104°F mineral springs in Wyoming's oldest state park in Thermopolis.

★ **Devils Tower:** Trek around Devils Tower to marvel at one of nature's most impressive monoliths.

★ **State fair:** Watch the rodeo, ride the Ferris wheel, and attend a chuck wagon breakfast at the Wyoming State Fair.

★ **Buffalo:** Check out Buffalo's history museums and the spectacular natural scenery of the surrounding Bighorn Mountains.

1 **Thermopolis.** The home of popular Hot Springs State Park offers a hint of the hydrothermal features you'll find at Yellowstone National Park, including mineral springs to soak in, without the crowds.

2 **Lovell.** This otherwise prosaic little town near the Montana border is a base for exploring Bighorn Canyon National Recreation Area.

3 **Cody.** The eastern gateway to Yellowstone National Park abounds with its own Western charms, including authentic dude ranches, a rollicking nightly rodeo, and exceptional museums.

4 **Sheridan.** From the largest city in the Powder River Basin, you can learn about the region's complicated Native American and cowboy history at several historic sites.

5 **Big Horn.** Home to the superb ranching exhibits of the Brinton Museum, this unincorporated hamlet offers easy access to the rugged Bighorn National Forest.

6 **Buffalo.** Stroll through the engaging historic downtown and museums of this fabled community in the eastern foothills of the scenic Bighorn Mountains.

7 **Gillette.** Northeastern Wyoming's largest and fastest-growing city and supply center lies at the edge of the Black Hills and is a hub of energy production with several noteworthy attractions.

8 **Devils Tower.** America's first national monument rises nearly 900 feet above the surrounding countryside

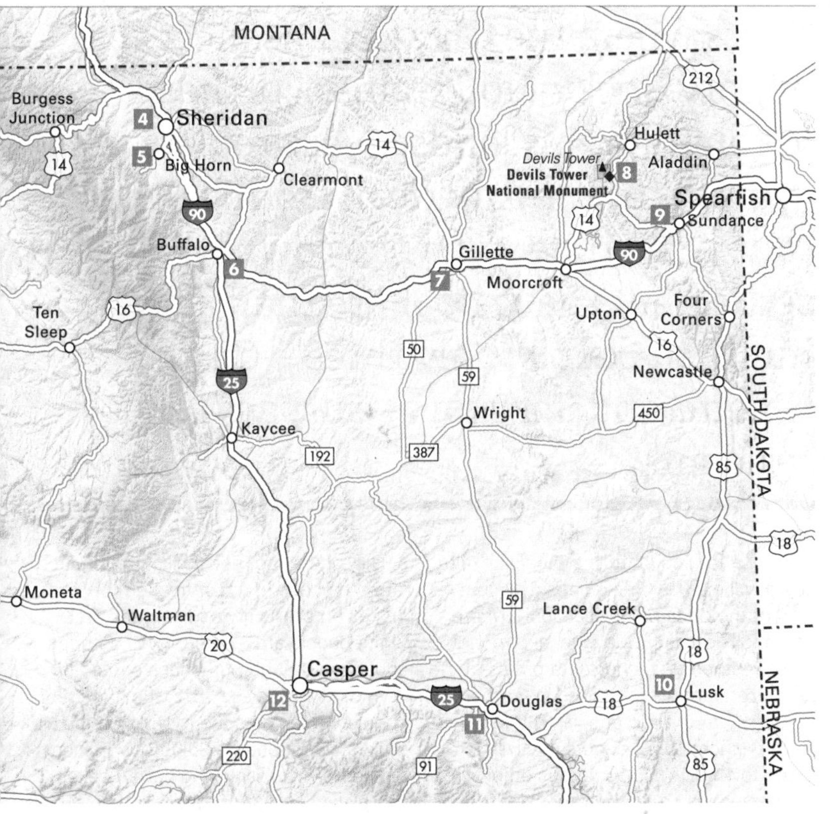

and makes for a fascinating short hike (only 1% of visitors make the technical climb to the top).

9 Sundance. This friendly little Black Hills town with an excellent history museum and a few colorful saloons gave the Sundance Kid his nickname.

10 Lusk. Learn about a key aspect of frontier history at the impressive Stagecoach Museum in this small high-plains town near the Nebraska border.

11 Douglas. Every August, the Wyoming State Fair draws thousands to this bustling railroad town on the North Platte River with some engaging history museums.

12 Casper. The state's second largest city is home to the exceptional National Historic Trails Interpretive Center and Tate Geological Museum and has an eclectic array of shops and restaurants.

Pine-carpeted hillsides and snowy mountain summits give way to windswept prairies and clean-flowing rivers where the Great Plains meet the mighty Rocky Mountains. Northern Wyoming's epic landscape is replete with symbols of the American frontier: the ranch, the rodeo, and the cowboy. Most settlements have no more than a few hundred people; only three—Casper, Gillette, and Sheridan—surpass 15,000 residents.

It may be that no state in the union exalts cowboy life as Wyoming does. The concept of the dude-ranch vacation—where urban folk learn to rope, ride, and rodeo with weathered ranchers and professional cattle drivers—started in northern Wyoming, at the still popular Eatons' Guest Ranch, 18 miles outside Sheridan in the town of Wolf. Numerous other guest ranches are strewn across the grassy plains here, from the dusty prairies east of Cody to the alpine meadows of the Big Horn Mountains. Most Big Horn–area dude ranches run pack trips into these high, rugged peaks, sometimes for days at a time. If you prefer a warm bed to sleeping under the stars, you'll find plenty of distinctive hotels and inns in the region's larger communities, especially Cody, the eastern gateway to Yellowstone National Park.

The outdoors is northern Wyoming's primary draw. Take the time to appreciate the wide-open spaces before you: take a hike, go fishing, ride a bike, or get out into the snow. Much of this territory is just as empty as it was when the first white people arrived here two centuries ago. Even though Europeans settled in Wyoming as early as 1812, the state's population remains the smallest in the nation, at just under 580,000 permanent residents. But many who have dwelt in this place have been history makers. This part of Wyoming has a rich and storied past that encompasses icons such as gunslingers, gamblers, miners, mule skinners, and warriors. Some of the most famous (and infamous) figures of the Old West passed through here, including Buffalo Bill Cody, Wild Bill Hickok, Calamity Jane, Chief Washakie, Butch Cassidy, and the Sundance Kid, the latter of whom took his name from one of the region's towns.

Planning

Getting Here and Around

AIR

The region has four small airports—Casper–Natrona County International Airport, Gillette's Northwest Wyoming Airport, Sheridan County Airport, and Cody's Yellowstone Regional Airport—with regularly scheduled commercial service to just two cities, although both of them are hubs. Delta Air Lines serves Casper and (in summer only) Cody from Salt Lake City. United Airlines flies from Denver into Casper, Cody, Gillette, and Sheridan.

CONTACTS Casper–Natrona County International Airport. ✉ *8500 Airport Pkwy., Casper* ☎ *307/472–6688* 🌐 *www.iflycasper.com.* **Northeast Wyoming Regional Airport.** ✉ *2000 Airport Rd., Gillette* ☎ *307/686–1042* 🌐 *www.ccgov.net.* **Sheridan County Airport.** ✉ *908 W. Brundage La., Sheridan* ☎ *307/674–4222* 🌐 *www.sheridancountyairport.com.* **Yellowstone Regional Airport.** ✉ *2101 Roger Sedam Dr., Cody* ☎ *307/587–5096* 🌐 *www.flyyra.com.*

CAR

Many people drive across northern Wyoming en route to visit the wonders of Yellowstone National Park, in the state's northwest corner. Try not to let the empty spaces between towns and the wide-open road tempt you to speed through the region too quickly. Give yourself enough time to check out the region's many intriguing attractions, and to overnight in both the small and larger towns in the region. If you're headed into Wyoming from the east along Interstate 90, be sure to stop in Sundance and make the short detour north to Devils Tower National Monument. The towns of Gillette, Buffalo, and Sheridan are good places to spend the night and have some excellent museums, too. Take either U.S. 14 or U.S. 16 through the mountains and stretch your legs in the Cloud Peak Wilderness Area, a prime spot for outdoor recreation, whether it's a 15-minute hike or a daylong ski trip. West of the Big Horns, the two highways meet up near Basin; from here, U.S. 14 is a straight shot to Cody and U.S. 310 is a scenic route through the arid plains around Lovell.

An alternative route for those interested in pioneer trails and stagecoach routes is to head south from Buffalo via Interstate 25 to the eastern Wyoming towns of Casper, Douglas, and Lusk. They lie in flatter landscape and—with the exception of Casper—offer less in the way of visitor services, but this is where you'll find the National Historic Trails Interpretive Center, Fort Fetterman State Historic Site, and other notable attractions. From here, head back north through dramatic Wind River Canyon on U.S. 20 to Thermopolis, then continue northeast into the Big Horns on U.S. 16 or northwest toward Cody and Yellowstone National Park via Highway 120.

Because the territory in this part of the world is so sparsely populated, it's almost impossible to find gas and repair shops at your convenience. There are few towns along the major routes here, even the interstates, so it's prudent to start out any trip with a full tank of gas and never to let the tank dip to below half full. Many small towns lack 24-hour credit-card gas pumps, and it's uncommon to find a gas station open past the early evening outside of Gillette, Sheridan, Casper, and Cody. If you're driving in a particularly remote region, it's wise to take along extra water. Although the communities here employ great fleets of snowplows in the winter, it can sometimes take them time to clear the upper elevations. Some passes in the Big Horns close entirely from as early as mid-November to as late as late May. Keep in mind, too, that locals are used to driving in a little snow and ice, so plows come out only if accumulations are substantial. Plan ahead, and note also that with the region's current energy-production boom, it can sometimes be difficult to get last-minute hotel reservations, especially in summer.

Hotels

Just as diverse as the area's landscape, which fades from small Western cities into vast expanses of open prairie and forested mountains, are its accommodations. In the population centers along the interstates, budget and midrange chain lodgings are the norm, but you'll also find a smattering of historic stone inns decorated with buffalo skins and Victorian furniture. Move beyond these larger communities, however, and you can find sprawling guest ranches alongside cold mountain-fed creeks. In the higher elevations, look for charming bed-and-breakfasts on mountain slopes with broad alpine vistas. And in a few historic towns, Cody in particular, you can find some interesting independent properties, from century-old hotels to inexpensive mom-and-pop motels and roadside cabin compounds. Even most simple budget accommodations offer good Wi-Fi and flat-screen TVs, but you will encounter some remote dude ranches and inns where Wi-Fi is spotty and cell service nonexistent; check in advance if this is important to you.

CAMPING

The opportunities to camp in this region are almost limitless. There are countless campgrounds in the Big Horns, and a few in the prairies below. Most of the public land within the national forests and parks is open for camping, provided that you don't light any fires. Keep in mind when selecting your campsite that the majestic peaks of the Big Horns are home to black bears and mountain lions.

Restaurants

In comparison to more touristy or trendy parts of the Rockies—like Bozeman, Jackson, and even laid-back Laramie—northern Wyoming remains behind the curve when it comes to the kind of dining that most food-driven travelers go out of their way for, the exception being steak houses that dole out impressive cuts of regionally raised beef, elk, bison, and trout, and small-town saloons and taverns where you can find tasty burgers, tacos, fried chicken, and other pub fare along with increasingly good selections of craft beer. In the larger communities along the interstates, chain restaurants dominate the landscape, but you will also find some independent Italian and Mexican restaurants, and a variety of Asian eateries, too. In smaller towns, homestyle taverns and diners are the main options, but it's becoming increasingly easier to find a hip brewpub, coffeehouse, Thai restaurant, or even a bistro with a seasonal menu.

Restaurant and hotel reviews have been shortened. For full information, visit Fodors.com.

HOTEL AND RESTAURANT PRICES

What it Costs			
$	$$	$$$	$$$$
RESTAURANTS			
under $10	$10–$18	$19–$30	over $30
HOTELS			
under $80	$80–$130	$131–$200	over $200

When to Go

People come to experience northern Wyoming in all four seasons—sometimes all in the same week. The weather here is notoriously difficult to predict, as warm Chinook winds can shoot

January temperatures into the 70s and freak storms can drop snow in July. On the whole, however, the area enjoys pleasantly warm summers and refreshingly snowy winters. Most travelers visit between June and September, a great time to pursue most outdoor activities. Others come to ski or snowmobile the pristine powder of the Big Horn Mountains in winter.

Temperatures in both seasons can be extreme, however. Thermometers often register a week of triple digits in August in the lower elevations. Snow begins to blanket the mountain slopes in late September and begins to recede only in late May, resulting in the seasonal closure of even some major roads over high-elevation mountain passes—always check conditions and forecasts when traveling in northern Wyoming this time of year. Spring, especially in the mountains, is sometimes nothing more than a week or two of rain and wind between the last winter snowfall and the warm sunshine of summer. Autumn, on the other hand, is full of pleasantly warm days, cooler nights, and vivid foliage. Additionally, the only crowds to fight are small pockets of hunters, anglers, and local leaf peepers.

★ Plains Indian Powwow
CULTURAL FESTIVALS | **FAMILY** | The two-day Plains Indian Powwow, in late June, brings together hoop dancers, traditional dancers, and jingle dancers from various tribes. The performances take place outdoors in the Buffalo Bill Center of the West's Robbie Powwow Garden. ✉ *720 Sheridan Ave., Cody* ☎ *307/587–4771* 🌐 *www.centerofthewest.org.*

Thermopolis

132 miles east of Dubois; 85 miles southeast of Cody; 130 miles northwest of Casper.

Native Americans, particularly the Shoshone, considered Thermopolis's hot mineral springs and surrounding land neutral territory. In 1896 they ceded the ground to the U.S. government as a "gift of the waters," stipulating that the springs remain available for the free use of all people. The springs and surrounding countryside were turned into Hot Springs State Park the following year, and you still take the waters gratis at the bathhouse, but a couple of commercially operated pools in the park charge a fee. A 10- to 15-minute walk west of the state park, the community's historic downtown has undergone a bit of a revitalization in recent years and has a handful of inviting eateries and shops. Thermopolis is also a good base for exploring scenic Wind River Canyon to the south and the Bighorn Mountains to the northeast.

GETTING HERE AND AROUND

Set along U.S. 20 between Shoshoni and Worland, Thermopolis is also the southeastern terminus of Highway 120, which leads northwest to Meeteetse and Cody. You'll need a car to get here, but downtown and the western side of the state park are easily managed on foot.

VISITOR INFORMATION

Thermopolis-Hot Springs Chamber of Commerce
✉ *220 Park St.* ☎ *307/864–3192* 🌐 *www.thermopolis.com.*

Sights

★ Hot Springs State Park
HOT SPRINGS | **FAMILY** | The land that became Wyoming's first state park in 1897 had always been sacred to Native Americans because of its healing natural hot springs. You can partake of these waters by soaking indoors or outside at the free 104°F mineral pools at the State Bath House, which is a central feature of this impressive 1,104-acre park that's also home to two waterparks (which charge admission fees) with more indoor and outdoor hot mineral pools, waterslides, and other amusements. You can

Wyoming's first state park, Hot Springs State Park, preserves the natural mineral pools and travertine terraces along the Big Horn River as well as over 1,000 acres of the surrounding area.

also hike or bike on 6 miles of trails, view the park's sizable bison herd, traipse across a swinging suspension bridge that traverses the Big Horn River, offering views of the dramatic travertine mineral terraces. ✉ *538 Park St.* ☎ *307/864–2176* 🌐 *wyoparks.wyo.gov* 🎫 *$12 per vehicle ($7 for Wyoming residents).*

Legend Rock State Petroglyph Site

ARCHAEOLOGICAL SITE | About 30 miles northwest of town, this state park preserves 92 petroglyph panels and more than 300 figures carved into a 1,312-foot-long sheer cliff face anywhere from a few hundred to 10,000 years ago. Interpretative trails lead to and describe the petroglyphs, and there's an informative visitor center and a picnic shelter as well. ✉ *2861 W. Cottonwood Rd.* ☎ *307/864–2176* 🌐 *www.wyoparks.wyo.gov* 🎫 *$12 per vehicle ($7 for Wyoming residents).*

Ten Sleep

TOWN | One of the region's quirkiest and most scenic little towns, Ten Sleep lies on the eastern edge of the Bighorn Basin, along scenic U.S. 16 before it climbs over 9,666-foot Powder Horn Pass en route to Buffalo. It's well worth a stop to stroll through the tiny downtown, stop by **Ten Sleep Mercantile**—a rollicking general store that opened in 1905—and grab a bite to eat or a drink at one of a handful of friendly taverns. You'll also find one of Wyoming's best craft breweries, **Ten Sleep Brewing**, on the west side of town. ✉ *U.S. 16, Ten Sleep* ✣ *60 miles northeast of Thermopolis, 65 miles southwest of Buffalo* 🌐 *www.townoftensleep.com.*

★ Wyoming Dinosaur Center

ARCHAEOLOGICAL SITE | **FAMILY** | Among the nearly 60 dinosaur skeletons displayed at this nonprofit museum and research center is the winged "Thermopolis Specimen," the only Archaeopteryx exhibited outside of Europe, and "Stan," one of the most complete Tyrannosaurus rex skeletons in the world, measuring 35 feet long and weighing in at nearly 6 tons. Special full-day programs allow kids and adults to try their hand at paleontology by digging in one of the several active dinosaur sites nearby (some 10,000 dinosaur bones have been excavated in the vicinity since 1993). Tours of the dig site are also offered daily in summer. ✉ *110 Carter Ranch Rd.* ☎ *307/864–2997* 🌐 *www.wyomingdinosaurcenter.org* 🎫 *From $10.*

★ Wyoming Whiskey
WINERY/DISTILLERY | The complex small-batch whiskeys produced by this craft distiller have received high marks from top spirits critics around the world. Fans of premium, barrel-age bourbon now flock to tiny Kirby (population 92, 13 miles north of Thermopolis) to sample and buy these smooth sippers and tour the handsome silo-style building in which they're distilled. ✉ *100 S. Nelson St., Kirby* ☎ *307/864–2116* 🌐 *www.wyomingwhiskey.com* ⏲ *Closed Sun.*

Restaurants

★ Bangkok Thai
$$ | **THAI** | You could be forgiven for not expecting to find legit Thai food in northern Wyoming, much less in tiny Thermopolis, but this simple downtown eatery turns out flavorful, authentic curries and stir-fries. Choose from the usual proteins along with duck and lamb—the avocado curry, drunken noodles, and steamed pork pot stickers are among the specialties. **Known for:** friendly, welcoming service; plenty of vegetarian options; mango sticky rice. *$ Average main: $16* ✉ *512 Broadway St.* ☎ *307/864–3565* ⏲ *Closed Mon.*

One Eyed Buffalo Brewing
$ | **AMERICAN** | As notable for its well-crafted IPA, whiskey stout, and peach blonde ale as for serving reliably good comfort fare, this convivial brewpub occupies a stately stone building downtown. You could make a meal of a few apps—fried pickle spears, potato skins, loaded nachos—or tackle one of the hearty entrées, like spinach-artichoke mac and cheese or a Cajun-rubbed spicy blackened burger. **Known for:** extensive mac and cheese selection; first-rate craft beer; boneless rib-eye steaks. *$ Average main: $14* ✉ *528 Broadway St.* ☎ *307/864–3555* 🌐 *www.oneeyedbuffalobrewingwyo.com* ⏲ *Closed Sun.–Tues. No lunch.*

Coffee and Quick Bites

Kirby Creek Mercantile
$ | **AMERICAN** | A bright, lively establishment set inside a vintage downtown storefront, the Mercantile is both a source of tasty breakfast, lunch, and dessert fare and craft gallery featuring works by regional artisans. Cuban sandwiches and build-your-own-omelets star among the savory offerings, while sweet tooths can indulge in gelato and fresh-baked goods. **Known for:** grilled cheese with roasted tomato soup; seasonal fruit pies; fun variety of toys, cards, and gifts. *$ Average main: $10* ✉ *535 Broadway St.* ☎ *307/864–3533* 🌐 *www.kirbycreekmercantile.com* ⏲ *No dinner.*

Hotels

★ Best Western Plus Plaza Hotel
$$$ | **HOTEL** | Located in Hot Springs State Park on the banks of the Big Horn River and by far the best hotel in town, this handsomely restored 1918 hotel has spacious rooms with attractive Western log-cabin-style furnishings, and suites have fireplaces. **Pros:** restored historic building; great location inside Hot Springs State Park; seasonal pool and year-round mineral springs hot tub. **Cons:** a 15-minute walk from downtown dining; bare-bones breakfast; no elevator. *$ Rooms from: $139* ✉ *116 E. Park St.* ☎ *307/864–2939* 🌐 *www.bestwestern.com* 🛏 *46 rooms* 🍽 *Free breakfast.*

RAFTING

Wind River Canyon Whitewater
WHITE-WATER RAFTING | FAMILY | This popular outfitter leads white-water floats—lasting from a couple of hours to a full day with lunch—down the Wind River. Scenic floats and fly-fishing trips are also offered. ✉ *210 Hwy. 20* ☎ *307/864–9343* ☞ *From $79.*

Lovell

49 miles northeast of Cody; 102 miles north of Thermopolis.

This small ranching community makes a convenient, if bare-bones, base for exploring the Bighorn Canyon National Recreation Area, which spans the Wyoming–Montana border. On the Wyoming side, Bighorn Lake is popular with boaters, anglers, and bird-watchers; most of the recreation area's main attractions, including the majority of the Pryor Mountain Wild Horse Range, lie on the Montana side.

GETTING HERE AND AROUND

Lovell lies at the junction of U.S. 14A and Highway 310, about an hour's drive northeast of Cody. Note that U.S. 14A east of town is steep and winding, though beautiful; it's closed due to snow from late November through late May. If you're traveling east toward Sheridan during these months, you'll have to detour south and then east via U.S. 14.

Bighorn Canyon National Recreation Area
NATIONAL/STATE PARK | To learn about this 120,000-acre national park wilderness that was established in 1966 following the creation of Yellowtail Dam, visit the South District's **Cal Taggart Visitor Center** in Lovell, where you can view geological and historical exhibits on the area, as well as a film about the canyon. Two shorter movies, one on the Pryor Mountain wild horses and the other about Medicine Wheel National Historic Landmark (east of Lovell), are shown on request, and there's a small gift and bookshop. The park's South District is reached by heading north on Highway 37 east of Lovell and encompasses Horseshoe Bend Marina, Devil Canyon Overlook, 12 hiking trails (in both Wyoming and southern Montana), four historic ranches that you can tour on your own, and three campgrounds. The park's North District is 120 miles north, in Fort Smith, Montana. Note that part of the park near Lovell is adjacent to Yellowtail Wildlife Management Area at the southern end of Bighorn Lake. More than 155 species of birds—including white pelicans, pheasants, bald eagles, and great blue herons—inhabit the 19,424-acre refuge, as do numerous other animal species, including red fox, mule deer, and cottontail rabbits. ✉ *20 U.S. 14A* ☎ *307/548–5406* 🌐 *www.nps.gov/bica* 🎫 *Free.*

★ **Medicine Wheel/Medicine Mountain National Historic Landmark**
NATIVE SITE | A ring of rocks 75 feet in diameter, this ancient site is the best preserved of nearly 150 Native American stone wheels found in Wyoming, South Dakota, Montana, Alberta, and Saskatchewan. Evidence such as the 28 spokes (one for each day of the lunar cycle) leading from the edge of the wheel to a central cairn has persuaded some that the wheel was an ancient spiritual observatory much like England's Stonehenge may have been. To protect the area, access to the wheel is restricted to foot travel; it's a 1½-mile hike on a well-maintained unpaved road to the site from the parking lot (people with disabilities may drive to the site). Up in the Big Horn Mountains, at an elevation of 9,642 feet, the site affords views of

The best preserved of nearly 150 Native American wheels is at Medicine Wheel/Medicine Mountain National Historic Landmark and may be 10,000 years old.

the entire Big Horn Basin. Dress warmly, as it's cool up here, even in summer. *✉ Forest Rd. 12, off U.S. 14A ✣ 35 miles east of Lovell ☎ 307/548–5406 🌐 www.nps.gov/bica 🎫 Free ⏲ Road closed mid-Sept.–mid-June.*

Pryor Mountain Wild Mustang Center

NATURE PRESERVE | At this interpretive center inside a modern log cabin just up the road from the Bighorn Canyon Visitor Center, photos, printed materials, and helpful volunteers introduce people to the 120 to 140 mustangs that roam over 38,000 acres of range. Although many of the mustangs will likely be up in the mountains, you're almost sure to see some right from the paved road, Highway 37, which is a short drive east of the center. This could include White Cloud, a stallion featured in two books by Ginger Kathrens. *✉ 1106 Rd. 12, off U.S. 14A ☎ 307/548–9453 🌐 www.pryormustangs.org ⏲ Closed Sun.*

Restaurants

Brandin' Iron

$$ | **AMERICAN** | This homey diner-style grill is a local favorite, where folks come for the kind of down-home cooking that sticks to your ribs: biscuits and gravy, ham-steak eggs Benedict, chicken-fried steaks, and shrimp scampi. For lighter meals, consider the several sandwich and salad options. **Known for:** down-home hospitality; steak-and-eggs breakfasts; build-your-own burgers. *$ Average main: $17 ✉ 483 Shoshone Ave. ☎ 307/548–9370.*

Hotels

★ Wyoming High Country Lodge

$$$$ | **B&B/INN** | **FAMILY** | Set amid verdant meadows at 9,000 feet elevation in the mountains of Bighorn National Forest, this peaceful compound of attractively outfitted contemporary cabins along with several spacious lodge rooms offers a charming, distinctive alternative to the handful of budget motels in downtown Lovell, about 30 miles away. **Pros:** tranquil location; close to a variety of outdoor activities, from hiking to snowshoeing trails; rates include well-prepared meals. **Cons:** no cell service and spotty Wi-Fi; main road to Lovell is closed in winter; extremely remote setting. *$ Rooms from: $220 ✉ Forest Rd. 13 ☎ 307/529–0914 🌐 www.wyhighcountry.com 🛏 12 rooms 🍴 All-inclusive.*

Cody

60 miles southeast of Red Lodge, MT; 52 miles east of Yellowstone.

Founded in 1896 and named for Pony Express rider, army scout, Freemason, and entertainer William F. "Buffalo Bill" Cody, Cody lies just east of the Absaroka Range in the high plains of the Bighorn Basin, about a mile above sea level. As the eastern gateway community for Yellowstone National Park, this town of about 9,800 sees a sharp influx of visitors during the summer months when Yellowstone's eastern entrance is open. But at any time of year, this easygoing community with a bustling downtown historic core offers plenty to see and do. Five superb museums under one roof make up the outstanding Buffalo Bill Historical Center, an affiliate of the Smithsonian, and the town exemplifies America's Western style and sensibility with its dude ranches and colorful shops specializing in everything from cowboy hats, landscape paintings, and hand-carved furniture to local beef jerky and outerwear. Part of the fun in Cody is sauntering down Sheridan Avenue, stopping by the Irma Hotel (built in 1902 by Buffalo Bill and named for his daughter) for an ice-cold beer, and attending the summertime nightly rodeo.

GETTING HERE AND AROUND

The North Fork Highway—as the region's span of U.S. 14/16/20 leading west to Yellowstone is known—follows the North Fork of the Shoshone River past barren rock formations strewn with tumbleweeds, then enters lush forests and green meadows as the elevation increases roughly 3,000 feet in 70 miles. Cody is within easy reach of the Shoshone National Forest, the Absaroka Range, the Washakie Wilderness, and the Buffalo Bill Reservoir. Although you can explore downtown, shops, restaurants, and even the Buffalo Bill Historical Center on foot, you need a car to explore the surrounding region.

VISITOR INFORMATION

Cody Country Chamber of Commerce
✉ 836 Sheridan Ave. ☎ 307/587–2777 🌐 www.codychamber.org.

TOURS

Cody Trolley Tours
TOUR—SIGHT | FAMILY | These hour-long tours on vintage trolley-style buses travel 22 miles and cover Cody's history dating back to the late-19th-century era of Buffalo Bill and Annie Oakley. Tours start at the fabled Irma Hotel, named for Buffalo Bill's daughter, and take in historic sites, scenery, and wildlife and other natural attractions. On summer evenings (except Sunday) at 6, stay to watch the amusing if cheesy 30-minute mock gunfights staged outside the Irma. The "Inside & Out Combo" package includes the tour and two-day admission to the Buffalo Bill Center of the West. *✉ Irma Hotel, 1192 Sheridan Ave. ☎ 307/527–7043 🌐 www.codytrolleytours.com 🎟 From $27.*

★ **Red Canyon Wild Mustang Tours**
SPECIAL-INTEREST | From mid-May through mid-October, the well-established outfitter offers morning and early-evening 2½- to 3-hour van excursions out to see the famed wild mustangs who roam freely throughout the McCullough Peaks Herd Management Area, about 20 miles east of Cody. You'll be provided binoculars,

Part of the Buffalo Bill Center of the West, the Plains Indian Museum focuses on the tribes of the Northern Plains, including the Arapaho, Lakota, Crow, Cheyenne, Blackfeet, and Pawnee.

and in addition to seeing these stately creatures running and playing in this vast badlands wilderness, you may spy pronghorn, coyotes, prairie dogs, and raptors. Red Canyon's tour menu also includes rafting, photography, and Yellowstone adventures. ✉ *Cody Wyoming Adventures, 1119 12th St.* ☎ *307/587–6988, 800/293–0148* 🌐 *www.codywyomingadventures.com.*

Sights

Bridal Veil Falls Trail

TRAIL | The best hiking in the region tends to be west of Cody and includes this moderately strenuous 4-mile round-trip trek to a dramatic waterfall in Shoshone National Forest, northwest of town. The trail starts out on a wide road that parallels the Clarks Fork of the Yellowstone River before cutting up alongside Falls Creek—the steep final half-mile to the falls will get your blood flowing. ✉ *Cody* ✣ *Trailhead: end of Hwy. 292, 11 miles west of Hwy. 120.*

★ **Buffalo Bill Center of the West**

MUSEUM | **FAMILY** | This extraordinary "five-in-one" complex, an affiliate of the Smithsonian Institution, contains the Buffalo Bill Museum, the Whitney Western Art Museum, the Plains Indian Museum, the Cody Firearms Museum, and the Draper Natural History Museum. All are well organized and mount superb exhibitions in their respective subject areas. The flagship Buffalo Bill Museum puts into context the life, era, and activities of its (and its town's) namesake, William F. "Buffalo Bill" Cody (1846–1917), whose numerous careers included guide, scout, actor, and entrepreneur. If you want to understand how the myth of the American West developed, this is the place to come. The other four museums—there's also a research library—are equally absorbing. Plan to spend at least four hours here—and to discover that this isn't enough time to take it all in. Luckily, your admission ticket is good for two consecutive days. ✉ *720 Sheridan Ave.* ☎ *307/587–4771* 🌐 *www.*

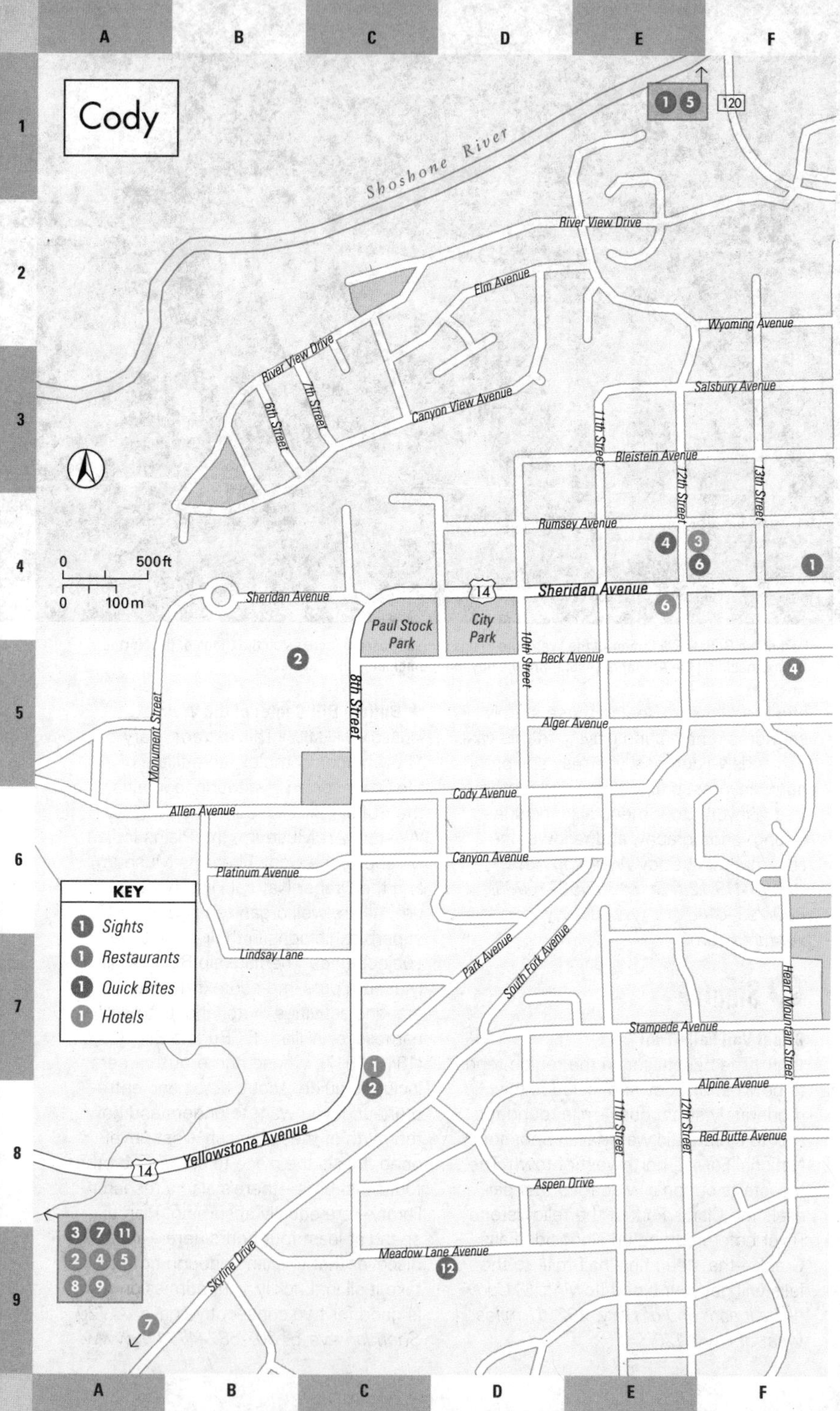

Cody
A
B
C
D
E
F
1
2
3
4
5
6
7
8
9
Shoshone River
River View Drive
Elm Avenue
Wyoming Avenue
Salsbury Avenue
Canyon View Avenue
6th Street
7th Street
11th Street
12th Street
13th Street
Bleistein Avenue
Rumsey Avenue
Sheridan Avenue
Paul Stock Park
City Park
10th Street
Beck Avenue
8th Street
Monument Street
Alger Avenue
Cody Avenue
Allen Avenue
Canyon Avenue
Platinum Avenue
Lindsay Lane
Park Avenue
South Fork Avenue
Heart Mountain Street
Stampede Avenue
Alpine Avenue
Red Butte Avenue
Yellowstone Avenue
Aspen Drive
Meadow Lane Avenue
Skyline Drive
120
14
0
500 ft
100 m
KEY
Sights
Restaurants
Quick Bites
Hotels

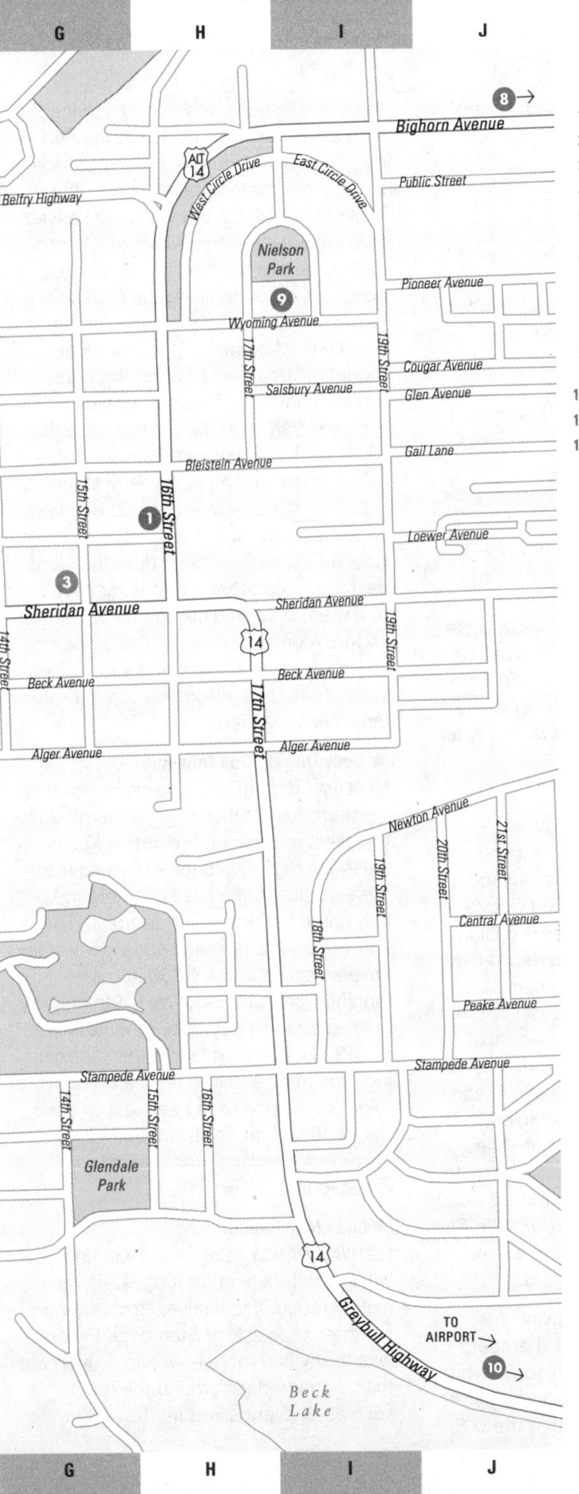

Sights

1 Bridal Veil Falls Trail E1
2 Buffalo Bill Center of the West... B5
3 Buffalo Bill State Park A9
4 By Western Hands E4
5 Chief Joseph Scenic Highway E1
6 Cody Dug Up Gun Museum........ E4
7 Cody Nite Rodeo.................. A9
8 Heart Mountain Interpretive Center J1
9 Historic Cody Mural & Museum.................... I2
10 Meeteetse Museums J9
11 Old Trail Town A9
12 Shoshone National Forest....... D9

Restaurants

1 Cody Steak House F4
2 8th Street at the Ivy................ C8
3 Pat O'Hara Brewing Company Pub & Grill G4
4 Trailhead Bar | Grill | Wood Fired Pizza F5

Quick Bites

1 The Station by Cody Coffee H4

Hotels

1 Best Western Premier Ivy Inn & Suites C7
2 Bill Cody Ranch A9
3 Chamberlin Inn...................... E4
4 Cody Cowboy Village............. A9
5 The Cody Hotel...................... A9
6 Irma Hotel E4
7 K3 Guest Ranch Bed and Breakfast................ A9
8 Rimrock Dude Ranch............. A9
9 Yellowstone Valley Inn & RV A9

centerofthewest.org *$20* *Closed Mon.–Wed. in Dec.–Feb.*

Buffalo Bill State Park

NATIONAL/STATE PARK | About 6 miles west of downtown on U.S. 14, you'll pass through the Shoshone Canyon Tunnel (the state's largest, at 2.8 miles) and emerge at the northeast end of Buffalo Bill Reservoir, which was formed in 1910 by the construction of a 350-foot-tall dam. The reservoir, which is popular for boating and fishing, forms the heart of Buffalo Bill State Park, which also has a campground and picnic area. Just after exiting the tunnel, you can also stop by the visitor center operated by the U.S. Bureau of Reclamation, where you can peer over this immense dam from a viewing platform, and watch a film and explore exhibits on this impressive feat of engineering and the region's natural and human history. ✉ *4192 N. Fork Hwy.* ☎ *307/587–9227* *$12 per vehicle ($7 for Wyoming residents)* *Visitor center closed Oct.–Apr.*

★ **By Western Hands**

MUSEUM | In a restored downtown hardware store, this nonprofit juried artisan guild and museum is devoted to preserving and showcasing Cody's profound influence on Western design as it applies to furniture and decorative arts. Inside the galleries you can view pieces by legendary Cody designers like Edward Bohlin who with his eventual Hollywood connections become known as the "saddle maker to the stars," and furniture craftsman Thomas Molesworth. Additionally, the showrooms are filled with ornately crafted works by the guild's members, who continue to further Cody's Western design legacy. ✉ *1007 12th St.* ☎ *307/586–1755* *www.bywestern-hands.org* *Closed Sun.–Wed.*

★ **Chief Joseph Scenic Highway**

SCENIC DRIVE | In 1877 a few members of the Nez Perce tribe killed some white settlers in Idaho as retribution for earlier killings by whites. Fearing that the U.S. Army would punish the guilty and innocent alike, hundreds of Nez Perce fled on a five-month journey toward Canada along what came to be known as the Nez Perce Trail. On the way they passed through what is now Yellowstone National Park, across the Sunlight Basin area north of Cody, and along the Clarks Fork of the Shoshone River before turning north into Montana. To see the rugged mountain area they traveled through, follow Highway 120 north 17 miles to Highway 296, the Chief Joseph Scenic Highway. The highway twists and turns for 46 miles, ending at similarly stunning U.S. 212, the Beartooth Scenic Highway, which leads west to the pretty hamlet of Cooke City, Montana and then the Northeast Entrance of Yellowstone, or east to the small ski and hiking hub of Red Lodge. Along the way you'll see open meadows, pine forests, and a sweeping vista of the region from the top of Dead Indian Pass. ✉ *Cody.*

★ **Cody Dug Up Gun Museum**

MUSEUM | The intriguing name of this museum fully states its unusual mission: to collect and exhibit firearms and other weapons that have been exhumed from the earth (or, in the case of an old musket, entombed inside a tree trunk). The knowledgeable husband-and-wife owners have amassed some 1,300 items, ranging from rusted-out mid-19th-century revolvers to rifles used by mobsters in the 1930s. Every artifact in this fascinating museum seems to tell a story that might otherwise have been lost to obscurity. ✉ *1020 12th St.* ☎ *307/587–3344* *www.codydugupgunmuseum.com* *Closed Oct.–Apr.*

★ **Cody Nite Rodeo**

FESTIVAL | FAMILY | Begun in 1938 and billing itself the world's longest-running nightly rodeo, this festive, family-friendly summer spectacle at Stampede Park is less flashy and more endearingly intimate than bigger rodeos around the region, such as Cheyenne Frontier Days. Kicking

The Chief Joseph Scenic Highway is one of the best drives in Wyoming, which roughly follows the route the Nez Pearce used to evade the U.S. Army in 1877.

off at 8 pm each evening from June through August, the Cody Nite Rodeo offers kids' competitions, such as goat roping and junior barrel racing, in addition to the regular adult events. Over early July's Independence Day weekend, the annual Cody Stampede features a full long weekend of events at the same venue. ✉ *Stampede Park, 519 W. Yellowstone Ave.* ☎ *307/587–5155* 🌐 *www.codystampederodeo.com* 🎫 *From $12.*

★ Heart Mountain Interpretive Center

MUSEUM | From 1942 through 1945, nearly 14,000 Japanese Americans were relocated to this hastily constructed incarceration center—one of 10 located throughout the country—at the foot of Heart Mountain, about 13 miles north of Cody. Evicted from their West Coast homes through an executive order issued by President Franklin D. Roosevelt shortly after the bombing of Pearl Harbor, the residents lived in small, tightly spaced barracks. In 2011, a poignant museum opened on the long-abandoned site. At the Heart Mountain Interpretive Center, you can learn about this shameful episode of U.S. history by watching an excellent short movie and touring both permanent and rotating exhibits that use photographs, letters, news clippings, and other artifacts to bring to life the powerful and often inspiring stories of Heart Mountain's inhabitants, who persevered in the face of anti-Asian prejudices and unjust conditions. ✉ *1539 Rd. 19, Powell* ☎ *307/754–8000* 🌐 *www.heartmountain.org* 🎫 *$9* 🕓 *Closed Sun.–Wed. in Oct.–mid-May.*

Historic Cody Mural & Museum

PUBLIC ART | The Cody Mural, at the Church of Jesus Christ of Latter-day Saints, presents a larger-than-life artistic interpretation of Mormon settlement in the West. Edward Grigware painted the 36-foot-diameter scene on the domed ceiling in the 1950s. A small museum contains historical artifacts as well as interactive kiosks where visitors can explore their genealogy. ✉ *1719 Wyoming Ave.* ☎ *307/587–3290* 🌐 *codymural.com.*

Meeteetse Museums

MUSEUM | Anchoring the historic downtown of this small community named for the Shoshone term for "meeting place," this collection of three free history museums is well worth a stop on the scenic drive along Highway 120 between Cody and Thermopolis. The most interesting of the group is the Charles Belden Museum of Western Photography, which occupies a 1919 former drugstore and contains photographs, Molesworth furniture, and other items that once belonged to the renowned early-20th-century photographer, whose works are featured prominently in *Life* magazine and *National Geographic*. The Bank Museum and Meeteetse Museum occupy other nearby vintage buildings and present engaging exhibits on the region's human and natural history. ✉ *1947 State St., Meeteetse* ☎ *307/868–2423* 🌐 *www.meeteetsemuseums.org* ⏲ *Closed Sun.–Tues.*

Old Trail Town

MUSEUM VILLAGE | **FAMILY** | A short drive west of downtown near the Stampede Park rodeo grounds, you can tour this living history museum that comprises about two-dozen historic buildings from Wyoming's frontier days—including a saloon and a blacksmith's shop—many of them housing photos and pioneer and Native American artifacts. The complex is situated on Cody's original townsite, and a small original cemetery serves as resting place for some of the region's famous mountain men, including Liver Eatin' Johnson, and about 100 horse-drawn vehicles are on display. ✉ *1831 Demaris Dr.* ☎ *307/587–5302* 🌐 *www.oldtrailtown.org* 🎟 *$10* ⏲ *Closed Oct.–mid-May.*

Shoshone National Forest

FOREST | Established in 1891 as the country's first designated national forest, this 2.4-million-acre tract of alpine woodland, sagebrush flats, and verdant meadows extends west from Cody to Yellowstone National Park (which is roughly the same size). At both the headquarters south of downtown and the Clarks Fork, Greybull, and Wapiti Ranger Districts office on the west side of Cody (✉ *203A Yellowstone Ave., Cody*), you can pick up maps, buy permits, and obtain advice on the many activities you can pursue in the forest—hiking, camping, fishing, mountain biking, horseback, snowshoeing, snowmobiling, cross-country skiing—and the best places to enjoy them. Some highlights include the well-preserved ghost town of Kirwin, about 65 miles south of Cody, and the Clarks Fork of the Yellowstone, a designated Wild and Scenic River during its 20½-mile course through the forest about 30 miles northwest of Cody. ✉ *Headquarters, 808 Meadow Lane Ave.* ☎ *307/527–6241* 🌐 *www.fs.usda.gov/shoshone* 🎟 *Free* ⏲ *Office closed weekends.*

Restaurants

Cody Steak House

$$$ | **STEAKHOUSE** | This handsome, clubby-feeling restaurant along Cody's main drag is a favorite of carnivores, but there's also a surprising variety of internationally inspired seafood and poultry dishes, including prawns with a spicy mango-jalapeño salsa. Among the meatier fare, consider the 16-ounce hand-cut buffalo rib-eye or 18-ounce T-bone Angus beef steak. **Known for:** prodigious portions; one of Cody's better wine and beer selections; rich chocolate brownie sandwiches topped with ice cream. 💲 *Average main: $25* ✉ *1367 Sheridan Ave.* ☎ *307/586–2550* 🌐 *www.codysteakhouse.com* ⏲ *Closed Mon. and Tues. No lunch.*

8th Street at the Ivy

$$$ | **AMERICAN** | A short drive west of downtown, this high-ceilinged regional American restaurant with deep booth seats and big windows looking out toward the mountains draws guests but also quite a few locals for breakfast, lunch, and dinner. Regionally sourced meat and seafood are the stars here,

Old Trail Town preserves some two dozen buildings and about 100 horse-drawn vehicles from the early frontier days on Cody's original townsite.

including fall-off-the-bone short ribs and flavorful grilled Idaho trout. **Known for:** well-curated wine list; creative entrée-size salads; buffalo burgers. *Average main: $21 ✉ 1800 8th St. ☎ 307/578–8444 🌐 www.8thstreet.co.*

Pat O'Hara Brewing Company Pub & Grill
$$ | **AMERICAN** | Stainless-steel brewing vats are the centerpiece of the bar and dining area of this friendly downtown Cody brewpub that also has a large dining patio. The kitchen turns out tasty gastropub fare, from bacon-wrapped grilled shrimp to amber-beer-battered fish-and-chips, and the ales on tap include both house brews and plenty of visiting craft beers from around the country. **Known for:** Irish-influenced classics like shepherd's pie; hefty cheeseburgers; seasonal brews. *Average main: $16 ✉ 1019 15th St. ☎ 307/586–5410 🌐 www.patoharabrewing.com ⏲ Closed Sun. and Mon.*

★ **Trailhead Bar | Grill | Wood Fired Pizza**
$$$ | **MODERN AMERICAN** | This hip neighborhood bistro a block off Cody's main drag serves some of the most creative fare in town—consider the starter of pork belly sliders with a kicky habanero-lingonberry aioli, followed by cured duck leg confit served on a bed of mascarpone-polenta with a cherry gastrique. There's also a full bar serving first-rate craft cocktails, like the Smoky Buck with mezcal, wood-fired strawberries, and lime. **Known for:** live music some evenings; wood-fired pizzas and grills; weekend brunches with a bloody Mary bar. *Average main: $21 ✉ 1326 Beck Ave. ☎ 307/578–8510 🌐 www.trailheadcody.com ⏲ No dinner Sun.–Mon.*

Coffee and Quick Bites

★ **The Station by Cody Coffee**
$ | **CAFÉ** | The downtown branch of this excellent small-batch coffee roaster with a flagship café by the airport occupies a colorfully restored and decorated former

gas station with a landscaped patio. In addition to well-crafted espresso drinks, both locations of Cody Coffee offer an extensive menu of sweet and savory crepes and triple-decker sandwiches. **Known for:** egg-ham-cheddar breakfast crepes; banana–bacon–peanut butter dessert crepes; mocha lattes. *Average main: $8 919 16th St. 307/578–6661 www.codycoffee.com No dinner.*

Hotels

Best Western Premier Ivy Inn & Suites

$$$$ | HOTEL | This newer and more upscale member of the ubiquitous Best Western brand offers among the most spacious and attractive rooms in town, in a handsome stone-and-timber building on the west side of town, making it convenient for making the 50-mile drive to Yellowstone's East Entrance. **Pros:** spacious and stylish rooms; good gym and indoor heated pool; full-service restaurant and bar. **Cons:** no pets; not within walking distance of town; on busy road. *Rooms from: $253 1800 8th St. 307/587–2572 www.bestwestern.com 70 rooms No meals.*

★ Bill Cody Ranch

$$$ | B&B/INN | FAMILY | A classic Wyoming dude ranch that retains its rugged and historic 1925 ambience, this sprawling property in the high country west of Cody offers inclusive packages that include meals in the Western-theme saloon and restaurant as well as daily four-hour horseback rides or less expensive lodging-only rates. **Pros:** stunning surroundings; guided horseback rides for guests of all ages; tasty food (with dining-inclusive packages available). **Cons:** no cell service; no laundry facilities; a half-hour drive from Cody. *Rooms from: $160 2604 North Fork Hwy. 307/587–2097 16 rooms No meals.*

★ Chamberlin Inn

$$$$ | B&B/INN | Named for Agnes Chamberlin, who opened a boardinghouse on this spot in 1904, this artfully restored redbrick inn a block off Cody's main street counts Ernest Hemingway and Marshall Field among its many past guests. **Pros:** filled with historic accents and furnishings; welcoming service; short walk to downtown dining. **Cons:** no elevator; summer rates are quite steep; no breakfast. *Rooms from: $285 1032 12th St. 307/587–0202, 888/587–0202 www.chamberlininn.com 22 rooms No meals.*

Cody Cowboy Village

$$$ | HOTEL | The simple but attractive single and duplex log cabins here are pure Western, right down to the pitched-roof beam ceilings, iron bedsteads with horseshoe designs, and bathroom wallpaper printed with boots and cowboy hats. **Pros:** large outdoor hot tub; cabin porches have nice mountain views; close to Cody Nite Rodeo and Old Trail Town. **Cons:** not within walking distance of town; breakfast is a bit meager; closed fall through spring. *Rooms from: $169 203 W. Yellowstone Ave. 307/587–7555 www.codycowboyvillage.com Closed mid Oct.–early May 50 rooms Free breakfast.*

The Cody Hotel

$$$$ | HOTEL | This upscale low-rise hotel on the west side of town abounds with comfy perks, including an indoor pool and hot tub, a well-equipped gym, a patio with a fire pit, and an inviting lobby and library with a fireplace. **Pros:** attractive common spaces; very good breakfast included; close to rodeo and Old Trail Town. **Cons:** on a busy road; rooms feel a bit cookie-cutter; a couple of miles west of downtown. *Rooms from: $229 232 W. Yellowstone Ave. 307/587–5915 www.thecody.com 75 rooms Free breakfast.*

Irma Hotel

$$$ | **HOTEL** | Built in 1902 by Buffalo Bill and named for his daughter, this striking downtown property retains both its frontier charm and rough edges, with period furniture and pull-chain commodes in many rooms, a large restaurant open all day, and an elaborate cherrywood bar said to have been a gift from Queen Victoria to Buffalo Bill. **Pros:** tons of character, history, and charm; affordable; in the heart of downtown historic district. **Cons:** in a busy area; a bit dated; restaurant is just so-so. *Rooms from: $147 1192 Sheridan Ave. 307/587–4221 www.irmahotel.com 40 rooms No meals.*

★ K3 Guest Ranch Bed and Breakfast

$$$ | **B&B/INN** | **FAMILY** | Here you have the chance to stay at an authentic, upscale 33-acre Western ranch, just a 15-minute drive from downtown Cody, without spending a mint or having to contend with a minimum-stay requirement. **Pros:** truly one-of-a-kind accommodations; a variety of tours around the region can be arranged; campfire breakfasts included in the rates. **Cons:** remote setting down well-posted gravel road; 15-minute drive into town; sheepherder's wagons have baths in separate location (though still private). *Rooms from: $179 30 Nielsen Tr. 307/587–2080 www.k3guestranch.com 7 rooms Free breakfast.*

★ Rimrock Dude Ranch

$$$$ | **RESORT** | **FAMILY** | One of the oldest ranches on the North Fork of the Shoshone River, Rimrock offers horseback-riding adventures into Shoshone National Forest's surrounding mountains, excursions to Cody Nite Rodeo and nearby Yellowstone National Park, fishing in a trout-stocked pond, rafting trips, and more—all for one set weekly price. **Pros:** cabins have exceptional views; lots of fun adventures and activities for families; friendly, gracious owners. **Cons:** half-hour drive from nearest town (Cody); one-week minimum stay; credit cards accepted for initial deposit only (not final balance). *Rooms from: $678 2728 N. Fork Hwy. 307/587–3970 www.rimrockranch.com Closed Oct.–May 9 cabins All-inclusive.*

Yellowstone Valley Inn & RV

$$$ | **HOTEL** | About 15 miles west of Cody and 30 miles east of Yellowstone National Park's east entrance, this sprawling property offers basic accommodations in a mountain setting on the Shoshone River. **Pros:** rustic but clean rooms; beautiful location between Cody and Yellowstone; pet-friendly. **Cons:** bar crowd can be noisy; same for live music in dance hall several nights a week; a half-hour drive to downtown Cody. *Rooms from: $145 3324 N. Fork Hwy. 307/587–3961, 877/587–3961 www.yellowstonevalleyinn.com 35 rooms Free breakfast.*

Nightlife

Cassie's

MUSIC CLUBS | A trip to Cody isn't complete without a chance to scoot your boots to live music, usually provided by the local group West the Band, at this rollicking supper club festooned with Western memorabilia and mounted taxidermy. The tunes are a mix of classic country, the band's Western originals, and today's hits. Opened in 1922 by a local "sportin' lady," Cassie's today has three levels with a steak house restaurant, a dance floor, and three bars. *214 Yellowstone Ave. 307/527–5500.*

★ Silver Dollar Bar

BARS/PUBS | Offering one of the region's largest selections of draft and bottled beer, a large patio, and live music on weekend evenings, this festive downtown bar is a fun place to shoot pool and meet the locals. The pub fare is pretty tasty, too, from Rocky Mountain "oysters" to prodigious burgers. *1313 Sheridan Ave. 307/527–7666 www.silverdollarcody.com.*

Performing Arts

On Thursday evenings from early July through late August, free jazz, country, and pop concerts and ice cream socials are held at **City Park on Sheridan Avenue.**

Cody Cattle Company Dinner Show
CONCERTS | **FAMILY** | Feast on a chuck wagon dinner of barbecue brisket or chicken (and freshly baked brownies for dessert) during these hour-long country-western shows that end at 7:30 pm, just in time for you to make the five-minute stroll to the Cody Night Rodeo, just down the road. Shows take place late May through mid-September. ✉ *1910 Demaris St.* ☎ *307/272–5770* 🌐 *www.thecodycattlecompany.com.*

Dan Miller's Cowboy Music Revue
CONCERTS | Monday through Saturday from June through September, head to this redbrick performance space behind the Irma Hotel to watch the popular country-cowboy variety shows led by Dan Miller, a popular radio and TV host, singer, and actor. ✉ *1131 12th St.* ☎ *307/899–2799* 🌐 *www.cowboymusicrevue.com.*

★ **Wild West Spectacular**
THEATER | **FAMILY** | Held in downtown's historic 1937 Cody Theater, this colorful western revue—held four nights weekly from late June through early August—uses comedy, dance, and music to tell the tale of Buffalo Bill Cody. ✉ *1171 Sheridan Ave.* ☎ *307/527–9973* 🌐 *www.codywildwestshow.com.*

Shopping

Sheridan Avenue, Cody's main drag, is a great place to browse and shop among its many Native American and Western-theme shops. Most carry high-quality goods, but if ever in doubt, confirm that the item you're interested in is made from natural rather than artificial materials.

ART GALLERIES

★ **Big Horn Galleries**
ART GALLERIES | At one of Wyoming's most respected galleries of Western and wildlife art, you'll find sculptures and paintings by more than 75 artists, including James Bama, Chris Navarro, and Vic Payne. ✉ *1167 Sheridan Ave.* ☎ *307/527–7587* 🌐 *www.bighorngalleries.com.*

Cody Country Art League
ART GALLERIES | Adjacent to the Cody Country Chamber of Commerce visitor center, this expansive and eclectic gallery displays paintings, wood carvings, bronzes, and pottery by both established and emerging regional artists, and at a wide range of prices. ✉ *836 Sheridan Ave.* ☎ *307/587–3597* 🌐 *www.codycountryartleague.com.*

Open Range Images
ART GALLERIES | This gallery in a handsome historic downtown building carries the work of some of the area's top photographers. Wyoming's wildlife, flora, and landscapes provide the primary scenes, but less traditional themes also are presented. ✉ *1201 Sheridan Ave.* ☎ *307/587–8870* 🌐 *www.openrangeimages.com.*

★ **Simpson Gallagher Gallery**
ART GALLERIES | Stop by this respected gallery to browse contemporary representational art by Harry Jackson, Kathy Wipfler, T.D. Kelsey, Kang Cho, and Greg Scheibel, as well as works for 19th- and early-20th-century luminaries like Carl Rungius. ✉ *1161 Sheridan Ave.* ☎ *307/587–4022* 🌐 *www.simpsongallaghergallery.com.*

BOOKS

Legends Bookstore
BOOKS/STATIONERY | In addition to stocking a wide selection of travel books, histories, and outdoor guides to Wyoming and the Rockies, this friendly independent bookshop is a good bet for distinctive local gifts. ✉ *1350 Sheridan Ave.*

☎ 307/586–2320 🌐 www.legendsbooks.com.

CLOTHING

★ Custom Cowboy Shop

CLOTHING | Stock up on top-quality cowboy gear and clothing, ranging from felt hats and bolo ties for men to women's paisley Western shirts and wool jackets; and there's a huge selection of gear for horses. You'll also find an impressive array of Western books and household and kitchen goods. ✉ *1286 Sheridan Ave.* ☎ *800/487–2692* 🌐 *www.customcowboyshop.com.*

Wayne's Boot Shop

SHOES/LUGGAGE/LEATHER GOODS | The Lundvall family has operated this beloved purveyor and repairer of traditional cowboy as well as hiking and work boots, plus many other brands of casual shoes. You'll find top boot brands like Nocona, Allen's, Justin, and Tony Lama. ✉ *1250 Sheridan Ave.* ☎ *307/587–5234* 🌐 *www.waynesbootshop.com.*

FOOD

Wyoming Buffalo Company

FOOD/CANDY | Stop by for buffalo-meat products, such as sausage and jerky, in addition to specialty foods such as huckleberry honey, barbecue sauces, candy, and other products made in the Cowboy State. ✉ *1270 Sheridan Ave.* ☎ *307/587–8708* 🌐 *www.wyobuffalo.com.*

SPORTING GOODS

★ Sunlight Sports

SPORTING GOODS | Whether you're prepping for a spring rafting trip or a summer hike at Yellowstone, or it's winter snowshoeing and skiing you're planning, this exceptionally well-stocked shop is an excellent place to pick up gear and advice on where to pursue your adventures. You'll find a terrific selection of camping supplies, outerwear, and backpacks by top brands like Osprey, Burton, Mountain Hardware, and Smartwool. ✉ *1131 Sheridan Ave.* ☎ *307/587–9517* 🌐 *www.sunlightsports.com.*

Activities

CAMPING

Absaroka Bay RV Park. This campground on the south side of downtown stands across the street from Beck Park, where lake fishing is free (though you need a Wyoming fishing license). All RV spots are pull-through, and there's a big tenting area, though tent sites are not individually marked off. The camp has picnic tables but no cabins or store, and Sheridan Avenue's shops and restaurants are a mile away. ✉ *2002 Mountain View, Cody* ☎ *307/527–7440 or 800/527–7440* 🌐 *www.cody-wy.com*

Cody KOA. At breakfast, this campground 3 miles southeast downtown serves free pancakes. With water jets at the pool, a giant checkers set, bike rentals, basketball courts, horseshoe pits, and a playground, this venue with RV and tent sides as well as cabins caters to families. ✉ *5561 Greybull Hwy., Cody* ☎ *307/587–2369, 800/562–8507* 🌐 *www.codykoa.com*

Dead Indian Campground. You can fish in the stream at this quiet 10-site tent campground in Shoshone National Forest, adjacent to the Chief Joseph Scenic Byway (Highway 296), 35 miles northwest of Cody. There are hiking and horseback-riding trails, plus nearby corrals for horses. The campground remains popular with visitors, but one hopes that the Forest Service will change the offensive name at some point. ✉ *2056 Hwy. 296, Cody* ☎ *307/527–6921* 🌐 *www.fs.usda.gov/recarea/shoshone/recreation/camping-cabins/recarea/?recid=35869&actid=29*

CANOEING, KAYAKING, AND RAFTING

Gradient Mountain Sports

CANOEING/ROWING/SKULLING | This outfitter provides kayaking excursions, as well as instruction, sales, and rentals of single and tandem kayaks, stand-up paddleboards, and canoes. ✉ *1390 Sheridan*

Ave. ☎ *307/587–4659* 🌐 *www.gradient-mountainsports.net.*

River Runners

WHITE-WATER RAFTING | Book two-hour and half-day whitewater rafting adventures on the Shoshone River with this popular outfitter. Excursions are offered from late May through August. ✉ *1491 Sheridan Ave.* ☎ *307/527–7238* 🌐 *www.riverrunnersofwyoming.com.*

Wyoming River Trips

WHITE-WATER RAFTING | **FAMILY** | The folks at Wyoming River Trips arrange several family-friendly rafting and float excursions along the Shoshone River, lasting from 1½ hours to a full day. ✉ *233 Yellowstone Ave.* ☎ *307/587–6661* 🌐 *www.wyomingrivertrips.com.*

FISHING

Casting into a clear stream or placid blue lake is a popular pastime all over Wyoming, with good reason: the waters of the entire state teem with trout, pike, whitefish, catfish, and bass of all kinds. Most fishing enthusiasts stick to the land near Yellowstone, leaving the blue-ribbon streams of northern Wyoming relatively underutilized. The Bighorn River, Powder River, Crazy Woman Creek, Keyhole Reservoir, and Buffalo Bill Reservoir are all excellent angling venues.

Fly-fishing is especially big here, and there's no shortage of outfitters to equip you, both in the towns and in the wilderness. Anyone with a pole—be it an experienced fly-fisher or novice worm dangler—is respected out here. All the same, if you're a beginner, you'd do well to hire a guide. Tackle-shop staff can direct you to some good fishing spots, but you're more likely to find the choicest locations if you have an experienced local at your side.

★ Tim Wade's North Fork Anglers

FISHING | You can buy fishing tackle, rent equipment, get information on fishing in the area, or take a guided half- or full-day trip through this outfitter run by Tim Wade, one of the most renowned fly-fishing experts in the West. ✉ *1107 Sheridan Ave.* ☎ *307/527–7274* 🌐 *www.northforkanglers.com.*

HORSEBACK RIDING

Cedar Mountain Trail Rides

HORSEBACK RIDING | **FAMILY** | From mid-May through mid-September, book trail rides of an hour to a full day through this company that also offers pack trips themed around fishing and photography. ✉ *W. Yellowstone Ave.* ✥ *1 mile west of rodeo grounds* ☎ *307/527–4966.*

Cody Country Outfitters and Guides Association

HORSEBACK RIDING | This local organization of Cody-area outfitters is a useful resource for planning horseback, hunting, fishing, and ranching adventures. ✉ *Cody* 🌐 *www.codycountryoutfitters.com.*

SKIING

Wood River Ski Touring Park

SKIING/SNOWBOARDING | In Shoshone National Forest's peaceful and secluded Wood River valley near Meeteetse, southeast of Cody, this Nordic ski area has 25 kilometers of groomed trails, a warming hut, rentals, and a basic cabin for overnight rentals. Use of the trails is free, but donations are appreciated. Check in with the town recreation office in downtown Meeteetse; the ski area is another 22 miles southwest. ✉ *Meeteetse Recreation District Office, 1010 Park Ave., Meeteetse* ☎ *307/868–2603* 🌐 *www.meetrec.org.*

Sheridan

147 miles north of Casper via I–25 and I–90.

Proximity to the Big Horn Mountains and Bighorn National Forest makes Sheridan (population 15,804) a good base for hiking, mountain biking, skiing, snowmobiling, and fly-fishing, and the small city's European-flavored cowboy heritage makes it an interesting stop for history buffs. Soon after trappers built a simple cabin along Little Goose Creek in 1873, the spot became a regional railroad center. Cattle barons, many of them English and Scottish noblemen, established ranches that remain the mainstay of the economy. Sheridan still has ties to Britain's aristocracy; in fact, Queen Elizabeth II herself has paid the town a visit. Recently, coal mines and oil wells to the east have brought much-needed jobs and tax income to this community of 16,429 residents.

The biggest annual draw remains the **Sheridan WYO Rodeo,** held each July since 1931. It's more than the nightly rodeo exhibitions of calf-roping and bronc busting. The whole town opens up for events and amusements, including a giant carnival. Besides the high professional standards of the riders and ropers who come, what distinguishes this rodeo is that it's also an important Native American event. There's always a Native American Pow Wow and Dance as well as the World Championship Indian Relay Race. For rodeo aficionados, this is one of the year's highlights.

GETTING HERE AND AROUND

Whether you're arriving from the northwest or east via Interstate 90 or the south via Interstate 25, the Big Horn Mountains provide an impressive backdrop to this decidedly Western town. Take the East 5th Street or East Brundage Lane exits to Big Horn Avenue and the downtown core, and then park and walk to a host of art galleries, Western stores, restaurants, and outfitters. You'll also discover 30 bronzes on permanent display and another 27 sculptures on extended display throughout downtown.

VISITOR INFORMATION

Located right off Exit 23 of I–90, this visitor center, which also houses a small museum, is the perfect first stop on your visit to Sheridan. The free museum offers exhibits on Wyoming wildlife, Native American battlefields, historic sites, and a diorama of the Big Horn Mountains. The visitor center has a plethora of free maps, brochures, and information about the area.

CONTACTS Sheridan Visitor Center. ✉ *1517 E. 5th St* ☎ *307/673–7120* 🌐 *www.sheridanwyoming.com.*

 Sights

King's Saddlery

STORE/MALL | Although local cowboy legend Don King died in 2007, his sons still operate King's Saddlery and King's Ropes, where they've been hand-tooling saddles since the 1940s. They also make high-quality equipment for area ranchers and professional rodeo performers. King's has crafted gear for many celebrities, including Queen Elizabeth II. Unless you're in the market for an expensive saddle, what makes this a worthy stop (and a real treat) is found across a small alley directly behind the store, where a small museum is chock-full of Western memorabilia, ranging from more than 400 vintage firearms and handcrafted spurs to historical photographs, wildlife mounts, and arguably the largest collection of Western saddles anywhere. ✉ *184 N. Main St.* ☎ *307/672–2702* 🌐 *www.kingssaddlery.com* ⏲ *Closed Sun.*

★ Sheridan Inn

HOTEL—SIGHT | **FAMILY** | Evidence of the area's old-world ties can be found at the Sheridan Inn, just a few blocks from downtown near the old railroad depot. Modeled after a hunting lodge in Scotland, the 1893 building sports 69 gables in a show of architectural splendor not often seen around these parts. On the National Register of Historic Places, the inn once lured the likes of Herbert Hoover, Will Rogers, and Ernest Hemingway, and Buffalo Bill auditioned performers here for his Wild West Show. The Inn underwent a $4.8 million restoration from 2006 to 2009, employing "green"

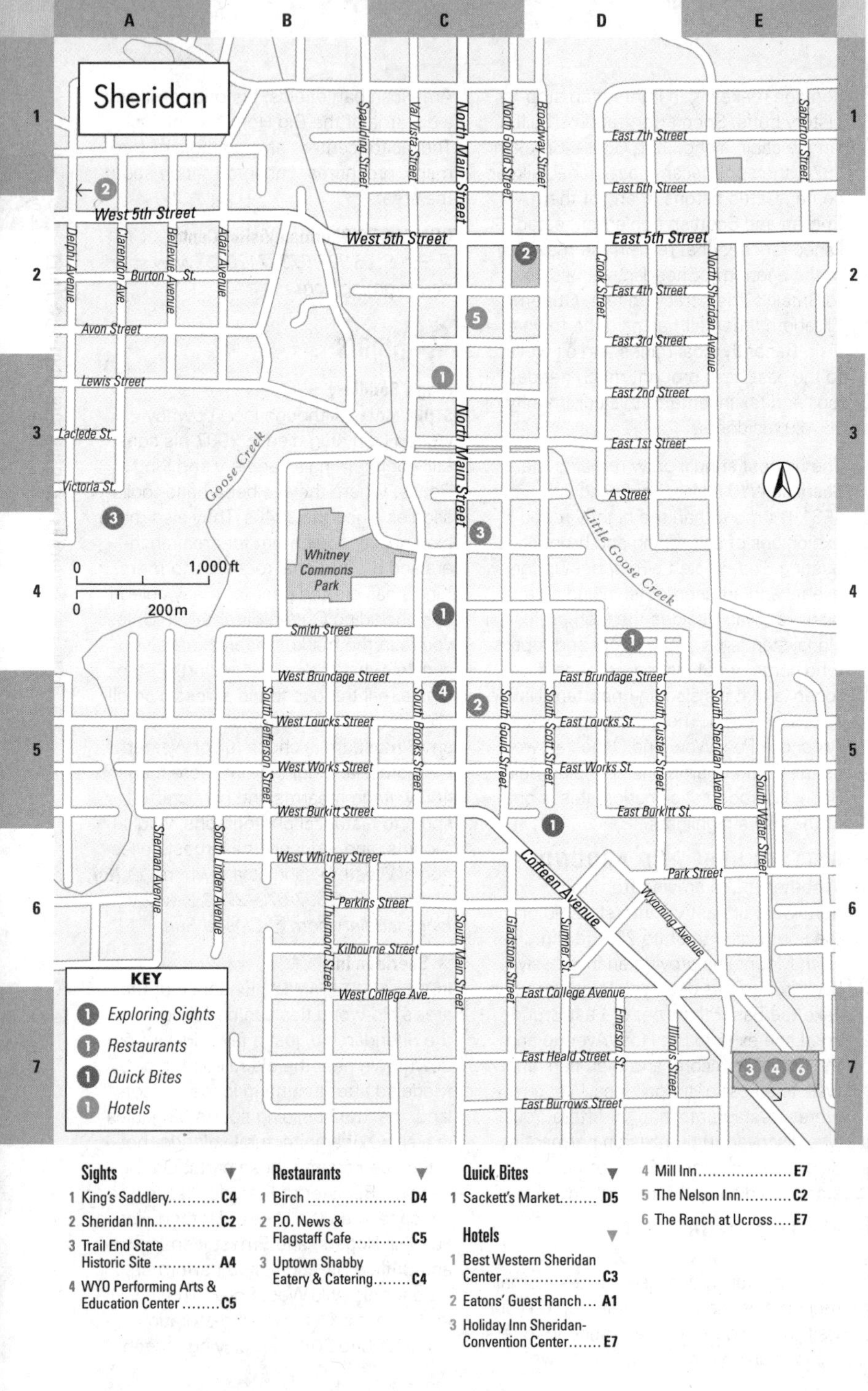

Sheridan
A
B
C
D
E
1
2
3
4
5
6
7
West 5th Street
East 5th Street
East 7th Street
East 6th Street
East 4th Street
East 3rd Street
East 2nd Street
East 1st Street
A Street
North Main Street
North Gould Street
Broadway Street
Spaulding Street
Val Vista Street
Crook Street
North Sheridan Avenue
Saberton Street
Delphi Avenue
Clarendon Ave.
Bellevue Avenue
Adair Avenue
Burton St.
Avon Street
Lewis Street
Laclede St.
Victoria St.
Goose Creek
Little Goose Creek
Whitney Commons Park
0
1,000 ft
0
200 m
Smith Street
West Brundage Street
East Brundage Street
West Loucks Street
East Loucks St.
West Works Street
East Works St.
West Burkitt Street
East Burkitt St.
West Whitney Street
Perkins Street
Kilbourne Street
West College Ave.
East College Avenue
East Heald Street
East Burrows Street
Park Street
South Jefferson Street
South Linden Avenue
Sherman Avenue
South Thurmond Street
South Brooks Street
South Main Street
South Gould Street
Gladstone Street
South Scott Street
Sumner St.
South Custer Street
South Sheridan Avenue
South Water Street
Coffeen Avenue
Wyoming Avenue
Emerson St.
Illinois Street
KEY
Exploring Sights
Restaurants
Quick Bites
Hotels
Sights
1 King's Saddlery C4
2 Sheridan Inn C2
3 Trail End State Historic Site A4
4 WYO Performing Arts & Education Center C5
Restaurants
1 Birch D4
2 P.O. News & Flagstaff Cafe C5
3 Uptown Shabby Eatery & Catering C4
Quick Bites
1 Sackett's Market D5
Hotels
1 Best Western Sheridan Center C3
2 Eatons' Guest Ranch A1
3 Holiday Inn Sheridan-Convention Center E7
4 Mill Inn E7
5 The Nelson Inn C2
6 The Ranch at Ucross E7

technologies, and an additional $2.8 million was spent in 2010 to refurbish the 22 guest rooms. The original Buffalo Bill Bar, an oak-and-mahogany monstrosity on the main floor, is purported to be a gift sent from England by Queen Victoria. ✉ *856 Broadway St.* ☎ *307/655–7861* 🌐 *www.sheridaninn.com.*

Trail End State Historic Site
HOUSE | A Flemish Revival mansion built in 1913 for John B. Kendrick, cattleman and one of Wyoming's first governors and senators, is now the Trail End State Historic Site. The furnishings and exhibits in the home are designed to depict early-20th-century ranching on the Plains. Highlights include elegant hand-carved woodwork and a third-floor ballroom. ✉ *400 Clarendon Ave.* ☎ *307/674–4589* 🌐 *www.trailend.org* 🎟 *$5.*

WYO Performing Arts and Education Center
ARTS VENUE | Built in 1923 as a vaudeville theater called the Lotus, the WYO Theater was closed and nearly demolished in the early 1980s. A strong show of support from the community saved the building, and now the refurbished art deco structure hosts everything from orchestras and ballets to lectures and Broadway revivals, especially in the summer. ✉ *42 N. Main St.* ☎ *307/672–9084* 🌐 *www.wyotheater.com.*

Restaurants

★ Birch
$$$ | **CONTEMPORARY** | This contemporary French-Asian restaurant displays a considerable amount of Wyoming flair, finding a home in a quaint yet elegant space away from the main strip. Ingredients are sourced locally whenever possible, and seafood is flown in fresh daily. **Known for:** in-house baker to make all of their buns and famous sourdough; cocktail tinctures all made from scratch and mixed mostly with Wyoming distilled spirits; Tuesday burger and beer night. 💲 *Average main: $25* ✉ *342 Whitney La.* ☎ *307/655–5551* 🌐 *www.birchsheridan.com* 🕓 *Closed Sun. and Mon. No lunch.*

P.O. News & Flagstaff Cafe
$$$ | **AMERICAN** | **FAMILY** | A tobacco store in the front and a casual restaurant in the back, the historic Flagstaff Cafe is one of the longest-running, continually operating businesses in Wyoming. This classic family-style menu offers hearty breakfast and lunch to weary travelers and locals alike. **Known for:** locally sourced Legerski sausage; all hamburgers ground fresh every day by the nearby Sacketts Market; convenient location in the heart of downtown Sheridan. 💲 *Average main: $19* ✉ *1 N. Main St.* ☎ *307/673–5333* 🌐 *ponews-flagstaffcafe.food93.com* 🕓 *Closed Sun. and Mon. No dinner.*

Uptown Shabby Eatery & Catering
$$ | **FRENCH FUSION** | **FAMILY** | With a farmhouse feel and an eclectic menu, this local favorite serves up iconic classics like skillet mac and cheese, flatbreads, and burgers, each with their own twists. You won't be leaving hungry here with meals like French PBC&B sandwich (peanut butter, chocolate, and banana served between French toast) or jalapeño popper mac and cheese. **Known for:** the famous blueberry cheesecake burger; weekend breakfast kabacos (kebab tacos); authentic French crepes. 💲 *Average main: $15* ✉ *1 E. Alger St.* ☎ *307/763–4133.*

Coffee and Quick Bites

Sackett's Market
$$ | **DELI** | With a back-to-basics approach to food, Sackett's sells freshly butchered meats and fresh-picked vegetables free from all chemicals, additives, and preservatives. But the market has become equally popular for its delicious sandwiches, salads, and a fresh soup of the day, all made for take-out. **Known for:** smoked meats made in-house; deli counter modeled after the original in Big Horn Mercantile; all products sourced from the

mountain states. *Average main:* *184 E. Burkitt St.* *307/672–3663* *www.sackettsmarket.com* *Closed Sun.*

Hotels

Best Western Sheridan Center
$$ | HOTEL | The rooms at this hotel are popular with tour groups to the region and are typical of chain motels, but some have lodgepole-pine furniture and earth and green tones. **Pros:** good restaurant on premises; friendly and helpful hospitality staff; nice pool area. **Cons:** travelers have complained about a lack of security; unimaginative, albeit free, breakfast options; conventioneers have felt ignored by hotel management. *Rooms from: $125* *612 N. Main St.* *307/674–7421* *www.bestwestern.com* *139 rooms* *Free breakfast.*

Eatons' Guest Ranch
$$$$ | ALL-INCLUSIVE | This spread is credited with inventing the dude ranch, back in the late 19th century, and it's still going strong, as well as being a working cattle ranch. **Pros:** a pleasantly rustic experience; plenty of chances to get in the saddle; attentive and friendly staff. **Cons:** with the minimum stay, if you find you don't like ranch life you're stuck for a few days; far from the amenities of downtown; cabins are basic. *Rooms from: $250* *270 Eatons' Ranch Rd., Wolf* *307/655–9285, 800/210–1049* *www.eatonsranch.com* *Closed Oct.–May* *51 rooms* *All-inclusive.*

Holiday Inn Sheridan–Convention Center
$$$ | HOTEL | The soaring atrium of this five-story hotel, which is five minutes from downtown by car, has a waterfall and is filled with overstuffed chairs and couches, as well as Scooter's Sports Bar. With white-and-blue accents and tan walls, the rooms are typical of chain hotels, but most have some Western-style touches, and some look out on the Big Horn Mountains. **Pros:** large and modern; good dining options; a fun and friendly staff. **Cons:** this is a big hotel with a business feel, even though it's not right downtown; breakfast is not included; rooms and ambiance has a dated, 1970s feel. *Rooms from: $150* *1809 Sugarland Dr.* *877/672–4011, 307/672–8931, 888/752–5338, 307/672–6388* *www.ihg.com* *212 rooms* *No meals.*

Mill Inn
$$ | HOTEL | A former flour mill near a bridge has been converted into this inviting small hotel, which is listed on the National Register of Historic Places. **Pros:** near downtown; complimentary breakfast; historic accents with great photography by L.A. Huffman. **Cons:** some think the inn is overpriced; bathrooms unaccommodating to those with disabilities; all rooms open directly to the outdoors, and those facing the street can be noisy. *Rooms from: $90* *2161 Coffeen Ave.* *307/672–6401, 888/357–6455* *www.sheridanmillinn.com* *42 rooms* *Free breakfast.*

★ The Nelson Inn
$$$ | HOTEL | FAMILY | Experience the industrial wild West while based in these spacious suites (almost all over 1,000 square feet) featuring high ceilings, natural light, bold style, and all the modern comforts of home. **Pros:** plenty of room to spread out; attention to detail, with beautiful modern touches in every room; walking distance to downtown, with plenty of shops and dining opportunities. **Cons:** no free breakfast, though each suite has a full kitchen; small and tends to book up quickly in the summer months; no pool or hot tub. *Rooms from: $185* *723 N. Main St.* *307/763–4414* *www.thenelsoninn.com* *9 suites* *No meals.*

The Ranch at Ucross
$$$$ | ALL-INCLUSIVE | If you're looking to get in touch with yourself—or your traveling companion—this Old West–style ranch on the banks of Piney Creek in the foothills of the Big Horns may well be the place. **Pros:** stay one night, and you'll

wish you owned the place; quiet and relaxing; great activities, like horseback riding, on-site. **Cons:** a long way from anywhere; some guests have noted the rooms have a dated appearance; not all rooms have Wi-Fi or TVs. $ *Rooms from: $200 ✉ 2673 U.S. Hwy. 14, 30 miles southwest of Sheridan, Clearmont ☎ 307/737–2281, 800/447–0194 ⊕ www.blairhotels.com ⇆ 31 rooms 🍽 All-inclusive.*

Shopping

The suburban malls that have drained so many downtowns are absent in Sheridan; instead, Main Street is lined with mostly homegrown—and sometimes quirky—shops.

Best Out West Mall

SHOPPING CENTERS/MALLS | In a break from typical gift stores stocked with rubber tomahawks, the Best Out West Mall is a two-story bazaar of Western paraphernalia, with booths hawking everything from spurs to rare books. Some items are new, but most are antiques. ✉ *109 N. Main St.* ☎ *307/674–5003.*

Bozeman Trail Gallery

ART GALLERIES | A stronghold of frontier culture, the Bozeman Trail Gallery has a varied collection of 19th- and 20th-century art and artifacts from the American West, ranging from vintage Colt revolvers and leather saddles to Cheyenne Sioux moccasins and Navajo rugs. The gallery also maintains a collection of significant Western paintings from artists such as Karen Vance and Ernest Martin Hennings. ✉ *190 N. Main St.* ☎ *307/672–3928* ⊕ *www.bozemantrailgallery.com.*

Crazy Woman Trading Company

ANTIQUES/COLLECTIBLES | The Crazy Woman Trading Company sells unique gifts and antiques, including deluxe coffees and T-shirts picturing a black bear doing yoga. Murphy McDougal, the store's CEO (and the owners' golden retriever), is usually sleeping near the front door. The store is closed on Sunday. ✉ *134 N. Main St.* ☎ *307/672–3939* ⊕ *www.crazywomantradingco.com.*

Activities

Like every other community on the edge of the Bighorn National Forest, Sheridan abounds with opportunities for outdoor recreation. A love of sports seems to be a common thread among people here, whether they're visitors or locals, winter enthusiasts or sunseekers, thrill hunters or quiet naturalists. Because of Sheridan's proximity to U.S. 14, a mountain highway near hundreds of miles of snowmobile trails and alpine streams, the town is especially popular among sledders in the winter and fly-fishers in the summer and autumn.

CAMPING

Big Horn Mountain KOA Campground. On the banks of Big Goose Creek minutes away from downtown Sheridan is this KOA, a well-developed campground with a basketball court, horseshoe pits, and a miniature-golf course. ✉ *63 Decker Rd.* ☎ *307/674–8766* ⊕ *www.koa.com* ⇆ *45 sites.*

FLY-FISHING

Angling Destinations

FISHING | More of a custom adventure company than an outfitter, **Angling Destinations** arranges multiday fishing trips to some of the most remote locations of Wyoming, Montana, and Idaho, as well as international destinations. ✉ *Wyoming 82801* ☎ *800/211–8530.*

Fly Shop of the Big Horns

FISHING | The full-service **Fly Shop of the Big Horns** offers rentals, fishing apparel and gear, guided trips on private and public waters, and a fly-fishing school, as well as the largest fly selection in the region. ✉ *334 N. Main St.* ☎ *800/253–5866, 307/672–5866.*

Big Horn

9 miles south of Sheridan via Hwy. 335.

Now a gateway to Bighorn National Forest, this tree-lined town with mountain views was originally a rest stop for emigrants heading west. An outpost on the Bozeman Trail, which crossed Bozeman Pass, Big Horn City in the mid-19th century was a lawless frontier town of saloons and roadhouses. After pioneers brought their families to the area in the late 1870s, the rowdy community quieted down. It never officially incorporated, so although it has a post office, fire department, and school, there is no bona-fide city government.

GETTING HERE AND AROUND

Located between the vast Bighorn National Forest and Interstate 90 south of Sheridan, the town of Big Horn can be reached via State Highway 335 south to County Road 28 East. It's a town of just 198 residents; you won't have trouble finding your way around.

Sights

Bighorn National Forest

FOREST | Big Horn is an access point to the 1.1-million-acre area, which has lush grasslands, alpine meadows, rugged mountaintops, canyons, and deserts. There are numerous hiking trails and camping spots for use in the summer, and it's a popular snowmobiling area in the winter. ✉ *2013 Eastside 2nd St.* ✣ *Ranger station* ☎ *307/674–2600* 🌐 *www.fs.usda.gov/bighorn.*

Bozeman Trail Museum

MUSEUM | FAMILY | A hand-hewn-log blacksmith shop, built in 1879 to serve pioneers on their way to the goldfields of Montana, houses the Bozeman Trail Museum, the town's historical repository and interpretive center. The jewel of its collection is the Cloud Peak Boulder, a stone with names and dates apparently carved by military scouts just two days before the Battle of the Little Bighorn, which was fought less than 100 miles to the north in 1876. The staff is very friendly to children, and there are some old pipe organs that kids are encouraged to play. ✉ *335 Johnson St.* ☎ *307/674–6363* 🎫 *Free* 🕓 *Closed weekdays and Sept.–May.*

The Brinton Museum

MUSEUM | If you're not staying at a ranch and you want to get a look at one of the West's finest, visit the south of Big Horn on the old Quarter Circle A Ranch. The Brinton family didn't exactly rough it in this 20-room clapboard home, complete with libraries, fine furniture, and silver and china services. A reception gallery displays changing exhibits from the Brinton art collection, which includes such Western artists as Charles M. Russell and Frederic Remington. ✉ *239 Brinton Rd.* ☎ *307/672–3173* 🌐 *thebrintonmuseum.org* 🎫 *Free* 🕓 *Closed late Dec.–mid-Feb.*

Restaurants

Bozeman Stable Grillroom and Saloon

$$ | AMERICAN | A wood-slat building with a false front and tin roof, this is the oldest operating bar in Wyoming, established in 1882. The inn's only sign is painted on a mock covered wagon that's perched above the door. **Known for:** Ernest Hemingway was a patron; small-town friendliness; options for everyone. 💲 *Average main: $18* ✉ *158 Johnson St.* ☎ *307/672–5837* 🌐 *thebozemanstable.com.*

Activities

POLO

Big Horn Equestrian Center

HORSE RACING/SHOW | Perhaps the most unexpected sport to be found in the outdoor playground of the Bighorn National Forest is polo. The game has been played at the Big Horn Equestrian Center ever since upper-class English and Scottish families settled the area in the 1890s, making these the oldest polo grounds in the United States. You can watch people at play for free on Sunday in the summer. The 65 acres here are also used for other events, including youth soccer and bronc riding. ✉ *352 Bird Farm Rd.* ✣ *Near state bird farm, on Hwy. 28, west of Big Horn* ☎ *307/673–0454* 🌐 *www.thebhec.org.*

Buffalo

34 miles south of Big Horn via I–90, U.S. 87, and Hwy. 335.

Buffalo is a trove of history and a hospitable little town in the foothills below Big Horn Pass. Here cattle barons who wanted free grazing and homesteaders who wanted to build fences fought it out in the Johnson County War of 1892. Nearby are the sites of several skirmishes between the U.S. military and Native Americans along the Bozeman Trail. Buffalo is 182 miles due west on I–90 of Sturgis, South Dakota. The first week of every August, Sturgis hosts a very popular and legendary bikers' conclave. So, if you're passing through at this time of year, don't be surprised to hear the occasional roar of hogs.

Buffalo's Occidental Hotel may be the best place to begin your visit to the Big Horn region, particularly on a Thursday night. That's when you'll find bluegrass music flowing through the doors of its Western-style saloon, and virtually the entire town assembled there. It's a good chance to meet the locals, enjoy some great music and refreshments, and contribute to local charities, for which the gathering has raised thousands of dollars. This is as friendly as the West gets.

GETTING HERE AND AROUND

Arriving in the region via Interstate 25, take the U.S. 87 or East Hart Street exit west to South Main Street and the downtown business district. Then park and explore area parks, shops, museums, and the famed Occidental Hotel. For a quiet, shaded picnic, check out City Park and Prosinski Park a block southwest of the Occidental.

VISITOR INFORMATION

CONTACTS Buffalo Chamber of Commerce. ✉ *55 N. Main St.* ☎ *307/684–5544, 800/227–5122* 🌐 *www.buffalowyo.com.*

Sights

Fetterman Massacre Monument

MILITARY SITE | The Fetterman Massacre Monument is a rock monolith dedicated to the memory of Lieutenant William J. Fetterman and his 80 men, who died in a December 21, 1866, battle against Lakota-Sioux warriors. Today, an interpretive trail with 21 signs spans the entire length of the battlefield, explaining the combatants, leaders, weapons, tactics, positions, and theories of a battle that lasted all of 30 minutes. This was the worst defeat for the U.S military on the Northern Plains until the Little Big Horn battle a decade later. Five miles west of the Fetterman site is the site of the Wagon Box Fight, which also has a short interpretive trail. Fort Phil Kearny is the starting point for both battle sites, providing brochures, guides, and an overview of the history of Red Cloud's War. ✉ *Buffalo* ✣ *18 miles north of Buffalo, off I–90; obtain directions at Fort Phil Kearny.*

Fort Phil Kearny State Historic Site

MILITARY SITE | Fort Phil Kearny State Historic Site was the focal point of Red Cloud's War, and Phil Kearny was probably the most fought-over fort in the West. This is the largest 8-foot stockaded, Hollywood-style fort ever built by the U.S. military, covering 17 acres; it experienced almost daily skirmishing against Cheyenne or Lakota warriors. Its location eventually led to major battles, including the December 21, 1866, Fetterman Fight, in which 81 soldiers were killed (the only time in American military history that a whole command was defeated to the last man) and the August 2, 1867, Wagon Box Fight, in which 32 men held their position in a daylong fight against more than 800 Lakota. This battle was considered a victory by both sides.

The fort's mission was to protect travelers on the Bozeman Trail going to the goldfields in southern Montana. However, there are theories that it may have been placed in what were the last and best hunting grounds of the Northern Plains tribes in order to draw them away from the railroad construction across southern Wyoming that was occurring at the same time. In the fall of 1868 the U.S. government signed the Fort Laramie Treaty, ending Red Cloud's War—the only war Native Americans won against the United States. The treaty closed the Bozeman Trail, making all the land between the Black Hill and Big Horn Mountains, and the land between the Yellowstone and North Platte rivers, unceded Indian land where whites could not go. However, it also for the first time established Indian Agencies along the Missouri River for the different Lakota tribes. So, although the Indians won the war, they lost the peace. As part of the treaty, Fort Phil Kearny was abandoned in August 1868. Within two weeks, it is believed, Cheyenne, under Two Moon, occupied and then burned the fort to the ground. No original buildings remain at the site, but fort building locations are marked, and the visitor center has good details. The stockade around the fort was re-created after archaeological digs in 1999. ✉ *528 Wagon Box Rd., Banner* ✣ *15 miles north of Buffalo on I–90* ☎ *307/684–7629* 🌐 *fortphilkearny.com* 🎫 *$5* ⏲ *By appointment only Nov.–Apr.*

★ Jim Gatchell Memorial Museum

MUSEUM | The Jim Gatchell Memorial Museum is the kind of small-town museum that's worth stopping for if you're interested in the frontier history of the region, including the Johnson County Cattle War. It contains Native American, military, outlaw, and ranching artifacts collected by a local pharmacist who was a close friend of area Native Americans. The museum completed a $300,000 renovation project in 2011. Visitors will discover new exhibits and interpretive opportunities. ✉ *100 Fort St.* ☎ *307/684–9331* 🌐 *www.jimgatchell.com* 🎫 *$7* ⏲ *Closed weekends.*

Restaurants

Bozeman Trail Steakhouse

$$$ | **AMERICAN** | This eatery, which is literally on the Bozeman Trail, serves decent food, from chicken, taco, and Cobb salads to local favorites such as prime-rib melts and club sandwiches or bison steak, burgers, and king-cut prime-rib plates amid Western memorabilia. You can also dine outdoors on the deck and sip from the large selection of microbrews. **Known for:** best place in town to try a bison steak; 19 beers on tap from around Wyoming and the country; diverse menu with something to please everyone. $ *Average main: $20* ✉ *675 E. Hart St.* ☎ *307/684–5555, 888/351–6732* 🌐 *www.thebozemantrailsteakhouse.com.*

★ The Virginian Restaurant

$$$ | **CONTEMPORARY** | Named for the 1902 Owen Wister novel that made Buffalo famous, this is the dining salon of the beautifully restored Occidental Hotel. Dishes made from organic beef range from buffalo rib eye to chateaubriand and filet mignon with béarnaise sauce. **Known for:** marvelous stained-glass accents in the saloon, dating from 1908; inspiration for Owen Wister's famous novel (and not much has changed since); decadent buffalo steaks. $ *Average main: $25* ✉ *The Occidental Hotel, 10 N. Main St.* ☎ *307/684–5976* 🌐 *www.occidentalwyoming.com.*

Winchester Steak House

$$$ | **STEAKHOUSE** | You can tie up your car in front of the hitching racks before this Western-style eatery in a false-front building. The Winchester has prime rib, steak, and more steak, plus appetizers, a good wine list, and a large rock fireplace and small bar. **Known for:** French onion soup (not to be missed); daily specials to keep you coming back; "Rocky Mountain oysters" (just use your imagination). *Average main: $25 117 Hwy. 16 E 307/684–8636 www.thewinchester-steakhouse.com Closed Mon. No lunch.*

Hotels

Hampton Inn Buffalo
$$$ | **HOTEL** | **FAMILY** | Enjoy the comfort of a solid chain hotel with a fitness room and a pool. **Pros:** big patio area to enjoy on summer mornings; hot breakfast bar with great offerings; 24-hour pool and fitness room. **Cons:** not walkable from downtown Buffalo; typical chain hotel; no hotel bar or restaurant. *Rooms from: $194 85 U.S. Hwy. 16 E 855/605–0317 www.hilton.com 75 rooms Free breakfast.*

★ The Occidental Hotel
$$$ | **B&B/INN** | This enchanting, fully restored grand hotel, founded in 1880, served emigrants on the Bozeman Trail, two U.S. presidents, and some of Wyoming's most colorful characters, and it remains in top form. **Pros:** well-stocked library; owners on premises offering gracious service; well-appointed rooms. **Cons:** no pool; old plumbing (but it doesn't leak); breakfast is not included. *Rooms from: $195 10 N. Main St. 307/684–0451 occidentalwyoming.com 19 rooms No meals.*

★ Paradise Guest Ranch
$$$$ | **ALL-INCLUSIVE** | **FAMILY** | Not only does this dude ranch have a stunning location at the base of some of the tallest mountains in the range, but it's also one of the oldest (circa 1907) and most progressive, as evidenced by its adults-only month (September) and two ladies' weeks. **Pros:** clean cabins with rustic, beautiful views; hospitable staff; good children's programs. **Cons:** minimum stays; not so close to Buffalo; no cell phone service at ranch. *Rooms from: $1985 282 Hunter Creek Rd. off U.S. 16, 13 miles west of Buffalo 307/684–7876 www.paradiseranch.com Closed Oct.–Apr. 18 rooms All-inclusive.*

SureStay Plus Hotel
$$ | **B&B/INN** | Several blocks from downtown, this motel is close to Clear Creek Trail, the city's bike and walking path. **Pros:** clean and contemporary; good breakfast; walking distance from shopping and dining options. **Cons:** standard chain hotel with no frills; some guests complained that the rooms were musty; hotel could use an update. *Rooms from: $95 65 U.S. Hwy. 16 E 307/684–9564, 800/424–6423 www.comfortinn.com 63 rooms Free breakfast.*

Activities

The forested canyons and pristine alpine meadows of the Big Horn Mountains teem with animal and plant life, making this an excellent area for hiking and pack trips by horseback. The quality and concentration of locals willing to outfit adventurers are high in Buffalo, making it a suitable base camp from which to launch an expedition.

ADVENTURE OUTFITTERS

South Fork Mountain Lodge & Outfitters
TOUR—SPORTS | The folks at **South Fork Mountain Lodge & Outfitters** can customize about any sort of adventure you'd like to undertake in the Big Horns, whether it's hiking, hunting, fishing, horseback riding, snowmobiling, or cross-country skiing. The company can arrange for all of your food and supplies and provide a guide, or render drop-camp services for more experienced thrill seekers. *7558 Hwy. 16 W 16 miles west of Buffalo on U.S.*

16 ☎ 307/267–2609 🌐 www.lodgesofthe-bighorns.com.

CAMPING

Deer Park Campground. Although one section of this campground is quiet and relaxed, reserved for campers over 55, the main campsites are busy. In addition to a heated pool and a hot tub, Deer Park offers ice-cream socials at night for $1. ✉ *146 U.S. 16* ☎ *307/684–5722, 800/222–9960* 🌐 *www.deerparkrv.com* *33 full hookups, 33 partial hookups, 34 tent sites, 3 cabins.*

HORSEBACK RIDING AND PACK TRIPS

Trails West Outfitters

HORSEBACK RIDING | Trails West Outfitters arranges multiday hunting, fishing, and pack trips in the Shoshone National Forest. The company also operates shorter wilderness excursions and drop camps for more independent adventurers. ✉ *140 Flagstaff Way* ☎ *307/684–5233, 888/283–9793* 🌐 *www.trailswestoutfitters.com.*

Gillette

70 miles east of Buffalo on I–90.

With a population that's boomed from 17,000 in 1981 to 32,000 in 2009, Gillette, the metropolis of the Powder River Basin, has many relatively new properties, restaurants, and shopping opportunities. Thanks to the region's huge coal mines, it's one of Wyoming's wealthiest cities, and as a result it has an excellent community infrastructure that includes the Cam-Plex, a multiuse events center that hosts everything from crafts bazaars and indoor rodeos to concerts and fine-arts exhibits. Gillette is also a gateway town for Devils Tower National Monument, the volcanic plug that is one of the nation's most distinctive geological features and a hot spot for rock climbers.

Gillette has worked hard to make itself presentable, but you don't have to look very hard to find a shovel bigger than a house at one of its giant strip mines. Once a major livestock center, from which ranchers shipped cattle and sheep to eastern markets, the city now mines millions of tons of coal each year and ships it out to coal-fired power plants. In fact, if Gillette (and surrounding Campbell County) were its own nation, it would be the world's sixth-greatest producer of coal. Currently the county turns out nearly a third of all American-mined coal. Gillette, however, is a big fish in a small pond, one of only two incorporated towns in the county (the other is Wright, population 1,347).

GETTING HERE AND AROUND

Gillette may well serve as the heartbeat of eastern Wyoming, with a new college, a new $45 million recreation center that opened in late 2009, new Interstate 90 overpasses, and 17 miles of new roadways built in town in 2008. Travelers will find new hotels, restaurants, shopping malls, and residential areas south of Interstate 90 on State Highway 59/South Douglas Highway. Heading north on the same route takes motorists directly downtown.

VISITOR INFORMATION

CONTACTD Gillette Visitor Center. ✉ *314 S. Gillette Ave.* ☎ *307/686–0040* 🌐 *visitgillettewright.com.*

Sights

Keyhole State Park

NATIONAL/STATE PARK | You can fish, boat, swim, and camp at Keyhole State Park. Bird-watching is a favorite activity here, as up to 225 species can be seen on the grounds. The park is 45 miles east of Gillette and 20 miles south of Devils Tower. ✉ *22 Marina Rd., Moorcroft* ☎ *307/756–3596* 🌐 *wyoparks.wyo.gov* *$9.*

Rockpile Museum

MUSEUM | Local artifacts, including mining tools, cattle brands, and rifles, make up the collection at the Campbell

County–run Rockpile Museum. The museum's name comes from its location next to a natural rock-pile formation that served as a landmark for pioneers and cattle drives. ✉ *900 W. 2nd St.* ☎ *307/682–5723* 🌐 *www.rockpilemuseum.com* 🎫 *Free* 🕑 *Closed Sun.*

Thunder Basin National Grassland
NATURE PRESERVE | A vast area that stretches from the edge of the Black Hills almost to the center of Wyoming, Thunder Basin truly is the outback of America. Except for a handful of tiny towns, deserted highways, and coal mines, it is entirely undeveloped. Farmers from the east settled this area at the end of the 19th century, hoping to raise crops in the semiarid soil. Experienced only with the more humid conditions east of the Rockies, the farmers failed, and the region deteriorated into a dust bowl. Most of the land has reverted to its natural state, creating millions of acres of grasslands filled with wildlife. Among the many species is one of the largest herds of pronghorn in the world (numbering approximately 26,000), prairie dogs, and burrowing owls that live in abandoned prairie-dog holes. Highway 116, Highway 59, and Highway 450 provide the best access; a few interior dirt roads are navigable only in dry weather. The grasslands, though, are most impressive away from the highways. Take a hike to get a real sense of the vast emptiness of this land. Stop by the District Forest Service Office in Douglas for maps, directions, and tips. ✉ *2250 E. Richards St., Douglas* ☎ *307/358–4690* 🌐 *www.fs.usda.gov* 🎫 *Free.*

Restaurants

Hong Kong
$ | **CHINESE** | Lunches here are served fast and cheap (between $7 and $8) and include more than 30 different dishes, such as Mongolian beef and cashew chicken. They're popular with the business crowd, so you might want to avoid the noon lunch rush. **Known for:** extensive menu; large portions; friendly service. *$ Average main: $8* ✉ *1612 W. 2nd St.* ☎ *307/682–5829.*

Hotels

Best Western Tower West Lodge
$$ | **HOTEL** | A range of earth tones decorates the comfortable rooms of this hotel on the west side of town. **Pros:** easy interstate access; restaurant on-site and several close by; cheap rates. **Cons:** located a fair distance from the downtown area; poor setting next to an industrial area; neighboring interstate is busy and noisy. *$ Rooms from: $90* ✉ *109 N. U.S. 14/16* ☎ *307/686–2210* 🌐 *www.bestwestern.com* *190 rooms* *No meals.*

Activities

Gillette is especially fitness conscious, and as a result, the town has invested in many new recreational facilities—including a massive $52 million city-schools recreation center and two health clubs—that cities of a similar size lack. There are also more than 37 miles of developed walking trails within the city limits, including paths on the north end of town, off West Warlow Drive, in McManamen Park, a prime bird-watching spot.

Devils Tower National Monument

65 miles northeast of Gillette via I–90 and U.S. 14; 32 miles northeast of Sundance via U.S. 14. 60 miles west of Spearfish, SD via U.S. 14 and I–90.

Devils Tower is a rocky, grooved butte that juts upward 1,280 feet above the plain of the Belle Fourche River. Native American legend has it that the tower was corrugated by the claws of a bear trying to reach some children on top, and some tribes still revere the site, which they call Bear Lodge.

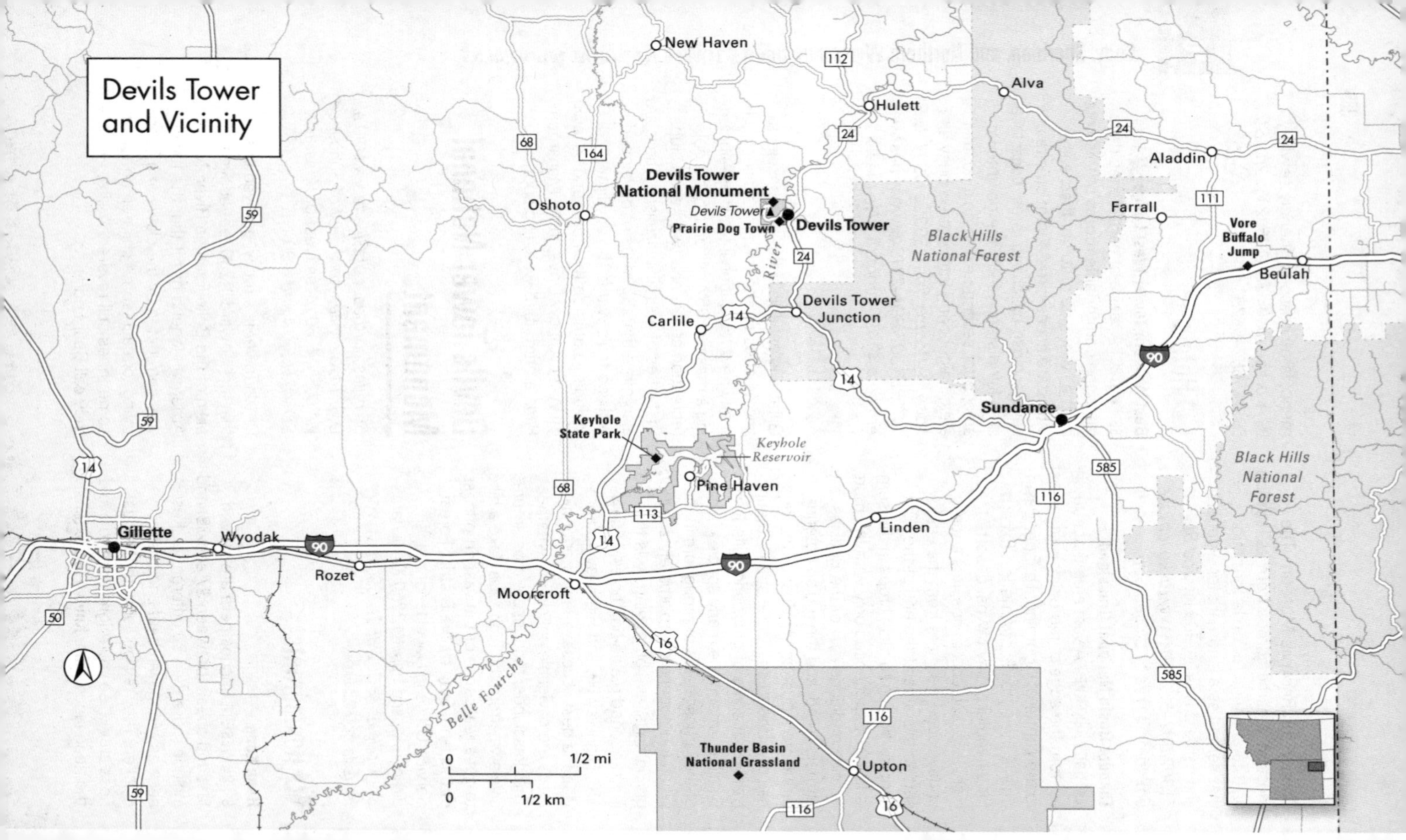
Devils Tower and Vicinity
New Haven
Hulett
Alva
Aladdin
Oshoto
Devils Tower National Monument
Devils Tower
Prairie Dog Town
Devils Tower
Farrall
Vore Buffalo Jump
Beulah
Black Hills National Forest
River
Devils Tower Junction
Carlile
Sundance
Keyhole State Park
Keyhole Reservoir
Pine Haven
Black Hills National Forest
Gillette
Wyodak
Rozet
Moorcroft
Linden
Belle Fourche
Thunder Basin National Grassland
Upton
0
1/2 mi
0
1/2 km
112
24
68
164
59
111
14
90
585
116
113
16
50

GETTING HERE AND AROUND

Located in extreme northeast Wyoming, America's first national monument can be accessed from several routes. Traveling from the west on Interstate 90, motorists may take U.S. 14 E at Moorcroft 25 miles, then Route 24 6 miles north to Devils Tower. After visiting the monument, travelers may then head south on Route 24, returning to U.S. 14 E to Sundance and I–90. Alternatively, after leaving the monument, stay on Route 24 for a scenic drive through Hulett to the small town of Aladdin and its quirky General Store, and then return south to I–90 via Route 111.

Sights

★ Devils Tower National Monument

MEMORIAL | As you drive east from Gillette, the highways begin to rise into the forested slopes of the Black Hills. A detour north will take you to Devils Tower. Geologists attribute the butte's strange existence to ancient volcanic activity. Rock climbers say it's one of the best crack-climbing areas on the continent. The tower was a tourist magnet long before a spaceship landed here in the movie *Close Encounters of the Third Kind.* Teddy Roosevelt made it the nation's first national monument in 1906, and it has attracted a steadily increasing throng of visitors ever since—up to nearly half a million people a year.

When you visit, take some time to stop at the visitor center. Exhibits here explain the geology, history, and cultural significance of the monument, and a bookstore carries a wide selection of materials relating to the park. Park rangers can provide updated information on hiking and climbing conditions. A short and easy walking path circles the tower. ✉ *Hwy. 110, Devils Tower* ☎ *307/467–5283* 🌐 *www.nps.gov/deto* 🎫 *$25 for a vehicle pass.*

Prairie Dog Town

NATURE PRESERVE | At the Prairie Dog Town on the monument grounds between Devils Tower and the Belle Fourche River, you can observe the burrowing, chirping rodents in their natural habitat. Prairie dogs were once plentiful on the Great Plains, but ranching and development have taken their toll; today, most sizeable populations of the animal are found on protected federal lands. ✉ *Hwy. 110, Devils Tower* ☎ *307/467–5283* 🌐 *www.nps.gov/deto* 🎫 *$25 per vehicle entrance to the monument.*

Shopping

Devils Tower Trading Post

GIFTS/SOUVENIRS | At the entrance to Devils Tower National Monument, you can purchase informative books, Western art, buffalo hides, clothing, knickknacks, and souvenirs. A giant Harley-Davidson flag (supposedly the world's largest) flies over the store, so it's no wonder that bikers overrun the place during the massive Sturgis Motorcycle Rally in August. The old-fashioned ice-cream parlor, which also serves a mean sarsaparilla, is a treat in the heat of summer. ✉ *57 Hwy. 110, Devils Tower* ☎ *307/467–5295* 🌐 *www.devilstowertradingpost.com.*

Activities

CAMPING

Belle Fourche Campground. Tucked away in a bend of the Belle Fourche River, this campground is small and spartan, but it is the only place in the park where camping is allowed. ✉ *Hwy. 110* ☎ *307/467–5283, 307/467–5350* 🌐 *www.nps.gov/deto* ⛺ *47 sites.*

Devils Tower KOA. Less than a mile from Devils Tower, this campground literally lies in the shadow of the famous stone monolith. The view of the sheer granite walls above red river bluffs is one of the property's greatest assets. Another is

President Thedore Roosevelt named Devils Tower the first U.S. national monument in 1906.

the bordering Belle Fourche River, which nurtures several stalwart cottonwood and ash trees that provide at least some areas with shade. Weather permitting, the campground stages a nightly outdoor showing of *Close Encounters of the Third Kind.* *✉ 60 Hwy. 110 ☎ 307/467–5395, 800/562–5785 🌐 www.koa.com ⛺ 80 sites.*

HIKING

Aside from affording excellent views of Devils Tower and the surrounding countryside, the hiking trails here are a good way to view some of the geology and wildlife of the Black Hills region. The terrain that surrounds the butte is relatively flat, so the popular **Tower Trail,** a paved 1.3-mile path that circles the monument, is far from strenuous. It's the most popular trail in the park, though, so if you're looking for more isolation, try the 1.5-mile **Joyner Ridge Trail** or the 3-mile **Red Beds Trail.** They're a bit more demanding, but the views from the top of Joyner Ridge and the banks of the Belle Fourche River are more than adequate rewards. Both the Tower and Red Beds trails start at the visitor center; Joyner Ridge Trail begins about a mile's drive north from there.

ROCK CLIMBING

Climbing is the premier sporting activity at Devils Tower. Acclaimed as one of the best crack-climbing areas in North America, the monument has attracted both beginners and experts for more than a century. There are few restrictions when it comes to ascending the granite cone. Although climbing is technically allowed all year, there is generally a voluntary moratorium in June to allow for peaceful religious rites performed by local Native American tribes. Additionally, the west face of the formation is closed intermittently in the summer to protect the prairie falcons that nest there. Before ascending Devils Tower you should sign in at the visitor center and discuss conditions with park officials. You can obtain a list of park-licensed guides here; courses are offered at all skill levels and sometimes include excursions into the Rockies or South Dakota. Some tour operators continue to guide climbs during the voluntary ban in June.

Sundance

31 miles southeast of Devils Tower National Monument via U.S. 14.

A combination of traditional reverence and an infamous outlaw's date with destiny put Sundance on Wyoming's map, and continues to draw visitors today. Native American tribes such as the Crow, Cheyenne, and Lakota consider Sundance Mountain and the Bear Lodge Mountains to be sacred. Before whites arrived in the 1870s the Native Americans congregated nearby each June for their Sun Dance, an important ceremonial gathering. The event gave its name to this small town, which in turn gave its name to the outlaw Harry Longabaugh, the Sundance Kid, who spent time in the local jail for stealing a horse. Ranch country and the western Black Hills surround the town. The Crook County Fair and Rodeo, held during the first week in August, offers live music shows, cook-offs, a ranch-style rodeo, and many other events; it's a popular draw for area residents.

GETTING HERE AND AROUND

This is a classic small Western town where you'll be tabbed as an outsider if you don't return a "hello" from a passerby on the street. To reach the downtown area, exit Interstate 90 on U.S. 14/E Cleveland Street or Route 585.

Sights

Vore Buffalo Jump

ARCHAEOLOGICAL SITE | Thousands of buffalo bones are piled atop each other at the Vore Buffalo Jump, where Native Americans herded bison over a cliff between the years 1500 and 1800, when hunting was done on foot rather than on horses imported from Europe. The site is open to visitors even as it continues to be excavated by archaeologists. ✉ *369 Old U.S. 14* ✥ *15 miles east of Sundance via I–90 or Old U.S. 14* ☎ *307/283–1000* 🌐 *www.vorebuffalojump.org* 🎫 *$9* 🕒 *Closed Oct.–May.*

Hotels

Bear Lodge Motel

$$ | **HOTEL** | A cozy lobby, a stone fireplace, and wildlife mounts on the walls distinguish this downtown motel. **Pros:** downtown location; close to restaurant, bars, lounges; short walk to a city park. **Cons:** slightly outdated appearance; no elevator for second-story rooms; long drive to most area attractions. $ *Rooms from: $120* ✉ *218 E. Cleveland St.* ☎ *307/283–1611* 🌐 *www.bearlodgemotel.com* *34 rooms* *Free breakfast.*

Serena Inn & Suites

$$$ | **HOTEL** | Brown carpeting and red drapes decorate the spacious rooms of this hotel. **Pros:** contemporary furnishings; easy access just off Interstate 90; gas and convenience store next door. **Cons:** just outside of town, not a walkable area; interstate noise; very basic rooms. $ *Rooms from: $150* ✉ *2719 Cleveland St.* ☎ *307/283–2800* 🌐 *serenainnsundance.com* *44 rooms* *Free breakfast.*

Activities

CAMPING

Mountain View RV Park. Clean and new, this contemporary RV park offers large pull-through sites ideal for the big rigs. Clean and new, this contemporary RV park offers large pull-through sites ideal for the big rigs. ✉ *117 Government Valley Rd.* ☎ *307/283–2270* 🌐 *www.mtview-campground.com* *Add # of sites.*

Lusk

140 miles northeast of Cheyenne via I–25 and U.S. 18.

Proudly rural, the 1,500 townspeople of Lusk often poke gentle fun at themselves, emblazoning T-shirts with phrases such as "End of the world, 12 miles. Lusk, 15 miles." You'll see what they mean if you visit this seat of Niobrara County, whose population density averages 524 acres of prairie per person. If you find yourself traveling the main route between the Black Hills and the Colorado Rockies, a stop in this tiny burg is worth the time for a quick lesson in frontier—particularly stagecoach—history. You can also find gasoline and food, rare commodities on the open plain.

Lusk owes its existence to rancher Frank S. Lusk, who cut a deal with the Wyoming Central Railroad in 1886. The railroad originally planned to build its route through central Wyoming along the Cheyenne–Deadwood Stage Line, which ran between the territorial capital and the Black Hills gold-rush town. Officials selected Silver Cliff, where Ellis Johnson ran a store, saloon, and hotel, as the area's station. When Johnson tried to raise the price for his land, the railroad changed its plans and bought from Lusk. The rail line bypassed Silver Cliff for the station named Lusk.

The stagecoach line that passed through Lusk played a role in the development of the Black Hills, but Lusk became a different sort of pioneering town in the 1990s. Town leaders installed fiber-optic cable lines and obtained computers for schools, public facilities, and homes, placing Lusk on the frontier of technology when other small Wyoming towns had barely even heard of the Internet. The media spotlight shone briefly on the town that led the state of Wyoming into the 21st century.

GETTING HERE AND AROUND

A vehicle is your only option for getting around in this part of the state, but Lusk is at the crossroads for U.S. 20 and U.S. 85.

Sights

Spanish Diggings

NATIVE SITE | FAMILY | A few miles east of Glendo State Park lies a vast stone quarry initially mistaken for the work of early Spanish explorers. Archaeologists later determined the site, known as the Spanish Diggings, to be the work of various indigenous tribes on and off for the past several thousand years. Tools and arrowheads carved from the stone quarried here, including quartzite, jasper, and agate, have been found as far away as the Ohio River valley. To see the diggings you'll have to drive through Glendo State Park. ✉ *397 Glendo Park Rd.* ☎ *307/735–4433* 🌐 *wyoparks.state.wy.us* 🎫 *\$7 for residents, \$12 for nonresidents.*

Stagecoach Museum

MUSEUM | FAMILY | Artifacts from early settlement days and the period when the Cheyenne–Deadwood Stage Line was in full swing are some of the displays at the Stagecoach Museum. You also can get information about the Texas Cattle Trail. ✉ *322 S. Main St.* ☎ *800/223–5875, 307/334–3444* 🎫 *Free (donations encouraged)* ⏲ *Closed Mon. and Tues.; by appointment only weekends. Closed Nov.–Apr.*

Restaurants

Pizza Place

\$\$ | PIZZA | FAMILY | A casual atmosphere and good food come together at this downtown eatery. Pizza, calzones, and sub sandwiches made with homemade bread are on the menu, and there's also a salad bar. **Known for:** from-scratch dinner rolls, and they'll even sell you a batch to take home; dough made fresh every day; sausage that's ground and seasoned in house daily. *Average main: $10 ✉ 218 S. Main St. ☎ 307/334–3000 Closed Sun.*

Hotels

Best Western Pioneer Lusk

$$$ | **HOTEL** | **FAMILY** | Although the exterior of this motel near downtown and the Stagecoach Museum is unremarkable, the lobby is attractive, with a ceramic-tile floor, hardwood trim, and wrought-iron tables and lamps. **Pros:** nice furnishings; omelet bar from an authentic 1890 chuck wagon from Memorial Day to Labor Day; pet friendly. **Cons:** outdoor pool open only part of the year; some guests complain about the rooms being smaller than average hotel rooms; more expensive than hotels in nearby towns. *Rooms from: $135 ✉ 731 S. Main St. ☎ 307/334–2640, 307/334–2660 www.bestwestern.com 30 rooms Free breakfast.*

Covered Wagon

$$ | **HOTEL** | **FAMILY** | With a covered wagon on the front portico, an indoor pool, and an outdoor playground, this U-shape motel is an inviting place for families with kids. **Pros:** newly installed playground for the kids; indoor headed pool and sauna; free breakfast. **Cons:** books up quickly in the summer, so plan ahead; dated furnishings in rooms; some guests complained of noisy rooms in rooms facing the street. *Rooms from: $100 ✉ 731 S. Main St. ☎ 800/341–8000, 307/334–2836, 888/338–2836 www.coveredwagonmotel.com 51 rooms Free breakfast.*

Rawhide Motel

$ | **HOTEL** | The standard-size rooms are rustic but warm, and service is friendly at this affordable, locally owned motel in downtown Lusk. **Pros:** good location; pet-friendly; guests noted this motel for its cleanliness. **Cons:** no pool; no frills; good for an overnight, but not great for extended stays. *Rooms from: $60 ✉ 805 S. Main St. ☎ 888/679–2558, 307/334–2440 rawhidemotel-lusk.com 18 rooms No meals.*

Douglas

55 miles west of Lusk via U.S. 18 and I–25.

Douglas is best known for two things: the Wyoming State Fair, which has been held here annually in early August since 1905, and the jackalope. A local taxidermist assembled the first example of the mythical cross between a jackrabbit and an antelope for display in a local hotel. There's an 8-foot-tall concrete jackalope statue in Jackalope Square in downtown Douglas, and many businesses sell jackalope figures and merchandise.

Surveyors plotted the town of Douglas (named for Stephen A. Douglas, the presidential candidate who lost to Abe Lincoln) in 1886, in preparation for the construction of the Fremont, Elkhorn, and Missouri Valley Railroad. The railroad, which owned the townsite, prohibited settlement before the rails arrived. Eager to take up residence, a few enterprising souls built shelters on Antelope Creek, outside the official boundaries. When the railroad arrived on August 22, they put their structures on wheels and moved them into town.

GETTING HERE AND AROUND

A car is required for transportation here. Douglas is right off I–25, about three-quarters of the way between Cheyenne and Casper.

Sights

Ayres Natural Bridge

NATURE SITE | Overland immigrants sometimes visited a rock outcrop that spans LaPrele Creek. It's now a small but popular picnic area and campsite where you can wade in the creek or simply enjoy the quiet. No pets are allowed at the campsite. ✉ *Douglas, WY.* ✢ *Off I–25* ☎ *307/358–3532.*

Fort Fetterman State Historic Site

MILITARY SITE | Built in 1867 to protect travelers headed west, the army post here is preserved today as the Fort Fetterman State Historic Site. Although the fort was never very large and had difficulty keeping its soldiers from deserting, its location on the fringes of the Great Sioux Indian Reservation made it an important outpost of civilization on the Western frontier. After white settlers overran the Black Hills and the government did away with the reservation, soldiers from here helped end armed Plains Indian resistance—and thus put an end to the fort's usefulness. Two buildings, the ordnance warehouse and officers' quarters, survived decades of abandonment and today house interpretive exhibits and artifacts related to the area's history and the fort's role in settling the West. The remains of other fort buildings can still be seen, as can the ruins of Fetterman City, which died out when Douglas was founded several miles to the south. ✉ *752 Hwy. 93* ☎ *307/358–9288* 🌐 *wyoparks.wyo.gov* 🎫 *$8* ⏲ *Closed Labor Day–Memorial Day.*

Medicine Bow National Forest, Douglas District

FOREST | The Medicine Bow National Forest, Douglas District, southwest of Douglas in the Laramie Peak area, includes four campgrounds ($5–$10 for camping; campground closed in winter) and areas where you can fish and hike. ✉ *2250 E. Richards St.* ✢ *Douglas Ranger District* ☎ *307/358–4690* 🌐 *fs.usda.gov/mbr.*

Wyoming Pioneer Memorial Museum

MUSEUM | **FAMILY** | At the Wyoming Pioneer Memorial Museum, the emphasis is on the Wyoming pioneer settlers and overland immigrants, but this small state-operated museum on the state fairgrounds also has displays on Native Americans and the frontier military. ✉ *400 W. Center St.* ☎ *307/358–9288* 🌐 *www.wyoparks.wyo.gov* 🎫 *$8* ⏲ *Closed Sun. and Mon., May–Oct. Closed Sun.–Thurs., Nov.–Apr.*

Restaurants

Plains Trading Post

$$ | **AMERICAN** | **FAMILY** | Antique furnishings and portions of old bank buildings set the scene at this restaurant, where the menu is diverse but basic—chicken, burgers, steaks—and the portions are large. It's open 24 hours a day, a rarity even in the larger cities. **Known for:** pie by the slice; open 24 hours a day; the Plains Burger. Ⓢ *Average main: $15* ✉ *628 Richards St.* ☎ *307/358–4489.*

Hotels

Douglas Inn and Conference Center

$$ | **HOTEL** | **FAMILY** | With its cathedral ceiling and fireplace, the atrium lobby is an impressive entranceway into this chain hotel. **Pros:** cozy atmosphere; pet-friendly; indoor pool. **Cons:** books up quickly; some guests have complained about cleanliness; breakfast selection is limited. Ⓢ *Rooms from: $105* ✉ *1450 Riverbend Dr.* ☎ *307/358–9790* 🌐 *www.douglasinnconferencecenter.com* *118 rooms* *Free breakfast.*

Activities

CAMPING

Esterbrook Campground. Nestled among pine trees near Laramie Peak, 30 miles south of Douglas, Esterbrook is only a few miles from Black Mountain Lookout, one of the few staffed fire lookouts remaining in the country. During fire season (generally mid-June through September) be sure to ask the ranger-in-residence before exploring his or her home. ✉ *Forest Rd. 633* ☎ *307/358–1604, 307/358–4690* 🌐 *www.fs.usda.gov/recarea/mbr* *12 sites.*

Casper

115 miles south of Buffalo via I–25; 180 miles north of Cheyenne via I–25.

Several excellent museums in Casper illuminate central Wyoming's pioneer and natural history. The state's second-largest city, it's also one of the oldest. Some of the first white people to venture across Wyoming spent the winter here in 1811, on their way east from Fort Astoria in Oregon. Although they didn't stay, they helped to forge several pioneer trails that crossed the North Platte River near present-day Casper. A permanent settlement eventually arose, and was named for Lieutenant Caspar Collins; the spelling error occurred early on, and it stuck. The town has grown largely as a result of oil and gas exploration, and sheep and cattle ranchers run their stock on lands all around the city.

GETTING HERE AND AROUND

A car is your best bet for transportation.

VISITOR INFORMATION

CONTACTS Casper Convention and Visitors Bureau. ✉ *139 W. 2nd St., Suite 1B* ☎ *307/234–5362, 800/852–1889* 🌐 *www.visitcasper.com.*

Sights

Casper Planetarium

OBSERVATORY | **FAMILY** | The Casper Planetarium has multimedia programs on astronomy. There are also interactive exhibits in the lobby and a gift shop. Public programs, which last an hour, are scheduled regularly year-round. ✉ *904 N. Poplar St.* ☎ *307/577–0310* 🌐 *casperplanetarium.com* 🎫 *$3* 🕒 *Closed Sun. and Mon.*

Edness Kimball Wilkins State Park

NATIONAL/STATE PARK | **FAMILY** | **Edness Kimball Wilkins State Park** is a day-use area with picnicking, swimming, fishing, and a 3-mile walking path. This park is along a migratory flyway, with more than 100 different species of birds frequenting the area. For this reason, Edness Kimball State Park has been designated one of Audubon Wyoming's important bird areas. ✉ *8700 E. Hwy. 20/26, Evansville* ✣ *6 miles east of Casper* ☎ *307/577–5150* 🌐 *wyoparks.wyo.gov* ☞ *$12 per vehicle for non-Wyoming residents, $7 per vehicle for Wyoming residents.*

Fort Caspar Historic Site

MUSEUM VILLAGE | **FAMILY** | The Fort Caspar Historic Site re-creates the post at Platte Bridge, which became Fort Caspar after the July 1865 battle that claimed the lives of several soldiers, including Lieutenant Caspar Collins. A post depicts life at a frontier station in the 1860s, and sometimes soldier reenactors go about their tasks. Museum exhibits show the migration trails. ✉ *4001 Fort Caspar Rd.* ☎ *307/235–8462* 🌐 *www.fortcasparwyoming.com* 🎫 *$4.*

★ National Historic Trails Interpretive Center

MUSEUM | **FAMILY** | Five major immigrant trails passed near or through Casper between 1843 and 1870. The best-known are the Oregon Trail and the Mormon Trail, both of which crossed the North Platte River in the vicinity of today's Casper. The National Historic Trails Interpretive Center examines the early history of the trails and the military's role in central Wyoming. Projected onto a series of screens 11 feet high and 55 feet wide, a film shows Wyoming trail sites and scenes of wagon travelers. You can climb into a wagon to see what it was like to cross the river, or learn about Mormon pioneers who traveled west with handcarts in 1856. ✉ *1501 N. Poplar St.* ☎ *307/265–8030, 307/261–7700* 🌐 *www.nhtcf.org* 🎫 *Free* 🕒 *Closed Sun. and Mon.*

Nicolaysen Art Museum

MUSEUM | **FAMILY** | A showcase for regional artists and mostly modern artwork, the Nicolaysen Art Museum also exhibits works by national artists.

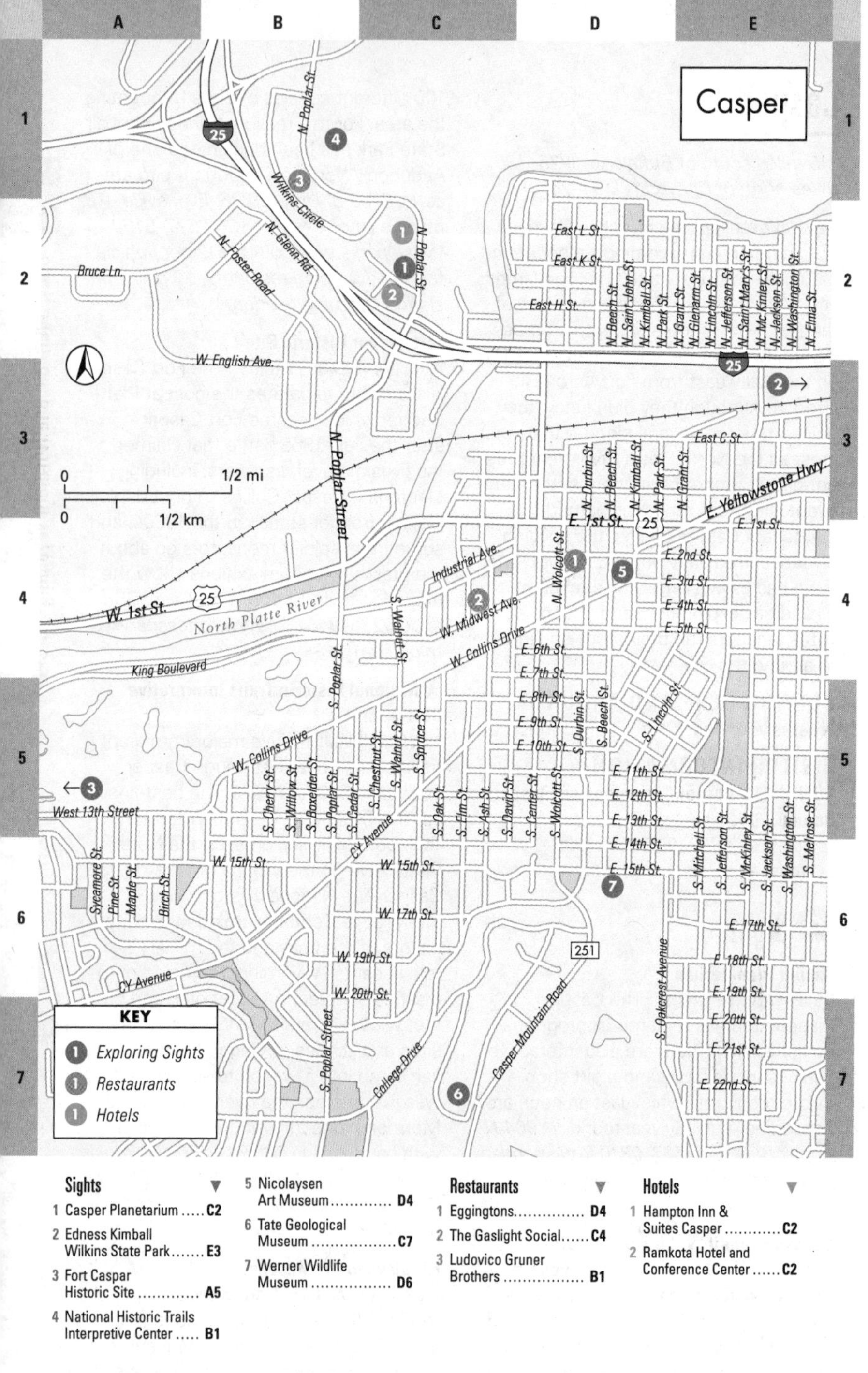

Sights

1 Casper Planetarium **C2**
2 Edness Kimball Wilkins State Park....... **E3**
3 Fort Caspar Historic Site **A5**
4 National Historic Trails Interpretive Center **B1**
5 Nicolaysen Art Museum............. **D4**
6 Tate Geological Museum **C7**
7 Werner Wildlife Museum **D6**

Restaurants

1 Eggingtons............... **D4**
2 The Gaslight Social...... **C4**
3 Ludovico Gruner Brothers **B1**

Hotels

1 Hampton Inn & Suites Casper **C2**
2 Ramkota Hotel and Conference Center **C2**

The building's early-20th-century redbrick exterior and contemporary interior are an odd combination, but this makes the museum all the more interesting. There are hands-on activities, classes, and children's programs, plus a research library and a Discovery Center. ✉ *400 E. Collins St.* ☎ *307/235–5247* 🌐 *www.thenic.org* 🎟 *$5* ⏲ *Closed Mon.*

★ Tate Geological Museum
MUSEUM | FAMILY | Casper College's Tate Geological Museum in the Tate Earth Science Center displays fossils, rocks, jade, and the fossilized remains of a brontosaurus, plus other dinosaur bones. The centerpiece for the Tate is Dee, an 11,600-year-old Columbian Mammoth. Dee is one of the largest complete Columbian Mammoths ever discovered. ✉ *125 College Dr.* ☎ *307/268–2100* 🌐 *www.caspercollege.edu* 🎟 *Free* ⏲ *Closed Sun.*

Werner Wildlife Museum
MUSEUM | FAMILY | The Werner Wildlife Museum, near the Casper College campus, has displays of birds and animals from Wyoming and around the world. There are more than 400 birds, fish, and animal species on display across 36 different exhibits. ✉ *405 E. 15th St.* ☎ *307/268–2676, 307/235–2108 for tours* 🎟 *Free* ⏲ *Closed weekends.*

Restaurants

Eggingtons
$$ | AMERICAN | FAMILY | It's not uncommon to see a line out the door here on weekend mornings. With a wide selection of breakfast and lunch options, there's something for everyone. **Known for:** 6 am opening time for the early birds; build-your-own breakfast tacos and omelets; nine staple burgers to choose from. 💲 *Average main: $11* ✉ *229 E. 2nd St.* ☎ *307/265–8700* 🌐 *www.eggingtons.com* ⏲ *No dinner.*

The Gaslight Social
$ | MEXICAN FUSION | FAMILY | This fun, open bar and grill has a build-your-own burrito amongst flavorful appetizers and a full drinks menu. Gaslight Social also functions as a concert venue and event complex. **Known for:** 31 beers on draft from around Wyoming and the country; big outdoor space with cornhole and other yard games; arcade games and golf simulator to bring out the kid in you. 💲 *Average main: $9* ✉ *314 W. Midwest Ave.* ☎ *307/337–1396* 🌐 *www.thegaslightsocial.com.*

★ Ludovico Gruner Brothers
$$$ | ITALIAN | FAMILY | Come for the beer and pizza, stay for the views. Gruner Brothers is run by two actual brothers who love making good beer to enjoy after a long day of work or play. **Known for:** incredible views of downtown, the North Platte River, and Casper Mountain; pizza made with local, fresh ingredients; good homemade cannoli for dessert. 💲 *Average main: $19* ✉ *1301 Wilkins Circle* ☎ *307/439–2222* 🌐 *ludovicocasper.com, grunerbrewing.com* ⏲ *Closed Sun. and Mon.*

Hotels

Hampton Inn & Suites Casper
$$$ | HOTEL | The rooms in this clean and very quiet lodging have coffeemakers, large cable TVs, white fluffy comforters, and easy chairs with ottomans. **Pros:** recently built structure; Cloud Nine beds give rooms a cozy feel; great pool and fitness center. **Cons:** doesn't allow pets; typical chain hotel; limited dining options within walking distance. 💲 *Rooms from: $145* ✉ *1100 N. Poplar Rd.* ☎ *307/235–6668* 🌐 *www.hamptoninn.com* 🛏 *120 rooms* 🍽 *Free breakfast.*

Ramkota Hotel and Conference Center
$$ | HOTEL | This full-service hotel, off I–25, has everything under one roof, from dining options to business services. **Pros:** neighboring Castaway Bay Water Park

is popular with kids; complimentary hot breakfast buffet; top-rated restaurant, the Remington, located within the hotel. **Cons:** typical chain hotel; thin walls; some guests noted the hotel design feels dated. *Rooms from: $116* *800 N. Poplar St.* *307/266-6000, 307/473-1010* *ramkotacasper.com* *229 rooms* *Free breakfast.*

Shopping

Eastridge Mall

SHOPPING CENTERS/MALLS | The largest shopping center in a 175-mile radius, the Eastridge Mall, anchored by such standbys as Sears, JCPenney, Target, and Macy's, is popular and important to locals. *601 S.E. Wyoming Blvd.* *307/265-9392* *www.shopeastridge.com.*

Activities

With thousands of acres of empty grassland and towering mountains only miles away, the landscape around Casper is full of possibilities for enjoying the outdoors. Casper Mountain rises up 8,000 feet no more than 20 minutes from downtown, providing prime skiing and hiking trails.

HIKING

★ Casper Mountain

HIKING/WALKING | Casper Mountain is an iconic landmark for residents and tourists alike. There are a number of hiking and mountain biking trails, camping spots, an archery range and even a small ski resort on the mountain. Contact the **Casper Convention and Visitors Bureau** for more information. *139 W. 2nd St.* *307/234-5362, 800/852-1889* *www.casperwyoming.info.*

Platte River Parkway

HIKING/WALKING | **FAMILY** | The **Platte River Parkway** hiking trail runs adjacent to the North Platte River in downtown Casper. Access points are at Amoco Park at 1st and Poplar streets, or at Crosswinds Park, on North Poplar Street near the Casper Events Center. Also at the Amoco Park is Casper's own white water park, with a man-made rock structure to simulate rapids for kayakers and boaters. *Casper.*

SKIING

Hogadon Ski Area

SKIING/SNOWBOARDING | **FAMILY** | Perched on Casper Mountain a few miles outside of town is **Hogadon Ski Area**, with a vertical drop of 600 feet. Less than a quarter of the runs are rated for beginners; the rest are evenly divided between intermediate and expert trails. Also here are a separate snowboard terrain park and a modest lodge. *2500 Hogadon Rd.* *Casper Mountain Rd.* *307/235-8499* *hogadon.net* *Day lift tickets $48 per day.*

Mountain Sports

SKIING/SNOWBOARDING | **Mountain Sports** provides more than just ski and snowboard sales. It also runs Wyomaps, which sells personal Global Positioning System products and provides custom mapping services. *543 S. Center* *307/266-1136, 800/426-1136* *www.caspermtnsports.com/.*

Chapter 11

CHEYENNE, LARAMIE, AND SOUTHERN WYOMING

Updated by
Stina Sieg

Sights ★★★☆☆

Restaurants ★★★☆☆

Hotels ★★★☆☆

Shopping ★★☆☆☆

Nightlife ★★☆☆☆

WELCOME TO CHEYENNE, LARAMIE, AND SOUTHERN WYOMING

TOP REASONS TO GO

★ **Botanic Gardens:** The Cheyenne Botanic Gardens are a great place to lose yourself in the scenery.

★ **Celebrate the Wild West:** Cheyenne Frontier Days is a blow-out celebration of the Wild West.

★ **Saratoga:** Public and private hot springs in little Saratoga offer relaxation to all.

★ **Laramie:** Laramie has a young, arty heart and the only state university in Wyoming.

★ **Leaf peeping on Battle Highway:** With hundreds of aspen trees, Battle Highway in the fall is an explosion of color.

1 **Cheyenne.** Wyoming's biggest city isn't all that big, but it's a major draw in the summer for Cheyenne Frontier Days, which has the state's biggest rodeo.

2 **Fort Laramie National Historic Site.** A major provisioning point for the Oregon Trail, Fort Laramie is about 100 miles northeast of Cheyenne.

3 **Laramie.** The University of Wyoming's home is the closest thing Wyoming has to a "hip" town.

4 **Medicine Bow.** Tiny town immortalized in the novel *The Virginian* is noteworthy these days mostly for the same-named hotel (built only after the novel was published).

5 **Centennial.** The quaint gateway to the Snowy Range Mountains is a good base if you plan on doing any summer hiking or winter skiing in the nearby mountains.

6 **Saratoga.** The small, rural spot known for its hot springs was named after the more famous town in upstate New York and has surprisingly sophisticated hotels and restaurants.

7 **Encampment.** The historic town on the outskirts of four major wilderness areas is popular with vacationers.

8 **Baggs.** A roadside community just over the Colorado border was once a hideout of Butch Cassidy.

9 **Rawlins.** The seat of Carbon County is full of history; despite downturns in sheep

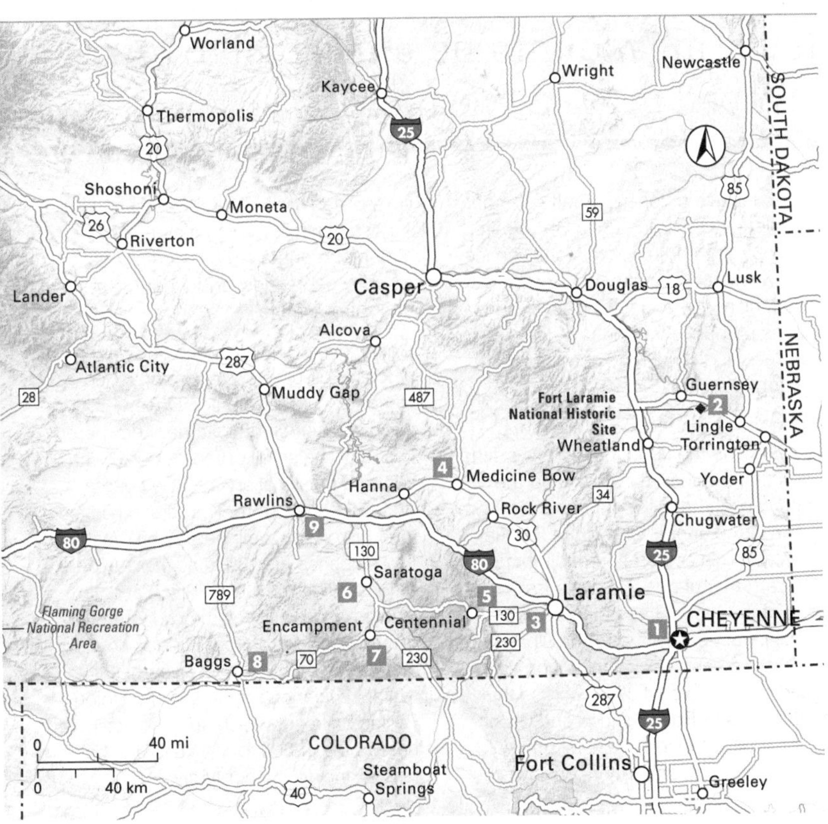

ranching and regional mineral production, it stays busy as the northern gateway to the Medicine Bow–Routt National Forest.

10 **Rock Springs.** Long a coal-mining town, Rock Springs is now better known for is proximity to the Red Desert just to the north and the Pilot Butte Wild Horse Sanctuary.

11 **Green River.** Seat of Sweetwater County, with the titular river running through it, the town is a gateway for Flaming Gorge National Recreation Area.

12 **Flaming Gorge National Recreation Area.** The beautiful area that gets its name from its red canyon walls straddles the Utah border, offering myriad recreational opportunities.

13 **Fort Bridger State Historic Site.** The well-preserved historic fort, originally a small trading post, dates back to the 1800s.

14 **Kemmerer.** The small town near Fossil Butte National Monument was also the hometown of retailer JCPenney.

Southern Wyoming is home to so much of what people love about this sparsely populated state: wide-open spaces, towering mountains, and small towns steeped in Wild West lore.

This is a place to lose yourself—but not completely. With long drives between communities and unreliable cell service, it's always good to carry physical maps, water, blankets, and food. The weather here is notoriously fickle, even in the summer, and good road conditions are never guaranteed.

Along the eastern edge of the state, Cheyenne is the largest city in Wyoming (though it's still pretty small) and the state capital. Its most popular event by a mile is the annual Cheyenne Frontier Days rodeo, a celebration of all things Western that brings in people from around the world. Less than an hour away, Laramie is home to the University of Wyoming and has a fun, young vibe. Heading west, you'll come across the small cities of Rock Springs and Green River, where museums detail their Old West, and sometimes outlaw, past.

I–80 is the main route through the region, but getting off the big road and into smaller communities is worth it. Many have cute downtowns and make good bases for skiing, hiking, and other recreational opportunities that take you deep into the backcountry. Medicine Bow has a well-known cowboy heritage portrayed in Owen Wister's 1902 Western novel *The Virginian* (and there's even a historical hotel there by the same name). Saratoga has a resort flavor, but with both public and private hot springs, doesn't feel too exclusive for comfort. Encampment and Centennial are little, slow-paced spots with storied histories. Across this rural region, catch re-creations of mountain-men rendezvous, cowboy gatherings, and other events that honor frontier life.

Once covered by an ocean and now rich in fossils, southwest Wyoming's Red Desert, or Little Colorado Desert, draws people in search of solitude. Kemmerer is one of the small outposts here, with a famed fossil gallery and the country's first JCPenney store. The region has a long history, as well: here John Wesley Powell began his 1869 and 1871 expeditions down the Green River, and Jim Bridger and Louis Vasquez constructed the trading post of Fort Bridger, now a state historic site. And all across the region, evidence remains of the Union Pacific Railroad, which spawned growth here in the 1860s as workers laid the iron rails spanning the continent.

Planning

Getting Here and Around

AIR

Cheyenne, Laramie, and Rock Springs' Southwest Wyoming Regional are the commercial airports in the area. Many visitors to southeastern Wyoming fly into Denver International Airport and drive the 100 miles north to Cheyenne.

CONTACTS Cheyenne Airport. ✉ *4020 Airport Pkwy. W, Cheyenne* ☎ *307/634–7071* 🌐 *www.cheyenneairport.com.* **Laramie Airport.** ✥ *3 miles west of Laramie off Hwy. 130* ☎ *307/742–4164* 🌐 *www.laramieairport.com.* **Southwest Wyoming Regional Airport.** ✉ *382 Hwy. 370, Rock Springs* ☎ *307/352–6880* 🌐 *www.sweet.wy.us.*

CAR

A car is essential for exploring southern Wyoming. I–80 is the major route through the region, bisecting it from east to west. In places it runs parallel to U.S. 30. Other major access roads include U.S. 287, connecting Laramie and Medicine Bow; Highway 130, serving Centennial and Saratoga; Highway 230, running through Encampment; and Highway 70, connecting Encampment and Baggs.

Although distances between towns can be long, gasoline and other automobile services are available in each community and at various points roughly 20 to 40 miles apart along I–80. When traveling here in winter, be prepared for whiteouts and road closings (sometimes for hours, occasionally for more than a day). Always carry a blanket and warm clothing when driving in winter, along with a safety kit that includes snack food and water. Cell service is getting better but is still sporadic in areas where mountains might interfere with cell towers.

Note that the Snowy Range Pass section of Highway 130, between Centennial and Saratoga, and the Battle Highway section of Highway 70, west of Encampment, close during cold weather, generally from mid-October until Memorial Day.

Planning Your Time

All across southern Wyoming you can immerse yourself in cowboy and Old West heritage. Some of your driving can take you along pioneer emigrant trails; you can hike or ride horses on other segments. A good place to start your explorations is at one of the two major frontier-era forts, Fort Laramie (northeast of Cheyenne) and Fort Bridger (in the southwest), that served emigrants heading to Oregon, California, and Utah. From Fort Laramie, drive to Cheyenne, where you can see one of America's most complete horse-drawn wagon collections. Continue west to learn about territorial and frontier justice at the historic prisons in Laramie and Rawlins. For a rare treat, spend some time visiting the region's small museums, which preserve evocative relics of the past. Start with the Grand Encampment Museum, Medicine Bow Museum, Little Snake River Valley Museum (in Baggs), and Carbon County Museum (in Rawlins), and then head west to tour the Sweetwater County Historical Center in Green River and Ulrich's Fossil Museum west of Kemmerer.

If you like to spend time in the outdoors, by all means take the scenic routes. From Cheyenne, follow Highway 210, which provides access to Curt Gowdy State Park. Traveling west of Laramie, head into the Snowy Range and Sierra Madre Mountains by taking Highway 130, which links to Saratoga by way of Centennial, or take Highway 230 to Encampment and then travel over Battle Highway (Highway 70) to Baggs. The mountain country of the Snowy Range and Sierra Madres provides plenty of opportunity for hiking, horseback riding, mountain biking, fishing, and camping. There are hundreds of thousands of acres to explore on trails ranging from wheelchair-accessible paths to incredibly difficult tracks for experienced backcountry travelers only. The action continues in winter, when snowmobilers ride freestyle across open country (rather than on trails), cross-country skiers glide through white landscapes, and snowshoers explore hushed forests. The lakes that attract anglers during summer are equally busy in winter, when ice fishing rules.

For a firsthand Western experience, stay at one of the guest ranches near Cheyenne, Laramie, or Saratoga, where you can take part in cowboy activities and ride horses. Wild horses range freely in southwest Wyoming's Red Desert, even though the area is being heavily developed for energy production. You can spot the magnificent creatures west of Baggs and north and south of Rock Springs.

Hotels

Because I–80 traverses this region, there are countless chain motels, but many other accommodations with more local flavor are also available. Southern Wyoming has a large number of independent lodging properties ranging from bed-and-breakfasts to lodges to historic hotels. Dude ranches are a unique lodging experience that let you sample a taste of wrangling life, and you can even stay in a remote mountain cabin in the heart of the national forest.

CAMPING

Just about every community in the region has private campgrounds and RV parks. The Wyoming Campground Association can provide information on these campgrounds.

You can also camp on public lands managed by the U.S. Forest Service and local Bureaus of Land Management; these camping opportunities range from dispersed camping with no facilities to campgrounds with water, fire pits, and picnic tables. Some of the best camping spots are in the Medicine Bow–Routt National Forest near the communities of Centennial, Saratoga, Encampment, and Baggs. Camping near lakes and reservoirs is possible west of Cheyenne at Curt Gowdy State Park and south of Green River at Flaming Gorge National Recreation Area.

Restaurants

Almost anywhere you dine in southern Wyoming, beef plays a prominent role on the menu; prime rib and steak are often specialties. Standard fare at many small-town restaurants includes burgers and sandwiches, and several eateries serve outstanding Mexican dishes. The pickings can be a bit slim for vegetarians, although most menus have at least one vegetable pasta dish or meatless entrée. You're bound to find the most veggie options in Laramie and Cheyenne. Jeans and a T-shirt are acceptable attire for most places (even if the folks at the next table happen to be dressed up). Cowboy hats are always welcome.

Restaurant and hotel reviews have been shortened. For full information, visit Fodors.com.

HOTEL AND RESTAURANT PRICES

What it Costs

	$	$$	$$$	$$$$
RESTAURANTS				
	under $10	$10–$18	$19–$30	over $30
HOTELS				
	under $80	$80–$130	$131–$200	over $200

When to Go

The best time to visit southern Wyoming is in summer or fall, when most lodging properties and attractions are open (some smaller museums, sights, and inns close between Labor Day and Memorial Day). Summer is the season for most local community celebrations, including the region's longest-running and biggest event, Cheyenne Frontier Days, held the last full week in July.

Some areas, particularly around Laramie, Centennial, Saratoga, and Encampment, are great for winter sports, including cross-country skiing, snowmobiling, and ice fishing. Bear in mind that in parts of southern Wyoming it can—and often does—snow every month of the year, so even if you're visiting in July, bring some warm clothes, such as a heavy jacket and sweater.

Cheyenne

Cheyenne is Wyoming's largest city, but at roughly 65,000 people it is not a place where you'll have to fight traffic or wait in lines—except during the last nine days in July, when the annual Cheyenne Frontier Days makes the city positively boom. Throughout the year it offers a decent variety of shopping, as well as art galleries, museums, and parks. Its small downtown is full of rambling, historic brick buildings, tall by Wyoming standards, some that have been lovingly repurposed into hip little shops. Many others seem to be permanently waiting for their second act.

Born in 1867 as the Union Pacific Railroad inched its way across the plains, Cheyenne began as a rowdy camp for railroad gangs, cowboys, prospectors heading for the Black Hills, and soldiers. It more than lived up to its nickname: "Hell on Wheels." But unlike some renegade railroad tent cities, which disappeared as the railroad tracks pushed farther west, Cheyenne established itself as a permanent city, becoming the territorial capital in 1868. Its wild beginnings gave way in the late 19th century to respectability with the coming of the enormously wealthy cattle barons, many of them English. They sipped brandy at the Cheyenne Club and hired hard cases such as Tom Horn (1860–1903) to take care of their competitors—which in many cases meant killing rustlers—on the open range.

Cheyenne became the state capital in 1890, at a time when the rule of the cattle barons was beginning to weaken after harsh winter storms in the late 1880s and financial downturns in the national economy. But Cheyenne's link to ranching didn't fade, and the community launched its first Cheyenne Frontier Days in 1897, an event that continues to this day. During the late July celebration—the world's largest outdoor rodeo extravaganza—the town is up to its neck in bucking broncs and bulls and joyful bluster. The parades, pageantry, and parties require the endurance of a cattle hand on a weeklong drive.

GETTING HERE AND AROUND

As with much of Wyoming, a car will be your primary mode of transportation here. Although the city has a public bus system, it can be difficult to navigate and is rarely used by tourists.

I–25 runs north–south through the city; I–80 runs east–west. Central Avenue and Warren Avenue are quick north–south routes; the former goes north one way and the latter runs south one way. Several major roads can get you across town fairly easily, including 16th Street (U.S. 30), which gives you easy access to downtown. Most places of interest are in the downtown area. Most shopping is also downtown or along Dell Range Boulevard on the north side of town. Note that there are a few one-way streets in the downtown area.

TOURS

The **Cheyenne Street Railway Trolley** (🌐 *www.cheyennetrolley.com*) takes a $12, 1½-hour tour of the historic downtown area, with a focus on the city's Wild West history. The trolley runs May to September. Tickets are sold at Visit Cheyenne, located inside the historic depot. While there, you can also pick up information on self-guided walking tours of the downtown and Capitol area.

VISITOR INFORMATION

CONTACTS Visit Cheyenne. ✉ *One Depot Square, 121 W. 15th St., Suite 212* ☎ *307/778–3133, 800/426–5009* 🌐 *www.cheyenne.org.*

Sights

★ Cheyenne Botanic Gardens

GARDEN | FAMILY | The gardens' greenhouse conservatory—several stories high—looks like a cathedral of plants and feels like a tropical oasis. It makes for an especially wonderful escape on winter days. The lush banana plants are the big star here; also look for cacti, bonsai, and perennial and annual plants. Kiddos will enjoy seeing the city through the periscope located at the top of the building (only open certain days), as well as exploring the whimsy of the Paul Smith Children's Village across the parking lot from the conservatory. The grounds are open daily from dusk to dawn. ✉ *710 S. Lions Park Dr.* ☎ *307/637–6458* 🌐 *www.botanic.org* 🎫 *Donations accepted* ⏲ *Conservatory closed Sun. and Mon.*

★ Cheyenne Frontier Days Old West Museum

MUSEUM | FAMILY | This spacious museum within Frontier Park houses some 60,000 artifacts related to rodeos, ranching, and the city's blockbuster of an annual event, Cheyenne Frontier Days. The museum's "rolling collection" of more than 150 carriages is the largest fleet of horse-drawn vehicles in the state (with many that still go on parade). In July, the carriages are swapped out for the Frontier Days Western Art Show & Sale, with works by top Western wildlife and landscape artists from across the country. Every spring, the Western Spirit Art Show & Sale features pieces that celebrate the heritage and heart of the American West. For young visitors, there's a children's room with hands-on exhibits open year-round, plus camps in the summer. ✉ *Frontier Park, 4610 N. Carey Ave.* ☎ *800/266–2696, 307/778–7290* 🌐 *www.oldwestmuseum.org* 🎫 *$12.*

★ Curt Gowdy State Park

NATIONAL/STATE PARK | FAMILY | You can fish, boat, hike, and picnic at this park named for Wyoming's most famous sportscaster, who got his start at local radio stations in the 1940s. The park, which is 24 miles west of the city, is especially popular with mountain bikers. There are more than 43 miles of hiking and biking trails, including an International Mountain Bicycling Association EPIC trail—a designation given to some of the most challenging and beautiful single-track trails in the country. ✉ *1264 Granite Springs Rd., off Hwy. 210 (Happy Jack Rd.)* ☎ *307/632–7946* 🌐 *wyoparks.wyo.gov* 🎫 *Daily use from $7 per vehicle; for camping add from $10.*

Wyoming Historic Governors' Mansion

HOUSE | Between 1905 and 1976 (when the state built a new residence for the governor), 19 Wyoming first families made their home in this Colonial Revival building. Period furnishings and ornate chandeliers remain in nearly every room. ✉ *300 E. 21st St.* ☎ *307/777–7878* 🌐 *wyoparks.wyo.gov/index.php/places-to-go/historic-governors-mansion* 🎫 *Free.*

Wyoming State Capitol

GOVERNMENT BUILDING | Construction on this Corinthian-style building, now on the National Register of Historic Places, was authorized by the Ninth Territorial Legislative Assembly in 1886. The dome, covered in 24-karat gold leaf and visible from all roads leading into the city, is 50 feet in diameter at the base and 146 feet high. Inside the building, you'll find a statue of Esther Hobart Morris, a proponent of women's suffrage. One of Wyoming's nicknames is the "Equality State" because of its early advocacy of women's rights. Thanks to Wyoming's informal ways, it's not unusual to find the governor wandering the halls of the capitol. You can take a self-guided tour of state

Coinciding with Cheyenne Fronter Days (the state's biggest rodeo), the Northern Arapaho and Eastern Shoshone tribes offer very popular dance presentations in a temporary village.

offices and the Senate and House chambers. Guided tours are also provided by appointment when time permits. ✉ *200 W. 24th St.* ☎ *307/777–7220* 🌐 *ai.wyo.gov/about-us/visit-the-capitol* 🎟 *Free.*

Wyoming State Museum

MUSEUM | FAMILY | Several permanent exhibits are dedicated to exploring the heritage, culture, and landscape of Wyoming, covering everything from natural resources to wildlife to historical events. There's a hands-on exhibit geared to children, and the museum hosts several additional temporary exhibits each year. Be sure to check out the semi-permanent exhibit of hundreds of whimsical wooden miniatures crafted by Earl Newell. His folk-art pieces from the 1930s show a micro version of Wyoming life, including farm animals, people, and itty-bitty tools. ✉ *Barrett Building, 2301 Central Ave.* ☎ *307/777–7022* 🌐 *wyomuseum.state.wy.us* 🎟 *Free* 🕒 *Closed Sun.*

Restaurants

The Albany

$$ | AMERICAN | Historic photographs of early Cheyenne set the tone for this downtown icon, a place that seems as old as the city itself (the structure was built circa 1900). It's a bit dark, and the booths are a bit shabby, but the American food is solid. **Known for:** local favorite since the 1940s; American staples like prime rib and chicken fried steak; located right next to the historic train depot. 💲 *Average main: $13* ✉ *1506 Capitol Ave.* ☎ *307/638–3507* 🌐 *www.albanycheyenne.com* 🕒 *Closed Sun.*

The Bunkhouse Bar & Grill

$$ | STEAKHOUSE | Locals and tourists alike make the 15-mile drive from Cheyenne for the live music and homey feel of this out-of-the-way spot. The dance floor is huge, and the menu is full of cowboy favorites, including steaks, burgers, and Rocky Mountain oysters. **Known for:** live music and a weekly jam session; steaks; walls filled with cowboy memorabilia.

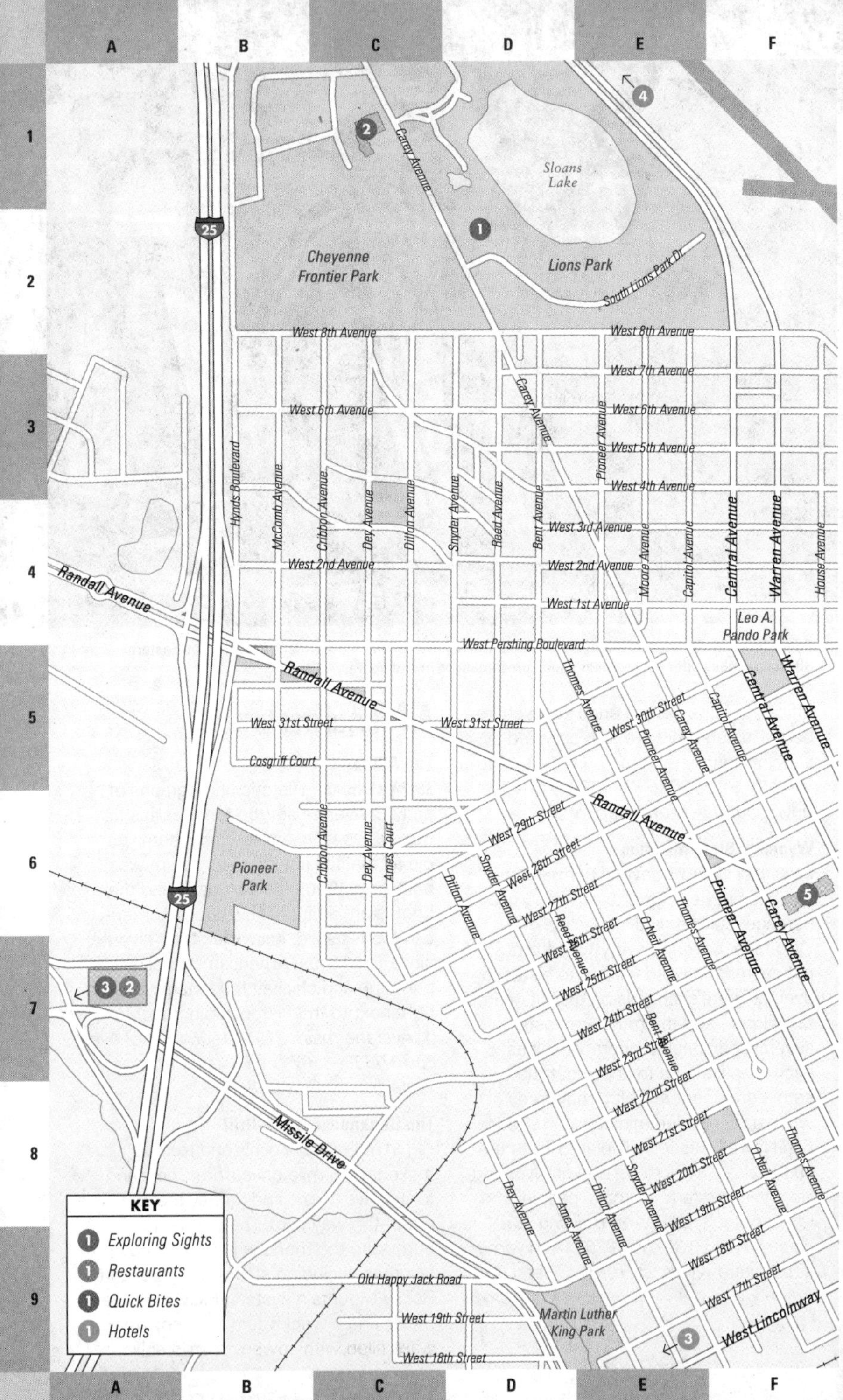

A
B
C
D
E
F
1
2
3
4
5
6
7
8
9
Sloans Lake
Cheyenne Frontier Park
Lions Park
South Lions Park Dr.
Carey Avenue
West 8th Avenue
West 7th Avenue
West 6th Avenue
West 5th Avenue
West 4th Avenue
West 3rd Avenue
West 2nd Avenue
West 1st Avenue
West Pershing Boulevard
Hynds Boulevard
McComb Avenue
Cribbon Avenue
Dey Avenue
Dillon Avenue
Snyder Avenue
Reed Avenue
Bent Avenue
Pioneer Avenue
Moore Avenue
Capitol Avenue
Central Avenue
Warren Avenue
House Avenue
Leo A. Pando Park
Randall Avenue
West 31st Street
Cosgriff Court
Thomes Avenue
West 30th Street
West 29th Street
West 28th Street
West 27th Street
West 26th Street
West 25th Street
West 24th Street
West 23rd Street
West 22nd Street
West 21st Street
West 20th Street
West 19th Street
West 18th Street
West 17th Street
West Lincolnway
O'Neil Avenue
Ames Avenue
Ames Court
Pioneer Park
Missile Drive
Old Happy Jack Road
Martin Luther King Park
25
KEY
Exploring Sights
Restaurants
Quick Bites
Hotels

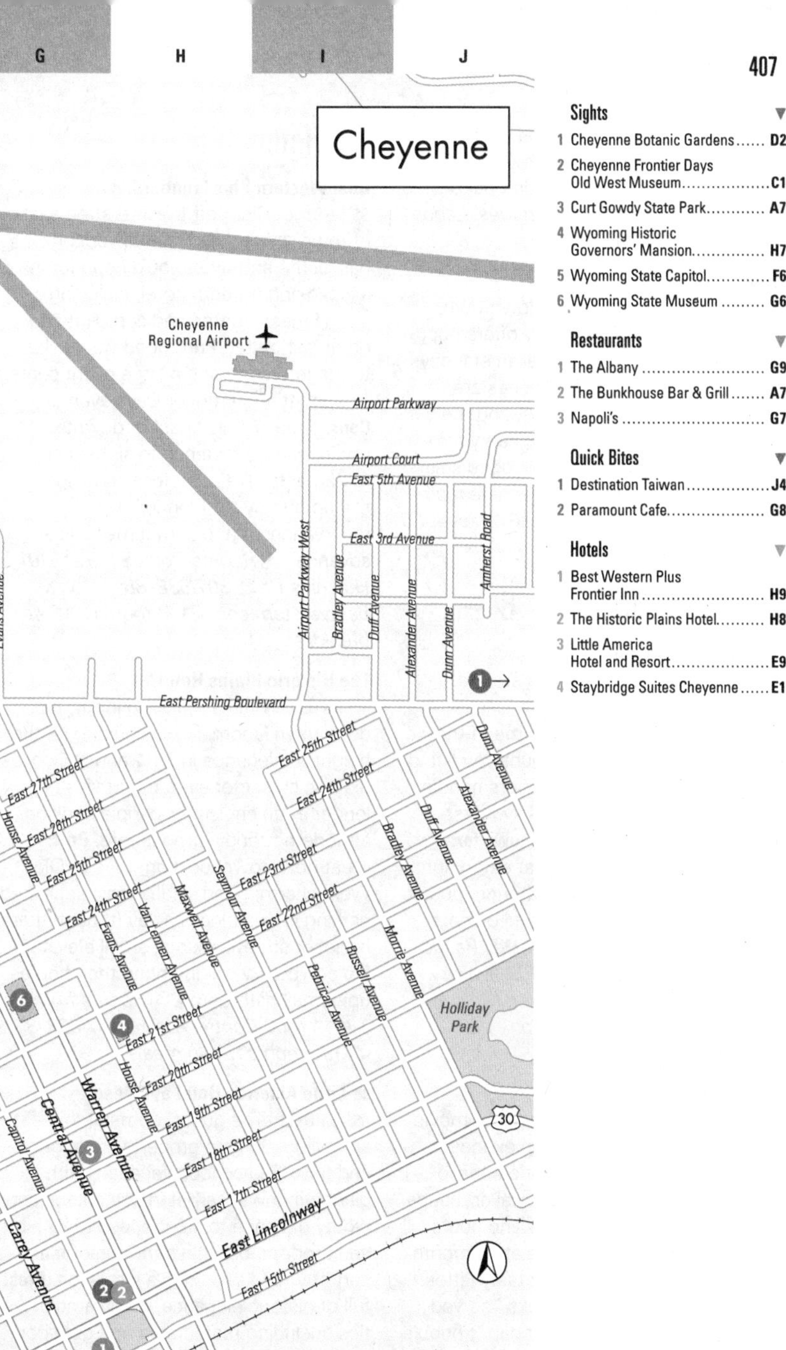

Sights

1 Cheyenne Botanic Gardens...... D2
2 Cheyenne Frontier Days Old West Museum.................C1
3 Curt Gowdy State Park........... A7
4 Wyoming Historic Governors' Mansion.............. H7
5 Wyoming State Capitol............ F6
6 Wyoming State Museum G6

Restaurants

1 The Albany G9
2 The Bunkhouse Bar & Grill....... A7
3 Napoli's G7

Quick Bites

1 Destination Taiwan.................J4
2 Paramount Cafe.................... G8

Hotels

1 Best Western Plus Frontier Inn H9
2 The Historic Plains Hotel.......... H8
3 Little America Hotel and Resort.....................E9
4 Staybridge Suites Cheyenne......E1

Ⓢ *Average main: $16* ✉ *1064 Happy Jack Rd.* ☎ *307/632–6184* 🌐 *www.bunkhouse-bar.com* ⏲ *Closed Mon. Memorial Day–Labor Day, closed Mon. and Tues. Labor Day–Memorial Day.*

Napoli's

$$ | **ITALIAN** | Located right downtown, this intimate, low-key eatery offers good pastas, pizzas, and other Italian standbys for lunch and dinner. The sauces are made-from-scratch delicious, and the bar is well stocked. **Known for:** creamy Alfredo sauce; homemade bread; good selection of seafood dishes. Ⓢ *Average main: $16* ✉ *1901 Central Ave.* ☎ *307/426–4300* ⏲ *Closed Mon.*

Coffee and Quick Bites

Destination Taiwan

$ | **TAIWANESE** | Don't let this stand's diminutive size and unromantic location fool you: it serves up some of the softest, fluffiest steamed buns you'll find anywhere. The menu also offers noodle and rice dishes, as well as Taiwanese pancakes and bubble tea. **Known for:** luscious steamed buns (best eaten right away, while piping hot); authentic food at budget prices; friendly, helpful owners. Ⓢ *Average main: $6* ✉ *2634 Dell Range Blvd., Unit A* ☎ *307/514–2702* 🌐 *www.shiuanskitchen.com* ⏲ *Closed Mon. and Tues., May–Dec. Closed Mon.–Wed. Jan.–Apr.*

Paramount Cafe

$ | **AMERICAN** | Located in a former movie theater, this airy coffee shop exudes a vintage vibe, a full array of espresso drinks, and a few snacks. Local art hangs on the walls, and musicians and poets take to the spot's tiny stage at its month open-mike night. **Known for:** tasty lattes with fun names; frozen drinks "served nice and cold like your ex's heart"; bubble tea in lots of flavors. Ⓢ *Average main: $5* ✉ *1607 Capitol Ave.* ☎ *307/634–2576* 🌐 *www.paramountcafecheyenne.com* ⏲ *No dinner.*

Hotels

Best Western Plus Frontier Inn

$$ | **HOTEL** | Right off the interstate east of town, this budget-friendly option has all the amenities you'd hope for in a clean and modern hotel, including a pool, fitness center, and complimentary breakfast buffet. **Pros:** good value; close to the interstate and a large event center; free shuttle to Frontier Days events. **Cons:** about 7 miles east of downtown; not in walking distance to sights and restaurants; like most local lodgings, fills up quickly for Frontier Days (with reservations made sometimes a year in advance). Ⓢ *Rooms from: $129* ✉ *8101 Hutchins Dr.* ☎ *307/638–8891* 🌐 *www.bestwestern.com* *74 rooms* 🍴 *Free breakfast.*

The Historic Plains Hotel

$ | **HOTEL** | With its stunning lobby, this downtown landmark was built to be the height of elegance in 1911 and still oozes historic character even though it's no longer a top choice for people seeking a modern, trendy atmosphere. **Pros:** great downtown location; tons of Old West charm; good value. **Cons:** dedicated parking is two blocks away (though there is closer street parking); small elevators (so cowboys wouldn't bring their horses up); small bathrooms. Ⓢ *Rooms from: $80* ✉ *1600 Central Ave.* ☎ *307/638–3311* *130 rooms* 🍴 *No meals.*

★ Little America Hotel and Resort

$$$ | **HOTEL** | The guest rooms at this sprawling, 80-acre property are large and full of old-school elegance, with giant windows, carpet in rich colors, and plenty of space to sit; it doesn't feel hip and modern, but that's the fun of it and part of what keeps this a local icon. **Pros:** full of historic elegance; many amenities, including restaurants and gift shop; largest convention center in Wyoming. **Cons:** golf course only has nine holes; many rooms not connected to main complex; outdoor pool only open seasonally.

Cheyenne Frontier Days

One of the premier events in the Cowboy State is Cheyenne Frontier Days, held the last full week of July since 1897. The event started as a rodeo for ranch-riding cowboys who liked to show off their skills; now it consumes all of Cheyenne for nine days, when 250,000 to 300,000 people come into town.

By the Numbers

Cheyenne Frontier Days includes nine afternoon rodeos; nine nighttime concerts; eight days of Native American dancing (Saturday–Saturday); four parades (Saturday, Tuesday, Thursday, and Saturday); three pancake breakfasts (Monday, Wednesday, and Friday); one U.S. Air Force air show (Wednesday); and one art show (all month).

The Rodeos

Dozens of the top Professional Rodeo Cowboys Association contenders come to Cheyenne to face off in bull riding, tie-down roping, saddle or bareback bronc riding, and steer wrestling. Women compete in barrel racing; and trick riders and rodeo clowns break up the action. In one of the most exciting events, three-man teams catch a wild horse and saddle it, and then one team member rides the horse around a track in a Wild West rendition of the Kentucky Derby. Frontier Days wraps up with the final Sunday rodeo, in which the top contestants in each event compete head-to-head for the coveted Cheyenne buckle.

Extracurriculars

Each night, concerts showcase top country entertainers such as Blake Shelton, Keith Urban, and Tim McGraw (be sure to buy tickets in advance). Members of the Northern Arapaho and Eastern Shoshone tribes from the Wind River Reservation perform dances at a temporary Native American village where they also drum, sing, and share their culture. The parades show off a huge collection of horse-drawn vehicles, and the free pancake breakfasts feed as many as 12,000 people in two hours. Crowds descend on the midway for carnival rides and games. At the Old West Museum, the expansive Frontier Days Western Art Show & Sale features pieces by top Western wildlife and landscape artists.

Boots and Books

Of course, there's plenty of shopping: at the Exhibition Hall, filled with Western wear and gear, you can buy everything from boots and belts to home furnishings and Western art. And you can pick up regional titles at book signings by members of the Western Writers of America.

Plan Ahead

Cheyenne Frontier Days entertains both kids and adults, in large numbers. It not only takes over Cheyenne but fills lodgings in nearby Laramie, Wheatland, Torrington, and even cities in northern Colorado. If you plan to attend, make your reservations early—some hotels book a year out.

For further information and to book rodeo and concert tickets, contact **Cheyenne Frontier Days** (☎ *800/227-6336 for the box office* 🌐 *www.cfdrodeo.com*). The website is a useful resource; you can buy tickets online, see a schedule of activities, and order a printed brochure, all well in advance of the event itself.

Rooms from: $159 ✉ 2800 W. Lincolnway ☎ 307/775–8400, 800/445–6945 🌐 www.littleamerica.com 188 rooms 🍽 No meals.*

Staybridge Suites Cheyenne
$$$ | HOTEL | FAMILY | The guest rooms in this all-suites hotel are infused with modern comfort and are especially geared toward longer stays, each with a good-size, fully stocked kitchen, desk, and pull-out couch. **Pros:** well-equipped rooms with all the comforts of home; free hot breakfast; large indoor pool and hot tub. **Cons:** not within walking distance to sights; fills up quickly during busy times; prices are higher than many hotels in the area (though you get a lot for your buck). *Rooms from: $169 ✉ 5109 Frontier Mall Dr. ☎ 307/634–6370 🌐 www.ihg.com 95 suites 🍽 Free breakfast.*

Shopping

Just Dandy
CLOTHING | For the best women's Western-style clothing in the city, ranging from belts, pants, shirts, and skirts to leather jackets, visit Just Dandy. *✉ 212 W. 17th St. ☎ 307/635–2565 🌐 www.justdandyonline.com Closed Sun.*

Manitou Galleries
ART GALLERIES | Original oil paintings, sculpture, jewelry, and other art are sold at Manitou Galleries, also located in the art mecca of Santa Fe, New Mexico. *✉ 1715 Carey Ave. ☎ 307/635–0019 🌐 www.manitougalleries.com.*

The Wrangler
CLOTHING | Now owned by Boot Barn, The Wrangler stocks a full line of traditional Western clothing, with sizes and styles for the entire family. *✉ 1518 Capitol Ave. ☎ 307/634–3048.*

Wyoming Home
HOUSEHOLD ITEMS/FURNITURE | Handcrafted furniture, artwork, and Western home items are available at Wyoming Home. *✉ 210 W. Lincolnway ☎ 307/638–2222 🌐 www.wyominghome.com Closed Sun. Labor Day–Memorial Day.*

Activities

CAMPING

Cheyenne KOA. Located about 7 miles east of downtown, this family-oriented campground has a seasonal heated pool and minigolf. *✉ 880 Hutchins Dr., I–80 Exit 367 ☎ 800/562–1507 🌐 koa.com/campgrounds/cheyenne/ 27 full hookups, 15 water and electric only, 11 tent sites, 6 cabins.*

Curt Gowdy State Park Campground. In rolling country with pine forest and a profusion of wildflowers during spring and summer, Curt Gowdy is a good camping spot 24 miles west of the city. The park has picnic sites and areas for swimming, boating, and fishing. Campsites can be used for tents or trailers. *✉ 1264 Granite Springs Rd., off Hwy. 210 ☎ 877/996–7275, 307/632–7946 🌐 wyoparks.state.wy.us/index.asp 178 sites, 4 cabins.*

Terry Bison Ranch. In addition to being a full-service campground and RV park with a restaurant and occasional entertainment, this is a working bison ranch, with a train tour that takes you right past the herd. *✉ I–25 Service Rd. near Colorado state line ☎ 307/634–4171, 307/634–9746 🌐 wwwterrybisonranch.com 102 full hookups, 100 tent sites, 7 cabins.*

Fort Laramie National Historic Site

105 miles northeast of Cheyenne via Hwys. 25 and 26.

The important and well-preserved 19th-century fort was an important stop along the Oregon Trail.

Historic Fort Laramie began as a way station for the Oregon Trail but became a military installation in 1849. The Treat of Fort Laramie was signed here in 1868, ending the First Sioux War.

Sights

★ Fort Laramie National Historic Site

HISTORIC SITE | FAMILY | Fort Laramie is one of the most important historic sites in Wyoming, in part because its original buildings are extremely well preserved, but also because it played a role in several significant periods in Western history. Near the confluence of the Laramie and North Platte rivers, the fort began as a trading post in 1834, and it was an important provisioning point for travelers on the Oregon Trail in 1843, the Mormon Trail in 1847, and the California Trail in 1849, when it also became a military site. The 1868 Treaty of Fort Laramie was signed here, leading to the end of the First Sioux War, also known as Red Cloud's War. National Park Service rangers interpret scenes of military life and talk about the fur trade, overland migration, and relations between settlers and Native Americans. ✉ *965 Gray Rocks Rd., Fort Laramie* ✣ *105 miles northeast of Laramie via WY 25 and 26* ☎ *307/837–2221* 🌐 *www.nps.gov/fola* 🎫 *Free.*

Happy Jack Road

SCENIC DRIVE | Although I–80 connects Cheyenne and Laramie more quickly, the drive between the two cities on Happy Jack Road (Highway 210) is very scenic, particularly in spring and early summer, when wildflowers are in full bloom. The road winds over the high plains, past Curt Gowdy State Park, and provides access to the Vedauwoo Recreation Area before linking back to I–80, 7 miles east of Laramie at the **Abraham Lincoln Memorial Monument.** At this state rest area you can obtain information about the region and view a larger-than-life sculpture of the 16th president's head looming above you.

Vedauwoo Recreation Areagoo

NATURE SITE | The Vedauwoo Recreation Area, in the Medicine Bow–Routt National Forest, is a particularly unusual area and a great place for a picnic. Springing out of high plains and open meadows are glacial remnants in the form of huge granite boulders piled skyward with reckless abandon. These one-of-a-kind rock formations, dreamscapes of gray stone, are great for hiking, climbing, and photography. There's also camping here. ✉ *27 miles west of Cheyenne off I–80 or Hwy. 210* ☎ *307/745–2300* 🌐 *www.fs.fed.us* 🎫 *Free, camping $10* ⏲ *Campground closed early-fall–late-spring.*

Laramie

51 miles west of Cheyenne via I–80.

At just over 30,000 people, Laramie is not a big city, but it is probably Wyoming's coolest. Home to the University of Wyoming, it has all the trappings you'd expect from a college town, from hip little stores, to a vibrant bar scene, to an excellent vegetarian restaurant. Its historic downtown has several quaint buildings, some of which date back to 1868, the year after the railroad arrived and the city was established. For a time it was a tough "end-of-the-rail" town. Vigilantes took care of lawbreakers, hanging them from convenient telegraph poles. Then in 1872 the city constructed the Wyoming Territorial Prison on the bank of the Little Laramie River. One of its most famous inmates was Butch Cassidy. The prison has been closed for more than a century now, but can still be toured during the summer, and like so much of Wyoming's Wild West past, still feels like it's flavoring the present.

GETTING HERE AND AROUND

I–80 skirts the south and then west sides of town; U.S. 287 (3rd Street within the city) bisects Laramie from north to south. Grand Avenue, which borders the University of Wyoming, is the primary east–west route through Laramie.

VISITOR INFORMATION

You can get brochures from the Laramie Area Visitor Center, on East Custer Street, for a self-guided tour of the late-19th-century Victorian architecture. Also available are self-guided tours of the city's historic downtown, murals, and more.

CONTACTS Laramie Area Visitor Center. ✉ *210 E. Custer St.* ☎ *307/745-4195, 800/445–5303* 🌐 *www.visitlaramie.org.*

Sights

American Heritage Center

LIBRARY | The center houses more than 90,000 cubic feet (or nearly 17 miles) of rare books, collections of papers, and memorabilia related to such subjects as American and Western history, the petroleum industry, conservation movements, transportation, and the performing arts. Permanent and temporary art displays also fill the museum space. ✉ *2111 Willet Dr.* ☎ *307/766–4114* 🌐 *www.uwyo.edu/ahc* 🎫 *Free* ⏲ *Closed weekends.*

Harry C. Vaughan Planetarium

OBSERVATORY | **FAMILY** | You can learn about the stars and watch science presentations that transport you to vast landscapes at the planetarium's full-dome theater. Entertainment shows, where images dance to music above you, are also sometimes offered. Public shows are typically on Tuesday, Friday, and Saturday, as well as certain holidays. Private bookings also available. ✉ *University of Wyoming, 10th and Fremont Sts., Physical Sciences Bldg. basement* ☎ *307/766–6506* 🌐 *www.uwyo.edu/physics/planetarium* 🎫 *$5* ⏲ *Closed when university is closed.*

Laramie Plains Museum at the Historic Ivinson Mansion

MUSEUM | This impressive, Queen Anne–style mansion is home to a growing collection of historical artifacts that help tell the history of the Laramie plains area. The home itself is a big part of the city's past. Its first owners, Edward and Jane Ivinson, were on the very first passenger train in 1868, and later constructed the mansion during Edward's run for governor of the new state of Wyoming.

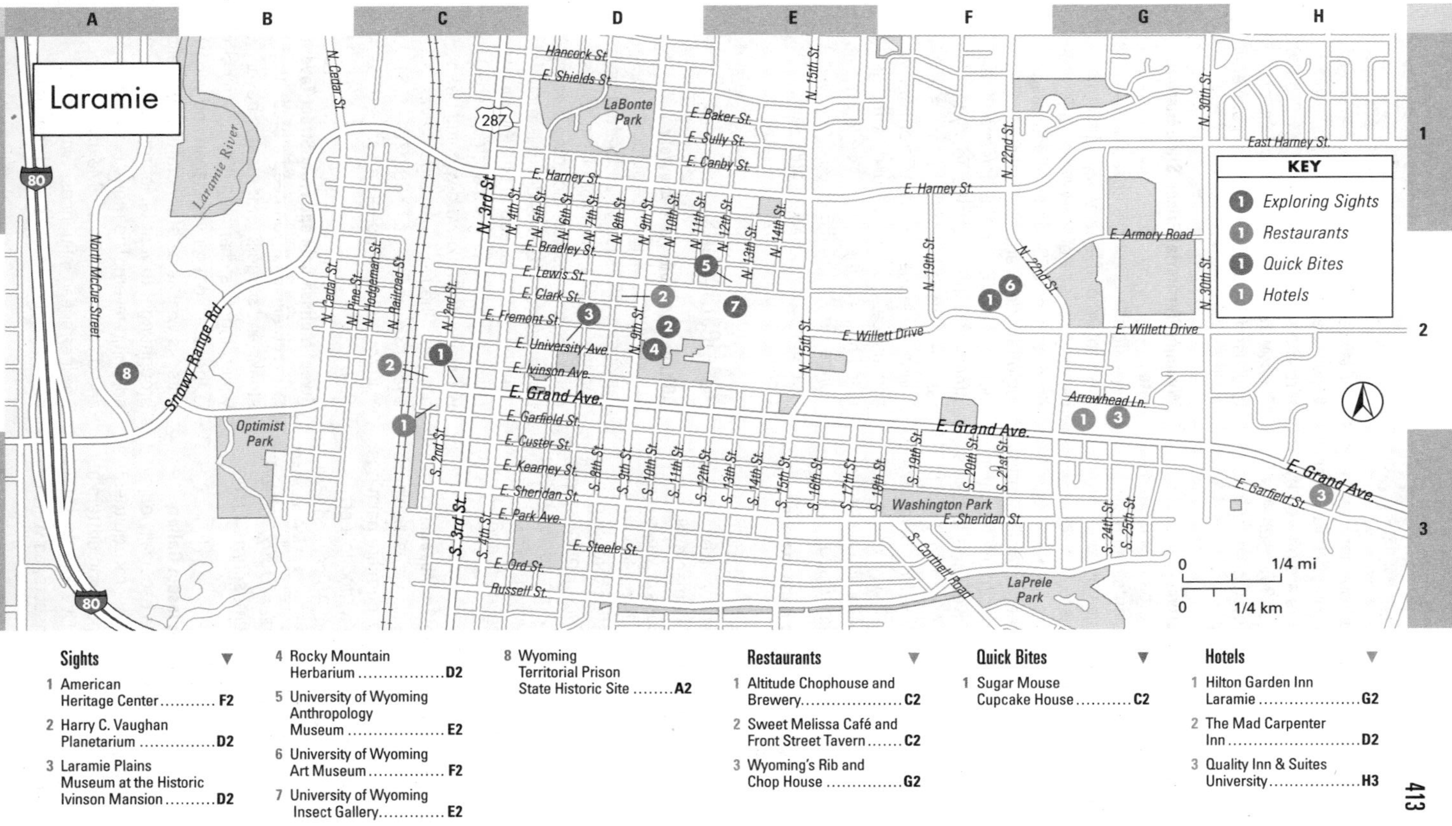

Sights

1 American Heritage Center F2

2 Harry C. Vaughan Planetarium D2

3 Laramie Plains Museum at the Historic Ivinson Mansion D2

4 Rocky Mountain Herbarium D2

5 University of Wyoming Anthropology Museum E2

6 University of Wyoming Art Museum F2

7 University of Wyoming Insect Gallery............. E2

8 Wyoming Territorial Prison State Historic Site A2

Restaurants

1 Altitude Chophouse and Brewery.................... C2

2 Sweet Melissa Café and Front Street Tavern....... C2

3 Wyoming's Rib and Chop House G2

Quick Bites

1 Sugar Mouse Cupcake House C2

Hotels

1 Hilton Garden Inn Laramie G2

2 The Mad Carpenter Inn D2

3 Quality Inn & Suites University.................... H3

The home was saved from demolition in 1972, and is on the National Register of Historic Places. Tours are offered by informed docents. ✉ *603 Ivinson Ave.* ☎ *307/742–4448* 🌐 *www.laramiemuseum.org* 🎟 *$10.*

Rocky Mountain Herbarium

LOCAL INTEREST | The herbarium focuses on Rocky Mountain plants, but also includes other examples of flora from the northern hemisphere. But don't expect any living plants here. This is a working dry plant research facility, and features 1.3 million specimens mounted on paper. Visitors are welcome to take a tour. ✉ *University of Wyoming, 9th St. at University Ave., Aven Nelson Bldg., 3rd fl.* ☎ *307/766–2236* 🌐 *www.rockymountainherbarium.org* ⏲ *Closed weekends and when university is closed.*

University of Wyoming Anthropology Museum

MUSEUM | **FAMILY** | The Anthropology Museum at the university takes visitors on a journey through human evolution, starting in Africa millions of years ago. Part of the museum also celebrates hunter-gatherer societies throughout world history. ✉ *University of Wyoming, 12th and Lewis Sts., Anthropology Bldg.* ☎ *307/766–5136* 🌐 *www.uwyo.edu* 🎟 *Free* ⏲ *Closed weekends and when university is closed.*

University of Wyoming Art Museum

MUSEUM | Among the artworks displayed in the campus art museum are paintings, sculpture, photography, and folk art from America, Europe, Africa, and Asia. ✉ *University of Wyoming, 2111 E. Willett Dr., Centennial Complex* ☎ *307/766–6622* 🌐 *www.uwyo.edu/artmuseum* 🎟 *Free* ⏲ *Closed Sat.–Mon.*

University of Wyoming Insect Gallery

MUSEUM | **FAMILY** | Kids especially enjoy looking at the butterflies, mosquitoes, and other crawling and flying critters at the Insect Gallery at UW. The collection includes preserved insects, as well as a small zoo of live ones. ✉ *University of Wyoming, 13th and Lewis Sts., Agriculture Bldg., Room 4018* ☎ *307/766–5338* 🌐 *www.naturalsciencecollections.org* ⏲ *Closed weekends and when university is closed.*

Wyoming Territorial Prison State Historic Site

HISTORIC SITE | Perhaps because of the bedlam of the early days, Laramie became the site of the Wyoming Territorial Prison in 1872. Until 1903 it was the region's federal and state penal facility, locking down Butch Cassidy and other infamous frontier outlaws. Today the restored prison is a state historic site that brings to life the legends of frontier law and justice. Open year-round, with curtailed hours in the winter. ✉ *975 Snowy Range Rd.* ☎ *307/745–3733* 🌐 *wyoparks.wyo.gov* 🎟 *$9* ⏲ *Closed Sun.–Tues. Oct.–Apr.*

Restaurants

Altitude Chophouse and Brewery

$$ | **AMERICAN** | A favorite of locals, this restaurant offers tasty handcrafted ales and fine cuisine, with surprising twists on American classics, including steaks, burgers, and pizza. The decor is mountain themed, with a beautiful bar. **Known for:** charred lime salmon; rib eye garnished with fried onions; award-winning beers brewed in-house. $ *Average main: $16* ✉ *320 S. 2nd St.* ☎ *307/721–4031* 🌐 *www.altitudechophouse.com* ⏲ *Closed Sun.*

Sweet Melissa Café and Front Street Tavern

$$ | **VEGETARIAN** | If you need a break from steaks and burgers (or if meat is never your thing) this charming downtown café is the local spot for vegetarian and vegan eats, as well as carefully crafted cocktails brought right to your table from the adjoining tavern. The menu is extensive and diverse, with Asian, Mexican, and Mediterranean influences, with a good selection of desserts and a menu for kids, too. **Known for:** clearly labeled vegetarian, vegan, and gluten-free options; delicious cauliflower "wings"; tasty cocktails, reasonably priced. *Average main: $11 213 S. 1st St. 307/742–9607 www.sweetmelissacafe.com Closed Sun.*

Wyoming's Rib and Chop House
$$$ | **STEAKHOUSE** | This fun and casual small chain has some of the best ribs, steaks, and seafood you'll find in the state. The portions are eye-popping in size, and there's a good selection of sides and desserts, plus a full bar. **Known for:** baby back ribs, marinated for 24 hours; hand-cut rib eyes; fried green tomatoes topped with crab and blue cheese. *Average main: $20 2415 Grand Ave. 307/460–9090 www.ribandchophouse.com.*

Coffee and Quick Bites

Sugar Mouse Cupcake House
$ | **BAKERY** | **FAMILY** | This pleasant downtown bakery is best known for its wide, changing selection of gourmet cupcakes. It also offers espresso drinks and items you'd expect in an English teahouse, including crumpets and biscuits. **Known for:** sumptuous cupcakes, with seasonal flavors; dairy- and gluten-free cupcake options; wide selection of tea, many imported from England. *Average main: $6 211 Grand Ave. 307/223–2147 www.thesugarmouse.net Closed Sun.*

Hotels

Hilton Garden Inn Laramie
$$$ | **HOTEL** | The nicest place to stay in the city, this modern hotel offers elegant, comfortable rooms decorated in warm tones. **Pros:** right by the university stadium (odd-numbered rooms have a view of it); only hotel in the area with a restaurant and bar; lovely pool and hot tub, open year-round. **Cons:** higher priced than many surrounding hotels; can book up early, especially during football season; made-to-order breakfast costs extra. *Rooms from: $189 2229 Grand Ave. 307/745–5500 www.hilton.com 135 rooms No meals.*

The Mad Carpenter Inn
$$ | **B&B/INN** | When you stay here, you'll likely meet the "Mad Carpenter" himself, Lawrence Thomas, who lovingly restored this historic home with the help of his wife, Danny Rue, whose fabulous homemade granola is available every morning with breakfast. **Pros:** great downtown location near the university; good value in a beautiful historic home; fabulous breakfast, including homemade cinnamon rolls. **Cons:** one room doesn't have an attached bath; like all local lodging, it fills up quickly during busy months; finding on-street parking can be a challenge (but owners do provide a pass). *Rooms from: $95 353 N. 8th St. 307/742–0870 www.madcarpenterinn.net 3 rooms Free breakfast.*

Quality Inn & Suites University
$ | **HOTEL** | On busy Grand Avenue, this a good budget option close to restaurants and fast-food chains, as well as War Memorial Stadium at the University of Wyoming. **Pros:** close to the stadium and conference center; indoor pool; all rooms have a mini-refrigerator and microwave. **Cons:** rooms fill up fast on game weekends; not pet-friendly; on a busy road. *Rooms from: $79 3420 Grand Ave. 307/ 721–8856 www.choicehotels.com 55 rooms Free breakfast.*

Nightlife

Buckhorn Bar & Parlor
MUSIC CLUBS | Kick up your heels to live country-and-western music or DJ tunes at the Buckhorn, Laramie's oldest bar. *114 Ivinson Ave. 307/742–3554.*

Cowboy Saloon
BARS/PUBS | Take a spin around the dance floor at the Cowboy Saloon Wednesday through Saturday. The bar has nightly

drink specials and frequent live music, including some performances open to adults under 21. ✉ *108 S. 2nd St.* ☎ *307/742–7788* 🌐 *www.thecowboysaloon.com* ☞ *Closed Sun.–Tues.*

Library Sports Grill and Brewery
BREWPUBS/BEER GARDENS | Stop by the Library Sports Grill and Brewery for beers brewed on-site. ✉ *1622 Grand Ave.* ☎ *307/745–0500* 🌐 *www.thelibrarybrewery.com.*

Mingles
BARS/PUBS | College students gather and shoot pool at Mingles. ✉ *3206 Grand Ave.* ☎ *307/721–2005.*

Laramie's most interesting shopping is found around Landmark Square, which is along Ivinson and Grand avenues. Stores here sell artwork, clothing, and handcrafted items.

BOOKS

The Second Story
BOOKS/STATIONERY | **FAMILY** | Located in a former brothel, this fun shop offers a wide range of books, segmented into different sections in the tiny rooms once frequented by ladies of the night. The adjacent Night Heron Books & Coffee House sells used books, as well as coffee and locally sourced eats, including sandwiches, soups, and pastries. A door divides the two spaces. ✉ *105 E. Ivinson Ave.* ☎ *307/745–4423* ⊙ *Closed Sun. (though Night Heron is open daily).*

CRAFTS AND GIFTS

Curiosity Shoppe
CRAFTS | Curiosity Shoppe sells antiques, pottery, and hand-embroidered and hand-crocheted items. ✉ *206 S. 2nd St.* ☎ *307/745–4401* 🌐 *www.curiosityshoppewy.com* ⊙ *Closed Sun.*

BIKING

Pedal House
BICYCLING | Mountain-biking trails are scattered throughout the Medicine Bow–Routt National Forest and the Happy Jack recreation area, east of Laramie. This popular bike store offers information, trail maps, and bike rentals. ✉ *207 S. 1st St.* ☎ *307/742–5533* 🌐 *www.pedalhouse.com.*

CAMPING

Laramie KOA. This campground on the west side of town has lots of grassy space and some trees, as well as two fenced-in pet areas. Satellite TV for your RV is included in the price, and free Wi-Fi is available throughout the campground. There are one- and two-bedroom cabins, and the rec center has ping pong, foosball, air hockey, and a laundry room. There are a few fenced-in pet areas. ✉ *1271 W. Baker St. (I–80 at Curtis St. exit)* ☎ *307/742–6553* 🌐 *www.koa.com* *156 full hookups, 30 tent sites, 8 cabins.*

Libby Creek Pine Campground. Wake up to the sound of Libby Creek as it rushes past your campsite. This campground is small and shady and tucked away from the main road. All sites are first-come, first-served and are open seasonally from June to mid-October, depending on the amount of snow. ✉ *32 miles west of Laramie on Hwy. 130 to Libby Recreation Area, then ½ mile on Forest Rd. 351* ☎ *307/745–2300, 877/444–6777* 🌐 *https://www.fs.usda.gov/recarea/mbr* *6 sites.*

Sugarloaf Campground. At 10,700 feet, this is the highest campground in Wyoming. Don't be surprised if you get snowed on in July. With stunning views of the mountains, getting a site here can be difficult, so plan accordingly. Heavy winter snows have prevented this area from opening until well into the summer, if at all, in some years. ✉ *40 miles west of Laramie* *on Hwy. 130 and then 1 mile north on Forest Service Rd. 346 ☎ 307/745–2300, 877/444–6777 🌐 www.reserveusa.com ➪ 16 sites.*

Medicine Bow

60 miles northwest of Laramie via U.S. 30.

When novelist Owen Wister (1860–1938) first visited Medicine Bow—the town he would immortalize in his 1902 classic Western tale *The Virginian*—he noted that the community looked "as if strewn there by the wind." Today the town still looks somewhat windblown, although the tiny business district is anchored by the Virginian Hotel, built in the early 1900s and named in honor of the book. This is a community of roughly 300 struggling for survival, with an economy based on agriculture and mining. Although the town sits at the intersection of U.S. 30 (Lincoln Highway) and Wyoming Route 487, you'll seldom encounter much traffic here, except during the fall hunting season (the area is particularly noted for its antelope hunting) and when there are football or basketball games at the University of Wyoming. On those days, expect a lots of folks on the road and fans talking about sports at the town's sole hotel.

Sights

Medicine Bow Museum

MUSEUM | You can learn about the history of this small dot of a town at the Medicine Bow Museum, housed in an old railroad depot built in 1913. The summer cabin belonging to famed fiction author Owen Wister was relocated and stands right next door. ✉ *405 Lincoln Hwy.* ☎ *307/703–8084* 🌐 *www.medbowmuseum.com* *Free* ⏱ *Closed Labor Day–Memorial Day.*

Hotels

Virginian Hotel

$$ | **HOTEL** | Inspired by the Owen Wister novel *The Virginian*, this sandstone hotel was built in 1909 and has been operating nearly continuously ever since; it's historic but pretty bare-bones. **Pros:** perfect for the history buff; down-home restaurant serves breakfast, lunch, and dinner; right by the museum and in the middle of the tiny town. **Cons:** local train tracks create a racket; most rooms in the main hotel don't have private bathrooms; a historic hotel showing signs of age. *$ Rooms from: $90* ✉ *404 Lincoln Hwy.* ☎ *307/379–2377* ➪ *56 rooms* 🍴 *No meals.*

Centennial

30 miles west of Laramie via Hwy. 130; 85 miles south of Medicine Bow via U.S. 30 and Hwy. 130.

Snuggled up against the mountains of the Snowy Range, Centennial lies at the head of the glacial Centennial Valley. As the community closest to the Snowy Range, the town makes a good base from which to take part in numerous recreational activities, including hiking, cross-country skiing, snowmobiling, and downhill skiing. This small town has a few hardy year-round residents, and many more people who summer in the area.

VISITOR INFORMATION

The local visitor center is sometimes closed starting in October through Memorial Day.

CONTACTS Centennial Snowy Range Visitor's Center . ✉ *Hwy. 130* ⊕ *1 mile west of Centennial* ☎ *307/742–9730.*

Medicine Bow–Routt National Forest, Laramie District

FOREST | You can hike, picnic, fish, ski, snowmobile, and take photographs in the 400,000 acres of Medicine Bow–Routt National Forest, Laramie District, and that is the short list. The Laramie District has 20 developed campgrounds, although some are closed for tree removal; dispersed camping is also allowed. Although the Laramie District administrative office is in Laramie, several of the most easily accessed campgrounds are along scenic Highway 130, just west of Centennial. Lodgings such as cabins, forest guard stations, and even a fire lookout tower high in the Snowy Range are available for rent in summer. Pole Mountain, located north of I–80 between Laramie and Cheyenne, is a popular area for recreation and is approximately 55,000 acres in size. ☎ *307/745–2300 administrative office in Laramie, 877/444–6777 for camping* 🌐 *www.fs.fed.us/r2/mbr/.*

Nici Self Museum

MUSEUM | The former Centennial Railroad Depot now houses this museum at the eastern edge of town. The museum displays ranching, farming, and mining equipment, plus artifacts typical of what you'd find in a pioneer home; there's also an outdoor-equipment exhibit. Most of the items have been donated by local families. The museum is open Memorial Day through September. ✉ *2734 Hwy. 130* ☎ *307/742–7763* 🌐 *www.niciself-museum.org* 🎟 *Donations accepted* ⏲ *Closed Labor Day–Memorial Day. Closed Tues. and Wed. Memorial Day–Labor Day. Closed weekdays in Sept.*

Snowy Range Scenic Byway

SCENIC DRIVE | Highway 130 between Centennial and Saratoga is known as the Snowy Range Scenic Byway. This paved road, which is in excellent condition, crosses through the Medicine Bow–Routt National Forest, providing views of 12,013-foot Medicine Bow Peak and access to hiking trails, 10 campgrounds (6 right near the road), picnic areas, and 100 alpine lakes and streams. Gravel roads lead off the route into the national forest.

At the top of the 10,847-foot Snowy Range Pass, about 10 miles west of Centennial, take a short walk to the Libby Flats Observation Site for views of the Snowy Range and, on clear days, Rocky Mountain National Park to the southwest in Colorado. Lake Marie, a jewel of a mountain lake at an elevation of approximately 10,000 feet, is also here. On the Saratoga side of the mountain the road passes through pine forest and descends to the North Platte River valley, with cattle ranches on both sides of the highway. Note that the byway is impassable in winter and therefore is closed between approximately mid-October and Memorial Day. ✉ *Centennial* ⏲ *Closed mid-Oct.–Memorial Day.*

Old Corral Hotel & Steak House

$$ | **HOTEL** | With its mountain views and classy cowboy vibe, this small-town log hotel makes for a comfortable escape from city life. **Pros:** just down the road from the Snowy Mountains; perfect location for snowmobilers; restaurant, best known for its steaks, has been open since the 1940s. **Cons:** hotel closings vary by season; restaurant not open during winter months; noise transmits easily through guest rooms. 💲 *Rooms from: $99* ✉ *2750 Hwy. 130* ☎ *307/745–5918* 🌐 *www.oldcorral.com* ⏲ *Closed mid-Oct.–mid-Dec. and mid-Apr.–mid-May* 🛏 *35 rooms* 🍽 *No meals.*

Vee Bar Guest Ranch

$$$$ | **ALL-INCLUSIVE** | This family-operated guest ranch along the Little Laramie River offers all-inclusive summer lodging

Summer hiking is a particularly popular activity in the Medicine Bow–Routt National Forest, and many trails can be easily accessed from scenic Highway 130 near Centennial.

in individual cabins that exude rustic luxury; winter accommodations are in the equally charming lodge suites, with breakfast-only included. **Pros:** vast, beautiful scenery; plenty activities to keep you busy; friendly, accommodating guides. **Cons:** located far from services (21 miles from Laramie and 9 miles from Centennial); in summer, only three- and six-day packages are available (except on Saturday, when a nightly stay is offered); horseback riding has a 260-lb weight limit. *Rooms from: $300* ⊠ *38 Vee Bar Ranch Rd.* ✣ *7 miles east of Centennial; 24 miles west of Laramie* ☎ *307/745–7036, 800/483–3227* ⊕ *www.veebar.com* *13 rooms* *All-inclusive.*

Activities

CAMPING

In addition to the campgrounds listed here, there are several others in both the Laramie and Brush Creek districts of the Medicine Bow–Routt. The Forest Service campsites are $10 per night.

Brooklyn Lake Campground. On the east side of Snowy Range Pass, at an elevation of 10,500 feet, this small campground sits beside Brooklyn Lake and is surrounded by pine forest. You can fish in the lake and use nonmotorized boats. There is a carry-down access for boats (no ramp). All campsites have views of the lake. The maximum length for a camping trailer is 22 feet. The campground generally opens in mid-July and closes in early September. No reservations are possible. ⊠ *Hwy. 130, 7 miles west of Centennial on Hwy. 130, then 2 miles east on Brooklyn Lake Rd./Forest Rd. 317* ☎ *307/745–2300* ⊕ *www.fs.fed.us/r2/mbr/* *19 sites.*

CROSS-COUNTRY SKIING

The same trails that serve hikers in summer cater to cross-country skiers in winter in the Lower Snowy Range trail system. You can access several trails on Highway 130 west of Centennial in the Medicine Bow–Routt National Forest, including the **Corner Mountain Trail** (3 miles west of Centennial), **Little Laramie**

Trail (4 miles west of Centennial), and the **Green Rock Trail** (7 miles west of Centennial). There is also a cross-country-skiing trail system at Snowy Range Ski and Recreation Area. Many of the trails are interconnected, so you can combine short trails for a longer ski trip.

HIKING

Dozens of miles of hiking trails slice through the Medicine Bow–Routt National Forest west of town. Major trailheads are on Highway 130, including trailheads for the 7-mile **Corner Mountain Trail** (3 miles west of Centennial), 7-mile **Little Laramie Trail** (4 miles west of Centennial), and 9-mile **Medicine Bow Peak Trail** (7 miles west of Centennial). The easy 1-mile **Centennial Trail** takes off from the Centennial Visitor Center at the forest boundary. More difficult is the 4½-mile **Barber Lake Trail**, which starts at Barber Lake and incorporates ski trails and old forest roads. Most hikers follow this trail downhill one way, and instead of doubling back use two vehicles to shuttle between Barber Lake and the Corner Mountain trailhead (the Barber Lake Trail hooks up with part of the Corner Mountain trail).

Trail maps and information are available at the Centennial Visitor's Center.

SKIING AND SNOWBOARDING

Snowy Range Ski Area

SKIING/SNOWBOARDING | **FAMILY** | Downhill skiing and snowboarding are available 5 miles west of Centennial at the family-oriented ski area, which offers lift tickets at much cheaper prices than the West's glitziest resorts. There are five ski lifts, with slopes for beginners and experienced skiers, plus some cross-country-skiing trails. Uphill traffic is allowed, with limited restrictions. ✉ *3254 Wyoming 130* ☎ *800/462–7669, 307/745–5750, 307/721–1114* 🌐 *www.snowyrangeski.com.*

Saratoga

49 miles west of Centennial via Hwy. 130 (Memorial Day–early Oct.); rest of year, 140 miles west of Centennial via Hwy. 130 east to Laramie, Hwy. 230 west to Encampment, and Hwy. 130 north or east to Laramie, I–80 west to Hwy. 130 and then south.

Tucked away in a valley formed by the Snowy Range and Sierra Madre Mountains, Saratoga is a rarely visited treasure. Fine shopping and dining happily combine with elegant lodging options and a landscape that's ideal for outdoor activities. This is a good spot for river floating and blue-ribbon fishing: the North Platte River bisects the region, and there are several lakes and streams nearby in the Medicine Bow–Routt National Forest. You can also cross-country ski and snowmobile in the area. The town first went by the name Warm Springs, but in an attempt to add an air of sophistication to the place, townsfolk changed the name to Saratoga (after Saratoga Springs, New York) in 1884.

VISITOR INFORMATION

CONTACTS Saratoga/Platte Valley Chamber of Commerce. ✉ *210 W. Elm St.* ☎ *307/326–8855* 🌐 *www.saratogachamber.info.*

Sights

Medicine Bow–Routt National Forest, Hayden District

FOREST | The Medicine Bow–Routt National Forest, Hayden District covers 586,000 acres, including the Continental Divide National Scenic Trail and the Encampment River, Huston Park, Savage Run, and Platte River wilderness areas. ✉ *Saratoga* 🌐 *www.fs.usda.gov.*

Saratoga Hobo Hot Springs

HOT SPRINGS | **FAMILY** | Hot mineral waters flow freely through the Saratoga Hobo Hot Springs, and the adjacent cooler swimming pool is heated by the springs. People have been coming here to soak for generations, including Native Americans, who considered the area neutral territory. Hardy folk can do as the Native Americans did and first soak in the hot water, then jump into the adjacent icy waters of the North Platte River. The free pools are open all day, every day. Bathing suits are required. ✉ *Walnut Ave.* ✣ *From 1st St. (Hwy 130), turn east on Walnut. Go 2 blocks to end of road* 🎫 *Free.*

Saratoga Museum

MUSEUM | The former Union Pacific Railroad depot houses the Saratoga Museum, with displays of local artifacts related to the history and geology of the area. Outdoor exhibits include a sheep wagon, caboose, and a one-bedroom cabin built by a local pioneer. ✉ *104 Constitution Ave.* ☎ *307/326–5511* 🌐 *www.saratoga-museum.com* 🎫 *Donations accepted* 🕒 *Closed Sun. and Mon.*

Restaurants

Bella's Bistro

$$$ | **ITALIAN** | Located in a little green house, Bella's cozy dining room is the place to head for a special occasion—and just any time you want some really good pasta, chicken Parmesan, or steak. The desserts, antipasti, soups, salads, and wine selection are also top-notch. **Known for:** classic Italian options, including lasagna, gnocchi, and spaghetti and meatballs; New York cheesecake and other house-made desserts; beautiful bar, with full selection of beer, wine and cocktails. 💲 *Average main: $20* ✉ *218 N. 1st St.* ☎ *307/326–8033* 🌐 *www.bellaswyoming.com* 🕒 *Closed Mon. and Tues. No lunch.*

The Grumpy Italian

$$ | **ITALIAN** | **FAMILY** | This casual, family-run eatery serves up big helpings of pasta, hefty sandwiches, and seriously good pizza. Despite the name, the service is always friendly and welcoming, and if you come back often enough, the owners might even put your picture up on the wall. **Known for:** delicious pizza, with a gluten-free crust option; fun vibe, with games at the tables; fabulous, authentic meatballs. 💲 *Average main: $14* ✉ *113 W. Bridge Ave.* ☎ *307/326–3210* 🌐 *www.thegrumpyitalian.com* 🕒 *Closed Sun. and Mon.*

Hotels

★ Brush Creek Ranch

$$$$ | **ALL-INCLUSIVE** | One of the best-regarded guest ranches in the country, this luxury getaway is also a working ranch on 30,000 acres of pristine, remote land with three distinct lodging options. **Pros:** a luxurious, all-inclusive resort with a Western heart; beautiful, rugged setting; plethora of activities, including horseback riding, yoga, and fishing. **Cons:** nearly 20 miles from the closest town; high-end comfort comes at a lofty price, plus a daily ranch fee that covers tipping; certain activities, experiences, and special menu offerings cost extra. 💲 *Rooms from: $1900* ✉ *66 Brush Creek Ranch Rd.* ☎ *307/327–5284* 🌐 *www.brushcreekranch.com* 🕒 *Closed mid-Apr.–mid-May, plus first few wks of Dec.* 🛏 *13 rooms, 29 cabins* 🍽 *All-inclusive.*

Hotel Wolf

$$ | **HOTEL** | This downtown 1893 hotel on the National Register of Historic Places is well-maintained by its proud owners, who have decorated each room differently, always maintaining the hotel's original simple Victorian charm. **Pros:** beautiful and historic rooms at a great price; family-run and friendly; delicious on-site restaurant serving Western favorites. **Cons:** steep stairs and no elevator; some rooms are small, with small bathrooms; no thermostat in room (it's possible to turn heat down, but not up, in each room). 💲 *Rooms from: $85* ✉ *101 E. Bridge Ave.* ☎ *307/326–5525* 🌐 *www.wolfhotel.com* 🛏 *10 rooms* 🍽 *No meals.*

Riviera Lodge

$$ | **HOTEL** | The rooms at this locally owned, riverside spot are large and simple and are a favorite with hunters, fishers, and snowmobilers. **Pros:** only two blocks from downtown; some rooms have a river view; pet-friendly. **Cons:** relatively few amenities; books up quickly in busy times; older rooms with small bathrooms. *Rooms from: $100* ✉ *104 E. Saratoga St.* ☎ *307/326–5651, 866/326–5651* *40 rooms* *No meals.*

★ **Saratoga Hot Springs Resort**

$$$ | **HOTEL** | With leather couches in the common areas, pole-frame beds, and Western art, this small-town inn is as nice as any place in Wyoming. **Pros:** 70-foot mineral-water pool; rentals available for outdoor adventure, including kayaks, paddleboards, and UTVs; on-site brewery and restaurant. **Cons:** feels disconnected from downtown, a 10-minute walk away; older property; pets are not allowed in rooms (though kennels are available for dogs). *Rooms from: $193* ✉ *601 E. Pic Pike Rd.* ☎ *307/326–5261* 🌐 *saratogahotspringsresort.com* *52 rooms* *No meals.*

Activities

CAMPING

Ryan Park Campground. During World War II this was the site of a camp for German prisoners, and you can still see some of the building foundations. The campground on the east side of Snowy Range Pass lies at an elevation of 8,000 feet. It has access to stream fishing as well as to hiking on forest trails and two-track roads. Just west of the small community of Ryan Park, it is 20 miles southeast of Saratoga. Check with the Brush Creek/Hayden district (307/326–5258) for closures because of tree removal. The campground is open June through September. ✉ *Hwy. 130, 20 miles southeast of Saratoga* ☎ *877/444–6777* 🌐 *www.recreation.gov* *47 sites.*

CROSS-COUNTRY SKIING

Hayden/Brush Creek Ranger District

SKIING/SNOWBOARDING | Extensive trail networks in the Medicine Bow–Routt National Forest are good for novice and experienced cross-country skiers and snowmobilers. For trail conditions, contact the **Hayden/Brush Creek Ranger District** of the Medicine Bow–Routt National Forest. ✉ *Saratoga* ☎ *307/326–5258* 🌐 *www.fs.fed.us/r2/mbr.*

FISHING

Brook trout are abundant in the lakes and streams of Medicine Bow–Routt National Forest, and you will also find rainbow, golden, cutthroat, and brown trout, as well as splake. You can also drop a fly in the North Platte River.

Drift

FISHING | This fly-fishing outfitter offers guided trips for all ability levels on sections of the North Platte and Encampment rivers. Scenic rafting trips are also available. It has no brick-and-mortar location in town, but all guides live in Carbon County. ☎ *307/223–2042* 🌐 *www.saratogaflyfishing.com.*

Encampment

18 miles south of Saratoga via Hwys. 130 and 230.

This is the gateway community to the Continental Divide National Scenic Trail, accessed at Battle Pass, 15 miles to the west on Highway 70. Hikers and horseback riders can take the rugged trail from Canada all the way south to Mexico along the Continental Divide, a total of 3,100 miles. Encampment is also a good place to launch trips into four nearby wilderness areas in the Hayden District of Medicine Bow–Routt National Forest—Platte River, Savage Run, Encampment River, and Huston Park—where you can go hiking, fishing, mountain biking, snowmobiling, and cross-country skiing. Although recreation is a quickly emerging industry, there's still a lot of quiet mountain country to explore, and it's not yet crowded in this town of about 400 residents. The tiny, adjacent community of Riverside has just a fraction of that population but also has some of the area's amenities.

Every July, the **Grand Encampment Cowboy Gathering** celebrates the Western lifestyle, with performances by cowboy musicians and poets. There's also stick-horse rodeo for children. Events take place at the Grand Encampment Museum and other venues around town.

Sights

Battle Highway

SCENIC DRIVE | As you make your way west to Baggs over the Battle Highway (Highway 70), you'll cross the Continental Divide and the Rocky Mountains. This route takes you through the mining country that was developed during the 1897–1908 copper-mining boom in the Sierra Madres; interpretive signs along the way point out historic sites. Legend has it that in 1878, Thomas Edison was fishing near Battle Pass with a bamboo rod when he began to ponder the idea of a filament, which led to his invention of the incandescent light bulb. Note that this section of the highway closes to car travel in winter, though it stays open for snowmobiles. ✉ *Encampment* ⏲ *Closed to cars Nov.–Memorial Day.*

★ Grand Encampment Museum

MUSEUM | **FAMILY** | The modern interpretive center at the Grand Encampment Museum holds exhibits on the history of the Grand Encampment copper district and logging and mining. A pioneer town of original buildings includes the Lake Creek stage station, the Big Creek tie-hack cabin, the Peryam homestead, the Slash Ridge fire tower, a blacksmith shop, a transportation barn, and a two-story outhouse. Among the other relics are three towers from a 16-mile-long aerial tramway built in 1903 to transport copper ore from mines in the Sierra Madres. You can take guided tours, and there's also a research area. A living-history day, with music, costumes, and events, takes place the third weekend in July. ✉ *807 Barnett Ave.* ☎ *307/327–5308* 🌐 *www.gemuseum.com* 🎫 *Donations accepted* ⏲ *Closed Sun. and Mon. Memorial Day–early Oct.; call or email ahead for winter hrs.*

Restaurants

Bear Trap Cafe & Bar

$$ | **AMERICAN** | People come for the large portions of hearty but basic food at this log building with the look and feel of a Western hunting lodge. The menu is strong on burgers, pizza, steaks, fish, and chicken. **Known for:** casual, friendly spot to grab a meal any day of the week; full bar; big portions. $ *Average main: $12* ✉ *120 E. Riverside Ave., Riverside* ☎ *307/327–5277.*

The Divide Restaurant & Lounge

$$ | **PIZZA** | This small spot has a little bit of everything and offers a comforting, nice dinner after a long day on the road or trail. While it's best known for its pizza, the pastas, Mexican dishes, sandwiches, and calzones are also excellent. **Known for:** pizza, including with a gluten-free crust option; breakfast on the weekends; full bar. $ *Average main: $12* ✉ *520 McCaffrey Ave.* ☎ *307/327–5064* 🌐 *www.the-divide-restaurant.com* ⏲ *Closed Mon.–Wed. No dinner Sun.*

Hotels

Cottonwood Cabins

$$ | **RENTAL** | **FAMILY** | In the quiet little hamlet of Riverside (immediately northeast of Encampment), just across the street from the town park, these cabins have wood furniture, country quilts, outdoor grills, picnic tables, and full kitchens. **Pros:** close to outdoor recreation; cabins have plenty of amenities; rustic interiors are full of character and comfort. **Cons:** open only through the summer; books up quickly; the area is sparse on restaurants and bars. *Rooms from: $80 ✉ 411 1st St., Riverside ☎ 307/327–5151 🌐 www.cottonwoodcabinswy.com ⏲ Closed Nov.–Apr. 3 cabins 🍽 No meals.*

★ Spirit West River Lodge

$$ | B&B/INN | Beside the Encampment River, this massive log structure has walls of lichen-covered rocks and large windows overlooking the water and surrounding scenery. **Pros:** quiet, secluded location; right on the river, with great views; owners R.G. and Lynn are warm and welcoming. **Cons:** its small number of rooms can fill up quickly; a 10-minute walk (or short drive) into downtown Riverside; only children 12 and older are allowed. *Rooms from: $90 ✉ Encampment ✣ ¼ mile east of Riverside on Hwy. 230 is sign that directs you to lodge ☎ 307/326–5753, 888/289–8321 for reservations 🌐 www.spiritwestriverlodge.com 6 rooms 🍽 Free breakfast.*

Activities

CAMPING

Hog Park Campground. In the Sierra Madres west of Encampment, this large campground sits beside a high mountain lake at 8,400 feet; some of the campsites have views of the water. You can use motorized boats and other watercraft on the lake. Hiking, horseback riding, and mountain-biking roads and trails abound, and there is a boat dock here as well. ✉ *20 miles southwest of Encampment, 5 miles west on Hwy. 70, then 15 miles southwest on Forest Rd. 550 ☎ 307/326–5258* www.recreation.gov *50 sites.*

Lazy Acres Campground. The Encampment River runs past this small campground with plenty of big cottonwood trees for shade. There are pull-through RV sites, tent sites, one small cabin (you provide bedding, stove, and cooking utensils), and four no-frills motel rooms, which have cable television and Wi-Fi. ✉ *110 Fields Ave., Riverside ☎ 307/327–5968 🌐 www.lazyacreswyo.com 17 full hookups, 14 partial hookups, 2 tent sites, 4 hotel rooms.*

Six Mile Gap Campground. There are only nine sites at this campground on a hillside above the North Platte River. Some are pull-through camper sites and others are walk-in tent sites. Trails follow the river, which you can cross during low water to reach the Platte River Wilderness Area. ✉ *Hwy. 230, 26 miles east of Encampment, then 2 miles east on Forest Rd. 492 ☎ 307/326–5258 🌐 www.fs.usda.gov 9 sites.*

CROSS-COUNTRY SKIING

Bottle Creek Ski Trails

SKIING/SNOWBOARDING | A network of cross-country trails in Medicine Bow–Routt National Forest, the **Bottle Creek Ski Trails** include several backcountry trails suitable only for expert skiers. There are also easier routes for skiers of all levels. Some trails double as snowmobile trails. All of them are free. ✉ *Hwy. 70 ✣ 6 miles southwest of Encampment ☎ 306/326–5258 🌐 www.fs.usda.gov.*

HIKING

There are extensive trails in the Sierra Madre range west of Encampment, ranging from developed paths around Bottle Creek to wilderness trails through Huston Park and along the Encampment River.

Medicine Bow–Routt National Forest, Brush Creek/Hayden District

HIKING/WALKING | For hiking information, contact the Forest Service office of the **Medicine Bow–Routt National Forest, Brush Creek/Hayden District**. ✉ *204 W. 9th St. ☎ 307/326–5258.*

Baggs

60 miles west of Encampment via Hwy. 70.

Settled by cattle and sheep ranchers, the Little Snake River valley—and its largest community, Baggs—is still ranch country. Two emigrant trails passed nearby: the south branch of the Cherokee Trail (circa 1849–50) crosses near the community, and the Overland Trail (1862–65) lies farther to the north. Notorious outlaw Butch Cassidy frequented the area, often hiding out here after pulling off a train or bank robbery. To the west of Baggs, large herds of wild horses range freely on public lands. The town is on the southern edge of what is now a major oil, gas, and coal-bed methane field, so large numbers of equipment trucks, big water trucks, and field workers ply the roads. The restaurants and one hotel in town stay busy.

Sights

Little Snake River Museum

MUSEUM VILLAGE | Ranch paraphernalia, handmade quilts, a doll collection, and the original 1870s-era cabin of mountain man Jim Baker are exhibited at the Little Snake River Museum in Savery. There are more than a dozen historic buildings at the site, including one that houses an exhibit completely dedicated to the history of sheep raising in Carbon County. At certain times in the past, it had more sheep than any other county in the country. The museum also has a nice gift shop, with a good selection of books. In nearby Baggs, the museum owns and operates The Outlaw Stop. Both museums are open from Memorial Day to "some cold day in October," which heralds the coming of winter. *13 CC Rd. 561 N, Savery 11.5 miles east of Baggs 307/383–7262 www.littlesnakerivermuseum.com Donations accepted Closed late Oct.–late May.*

The Outlaw Stop

MUSEUM VILLAGE | The Outlaw Stop, which is owned and operated by the Little Snake River Museum in Savery, has two historic buildings: one that functioned as a home, the other as a town hall/fire station/jail. There's also a picnic area. *250 N. Penland St. 307/383–7262 Little Snake River Museum in Savery Closed late Oct.–late May.*

Restaurants

Brenda's Home Cooking

$$ | **AMERICAN** | This small, casual spot makes almost everything from scratch, including the breads and other baked goods. The menu is all-American, filled with burgers and steaks, served with a big helping of down-home friendliness. **Known for:** opens at 5 am; tasty breakfast burritos; boneless wings in a homemade chokecherry barbecue sauce. *Average main: $11 1459 Penland St. 307/383–6369 Closed Sun.*

Hotels

The Cowboy Inn

$$ | **HOTEL** | Big, no-frills rooms are well-kept, and there's an adjacent restaurant ($$) and full bar. **Pros:** the attached restaurant is reliable and tasty, open for three meals a day; rooms are big and well-kept; this is a good place to rest and recharge after a long drive. **Cons:** this is pretty much the only game in town; more than an hour from Rawlins, the next-closest city; spotty cell service in the area (Verizon, in particular, doesn't work in town). *Rooms from: $110 210 Penland St. 307/383–2200 www.thecowboyinn.com 45 rooms No meals.*

Rawlins

70 miles northeast of Baggs via Hwy. 789 and I–80.

The northern gateway to the Medicine Bow–Routt National Forest, Rawlins stands at the junction of U.S. 287 and I–80. Started as one of the Union Pacific's hell-on-wheels towns, this was an important transportation center as early as 1868, when miners heading for the goldfields at South Pass to the north rode the rails to Rawlins or points nearby, then went overland to the gold diggings. The town became a large sheep-raising center at the turn of the 20th century. Kingpins in the sheep industry, such as George Ferris and Robert Deal, also backed the development of the Grand Encampment Copper Mining District in the Sierra Madres after miner Ed Haggarty discovered copper there in 1897.

Declines in sheep raising, long Rawlins's mainstay industry, have hurt the community economically, as have downturns in regional mineral production. But the city of 10,000 is still home to many railroad workers and employees of the Wyoming State Penitentiary outside of town. In summer there are weekly free concerts in the park.

VISITOR INFORMATION

CONTACTS Carbon County Visitors' Council. *508 W. Cedar St. 307/324–3020 www.wyomingcarboncounty.com.*

Sights

Carbon County Museum

MUSEUM | FAMILY | This expansive museum tells the history of Carbon County through stories, artifacts, and photos spread across several gallery spaces and a garage. Some notable collections focus on the history of women in the area, Native Americans, and the military. There's a hands-on space for kids, and for railroad buffs there's one of the largest exhibits of Union Pacific memorabilia and history in the state. Many people come to see the original Wyoming flag, as well as a much more gruesome historical memento: a pair of shoes crafted out of human skin; Dr. John Osborne made them from the body of outlaw Big Nose George Parrott, who was lynched here in 1881. Legend has it that Dr. Osborne wore those very shoes several years later to his inauguration as Wyoming's governor. *904 W. Walnut St. 307/328–2740 www.carboncountymuseum.org Free Closed Sun. and Mon.*

Seminoe State Park

BODY OF WATER | You can fish, boat, and water-ski on the Seminoe Reservoir, the primary attraction within Seminoe State Park. This is also a popular spot for camping and picnicking. It's on a Bureau of Land Management backcountry byway, Carbon County Road 351, which links Sinclair with Alcova. *County Rd. 351, Sinclair 307/320–3013 wyoparks.state.wy.us From $7 vehicle; from $10 camping.*

Wyoming Frontier Prison

JAIL | FAMILY | Cold steel and concrete, the Death House, and the Yard are all part of the tour of the Wyoming Frontier Prison, which served as the state's penitentiary from 1901 until 1981. There are occasional midnight tours, and there's a Halloween tour. During the summer months, the prison is open every day of the week. *500 W. Walnut St. 307/324–4422 www.wyomingfrontierprison.org $10 Closed Fri.–Sun. Labor Day–Memorial Day.*

Restaurants

Anong's Thai Cuisine

$$ | THAI | There are three Anong's locations across Wyoming, but this friendly spot is the original. Anong, the restaurant's founder, is originally from Thailand and her menu has all the authentic specialties you would hope for,

Wyoming's Cowboy Symbol

Ask any old-timer in Cheyenne, Laramie, Lander, or Pinedale who the cowboy is on the Wyoming license plate's bucking-horse symbol, and you'll probably get four different answers. Artist Allen True, who designed the symbol, once said he had no particular rider in mind, but that hasn't stopped Wyoming residents from attributing the rider to regional favorites. Several well-known cowboys are often mentioned, including Stub Farlow of Lander and Guy Holt of Cheyenne (who later ranched near Pinedale).

True was not the first person to create this bucking-horse design, however. The symbol evolved over a number of years, beginning with a 1903 photograph by Professor B.C. Buffum of cowboy Guy Holt riding Steamboat, one of five horses recognized as the most difficult bucking horses of all time. In 1921 the University of Wyoming used that photograph as a model for the bucking-horse-and-cowboy logo on its sports uniforms.

But by that time there was already another Wyoming bucking-horse symbol. During World War I George Ostrom, a member of the Wyoming National Guard serving in Germany, had a bucking-horse-and-rider design painted on a brass drum. His 148th Field Artillery unit soon adopted the logo for its vehicles as well, and it became known as the Bucking Bronco Regiment from Wyoming. And which horse was the symbol modeled after? In the case of the Wyoming National Guard logo, the horse was Ostrom's own mount, Red Wing.

Using Allen True's design, the state of Wyoming first put the bucking bronco on its license plate in 1936, and the well-known, trademarked symbol has been there ever since.

bursting with flavor and made from fresh ingredients. **Known for:** also has locations in Laramie and Cheyenne; delicious tom kha (coconut chicken) soup; especially tasty pad see ew (stir-fried wide rice noodles). *Average main: $13 ✉ 210 5th St. ☎ 307/324–6262 🌐 www.anong-thai.com.*

Aspen House

$$$ | STEAKHOUSE | The fanciest restaurant in Rawlins, this little steak house in a Victorian home serves hand-cut meat, seafood, and pasta, with a few Asian fusion dishes, to boot. Co-owner Lena Dirck grew up in Singapore and opened the restaurant with her husband James in the mid-1990s, back when it was hard to find a variety of restaurants in Rawlins. **Known for:** cozy, intimate atmosphere; hand-cut steaks; large portions (which is definitely the Wyoming way). *Average main: $23 ✉ 318 5th St. ☎ 307/324–4787 🌐 www.aspenhouserestaurant.com ⏲ No lunch.*

Su Casa

$$ | MEXICAN | One of Wyoming's best Mexican restaurants is in the tiny refinery town of Sinclair, 6 miles east of Rawlins. Green chili is a big draw here, and the menu is full of Mexican favorites, as well as Navajo tacos. **Known for:** chiles rellenos (fried cheese-stuffed peppers); shredded beef enchiladas; famed green chili that you can take home by the gallon. *Average main: $11 ✉ 705 Lincoln Ave., Sinclair ☎ 307/328–1745.*

Best Western CottonTree Inn
$$$$ | **HOTEL** | The rooms in this pleasant hotel have a classic elegance to them, as well as a lot of practicality—all with a microwave, fridge, and desk. **Pros:** welcoming atmosphere; large, attractive pool and hot tub area; hot breakfast buffet. **Cons:** located in a commercial part of town, not in walking distance to most amenities; small bathrooms; priced higher than most other local hotels. *Rooms from: $210* *2221 W. Spruce St.* *307/324–2737* *www.cottontreeinns.com* *122 rooms* *Free breakfast.*

Fairfield Inn & Suites Rawlins
$$$ | **HOTEL** | The nicest (and newest) hotel in town offers rooms that are tastefully decorated with warm walls and dark carpeting, each with a microwave and fridge. **Pros:** modern and inviting; large bathrooms, with walk-in showers; tasty hot breakfast buffet included. **Cons:** no pets; fills up quickly in the summer (book at least two weeks in advance); nearby train tracks can be loud at times. *Rooms from: $159* *2370 E. Cedar St.* *307/328–5991* *www.marriott.com* *77 rooms* *Free breakfast.*

Windswept Goods
HOUSEHOLD ITEMS/FURNITURE | Located in the town's historic core, this spacious, hip shop is the kind of thing you'd expect in a much bigger city. There's a little bit of everything here: contemporary clothing and accessories, home decor, gifts, and art. *410 W. Cedar St.* *307/321–2667* *www.windsweptgoods.com* *Closed Sun.*

CAMPING

Red Desert Rose Campground. There are pull-through RV sites and tent sites at this year-round campground on the west side of Rawlins. Full hookups are available (some with cable), as well as sites with just electric and water. There's a playground and a fenced pet run. Mini golf and pedal carts are available. *3101 Wagon Circle Rd.* *307/328–1091* *www.reddesertrose.com* *113 hookups, 12 tent sites.*

Western Hills Campground. There are pull-through RV sites, grassy tent sites, and an 18-hole miniature golf course at a seasonal campground on the west side of Rawlins. Barbecue, play horseshoes, or browse the gift shop. The campground closes from November through March. *2500 Wagon Circle Rd.* *307/324–2592* *www.westernhillscampground.com* *115 full hookups, 80 tent sites.*

Rock Springs

106 miles west of Rawlins via I–80.

Thousands of acres of public land attract people to this area to see wild horses, hike, and explore 19th-century emigrant trails. Coal mining has always defined the community of Rock Springs, established when the Union Pacific Railroad pushed through the area in the late 1860s. The mines drew laborers from a variety of nationalities, making this a real melting pot of cultures. Sprawled at the base of White Mountain, this city of about 23,000 people is the site of Western Wyoming Community College, a facility known for its paleontological resources.

The Red Desert to the north and east is home to a gigantic sand dune field as well as hundreds of wild horses; you can often catch a glimpse of them from area highways.

Community Fine Arts Center
MUSEUM | **FAMILY** | The center's Halseth Gallery houses a permanent collection of nearly 500 mostly American paintings,

prints, drawings, and photographs, including works by Norman Rockwell, Grandma Moses, and Rufino Tamayo. The center also draws some of the best traveling art exhibitions from around the country. Concerts and other programs are presented throughout the year as well. ✉ *400 C St.* ☎ *307/362–6212* 🌐 *www.cfac4art.com* ☞ *Closed Sun.*

Killpecker Sand Dunes

LOCAL INTEREST | **FAMILY** | The second largest active sand dune field in the world, these otherworldly mountains and valleys of sand stretch for more than 100 miles. Pay attention to signage: some areas are friendly to off-roading, while others are federally protected and do not allow motorized vehicles. The ADA-accessible Killpecker Sand Dunes Open Play Area Campground is located 32 miles north of Rock Springs and has a vault toilet and fire rings. ✉ *Rock Springs* ✥ *From Rock Springs, take U.S. 191 about 10 miles north, then turn right at CR 4-18 (the sign reads "Petroglyphs, Sand Dunes, Boar's Tusk"), then turn left at CR 4-18* ☎ *307/352–0256* 🌐 *www.blm.gov/wyoming.*

Pilot Butte Wild Horse Scenic Loop Tour

SCENIC DRIVE | Wild horses, antelope, desert elk, coyotes, hawks, and sage grouse are among the wild animals you might see on the Pilot Butte Wild Horse Scenic Loop Tour, which also takes you past such prominent features as Pilot Butte, the Killpecker Sand Dunes, and segments of the Overland Trail. Along the route there are pullouts with interpretive panels.

This loop links Rock Springs and Green River; it takes two to three hours to drive the full 50-mile route, half of which is on gravel roads, between the two towns. From Rock Springs, travel north for 14 miles on Highway 191. Turn left onto Sweetwater County Road 4-14 and follow the route for 2½ miles before turning left onto Sweetwater County Road 4-53, which will take you to Green River, 33½ miles away. ✉ *Rock Springs* ☎ *307/362–3771.*

Rock Springs Historical Museum

MUSEUM | **FAMILY** | Countless artifacts here illustrate the beauty and ugliness of Rock Springs's past, which dates back to the mid-1800s. Learn about how the railroad and coal mines built the community and contributed to the incredible diversity of its population (with 56 nationalities represented here at one time). The companies' hiring practices were not pure, however, and they hoped that all these different languages and cultures would keep workers from organizing. The museum has permanent exhibits with period clothing and military uniforms, as well as an explanation of the 1885 Chinese massacre, when at least 28 people died. Jail cells dating back to the late 1800s are on-site, as is an old fire station, complete with a working door. ✉ *201 B St.* ☎ *307/362–3138* 🌐 *www.rswy.net* 🎫 *Free* ⏲ *Closed Sun.*

Western Wyoming Community College Natural History Museum

MUSEUM | **FAMILY** | Dinosaurs, placed throughout the building, are among the prehistoric animal and plant specimens on display at the WWCC Natural History Museum. Species range in age from 67 million to 180 million years old. Don't miss the fossilized fish and the baby alligator. The museum also has rotating exhibits. ✉ *2500 College Dr.* ☎ *307/382–1600* 🌐 *www.westernwyoming.edu* 🎫 *Free* ⏲ *Closed Fri.–Sun. during summer (June–Aug.). Otherwise, open daily.*

 Restaurants

Bitter Creek Brewing

$$ | **AMERICAN** | This welcoming, low-key brewery has a good selection of burgers and sandwiches and slings its own award-winning brews. There are also soups, steaks, pasta, and massive salads on the menu. **Known for:** creamy capelli pasta with Cajun shrimp and andouille sausage; clam chowder; "Coal Porter" (a beer named in honor of the area's mining history). *Average main: $13* *604 Broadway St.* *307/362-4782* *www.bittercreekbrewing.com* *Closed Sun. and Mon.*

Hotels

Homewood Suites by Hilton Rock Springs
$$ | **HOTEL** | Each spacious room in this extended-stay hotel is packed with amenities, including a full kitchen, couch, chair, desk, and table. **Pros:** comfortable and modern; free hot breakfast; indoor pool and hot tub. **Cons:** not within walking distance to anything else; books up quickly; pool and hot tub don't open until 8 am. *Rooms from: $119* *60 Winston Dr.* *307/382-0764* *www.hilton.com* *84 rooms* *Free breakfast.*

Activities

CAMPING

Rock Springs KOA. Tent sites, camping cabins, and plenty of RV space make up this campground on the west side of the city. There's plenty to keep you busy here, including a pool, basketball, and an exercise room. *86 Foothill Blvd., Rock Springs* *307/362-3063* *www.koa.com* *85 full hookups, 20 tent sites, 6 cabins, 5 lodges.*

Green River

120 miles west of Rawlins via I–80.

A town of about 13,000, Green River attracts those who want to explore the waterways of the Green River drainage in the nearby Flaming Gorge National Recreation Area. Of all the towns along the Union Pacific Railroad, this is the only one that predated the arrival of the rails in the late 1860s. It began as a Pony Express and stage station on the Overland Trail. In 1869 and again in 1871, explorer John Wesley Powell (1834–1902) launched expeditions down the Green and Colorado rivers from nearby sites.

Every June, the town hosts a several-day celebration known as **Flaming Gorge Days,** with a parade, arts festival, sports tournaments, and concerts.

VISITOR INFORMATION

CONTACTS Green River Chamber of Commerce. *1155 W. Flaming Gorge Way* *307/875-5711* *www.grchamber.com.*

Sights

Seedskadee National Wildlife Refuge
NATURE PRESERVE | Prairie and peregrine falcons, Canada geese, and various species of hawks and owls inhabit this refuge, which stretches more than 25,000 acres. Trumpeter swans also occasionally use the area. Within or near the refuge there are homestead and ranch sites, Oregon Trail crossings, and ferries that cross the Green River, as well as the spot where Jim Bridger and Henry Fraeb built a trading post in 1839. Visitor information and restrooms are available during daylight hours. *37 miles north of Green River on Hwy. 372* *307/875-2187* *www.fws.gov/seedskadee* *Free.*

Sweetwater County Museum
MUSEUM | **FAMILY** | Learn about the history of southwestern Wyoming in this renovated post office in downtown Green River. Permanent exhibits go in-depth about the Shoshone and Ute tribes who once lived here, as well as the cowboys, explorers, railroad workers, miners, and fur traders who later called the area home. Sweetwater County hosted the first Rocky Mountain Rendezvous in 1825, and several emigrant trails passed through these parts, including the Oregon, California, and Overland. *3 E. Flaming Gorge Way* *307/872-6435* *www.sweetwatermuseum.org* *Closed Sun. Closed Sun. and Mon. mid-Oct.–mid.-Mar.*

Restaurants

Guidino's Café

$$ | **AMERICAN** | This low-key restaurant offers breakfast, lunch, and dinner—not to mention homemade pies—seven days a week. Prices are a little higher than other nearby restaurants, but portions are generous, with a large selection of burgers, sandwiches, and steaks, plus some Mexican options. **Known for:** all-day breakfast; great burgers; friendly service. *Average main: $13 ✉ 211 E. Flaming Gorge Way ☎ 307/875–3860.*

Hotels

Hampton Inn & Suites Green River

$$$ | **HOTEL** | Underneath towering rock formations, this modern hotel has comfortable rooms with a few fun cowboy touches, including rustic headboards and swivel chairs covered in faux cow hide. **Pros:** classiest hotel in town; nice pool and hot tub; located on Pilot Butte Wild Horse Scenic Loop. **Cons:** not in walking distance to town; not all rooms have bathtubs; more expensive than other nearby hotels. *Rooms from: $149 ✉ 1055 Wild Horse Canyon Rd. ☎ 307/875–5300 🌐 www.hilton.com 106 rooms Free breakfast.*

Little America

$ | **HOTEL** | This one-stop facility stands alone in the Red Desert, and its large, comfortable rooms can be a real haven if the weather becomes inclement. **Pros:** rooms have a historic elegance to them; located in a full-service travel center open 24 hours a day; large gift shop and convenience store. **Cons:** closest town is 20 miles away; some rooms only have showers and no tubs; not a modern hotel, if that's what you're seeking. *Rooms from: $71 ✉ I–80, Exit 68, Little America ✣ 20 miles west of Green River ☎ 307/875–2400, 888/652–9042 for reservations 🌐 littleamerica.com 140 rooms No meals.*

Activities

A stroll on the paved path by the Green River takes you along the route that John Wesley Powell followed on his expedition down the waterway in 1869. Along the way you can visit Expedition Island, the Green Belt Nature Area, and the Scotts Bottom Nature Area. Access **Expedition Island** off 2nd Street, southwest of the railroad yard in Green River; wild birds, squirrels, and rabbits inhabit the grassy, tree-shaded island. Downstream from Expedition Island on the south bank of the river is the **Green Belt Nature Area,** with interpretive signs, nature paths, and numerous birds, including waterfowl. Farther south is **Scotts Bottom Nature Area,** where you'll find more interpretive signs related to the wildlife that lives in this riparian habitat.

Flaming Gorge National Recreation Area

20 miles south of Green River via Hwy. 530 or Hwy. 191.

The Flaming Gorge Reservoir of the Flaming Gorge National Recreation Area is formed by Green River water held back by Flaming Gorge Dam. Here you can boat and fish, as well as watch for wildlife.

Sights

Flaming Gorge National Recreation Area

NATIONAL/STATE PARK | **FAMILY** | The Flaming Gorge area is as rich in history as it is spectacularly beautiful. Mountain men such as Jim Bridger and outlaws such as Butch Cassidy found haven here, and in 1869, on his first exploration down the Green River, John Wesley Powell named many local landmarks: Flaming Gorge, Horseshoe Canyon, Red Canyon, and the Gates of Lodore. The recreation area straddles the border between Wyoming and Utah; most of the park's visitor services are in Utah. There are marinas, campgrounds, places to rent horses and snowmobiles, and trails for mountain bikes, as well as lodging and food. The Ashley National Forest administers the area. ✉ *Flaming Gorge National Recreation Area* ☎ *435/784–3445, 800/752–8525 for information on reservoir elevations and river flows, 877/444–6777 for campground reservations, 877/833–6777 TDD camping reservations* 🌐 *www.fs.usda.gov/ashley* *Free; day-use areas $5 (including boat ramp and swimming areas).*

Activities

BOATING

Buckboard Marina

BOATING | **Buckboard Marina** provides full marina services, including boat rentals, a marina store, and an RV park. ✉ *Hwy. 530, 25 miles south of Green River* ☎ *307/875–6927* 🌐 *www.buckboardmarina.net.*

CAMPING

Buckboard Crossing Campground. The campsites at this campground on the west side of Flaming Gorge can be used for tents or RVs, though only a few sites have electrical hookups for RVs. There's a boat dock here. ✉ *23 miles southwest of Green River on Hwy. 530, then 2 miles east on Forest Rd. 009* ☎ *435/784–3445 for information, 877/444–6777 for reservations* 🌐 *www.recreation.gov* *66 sites.*

Firehole Canyon Campground. Located in the Flaming Gorge National Recreation Area, this campground has great canyon views. You can pitch a tent or park an RV on the campsites here, but there are no hookups for RVs. There's a beach area nearby, plus a boat ramp. ✉ *13 miles south of Green River on Hwy. 191, then 10 miles west on Forest Rd. 106* ☎ *435/784–3445 for information, 877/444–6777 for reservations* 🌐 *www.recreation.gov* *40 sites.*

Fort Bridger State Historic Site

51 miles west of Green River via I–80.

Started in 1843 as a trading post by mountain man Jim Bridger and his partner Louis Vasquez, Fort Bridger was under the control of Mormons by 1853, then served as a frontier military post until it was abandoned in 1890.

Sights

Fort Bridger State Historic Site

HISTORIC SITE | **FAMILY** | Historians aren't sure how Mormons came to control Fort Bridger trading post. They may have purchased Fort Bridger from Jim Bridger and Louis Vasquez or forced the original owners to leave. As the U.S. Army approached during a conflict known as the Mormon War of 1857, the Mormons deserted the area and burned the original Bridger post. Fort Bridger was rebuilt and then served as a frontier military post until it was abandoned in 1890, and many of the military-era buildings remain. You can attend interpretive programs and living-history demonstrations during the summer, and the museum has exhibits about the fort's history. The largest mountain-man rendezvous in the intermountain West occurs annually at Fort Bridger over Labor Day weekend, attracting hundreds of buckskinners and Native Americans, plus thousands of visitors. The grounds are open daily, and the historic buildings are open in the warmer months. ✉ *Exit 34 off I–80, Fort Bridger* ☎ *307/782–3842* 🌐 *wyoparks.state.wy.us* *$4 vehicle (resident), $8 (nonresident)* ⏲ *Historic buildings are closed Oct.–Apr.*

Although the fort was abandoned by the army in 1890, many of Fort Bridger's historic buildings remain, and some have been restored.

CAMPING

Fort Bridger RV Camp. There's plenty of grass for tents and room for RVs as well at this campground within walking distance to Fort Bridger. ✉ *64 Groshon Rd., at S. Main St.* ☎ *307/782–3150* 🌐 *www.reserveamerica.com* *38 full hookups.*

Kemmerer

34 miles north of Fort Bridger via Hwy. 412; 35 miles north of Evanston via Hwy. 189.

This small city serves as a gateway to Fossil Butte National Monument. Probably the most important person in Kemmerer's history was James Cash Penney, who in 1902 started the Golden Rule chain of stores here. He later used the name J.C. Penney Company, which by 1929 had 1,395 outlets. Penney revolutionized merchandising in western Wyoming. Before the opening of Penney's stores, the coal-mining industry dominated the region, and miners were used to working for the company and purchasing their supplies at the company store—which often charged whatever it wanted, managing to keep employees in debt. But when Penney opened his Golden Rule, he set one price for each item and stuck to it. Later he developed a catalog, selling to people unable to get to town easily.

Fossil Butte National Monument

ARCHAEOLOGICAL SITE | A unique concentration of creatures is embedded in the natural limestone outcrop at Fossil Butte National Monument, indicating clearly that this area was a freshwater lake more than 50 million years ago. Many of the fossils—which include fish, insects, and plants—are remarkably clear and detailed. Pronghorn, coyotes, prairie dogs, and other mammals find shelter within the 8,198-acre park, along with numerous birds, such as eagles and falcons. You can hike two trails and unwind at the picnic area. A visitor center here houses an information desk and fossil exhibits, including a 13-foot crocodilian, long since extinct but related to the modern crocodile. ✉ *864 Chicken Creek Rd.* ✢ *15 miles west of Kemmerer via U.S. 30* ☎ *307/877–4455* 🌐 *www.nps.gov/fobu* 🎟 *Free* ⏲ *Visitor center closed Sun.*

Fossil Country Frontier Museum

MUSEUM | **FAMILY** | This small but charming window into the past is housed in a former church and features fossils and displays related to early settlement in the area. See an old still and wine vat, as well as a taxidermied two-headed calf. ✉ *400 Pine Ave.* ☎ *307/877–6551* 🎟 *Free* ⏲ *Closed Sun.–Wed.*

Ulrich's Fossil Gallery

MUSEUM | **FAMILY** | In business since the 1950s, Ulrich's Fossil Gallery has fossils from around the world on display. You can even buy some specimens, particularly fish fossils. Ulrich's also runs fossil-digging excursions at private quarries; call for more information. ✉ *4400 Fossil Butte County Rd.* ☎ *307/877–6466* 🌐 *www.ulrichsfossilgallery.com* 🎟 *Gallery free, fossil-digging excursions $125. Reservations recommended for trips* ⏲ *Closed weekends Nov.–Apr.*

El Jaliciense

$$ | **MEXICAN** | Locals love this small Mexican joint that serves up big portions at reasonable prices. The menu has such staples as enchiladas, tacos, and burritos, plus a large selection of chicken, beef, and seafood dishes. **Known for:** enchiladas suizas; friendly service; many types of delicious burritos. 💲 *Average main: $12* ✉ *1433 Central Ave.* ☎ *307/877–2948* ⏲ *Closed Sun.*

Best Western Plus Fossil Country Inn & Suites

$$$ | **HOTEL** | The nicest lodging around by far, this modern hotel offers spacious rooms with an elegant feel, each with a desk, microwave, and refrigerator. **Pros:** best hotel in a small, rural town; delicious (and free) made-to-order breakfast; indoor, heated pool and hot tub. **Cons:** not in walking distance to amenities; entrance is by a long, narrow driveway that's easy to miss; only four pet rooms available (with a $20 fee for the first dog). 💲 *Rooms from: $140* ✉ *760 Hwy. 189/30* ☎ *307/877–3388* 🌐 *www.bestwestern.com* 🛏 *80 rooms* 🍽 *Free breakfast.*

JCPenney "mother" store and historic J.C. Penney House

DEPARTMENT STORES | To understand Kemmerer's roots, stop at the JCPenney store, which is where James Cash Penney began his merchandising career. This small retail establishment, known as the "mother store," sells clothing. Just down the street, Penney's historic home is open to visitors in the summer. ✉ *722 JC Penney Dr.* ☎ *307/877–3164* ⏲ *Closed Sun.*

Index

A

B

C

D

E

I

J

K

L

P

R

S

Photo Credits

Front Cover: A.J. Rich. [Description: The silhouette of a hiker and backpacker takes in the beautiful view along the Highline Trail during an early morning hike. Image taken at Glacier National Park, Montana, USA.]. **Back cover, from left to right:** Lorcel/Shutterstock, Krasnova Ekaterina/Shutterstock, Galyna Andrushko/Shutterstock. **Spine:** Andrew S/Shutterstock. **Interior, from left to right:** Visit Montana (1). Traveller70/Shutterstock (2). Jeff Vanuga (5). **Chapter 1: Experience Montana and Wyoming:** Lorcel/Shutterstock (8-9). Bertl123/Shutterstock (10). Atmosphere1/Shutterstock (11). Alexey Kamenskiy/Shutterstock (11). FrancesFiestaa/Shutterstock (12). Anh Luu/Shutterstock (12). Courtesy_Grand Targhee Resort (13). Sandra Foyt/Shutterstock (14). Silken Eye Photography (14). Jason Lindsey/Wyoming Office of Tourism (14). Glowimages RM / Alamy Stock Photo (14). Lincoln Rogers/Shutterstock (15). Sue Smith/Shutterstock (15). Dan Schreiber/shutterstock (15). Victoria Ditkovsky/shutterstock (15). Edgar G Biehle/Shutterstock (16). David R Butler/shutterstock (16). AlexBuess/Shutterstock (16). Regien Paassen/Shutterstock (16). Jackson Hole Mountain Resort (17). Jess Kraft/Shutterstock (17). brown54486/iStockphoto (18). Ericliu08/iStockphoto (18). Master1305/Shutterstock (18). Frank L Junior/Shutterstock (18). Mendenhall Olga/Shutterstock (19). Adrian Sanchez-Gonzalez/MSU (24). Donyanedomam | Dreamstime.com (24). Zrfphoto | Dreamstime.com (24). Visit Montana (25). Brittany Mumma (25). Wildnerdpix/Shutterstock (26). Robert Mutch/Shutterstock (26). Danita Delimont/shutterstock (26). Adam Reck/Shutterstock (26). Zack Frank/Shutterstock (27). Larson755 | Dreamstime.com (27). Jim Parkin/Shutterstock (27). Michelle Holihan/Shutterstock (27). Sulae/shutterstock (28). Pncpchw7 | Dreamstime.com (28). Alexey Kamenskiy/Shutterstock (28). Don Mammoser/shutterstock (29). Laurens Hoddenbagh/Shutterstock (29). **Chapter 3: Yellowstone National Park:** funtravlr (55). Paul Stoloff (74). Jeff Vanuga (78-86). **Chapter 4: Bozeman, Helena, and Southwest Montana:** Rob Crandall/Shutterstock (101). Edgloris Marys/Shutterstock (110). Mandritoiu | Dreamstime.com (119). Mendenhall Olga/Shutterstock (125). Americanspirit | Dreamstime.com (130). Philipbird123 | Dreamstime.com (133). bmswanson/iStockphoto (145). Rob Crandall/Shutterstock (156). Mtsue | Dreamstime.com (159). Bruce Ellis/Shutterstock (161). **Chapter 5: Glacier and Waterton Lakes National Parks:** alfwilde (163). chip phillips/iStockphoto (177). **Chapter 6: Missoula, Kalispell, and Northwest Montana:** Oliver1803 | Dreamstime.com (193). Debraansky/iStockphoto (201). 11jasons/iStockphoto (206). Ronnie Chua/Shutterstock (216). Marty Nelson/Shutterstock (228). Marty Nelson/Shutterstock (238). **Chapter 7: Great Falls, Billings, and the Montana Plains:** Reid Morth / Morth Photography (243). Nikki Yancey/Shutterstock. (252). Jacob Boomsma/Shutterstock (265). Mendenhall Olga/Shutterstock (274). Steve & Nancy Cerroni, PryorWild (276). Visit Montana (279). Rinusbaak | Dreamstime.com (284). **Chapter 8: Grand Teton National Park:** jack-sooksan/Shutterstock (289). **Chapter 9: Jackson and the Wind River Range:** Steve Price/Shutterstock (311). Sopotnicki/Shutterstock (322). EQRoy/Shutterstock (327). Cavan Images / Alamy Stock Photo (332). CSNafzger/Shutterstock (339). Tobin Akehurst/Shutterstock (342). **Chapter 10: Cody, Sheridan, and Northern Wyoming:** Jason Koperski (351). melissamn/Shutterstock (358). DC_Colombia/iStockphoto (361). Courtesy of Buffalo Bill Center of the West (363). Jimsphotos | Dreamstime.com (367). Milosk50 | Dreamstime.com (369). anthony heflin/Shutterstock (388). **Chapter 11: Cheyenne, Laramie, and Southern Wyoming:** AquaSage/iStockphoto (397). Bdingman | Dreamstime.com (405). B-A Graphix/Shutterstock (411). Alexeykamenskiy | Dreamstime.com (419). Dtkell1392 | Dreamstime.com (433). **About Our Writers:** All photos are courtesy of the writers except for the following: Katie Jackson, courtesy of Eric Baumann.

*Every effort has been made to trace the copyright holders, and we apologize in advance for any accidental errors. We would be happy to apply the corrections in the following edition of this publication.

Notes

Notes

Notes